Management Informati

Second Edition

Management Information Systems

Second Edition

A EARDLEY, D V MARSHALL and R L RITCHIE

The Chartered Association of Certified Accountants

LONGMAN

PUBLISHED BY LONGMAN GROUP UK LTD IN CO-OPERATION
WITH THE CHARTERED ASSOCIATION OF
CERTIFIED ACCOUNTANTS

ISBN 0 85121 715X

Published by

Longman Law, Tax & Finance
Longman Group UK Limited
21-27 Lamb's Conduit Street, London WC1N 3NJ

Associated Offices

Australia	Longman Professional Publishing (Pty) Limited 130 Phillip Street, Sydney, NSW 2000
Hong Kong	Longman Group (Far East) Limited Cornwall House, 18th Floor, Taikoo Trading Estate, Tong Chong Street, Quarry Bay
Malaysia	Longman Malaysia Sdn Bhd No 3 Jalan Kilang A, Off Jalan Penchala, Petaling Jaya, Selangor, Malaysia
Singapore	Longman Singapore Publishers (Pte) Ltd 25 First Lok Yang Road, Singapore 2262
USA	Longman Group (USA) Inc 500 North Dearborn Street, Chicago, Illinois 60610

A CIP catalogue record for this book is available from the British Library.

Printed in Great Britain by Loader Jackson

For further information and enquiries please contact your local Longman office.

Europe, Latin America, Iran
Please contact our International
Sales Department
Longman House
Burnt Mill
Harlow
Essex CM20 2JE

Arab World
Longman Arab World Centre
Butros Bustani Street
Zokak el Blat
PO Box 11-945
Beirut
Lebanon

New Sphinx Publishing Co. Ltd.
3 Shawarby Street
Kasr el Nil
Cairo
Egypt

Librairie Sayegh
Salhie Street
PO Box 704
Damascus
Syria

Longman Arab World Centre
Al-Hajairi Building
Amir Mohammed Street
PO Box 6587
Amman
Jordan

Longman Arab World Centre
15th Street
PO Box 1391
Khartoum
Sudan

Cameroon
M A W Ngoumbah
BP 537
Limbe
Cameroon

Australia
Longman Cheshire Pty Ltd
Longman Cheshire House
Kings Gardens
91-97 Coventry Street
South Melbourne
Victoria 3205

Botswana
Longman Botswana (Pty) Ltd.
PO Box 1083
Gaborone

Canada
James D Lang
Marketing Manager
Carswell Legal Publications
2330 Midland Avenue
Agincourt
Ontario
M1S 1P7

Ghana
Sedco Publishing Co. Ltd.
Sedco House
PO Box 2051
Tabon Street
North Ridge
Accra

Hong Kong
Longman Group (Far East) Ltd.
Cornwall House 18th Floor
Taikoo Trading Estate
Tong Chong Street
Quarry Bay

India
Orient Longman Limited
5-9-41/1 Bashir Bagh
Hyderabad 500 029

UBS Publishers Distributors
5 Ansari Road
PO Box 7051
New Delhi 110 002

Japan
Longman Penguin Japan Co. Ltd.
Yamaguchi Building
2-12-9 Kanda Jimbocho
Chiyoda-ku
Tokyo 101

Kenya
Longman Kenya Ltd.
PO Box 18033
Funzi Road, Industrial Area
Nairobi

Lesotho
Longman Lesotho (Pty) Ltd.
PO Box 1174
Maseru, 100

Malawi
Dzuka Publishing Co. Ltd.
Blantyre Printing & Publishing
Co Ltd. PMB 39
Blantyre

Malaysia
Longman Malaysia Sdn Berhad
No 3 Jalan Kilang A
Off Jalan Penchala
Petaling Jaya
Selangor

New Zealand
Longman Paul Ltd.
Private Bag
Takapuna
Auckland 9

Nigeria
Longman Nigeria Ltd.
52 Oba Akran Avenue
Private Mail Bag 21036
Ikeja
Lagos

Pakistan
Tahir M Lodhi
Regional Manager
Butterworths
7 Jahangir Street
Islamia Park
Poonch Road
Lahore

Singapore
Longman Singapore
Publishers Pte Ltd.
25 First Lok Yang Road
Off International Road
Jurong Town
Singapore 2262

South Africa
Maskew Miller Longman (Pty) Ltd.
PO Box 396
Howard Drive
Pinelands 7405
Cape Town 8000

Swaziland
Longman Swaziland Ltd.
PO Box 2207
Manzini

Tanzania
Ben & Co. Ltd.
PO Box 3164
Dar-es-Salaam

USA
Longman Trade USA.
Caroline House Inc.
520 North Dearborn Street
Chicago
Illinois 60610

Transnational Publishers Inc.
PO Box 7282
Ardsley-on-Hudson
NY 10503

West Indies
Longman Caribbean (Trinidad) Ltd.
Boundary Road
San Juan
Trinidad

Longman Jamaica Ltd.
PO Box 489
95 Newport Boulevard
Newport West
Kingston 10
Jamaica

Mr Louis A Forde
'Suncrest'
Sunrise Drive
Pine Gardens
St Michael
Barbados

Zimbabwe
Longman Zimbabwe (PVT) Ltd.
PO Box ST 125
Southerton
Harare

The content of this title has been fully approved and endorsed by a specially constituted Advisory Board, whose members are:

Professor Susan Dev, MSc, FCCA, ATII, Professor Emeritus at the London School of Economics and Political Science
Professor Roger Groves, B Comm, MSc, Phd, FCA, Professor of Accounting at the Cardiff Business School
Hymie Lipman, BA, MSc (Econ), FCCA, FCA, Head of Accounting and Finance at the Kingston Business School
Anthea Rose, MA, Deputy Secretary of the Chartered Association of Certified Accountants

Preface

Data holdings and the information that may be extracted from them are now recognised as a key resource for all organisations, providing potential opportunities for competitive advantage, enhanced performance and greater efficiency in operations. Today, few organisations, whether commercially orientated or not-for-profit, can afford to ignore either these potential opportunities or the contribution that a technological approach to the management of the information may provide towards their realisation.

Two major themes are explored in this text. Firstly, if organisations are to seek to exploit the full potential of the markets which they serve, the senior managers must manage the information resource effectively at the strategic level. Secondly, the contribution that management and staff at all levels can make towards the effectiveness and efficiency of the organisation's information systems is crucial in the optimisation of overall performance. Hence, it is no longer sufficient to leave the planning, development and management of information systems to the so-called experts. Indeed, more recent developments in the information technologies have made information systems more accessible to all users, and encouraged the phenomenon of user computing. Thus, the contemporary concept of Information Technology (IT) comprises the integration of the services available through the use of computer hardware, software and communications technologies, and the relationship between these services and human users—the interface being achieved through the development of information systems.

The primary orientation of the text reflects these themes and approaches information systems planning, development and control from the management perspective. The initial chapters analyse and develop the role of information within the organisation, the major characteristics of the systems which are used to handle the information resource, and the primary issues involved in managing the resource and the associated systems. Because information usage is common to all organisations, the material covered up to this point may be applied equally well in the context of manual as opposed to computer-based information systems. Thereafter, the emphasis shifts to the theme of automating the resource. The major dimensions and developments in the information technologies are outlined in Chapter 5, but the emphasis is placed on both the contribution made, and the problems encountered, in their application to practical information systems, rather than on the technical and operational characteristics.

The importance of the strategic approach to systems development is then highlighted prior to focusing on the more detailed approaches to the analysis and design of individual systems. The tools and techniques used in supporting the systems analysis and design process are explored in Chapter 8 (illustrated by the use of an example relating to student admissions to college). Managing the implementation and maintenance of the systems (Chapter 9) provides an appropriate introduction to the wider issues and approaches to managing the total systems development project outlined in Chapter 10.

The advances in computing and communications technologies have resulted in the potential for significantly larger volumes of data to be made available to a wider body of users, both within and outside the organisation. While such developments may provide considerable benefits and improved efficiency, they also represent significant threats to the security of the data, the information systems and ultimately the organisation itself. These threats and the increased risks which face the organisation, now require management to develop effective security and control systems. These issues and the potential responses are addressed in the concluding chapters.

The text has been specifically designed to meet the requirements of the syllabus laid down by The Chartered Association of Certified Accountants on Information Systems Development and Operation. However, the nature of the material covered, the primary orientation and the level would make this text appropriate both for courses concerning the management of information systems at the level of BTEC Higher National, and for undergraduate courses in Business Studies, Accountancy or Information Systems.

In keeping with the writers' broad yet sometimes guarded view of information systems and the associated technologies that drive them, all possible technologies were called into play in creating this text. Hence, a proportion of the drafting was undertaken on the latest word processing and graphics technology available, while the remainder exploited the fail-safe system of pencil and paper (a user-driven technological advance designed to avoid the blotting caused when using a quill pen).

Contents

Chapter 1

The Nature of Information Systems

CHAPTER OBJECTIVES

The primary objective of this chapter is to introduce the concept of an information system and to provide the necessary framework and foundations for the subsequent treatment of information systems and their development in later chapters of the text. The detailed objectives of this chapter are to:

1. provide an overview of information systems within organisations;
2. develop a model of the organisation which will identify the major components of an organisation in terms of its resources, activities and structure, and help to highlight the major types of information and their uses;
3. distinguish between the terms data and information and establish the requirements for the conversion of data into information;
4. outline the general functions that information performs with particular reference to the role of information both as a key tactical and strategic resource and as a source of added value;
5. identify the underlying reasons for the rapid expansion of data processing activities within organisations;
6. define the term **information systems** within the context of organisations;
7. review the previous, current and likely future developments in Information Technology (IT). This involves the recognition of the view that IT is a convergent technology, and so it will be necessary to identify the main components of IT, and the nature of their interaction;
8. construct a model of the information systems development process, identifying the key stages and their purpose. This model will be used to outline the structure and composition of the remainder of the text.

1.1 COMPONENTS OF AN ORGANISATION

The primary theme of this book is the development, implementation and operation of **information systems** within the modern organisation. Throughout the text, the term organisation will be used to refer both to profit-orientated business and commercial organisations, and to the 'not-for-profit' organisations such as public authorities, charities and voluntary organisations. As a first step, it is therefore necessary to introduce the major component elements of an organisation so that there is an adequate foundation for subsequent discussions of the most common information systems. This chapter is intended only as an introduction to these major components, with later chapters filling in the detail when the context requires it.

Organisations depend upon, and are the product of, the following major components:

(a) purpose and objectives,
(b) environment,
(c) resource inputs, activities, infrastructure, tools and techniques, and resource outputs.

1.1.1 Purpose and objectives of an organisation

The primary purpose of an organisation is to satisfy the needs of its market or clients. If it is to survive, it ought to act both effectively and efficiently. This applies whether or not the organisation is profit-motivated because, in both cases, it should actively seek to meet the needs of its existing and potential clients, whether or not those clients make a financial payment for the goods or services provided. In broad terms, the explicit purpose will reflect the reasons underlying the initial establishment of the organisation although that purpose may have been modified in the light of the experience gained through its continued existence. For instance:

(a) In the profit-orientated organisation—an example might be the design, manufacture and marketing of high quality ladies footwear in such a way as to provide secure and satisfying employment conditions for all employees, consistent with the need to provide a satisfactory return to the shareholders and owners of the business.
(b) In the not-for-profit orientated organisation—an example might be the provision of care, welfare and support facilities for mentally handicapped children and their parents in a way which is sensitive and humane to the recipients, while being a socially acceptable use of that scale of resource.

The purpose of an organisation should be seen as a dynamic element which is likely to evolve over time as the needs of the clients, owners and employees change. It should also be recognised that the purpose may not be particularly well articulated or indeed explicitly stated by the organisation, and may have to be inferred from the current declared values and beliefs of those managers with the power to influence the affairs of the organisation.

While the purpose reflects the longer-term nature and characteristics of the organisation, the objectives of the organisation usually provide an indication of the direction and level of achievement sought within a more foreseeable timescale. These objectives are typically divided into three categories relating to the period of time during which they are to be put into operation, ie:

Category of objective	*Typical timescale*
Long-term	up to 7 years
Medium-term	up to 3 years
Short-term	up to 1 year

These categories of objectives and their timescales reflect the major levels of planning and decision-making activity within most organisations (covered more fully in 2.7). These categories are not absolute, but provide examples of the typical life span of objectives which may vary depending on the nature of the product or service provided by the organisation. For example, in the nuclear power generation industry, the long-term planning issues and objectives may cover a period of up to 20 years or more, because this is approximately the period required to gain approval for the concept, and then to design and construct a new power station. However, the medium and short-term operating objectives and planning periods in this industry may cover a similar period to those illustrated above. Alternatively, in the case of ladies' fashion-related industries, the short-term and medium-term timescales may be more condensed given that changes in product designs may alter several times in a given year.

The objectives formulated by each organisation will reflect a number of different dimensions which will tend to be particular to each organisation and its operations, but which will broadly encompass the following:

1 **The environment**—at an early stage in its development, each organisation must take decisions about how it intends to relate to the main elements of its environment both internal and external to the organisation, eg its effect on the local ecology in terms of waste disposal or noise, or its attitude towards relevant trades unions or staff associations.
2 **Competitiveness**—by establishing the degree of competitiveness to be adopted, the organisation sets the tone for the way in which it will seek to satisfy the needs of its clients and/or the market, eg will it seek to attain high levels of technical excellence, low prices and/or high quality in the product or services provided, or will other less tangible criteria prevail?
3 **External performance measurement**—the management team, in consultation with affected third parties, must decide the basis upon which to judge the effectiveness or otherwise of the organisation in terms of the number of satisfied clients or customers, market share or sales revenues generated, etc.
4 **Internal performance measurement**—whether at an organisational or cost-centre level, decisions must be taken to set the level of internal efficiency sought. This will ultimately be

reflected in the scale of profitability, or the declared costs of providing a service, or by reference to some other measure of resource productivity.

5 **The people**—employees represent a resource within the organisation and, if the organisation is to effectively exploit that resource, it must encourage a constructive framework within which the staff may make their contribution. Equally, the end consumers are people whose needs and aspirations must be taken into account if the organisation is to fulfil its purpose.

It is the norm for the objectives of an organisation to be primarily related to practical performance criteria measured against a given timescale, and they are likely to be specified within one or more of the broad dimensions outlined above. Consequently, organisations tend to be simultaneously pursuing multiple objectives, each related to these dimensions. But, in a number of cases, the objectives pursued by an organisation will not be mutually consistent. This arises because the achievement of one objective may be at the expense of achieving another, eg achieving a given percentage market share may be at the expense of profitability targets and inconsistent with objectives related to the welfare of key employees. Given that organisations frequently pursue multiple and often inconsistent objectives, the management of the organisation must therefore make all the objectives explicit, and then prioritise these objectives, recognising the practical limits on achieving any single objective.

1.1.2 Organisational environment

All organisations operate in an environment which has many components, each of which may place different demands and constraints on the organisation. The major elements which the environment comprises are:

(a) **macro-economic**—factors such as the rate of inflation, the level of growth in the economy and the level of employment;
(b) **financial**—eg currency exchange rates, interest rates and corporation tax rates;
(c) **political**—the political party in power and their policies that affect the operation of the organisation or its markets;
(d) **market-based**—trends in product design, consumer tastes and distribution channels;
(e) **the competition**—the existing competitors' pricing and promotional strategies, and the potential entry of new competitors;
(f) **technological**—changes in technology which affect the technical specification of the product, the manufacturing processes, or the manner in which the organisation conducts its operations;
(g) **social**—developments in the structure, expectations and behaviour of society;
(h) **demographic**—changes in the total size and composition of the population;
(i) **legal**—existing or prospective laws, both statutory and case law, which may directly or indirectly constrain the operations of the organisation, and shifts in the pattern of social attitude, eg in the willingness of people to use the courts as a remedy; and
(j) **ecological**—the effects of the organisation's operations on the natural environment.

It is impossible to reflect diagrammatically the full complexity of the organisation-environment interaction, and each of the above components are likely to interact with each other to an extent greater than implied in the drawing of the diagram. For example, changes in technology may produce unfavourable effects on the ecology or social environment, causing sections of society to put pressure on the political component. This in turn may generate legislation to limit the unfavourable consequences of the technological development. Such changes may then influence the potential of the market and the nature of the competitive interactions between organisations in the market. Figure 1.1 therefore provides a simplified illustration of the interaction between these environmental factors and the organisation.

The key point to remember is that, because of the number of dimensions involved, the environment in which organisations operate is highly complex. It should also be recognised that the organisation itself is an active participant in the environment, and that many of its decisions and actions may well have an impact on individual components in the environment. For most organisations, these effects will be limited either to the local environment or to the industry and

FIGURE 1.1 **The organisation and its environment**

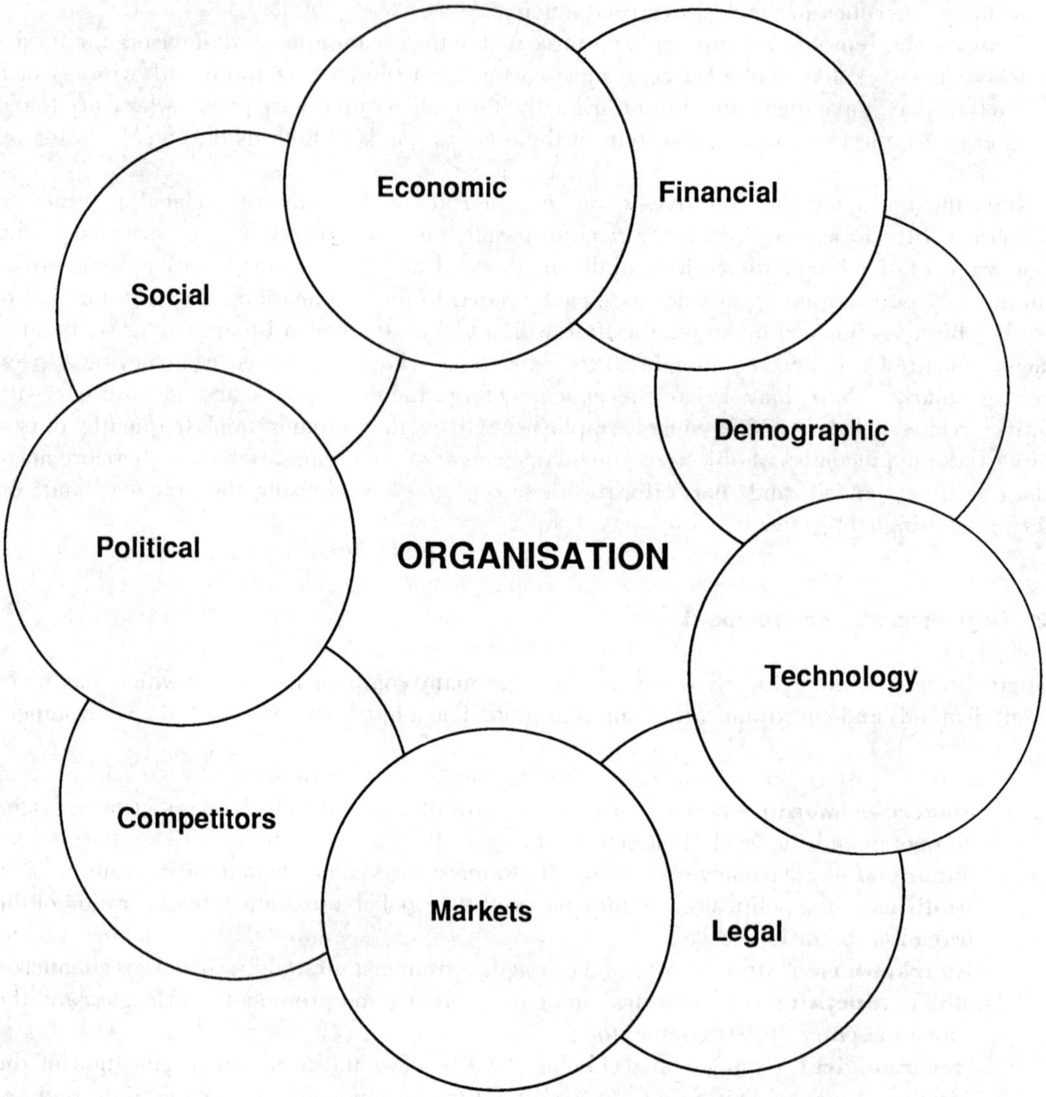

markets within which it operates, and there will be no material change in the national or international dimension. The exception to this will be the large multi-national organisations such as the Ford Motor Company or IBM, whose scale of operations and world market position would allow them to have some influence on the national and international environment.

A further important feature of the organisation's environment is its dynamic nature, ie all dimensions of the environment are subject to continuous change. The rate of that change is variable. Hence, some dimensions may change only relatively slowly, eg demographic and social factors, while other dimensions are likely to change more rapidly, eg the economic and financial components or the actions of competitors in the market. Because our understanding of the underlying causes and mechanisms for change are still inadequate, it is not possible to predict accurately either the direction or the rate of change for each of the various components. There is also evidence that certain dimensions of the environment that previously were relatively stable and predictable are increasingly becoming subject to more rapid and often dramatic change. Examples of this may be found in both the social and ecological areas of the environment.

Finally, it should be recognised that different organisations will be influenced by changes in particular environmental components to differing degrees. For example, changes in currency exchange rates may have a significant impact on a UK distributor for imported cars but have minimal effect on the local hairdressing salon. Whereas changes in the methods of charging for water consumption are likely to have a greater impact on the latter organisation if it is assumed that the washing of hair has a greater percentage impact on variable overheads than the washing of cars for display purposes.

The environment and the changes which occur, provide the organisation with both potential threats and opportunities. Potential threats may be in the form of changes in technology or in the manner and scale of the competition which challenge either the organisation's products or position in the market. Similarly, potential opportunities may arise from changes in technology, consumer tastes or the actions of competitors. Broadly, the management of the organisation needs to be able to respond positively to the threats and opportunities posed by the environment, while seeking to maintain and achieve the declared objectives. This balancing programme must be carried out in the knowledge that the type and scope of the actions that the management may take are themselves constrained by various elements in the environment.

The environment can therefore be summarised as follows:

(a) it contains a very large number of components;
(b) these components dynamically interact with each other and this results in very complex inter-relationships;
(c) the organisation is itself an active participant in the environment although its sphere of influence may be somewhat limited;
(d) the components are dynamic, but the scale and direction of change are difficult to predict;
(e) different components will influence different organisations to different extents;
(f) there is likely to be a simultaneous presentation of potential threats and opportunities to the organisation which may assist or impede the achievement of its objectives; and
(g) the complexity of factors will constrain both the type and scope of actions that management may take in responding to threats and opportunities.

THE ROLE OF ENVIRONMENTAL INFORMATION

The organisation needs a structure which will allow ready access to information on what is happening in its environment. This process of environmental scanning, ie of collecting, interpreting and analysing information about the external environment, is an important and continuing part of any organisation's overall information system, and should involve most members of the organisation. A more detailed treatment of this element of the information system is provided in 3.1.2. The dynamic nature of the environment requires that the organisation's information and decision-making systems are themselves sufficiently flexible, sensitive and dynamic to respond effectively to the changing needs of the organisation and its environment.

1.2 ORGANISATION COMPONENTS AND STRUCTURE

Any organisation consists of a number of components which have been found necessary for its functioning and the achievement of its objectives. These components may be broadly classified into:

1 resource inputs,
2 activities,
3 infrastructure,
4 tools and techniques,
5 resource outputs.

The role of management is to integrate these components effectively and efficiently in the delivery of the optimum level of value to the organisation's clients/customers, employees and owners/supervisory bodies. Figure 1.2 provides a schematic model of an organisation illustrating these five main components.

The organisation receives resource inputs which it seeks to integrate and process to enhance the value of the individual inputs and to deliver products and services to its customers and clients. This is often termed the **added value process**, and the objective of most organisations is to provide the maximum value to their customers, consistent with the need to make some return on each transaction. In the case of profit-orientated organisations, the aim is to undertake this resource conversion process with sufficient efficiency to generate profits which will reward the owners of the business for the risk involved and which will provide additional capital for the future development and growth of the organisation. In the case of the not-for-profit organisations, the objective may be to

FIGURE 1.2 **Key elements of an organisation**

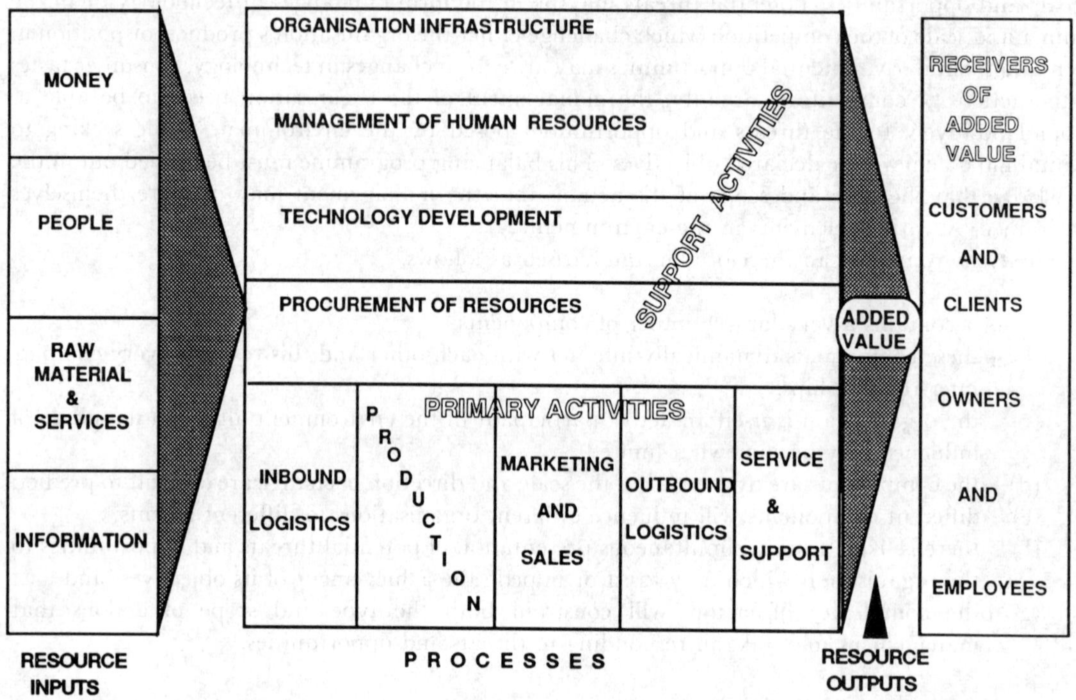

generate a sufficient operating surplus from the process to facilitate its continued existence and development, and to achieve its other objectives.

1.2.1 Resource inputs

The main categories of resource inputs are :

1 **Money** or capital—this represents a key resource input as it enables the purchase of all other resource inputs. An organisation not only requires the initial capital to establish its operations and to acquire the initial resources, but it also needs to generate a sufficient and continuous flow of capital to sustain its operations. This flow of capital, or cash flow as it is more commonly termed, is considered in more detail in later chapters, together with its implications for the information system.

2 **People**—provide the necessary knowledge, skills and expertise to operate and manage the resource conversion process and to ensure the satisfaction of the needs of the organisation's customers and clients. This is arguably the most important resource as it provides creativity and ingenuity, but it is also the most difficult resource to manage effectively.

3 **Raw materials and services**—these represent the basic inputs required for the resource conversion process. Some of these inputs, eg components, sub-assemblies and energy, may be used directly in the production of the products or services. Others, eg catering facilities and professional auditing services, provide a less direct contribution to the value-added process. These inputs will generally be acquired from other organisations and will require payment for the inputs supplied from the organisation's capital.

4 **Information**—inputs in this context relate to information which concerns the external environment (see 1.1.2). The organisation would also require information about the three other categories of resource inputs outlined above. For example, information on the potential sources of capital available and their respective costs; the availability of particular skilled people and the costs of recruiting and retaining them; and the alternative sources of particular materials or services and their relative merits in terms of quality, costs, delivery etc.

1.2.2 Activities

The activities of the organisation can be broadly divided into two: **primary activities** and **support**

activities. The support activities will be covered in the next sub-section related to organisational infrastructure.

Primary activities are those which are directly concerned with the production and delivery of the product or service to the customer or client, including:

1 **Inbound logistics**—purchasing, goods receiving, quality inspection, warehousing and stock control of materials, and acquiring the necessary services;
2 **Operations**—those activities involved in the conversion of the resource inputs into the desired products or services;
3 **Marketing and sales**—market research, promotion, advertising and selling activities;
4 **Outbound logistics**—quality inspection, warehousing, packaging, and either the delivery and installation of finished goods or the supply of the given service; and
5 **Service and support**—provision of after-sales service and support activities including training, fault clearance and maintenance, etc.

1.2.3 Infrastructure

Support activities are those not directly involved in the production process, but which play an essential role in facilitating and supporting the primary activities outlined above, and which contribute to the overall value added process. These support activities have been classified into four broad groups in Figure 1.2:

1 **Procurement of resources**—this includes the development of policies, procedures and guidelines for the acquisition of resources, as well as the purchasing of materials and services, raising finance, and the recruitment of personnel.
2 **Technology development**—the research, development and design of new products, manufacturing processes, and information systems.
3 **Human resource management**—the development of policies, procedures, structures and systems for the training, management and control of human resources within the organisation.
4 **Organisation infrastructure**—the preparation of strategic plans and corporate policies to meet the desired objectives; the development and implementation of appropriate organisation structures; and decision-making, planning and control systems to achieve these.

It should be recognised that these support activities provide as important a contribution as the primary activities to the effective and efficient operation of the organisation, even though they are not directly involved in the production operations.

1.2.4 Tools and techniques

A wide range of tools and techniques have been developed to assist decision-makers at all levels in the organisation with those activities related to analysis, decision-making, planning, scheduling, and the monitoring and control of the resources and operations of the organisation. In some cases, these techniques have been transformed into routine operating procedures and guidelines, while in other cases, the decision-maker is required to apply the technique or tool to a particular situation. Examples of the former would include quality control procedures and stock control guidelines, while the latter would include capital investment appraisal decisions and product pricing policies.

It is important to recognise that all of these tools or techniques demand that information inputs operate effectively and, in most instances, the quality of the information input is a critical determinant of the potential quality of the decisions taken. Information is also required to provide the decision-makers with appropriate feedback on the effects of their decisions.

1.2.5 Resource outputs

As explained earlier in this chapter, the purpose of any organisation is to produce some form of resource output. The precise nature of the resources output, in terms of goods or services, and the recipients of these resources will depend on the nature of the organisation and its purpose. It is possible to identify four broad groups of recipient for the organisation's resource outputs:

1 **Customers or clients**—typically they receive tangible products or services, and provide some form of payment in return to the organisation. The exception to this may be the case of charitable and many not-for-profit organisations, where the clients provide no compensation for the products or services received.
2 **Owners or shareholders**—in the case of profit-orientated organisations, the shareholders or owners would expect to receive a share of the profits generated by the operations. In the case of not-for-profit, the subscribers or owners may be satisfied with the knowledge that their financial contribution has provided some assistance to the organisation's cause.
3 **Employees**—in any organisation those employed would expect rewards for their contribution either in the form of financial payments and/or non-financial elements, eg job satisfaction.
4 **Society**—the state as a whole may benefit from the resources produced by organisations through either the increased wealth generated or the benefits created from the services provided by the organisation.

1.3 ORGANISATIONAL LINKAGES

A further feature inherent in the conduct of both the primary and secondary activities is illustrated in Figure 1.3. These are termed the linkages between the various activities. Only a few of the many linkages which may exist between particular groups of activities have been shown in the diagram. An example of the more obvious linkages between the primary activities (linkage 1 in the diagram) would be the marketing and sales activities which provide information both on future demand to the production activities and on the earlier activities involved in inbound logistics. A second example (linkage 2 in the diagram) may be the feedback of information from the customer service staff to the purchasing and quality inspection activities (inbound logistics) as to the incidence of faults on particular components in the product during its use. There would also typically be a number of linkages between the support activities and the primary activities (eg linkage 3 in the diagram where developments in the manufacturing technology resulting from the organisation's research and development activities may have implications for all of the primary activities). There are also linkages between the different groups of support activities (eg linkage 4 in the diagram shows that the changes in manufacturing technology would clearly have implications for the management of human resources, in particular the staff training elements).

An important aspect of the model presented is that the particular types of activities within each block may vary between organisations, and certainly the importance and number of linkages between different activities will vary depending on the particular nature of the organisation and its operations. Moreover, while there may be similarities between different organisations in terms of the primary activities, secondary activities and linkages between them, it should be recognised that each organisation is likely to have a unique configuration of these components. The exact configuration of the components in a particular organisation will be a function of a variety of factors including the scale of the organisation, the nature of the product and production processes involved, the type of technology employed, the nature of the market and its competitive situation, the previous history of the organisation, and the personnel employed. In addition to this potential uniqueness of organisational configuration, the rate and direction of change in this configuration is likely to differ between organisations.

The important conclusion for those engaged in information systems development is that there is no standard information system that may effectively be applied to all organisations. The essence of information systems development is therefore tailoring the information systems to meet the needs of each individual organisation and to suit each organisation's configuration.

1.3.1 Information flows and systems

The previous division of an organisation into a number of discrete groups of activities or functional units, each having the necessary linkages between them to achieve effective and efficient operations, is of particular importance in the development of information systems. In essence, the information

FIGURE 1.3 **Key elements of an organisation: linkages**

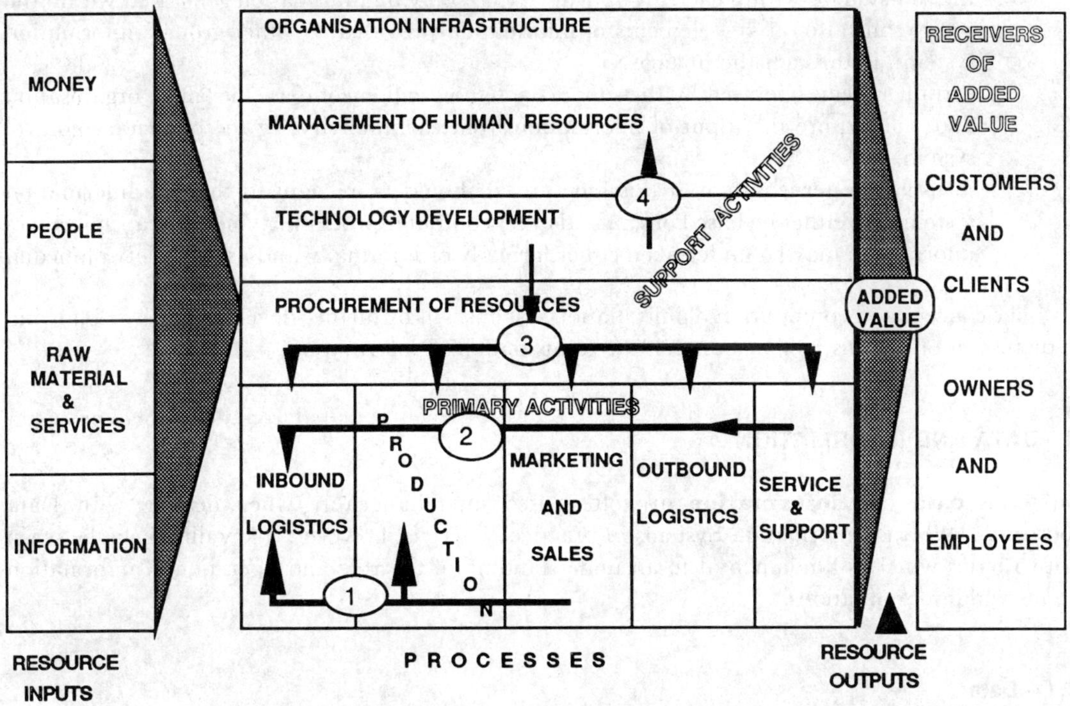

FIGURE 1.4 **Key elements of an organisation: information systems**

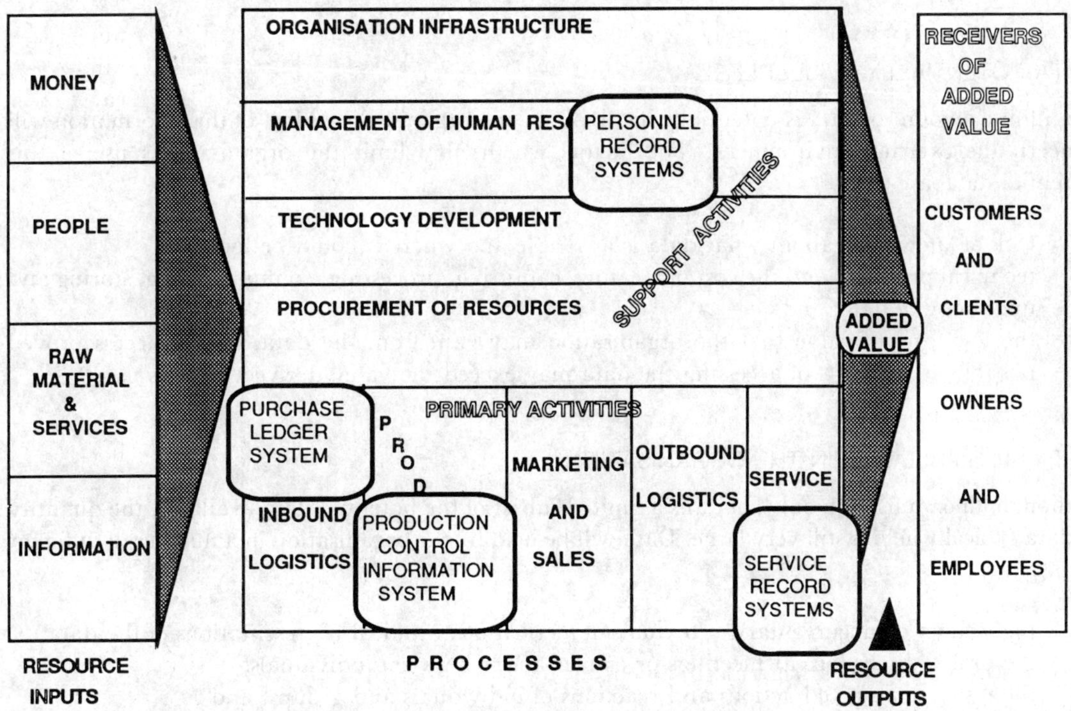

system in an organisation could equally be mapped on to Figure 1.3 or on to Figure 1.4. Again, for the sake of clarity, only a few examples of the information systems within an organisation have been shown in the diagram.

The essential features of this model of the information systems are that:

(a) each of the primary and support activity groupings will develop their own information system which will be sufficient to support the operations of that activity;

(b) within each of these groups there will be a number of information sub-systems;
(c) the sub-systems within each group will rely not only on information generated within the group, but also on key elements of information provided by other groups' information systems, ie through the linkages;
(d) certain systems operated by the support activities will encompass the whole organisation and will require the input of information from each activity, eg the budgetary control system; and
(e) in using the term system at this juncture, it should be recognised that the information system may either be based on manual or on computer processing, and the transmission of information may be undertaken either formally or informally and use a variety of media.

The concept and composition of information systems will be further developed in 1.5, following the discussion on the distinction between the terms data and information.

1.4 DATA AND INFORMATION

The terms **data** and **information** are often used interchangeably when dealing with Data Processing (DP) and Information Systems in practice. There is, however, a key difference between the two terms which is fundamental to an understanding of the role and operation of information systems within organisations.

1.4.1 Data

The term **data** refers to the complete range of facts, events, measurements, opinions and value judgments, etc that exist both within and outside the organisation. It is possible to classify data within an organisational context into a number of different categories or levels, as illustrated in Figure 1.5.

DATA POTENTIALLY AVAILABLE

An infinite amount of data is potentially available to any organisation. Most of this information will concern the external environment. The factors which may limit the organisation's use of this potential database are:

1 lack of knowledge about what data is available and where it could be located;
2 technical problems and the cost of locating, capturing, processing, communicating, storing and updating the data; and
3 the low level of value that the organisation may gain from the data, even if access proved possible, ie the costs of accessing the data may exceed the value derived from its use.

DATA AVAILABLE WITHIN THE ORGANISATION

Although an organisation only contains a limited subset of the potential data available, the quantity of data typically held is still very large. Data will be held by the organisation in a number of different forms:

1 the written or documentary—textual, numerical or graphical representations of the data;
2 the oral—discussions at meetings or conversations between individuals;
3 the visual—observed actions and reactions of individuals and groups; and
4 the subconscious—knowledge, experience and opinions of the individual members of the organisation, which they may apply in conducting their roles and activities within the organisation.

DATA RECORDED WITHIN THE ORGANISATION

Only a proportion of the data available within the organisation will be formally recorded and processed within the data processing activities. The reasons for this are identical to those identified

FIGURE 1.5 **Schematic view of data and information**

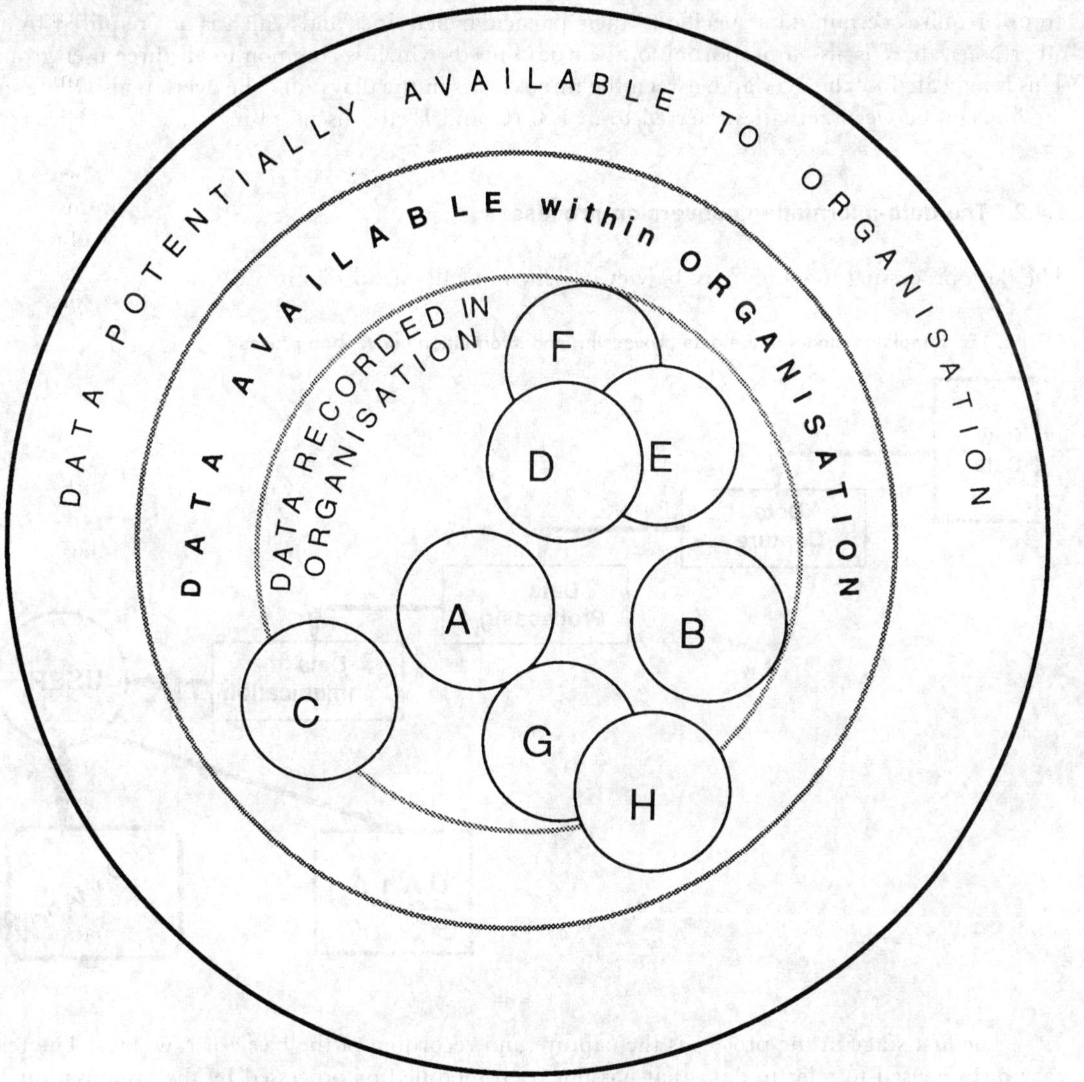

above for the organisation's limited use of the total potential database available. While the most common media for recording data is the written form, there are situations where a particular organisation may find it valuable to record oral and visual forms of data. For example, it is common practice for organisations trading in financial securities to record all staff telephone conversations, as the majority of the organisations' business is conducted over the telephone and this provides evidence of the terms and conditions of contracts made or of insider dealing. Other organisations may exploit video recording equipment either for security monitoring or for monitoring production operations. Typical examples of potentially valuable data held in written or graphical form within an organisation would include:

(a) the quantities of products sold during each month,
(b) the stock levels of particular products,
(c) the minutes of meetings held by staff at all levels,
(d) a full employee profile including age, salary and employment records and skills,
(e) reponses to consumer research surveys, and
(f) forecasts of future market demand.

In Figure 1.5, the groups of activities or users represented by the circles A and B indicate the uses of data which are formally recorded in the organisation. Group C indicates the use of some data which is formally recorded together with other data available within the organisation, but which is not formally recorded, eg as expertise personal to individuals. A more common situation in practice would be that represented by the user groups D, E and F. This indicates that while each of these user groups requires certain data specific to their particular activities and which is not required by the other users, there is also a proportion of their data needs which is common to all three user groups. This is indicated by the overlap between the three circles in the diagram. The overlap also represents the linkages between activities referred to in 1.3. (G and H are discussed in 1.4.3.)

1.4.2 The data-information conversion process

The data processing function may be viewed schematically as in Figure 1.6.

FIGURE 1.6 **Simplified model of the data processing and information conversion process**

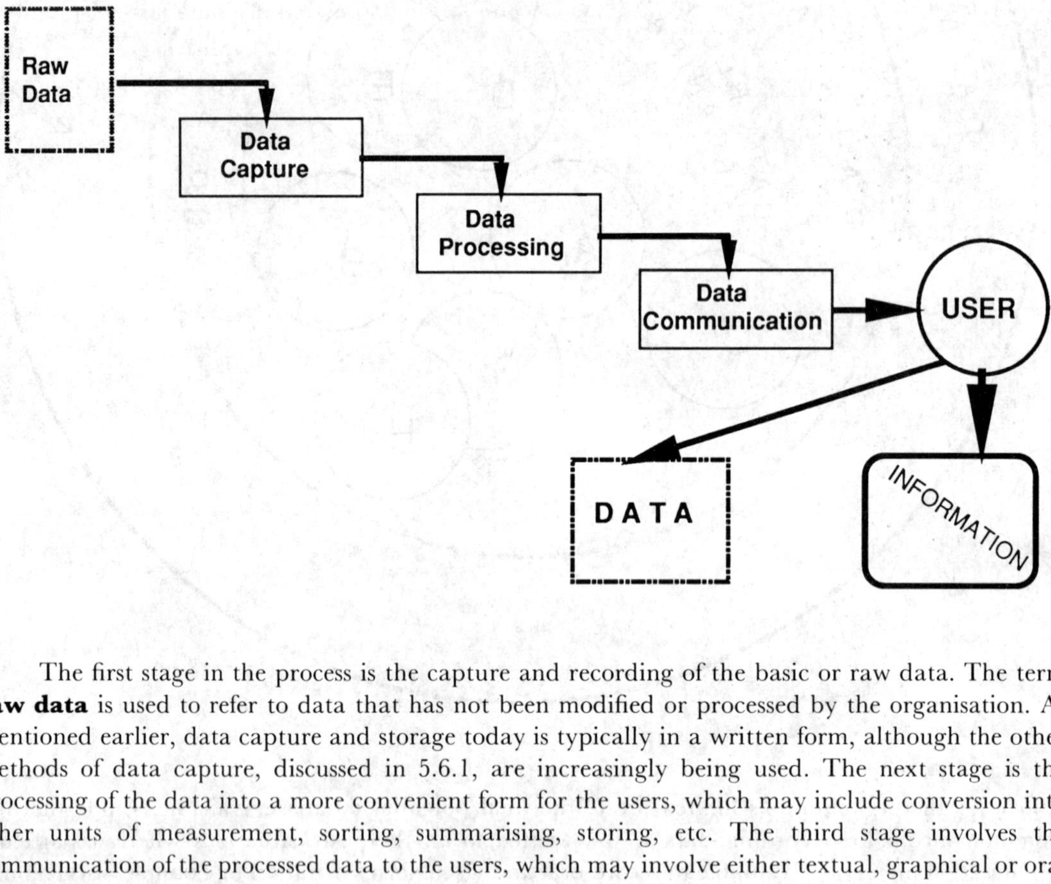

The first stage in the process is the capture and recording of the basic or raw data. The term **raw data** is used to refer to data that has not been modified or processed by the organisation. As mentioned earlier, data capture and storage today is typically in a written form, although the other methods of data capture, discussed in 5.6.1, are increasingly being used. The next stage is the processing of the data into a more convenient form for the users, which may include conversion into other units of measurement, sorting, summarising, storing, etc. The third stage involves the communication of the processed data to the users, which may involve either textual, graphical or oral methods of communication. Up to this point, the process is still only concerned with data, although the process is developing the data into a form in which it can potentially become information. The general term applied to these activities is data processing.

1.4.3 Information

Information, as shown in Figure 1.6, can be viewed as a subset of the data held within the organisation. This indicates that although the data processing system delivers data to the user in a processed form, only a part of this data will be converted into information, the remainder being discarded by the particular user. In other words, all members of an organisation will receive a stream of data inputs in the form of instructions, letters, statistics, internal memoranda, etc. A proportion of this data will be either filed away automatically and never referred to, or alternatively deposited in the waste paper bin. Only a proportion of the data received will be read, used or acted upon by the receiver and this would then be classified as information rather than data. Information is that part of the total data available which is appropriate to the requirements of a particular user or group of users. It should therefore be acknowledged that an effective information system would be one which minimised the amount of data passing through the hands of the user without becoming information, ie which reduced or eliminated the contents of the data box in Figure 1.6, and increased the contents of the information box.

Certain parts of the data may be appropriate to only one user in the organisation, as in the case of users A, B, and C illustrated previously in Figure 1.5. Alternatively, as in the case of users D, E, and F, parts of the data are appropriate or common to all three users while other data is specific to each individually. The third case illustrated in Figure 1.5 indicates that user H only requires part of the information that user G requires, even though they are members of the same activity group. This may represent, for example, the situation of the Chief Accountant as user H and the Payroll Clerk as user G. Further, it should be noted that user H, the Chief Accountant in this example, also relies on both formally recorded and unrecorded data from other sources in the organisation outside the accounting activity or function. It is also important to recognise that the way in which the data is presented to the various users may be different to suit their particular needs. Hence, the Chief Accountant may only require summarised statements of salary and wage expenditures, whereas the Payroll Clerk will require detailed data on each member of staff. However, neither the relevance of items of data to the user's situation nor the problem faced, nor the effectiveness of the data processing are, in themselves, sufficient to ensure the conversion of data to information. The other key element in the conversion process of data to information is the user or receiver of the data.

WHEN IS DATA INFORMATIVE?

The outline model of the data processing system (Figure 1.6) indicates that only a part of the data transmitted to the user becomes information. The remainder stays in the form of data and is essentially unused or redundant as far as the particular user is concerned. It is important to stress that this does not necessarily imply that the data is redundant for the organisation as a whole, but merely from the perspective of that particular user. However, the issue of **data redundancy** is of particular importance to the field of systems analysis and design, as high levels of data redundancy are often a consequence of poor quality systems design. If levels of data redundancy are excessive, it would also imply both higher than necessary data processing costs and potentially reduced quality of decision-making because the users may be required to sift through large volumes of superfluous data to find the appropriate information which they require to optimise a decision.

The conversion of data to information will occur when the data received by the user enhances his or her knowledge or understanding of a situation. For this to happen, the user would need to:

(a) recognise that the data received is relevant to their particular situation, and
(b) have a sufficient level of prior knowledge and experience to be able to use that data to enhance their knowledge and understanding.

Given that different users in an organisation possess different levels of prior knowledge and experience, it follows that the same data input received by such users will not always become information. Thus:

Data is only information to some of the people some of the time, and not to all of the people all of the time!

For example, consider the following data items:

1 0111
2 Net Present Value = – £360,000

What meaning is conveyed? The first item is the binary representation of the number 7, which would probably be understood by those familiar with the binary numbering system. The second item represents the result from a discounted cash flow appraisal of an investment, indicating that the investment concerned would generate a loss of around £360,000. Again prior knowledge or understanding of this particular approach to investment appraisal would convert this from an item of data to information.

Apart from the issues related to the user's prior knowledge, the conversion of data to information faces a number of other hurdles:

1 **The quality of source data** A basic issue related to the quality of the information received by the user concerns the quality of the initial data input into the system. If, for example, the data input is poor in terms of accuracy or detail, the resulting information received by the user will be of a similarly poor quality. No matter how good the data processing system is, it will never be able to compensate for poor quality data input. This lack of quality may result either from the quality of the data that is available to the organisation and over which it may have little or no control, or from defective data capture methods which are generally within its control. A common way of expressing this phenomenon is,

RUBBISH IN = RUBBISH OUT

2 **The processing activities** This refers to the various ways in which the data is manipulated within the data processing system, and includes both manual and mechanical/electronic activities. Despite the extensive development and application of electronic data processing technology, it should be recognised that there are still a significant number of processing activities carried out manually in any system. These manual activities are frequently the source of loss of quality in the data during processing, because humans are notoriously fallible when asked to undertake activities consistently and accurately. Although many of these manual activities are being replaced by automatic systems (eg electronic point-of-sale recording systems), it should be recognised that automatic systems may also lead to reductions in quality if they either malfunction technically, or their processing activities are poorly designed.

3 **Time** When the data is presented to the user, it may be inappropriate to the issues or circumstances facing the user at that particular time, but may become more appropriate at some future time. This issue of timing, in the sense of users being able to rapidly access the appropriate information as and when they require it for a particular aspect of their work, is a major reason for the development of large database storage systems and real-time computing facilities. This aspect of timing and the resulting issues of databases and real-time computing are discussed more fully in Chapters 5 and 7.

4 **Communications** In addition to the quality of presentation, the media used to communicate the data will also have an impact on the effectiveness of the data conversion process. In addition to the technical quality of the communications system, the use of printed documents, screen displays or voice communications may be more effective for particular users in particular situations.

5 **Presentation** The way in which the information is presented to the user may result in a failure to recognise the informative value of the data, eg if the data is poorly presented in terms of the quality of the layout or contains too much detail, the user may either miss the significant data or possibly abandon the task of searching for it in a mass of detail. The development of graphical and colour display systems provide considerable potential to improve the quality of the presentation.

6 **User interface** The quality of the interface between the user and the technology and systems providing the data, have a significant impact on the effectiveness of the conversion process. In essence, this concerns the ease with which users can use or interact with the technology to define their information needs and to receive the necessary information. This aspect is normally described as the user friendliness of the system, and is a critical feature of effective systems design.

In summary, the key factors which influence the effectiveness of the data to information conversion process are:

(a) the quality of the source data,
(b) the effectiveness of the processing activities,
(c) the quality of the communications,
(d) the degree of user friendliness in the interface,
(e) the level of accessibility in the presentation,
(f) the ability of the user to gain access to the information at the right time, and
(g) the adequacy of each user's knowledge, skill and expertise to make the best use of the data.

These factors will be discussed more fully in subsequent chapters dealing with the design and development of information systems.

1.4.4 The value of information

When considering the information received by each user, it is possible to attribute different levels of value to each piece of information. An example of how the value of information may be categorised is shown in Table 1.1. While the table does not attempt to cover every conceivable permutation of levels of understanding and relevance to the user's situation, it does illustrate that the value of information is a function of both the user's understanding and the relevance of the data to the situation. Thus, no matter how important it might be to the situation if it happened to be in the right hands, it will remain as data if it is not understood by the immediate user. Alternatively, where there is understanding, the greater the degree of relevance of the data provided to the user's situation and the greater the user's level of understanding of both the situation and the data provided, then the higher the information value that can be extracted from the data provided will be. This will be explored in more detail in Chapter 2.

TABLE 1.1 **Value of information: outline classification**

Level of user understanding	*Relevance/importance to user's situation*	*Information value*
None	None	⇒None remains as data
None	High	⇒None remains as data
Some	None	⇒Low value
Good	Some	⇒Moderate value
Good	High	⇒High value
Good	Critical	⇒Maximum value

1.4.5 What function does information perform?

Table 1.1 indicates that there are different levels of value in the information received. In essence, if users possessed perfect knowledge about each situation faced, then there would be no requirement for information. However, given that in the more typical situations faced by users, they have less than perfect knowledge, all relevant information provides the opportunity to improve the response to the situation. Within this broad role of enhancing knowledge, information may be considered to fulfil the following functions:

(a) the reduction of uncertainty in decision-making, though it ought to be recognised that more information may add other possible outcomes to a situation not previously considered, thus increasing the uncertainty;
(b) the provision of error signals which indicate any deviation from planned performance or operation, thus aiding control activities;
(c) the provision of a mechanism for the communication of plans, forecasts, procedures, guidelines, etc;
(d) the supply of historical evidence of transactions, levels of performance, results of decisions, etc; and
(e) the reduction of complexity through enhancing the user's knowledge and understanding of a situation.

PRESSURES FOR MORE INFORMATION

There have been a number of developments which have generated increased demands for data and information processing within most organisations. These include:

(a) Advances in processing technologies which improve the technical capacity to capture and process data which previously proved difficult or time consuming. For example, meteorologists are now able to capture data from weather satellites and to process weather patterns across the country within fractions of a second. Reference to Figure 1.5 earlier in this chapter will help to illustrate the effect of these developments. Organisations are becoming increasingly able to extend the volume of data formally recorded in the organisation (ie the inner circle is expanding outwards), as well as increasing their coverage of the data potentially available outside the organisation (ie the second circle is also expanding outwards).

(b) Improved methods of communication—the developments in communications technologies have provided increased scope for improved effectiveness in the distribution and exchange of information, both within and between organisations.

(c) Reduced costs of processing, storing, retrieving and communicating data. A consequence of the developments in the information technologies has been the significant reduction in the costs of processing a unit of data.

(d) Developments in information technology while making the technical operation of data processing inherently more complex, have also been directed towards improving the interface between the technology and the users. The primary objective has been to make the technology more user friendly, ie to make the use of the technology simpler and more adaptable to the style of normal human modes of operation and thought processes. A variety of devices including menus, graphical displays (icons), windows and the mouse, are all examples of developments to improve the user interface with the technology. These and other similar developments which are enhancing the use and hence the demand for information are discussed in more detail in Chapters 5 and 8.

(e) Increased complexity of the environment within which organisations operate and in which decisions are made. Decision-makers now need to consider a wider range of factors in making their decisions, which in turn generates a demand for greater information.

(f) In addition to the increasing complexity of the external environment, the increased scale and complexity of organisations themselves is creating a demand for more information. This has resulted from the increased scale of many organisations, their diversification into a number of different product/market sectors, the increasing specialisation of activities within the organisation's functions, and the development of alternative organisation structures to facilitate effective management and control of the organisation. It should be recognised that many business and commercial organisations operate on a multinational basis, extending the problems of management, control and communications across national boundaries.

(g) The improved knowledge, education and training of decision-makers and users of information have resulted in the demand for more comprehensive and detailed information to assist in their organisational activities. Associated with this development have been the significant improvements in the fields of management and organisational research, which have produced more comprehensive models to assist in the management and control of business organisations. Such models have resulted in the development of a range of tools and techniques to aid decision-making, which invariably require more comprehensive, more detailed and better quality information in their application.

(h) Greater demands have been made of the organisation to provide more information on its operations to outside agencies and regulatory bodies. For example, the disclosure of information to shareholders and employees has been significantly enhanced, as have the demands of the government in terms of its revenue, employment and statistical departments. It should also be acknowledged that many organisations have increased their disclosure of information independently of the mandatory requirements, because they have recognised the potential benefits to be gained from voluntarily providing interested parties (eg employees) with information about the organisation.

In summarising the above reasons for the increased level of data processing and information use within organisations, it is possible to reduce these to two primary causes:

1 the increased demand from users, both from within and outside the organisation, and
2 the developments in information processing technologies and their application to meet these demands.

While it may be interesting to speculate as to whether user demand or technological development is the primary motivating factor in increasing information usage, it is inappropriate to the current discussion. Subsequent chapters of this text will engage in a more detailed exploration of user needs and demands for information, the developments in the information technologies and, more particularly, the methods for attempting to ensure the successful application of the technology to meeting the users' information needs.

1.4.6 Information as a tactical resource

More recently, information has increasingly been recognised both as a key tactical and strategic resource in the organisation, and as a significant source of potential added value (for a full development of the distinction between the terms tactical and strategic see 2.7). This has always been true of information as it provides a source of competitive advantage in the business context. For example, up-to-date information on the prices charged by competitors for their products and services will enable an organisation to respond rapidly with its own price changes. If effectively communicated to potential customers, this may give the organisation an advantage over other competitors whose pricing information is less up-to-date. But the real change that has occurred and that enhances the potential value of information, is the ability of the organisation to exploit more fully this source of advantage through the use of the new technologies. Thus, price lists and brochures can be amended instantly using desk top publishing facilities, and the high quality results sent by post or fax to a hit list of addresses culled from a selective database search for prospective buyers.

Information is an invaluable resource in supporting the short-term tactical decisions involved in the on-going operations of the organisation. For example, in the food retailing business it has long been recognised that an important source of advantage over competitors and of ensuring higher profits, is up-to-date information on demand for individual products. This enables management to improve their demand forecasts and ordering policies to ensure that fast selling items are always in stock and that slow selling items are either withdrawn or reduced in quantities stocked, thereby providing more shelf space for the faster moving products. A key performance variable in food retailing is the sales revenue and profit per square metre. Previously, a supermarket with over 1,000 product lines in stock would find it both time-consuming and expensive to monitor the stock levels of each item regularly, as this would involve the manual counting and processing of the data prior to taking decisions. The development of electronic tally systems and, subsequently, Electronic Point-of-Sale (EPOS) systems now provides store management with accurate data on the current stock levels and sales volumes of all items at any time during the day. This provides the management with the necessary information on which to make decisions which may gain an advantage over their competitors. EPOS, in addition to improving information on stock movements, also increases the flexibility and speed with which the organisation can change its product prices in relation to demand patterns and competitors' prices.

There are, however, a number of potential problems associated with the potential tactical and strategic benefits of improved information, including:

1 The scale of such an advantage will tend to narrow as other competitors introduce similar technology and gain access to information of similar quality.
2 The costs of providing the information need to be offset against the benefits gained from increased revenues and profits and reduced operating costs.
3 The provision of improved quality of information to the management is no guarantee that the quality of the resulting decisions will be sufficient to maximise the potential competitive advantage.

Important points from this example are that:

1 Information technology merely provides an opportunity to gain competitive advantage and improve operational efficiency, it does not guarantee results.
2 There are significant costs associated with the application of information technology, not only in the equipment used, but in its application and implementation within the organisation.
3 The potential advantages that information technology offers are available to all organisations including competitors. Thus the real advantage to an organisation necessarily arises from both

the successful initial implementation and from the sustained management development of that information system within the organisation.

4 Investment in the better information systems will produce the process and supply of data which can be the source of better quality information, but there can be no guarantees of success through better decisions. The quality of management decision-making ultimately depends upon the skill and experience of the employees and upon their ability to use the information system effectively.

These issues will be further developed in subsequent chapters of this text.

1.4.7 Information as a source of added value

Information also provides a potential source of added value to the clients and customers of the organisation. The term added value in this context refers to the bundle of consumer needs and aspirations that the product or service is intended to satisfy, ie the value to be derived by the consumer from the product or service. The consumer will normally be seeking a product or service which will provide the greatest value for the least cost. The organisation must therefore seek to identify these perceived sources of value and to find ways of adding to the product or service's total value while still making a profit. For example, the following sources of information may be exploited both in the medium-term (tactical), and in the longer-term (strategic), situations:

(a) Information on consumers' needs and their opinions on the organisation's current products and services could lead to improvements in product design. Market and consumer research studies together with capturing the data held by sales personnel may provide this information.
(b) Information concerning the current developments in materials, design and process technologies could lead to improved product design and quality.
(c) Quality may also be enhanced through improved communications between customer service staff and the product design and manufacturing functions, highlighting problems and defects encountered in installation and operation in the field.
(d) Improved information flows between the sales and manufacturing functions may improve forecasting and production scheduling activities, resulting in reduced delivery times.
(e) The availability of better quality information to management concerning the operations of the business may lead to better resource allocation decisions and greater efficiency, with consequent reduction in costs, improvement in profit margins, and potential reductions in product prices.

These are some examples of the ways in which information may provide added value to the customers of the organisation, resulting in greater customer satisfaction and potentially enhanced market share and profitability for the organisation.

1.4.8 Information as a strategic resource

In addition to the short- and medium-term contribution to the organisation, information also provides a significant contribution to the strategic development of the organisation. Strategically-orientated components of the organisation broadly look towards the markets of the future, and usually plan over a timescale of the next five to seven years. Planning on this timescale obviously entails higher levels of uncertainty and risk, but if the management can maintain the quality of their information about potential developments and trends in the external environment, this will assist in reducing, though not eliminating, the risk elements. Equally, the availability of techniques and packages to produce rapid evaluations of the likely impact of alternative scenarios and forecasts, or to simulate the business and market operations of the future, will provide the potential for improved strategic decisions. (For more detail, see Chapter 2.)

Information provides an organisation with potential sources of:

(a) improved efficiency in resource usage,

(b) cost reduction,
(c) added value,
(d) competitive advantage,
(e) improved effectiveness,
(f) enhanced profitability.

1.5 INFORMATION SYSTEM—AN OUTLINE MODEL

An **information system** may be broadly defined as a series of inter-related activities concerned with the capture, processing, communication and conversion of data to information. The main groups of activities in an information system are shown in Figure 1.7, and are briefly described below.

1.5.1 Situation or problem

An information system is typically concerned with providing data on a particular situation or problem of concern to the user or organisation. Some systems will be **permanent systems**, and will continuously and regularly collect data relating to a particular situation, eg a sales order processing system will continually provide data on the organisation's sales. Other systems, **transient systems**, may be established in response to particular needs of the organisation or its users, and will continue to operate only while that need remains. An example of a transient system would be the collection of data concerning the effects of a disruption in the supply of key components due to an industrial dispute at the primary supplier.

It may often be the case that a transient system will be established on the basis of data provided by the permanent information system which identifies a particular problem requiring more detailed data and investigation prior to providing a solution. In many respects, it would be preferable to design a system which already contained all the necessary data for particular problems that arise. However, it is clearly not possible to identify in advance the nature of all problems likely to be faced by the organisation.

1.5.2 Data

As observed previously, any situation will contain a wealth of data varying in terms of relevance to the user's particular needs and situation. An important element in the design of information systems is establishing clearly what the data needs are for each user and designing the system to effectively segregate the most relevant data from the less relevant or irrelevent data.

1.5.3 Data capture

Data capture concerns the processes of finding the relevant data, recording it and converting it into a suitable form for further processing and eventual communication to the user. For example, the doctor in seeking to diagnose the patient's illness uses a variety of devices to measure and identify the symptoms, eg thermometer, sphygmomanometer (for blood pressure readings), etc. The measurements are then converted to numeric values for further processing. It is evident that the quality of the measuring devices and the conversion processes used are crucial both to the quality of the data provided, and to the consequent diagnoses and remedial actions. This is equally true in organisations where the problems of measurement and diagnosis are often as complex as those facing the medical practitioner.

1.5.4 Processing

This term encapsulates a range of actions which may be performed on the data to improve its usefulness or utility to the users, and could include:

FIGURE 1.7 **Information system: an outline model**

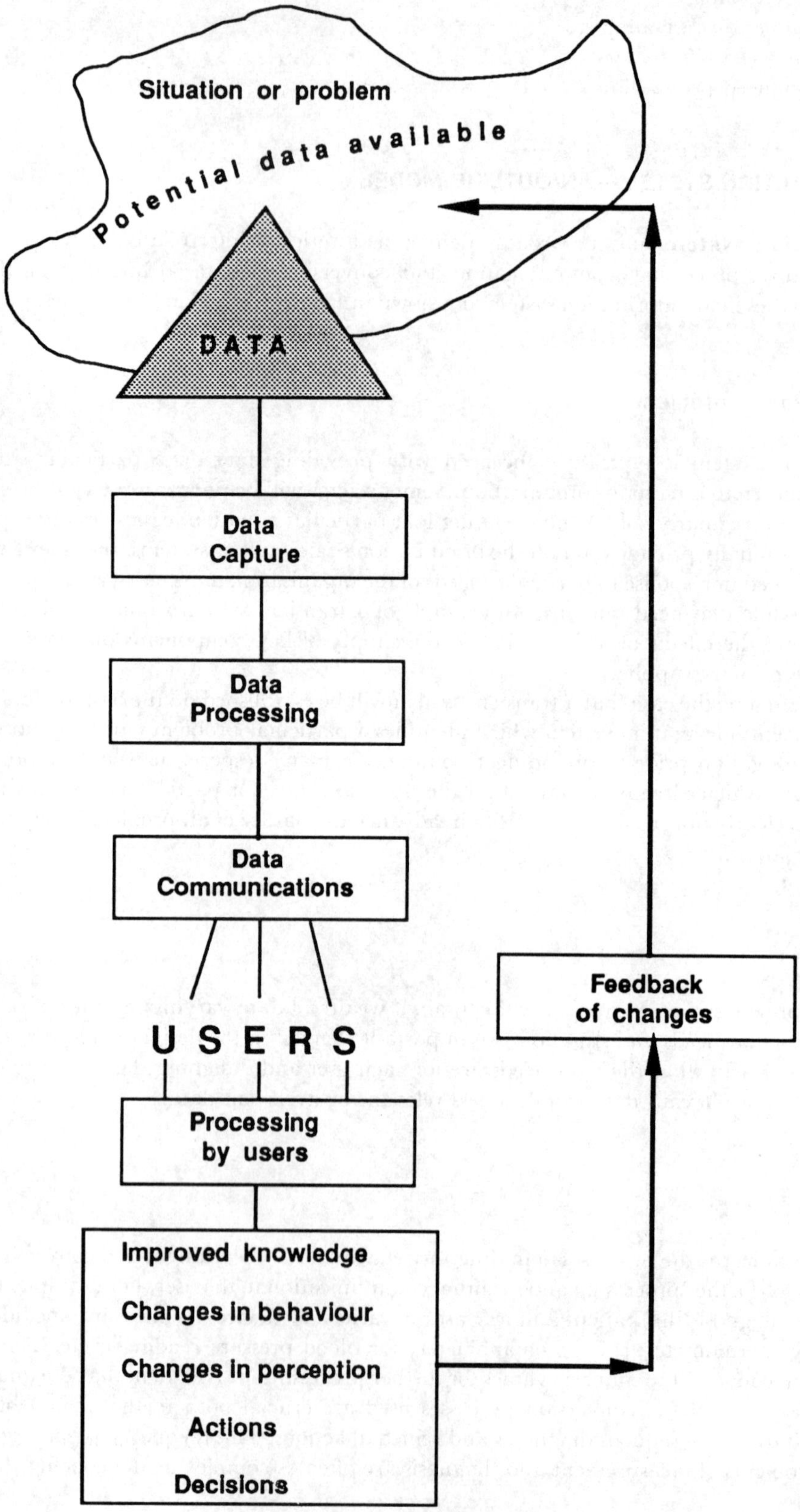

(a) **summarising**—reducing the level of detail,
(b) **arranging** or **sorting** into a more appropriate order, ie alphabetically or in order of size,
(c) **storing**—collecting the data until an appropriate volume has been acquired prior to transmission to the user,
(d) **calculating**—performing numerical calculations on the data, or converting them into more usable units, ie converting weights of inputs into monetary values,
(e) **selecting**—providing only those data items or events which meet a particular requirement, eg details on all financial transactions exceeding £10,000.

1.5.5 Communications

Communication of the processed data to the user is only part of the overall communications within the system, as communications are effectively taking place between each stage identified in the diagram. However, the communications with the users is the area which can be most clearly identified in practice. Communications with the human user may be by any of the human senses of sight, hearing, touch or smell, or indeed a combination of these senses simultaneously. The more usual forms of communication are visual and sound, as these senses are more fully developed and responsive in most individuals. However, individuals suffering sight or hearing handicaps often develop very responsive alternative senses to compensate for their loss of sight or hearing.

1.5.6 Users

The users are themselves a critical element in the overall information system. Not only are they the primary focus of the data processing activities outlined above, but they are the essential ingredient which converts data to information and information to action through the knowledge, understanding and skills which they bring to bear on the data provided. It is only at the level of the user that the information system actually provides benefit or value to the organisation, as prior to this the data processing has only been incurring costs.

USER PROCESSING

The users in any information system will themselves undertake further processing of the information received. In some cases, they will undertake processing activities along the lines outlined under the processing stage above, **primary processing**, ie calculating, sorting, selecting, etc. In other cases, the processing activities will be related more to interpretation, application to the specific circumstances, judgment and reasoning, etc, ie **secondary processing**. A good quality information system ought to minimise the amount of the primary level of information processing that the users are required to undertake, allowing them to devote their skills and time to the secondary level of processing. Developments in the field of the so-called expert systems are beginning to provide valuable support from the information system into this second level of user processing, particularly in situations where the user applies a logical sequence of rules or procedures in arriving at his/her decisions.

1.5.7 Outcomes

The end product of any information system must be represented in some form of outcome. The range of outcomes will vary and may include:

(a) actions or decisions,
(b) change in a situation, or change in either individual or group behaviour,
(c) improved knowledge and understanding,
(d) a change in the users' perception of a situation.

Ideally, the value of an information system ought to be measured in terms of the value of these outcomes. However, it is difficult to quantify the benefits derived from improved knowledge and understanding because such intangible improvements may not appear to provide any immediate ecomomic advantage, but may only be evidenced by implication through improved performance in future time periods.

1.5.8 Feedback

In the situations where the outcome of the information system is a specific action or decision, the user requires some means of assessing the effectiveness of the action or decision taken. This is achieved through the monitoring function of the information system which provides essential feedback of the results to the user. This feedback activity provides the necessary loop back to the start of the outline model of the information system. The sequence of stages is continually repeated with the capture, processing and communication of further data through the system, reflecting the changing situation and problems facing the organisation and its users.

1.6 INFORMATION TECHNOLOGIES

Information systems have been, and to a large extent continue to be, dependent on manual processing methods and procedures. However, the continuing development of technologies which have been applied to the processing of information in organisations, are increasingly revolutionising both the data processing and information systems. The major impact of these technologies today and in the future is derived from the convergence of the following technology areas:

1 computer hardware,
2 computer software, and
3 communications.

The developments in each of these technology areas have been very significant in the last decade. The most dramatic advances have been achieved through the increased potential for each of these areas to interact more effectively and efficiently with the others, thereby producing a synergistic effect, ie through convergence, the overall benefits derived have exceeded the benefits that would have been derived if the technological developments had taken place in isolation of each other.

The unstated fourth element in this synergy is the human dimension. While the developments in technology create the potential for more efficient and effective information systems, the realisation of this potential is dependent on the degree to which people are prepared to interact with, or use, the new systems. Unless organisations make adequate plans for the implementation of new systems, ie aim to re-orientate attitudes to changing work patterns through training and skill development, the actual changes in the structure and culture of organisations are unlikely to maximise the potential of the technology. Indeed, this fourth element may be the most important because it can often act as a constraint on realisation of the full potential of the developments made in the other three areas. Hence, a considerable proportion of the work involved in developing, implementing and maintaining information systems revolves around the interface between the human dimension and the other three technological dimensions, and a considerable proportion of this text will address these issues.

1.6.1 Potential benefits to be derived from the increased use of information technologies

(a) Improved efficiency in terms of time, human resource usage and costs, in all stages of data processing and transmission from the data source to the users.
(b) Improved quality of information, eg in terms of accuracy, level of detail, timeliness, etc.
(c) Greater flexibility and responsiveness to particular user needs, ie information systems may more readily be tailored to specific user needs.
(d) Increased access for users to all information sources within and external to the organisation.
(e) Increased efficiency through the sharing of common databases, either within the organisation or by using external database sources.
(f) An enhanced degree of user interaction to specify information and processing needs, and to review and modify these needs as the problem/situation develops or unfolds.
(g) Improved effectiveness of communications both between members of the organisation, and with outside organisations and agencies.

1.6.2 Dangers inherent in the increasing use of information technologies

(a) The ease with which data may be captured and stored may result in a less selective approach to identifying the information needs of users. Possible consequences of this are high levels of redundant data within the system, and the likelihood that users will be provided with large volumes of superfluous data, making the information system less effective.

(b) The apparently limitless capacity of the technology in terms of storage and processing may result in less cost-sensitive approaches to designing and using the information system.

(c) The sophistication and complexity of the interfaces with the users may be in advance of the skill and training levels of the personnel, resulting in reduced levels of total system effectiveness and efficiency.

(d) The functions of system design, development and maintenance are becoming increasingly specialist functions, with the potential danger that the specialists in such fields lose touch with the needs and expectations of the users.

(e) The enhanced potential for flexibility in designing systems for particular user needs may result in the loss of common standards and approaches within an organisation, thereby reducing the transferability of information processing skills within the organisation.

(f) Improved access to databases and information sources carries with it the major problem of security, ie limiting access to data that may be considered either sensitive or confidential, and preventing fraudulent transactions or deliberate acts of sabotage against the system.

(g) The decentralisation of user access and interaction with the processing and data sources also exacerbates the issues of the effective management of the total system. In earlier times, when all the processing of user data was physically handled by the computer operations staff, eg packs of punched cards in batch run systems, the computer services function could monitor directly the type and volume of activity taking place. Today, however, with users accessing central data sources from remote locations, and often processing the data at the remote location, the computer services function has less opportunity to monitor activity.

1.6.3 Thematic conclusions

Analysis of the potential benefits and dangers from the application of information technologies signals the following fundamental issues which underlie the approach adopted in this text:

(a) Development and design of information systems must integrate user needs fully with the technology available, ie system design should be user-driven and not technology-driven.

(b) System development and design should be planned and managed at the strategic, management and operational levels. Information systems development must be related to the organisation's objectives and incorporated within the strategic plans.

(c) To maximise the potential benefits and minimise the potential problems, the information system requires effective management at all stages in its development, implementation and continued operation.

(d) Information systems must reflect both the changes in the information technologies and the changing requirements of the organisation and its users. Hence, information systems need to be continually monitored and updated.

1.7 INFORMATION SYSTEMS DEVELOPMENT MODEL

Figure 1.8 provides an overview of the main areas and issues involved in the development, operation and maintenance of information systems within organisations. The model views information and the systems which deliver this information as key elements in the process of achieving organisational integration, which is essential to achieving general efficiency and effectiveness. The major features of this model are outlined in the following paragraphs, with more detailed treatment of each of the areas in subsequent chapters of the text.

FIGURE 1.8 **Information systems development model**

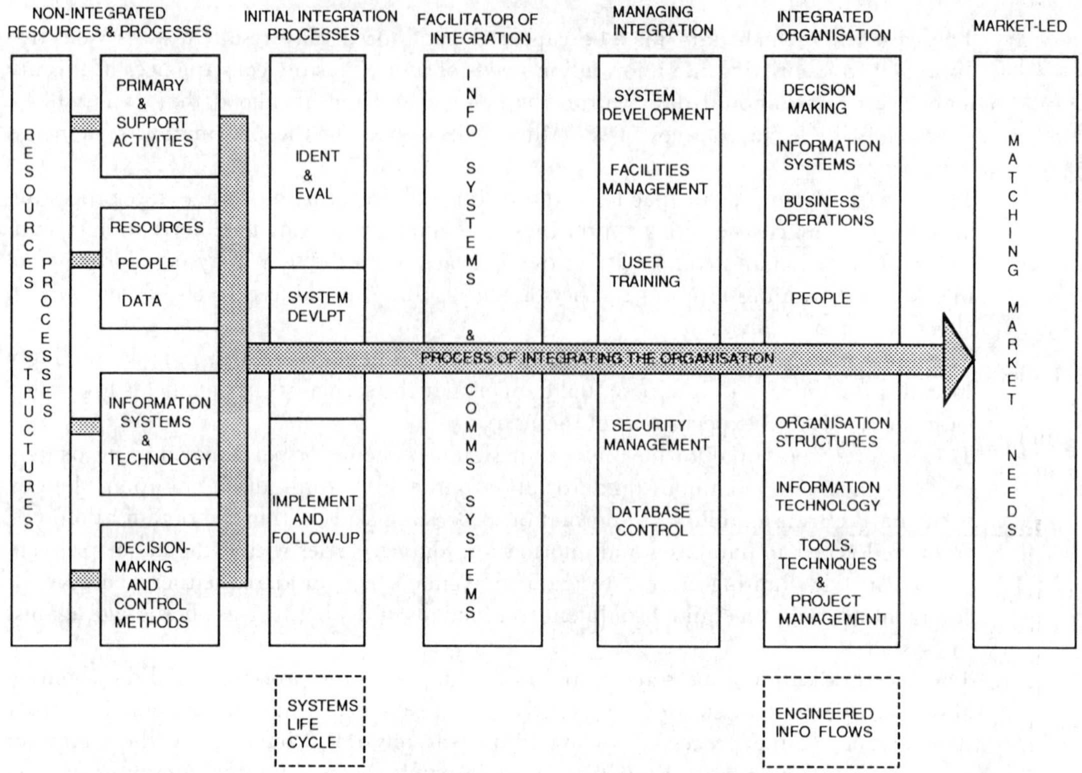

MARKET-LED

The primary purpose of any organisation is to meet the needs of its market or clients. This applies both to profit-orientated and to not-for-profit orientated organisations. The broad aim of all management is to produce an optimised organisation in terms of structure, resources and operations to achieve effectiveness and efficiency in meeting the needs of the market and in satisfying the purposes and objectives. The primary function of an information system in this context is to support the organisation, its management and employees in meeting this broad aim.

An important point to note at this stage, is that the strategic development of information systems should be primarily dictated by the needs of the market, the organisation's objectives, and the requirements of the users within the organisation. The systems development strategy should not be dictated by the developments in the information technologies themselves, as such developments may not be consistent with the needs of the market, the organisation or its users. There are many examples of organisations which have based their systems development strategies on current technological developments, only to find that the organisation has performed less effectively and efficiently. In many cases this is due to the technology being in advance of the capacity of the organisation or its users to employ or apply the latest facilities effectively.

NON-INTEGRATED RESOURCES AND PROCESSES

An organisation essentially comprises a series of resources, processes and structures.

1 **Resources**—comprising finance, people, land, buildings, equipment, raw materials, and technical and professional services.
2 **Processes**—a range of activities, classified earlier in this chapter as primary and support activities, encompassing the production operations, decision-making, planning and control. Organisations have developed a battery of procedures, tools and techniques to assist in these activities and in the general management of the processes and resources involved.
3 **Structures**—organisations also develop a variety of structures to improve the effectiveness and efficiency of the resource utilisation and the management of the processes. The more

obvious of such structures are the division of the organisation into specialist functions, each responsible for managing particular aspects of the organisation's resources and processes. Such structures may take a number of different forms as indicated in the detailed discussion of this in Chapter 2.

The key elements from these groups in terms of information systems development are:

(a) the needs of the primary and support activities,
(b) the resources available, ie people, data, etc,
(c) the management, control and decision-making requirements, and
(d) the information systems and the technology available.

1.7.1 Initial integration processes

The initial stages in achieving organisational integration involve the development and design of the organisation's information systems.

1 **Identification and evaluation** The analysis of the organisation's information requirements is the first stage in the integration process. It is important that this process is focused on the actual requirements of the individual users or groups of users, as opposed to merely assessing their likely requirements. Indeed, the whole process of systems development needs to be orientated towards user requirements from the outset, and should actively involve users in the overall process. This links to the key areas identified in the previous paragraph of understanding the needs of the primary and support activities, the management and control requirements, and the people in the organisation.

2 **Systems development** Generally, the systems development process is concerned with matching user requirements with the potential of the technology and the data available in the most effective and efficient manner possible.

3 **Implementation and follow-up** The inclusion of this stage in the integration process recognises both the importance of the initial implementation of an information system or sub-system, and the need to continually review the effectiveness of the system once operational. An earlier section of this chapter highlighted the dynamic nature of the environment in which organisations operate. In this situation it is likely that the issues and problems faced by the organisation and its members will be subject to a process of continual change, resulting in changing information requirements.

4 **Systems life cycle (SLC)** The process of change in the situation, issues and problems facing the organisation also suggests that an information system will only have a limited life-cycle. The SLC concept, which is discussed in detail in Chapter 6, reflects this point, suggesting that the value of the contribution made by an information system will change as time progresses and the situation changes.

5 **Facilitating integration** The development of information and communication systems within an organisation provide the potential to achieve integration. These facilities create the opportunity for the effective exchange and flow of information between users, and between the organisation and its environment.

6 **Managing integration** While the development of information and communication systems provides the facilities for potential integration, the realisation of this potential requires that these systems are effectively managed. There is an important functional responsibility for the overall planning, development, management and maintenance of these systems. This relates not only to the computer facilities and the software, but also to the overall management of organisational data and information flows, system security, and training and support of users.

1.7.2 The integrated organisation

The outcome of the integration process based on the information systems development will be an integrated organisation, in which:

(a) problems and issues are identified at an early stage;

(b) relevant information may be accessed easily and quickly to analyse such decisions, and the decision-maker has the necessary decision support tools to aid in this analysis;
(c) decisions can be taken quickly and effectively on the basis of high quality information;
(d) effective communications structure enables the involvement of all appropriate people in the decision-making process;
(e) decisions are communicated quickly and effectively in terms of new policies, guidelines, etc, allowing speedy response to problems that arise;
(f) activities in diverse parts of the organisation are co-ordinated more effectively with each other;
(g) the organisation is receptive and responsive to change, and new systems, processes and structures may be developed and implemented rapidly and effectively in response to changing needs; and
(h) performance measurement systems are sufficiently responsive and accurate to identify early deviations from planned performance levels or objectives.

The key to the achievement of an integrated organisation is effective information systems development, supported by continuing maintenance and sympathetic management. The achievement of this requires support and commitment from all members of the organisation.

SUMMARY

The key points covered in this chapter are that:

1 The primary purpose and objectives of an organisation relate to satisfying the needs of their customers and clients.
2 Organisations operate in a complex environment which is subject to continuous change, and which poses new threats and opportunities.
3 The role of management is to integrate resource inputs, activities, processes and structures both effectively and efficiently while maximising the added value to the customer.
4 Information systems provide a key role in facilitating the integration process and in supporting management.
5 Information itself is a key resource for tactical and strategic decision-making, and is a potential source of added value.
6 Information technology is essentially a convergence of technological developments in computer hardware, computer software and communications, which constructively interwork and interact with the potential information users in the organisation; and
7 Effective information systems are user-orientated rather than technology-orientated.

QUESTIONS *Solutions to questions of an examination standard start on p 395*

Write brief notes on the following:

(a) the purpose and objectives of an organisation;
(b) the added value process;
(c) the characteristics of data and information;
(d) the use of information as a strategic resource.

Questions of an examination standard

1 The objectives formulated by an organisation will be affected by a number of factors which will be particular to that organisation and its operations.

Briefly describe FIVE dimensions which may impinge on an organisation when formulating its objectives.

2 An information system may be defined as a series of inter-related activities concerned with the conversion of data to information.

Briefly discuss an outline model of this conversion process.

3 The continuing development of technologies are increasingly revolutionising both the data processing and management information systems.

Discuss the potential benefits and dangers from the increasing use of information technologies.

Chapter 2
Information Usage Within the Organisation

CHAPTER OBJECTIVES

Information has been identified as a key resource within the organisation. This chapter focuses on the information resource and the contribution which it makes to the operations and processes performed by the organisation. Initially, the concern is primarily with the identification and evaluation of the uses of this resource, and of the way in which the nature and quality of the information required varies with the type of usage. Subsequently, attention will be directed towards the influence that the organisation's structure and culture have in dictating the quantity and quality of the information resource required, and its usage. This chapter seeks to:

1 identify and evaluate the usage of information within an organisation, and recognise the reasons for information processing activities;
2 outline the commonly observed stages in the decision-making process;
3 examine the differences between the decision-making levels in organisations, and to highlight their differential information requirements;
4 identify the qualitative dimensions of information and relate these to the needs of the decision-making levels;
5 provide an outline description and evaluation of commonly used generic, and the more situation-specific information processing systems and their role in supporting decisions in the organisation;
6 outline alternative organisation structures and to evaluate the implications of these structures for the effective and efficient usage of the information resource.

2.1 USES OF INFORMATION

The usage of information within any organisation may be divided into the following categories:

(a) recording transactions,
(b) decision-making,
(c) planning,
(d) performance measurement,
(e) control, and
(f) communications.

The way in which information is used in each of these activities is described in the following paragraphs.

2.2 RECORDING TRANSACTIONS

The overall process of producing and delivering goods or services to the customer or client may be viewed as an interdependent sequence of transactions or activities. In judging the nature of the process, the organisation cannot be viewed in the abstract. It must be seen as an integral part of the environment. Thus, the range of the transactions and activities encompasses both the relationships with external organisations and persons, and the internal operations of the organisation itself. Recording details of each of all these transactions is necessary for the following reasons;

1 It provides a way of evidencing the nature and content of the transactions with other organisations and individuals, including suppliers, customers, shareholders and employees. On some occasions, there will be positive legal duties to keep this information, eg a register of shareholders, but generally it is merely an advisable step and reduces the risks of a subsequent dispute resulting in doubt and being resolved against the organisation with poor records.
2 It allows the organisation to monitor levels of resource availability and usage at various stages in the production or supply process.
3 It potentially enables the organisation to identify the costs and revenues associated with each particular transaction or activity, and to attribute these to the final unit of production or service delivered to the customer or client.
4 After the event, it provides recorded evidence of the transactions for the purposes of accounting, auditing and, where appropriate, tax assessment.
5 The quality of the record keeping and of the way in which that data is used to image the organisation, ie to present or represent the organisation to the public, is one of the main methods of assuring the shareholders and other suppliers of capital about the safety and stewardship of their capital — this also applies to the state-based and nationalised organisations which may be considered custodians of capital from the public purse.

The process of recording transactions within an organisation may be divided between the primary and the support activities involved. The distinction between these two groups of activities was presented in 1.2.2 and 1.2.3. Figure 2.1 presents an outline schematic flowchart of the major sub-groups of primary activities conducted in an organisation.

The function of **transaction processing** is concerned with recording, processing and communicating data relating to the primary and support activities involved in converting input resources into goods and services to meet customer needs. The dimensions of this data include quantitative, qualitative and financial aspects.

2.2.1 Purchasing transactions

Every organisation has some degree of involvement in the activity of purchasing or otherwise legitimately acquiring resource inputs from outside sources. These inputs may be conveniently grouped under the headings of:

(a) materials,
(b) services,
(c) labour, and
(d) capital.

In all of these cases there will be some form of contractual or commercial transaction between the organisation and the supplier. It is necessary to record these transactions for the reasons outlined earlier, and to identify both the costs of the resources acquired, and the costs of making the transaction.

2.2.2 Resource stocks

The resources acquired through the purchasing activities will not always enter the first stage of the primary processing operations immediately and will be stocked until such time as they are required. In essence, stocks of resource inputs may be viewed as a buffer between the purchase transactions and the primary operations of the business. This helps to ensure continuity in the operations in the event of delays or interruptions in the supply of inputs. Stocks are also a reflection of the economic factors involved in the buying transactions as it may prove more cost-effective for the organisation to use its purchasing power to order large quantities on an infrequent basis at high discount rates and on longer periods of credit, than small quantities on a more frequent basis but less favourable terms.

Information concerning the current quantities and the changes in stock levels is important because:

FIGURE 2.1 **Transaction processing in the information system**

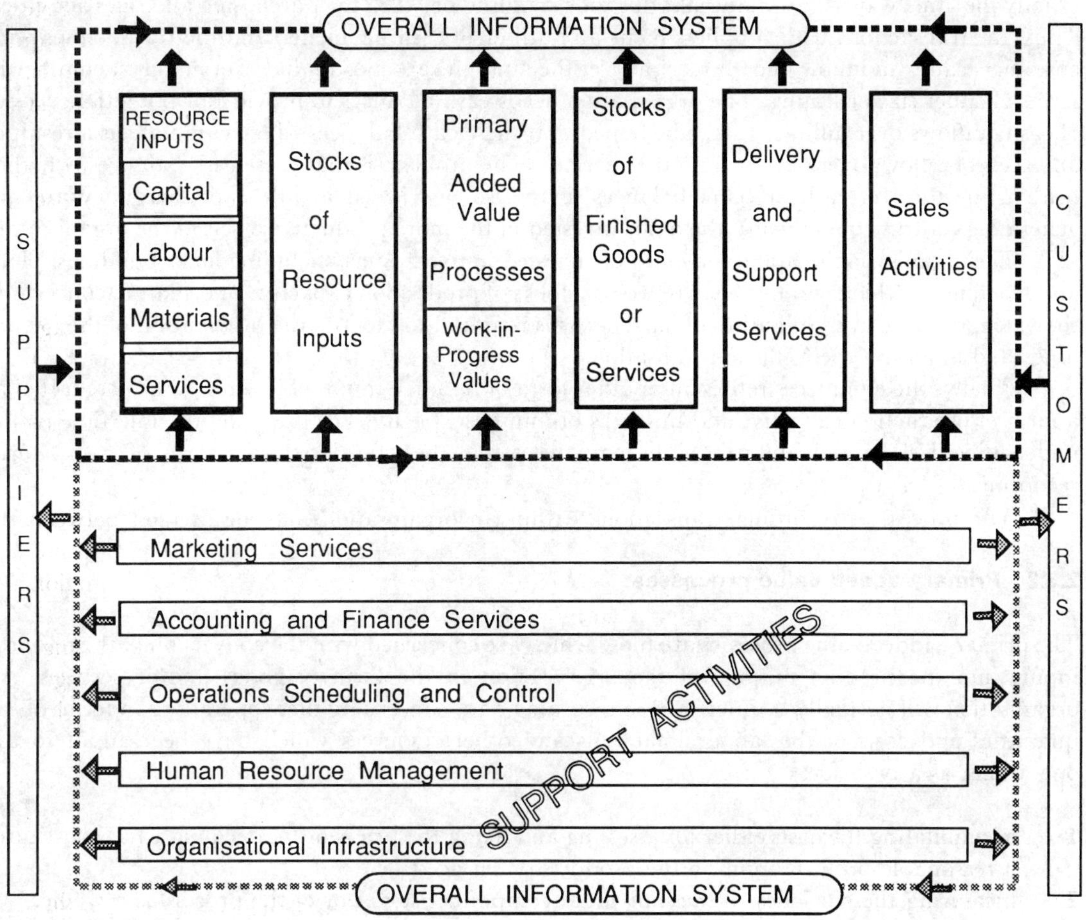

1 it enables the organisation to assess the quantity of particular items currently held in stock, and to trigger off the purchasing process when these levels reach some predetermined minimum level, set in the knowledge of the time usually taken to restock;

2 it provides an indication of the percentage value of the organisation's circulating resources held in that form, and of the cost of financing that investment; and

3 it allows the organisation to monitor the level of risk of dislocation to its functions and operations through the potential shortage of input resources.

Most organisations recognise the significant potential value of the capital resources invested in stocks. But this may equally be viewed as idle capital. The problem is that stocks represent an accumulation of resources and added value which the organisation has paid for, but which remain an unrealised investment. In addition to the direct financing costs involved in providing this idle capital, it may also be argued that there is an opportunity cost in terms of the return that could be generated from the capital if it were in more immediately productive use. As a result, close attention has been given to improving the efficiency of the purchasing transactions in terms of creating a continuous, regular and uninterrupted flow of inputs from suppliers. This may significantly reduce the level of investment in stocks of resources, reduce the financing costs and release capital for more productive purposes. An example of this in manufacturing industry is the just-in-time supply systems developed by the motor vehicle manufacturers. This involves a continuous flow of input components to the vehicle assembly plants such that only a few hours of key resource inputs are held in stock at any time by the manufacturer. The importance of information monitoring in respect of these flows and stocks of resources is obvious in such situations, particularly as such systems expose the production operations to higher risks of interruption due to delays in supplies.

The definition of resource stocks is not limited to materials and components used directly in the production operations. It must also include capital. Capital stocks may be represented by cash balances held in the organisation itself or in its bank accounts. These stocks represent a buffer in exactly the same way as raw materials, this time standing between the purchasing and sales activities. Thus, the transactions with suppliers incur an outflow of cash payments, and the transactions with customers cause an inflow of cash receipts, yet the amounts are most unlikely to match each other in terms of either size or timing. The organisation needs cash balances to provide for potential excesses of cash outflows over inflows. It is to be hoped that these cash balances will accumulate as a result of an excess of inflows over outflows at other periods. The problem is that these cash balances, whether held in the form of cash or bank balances, may also be viewed as idle capital as they are not generating returns equivalent to the funds invested in the more productive assets of the organisation.

The organisation's capital may also be invested in fixed assets, including land, buildings, plant and machinery, which cumulatively represent stocks of production capacity. Information concerning the value, location and utilisation of fixed assets is required to identify the distribution of the capital funds and to ensure their efficient utilisation.

Finally, the employees represent another form of resource input which may also be reflected as a form of production capacity, and in stocks of unused capacity. For example, the idle time or the under-utilised skills and abilities of the employees may be considered as a form of stock worth recording.

2.2.3 Primary added value processes

The primary added value processes are those which are concerned with the conversion of the resource inputs into the product outputs of the organisation in the form of goods and/or services. An organisation will normally be interested in recording data concerning these operations in terms of the quantities and costs of the labour, materials and other resources which have been input to the operations, as a basis for:

1 accumulating the costs either for assessing and fixing the prices or for deciding what constitutes a reasonable profit margin on the products or services;
2 measuring the efficiency of the individual component stages or of the process as a whole.

The type and quality of the information collected on this group of transaction activites will be determined by the nature of the production processes employed. These may be classified into three groups:

1 **Job processing**—this makes a single product unit the focus of attention. The organisation follows the production of a single identifiable item through each of the processing stages, creating the option that the costs of resource inputs used at each stage may be charged (recorded) directly to each item or job. Each job is usually allocated a unique reference number, ie Job Number, and will often be related to a specific customer's order.
2 **Batch processing**—identical product items are processed as a group through each of the processing stages. The products in each batch may be associated with the same customer's order or may relate to orders for several different customers. The usual reason advanced for batch processing is that there may be variations in the production operations required to produce either completely different products or variations on the same product design. The costs associated with preparing the machinery for each new product type or variation may make it more efficient to process a number of similar items before adjusting the machinery for the next type of product. It is clearly more efficient to paint all the blue cars consecutively before spending time in cleaning the spray gun and changing the paint supply to paint the red cars, as opposed to undertaking these operations after every car is sprayed if they are not batched in similar colour requirements. The data on the costs of those resources used in the production operations are collected and charged to each batch of items processed. The cost of individual items would normally be assessed from the average cost of the batch produced.
3 **Flow-line or process**—this represents situations either where all of the product output is the same, or where it is difficult and not cost-effective to separate the output into identifiable units. Examples include the manufacture of chemicals, nuts and bolts, and confectionary products, or the provision of banking services. Costs in such cases are usually averaged over the total volume

of output produced in a given time period. Efficiency measurements would also be related to the resource inputs required to produce a particular volume of outputs.

Different product costing systems have been developed to cater for each of these three types of production operations. In some organisations, it is likely that there will be a combination of two or more of these types applying to different stages of the total manufacturing or service supply process. The manufacture of mainframe computers, for example, may incorporate the following:

1 **Process**—the manufacture of small transistors, capacitors and other electronic components which are used in the computer hardware, will typically involve the production of a large volume of similar components.
2 **Batch**—the assembly of printed circuit boards containing these electronic components. The manufacturer will assemble a variety of boards in different quantities depending on the particular functions that each board is required to perform. Each board is likely to use the same basic components, albeit in different design configurations.
3 **Job**—the printed circuit boards, along with other components, will then be used to assemble the mainframe computer. Some computers may be made for stock, others may be made to order. Each of the computers which are being made to order is likely to vary in terms of the composition of boards and components, depending on the customer's particular requirements, though the scale and the nature of the assembly processes would enable each item to be identified and charged against each customer's order.

The mainframe computer manufacturer in this situation may be interested in the following types of information.

COST INFORMATION

This will be determined by reference to the following elements:

1 the cost of all the components used in assembling each computer, eg transistors, printed circuit boards, wiring, cabinets, etc;
2 the labour costs involved in each stage of the manufacturing and assembly process;
3 the time required on each piece of plant and equipment to assess the proportion of capital costs that it may be appropriate to allocate to the particular product;
4 the degree to which the organisation's support and other services are used as a basis for assessing the appropriate level of overhead costs to charge to each computer.

EFFICIENCY MEASUREMENT

The organisation will be able to assess efficiency by referring to the following types of performance indicator:

1 the quantity of those components wasted or rejected as faulty;
2 the labour and machine time taken for each stage of the assembly process, often measured against a pre-determined standard for the type of product;
3 the quantity of defects found in the finished computers which require correction or further working, and the cost of this work;
4 the percentage utilisation of plant and equipment capacity, and data on breakdowns of plant.

The value of the resources currently committed to the process of production, commonly termed work-in-progress, is also of importance in calculating the level of value added by the organisation. The valuation process for work-in-progress is equally applicable to both manufacturing and service organisations, with the latter requiring some assessment of the proportion which each task in hand represents of the total service provided at a particular stage in time.

2.2.4 Finished goods stocks

Products completing the phases of the production operations will usually become part of the finished goods stocks. As with the stocks of input resources, the finished goods stocks represent a buffer between the primary activities of the organisation and outside agencies. These agencies are usually the customers or clients of the organisation. The maintenance of such stocks is necessary to:

1 enable the organisation to respond quickly to customer requirements for particular products, which may represent an important element in the total service and added value provided to the customer;
2 provide for fluctuations in demand from the market, if the pattern of market demand is likely to be uneven due to seasonal effects or unexpected variations. Failure to maintain stocks may result in the loss of sales, particularly if the lead-times required to manufacture and deliver the products are lengthy;
3 maintain an even level of production activity or to ensure the full utilisation of production capacity.

As with stocks of input resources, information concerning quantities and the changes in stock levels is important in terms of:

1 assessing the quantity of particular items held in stock, and triggering off the production process to replenish stocks when these reach some specified minimum level;
2 providing an indication of the value of capital resources invested, and the associated financing opportunity costs;
3 monitoring the level of risk of dislocation to the organisation's sales operations and revenue generation should products or stimulus materials, eg catalogues and brochures, be out of stock.

Some organisations operate their activities on the basis of only producing goods to customer orders received, which would mean that every product in the production process is designated for a particular customer, eg shipbuilders. However, except in the most extreme cases, there are likely to be stocks of finished goods either awaiting completion of other goods in the same order, or awaiting delivery to the customer.

2.2.5 Delivery and support activities

From the customer's perspective, the most important features of an organisation's performance, apart from the quality of the product itself, are often the delivery, installation, maintenance and general after-sales support that goes with the product. The organisation will require information to monitor the costs, efficiency and effectiveness of these activities. For this purpose, the information requirements may include:

1 the delivery schedules, times, routes and transport costs;
2 if appropriate, the length of time required to install the product at a place selected by the purchaser or service receiver, and the level of any training provided to those who are to use the product;
3 the frequency and cost of maintenance or fault-repair visits to each customer site;
4 the nature of the problems encountered and the general quality of the after-sales support services provided.

2.2.6 Sales activities

In practice, sales activities may be involved at a number of different stages in the sequence of primary activities, with the agreement by the customer to purchase occurring early in the sequence, and post-delivery follow-up at the end. However, to simplify the model used and our discussion, all these sales activities are dealt with together at this stage. The sales activities reflect a series of transactions with the existing customers of the organisation, as well as its potential customers. Recording the details of the commercial transaction with the customer is important to the organisation because it provides information concerning the:

1 nature of the contractual rights and obligations incurred by both the seller and the buyer—this can be particularly important, say, if the selling organisation has attempted to protect its position by reserving ownership of the goods pending payment of the price by using a Romalpa clause;
2 specification of the customer's requirements which are to be met:
   (a) from existing stock,
   (b) by modifying existing stock,
   (c) through the primary production operations;
3 possible demand for resource inputs necessary to complete the order, and identification of shortages resulting from the satisfaction of the order which require replacement purchasing;
4 quantities, prices and discounts agreed to facilitate the preparation of accounting records and initiate other accounting and support activities;
5 where appropriate, the delivery destination(s), and any other arrangements for installation and training, etc;
6 purchase activities of the particular customer to assist the sales department's customer monitoring and progressing activities;
7 transaction itself for other external purposes including auditing and tax assessment.

The organisation will also be interested in measuring the costs involved in the sales activities, their level of efficiency and effectiveness.

The information system in aggregate terms for an organisation will be receiving data inputs from and transmitting to each of the six broad groups of primary activities. This data flow will be both concurrent and continuous across each of these groups. Figure 2.1 was designed primarily to highlight the overall transaction-based information system and its main components, and as such omits details of the essential information flows both between and within the groups. These inter-group and intra-group information flows represent the organisational linkages explained in Chapter 1. The examples earlier in this sub-section should indicate that the information flows occur not only between adjacent activity groups, but between all of the activity groups illustrated in the diagram.

2.2.7 Support activities

The other activities in an organisation which support the primary activities outlined above have been added to the primary activities in the previous diagram, as shown in Figure 2.2.

Some of the support activities in an organisation are involved in directly supporting the individual primary activities or the general operation of the organisation's affairs, while others are concerned with the more general aspects of planning, decision-making and performance measurement. These latter activities will be discussed under the corresponding headings later in this section. The activities involved in supporting the primary activities include:

1 **Marketing services**—because commercial organisations only survive by identifying and satisfying the market, it is debatable whether this is properly a support activity. It may be better to view it as a major part of the strategic planning effort of the organisation. However, pending resolution of this debate, the services comprise:
   (a) researching customer needs and market trends,
   (b) planning, implementing and controlling product development, distribution channels, pricing policies, advertising and promotional strategies and other similar activities associated with identifying and satisfying consumer needs.
2 **Accounting and financial services**—these are clearly support activities and include:
   (a) the routine recording of purchases and the arrangement of payment for resource inputs and services;
   (b) the raising of invoices for sales, controlling credit and progressing payment;
   (c) ensuring that adequate funds are available at the appropriate time to make wage and salary payments for the labour resources used;

FIGURE 2.2 **Transaction processing and the information system**

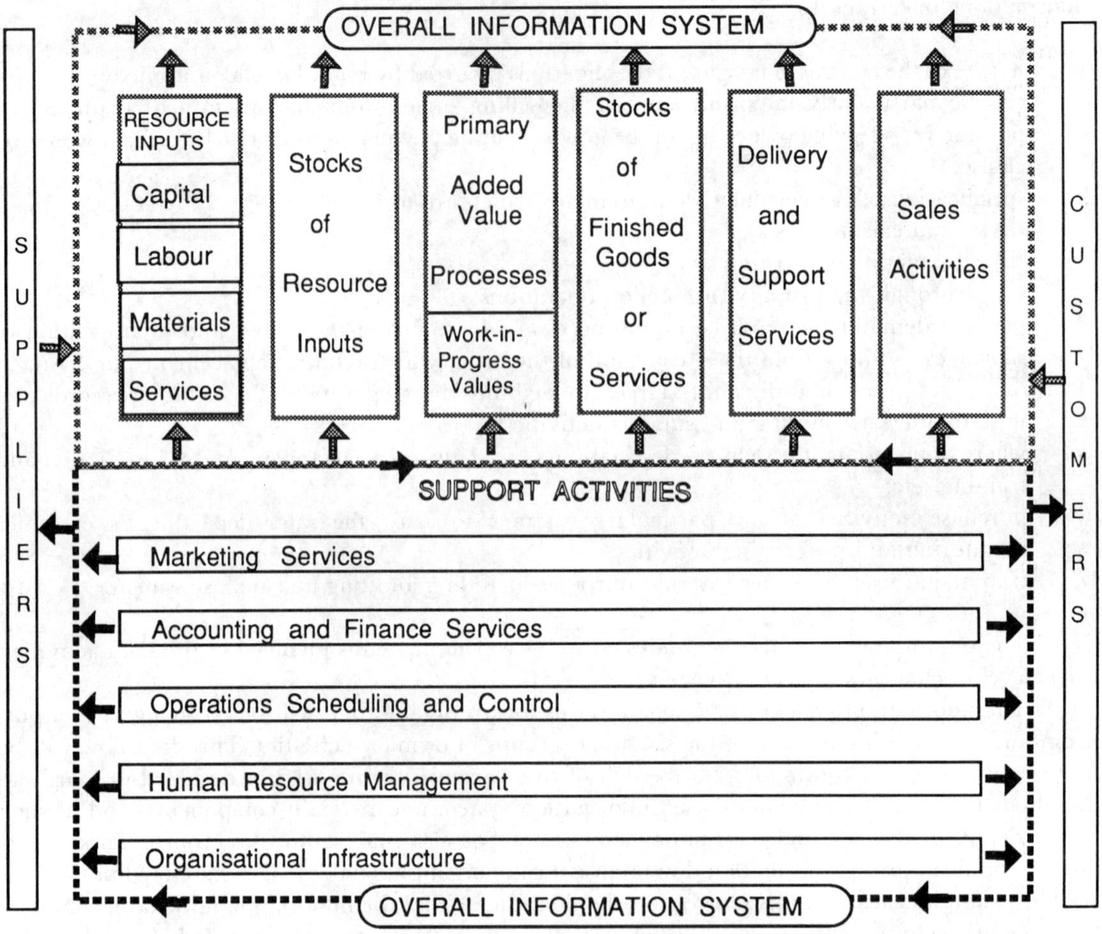

(d) monitoring the percentage of capital resources used effectively within the organisation, and paying for all the resources in use.

3 **Operations scheduling and control**—these activities include:

(a) planning and co-ordinating the various primary activities involved in the production process;

(b) establishing processing priorities for particular orders.

4 **Human resource management (personnel)**—these activities are now being recognised as increasingly important as organisations seek to optimise their investment in human skills. The services include:

(a) recruitment and training of the required personnel resources;

(b) providing the necessary support services such as medical, safety, catering services, etc, to maintain the effectiveness and skills of the labour force;

(c) ensuring that proper staff development is maintained by providing continuing training, and maintaining morale by seeking to ensure proper career development and advancement.

5 **Organisational infrastructure**—this comprises:

(a) the practical activities of planning, developing and administering the organisation's fixed capital resources (eg buildings and plant), and

(b) the less tangible, but equally necessary, resources such as the organisation's structures, systems and processes which facilitate the effective operation of both the primary and other support activities.

2.2.8 Cash flows

One dimension of the primary and support activities not reflected in the diagram, but which necessarily has a significant effect on every organisation, is the cash flow associated with the various operations undertaken by the organisation. The overall flow of cash within the cycle of operations is a reflection in summarised form, of all the primary and support activities. The aggregate cash flow position is compiled from data inputs which are derived from all of the activities outlined above. In addition to recording the financial value of each transaction involved, cash flow accounting necessitates the recording of details on the timing of all the cash receipts and payments including:

(a) materials, labour and services acquired for primary and support operations;
(b) purchases of capital equipment and/or the leasing and rental charges;
(c) payments for capital resources used including interest charges and dividend payments;
(d) receipts from the sales of goods and services.

2.3 DECISION-MAKING

This section considers decision-making in general terms, incorporating all the types and levels of decisions in the organisation. The next section develops this further by distinguishing between the different levels or types of decisions and examining the consequences for the information requirement.

The importance of information to the decision-making process cannot be overestimated. Indeed, 'The entire decision-making process can be viewed as the acquisition and processing of information.' (MacCrimmon, 1974) For these purposes, the term **decision** may be defined in a number of different ways, often reflecting the situation in which the decision is taking place. However, a broad definition of the term for the purposes of the current discussion would be: A decision is a process or a sequence of activities undertaken by an individual or group(s) with a view to establishing and implementing a solution to an existing or potential problem. Three features of this definition are worth stressing:

1 Decision-making is a process or a sequence of activities which will not always take place in a continuous or uninterrupted fashion.
2 The taking of decisions is both an individual and a group activity, with the latter likely to be more common in most organisations.
3 Decisions may be taken in a pro-active stance for solving or preparing solutions to potential future problems, as well as a reactive stance for resolving existing problems.

Figure 2.3 provides an outline of the main stages in the decision-making process and identifies the information inputs associated with each of them.

2.3.1 Decision trigger

Every decision process requires some factor to trigger or initiate the process. Data/information is the input most likely to trigger the process. For example:

1 Information identifying defects in components purchased ought to trigger an examination of the quality standards maintained by the particular supplier and might lead to a decision to change suppliers.
2 Information revealing increasingly high stock levels of certain finished goods may trigger an evaluation of market demands and production levels for the product with a view to deciding on future changes in pricing, promotional or production policies for the product.
3 Information concerning future changes may also initiate the decision process. Thus, a proposal to change the technology that is used to produce the organisation's products may require decisions on financing the capital investment, on amending the marketing policies to reflect the modernisation of plant and/or product, and on training the staff who will be associated with the new technology implementation.

2.3.2 Problem definition

Having initiated the decision-making process, it may then prove necessary to define the cause of the problem. The important issue at this stage is to differentiate between cause and effect. While the

FIGURE 2.3 **Stages in the decision-making process**

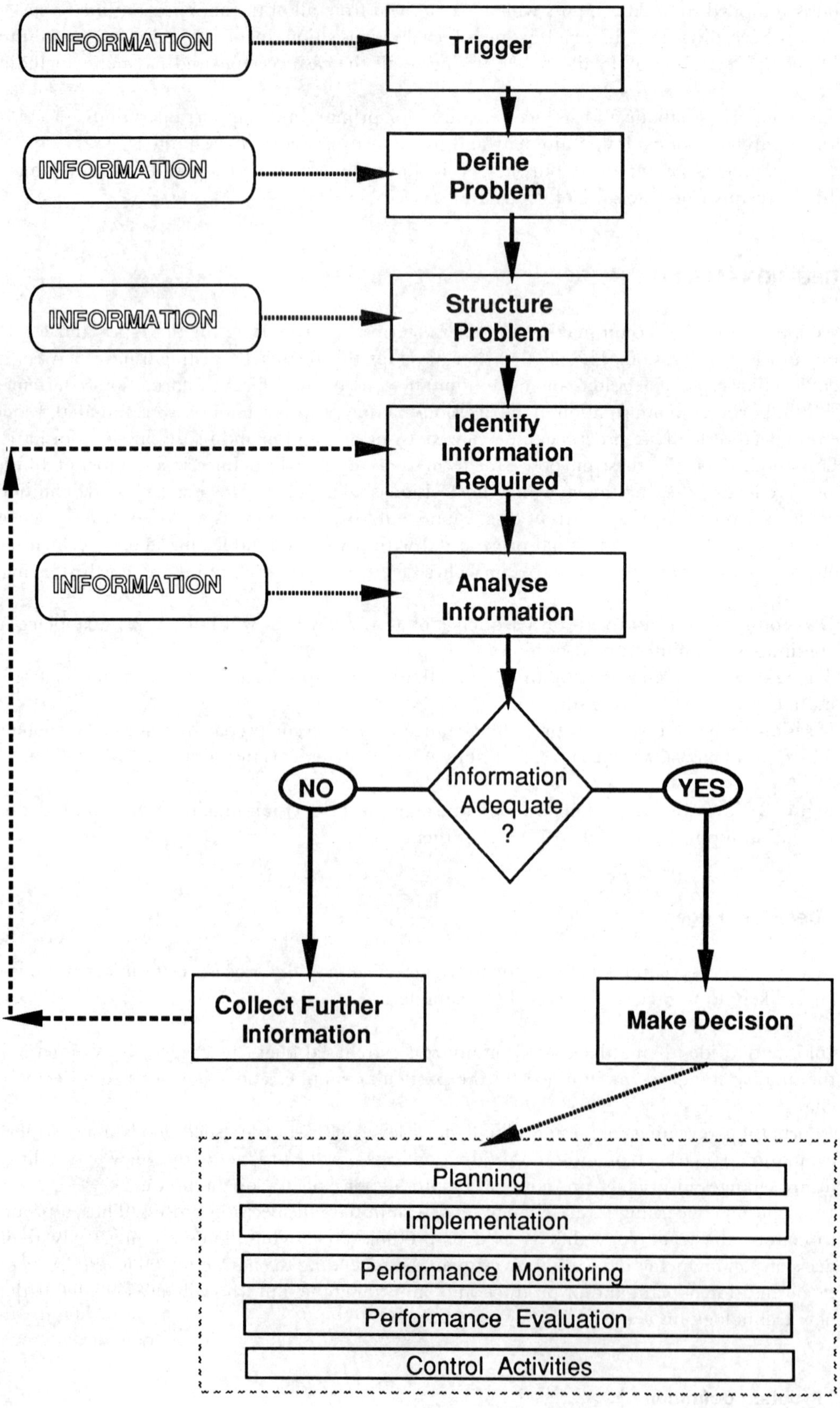

decision-maker may be only too aware of the effect of particular problems on the running of the organisation, the effectiveness of the proposed solution(s) will depend on how well the root causal factors have been identified and understood. For example, a reduction in the level of sales revenue may be caused by any number of factors including changes in the total size of market, changing consumer needs, competitors' actions influencing both price and quantity of sales, and an increase in customer dissatisfaction due to poor quality products or support services.

The problems encountered in practice are typically complex in the sense that there are usually several causal factors involved. Further, each factor is likely to interact with one or more of the others, making the effects of any individual factor difficult to assess. Time is also a vital variable as the importance of individual factors may change as the organisation's situation changes. Thus, even as the decision-maker is defining the current problem, the nature of the problem may itself be changing due to changes in the external environment. In the sales revenue example above, the primary causal factors may have been established as the competitors' pricing policies and customer dissatisfaction with quality standards. Competitors' lower prices alone would have some effect on sales revenues, but when combined with customer dissatisfaction, the reduction in sales may be considerably greater than if the quality standards were high. Continual changes in competitors' prices will result in a dynamic as well as a complex problem situation. In these situations, the decision-makers not only require the initial information to establish the relevant causal factors, but require that this information is continually updated to reflect changes in the problem situation.

2.3.3 Problem structuring

Defining the problem in terms of the primary causal factors provides the basis upon which to structure the problem. This may take the form of constructing a model of the problem, highlighting the important dimensions, the scope of the analysis required and the possible types of solution. Continuing the sales revenue example above, and assuming that the problem is defined primarily as competitors' actions, the problem may be structured in terms of which competitors to consider, the parts of their activities which have some relevance to the problem, and the markets and products involved. Once this has been done, it becomes easier to make decisions as to which techniques and tools are appropriate for analysing and resolving the situation. Two fundamental issues arise at this point.

MODELS

The term as used in the context of problem structuring may be defined in a number of ways:

(a) **Physical model**—a two-dimensional or three-dimensional drawing or physical representation of the decision problem. For example, a graph showing the sales revenues of competitors in the market over the last three years, or a model of a proposed plant layout incorporating new technology features.

(b) **Symbolic model**—a representation of the problem situation using symbols, equations or mathematical formulae. An example would be the use of regression analysis methods to identify and express the trends in sales revenue.

(c) **Conceptual model**—a representation of the situation in a less specific form, often in the mind of the decision-maker, and exploiting the available knowledge and experience of those involved. For example, the previous experience of the decision-maker may suggest the most likely reactions of the competitors to changes in price or to promotional activities undertaken by the organisation. This experience may be difficult to capture in either a physical or symbolic type of model. However, as will be seen later, many of the developments in supporting decision-makers are increasingly focusing on methods to capture and represent such models in a form suitable for analytical appraisal. The advance in spreadsheet software packages has provided one such vehicle for these developments.

OBJECTIVES

A vital element in structuring the problem situation is a clear and explicit understanding of the objectives which the decision is seeking to achieve. These objectives may be expressed in a number of different ways for a given decision situation. For example, in the declining sales revenue situation referred to above, the objectives may be expressed as:

(a) prevent any further decline in sales revenue in the future;
(b) redress the decline in sales revenue to the previous levels;
(c) achieve a 5% increase on the previous levels of sales prior to the decline.

Each of these objectives may be further qualified in terms of, say, the requirement that the objective should be achieved without any reduction in the profit margins per unit, or within the current sales and marketing budgets. It will be evident that the objectives determine not only the broad parameters of the potential solutions and the criteria against which each potential solution should be judged, but also indicate the type and quality of information required and the depth of analysis which must be performed to verify which of the proposed solutions is the one most likely to succeed.

2.3.4 Information requirements

The major by-product from the structuring of the problem is an identification, at least initially, of the information required to analyse those aspects or dimensions of the problem that are seen as important, and the information required to evaluate possible alternative solutions to the situation.

Continuing the sales revenue example from above, the decision-maker may identify the initial information required as:

1. the sales patterns for the product over the last two years;
2. the market shares of the organisation and of each major competitor;
3. the organisation's pricing levels over this period;
4. the prices of, say, the three major competitor's products over a similar period; and
5. the cost structure of the product and the resulting profit margins.

The key factor in this identification process is the definition of the type and quality of information that will be required to support the decision-making. There are many possible dimensions to information quality, including variables such as the level of detail and the degree of accuracy and reliability in the initial data. In certain cases, detailed and accurate costs and financial information may be required to support decisions on changes to product pricing structures, while in other cases, broad estimates of costs and margins may prove sufficient. This aspect of the different qualitative dimensions of the information required for different decisions will be outlined in 2.8.

2.3.5 Information analysis

The analysis of the information specified is undertaken by the decision-maker, and will involve both quantitative and qualitative approaches. Quantitative approaches may include statistical methods such as graphical trend plotting, regression analysis or correlation analysis. This process need not be automated, and the analysis may involve a series of manual data processing activities including the sorting, coding, selection and summarising of the data available. Following this analysis the decision-maker may apply pre-determined criteria in evaluating the situation and/or undertake some degree of subjective evaluation of the results produced in relation to the situation.

2.3.6 Adequacy of information

An integral part of the process is an evaluation by those involved in taking the decision as to whether or not the information presently available is adequate to enable the decision to be made. If the decision-maker considers that the information is inadequate, then he/she will specify the further information required and arrange for its collection and subsequent analysis. This is represented by the loop (dotted line) in Figure 2.3. Requests for further information may be the result of one or more of the following:

1 Identifying a lack of data concerning certain dimensions of the problem. This may be due to poor initial problem specification, to inadequate information collection, or to the subsequent appreciation of the importance of the particular factors.
2 The poor quality of the information provided, an issue addressed more fully later in this chapter.
3 A recognition that it is necessary to search for further information to support and confirm a tentative decision already taken.
4 A deliberate action to delay the decision and its implementation pending an assessment of potential reactions internally and externally. This may involve the decision-maker in requesting additional information that is unlikely to influence the decision taken to any significant extent.

This assessment of the adequacy of the information that is available should also be considered in cost-benefit terms. The decision-maker should assess the likely costs and the feasibility of collecting further information against the potential benefits arising from the above list. However, it is most unlikely in practice that the decision-maker will ever achieve the state in which there is perfect information about all the relevant dimensions of the problem situation. The primary difficulty in practice is that the greater the level of information quality specified by the decision-maker, the greater the cost of producing it is likely to be. When it comes to the justification of this high level of cost, it is then recognised that it is difficult to assess the potential benefits that will be derived from the additional information. It is common for the decision-maker to make subjective approximations, asserting that the additional information may be useful in helping to make the decision. But it will usually be impossible to quantify this value or usefulness in advance, and it may not even be possible to do so after receiving the information. The reason for this difficulty is that additional information will probably only have a marginal effect on the decision taken, often doing no more than providing confirmation of the decision already taken. Thus, while it may be argued that decision-makers ought to continue to collect and analyse additional information until the marginal benefit derived from the last item of information received equates to the cost of providing that information, in practice, decision-makers are unable to achieve this through their inability to quantify the marginal costs and benefits.

2.3.7 Decision taking

At some stage in this process, the decision-maker will proceed to the decision taking stage. Arrival at this moment may be at the natural conclusion of an exhaustive analytical process, or it may be more premature. Decisions are often hurried because:

(a) a deadline has been set or the decision-maker is reacting to other less formal time pressures which make it expedient to produce a solution even though it is known to be sub-optimal;
(b) there may be no further information or analytical methods easily and quickly available;
(c) the decision-maker may be too tired to continue;
(d) more pressing problems may have appeared and require attention.

Sadly, in these more competitive times, the premature rather than the exhaustive response is likely to be the norm in the practical business situation. The concluding decisions are taken because it is considered inexpedient and uneconomic to take no decision. They may be a positive response in terms of a particular action proposed, or a more negative or passive response by deciding not to take any action.

In summary, information in the context of the decision-making process contributes as a:

1 trigger to initiate the process;
2 resource to facilitate the definition and structuring of the problem situation;
3 resource to aid the evaluation of the proposed decision;
4 vehicle to communicate the decision to others and to provide a basis for implementing the decision; and
5 basis for feeding back the results of a decision to facilitate performance monitoring and control during the implementation and subsequent running of the planned responses.

2.3.8 Programmable and non-programmable decisions

A further distinction should be made which has important implications for an organisation's information requirements. Decisions may be classified as either **programmable**, highly structured decisions, or **non-programmable**, highly unstructured decisions. In the case of programmable decisions, the problem situations are generally predictable and so the decision-making activities of problem definition, structuring, analysis and resolution may be specified or programmed in advance. The solution will normally depend upon the application of **algorithms**.

Programmable decisions are usually those which:

(a) occur relatively frequently;
(b) require the consideration of only a few factors which may be incorporated in a pre-determined structure;
(c) display relatively simple inter-relationships between the various factors;
(d) have a limited and predictable range of possible solutions;
(e) have decision criteria that may be explicitly stated and easily applied to selecting the most appropriate solution from the limited range.

Examples of programmable decisions would include the credit rating of new customers, quality control inspection, equipment maintenance and delivery scheduling. If the organisation is able to develop suitable algorithms (ie formalistic rules) for each general decision-making situation, the information requirements will be readily identifiable in advance and, given the frequency with which such decisions are likely to occur, the organisation would probably incorporate the collection of the necessary information as part of the routine transaction information system outlined in 2.2. An alternative term for programmable decisions is **routine decisions**.

Non-programmable decisions are usually less routine, and less predictable in at least one of the stages in the decision process. They may, for example, require novel approaches to defining, structuring or analysing the problem situation, and require the decision-maker to develop and formulate the criteria to be used in selecting the best solution strategy. This involves the application of **heuristics** (ie a system of making choices using non-linear methods). Examples of such decisions may include fixing the pricing policy for a new product, selecting the most appropriate location for a new warehouse and distribution outlet, and evaluating a proposal to acquire another organisation to provide the capacity to expand market share and production capacity. Each of these decisions will have one or more unique features in that, for example, the prospective sites for creating a new warehouse will all have different attributes, some of which, upon investigation, will prove to be advantageous, others disadvantageous. Although it would be possible to lay down general information requirement guidelines in advance, the decision-makers are only able to specify the actual information requirements for each decision when the preliminary problem analysis has taken place. This means that the information system must have a degree of flexibility in its design and operation to enable it to respond to the variable information demands of the non-programmable decisions. An alternative term for this type of decision is **non-routine**.

This distinction between programmable and non-programmable decisions and their information requirements will be developed further in 2.7

2.4 PLANNING AND IMPLEMENTATION

Having selected what appears to be the appropriate solution strategy for the particular problem situation, the next stage in the decision process involves planning and implementing the necessary steps to make the decision effective. Figure 2.4 illustrates the main stages involved in this planning and implementation phase. Planning involves:

1 determining the sequence (logical or otherwise) of action and/or inaction which will be required;
2 establishing the dates or times required for the completion of each step in the plan;
3 estimating the resources which will be required for, and the durations of, the individual steps;
4 scheduling the programme of necessary activities.

Although planning and implementation are concerned with the detail of putting a decision into practice, the process itself incorporates a series of second-order decisions involving, for example, establishing priorities of resource usage within the organisation as a whole, and making commercial judgments as to the timing of the implemention. A more detailed treatment of the issues and methods involved is provided in Chapter 10 which deals with project management.

2.5 PERFORMANCE MEASUREMENT, MONITORING AND CONTROL

The final stage in the decision-making process, as illustrated in Figure 2.4, involves the measurement of the levels of performance achieved against those set as the justification for the project in the decision-making and planning stages. The measurement of actual performance against the planned or budgeted performance is a fairly common approach and it is used in most of the standard planning approaches and techniques. Performance measures may include time scales, target completion dates, resource usage, costs incurred, or other similar measures of efficiency and effectiveness. The original decision-maker, or those subsequently responsible and accountable for its implementation, will continuously monitor the performance levels achieved during both the implementation phase, and in its initial and subsequent operation. For these purposes, the monitoring may be directed towards the assessment of both effectiveness and efficiency. Given that commercial organisations depend upon the efficiency of their systems to maintain or enhance profitability, a considerable proportion of any organisation's information processing activities is necessarily devoted to supporting performance measurement and monitoring activities. These activities may either be related to specific projects or to the ongoing operations of the primary and support activities.

In a number of areas, the organisation will incorporate a continuous process of performance monitoring as a part of the transaction processing system. This may involve the regular recording of costs, revenues, time spent, resources used, etc, in its operations. A prerequisite of performance measurement is the establishment of clearly defined objectives or targets which can be related to the desired performance levels as the key parameters (eg profit levels, budgets or standard costs). There are three possibilities:

1 the actual levels of performance required will be explicitly stated;
2 some minimum acceptable levels of performance may be indicated;
3 the targets may be implicit rather than explicitly stated.

Irrespective of the method adopted for setting the performance requirements, the information received will be used to indicate whether performance is adhering to planned targets or deviating from those targets. The scale of any deviation detected will influence both the degree of urgency perceived necessary, and the scope of any corrective action to keep the operation under control, ie within the planned performance parameters.

The control process is a consequence of performance monitoring and involves taking actions either to prevent anticipated deviations from planned performance, or to correct deviations after they have occurred. Control will encompass decision-making elements together with planning elements, and may involve:

1 applying corrective action to existing operations or to stages in the planned implementation;
2 modifying future plans to reflect changes in circumstances or current performance levels;
3 re-appraising objectives, plans and performance targets in the light of current performance.

It is important to recognise the distinction between the **reactive** and the **pro-active** approaches to control, as these have differing implications for the organisation's information system. In the former approach, the organisation's management is responding to existing deviations from the planned activities or performance levels. Managers will act with a view to correcting the deviations, or to preventing those deviations from damaging the future interests of the organisation if left unchecked. In the pro-active approach, the management is consciously exploring the potential sources of future deviations with a view to instituting the necessary avoidance or damage limitation measures in advance. The implications for the information system of a pro-active approach are that the information requirements will be orientated more to future events, and the decision support tools and software will be directed more towards forecasting, model building and sensitivity analysis,

FIGURE 2.4 **Stages in planning, implementation and control**

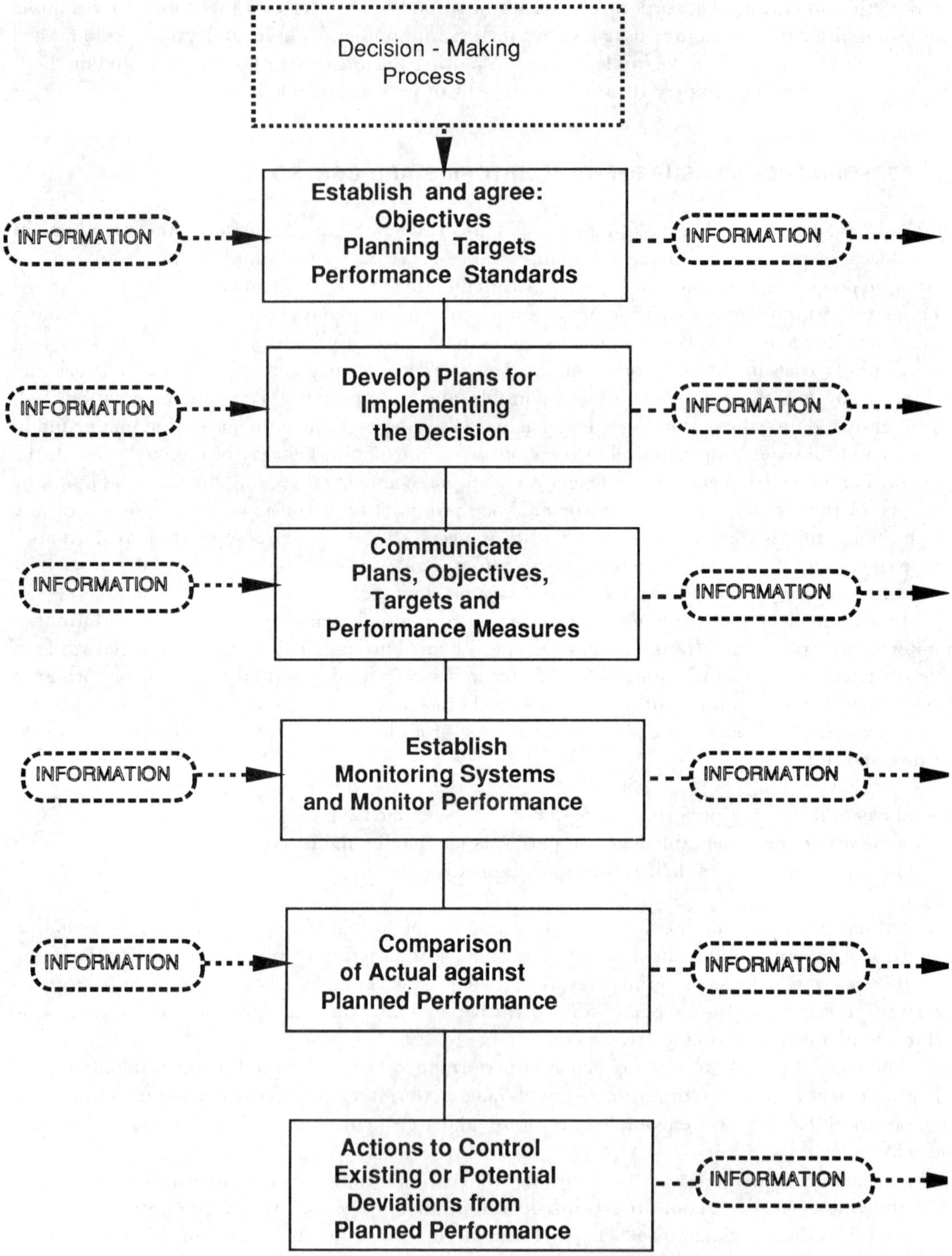

providing the management with assessments which will help to answer the *what if?* type of question. Reactive approaches will rely more heavily on historical data although again, the management will require decision support tools to support the analysis of alternative solutions and their implications. It is likely that both approaches will co-exist in most organisations. This reflects the fact that the development of paranoia in management is not a viable strategy. If an organisation continually plans on the basis of the worst possible case, and seeks to predict every potential deviation in advance, a substantial amount of redundant activity and expenditure will be achieved. Responsible management acknowledges that the organisation must be able to respond flexibly to the existing, the realistically predictable and the unpredicted problems. The result is that the emphasis in management development and training is moving strongly towards the need to adopt a more pro-active approach, and this trend is being increasingly supported and facilitated by developments in information technologies.

The ability to control a situation is heavily dependent on the receipt of timely and good quality performance information. Should symptoms of the deviation from planned or anticipated performance targets not be clearly signalled in time, the necessary trigger to initiate the decision-making activities within the control process will not arise. One of the difficulties in designing an effective control system is the potential volume of information which may be generated on the organisation's activities. The greater the volume, the greater the level of resources that must be devoted to analysing and reviewing it. An important principle adopted by many organisations is therefore that of exception reporting or management by exception. This operates on the presumption that actual performance levels either matching or closely matching the planned levels are under control and do not require special attention. Thus, management only requires information on those areas of performance that are failing to meet the planned levels by a significant margin as these may be considered to be out of control and require management's attention. This principle has important implications for the design and operation of management information systems.

2.6 COMMUNICATIONS

The communication system in any organisation is essentially concerned with the movement of data between one area or element in the organisation and another. It should be considered the system of veins and arteries which carries the life blood of data to all parts of the organisation. In the strategic brain of the organisation, decisions are made which must be circulated to all parts of the organisation. But to function efficiently, the brain must be refreshed by the oxygen of data drawn from the external and internal monitoring senses. To that extent, the communication system is the heart of the organisation's information system, providing the channels for the effective and efficient transfer of data to the right person in the right place so that quality information may be transmitted. The communication of information in an organisation may classified into two broad forms:

1 **Hard communications** where there is some physical, tangible or hard copy of the information being transmitted, eg a written memorandum or letter, minutes of a meeting, tape recording of a telephone conversation, or an electronic recording on a computer's magnetic disk. In each of these cases there is a tangible record of the information which may be passed to the receiver and, if required, provide a permanent record of that information.
2 **Soft communications** where the information is transmitted in a less tangible form, eg the tone of voice, the facial expression or other mannerisms used while orally transmitting the information, or the general atmosphere in which the communication takes place. These less tangible features may be particularly important to the correct interpretation of the information. They may equally be responsible for the incorrect interpretation of the information by the receiver, by giving undue weight to certain dimensions or elements.

Both types of communication co-exist in almost every organisation. From the information systems development and design point of view, however, the emphasis tends to centre on the mechanisms for delivering the hard forms of the organisation's information. This is mainly due to the fact that economical methods have been developed to capture, store, process and transmit this type of information by using the electronic media. The development of cost-effective processing methods for the soft elements is less readily available. This would take the form of teleconferencing systems incorporating live CCTV links, and electronic messaging systems that convert the video images into electronic media prior to storage, and re-convert when subsequently required. There is little doubt that the handling of these soft elements is technically feasible, and that they are likely to become increasingly cost-effective and hence useful in the future.

2.7 NATURE AND LEVELS OF DECISION-MAKING

2.7.1 Decision-making levels

The activities of decision-making, planning, communicating, performance monitoring and control occur extensively and continuously in almost every organisation. It is possible to differentiate these activities within an organisation in a number of ways, the most common of which are by reference to:

(a) the functions involved, eg marketing or financing;
(b) the aspects of the operations to which the decisions relate, eg pricing or employee remuneration;
(c) the time period which they concern, eg short-term, medium-term or long-term.

There is a further generally accepted division of the range of decision-making activities in an organisation which is illustrated in Figure 2.5.

FIGURE 2.5 **Levels of organisational decision-making**

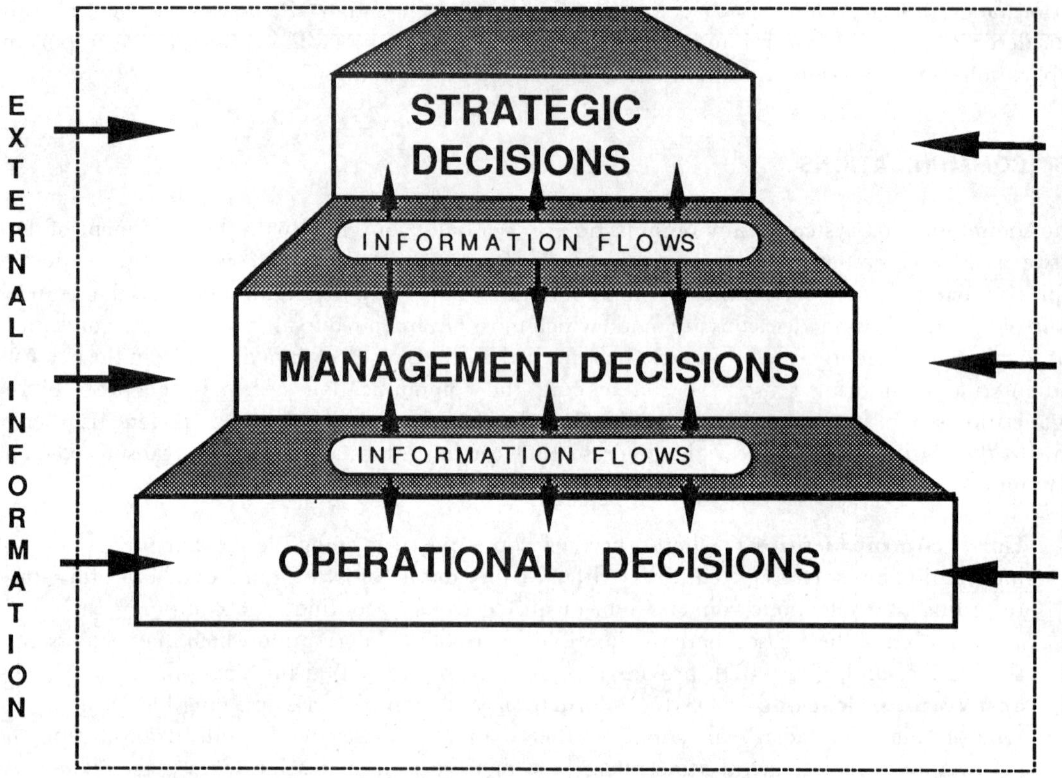

EXTERNAL ENVIRONMENT

The three levels of decision-making illustrated reflect essential differences in the nature of the decisions being taken, and consequently the position of the potential decision-maker in the hierarchy gives rise to different information requirements to support the decisions. The differences in the type and quality of the information required for each of these levels are explained in more detail in 2.8.

When judging the volume or the frequency of occurrence of each type of decision, the **operational** decisions are the most prevalent in an organisation, with the **strategic** decisions being the least prevalent. Conversely, as a measure of the significance of the consequences for the whole organisation, the strategic decisions are potentially the most significant, while operational decisions have little potential impact on the organisation as a whole.

It would not be safe to assume that the clarity of the distinction between the three levels represented in Figure 2.5 is reflected in the practical situation in organisations. The distinction between **operational** and **management** level decisions on the one hand, and management and strategic on the other, is often a matter of interpretation within a specific organisational situation, and usually reflects the nature of the particular processes employed in managing the organisation. The distinction between operational and strategic level decisions is usually more clearly observable in practice. The following paragraphs seek to elaborate on the nature of these three levels of decision-making, and to provide some examples of the types of decisions involved in each of the groups. The discussion of the management level is reserved to the end because it interacts significantly with the other two levels.

2.7.2 Operational decisions

Operational decisions are concerned with the on-going daily or routine operations of the organisation, relating mainly to its primary activities. Figure 2.6 illustrates the main groups of primary activities and shows a few examples of the decisions associated with each of them. The list of examples is not exhaustive, and relates to a manufacturing organisation, although some features would also be found in the operations of a service sector organisation, eg the sales ledger system.

FIGURE 2.6 **Operational decisions in an organisation**

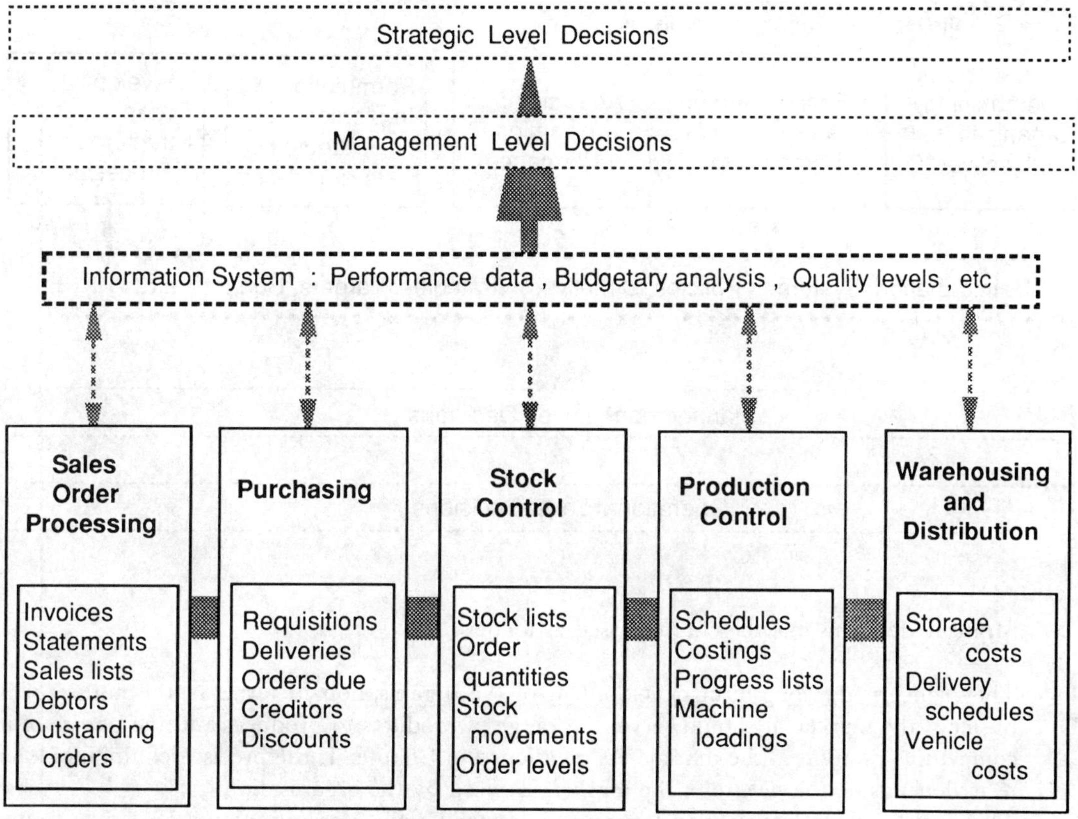

Each of these groups represents a major sub-system in the organisation's overall information system. It should be recognised that the sequence of activities and decisions indicated in Figure 2.6 is not necessarily the order in which they would occur in practice. Indeed, many of the activities shown will take place simultaneously. Another important feature highlighted in the Figure is the linkages between each of these primary sub-systems. They usually reflect some flow of data between each of the sub-systems. The Figure also indicates the two-way flow of data between the operational sub-systems and the corresponding elements in the management level.

Operational decisions are concerned primarily with:

1 Short timescale and routine programmes to promote the effectiveness and efficiency of the daily operations including sales and customer order taking, the acquisition and stocking of raw materials, production operations, delivery and installation of goods and services, and the invoicing and collection of payment for the goods and services.

2 Explicit and specific performance objectives facilitating direct and often very objective measurement of efficiency and effectiveness. For example, the number of items manufactured in a particular day, or the number of transactions processed by the sales order staff in a day.

3 Highly programmable and well documented decision-making procedures, which are frequently encapsulated in operating procedures, operations manuals and specific instructions.

4 Decisions where there are relatively low levels of uncertainty and risk, and decision-makers use mainly objective analysis methods and simplified selection criteria in making their decisions.

5 Highly predictable information demands in terms of the information required to make the decision and to monitor its consequences.

2.7.3 Strategic decisions

Strategic decisions are concerned with the the long-term development and planning for the whole organisation as opposed to specific functional areas or individual operations. The major groups of decision activity within this level are shown in Figure 2.7.

FIGURE 2.7 **Strategic decisions in an organisation**

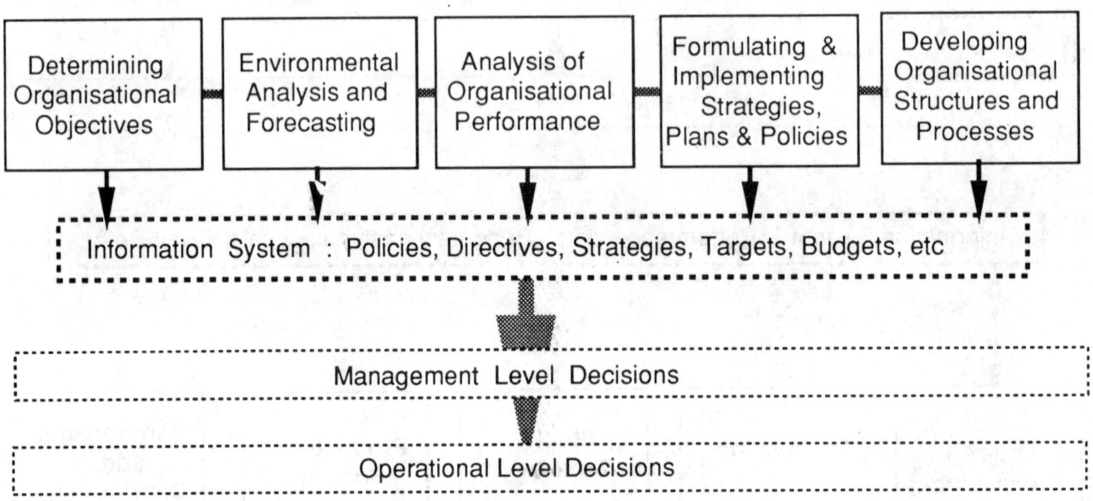

Strategic decisions may be characterised as follows:

1 They concern the long-term development of the organisation in terms of the nature of its business, the markets it should serve, the range of products to produce, and the nature of its competitive position in the market. As mentioned in Chapter 1, the precise definition of long-term depends on the nature of the markets serviced by the organisation.

2 They involve the selection, development and articulation of organisational objectives from a range of potential objectives against a background of the constraints imposed by the external environment and by the internal structure and operations.

3 They tend to be highly unstructured or non-programmable, and are often novel to the organisation and its decision-makers, with no guarantee that they will recur in a similar context.

4 They involve high levels of uncertainty and risk, requiring significant levels of personal and subjective analysis, appraisal and choice within the decisions.

5 The information demands to support this level of decision-making are not generally predictable, although certain types of external and internal information will be regularly processed for this decision-making group as a general part of the organisation's need to develop good sources of intelligence and broad performance indicators.

2.7.4 Management decisions

The level of management decision-making may be considered as filling the centre spread of the spectrum of decision types between operational at one extreme and strategic at the other. An alternative term used for management level decisions is tactical decisions. This level shares a number of features with both the operational and strategic levels, and has been discussed last for this reason. Figure 2.8 indicates the broad areas of decision handled at this level.

The role of the individual managers in this section of the decision hierarchy also needs to be recognised to appreciate that in addition to decision-making, this level of management also has the

FIGURE 2.8 **Management level decisions in an organisation**

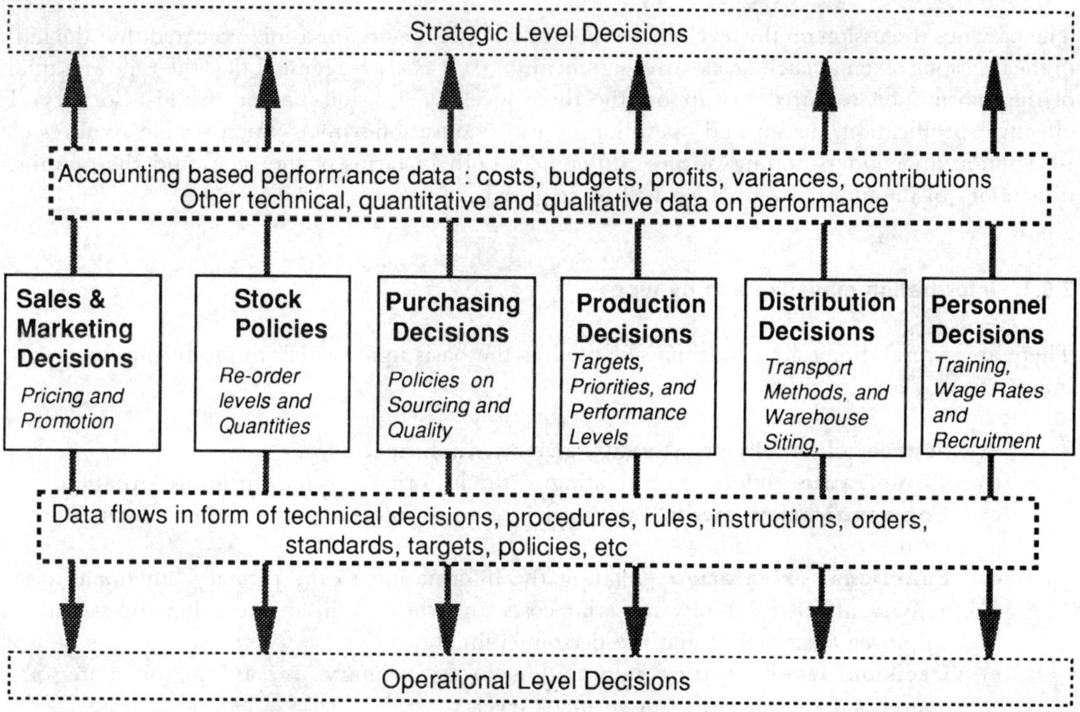

task of integrating and co-ordinating activity and communication between the strategic and operational levels. The function of these managers is to interpret, implement, monitor and control the strategic objectives, plans and policies established by the organisation. This may involve developing plans, performance levels, guidelines, procedures and operating instructions for the operational levels in the organisation.

In addition to this enabling link from the strategic to the operational levels for implementation purposes, the management level also has a responsibility to monitor the operations of the organisation and to feed back summarised performance data to the strategic level. It is argued that this management role is the most crucial element in the organisation's operation as it provides a vital interface between the long-term plans of the organisation and their more immediate implementation and control.

Management level decisions may be characterised in terms of:

1 A practical concern with the short-, medium- and long-term perspectives of organisational performance, although the predominant emphasis will tend to be medium-term.
2 The need to relate primarily to the functional elements in the organisation while recognising the overall strategic objectives, strategies and development proposals.
3 The involvement of moderate degrees of uncertainty and risk in appraising the decision options and the alternative solutions available.
4 The semi-structured nature of the problems encountered, since there will be some elements in each problem which may be relatively common, while other elements are novel both to the decision-maker and to the organisation. A core of standard analytical techniques has been developed to provide some basic tools to tackle different problem situations. Examples of these would include operational research methods (eg linear programming or queuing algorithms), statistical methods, variance analysis methods in budgetary control, and spread sheet software packages. The real skill at this level of decision-making is the ability to structure the problem encountered into an appropriate form and to select the correct decision tools to assist in the analysis and selection of the best solution strategy.
5 The information requirements which are only partially predictable, eg the regular performance monitoring requirements and reports. The unpredictable elements reflect the need for management to focus on particular novel issues and problems as they arise, and to use standard-purpose analytical tools to evaluate the alternatives and to take decisions.

2.8 TYPES AND QUALITY OF INFORMATION

The previous discussion on the levels of decision-making in the organisation indicated that the nature of the decisions taken at each level varies significantly. It was also suggested that the type and quality of the information required to support the three levels of decision-making would also vary. The effective specification, design and operation of an organisation's information system requires clear recognition and understanding of these differences both in terms of the types and the qualitative dimensions of the information which will be required.

2.8.1 Information classification by type

There are several dimensions that may be used as the basis upon which to produce a taxonomy of information. These include:

(a) **Source**—internally or externally generated information.
(b) **Time-frame**—information relating to the historical, current or future situation.
(c) **Communication media**—the presentation of information in either a written or oral form.
(d) **Functional orientation**—relating the information to the primary functional area or activity affected, eg raw material costs and the purchasing function, or statistics on employee absenteeism and the personnel function.
(e) **Decision level**—relating information to its primary use at one or more of the operational, management or strategic levels.

These classifications are not mutually exclusive, and a particular item of information may be classified using each of these dimensions. For example, information on the sales achieved by a particular product in a given month may be classified as internally-generated, historical, written and appropriate to management level decisions in the sales function. Whereas, forecasts of market demand for the product may be externally generated, futuristic, written and primarily for use in strategic level decisions in the marketing function.

2.8.2 Qualitative dimensions of information

In addition to classifying by type, information may also be differentiated on the basis of its quality. The term quality in this context refers to the dimensions which enhance the value of the information to the user. Figure 2.9 illustrates a number of the more important quality dimensions of information.

There are a number of points which need to be stressed in relation to these quality dimensions:

1 not all the dimensions will be relevant in any given decision situation;
2 each dimension may be represented by a range of potential levels of quality;
3 even in the situation where there are several relevant dimensions, certain dimensions may be more important than others. In the case of financial accounting information, for example, a high degree of accuracy may be more important than the timeliness or currency of the information received;
4 the importance of a particular dimension in a given decision situation is a reflection of the decision situation, the nature of the problem faced, and the skills of the individual decision-maker(s). In the case of a decision-maker with strong analytical abilities, the provision of detailed and comprehensive information as opposed to summarised and partial information may enhance the decision taken. However, if the decision-maker's analytical abilities are less well developed, a more summarised version of the information may yield higher value in terms of the decision taken.

The improvement of quality or the enhancement of the value received by the user from the information will normally necessitate additional information processing costs. Each of the qualitative dimensions listed has a cost associated with the improvement of the quality of the information in that particular dimension. Thus, if the production planning and control section operated on the basis of

FIGURE 2.9 **Qualitative dimensions of information**

Attribute	← Range of attributes →		
Level of detail	detailed	↔	summarised
Accuracy	highly accurate	↔	inaccurate
Accessability	readily available	↔	delayed availability
Time perspective	current	↔	historic
Completeness	fully comprehensive	↔	partial outline
Relevance	appropriate to current needs	↔	inappropriate to current needs
Bias	objective	↔	subjective
Verifiable	self-verifiable	↔	no means of checking
Quantifiable	quantified	↔	not amenable to numeric expression
Degree of uncertainty	certain	↔	highly uncertain
Clarity	clearly expressed	↔	ambiguous

reports received at the end of each day, the proposal might be made to improve the timeliness of the information received by providing information on a real-time or immediate response basis throughout the day. This would involve considerable investment in the computer hardware and communications equipment needed to capture and transmit the data from the shopfloor, in the development or acquisition of appropriate software to process the information, and in increased staff time both in capturing the primary data and in accessing the resulting information. Systems designers need, therefore, to fully understand the needs of the user and to translate these into the appropriate levels of information quality provision.

While accepting that additional expenditure on information processing may improve the quality of the information provided, it should also be recognised that there are limitations on the degree to which quality may be improved, apart from the cost limitations. The quality of the source data used will dictate the potential to improve the qualitative dimensions. For example, market survey data which failed to record the age of the respondents could not have this detail added later. Similarly, costing information recorded in units of hundreds of pounds could not be provided in greater accuracy, say, in terms of pounds and pence. Technical limitations may also restrict the potential improvements in quality as the ability to capture, store and process the volume of data necessary to provide a comprehensive statement of the organisation's markets may be limited. Another important limiting factor is the cognitive capacity of the users. While it may prove possible to improve the detail and comprehensiveness of the data provided, the capacity of the overworked user to use this effectively may be constrained in terms of the sheer volume of information provided. Thus, although the inherent quality of the information has been enhanced, it does not add value to the user in the decision-making or control activities. Alternatively and more bluntly, no matter how much time is available, good quality information on its own does not convert a bad decision-maker into a good decision-maker.

2.8.3 Decision levels and information needs

Differences in the nature of the decisions at different levels in the organisation will be an important determinant of both the type of information required and its quality. Figure 2.10 provides an illustration of the differential nature of type and quality for the three broad levels of decision-making outlined earlier.

FIGURE 2.10 **Decision levels and information type and quality**

Information Attributes	Operational	Management	Strategic
Orientation	primarily internal	internal and external data utilised	greater orientation to external data
Planning horizon	immediate to next few days	short to medium- term (weeks and months)	medium to long - term (months and years)
Performance focus	focus on current activities	historic and current activities	focus on predictive rather than historic performance
Coverage	relates to specific activities	relates to groups of activities within department / function	coverage of total organisation
Level of detail	highly detailed	mixture of detailed and summarised reports	data typically presented in highly summarised form
Uncertainty levels	low uncertainty levels	moderate levels of uncertainty	high levels of uncertainty as focussing on longer term
Degree of objectivity	objectively measured data normally	combination of objective and subjective data	data incorporates higher proportion of subjective valuations
Level of accuracy	high levels of accuracy usually required	moderate accuracy levels	accuracy less critical to decisions at this level

Strategic decisions are concerned primarily with positioning the organisation in the optimum position in the environment to meet targets and objectives, while planning to allow the organisation to develop dynamically in response to changes in that environment. Such decisions typically involve a higher proportion of externally-generated data. This will often be presented in a summarised form and relate more to future developments than to historical or current developments. The information required will also generally be less accurate in the pedantic sense, and incorporate more subjective valuations of future trends and developments. This will tend to make the contents less predictable as the information needs will be dictated to a large extent by the developments in the external environment which, by definition, are largely outside the control of the organisation.

Operational decisions will tend to be based upon information which originates primarily within the organisation, and relates to either historical or current activities. The conduct of the decision-making at this level will also require detailed and accurate information which is often pre-determined in terms of both the content and quality necessary to be incorporated into the highly structured decisions.

Management decisions are concerned with the tactical planning and control of the organisation. A significant proportion of the information inputs to this level will comprise summarised statements capturing the performance of the organisation's primary activities, usually on a periodic basis. In such cases, the information inputs will be highly structured and predictable in terms of content, level of detail and accuracy required.

It should be recognised that the above summaries are intended to illustrate the general distinctions in the type and quality of information at each of the three levels. It should also be recognised that in any organisation, the differentiation between the three levels is often blurred and consequently the differentiation in the type and quality of information used may be similarly blurred.

2.9 ORGANISATION STRUCTURE AND INFORMATION REQUIREMENTS

2.9.1 Primary issues involved

All organisations are built up from standard resource-based components, but the individual motives, pressures and constraints which operate at the time of construction tend to produce strongly differentiated organisational structures, even where the organisations to be compared seek to serve the same market. However, there are a number of common denominator themes which emerge in the structuring period, regardless of whether the organisation is taking decisions explicitly or implicitly. At a macro level, the organisation will seek to structure its human resources and operations in the most effective and efficient manner to achieve its objectives. To make these objectives operational, the organisation must:

(a) formally identify and structure the available resources,
(b) establish efficient information and communication systems,
(c) create processes for effective decision-making, planning and control.

The strength of all organisations ultimately lies in its human resources. But if the optimum use of these resources is to be achieved, the organisation must take key decisions to allocate authority and responsibility. Without properly defined roles and a career structure which is likely to develop and maintain staff morale, it will be difficult to make effective use of the other resources, no matter how easy it may actually be to exploit them, and management skills will fade. This depends in turn, upon the development and communication of a personnel policy which is perceived as co-ordinated with the more general policies of the organisation. Thus, training must be planned to introduce new skills and enhance the old, and a pathway of promotion must lead to a gathering of experience which will allow each manager to gain a real insight into the aims and methods of the organisation.

The ways in which an organisation may be controlled vary from the autocratic excesses of an aggressive entrepreneur, to an open and democratic system of decision-making. The power structures which are developed will come to represent the culture of the organisation and be a vital factor in setting the tone and feel of employment. Key factors in maintaining motivation are the extent to which each manager is allowed to participate in the decision-making acknowledged to be significant, and the degree of authority delegation. If a manager is trusted with the responsibility and found to be competent, this reinforces the mutual confidence between manager and organisation, and should lead to better performance.

But no organisation can afford to accept success uncritically. The predicted outcomes may have arisen through circumstances entirely outside the control of the organisation, eg blind luck, and survival depends upon recognising that the current organisational structure is not necessarily the most effective and efficient. Thus, structural appraisal and evaluation may lead the organisation to propose changes in the form of organisation which will allow greater control or better decision-making. But all change is a threat to the established power structures, and where individuals have had responsibility and authority, it can be difficult to make the change effective. To that extent, all managements need to be aware of the political structure within the organisation so that the process of change can be steered through the matrix of entrenched self-interest. The political structure may map directly on to the formal decision-making structure, with power and influence controlled by the largest departments, or the most productive and/or profitable departments. Sometimes, the survival of power is an anachronism. The original managers of the first form of the organisation retain influence even though new parts of the business have long since outstripped them in terms of performance. This inevitably means addressing the issues of the size of organisation and of its component elements. Empire building by one or two ambitious individuals can be a way of promoting rapid growth, but it does not necessarily lead to a better quality of management or an organisation with the right balance of activities.

2.9.2 The information required

Up to this point, it has been assumed that the primary information requirements are to permit the organisation to monitor and control the way in which its processing systems interwork to meet the demands of the external environment. Thus, production must supply sufficient stock so that the sales force can confidently locate buyers and thereby generate revenue. The data required to build up a picture of these processes is limited in its potential information content. So when the production department supplies data on the number of units manufactured in each time period, the following data would also be desirable:

1 **Costing data**—what volume of raw materials and consummables was used and what was the level of wastage? how many man hours was required to produce the given level of output? what is the value of capital resource tied up in the plant and equipment used for this output? etc.
2 **Scheduling and production data**—what is the percentage of productive capacity utilisation, ie what is the level of plant and equipment reliability? how frequently does it break down? how long does it take to restore production? how long does it take to retool between different production runs? what are the shift arrangements? what is the accident record? is there any record of sabotage? etc.
3 **Personnel data**—what is the absenteeism record? in comparing the different manufacturing processes, where the equipment is comparable, are there significant differences in the output performance per man hour? are the staff prepared to work overtime? are the staff prepared to engage in further training? etc.
4 **Predictive data**—the what if? data which asks the questions: if particular work practices were modified, what would output be? if the scheduling was changed, would retooling times be reduced? if parts of the equipment were upgraded, what might output be? etc.

By analysing this data, it would be possible to draw a variety of conclusions. Thus, it might appear that there is a high absenteeism rate in certain areas of production. The plant may be old and temperamental, the wastage rates high and staff morale low. By improving the production environment and upgrading the equipment, the opportunity to improve performance may be gained. Should the plant be new, it is obvious that there may be a problem in training, or that the design of the human-machine interface is defective. If it appears that either situation has been going on for some time, why have none of the operational or managerial level staff pressed for change? Thus, the data may supply hard information in terms of real numbers which can be processed or analysed. It may also permit soft information to be inferred or deduced. This latter category is the more important when it comes to a self-critical appraisal of organisational structure. Power brokers who play the political game will not freely give information which will show managerial inadequacy. The information requirement should therefore be specified to extract information which is either:

(a) evidential—positive data on actual performance; or
(b) inferential—data which allows the organisation to appraise performance indirectly, eg through the failures to supply evidence of performance or to take action, etc.

By using both sets of data together, an information picture of the organisational structure can be built up which should reveal those issues which justify further examination by more direct methods of investigation.

SUMMARY

The key points covered in this chapter are that:

1 Information is recorded data which may be used to support the planning function in particular, and decision-making in general. It also allows the organisation the opportunity to monitor and control every aspect of its operation.

2 When problem situations have been structured, it is possible to identify the information requirements for their possible resolution.

3 The management must ensure that data flows support good communication links between the different parts of the organisation.

4 Decision-making within an organisation will be strategic, management or operational, depending on the timescale involved and the nature of the decision to be taken. It is important to ensure that information is of the right type and quality for each level of decision-making.

QUESTIONS *Solutions to questions of an examination standard start on p 395*

Write brief notes on the following:

(a) programmable and non-programmable decisions;
(b) transaction processing within an organisation;
(c) organisation structure and information requirements;
(d) types and quality of information.

Questions of an examination standard

1 The entire decision-making process can be viewed as the acquisition and processing of information.

List and briefly describe the stages in the decision-making process.

2 It is a commonly accepted model that organisational decision-making has three levels.

Briefly describe the three levels of decision-making, indicating the character of the decision made at each level, using examples where appropriate.

Chapter 3
Information Systems

CHAPTER OBJECTIVES

Information systems are only one of an almost infinite variety of systems which may operate within an organisation. An important pre-requisite to understanding the specific role and operation of information systems in an organisation is therefore an appreciation of the significance of the term system and of the major components of any system, irrespective of whether the system relates to information or some other resource in the organisation. The main purpose of this chapter is to introduce the major concepts involved in **systems theory**—the general theory which applies to systems of all types. These concepts will then be related and applied specifically to information systems within organisations. This chapter seeks to:

1 provide a general outline and understanding of the primary principles and concepts underlying the general systems theory;

2 highlight some key issues faced in dealing with systems including the definition of system boundaries, the systems hierarchy, the required level of system definition, and the interaction and integration of systems and sub-systems;

3 examine the issues of communications, feedback and control as they apply to systems;

4 relate the concepts, principles and findings from the general systems theory to the area of organisational information systems;

5 identify and evaluate the contribution of certain generic system components in organisational information systems including text processing, spreadsheets, databases and expert system shells;

6 introduce the different areas in the organisational information system outlining the key sources of interaction and integration between them;

7 examine in greater detail a particular sub-system within the overall business information system to illustrate and integrate the concepts and issues developed earlier in the chapter.

3.1 SYSTEMS THEORY AND CONCEPTS

In general terms, the **systems theory** or the **systems approach** is a structured method for developing a model or a conceptual framework to assist in the analysis and exploration of a given situation. The method may be applied in a diversity of fields including:

(a) manufacturing systems,
(b) telecommunications systems,
(c) central heating systems,
(d) traffic systems,
(e) human behaviour systems,
(f) waste disposal systems,
(g) information systems,
(h) accounting systems,
(i) education systems.

Basically, any situation which involves the handling or manipulation of materials or resources of any kind whether human, financial or informative, may be structured and represented in the form of a system. This is achieved by adopting a logical approach to the classification into one of the four groups outlined in 3.1.1, of each of the major elements or components identified in the given situation. It should be noted that this approach is not dependent on the application of computer or information technology. Indeed, the development of systems theory predates the extensive use of computer technology in business and commerce. Moreover, this approach may be applied equally effectively to both manual and computer-based information or other systems within an organisation. However, in an attempt to ensure the effective and efficient application of computer technology to business and commercial, or other organisational, situations, a logical approach to the modelling of the situation, as incorporated in the systems approach, is essential.

The usual purpose behind the development of a system model is to assist in the improvement of the level of efficiency and effectiveness in the given situation or set of operations. It must first be recognised that no organisation can permit activities, processes, decisions and resources to exist completely independently of each other. The analysis is therefore aimed at producing a pictorial representation of the relationship between each important component element which comprises the organisation. It is an attempt to map even the most inaccessible regions of the organisation and the resulting charts should allow the observers to:

(a) gain an improved understanding of the situation by using a structured approach to the analysis;
(b) identify and classify the important elements or components;
(c) more effectively disclose the interaction of these system components with each other within the part of the system being represented;
(d) analyse the interaction and integration of the system components with components in other systems or sub-systems.

This latter point is one which is particularly highlighted through the systems approach, as opposed to other forms of structured analysis.

3.1.1 The elements of a system

The first step in the systems approach involves a functional decomposition of the given situation or activity into the four basic elements shown in Figure 3.1.

The four main elements may be defined as:

1 **Inputs**—Here the part of the system under study receives some form of resource input material which might take the form of people, finance, energy, or information. These resources may be received either individually or in combination, and they may also originate from a number of different sources. Further, they may occur as discrete and sometimes infrequent events or as a continuous and regular flow of inputs.

2 **Process**—Some form of activity takes place as a response to the inputs received, which typically, though not exclusively, enhances the value of those resource inputs. These activities may include:
(a) recording,
(b) storing,
(c) machining,
(d) heating,
(e) transmitting,
(f) calculating,
(g) assembling.

3 **Outputs**—Once the process is complete, the perhaps modified resources will be output into the organisational environment. This may involve the return of the resources to their original source (eg the data elements are returned to the central database), or their transmission on to a new system or sub-system (eg sales data is transmitted to the marketing department for consolidation and analysis). At some point, the resources may leave the organisation and reach the consumers of the product or service. Typically, the value of the output resources will be greater than the value of the input resources as a result of the processing within the system. In the more usual sense, the system is seen to add value to the resources used. Some care needs to be exercised in defining the precise nature of the value which is added, as the term value may mistakenly be taken as confined to the needs of particular output recipients and not applied to all recipients. For example, the provision of a new motorway system may provide considerable added value to the car users able to use the new roads, but the roads provide no added value, or

FIGURE 3.1 **Elements of a system**

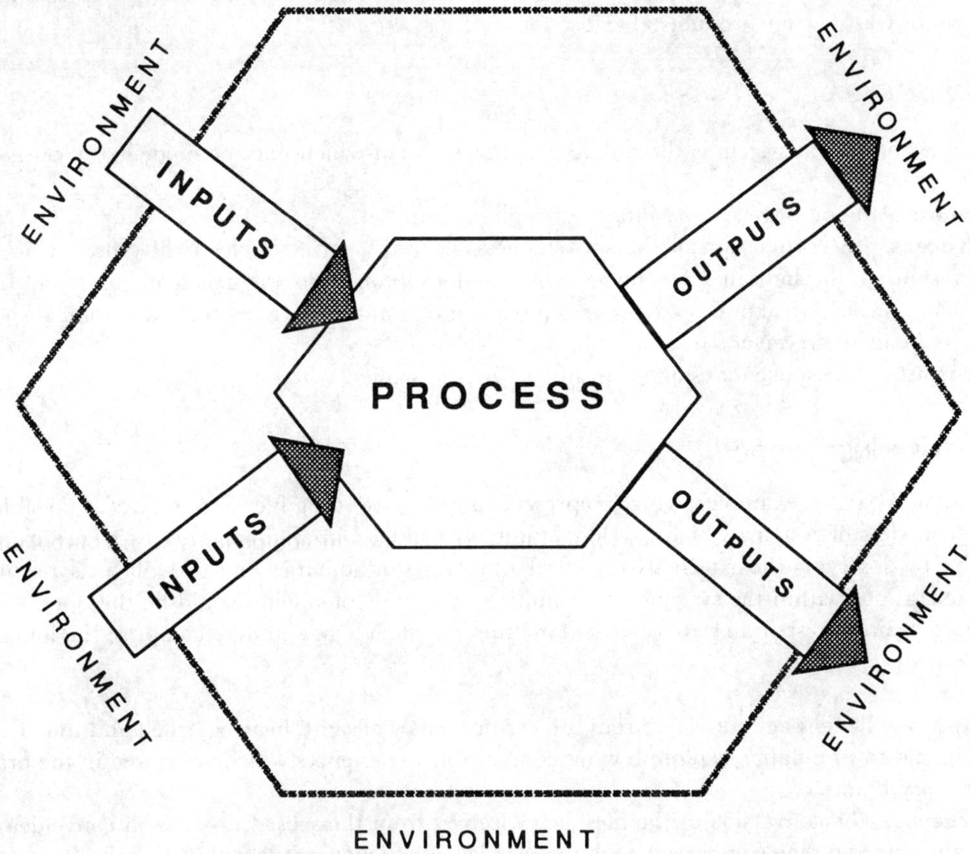

indeed negative value, to the local residents in terms of increased noise and pollution. Hence, a system may add value to only part of the total environment that it relates to.

4 **Environment**—The environment represents the context or framework of organisations, institutions, structures, procedures and constraints within which a system operates. In essence, the system will be receiving and responding to various inputs from the environment and providing outputs and responses to the environment. This dimension and the system's interaction within it are discussed in more detail in 3.1.2.

To illustrate the first three elements of a system in a more general context prior to applying them to the more specific information system, three different examples of a system are provided:

(a) domestic heating system,
(b) telephone system, and
(c) human response system.

DOMESTIC HEATING SYSTEM

The first example of a system is the domestic heating system which may be decomposed into the three basic elements:

1 **Inputs**—energy in the form of fuel such as coal, oil, electricity and/or gas. For installation or implementation purposes, there must also be conductor, carrier or distributor elements to deliver the heat created to the users. This may take the form of the boiler and associated system of pipework and radiators, and water as the circulating medium.

2 **Process**—conversion of the fuel inputs into energy, usually by a process of burning, to release energy in the form of heat, and then pumping the heat through the distribution system to heat the house.

3 **Outputs**—may be direct in the form of heat within each room of the house, hot water for washing, waste products from the fuel combustion processes involved, etc, or indirect in the form of waste water products after use for washing, etc.

TELEPHONE SYSTEM

A second example of a system is the public telephone system which may be modelled in terms of:

1 **Inputs**—the message spoken into the telephone handset.
2 **Process**—the conversion of the spoken message into a series of electrical pulses which are transmitted through the telephone cables and exchanges to the receiving handset. Upon receipt, the electrical pulses are converted back into sound waves to recreate the original spoken message in the receiver's handset.
3 **Outputs**—the spoken message transmitted by the sender.

HUMAN RESPONSE SYSTEM

In addition to these examples which represent physical or tangible systems, it is possible to construct models of systems which are less tangible or indeed intangible. These systems are only detectable by observing the externally manifested processes or activities that take place as a result of hidden operations within the system. An example of this type of system would be the operation of the human brain in responding to a particular stimulus. Such a system may comprise the following elements:

1 **Inputs**—the messages received from the various senses of sight, hearing, smell and touch. This will tend to stimulate recall of previous comparable experiences which are stored in the brain's memory banks.
2 **Process**—the conversion of the messages received from the senses into a form convenient for evaluation and then comparison with the recalled experiences to create images or perceptions of the situation immediately faced. This should lead to the generation of appropriate signals to other components of the body which are designed to make the necessary responses.
3 **Outputs**—a set of views, opinions, perceptions and conclusions which relate to the situation faced, with decisions to act or not to act based on those conclusions as to the necessary responses required.

A simple example of the operation of this system would be the driver who approaches a traffic light at red. The visual message of the red light is transmitted to the brain. This is matched against previous knowledge and experiences stored in the brain which suggest that the red light means danger and that the law requires the driver to stop the vehicle (even a fire engine on the way to a major disaster will technically break the law if the instruction of the red light is ignored). Following this processing, a series of output commands are transmitted which result in the necessary actions of the driver's limbs to halt or not to halt the vehicle.

3.1.2 System environment

The fourth element in the modelling of a system in addition to the input, output and process elements is the environment. This was shown in Figure 3.1, but it has not been referred to specifically in the previous examples. In fact, every system must operate within a context or environment and, if it is to function effectively, it will interact with this environment by receiving inputs and delivering outputs. But the parts of the environment from which the system receives its inputs are not necessarily the same as those to which it delivers its outputs. Hence, the retail food shop as a system will receive its primary inputs from the food manufacturers in the environment, and the outputs will be collected by, or delivered to, the customers in the environment. Similarly in the domestic heating example, the fuel input will be received from the energy suppliers, but it produces an output for the customer and not the supplier.

The other components of the environment with which the given system interacts may themselves be classified as systems. Figure 3.2 provides a schematic view of the interdependence of a

FIGURE 3.2 **Layers of interacting systems in the system's environment**

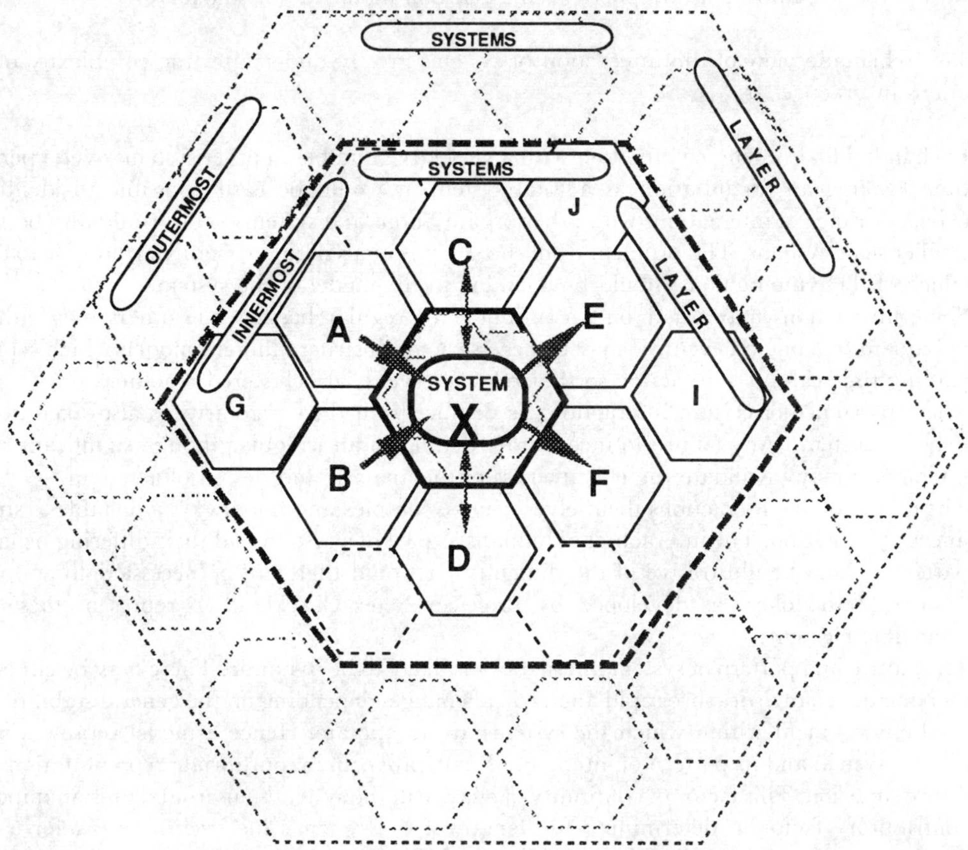

system with the other systems in its environment. In conceptual terms, the environment may be viewed as a series of levels or layers of systems which surrounds and supports the primary system under consideration. The innermost layer represents those elements or systems within the environment which have the most direct and positive effect upon the system. Other systems or elements in the outer layers have progressively less direct interaction with and, therefore, less effect upon, the system at the centre. Indeed, the more remote the systems in the outer layers, the less likely it is that their influence will be felt in the inner layers. Thus, when a systems analyst is called upon to map a system's environment, only those systems in the innermost layer would normally be considered, although in planning damage limitation strategies, the analyst needs to recognise that systems in the outer layers may, by a form of domino effect, occasionally produce a significant and unexpected impact on the centre system.

System X (not to be confused with the telephone system) in Figure 3.2 may interact directly with each of the other six systems shown in the inner layer of its environment. In a practical situation, the degree of interaction or the nature of the interdependence is likely to vary in each of the relationships between the various systems. For example, Systems A and B may only provide inputs to System X and receive no outputs, while Systems E and F may only receive outputs from System X without contributing any inputs. Systems C and D provide a model of the third possibility in that they provide inputs to, and receive outputs from, System X following processing. In the earlier example of the domestic heating system, the systems would match up as follows:

— (A and B) = the fuel supply system which provides the basic inputs.
— (C and D) = the system of pipework and radiators which receives the heated water for distribution and returns the water to System X for further processing or reheating.
— (E and F) = the flue system designed to extract the waste and often harmful products from the fuel combustion process and to dispose of these safely into the atmosphere.
— (G, I and J) = systems which do not interact directly with System X, but may have an indirect impact on its inputs, processes or outputs through the other systems. In the domestic heating situation this may be represented by dislocations in the primary processing or distribution of the

fuel used, eg a power cut, or the enactment of legislation to control the emission of harmful waste products into the atmosphere such as carbon monoxide or smoke.

This schematic view of the interaction of systems grossly understates the complexity of such interactions in practice, as:

1 Each individual system may interact with a very large number of other systems over a period of time. Taking an organisation as a total system, it would be easily possible to identify an extensive range of interactions with other organisations and systems. This would also be true of smaller scale systems. The problem from the systems analysis and design viewpoint is to decide which of these interactions should be included in the model of the system.

2 Some interactions may occur on a continuous or regular basis, while others may either be infrequent or a one-off event. It may be necessary to construct different models which represent varying timescales of interaction so that relevant events are clustered together.

3 The importance of certain interactions as distinct from their regularity is also likely to vary between systems. Any failure to incorporate details on an irregular though significant system interaction may invalidate the effectiveness of the analysis and design of a system.

4 The nature of the interactions themselves may be complex and not always amenable to straight line representation. The interaction of humans as part of a system and their differing behaviour patterns would be illustrative of the difficulty. It would therefore be necessary to adopt Soft System Methodology as developed by Professor Peter Checkland to represent these more intangible elements.

5 The nature and pattern of system interactions is likely to be dynamic. There may be either slow incremental change or more rapid and radical changes depending on the general stability of the total environment within which the systems are to operate. Hence a model representing the current system and its pattern of interactions may prove an inappropriate representation of the future situation. This factor of continuity of change in the system's environment is an important contributory factor in determining the length of the system's life cycle (see 6.2 for a fuller treatment of the system's life cycle concept).

3.1.3 Systems, sub-systems and the system hierarchy

Another approach to describing the situation shown in Figure 3.2 is to use the terms **system** and **sub-system**. By using these terms, it is usually possible to develop a **systems hierarchy** for any given situation such that any system can be seen to be made up of several sub-systems, each of which in turn may comprise further sets of sub-systems. Further, the immediate system may be viewed as a sub-system of a larger system. In Figure 3.2, all of the systems lettered A to E and X may be classified as sub-systems of the larger system, a possibility represented by the dotted line embracing them. In turn, each of these sub-systems may be represented by a number of sub-systems. Thus, in the domestic heating example, System X in the figure may represent the energy conversion process and may itself comprise the following sub-systems:

(a) ignition system,
(b) temperature control system,
(c) timing system, and
(d) safety cut-out system.

Each of these sub-systems could potentially be further decomposed into sub-systems which would more particularly relate to their constituent parts or activities in undertaking their function. The energy conversion process of which they are part is itself only a sub-system of the total domestic heating system.

Thus, because it is almost impossible to conceive of the nature of the last or highest element in the hierarchy of systems, every system is almost inevitably a sub-system of a larger system. The actual decisions in the modelling process to select elements for inclusion as being either a system in its own right or as part of a larger system will depend on the purpose behind developing the model of that system, and generally relates to the level of detailed analysis and investigation that can be cost-justified. Progressing down the system hierarchy, the level of detail successively increases allowing more detailed analysis and design to be undertaken of the various sub-systems. Conversely, progressing up the systems hierarchy provides a successively broader view of the systems and the sub-systems operating within them. The advantages of viewing the system hierarchy at differing levels will be illustrated through consideration of an organisation's system hierarchy.

3.1.4 The organisation as an example of a system hierarchy

Any organisation ought to be viewed as part of an overall system operating within an environment comprising a number of other systems. For example, the business organisation may be viewed as operating within an overall system of business and interfacing with other systems including the prevailing:

(a) economic system(s),
(b) political system(s),
(c) government policy-making or legislative system(s),
(d) financial system(s),
(e) social system(s),
(f) technology system,
(g) market system(s),
(h) competitive system.

At a macro level, the organisation may interact with each of these broad systems at a number of different levels including local, national and international. At a micro level, the organisation itself may be viewed as a system comprising a number of levels of sub-systems as shown in Figure 3.3.

The five levels of the system hierarchy identified in the diagram may be summarised as:

1 **Corporate/strategic**—these are systems concerned with supporting the direction, co-ordination and management of the organisation as a corporate unit in terms of its objectives, policies, strategies and relationships with the key systems in the external environment. Systems at this level are often termed **strategic support systems**. Examples of systems at this level would include:
(a) business/economic/market forecasting,
(b) corporate budgets and performance analysis,
(c) financial planning and modelling.

2 **Business unit**—many of the larger organisations comprise a number of distinct units which operate within different areas of technology, and with different product lines or serving different markets or elements of the environment. These units may either be identified as divisions within the organisation or they will operate as subsidiary companies within a holding company arrangement. The systems which are designed to support this level are also primarily related to the strategic management issues, although in this context, they tend to be more concerned with the specific product, than the technology or market aspects of the unit itself. Such systems are also likely to be termed strategic decision support systems (DSSs), even though their content will differ in some respects from the corporate level systems. Examples of the type of system at this level would be:
(a) market research and forecasting for specific products and markets,
(b) competitor intelligence and performance,
(c) performance analysis of particular product lines.

3 **Functions**—systems at this level will be designed to support the management of the primary functions of the organisation and to incorporate systems concerned with aspects of strategic and medium-term planning as well as co-ordination, performance monitoring, evaluation and control. The more general term for this type of system is a DSS. Systems at this level may incorporate:
(a) financial planning and budgeting,
(b) manufacturing performance analysis,
(c) profit/volume/pricing analysis.

4 **Departmental**—the primary issues at the departmental level are related to the implementa-

FIGURE 3.3 **Hierarchy of systems in an organisation**

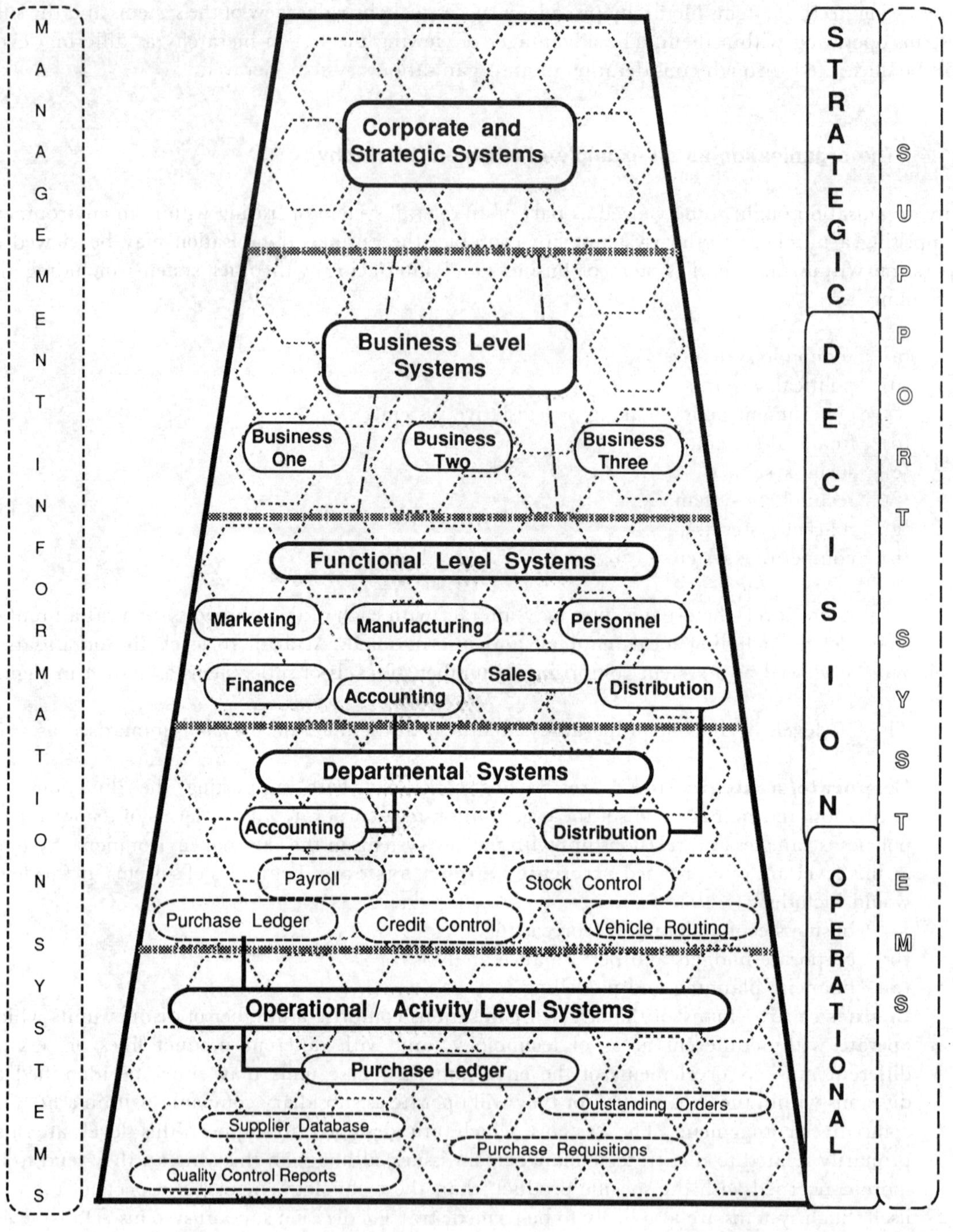

tion of strategic plans and the management of the resources and operations within the department. Typically the time-horizon is short to medium-term, and the systems used are often similar to the DSSs, although the term applied to these is often **operational control systems**, as they focus more on the planning and control of operational activities as opposed to the analysis, planning and control of tactical or strategic issues. Typical examples of these systems would be:

(a) credit management and control,

(b) stock control,

(c) quality control.

5 **Operational**—the operational level systems are designed to support the individual day-to-day operations of the organisation, and they appear in a wide variety of forms depending on the nature of the operations or transactions concerned (for an example, see the sales order

processing system described in 3.4). The terms **operational support systems** or **transaction processing systems** are frequently used to refer to systems at this level. Examples of this level of system include:

(a) sales order processing,
(b) stock requisitioning,
(c) production progress chasing.

Although it is true that a number of terms have been developed to assist in distinguishing between the systems which appear at different levels in the hierarchy, in practice the degree of distinction is less obvious because:

1 **Common data**—systems at different levels frequently use the same data sources, and the processing of the data relevant to each level is undertaken simultaneously. This follows from the fact that the information used at a higher level is often little more than a summarised form of the information used for activities at the lower levels.
2 **Decision interdependence**—the nature of the activities between the levels is often interlocking as it is rarely possible, say, to make strategic decisions without also considering the management, or operational implications. Moreover, the analysis of strategic alternatives may often require detailed investigations of certain dimensions of the operations to test the feasibility of each possible alternative.
3 **Common decision-makers**—in smaller organisations many of the levels of decision-making and control which are differentiated in Figure 3.3 are undertaken by the same individual, who may be simultaneously responsible for the strategic, management and operational control in a certain functional area of the organisation.

A broad term used to define all of the systems designed to support the management and control of the organisation at all levels is Management Information systems (MISs), which generally encompasses strategic support systems, DSSs, and some elements of the operational support systems concerned with the monitoring and control of departmental operations.

It should be recognised that while a number of these sub-systems may operate within clearly identified functional or departmental boundaries, there are also a number of sub-systems which necessarily operate across several functions or departments within the organisation. To simplify the management's decision-making task by reducing the number of variables to be considered, the various internal sub-systems in the organisation will usually be organised so that they interact with only a limited number of the other systems in the organisation's external environment, and often with only a part or sub-system of the total system in the environment. For example, the payroll sub-system in an organisation may have links with the income tax sub-system in the overall government/legislative system and with the local banking sub-system within the overall financial system, but have little or no links with any of the other environmental systems identified earlier.

Recognition of this hierarchy of systems and sub-systems is of particular importance to the activities of analysis, evaluation, development and design as applied to systems. Viewing a system and its component sub-systems at different levels provides differing and valuable perspectives for these activities. For example:

1 **The total system level** provides an overview of the entire system, indicating the major interactions with other systems in the environment, the overall balance and structure of the system and the major component sub-systems. The systems analyst or designer requires this view as it provides the perspective within which the overall or strategic development of the system may be viewed, and it also assists in locating or putting into context, the specific sub-systems which are of more immediate or tactical concern.
2 **The functional/departmental sub-systems level** provides an understanding of the major sub-systems within a particular function or department, and the nature and extent of the interactions between each of these sub-systems. The tactical or short- to medium-term system development activities need to be aware of these interfaces and seek to maximise the efficiency and effectiveness of these interactions.
3 **The individual operational sub-systems level** within functions, departments or areas of activity provides the basis for the detailed analysis and design activities concerning the

operation of the system and its effective interaction or interface with humans whether as operatives inputting resources or controlling the processing, or receiving the resource output.

3.1.5 System boundaries

While the analyst may be able to separate systems and sub-systems on a conceptual basis, either in terms of their different levels in the hierarchy, or in terms of some functional division between those operating at the same level, the practice is far more difficult. The primary difficulty lies in identifying where one system or sub-system ends in terms of its outputs, and where the next system begins. This applies equally at both the horizontal and vertical levels of system interfaces, and it is evident in both the physical processing systems as well as the information systems. An example of this problem of boundary definition in the context of information systems would be the situation in which two sub-systems require the same basic input data, but process this data in different ways to produce different outputs.

Hence, an organisation may create a manufacturing reporting system. Its purpose may be the recording, collection and processing of the production output levels achieved by individual employees, and it is likely to function as a sub-system of the performance monitoring process for employees as productive workers, and for operations in general. The wages system may equally use this data as the basis upon which to calculate the wages due to each employee, say, on a piece work rate. The data as used is the same for both systems, but the nature of the processing and the outputs may differ. The issue is whether, in analysing or constructing a model of the wages system, the analyst should incorporate the activities of recording and processing the basic data currently undertaken within the manufacturing reporting system. In practice, this involves fairly pragmatic decisions by the systems analyst based on:

(a) the nature and scope of the analysis and design task in terms of the detail required,
(b) the stage in the overall systems development process,
(c) the importance of data input or output quality and the need to exercise control over assuring this quality,
(d) the degree of integration proposed between the appropriate sub-systems and the importance of ensuring effective interaction.

3.1.6 System interfaces

The essential feature inherent in the interface between the various sub-systems, both internal and external to the organisation, is that there is some form of resource exchange. This resource exchange is normally in the form of an input/output relationship and, in the business and commercial context, it will be a reciprocal exchange. Thus, the provision of raw materials by a supplier usually involves the reciprocal supply of money or equivalent value to pay for those materials. Similarly, the delivery of processed outputs to another system, eg to the wholesale distributor, will usually be reciprocated by payment for the goods or services delivered. The overall objective of the business or commercial system as outlined in Chapter 1, is to undertake each system represented by the input-process-output cycle of operations at a level which yields an economic reward or profit. In the not-for-profit organisation, the incidence of financial compensation in return for resources received or delivered is likely to be less evident, although there will still often be a reciprocal exchange of other resources or services to assist in meeting variable costs. In a number of general situations, the financial compensation provided will be less than the value of the resources exchanged, as in the present structure of public benefit provision through local education or the health services.

Other systems also involve the exchange of resources or value between the various sub-systems. The domestic heating example, outlined under 3.1.1, involves an exchange between the unprocessed fuels, heated water and waste products. In this system there is less evidence of the exchange of financial compensation other than to the supplier of the unprocessed fuel and, if it is efficient, the ability to avoid other payments to create or run an alternative or supplementary heating system. Similarly, the example of the telephone system involves the exchange of resources between the various sub-systems, though the level of reciprocity between the sub-systems is less evident and financial compensation is usually paid to the supplier of the telephone company which makes the communication possible and, if different, to the company which supplies the telephone-based service, eg the chat-line service which provides the value of friendly conversation to relieve boredom or loneliness for a fee. In the third example of the human brain system, there is an exchange of resources between the various human sub-systems, though no evidence of financial compensation for the supply of the resources other than payment to the present holder of the brain if the output is marketable!

3.1.7 Communications

The reliability of the interface between systems depends upon the effectiveness and robustness of the communications. The quality of the integration and interaction achievable between the various systems will largely be determined by the following factors:

(a) the quality of the original data,
(b) the quality of the transmitter and receiver,
(c) the quality of the channel, and
(d) the effectiveness of the feedback loops employed.

The main elements which comprise the communications system are shown in Figure 3.4, and the analysis of the figure is followed by three illustrative examples relating to voice, written and electronic communications.

1 **Quality of original data**—the quality of the data available will be judged either by the content or by reference to the other qualitative dimensions outlined in 2.8. There is a direct relationship between the initial data quality and the maximum quality level of data that may be produced by a system. A commonly used expression for this situation is:

Rubbish In = Rubbish Out

which indicates that poor quality input data may only produce poor quality output data. In one sense, there is no doubt that if the initial data is corrupted, little can be made of it. But if the data is merely inadequate to support decision-making in its initial form, processing may enhance its quality. The question is as to the degree of improvement achievable. This will always be limited by the quality and detail of the input data as obtained and recorded.

Issues related to quality are those of **data redundancy** and **data reduction**. Data redundancy implies that parts of the data collected and input are unnecessary for the processing required to produce the desired outputs. Generally, this would suggest inefficiency as additional units of unwanted data are being collected, stored, transmitted, sorted out and, possibly, discarded. This may considerably add to the overall communication, handling and processing costs. There are some situations in which data redundancy is deliberately introduced. Here, additional or duplicate data elements are created to assist in assuring the quality of the overall communication process (see later in this sub-section under feedback systems). Data reduction, on the other hand, usually represents a deliberate policy of reducing these costs by only transmitting a summarised or truncated version of the complete data. The use of abbreviated words in telex transmissions is an example of data reduction. While this technique may improve the speed of data transfer and reduce the cost because of the lower volume of data, an obvious danger is the greater potential impact that interference or noise may have on the quality of the data received. In the worst case, the transmission of only key characters or data elements may result in either unintelligible or misleading data being received depending on the nature and severity of the interference or noise in the communications system (see paragraph 3 on channel quality).

2 **Transmission or receiver quality**—the quality of the devices used to transmit and receive the data at either end of the communications channel will also influence the effectiveness of the communications. It ought to be recognised that the transmitting or encoding systems largely involve some form of human interface, eg the use of a telephone, transcription by typewriter to hard copy, or the use of a keyboard by stock control operatives to input data. Such human interfaces are frequently the source of the greatest loss of data quality and, as a result, considerable research and development has been undertaken to improve or often eliminate this

FIGURE 3.4 **System communications**

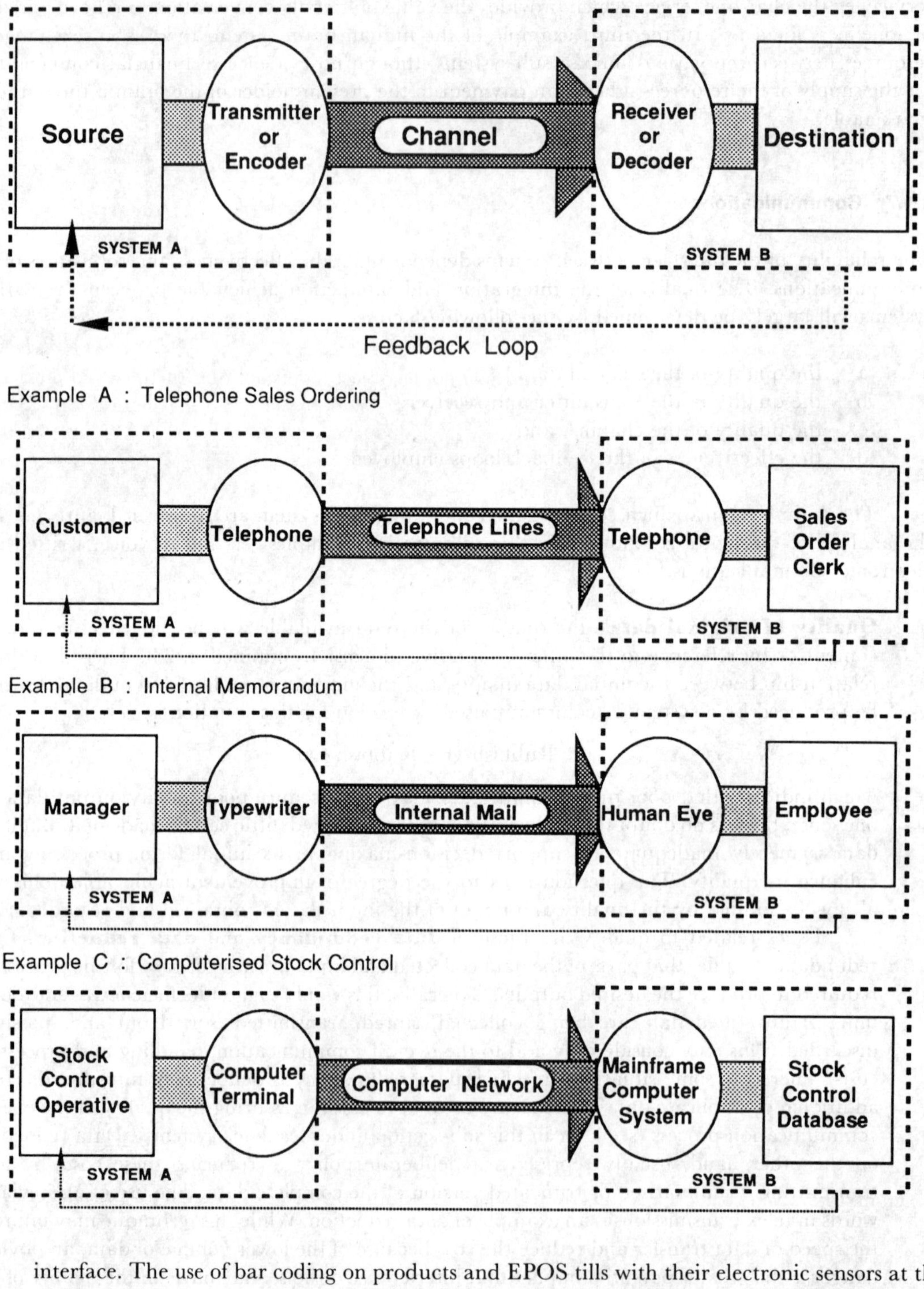

interface. The use of bar coding on products and EPOS tills with their electronic sensors at the supermarket instead of relying on the checkout assistant to accurately key in the identity and price of every item sold is an example of such a development. A similar problem exists at the receiver/decoder end of the communications channel, as in the cases of the telephone sales clerk who is employed to hear and then record the data received, or the human eye of the employee which must read the memorandum from the manager. Technological developments have made a larger impact here. The primary reason for this is that, providing the data has been transmitted in an electronic form, it may be input directly into the electronic processing system without further human involvement. The example of a network of terminals linked to a mainframe computer system, as in the stock control example in Figure 3.4, is illustrative of this.

3 **Channel quality**—the type and quality of the media used to channel the data from the transmitting system to the receiving system will influence the quality of the communications.

To adopt engineering terminology, the channel may be affected by interference, distortion and noise. **Interference** is often associated with some form of technical difficulty, eg inadequate shielding in the cabling used (see 5.12.3 and 12.4.6). **Distortion** is where a material change occurs in the form of the data during transmission. Any reduction in the volume of a telephone message during transmission would be a form of distortion. The term often refers to changes which have qualities of predictability and uniformity of effect, so that the data can be restored by an inverse operation at the receiving end, eg by increasing the volume on a telephone receiver. **Noise**, as distinct from distortion, represents a more random and unpredictable form of interference or change in the message transmitted. In the case of noise, any part of the message as transmitted may be altered, corrupted or misinterpreted by the receiving system. The term may also apply to the superfluous data content in the message transmitted which obscures the intended meaning, or to the use of language or a writing style in a document which may be misunderstood by the recipient.

4 **Feedback loops**—a fairly common method of ensuring the integrity of any communication between two systems is to institute some form of feedback loop such that the received message, or parts of it, may be transmitted in the reverse direction and checked by the originator. The telephone sales-order clerk may, for instance, repeat the full details of the order to the customer prior to completing the transaction, the employee may telephone the manager to verify the intended interpretation of the instructions in the memorandum, and the mainframe computer may retransmit the message received on to the computer terminal screen for final validation by the stock control clerk.

Another method of improving the integrity of the communications is to incorporate extra elements of data which may be used to verify specific dimensions of the data transmitted, eg batch totals provide a check that all the items transmitted have been received, while column and hash totals provide some check on the integrity of the data within the records. The incorporation of check digits or other coding systems may also be used to improve the quality and accuracy of the communication process (see 15.2). Each of these methods invariably increases the amount of data to be handled and transmitted and therefore adds to data redundancy. The irony is that the more data that requires transmission, the greater the potential incidence of interference, distortion and noise, thus counteracting some of the benefits to data integrity achieved through their use.

While these feedback and other methods of verifying the integrity of the data will probably improve the quality of the communications and reduce the problems associated with transmission, receiver and channel quality, they are not infallible. Equally, they will not be capable of improving the quality of the original data prior to transmission given that, at best, they can only produce a perfect reproduction of the original data. It should also be recognised that each of these mechanisms involves additional costs both in the initial design and to operate, and may also reduce the efficiency of the communications system even though improving its effectiveness.

3.1.8 System control

A feature of many systems is the incorporation of some form of regulatory or control mechanism which monitors and corrects any deviations in the desired performance of the system. This may either be internal to the system so that the system is self-correcting, or it may be external to the system and require action by another system to provide the necessary corrective actions. In addition to correcting any detected deviations in the internal processing elements, a system may also have to respond to changes in the environment both in terms of inputs received and outputs required. Most naturally occurring systems have in-built control systems which take corrective actions either for changes in the environment or for deviations in the normal system processes. In the case of human-generated systems, these control features need to be designed into the system itself. Hence, excessive increases in the temperature of the fuel core in a nuclear power station ought to result in a sequence of activities to control the deviation, although the nature of these activities and their effectiveness will depend on the quality of the design process.

The basic issue from the systems design point of view is the degree to which potential changes in the environment and the difficulties which may be encountered in the processing and communications systems, may be accurately predicted or foreseen. The designer also needs to establish the extent to which the system should be capable of responding to changes in the environment. Because of the additional capacities, the design of systems which are highly responsive or flexible often incurs significantly higher design and operating costs than those designed to meet only the more obvious demands of the environment. Failure to predict certain situations, inadequate detection systems, ineffective feedback systems, or poorly designed features to respond to the situation could have serious consequences for the overall system's effectiveness and efficiency. The organisation must therefore make design decisions based on accurate cost-benefit analysis.

An **open-loop control system** refers to those systems which are not responsive to changes in the environment. Such a system, as outlined in Figure 3.5, has a one-way relationship with its environment, having no mechanisms to monitor the effect of its outputs on the environment and hence no means of adapting to changes in this environment. If the environment is relatively stable then such systems may operate effectively for long periods of time. In more dynamic environments, such systems will rapidly disintegrate or become obsolete relative to the requirements of their environment. Systems which are completely immune to the needs of their environment are becoming increasingly rare, particularly in the field of information systems, where changes in the technological and the general organisational operating environments are becoming increasingly rapid and dramatic.

FIGURE 3.5 **Control systems**

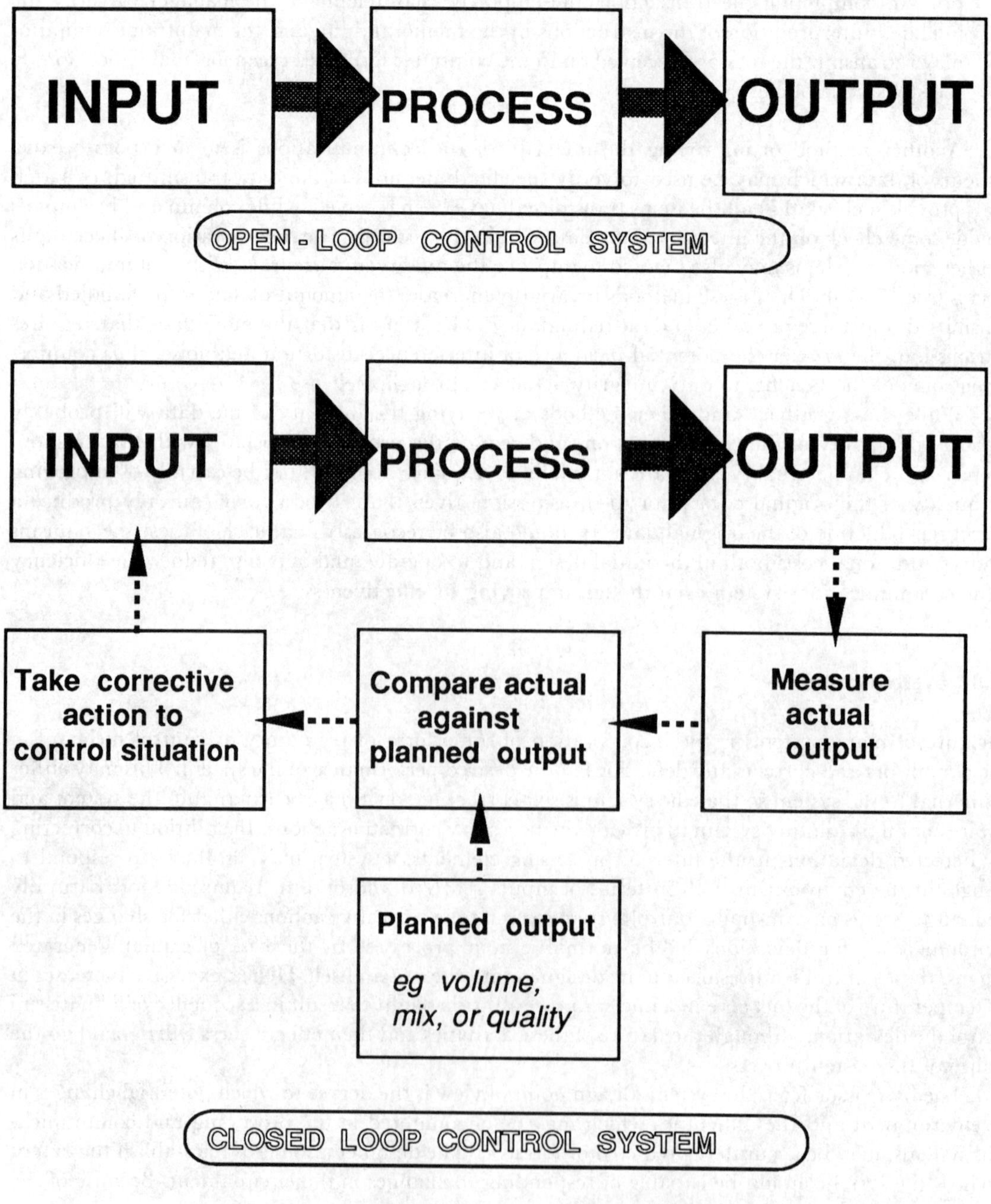

A **closed-loop control system** is the term applied to systems which are responsive or adaptive to the environment within which the system operates. Usually the system would incorporate desired or planned performance parameters, which may be specified in terms of the different anticipated environmental situations that may be encountered. The system design would also incorporate some mechanism for testing both the environment and the system's performance and feeding back the findings to the system itself. Figure 3.5 provides a schematic outline of the main components of the control system. Control mechanisms within the system would then institute the necessary changes to respond to the changing environmental situation. It should be recognised that few human-generated systems are completely responsive to changes in the environment. Thus, systems will differ in terms of their degree of responsiveness, a factor often determined by the effectiveness and quality of the control system in operation.

3.2 ORGANISATIONAL INFORMATION SYSTEMS

3.2.1 Functions of an information system

The development of the concepts and approaches of systems theory outlined above may be applied to any system which deals with resources, including the information resource. An information system in an organisation may be represented by one or more of the following functions:

1. Recording transactions between particular systems and sub-systems in terms of the inputs and outputs. This may be between the organisation and other external systems, or internally between the organisation's various sub-systems.
2. Recording or monitoring the processing activities within a system or sub-system with a view to providing information on the efficiency and effectiveness of the operations or activities involved.
3. Processing the information itself as the basic resource. Examples of this include market research and intelligence systems, library catalogue systems and teletext services.

In the first two functions the information system is operating in parallel to the other operational systems within the organisation, and is providing information on the activities involved. In a sense, the information system and its sub-systems are essentially shadow systems designed to monitor the performance of the other (productive) systems. This would be true even in the third function where the primary resource being processed is information itself. The situation is complicated further by the existence of information sub-systems which are designed to monitor the development and operational performance of the organisation's information systems themselves. These latter information systems will be explained later in the text.

3.2.2 Elements of an information system

A model of an information system can be produced by applying the elements from the general systems approach. From a functional point of view, an information system is a system primarily concerned with the conversion of data into information, as discussed in Chapter 2. The contribution that such a systems model makes to the analysis and design process is outlined below in relation to each of the major system elements discussed earlier. Only a broad view of the contribution of the systems approach is provided at this stage as a more detailed view is provided in the later chapters dealing specifically with the development, analysis and design of information systems.

The contribution of the general systems approach to the analysis and design of information systems, may be summarised as:

INPUTS

1. the identification both of the data available in other sub-systems and of the data that may have to be originated by the system itself;

2 the evaluation of the potential to interface with other sub-systems, either in the technological/technical sense of the compatibility of the systems, or in the commercial sense of feasibility and costs;
3 the assessment of both the content and quality of the information available and the degree to which this matches the needs of the information system's users.

PROCESS

1 the analysis of the processing activities required to convert the input received into the outputs required, which may include a selection from:
 (a) recording,
 (b) conversion into other units or media,
 (c) storage,
 (d) calculation,
 (e) summarisation,
 (f) retrieval,
 (g) communication.
2 an assessment of the quality standards required in terms of processing to maintain the content and quality of the data input;
3 an evaluation of the potential effectiveness and efficiency of the processing activities involved;
4 an investigation of the interaction between the various sub-systems involved in the processing of the data.

OUTPUT

1 the analysis and evaluation of the potential users of the information and their requirements in terms of content and quality;
2 an investigation of the alternative means of communicating to the users in terms of media used, frequency, content and style;
3 an examination of the nature of the interaction process between the system, its users and other sub-systems in terms of regular communications or *ad hoc* enquiries.

ENVIRONMENT

1 the identification and assessment of the interaction between the system, as both currently and potentially constituted, and other external systems or sub-systems. This aspect is becoming increasingly important as the developments in technology facilitate rapid and cost-effective communications through the networking of information systems.
2 the evaluation of the appropriate methods for assessing the quality of the output from the system.

COMMUNICATION CHANNELS

1 the recognition of the potential communication channels and alternative media, and the selection of the most appropriate for the given situation in terms of volume and quality of data transmission required;
2 the identification of likely sources of interference, distortion and noise on the channels used and an evaluation of the possible means of overcoming these difficulties.

FEEDBACK AND CONTROL SYSTEMS

1 the analysis and development of appropriate feedback systems which will record the quality, effectiveness and efficiency of the input and processing stages in the system, and monitor the environmental responses to outputs;
2 an appraisal of the likely situations requiring control actions, and the development and evaluation of automatic control routines or the provision of information to facilitate effective human control.

3.2.3 Major components in the organisation's information system

The major components in a typical business or commercial organisation are shown in Figure 3.6. The not-for-profit organisations will have a number of similar components though the terminology used and the nature of their functions may vary from the model shown.

FIGURE 3.6 **Components of a business organisation's information system**

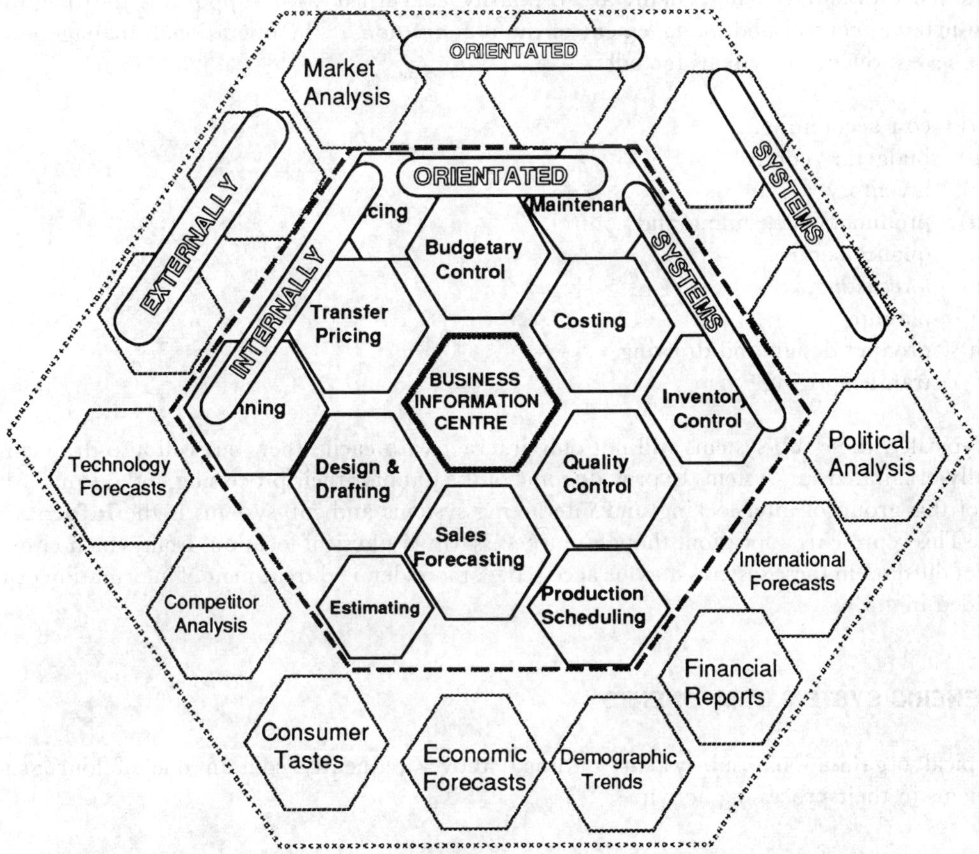

The sub-systems in the overall information system have been divided into two groups according to the degree with which they interact with the external environment and its sub-systems.

EXTERNALLY-ORIENTATED SUB-SYSTEMS

These sub-systems record the transactions between the organisation and the systems within its environment in terms of suppliers, customers and other agencies, incorporating:

(a) purchasing,
(b) goods received,
(c) purchase payments/ledger,
(d) marketing,
(e) sales,
(f) distribution,
(g) sales invoicing,
(h) sales receipts,
(i) personnel,
(j) wages and salaries,
(k) research and development.

Many of these sub-systems reflect the primary activities of the organisation. As such, there is likely to be interaction both internally and externally as data is transferred between each sub-system to facilitate co-ordinated actions relating to the suppliers, customers or other agencies in the environment. For example, the transfer of customer order and credit details from the sales sub-system is essential for the preparation of sales invoices and the subsequent collection of monies owing.

INTERNALLY-ORIENTATED SUB-SYSTEMS

The internally orientated sub-systems are primarily concerned with supporting the operations, decision-making, control and management of the organisation at the operational, managerial and strategic levels. Such sub-systems include:

(a) cost accounting,
(b) budgetary control,
(c) inventory,
(d) production scheduling and control,
(e) quality control,
(f) forecasting,
(g) planning,
(h) product design and drawing,
(i) transfer pricing.

Typically, these sub-systems will not only interact with each other, but will also draw on the externally-orientated sub-systems to provide some of the data for their processing and output. At the centre of this group of inter-locking and interacting systems and sub-systems is the **information centre**. This represents a location, though not necessarily a physical location, from which either all or part of the data in these systems may be accessed. A more detailed treatment of information centres is provided in 4.3.1.

3.3 GENERIC SYSTEM COMPONENTS

The typical organisational sub-systems outlined above frequently contain one of four generic components in their processing activities:

1 text or word processing,
2 spreadsheet manipulation,
3 database storage and retrieval, and
4 expert system operations.

These activities are equally likely to be found in either the externally or the internally-orientated sub-systems. A number of the applications are also likely to be found in systems which rely more on the manual processing of data than on electronic technology. This should not conceal the fact that the advent of powerful and rapid data processing technology has considerably enhanced the power and potential contribution of each of these components. The basic elements of each of these will be introduced in the following paragraphs with more detailed treatment included in Chapters 4, 5 and 7.

3.3.1 Word processing

Text or word processing concerns the manipulation of data in the form of text by the processes of creation, storage and modification. The efficient application of these processes does require appropriate computer or word processing technology, although systems of standard format letters and correspondence have permitted the modest application of such processes in manual systems. Such processes may prove efficient in situations where:

1 the original data or text entered may require significant modification prior to final output and distribution;

2 the bulk of the data or text remains the same for a large volume of potential recipients with only minor modifications required for the different recipients, eg changes in name, address and title for the recipients of a standard letter;

3 different documents may be created for communication (whether electronic or manual) by selecting from a series of standard paragraphs or blocks of text. Thus, different combinations or sequences are prepared to meet the particular needs of a given situation, eg the compilation of contractual agreements and conditions of employment for differing groups of employees in an organisation by abstracting, and perhaps modifying, the most appropriate clauses from a databank of precedents.

The application processes associated with or developing from word processing include:

1 **Desk-Top Publishing (DTP)** which provides a range of specialist facilities to design and modify the layout of the text to improve its appearance and communications effectiveness.

2 **Mailing list applications** provide a constructive link between word processing facilities and databases. The best results are achieved when powerful facilities are created to tailor the contents and layout of correspondence to the needs of particular recipients.

3 **Business graphics** represents a link between the text processing and spreadsheet components, allowing sometimes complex information to be displayed in a form more easily understood. This may be screen-based or modern printers may reproduce the output in a form which can be incorported into reports and other textual material, thereby enhancing the effectiveness of the communication. DTP software facilities now provide sophisticated packages to manipulate the presentation of text and graphics on the printed page. Common examples of PC-based word processing packages include Wordperfect and Microsoft Word. More sophisticated DTP packages include Ventura and Aldus Pagemaker. An example of a popular business graphics package would be Harvard Graphics. The majority of the more sophisticated packages require a high specification PC and monitor.

3.3.2 Spreadsheets

Spreadsheet processing primarily concerns the manipulation of numeric data, though textual data may be incorporated to facilitate titling and other forms of brief commentary relating to the data. The layout of a spreadsheet is in the form of a matrix with a series of rows and columns as shown in Figure 3.7.

The operation of a spreadsheet simulates the sequence of manual processes or calculations that may be performed on a set of data. The application of spreadsheet processing is particularly appropriate in cases where:

1 A set of identical or standard calculations or manipulations needs to be repeated several times for different sets of data, for example, technical calculations in the engineering design department to establish the precise composition and tolerances required in the manufacture of a particular component to meet differing customer requirements.

2 The data is to be processed using a continuous sequence of calculations, such that the output from one calculation represents the input to the next calculation in the sequence. The calculation of profit within an income statement would represent this type of application, or the preparation of monthly budget forecasts as shown in Figure 3.7.

3 The use of spreadsheets to support forecasting is significant. This may be achieved either by analysing the effect of changes in a single variable in a given situation or by simulating the effects of changes in a variety of the parameters. This is normally termed **sensitivity analysis**. Its utility lies in the scientific testing of the robustness of the predicted model. Measuring the effect on the profitability of a capital investment under differing assumptions of rates of interest, market growth rates or inflation rates is representative of the type of application involved.

FIGURE 3.7 **Spreadsheet application**

	Sales forecasts / income and expenditure budgets						
	January	February	March	April	May	June	Total
Sales Revenue Forecasts							
Product A							
Units	1200	1253	1246	1368	1413	1395	7875
Price (£)	20	20	20	20	22	24	
Revenue (£)	24000	25060	24920	27360	31086	33480	165906
Product B							
Units	960	950	1005	1010	1020	1100	6045
Price (£)	35	35	35	35	35	35	
Revenue (£)	33600	33250	35175	35350	35700	38500	211575
Total Revenue (£)	57600	58310	60095	62710	66786	71980	377481
Expenditure Forecasts							
Wages & Salaries	27000	27000	28600	28750	28900	29000	169250
Materials	12000	12400	12560	12760	12850	13505	76075
Direct Overheads	4000	4500	4500	4600	4200	4300	26100
Indirect Overheads	7000	7500	7500	8000	8500	9000	47500
Total Expenditure (£)	50000	51400	53160	54110	54450	55805	318925
Profit Forecast (£)	7600	6910	6935	8600	12336	16175	58556
If Sales Volume and Price Increase by 10% (costs remaining constant)							
Profit Forecast (£)	18096	17465	17849	20033	24656	29510	127609
If Sales Volume and Price Decrease by 10% (costs remaining constant)							
Profit Forecast (£)	-1744	-2479	-2777	-1579	1352	4279	-2948

Although the spreadsheet approach may be applied in manual systems, the true power of this system tool may only be realised in conjunction with a computer system which facilitates the rapid calculation of the many formulae incorporated in the construction of such models. Manual calculation often proves too time consuming to enable more than a few modifications to the model parameters to be considered effectively. The trend for PC-based packages was set by Computer Associates' Visicalc. Packages introduced since have tended to concentrate on the following enhancements to the original concept:

1 Increasing the maximum size of the matrix which can be manipulated.
2 Producing more attractive graphical displays from the results of the calculations.
3 Exchanging data with stand-alone database and word processing packages.
4 Producing more user friendly interfaces.
5 Providing availability for mini and mainframe computer platforms.

Examples of popular spreadsheet packages include Lotus 1-2-3 which became very popular on the IBM PC, and Microsoft Excel which proved equally popular with Apple Macintosh users. Borland QuattroPro is another package which contains many advanced features. An example of a spreadsheet package for mini or mainframe computers would be Oracle SQL*Calc which interfaces with the Oracle relational database and fourth generation language (4GL).

3.3.3 Databases

The database component essentially collects data together into convenient groupings, and provides a facility to achieve rapid access to retrieve the data elements which are required for processing by other system components. These sets of data or records may be classified by contents as the customer database, the product database, the employee database, etc. In the manual system such databases would normally be housed in filing cabinets, whereas in the computer-based systems, the larger databases will be stored on disk packs. In addition to providing storage for the data records, the database system typically incorporates facilities for adding to or maintaining the existing records, and a facility for retrieving the particular data required. It is the speed of response and the sophistication of the retrieval through the use of Boolean connectors which make the computer-based system significantly more powerful than the equivalent manual systems.

PC databases share the same type of user friendly interface as the spreadsheet and word processing packages. Although obviously not able to hold as many data items as a large mini or mainframe database, a PC package such as Ashton-Tate's dBase IV or Foxbase will allow the user to carry out the basic operations of data insertion, amendment, review and deletion, and allow simple tabular reports to be produced. Examples of mini or mainframe databases which could supply the information needs of a large organisation include Oracle and Relational Technology's Ingres.

3.3.4 Expert systems

Expert system components essentially comprise routines or sets of instructions relating to the data processing and analysis tools and techniques available for use by the organisation, and for supporting the organisation's decision-making. Typically such systems are designed to emulate the analytical and choice processes undertaken by human decision-makers, and to incorporate some of the knowledge elements and choice criteria that would be applied in specified decision situations. These systems may either be allowed the responsibility of taking the complete decision (eg electronic share dealing systems buy and sell on world markets without immediate human supervision) or be used to screen or filter out the unacceptable decision alternatives on given criteria before the human decision-maker makes the final judgment based on a wider set of less predictable or quantifiable criteria. The role of expert systems, their construction and issues associated with their application in organisations are developed in 4.3.3.

3.3.5 Integrated packages

It is possible to buy packages which integrate the features of word processor, spreadsheet and small database. An example of such a package would be Lotus Symphony. The advantages which are claimed for such a package, as against separate packages, include the following:

1. The user has only one interface or set of commands to learn. The overall time taken to make use of all three components is thereby reduced.
2. The problems of exchanging data between three separate packages are eliminated. Adding spreadsheet results to reports (eg a cash budget proposal) or merging a report from the database into a word-processed letter (eg an 'overdue' letter sent to a defaulting creditor) would be much easier.
3. An integrated package may be cheaper than three separate packages. This is because the marketing and support costs will not be tripled and the amount of programming involved in producing the package is generally less.
4. The user only has to deal with one supplier for maintenance and support.

All of these features would appear to make a strong case for the integrated PC package. However, the following disadvantages should be borne in mind before selecting such a package:

1. The separate package approach may be more flexible. A single package may be upgraded if a new version is released or even changed if later another package is found preferable,

whereas an integrated package may be upgraded less frequently and component packages cannot easily be replaced by packages from other manufacturers.

2 An integrated package usually only proves useful to someone whose job includes data storage, manipulation and calculation. While this rules out many managerial and clerical workers, it describes an accountant's role quite accurately!

3 There may have to be design compromises in terms of the features or performance of one of the components of the integrated package, striking a balance between the size of the package itself and its data handling capacities. The word processing component of an integrated package is the one most usually sacrificed by the manufacturer, and it will rarely be as powerful as a specialist word processor. This may be of importance if the intention would be to produce significant amounts of text or to perform a general secretarial function.

4 Separate packages may be more flexible. The user can tailor a mixture of separate packages to his or her own requirements. For example, an accountant may place less importance on the word processor and therefore require fewer features in this component.

A formal method of carrying out a comparison to determine the merits of an integrated package as against separate packages would be to use the weighted ranking technique (see 5.10.6).

3.4 COMPONENTS OF A TYPICAL BUSINESS INFORMATION SUB-SYSTEM

The scale and complexity of the total information system within even small organisations makes a detailed description impossible in this text. However, a particular sub-system of the total information system, which itself comprises a number of identifiable sub-systems has been selected to illustrate and consolidate a number of the concepts and issues relating to the systems approach developed in this chapter, including:

(a) Data inputs—distinguishing between those that are internally generated and those that are externally generated.

(b) Processes—illustrating a number of the typical data processing activities, and showing how they combine within an information system.

(c) Outputs—identifying those that are directed towards users outside of the environment, those that are used internally, and those that essentially provide an input into another processing sub-system.

(d) Communications and the nature of the channels used.

(e) Interaction between a particular sub-system and other sub-systems.

(f) Hierarchy of levels within the organisation's decision-making system and the way in which the same data may be successively re-processed to meet the needs of users at each different level.

The system used to illustrate these points is the sales order processing system which, in its general operation and components, is fairly common to most types of business and commercial organisations. A schematic representation of this type of system is provided in Figure 3.8.

3.4.1 Operational level

The function of the system at the operational level is to facilitate and support:

1 the effective processing of each sales order transaction and to produce the necessary outputs for both internal and external users to facilitate the completion of the sales transaction;

2 the monitoring and control of the transaction operations on an on-going basis.

INPUTS

In addition to the receipt of the customer's order, the system requires inputs from internal sources identifying, say, the customer's address, any special delivery instructions or discount arrangements (held in the customer database); the product descriptions, specifications and prices (held in the product database); details of the amount already owed by the customer and of the credit limits allowed (held in the sales ledger); and the availability of the items ordered (held in the stock database).

FIGURE 3.8 **Sales order processing system**

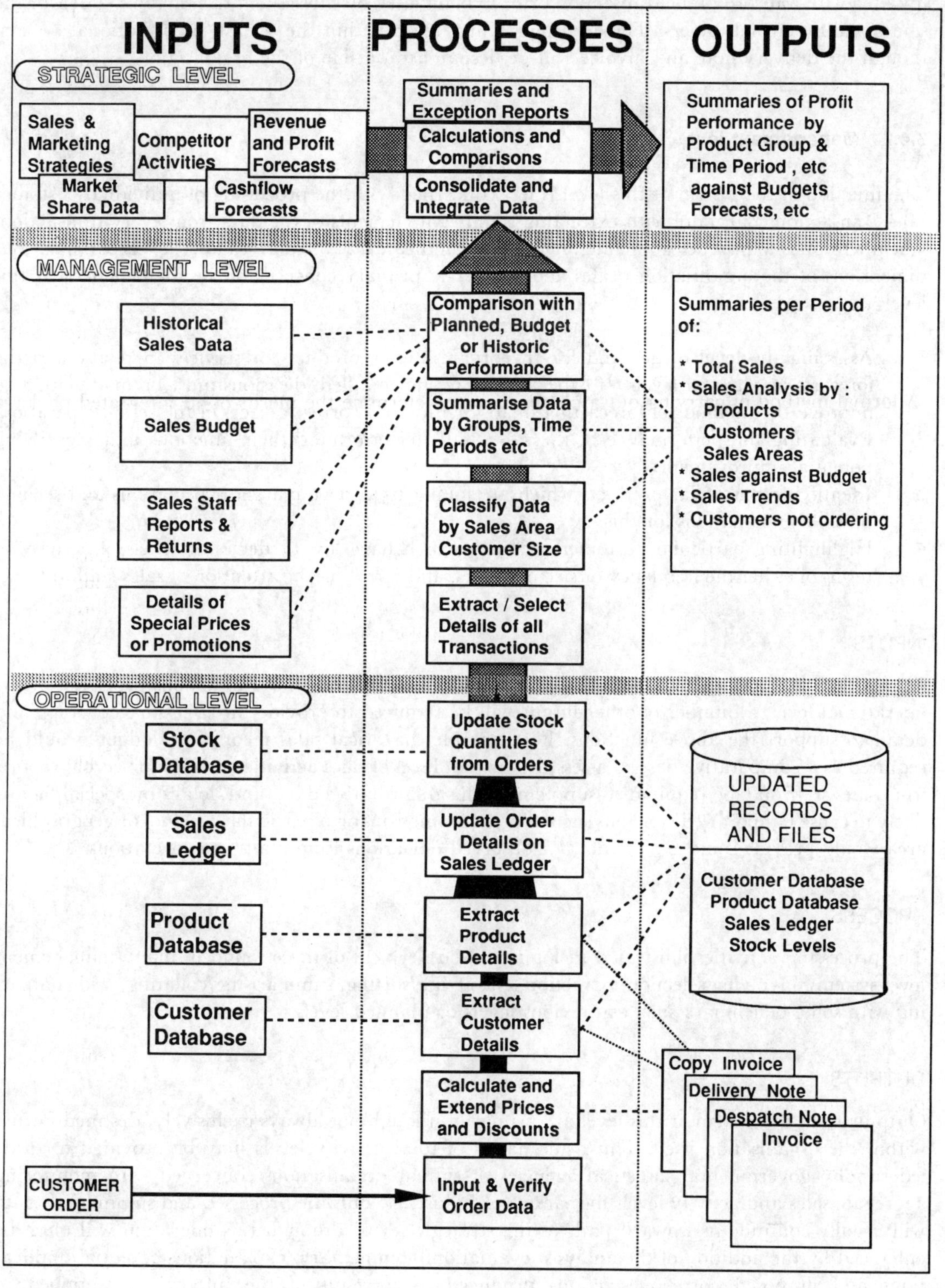

PROCESS

Typical activities involved in the processing of the order as received are the preparation of the necessary instructions to fulfil the order, requesting payment from the customer, recording the transaction details and updating its effects on the other activities in the business. It should be recognised that these broad processing activities in themselves comprise a number of individual activities each using parts of the data inputs.

OUTPUTS

At this level, the primary outputs are internal instructions (or inputs) to other systems in the organisation (not shown in Figure 3.8) to undertake the prescribed processing or activities required to fulfil the customer's order. The input resources used in processing the sales transaction are also updated with a record of the transaction prior to being used on subsequent transactions either for the same or different customers. These outputs will remain within the overall organisational system, though the delivery note and invoice will be despatched outside of the organisation.

3.4.2 Management level

The function of the system at this level is less concerned with the processing of individual customer sales transactions but more with extracting significant elements of the data from every transaction. The intention is to produce guidelines, measures or indicators of the performance levels of the various dimensions of the organisation's sales activities. The primary concerns of the management at this level are:

1. Assessing the level of demand for the organisation's products or services in relation to the forecasts or planned levels. If expectations are not fulfilled, decisions must be made either to improve the methods of forecasting or to identify and correct defects in the selling operation.
2. Evaluating the performance of the sales staff in performing their functions and identifying potential improvements.
3. Identifying particular products which are failing to achieve market expectations and seeking possible explanations for this.
4. Highlighting particular customer accounts which have low or declining levels of activity in terms of either the frequency or size of orders, and directing the attention of sales staff to these.

INPUTS

In addition to the extracted and summarised data elements from the transactions processed at the operational level, a number of other inputs will be required to provide the necessary coverage and detail to support the above functions. For example, historical sales records or budgets would be required as a comparative base to assess the current level of sales activities; written or verbal reports from sales staff may be required to supplement this quantitative data; and details on special factors likely to cause temporary distortions such as price promotions on a particular product or geographical area would provide some explanation for observed deviations from plans or expectations.

PROCESS

The processing activities illustrated in Figure 3.8 are typical of those found in many management level systems, involving selection/extraction, classifying/sorting, summarising/collating, and comparing with some benchmark such as previous levels or planned levels.

OUTPUTS

Outputs from the system at this level are primarily, though not always exclusively, destined for use within the organisation itself. Thus, summaries of total activity levels may be provided to trade federations, governmental statistical agencies or similar organisations concerned with monitoring aggregate sales and activity levels in markets or industries. But, the processed and summarised data will usually continue its upward path to the strategic level, although this migration will often be enhanced by the addition of the analysis, evaluation, commentary, explanation, potential implications and proposed corrective actions produced as a result of the information supplied to management for performance monitoring, control and decision-making. The transfer of this information to the next level will typically be in report form, often more selective and summarised than at the management level.

3.4.3 Strategic level

Systems at the strategic level are primarily concerned with providing an overview of the performance of the total organisation, highlighting any potential deficiencies, and providing information to guide and support the strategic development, planning and control.

INPUTS

The data captured in the sales order processing system at the operational level, and subsequently aggregated and summarised at the management level, provides an important contribution towards this strategic analysis and development by providing data on the performance of the company in the market. The sales revenue data is also consolidated and integrated with cost and expenditure data generated from other operational information systems to provide assessments of profit performance and the cash flow implications. In addition to the use of internally generated information, the strategic appraisal process utilises a significant volume of externally generated data, as illustrated in Figure 3.8, to facilitate comparative analysis of the organisation's performance with its competitors in terms of sales growth trends, market shares, profitability and other appropriate performance criteria. The strategic level is typified not only by the increased reliance on externally-generated data, but also on the diversity of data sources used internally.

PROCESS

The data processing activities at this level are primarily concerned with integrating performance data from the different functions and operations in the business to provide a consolidated view of overall performance. For example, consolidation of revenue and cost data to provide a monthly income statement or budget summary. Other typical processing activities are the summarisation of the data, identification of exceptional elements, and the comparison of actual performance against plans or targets.

OUTPUTS

The format and content of the outputs from this processing stage will invariably be more summarised, more integrated across all the operations or functions of the business, and concerned more with the implications of the observed trends for the future of the organisation. In the context of the sales order processing system, the output would identify the broad pattern of sales trends for each product, comparing these with the sales forecast, and the planned levels or competitors' sales, and extrapolating these trends into the future.

COMMUNICATIONS WITHIN THE SYSTEM

A feature of most systems which operate in a hierarchical organisational system is the successive filtering of the data as it progresses up the hierarchy. The key implication of this data reduction is the loss of detail. The greater the degree of abstraction from the source data, the more likely is the loss of accuracy. Counteracting this, however, is the potential reduction in the incidence of interference, distortion or noise as the volume of data being transmitted reduces as it progresses up the hierarchy. In this context, it should be recognised that the impact of information technologies is greater at the operational levels than at the management or strategic levels. Hence, there is likely to be greater use of electronic capture, processing, communications and output at the operational level than at the higher levels. For example, in many sales order processing systems the first task is capturing and converting the data into an electronic format via electronic tills, keyboards or electronic scanners. Once converted into the electronic form, all of the subsequent processing at the operational level may take place without further manual manipulation, thereby reducing the labour content which is revenue expensive, and minimising the chances of error. Subsequent processing at the management or strategic levels may involve manually orientated processes of selection, integration and analysis. The results may appear in the form of written reports, and the preparation will be demanding where the format and content is to vary each period. If the content and format are relatively static, then the automatic production of these outputs by utilising the electronically stored data becomes technically and economically viable.

SUMMARY

The key points covered in this chapter are that:

1 Any situation, operation or activity may be expressed in the form of a system. The

decomposition of a given situation into the key system elements of inputs, processes and outputs aids the analysis and design of the situation.

2 A key feature of the systems approach to analysis is the recognition of the interactions between a system and other systems in its environment. This is particularly appropriate to systems in the organisational context.

3 Any system itself may be further divided into sub-systems each of which interact and integrate with each other to provide the aggregate performance of the total system. This is particularly relevant to the operation of information systems within organisations.

4 The quality of the communications or linkages between systems is vitally important in determining the overall quality of an information system. Effective communications channels should be designed to minimise interference, distortion and noise.

5 Control systems may be developed within a system to test both the appropriateness of the system's outputs in relation to the environment's needs, and the effectiveness and efficiency of the communications channels. Systems which have the facility to monitor and feedback responses from the environment and to modify their operations to meet the changing situation are termed **closed-loop** as opposed to **open-loop control systems** which have no interaction with their environment.

6 Information systems contain a number of generic components (word processing, spreadsheet, databases, expert systems), which are frequently combined to facilitate specific types of data processing.

QUESTIONS *Solutions to questions of an examination standard start on p 395*

Write brief notes on the following:

(a) the four main elements of a system;
(b) system boundaries;
(c) open-loop and closed-loop control systems;
(d) externally-orientated sub-systems.

Questions of an examination standard

1 At a macro level, the organisation itself may be viewed as a system comprising a number of levels of sub-system.

List and briefly describe the FIVE levels of the system hierarchy which may be found in a large commercial organisation.

2 The reliability of the interface between systems depends upon the effectiveness and robustness of the communications.

List and briefly discuss FOUR factors which largely determine the quality of integration and interaction between systems.

3 A model of an information system can be produced by applying the elements from the general systems approach.

Briefly list the components of an information system and apply to them the contribution of the general systems approach.

Chapter 4
The Management of Information Systems

CHAPTER OBJECTIVES

The chapter seeks to identify and discuss the primary management issues which affect the organisational decision-making in the handling of information and the management of information systems. In particular, it examines:

1. the way in which organisations plan for change in the use and exploitation of information;
2. the extent to which Information Technology (IT) should be seen as a capital resource, and how the organisation should fix a transfer pricing policy;
3. how an organisation establishes its objectives and then manages the process of achieving them; and
4. the organisational structures which will allow the organisation to manage the information resource most effectively, ie the nature of an information centre, the role of the management services department, and the changes which have overtaken the data processing department.

4.1 GENERAL MANAGEMENT ISSUES

At the simplest possible level, the range of management issues may be classified by function as either:

1. identification, ie
   (a) of what the organisation has, and
   (b) what the organisation needs; or
2. planning, ie the organisation decides how to get from what it has to what it believes that it needs.

When it is put this simply, the decision-making process requires the degree of organisational overview which is only to be found at a strategic level rather than either the managerial/tactical or the merely operational levels. Once made, the responsibility for the implementation of those idealised decisions will filter down through the management system to a tactical and operational level. This downward migration will be paralleled by a necessary shortening of the time horizon. As a result, the managers will be required to identify sub-goals and aims which can be taken as acceptable in the short-term, because they facilitate the organisation's general progress towards a total or partial realisation of the preferred long-term aims. Institutionally, this may be seen as management from the top down. But conceptually, it must also be matched to the general patterns of life cycles within the organisation —for a more detailed explanation of life cycles, see 11.3.1.

However, it must not be assumed that all management is direction from the top. More particularly and conversely, the traditional structured methodologies which have been exploited for the process of system design, grew out of the technology which was exploited at the operational levels. In a sense, the development of these tools and techniques arose because management recognised the value of observation and feedback from the operational level. In fact, historically, the earliest forms of information systems were the payroll and accounting systems, ie the partial or total automation of routine and mechanical functions was ideally suited to the then limited capacities of the technology. These limitations tended to predispose the decision-makers to a somewhat pedantic and restricted view of information systems at large, ie in a commercial environment, the planning activity was aimed at optimising the practical results to be derived from the money invested and not at promoting blue sky projects, ie those pure research projects which speculate on being able to exploit machine capacities not immediately available.

It is a sad reflection on the quality of management decision-making available to many organisations to note that although machine-supported systems have developed significantly improved capacities, many organisations still fail to satisfactorily apply those capacities to support those areas of activity which may be classified as either strategic or tactical, ie through the development of decision support systems or by a programme of knowledge elicitation for incorporation into one or more expert systems. In part, this must be seen against the human resource management background. Whereas senior management is sanguine, if not cynical, when considering the issue of automation as it affects employment at the operational level, there can be reluctance to consider issues which might affect the more senior management levels. Such decisions would threaten the organisation's culture with its embedded power structures.

4.1.1 Organisational culture as a factor in change

Amending the bureaucracy of an organisation inevitably affects the culture of organisations and potentially shifts power. 'Power is a manifestation of individuals wishing to control their environment... Control is used here in the control engineering sense, as a means of attaining stability.' (Stowell p182) One of the ways in which this amendment may arise is through the decentralisation of data and a corresponding increase in access to it. This destabilises the environment by potentially democratising the decision-making activity. This would be achieved if there were to be a progressive expansion of the extent to which management information is shared, and by the frequency with which feedback of economic results of known decisions is made to employees. The more both task and resource decision-making is localised and operates on a participatory basis, the more the traditional conceptions of managerial roles will be distorted at all levels of the organisation.

This arises because there will be greater group identification and improved self-esteem and morale if local decision-making is shown to be effective. The intermediate managerial class in a hierarchy will therefore lose a part of their supervisory and control function, but gain through their ability to co-ordinate each group's activities and input to enable proper tactical (and ultimately, strategic) decisions to be made. The essence of the result of greater co-operation is the downward migration of power through a redistribution of knowledge. All information systems design must therefore recognise that the proposals are ultimately to be made operational within the reality of each organisation's political and cultural framework.

This factor is also fundamental in the processes adopted by organisations to agree upon their purposes and objectives (see 1.1.1). As indicated in 1.5, the organisation will then seek to achieve a better integration of resources and processes by making decisions about information systems. The decision whether to automate, and if so, to what degree to automate, is inevitably a strategic decision, being based upon the organisation's perceptions about its needs. The meaning given to **needs** should not be restricted to information, but must be understood in the sense of all the aspects of the organisation's activities, resources, methods and technologies. To that extent, the organisation must identify what it needs in the most general sense. That means a market analysis in commercial terms, assuming that the organisation is market-led. This may be summed up in the market rallying cries,

IT for commercial advantage, or
IT as a competitive weapon.

In the commercial world, and to some extent in the newly accountable public sector, all business is a form of warfare, and all organisations should be appropriately armed for today's conditions.

4.1.2 Planning for the future

As a result of analysis, the organisation will know what it has in resource terms, including its existing data holdings. It should also have a clear idea of its market share and/or performance levels in comparison with peer organisations. Having established a picture of current reality, planning may then be seen as the process whereby the organisation looks to the future to identify those objectives which it is most realistic to pursue. Once these decisions have been taken, it should be possible for the managers to define what resources, including data holdings, are going to be required to best support the organisation while in pursuit of those objectives, and to ensure that the organisation is in an optimal condition upon arrival. This means that the management has unequivocally accepted that data is a resource from which a broad spectrum of information can be extracted to support a variety of purposes.

This planning ahead takes place at a strategic organisational level. The result is **corporate strategy**, which draws its force from a market analysis, and then feeds down into the **information strategy**. The corporate and information strategy then interact in a process of feedback, and dynamic development and change. Indeed such is the degree of mutual dependence between the two strategies, that in an ideal organisation, it may be preferable to say that they interwork rather than merely interact. It is a case of checks and balances. At a corporate level, the organisation knows what it wants to achieve but recognises that there may be limitations in the information which it can extract from the data resource which can be made available. This may represent a check to a part of the corporate strategy, and necessitate a modification to the plan. Equally, when the data actually available is analysed, it may allow an extension to, or indeed a complete amendment of, both strategies because the analysis of the information strategy has been a form of feasibility study for the corporate strategy. Once it is recognised that these data resources can be made available, it may allow the organisation to develop in a previously unsuspected direction.

Hence, the organisation might identify a commercial market for some of the information which it can extract from the data already held. It therefore generates revenue by marketing that information as a new product in its own right. Alternatively, by looking at the market generally to seek the elusive commercial advantage, it might become apparent that certain types of information are going to be required. To that extent, the information strategy may create new types of data holding within the organisation. This, in turn, may lead to new strategies as the organisation becomes more expert in the manipulation of this new resource. In appraising its options, the organisation might wish to:

1 create internal facilities through which to generate the required data,
2 devise new methods and techniques by which to extract the information from the existing data, or
3 subject to commercial criteria of confidentiality, to identify sources for that information at a rate which is economically viable.

Whichever option is selected, the decision is tactical. The strategic decision is whether to regard the data and the information which it represents as a corporate resource. Once that decision has been taken, the organisation then addresses the practical details. Thus, for example, should every department eg accounts and sales, within the organisation be allowed to collect and store their own data, or should the organisation choose to generate a centralised resource from which all those with an appropriate access clearance may take their information? This requires the organisation to consider data flow in a root and branch information structure.

Every member of staff within the organisation must have an ascertained responsibility for the data which either they generate and develop or which they, for the time being, manage (see 16.3 for a discussion of what dangers are represented by different grades of staff). Arrangements must then be made for the localised data to feed into the corporate resource. So there are strategic decisions to be made about how the information at the periphery of the organisation is going to be consolidated, and the extent to which it is going to be broken down for security purposes so that people cannot get an overview of what is happening, and of what might be confidential (see 15.1 and 15.2)

4.1.3 What is contained in an information strategy?

Information strategy consists of the following elements:

1 a definition of the nature of the data available within the organisation and a list of who has control over it;
2 who has access to each part of the data;
3 who is responsible for generating and maintaining the data;

4 every part of the organisation may have control over separate islands of information, so if the organisation is to gain the prospective commercial advantage, the strategy must address the issue of data consolidation and the continous monitoring and management of that function. This consolidation might take place through one or more of the following techniques, ie by:
(a) summarising the data,
(b) sampling the data,
(c) extrapolating from the data, or
(d) by producing some form of tiered approach whereby the data is reformatted to produce more strategically useful views of the data. This is a part of the general issue of communications. At one level, this means that the organisation must identify the data flows so that the communication mechanisms within the organisation can be mapped on to the information-producing and handling parts of the organisation. This is a facet of the more general phenomenon of organisation design.

Access to information must be defined in relation to people, defining each individual's security clearance. This must be seen against the general background need of the organisation to train its staff, to identify the skills of the workforce and to seek to optimise their performance levels. Future development is also a necessary part of the strategy, to enable the organisation to make the most effective migration from one use of information to another, or from one technology to another.

4.1.4 The post of information manager

Within all organisations of substance, there should be an identified post with responsibility for information management. This individual would almost inevitably work through a committee structure which was established to represent both the interests of the organisation as a whole, and of the individual users. It is difficult for an organisation to survive by using a committee structure on its own. The trouble with committees is that they can be headless wonders, so it may be advantageous if the organisation is to address the full range of issues, ie:

1 the development of existing information resources,
2 the initiation of new information resources,
3 the migration from one set of uses of that information to another set.

This must all be part of a continuing policy for the optimum development in the use of data. The organisation must be able to take a given amount of data, and to plan a phased development in the utilisation of that data. For these purposes, the move might be from a simplistic to a complex use, or from one use through to a quite separate innovatory use. The development process has sometimes operated in reverse and produced a less technologically sophisticated system. Thus, it might be argued that the use of information at an office level as a result of using PC technology is a return to the old days where every clerk had a filing cabinet full of data. Because of the inherent hardware limitations of the then PC systems, the implementation actually ignored and (temporarily) scrapped a substantial part of the technological development which occurred in the 1970s. But the fact that it happened demonstrates the sad fact that a significant number of organisations blindly rush into each technology-led environment without properly considering the effect in organisational terms. Thus, the assumption was that the incremental centralisation of the data processing function could suddenly be reversed at an economical rate, and that the reversal could achieve improvements in organisational performance which would more than offset the cost.

The IT provision should be managed by a senior board member. Because the organisation should be addressing the issues at a strategic decision-making level, the whole resource should be under the control of a senior strategic manager as opposed to a tactical data processing manager. The role of the strategic manager becomes even more important when the organisation begins to decentralise the information system and to produce separate information centres within the organisation. Clearly, the person who is to co-ordinate the activity and to contend with the general managerial implications must have a superior position to the individual who is to arrange an appropriate hardware configuration with good communications, and portable software and data.

4.1.5 Information technology as a capital resource

The information strategy must also address the issue of IT as a capital resource. A significant percentage of an organisation's capital and revenue may be committed both to providing the equipment and in employing the people who will manage the equipment. This is of prime importance in the project selection phase of the Systems Development Life Cycle (SDLC)—(see 6.2). Money to be spent on computer systems is only won in competition with other departments for fleets of delivery vehicles, production machinery, the chairperson's Rolls Royce, or the redecoration of the canteen. It is of fundamental importance that whoever is sponsoring the information system's cause in this competitive arena, is of the right calibre to ensure that the case is given proper weight in the overall allocation of resources within the organisation. The capital resource is crucial. The organisation must make value judgments about what it can afford in each year, bearing in mind that all equipment is to a greater or lesser extent obsolescent, and will have to be replaced. The payback period for each component element must be matched to the life cycle of the relevant part of the organisation.

Unless the organisation has very strong initial capitalisation and can afford to install an information system from scratch, it is customary to find that the strategic plan calls for the development of the information resource to be phased in over a number of years. For these purposes, the organisation must be seen as a series of meta-processes and activities (ie superior systems, each one built up from dependent sub-processes and activities. It is entirely possible that each component element may have a different period of expected life within its cycle. The problem with the standard techniques of decomposition is that they are essentially two dimensional, ie they map processes and activities in a hierarchical or other literal relationship (see 6.1.6, 8.1.2 and 8.1.3). If time is built in, a three dimensional and therefore more usefully real picture is achieved.

There is an argument for producing a hierarchical analysis of all the different life cycles because the managers ought to be in a position to show that, subsumed within the overall processes and activities which the organisation is conducting, there may be many other activites and processes, each one with its own individual life cycle. Premature obsolescence in one component element may bring an unexpected end to an otherwise profitable activity. Some of these life cycles will relate to the system in hardware terms, some to the system in human resource terms, and some to the system in the form of circulating assets from raw materials through to the finished product or services offered by the organisation (see 11.3.1). At a conceptual level, it may also be found that life cycles are an integral part, because once the organisation begins to think constructively in terms of the temporal fitness of each part of the whole, it may conclude that some practices and processes have outlived their market viability and should therefore be wound down. Other processes and practices may still be considered acceptable, but if they are to be continued, and if the organisation is going to continue to develop strategically, it must plan for obsolescence at different points within the overall processes and activities being conducted. This means that the managers will have to very carefully monitor the passage of time within all of the life cycles which are subsumed within the whole, with capital made available for repair and replacement at the appropriate moment.

If organisations are to plan their expenditure on plant and equipment properly, it must be seen as an accounting exercise which takes place both above and below the line. Particularly from an accountant's point of view, equipment expenditure has to be seen against a background of depreciation and obsolescence. The organisation must establish the periodicity of the payback and replacement cycle for each item of plant. Proper planning in financial terms can then take place. Conceptually, there is a question over some of the methodologies of depreciation eg discounted cash flow, but whatever the theoretical debate, the organisation still has to write off the cost of the equipment in accounting terms. One of the reasons for the decline in the acceptability of some of these more detailed methods is that the Chancellor of the Exchequer has restricted and withdrawn many of the capital allowances which used to favour this aspect of the organisation's capital and revenue planning exercise. This cannot change the organisation's need to plan to write off the expenditure, the usual period being four to five years.

But when it comes to the system elements and the human resource implications for recruitment and training, the cost elements are not as easily identified. The problem is that many of the cost elements are subsumed within the organisation's general overhead. Because it is an included cost within the general running costs, it is more difficult to separate out the strands of expenditure which it is proper to attribute to each activity and process supported by the organisation. Indeed, the difficulty in pulling the figures out is often used as an excuse for not properly cost-justifying IT implementation. Initially, many organisations made investment judgments based on the article of faith that automation was a good thing. This arose because it was difficult to put a value on alleged qualitative improvements in control, faster processing and more accurate information. One of the reasons for the general slow down in IT implementation is that organisations are no longer so willing to act solely on the basis of faith. Proper justification is required. This can only be achieved by a full and proper evaluation of the organisation's activities to identify at a level of individual contribution, which aspects are most critical to the success of the organisation. Once this has been done, a cost base has been established against which to project possible savings. At this point, organisations tend to encounter difficulty because the new technology will be seen as likely to reduce or remove unnecessary activity. Given that most of the organisation's overhead is likely to be in the form of staffing, the projected saving will almost certainly be in the form of jobs. Such proposals tend to meet with a hostile reaction from the staff whose functions are threatened.

4.1.6 Transfer pricing

The cost-justification exercise is an aspect of a further element within the organisation's financial brief. This reflects the opportunity that, given that at an individual employee level, the cost of employment will be potentially attributable to a data source or processing activity, it is possible to produce a more scientific basis upon which to charge the information system out to the departments which seek to exploit it. Each organisation's transfer pricing policy will depend upon the functions performed by the organisation and the rationale for its operation. This is a strategic issue because the policy must determine whether prices are to be transferred at cost, or whether the departments which operate or maintain the information system are allowed a cost-plus approach which would notionally allow a profit element. If such a profit is to be allowed, the organisation must determine what margin is to be allowed and what limits to impose on the discretion of the receiving department to use that surplus. It is not necessarily financially healthy to have departmental slush funds which can be used without proper accountability to the whole organisation.

If the data resources are shared between several different user departments, the policy must also lay down a formula by which to determine how the price is to be distributed between them. It could be done on a simple quantitative basis, the price being divided in line with the proportion of on-line time used. But one department might have a substantial call for time simply to keep the organisation running, eg to process invoices and control credit, while other uses might be more profitable, eg to extract a list of customers who pay quickly as the basis of a mail shot marketing campaign. Once one acknowledges that there are significant qualitative uses of the same data, the political thorniness of the policy making becomes more clear.

Taking the converse, sales departments are going to have sales representatives out in the field. A proportion of their activity will be the collection of orders for processing, but a part of their activity is necessarily the collection of data that will be useful to the organisation for other purposes, and could even be marketable in its own right. The representatives produce data from which invoices are prepared for income-producing purposes, but the data can also be used to identify general market trends and individual product trends which help the organisation at a strategic level. If an organisation is going to charge the sales department for their use of the data handling and manipulation system —their use of the resource is inevitable whether to extract information on who to call on next, or to input the latest marketing data—the setting of the price must be seen against the apparent right of that department to make a charge for the data collection which may be so valuable to the organisation. In the last analysis, this part of the decision-making process lies at the heart of the organisational culture (see 4.1.1). The organisation must therefore make a range of both strategic and tactical decisions which will affect the power structures within their organisation. This arises because both access to and contribution to the information resource available to the organisation is the basis upon which power is divided within the organisation. It is therefore likely that whatever charges are explicitly made will reflect the existing culture.

To avoid the problems which might arise through explicit decision-making, many organisations simply take the cost of the resource off the top, ie the expenditure is simply defrayed out of gross income without attempting to allocate that cost to individuals or their departments. But, when seeking to cost-justify future projects for the improvement of the whole, or part of the organisation's activities, the organisation then runs into further problems because it has no immediate and agreed basis upon which to make an apparently more objective appraisal. The organisation must then consider whether it wishes to find some way of allocating the proposed increase in the overhead. This might be done on a proportional basis. So at some point, each organisation could formally allocate a proportion of its salaries and hardware costs to that particular function. Alternatively, it could attribute the new costs to the sponsoring user department, or group of users if the new resource is to be shared. Thus, the organisation maintains the status quo on the present expenditure, but gradually allocates cost over a period of time as the old system becomes obsolete and is replaced.

4.2 ORGANISATIONAL OBJECTIVES

Each individual division within the organisation, or group of departments within that division, is going to establish both internal and external objectives at both tactical and operational levels. This is an inevitable part of the process of implementing the corporate strategy. To promote this process, the organisation must take decisions about the management style to be adopted. The tone could be autocratic and oligarchical with minimal opportunity given for consultation, or it could be very democratic with a decentralised or modular approach. If the organisation intends to be responsive to positive feedback from the tactical and operational levels, and to that extent, many employees may become involved in helping to formulate the organisation's objectives as a whole, all sorts of nice judgments must be made in the cultural, power-sharing sense, about who should be allowed to make this contribution. This applies not just to the information system objectives, but also to the objectives of the organisation at large, the two often being inextricably linked together (see 4.1.2). Each organisation must therefore establish and identify:

1. the objectives which are the present basis of the organisation's activities at each management level, ie strategic, tactical and operational;
2. the processes whereby objectives are to be set at each of the levels within the organisation (different processes might be established for separately identified purposes);
3. the detailed objectives for the information system which will be allowed to feed up through the organisation and into the strategic plans.

4.2.1 How do affected users make their contribution?

It is customary for organisations to create and maintain some form of committee structure which would offer a reasonable opportunity for consultation and discussion. There would be departmental representation within this committee structure which would seek to identify and promote the needs of those users wishing to promote projects. If the committees are not fully representative in the sense that not all the interest groups and affected parties can be allowed membership because otherwise the committees would be too unwieldy, the committees would either have to approach the users directly to ask for their views and comments, or would allow users to submit projects for their consideration. In the latter case, the committee receiving the proposal could co-opt the user on to the committee so that the case for the project could be properly argued, or the price of being allowed to submit a project might be the necessity of convincing an existing member that he/she ought to sponsor it.

At the simplest level, one of the primary objectives of the information system is to inform, yet the simplicity of this statement conceals a wealth of complexity. The term **inform** might be taken in the sense of simply allowing people to recognise current reality, or it could be taken in a broader sense to mean information which is going to properly support the decision-making of the organisation. In return, the information system ought to be supported by all the primary departments within the organisation. A part of this support will come through the routine task of creating some part of the data. In such cases, the process and the content will be inextricably linked. But others will more positively create the information out of the data holding, adding to the capacity of the organisation through the novelty of the insights thereby achieved. In such cases, the processes engaged in will develop the informative content of the data.

Some people within the organisation will have quite legitimate objectives for the information system which do nothing more than reflect their limited personal perspectives and ambitions, eg to stabilise existing power structures or to encroach on other power structures. These objectives will be quite different from the objectives of those managers within the organisation who can gain a better perspective of, and sense of identification with, the direction and thrust of the organisation's endeavours. But, no matter what the content of the individual objectives at an intermediate level, the organisation ignores them at its peril if it wishes to achieve co-ordinated action to identify and pursue a set of corporate objectives. If there is too much warfare between aggressive interest groups within the organisation, then the organisation cannot relate properly to the outside world.

IT is the one area which is likely to give rise to a great deal of conflict because access to the information system and the data which it contains is access to power. So there are two basic classifications of objective which are likely to be developed. The first reflects the open agenda of declared organisational policy, and the second relates to the hidden agenda of power broking. The broad and legitimate corporate objectives might be the development of IT to provide commercial advantage or to underpin operational effectiveness. But that is not sufficient to drive a policy on information strategy because it lacks the requisite level of specificity. It is too organisational in its intent. It would not tell the organisation why it was to adopt a particular objective, nor would it indicate how the advantages or effectiveness were to be achieved. In fact, the key issue in information terms is the extent to which the data which is to be made available through the information system is going to support and inform decision-making at all the relevant levels within the organisation.

There will be differing data needs at each identified level of decision-making within the organisation. The immediate task of the organisation is to qualitatively define those data needs so that the best support possible is provided to the decision-making function. This represents the operationalisation of the primary strategic policy objective which is to optimise decision-making. It is achieved by having data available at the right place and at the right time so that the best person can take the decision. The organisation needs to examine and appraise its decision-making structure, carefully defining the roles which each individual plays or ought to play in taking decisions. At this point, the organisation will know which decisions each individual is actually going to take, and to specify which further decisions he/she ought to take. By then re-examining the job specification against the background of the organisation as a whole and in the light of the identified information resources, the organisation can begin to say which data units ought to be made available if each person's decision-making is to be optimised.

4.2.2 How is the consultation managed?

The organisation can represent the process in tabular form to show the objectives in a dynamic relationship with the activities of planning, systems design and implementation. All of these stages are in a sense interchangeable, because there may well be issues which force a reappraisal of fundamental assumptions no matter how far through the process the organisation might be. This reappraisal may involve going back to reassess one or more of the more fundamental organisational objectives. Indeed, if the consultation process has not been effective in addressing the organisational culture within which each aspect of the corporate and information strategy is to be made to work, the reappraisal during implementation will be stimulated because that is the moment at which the empire builders must face the reality of any proposed changes in their power relationships. This is the moment when the in-fighting really starts. This goes to emphasise the crucial role of senior managers in the management of change. IT is a tremendous catalyst for change in forcing individuals to re-evaluate the role which they have within the organisation and the way in which that role contributes to the well-being of the organisation. If change is approached simply on the basis that it is the automation of work practices, it will fail to address the real issues.

In a sense, the real issues which are involved in this process form a part of the more general consideration of obsolescence. It is quite wrong to restrict the interpretation of obsolescence to simple deterioration of machines. It may equally be applied to people. Hence, as a part of the resources available to the organisation, the roles and responsibilities which people adopt may become less relevant to the organisation, or as defined, make a sub-optimum contribution to the organisation's well-being. This may first become apparent at an operational level where more easily measurable performance criteria can be applied. The greater the impact of the change at an operational level, the greater the upward pressure for change. Controlling this pressure from the bottom up may well start with a redefinition of the work practices at an operational level. This feeds into a consideration of the responsibilities of supervising departments. Such a consideration may lead to changes in departmental structures to accommodate the newly identified or emerging roles. This inevitably leads to changes in divisional or organisational structures.

4.2.3 Centralisation or decentralisation

The development of networking becomes a critical element in this process of change because it provides a means whereby decision-making may be decentralised by allowing wider access to, and availability of, the data relevant to support decision-making at a strategic level. In a centralised and hierarchical organisation, it is possible to achieve efficient operation and control through the exploitation of a secure central data resource. If a functional data resource is established in each operating unit within the organisation, it may lead to more effective decision-making, but there are a number of problems:

1. In a centralised resource, there can be a better co-ordinated approach to system development and to the creation of corporate databases, and by avoiding the duplication of effort, the staff are better placed to manage the large projects. In a decentralised organisation, there may be significant duplication of effort and resources.
2. In a single department, computing staff can be given better career development opportunities which enhance motivation. In a decentralised environment, a large number of less skilled users must be given individual assistance. This is inefficient and comparatively expensive. It can also be frustrating and unfulfilling for the specialist staff.
3. In a multiuser system, access to centralised files can be significantly slowed down at peak operating times, and data transmission costs are higher. It can also lead to a data hoarding phenomenon whereby interest groups sit on pockets of data instead of allowing them to be properly consolidated. This leads to a fragmentation of decision-making and an increasing lack of co-ordination between the different activities pursued by the organisation. Independently of the phenomenon of deliberate hoarding, the more decentralised the system becomes, the more difficult it becomes to ensure that each individual's holding of data is updated. It may well be that each user is supplied with perfectly contemporaneous data when the initial decentralisation or dissemination of data takes place. But the intrinsic nature of data is dynamic and each department will be adding to or amending the data. This is not a problem if all of the significant additions or alterations to that data are circulated and consolidated on a regular basis, or upon need. Any failure in this area means that not all departments are taking decisions based on the best data.
4. Although costs are higher, user departments are prepared to pay to gain greater control over the operation of the system. But this may equally lead to amendments being made to the centrally provided packages, limiting compatibility and portability. The degree of control must also be limited to issues of data validation and other in-house administrative matters. When dealing with a central department, each user competes for attention. If a fair administration is in place, all those projects which will benefit the organisation will be given priority. In a decentralised environment, the right of control is limited to the immediate section of the system. If there could be benefits to the organisation by making co-ordinated changes to several separately controlled sections of the system, there could be real political difficulty in getting agreement. Thus, even though the department may be paying for the privilege of control, the organisation must have the right to override local interest for the greater good.

Although the new technology gives the organisation the opportunity to decentralise, it allows far greater damage to be caused to the organisation through lack of proper co-ordination of effort because of the speed at which events may proceed when systems are automated. However, the speed of communication and the capacity to exchange information available through automation also provide the means to sustain co-ordinated activity and therefore to reduce the problems. This assumes that in the information strategy, the organisation has ensured system compatibility between all the different parts of the whole to ensure that the proper exchange of data can take place, and that, more critically, the updating of that data can be guaranteed without significantly affecting each departments' holdings.

The practice of updating can be very problematical. Each department will be planning on the basis of the data held. If an external user gains access to the database without warning the holder, and amends one or more critical elements in the data while the planning process is only partially complete, that can completely throw the decision-making process. There must be a system which tells decision-makers that there is going to be an update, and possibly provides some form of holding file system where data can be held pending completion of the matter in hand. As a security measure, this allows the data to be validated before it is consolidated into each department's holding and reduces the chances of damage to data integrity. Moreover, it can be important in, say, the handling of budgeting resources data. If budgetary data is regularly updated, then all departments know what the present state of the organisation's support might be. But if a department starts to budget on the basis of old data, levels of expenditure might be set which cannot later be sustained.

4.2.4 The role of a data librarian

Although the new technology can be used to create a whole range of new opportunities for the organisation, the organisation must create a mechanism which alerts the users to the extent of the information which can be made available. Even if the technology is in place and adequate communication exists between all the relevant parts of the system, the organisation must identify what data holding might represent useful information to its users, and take steps to notify users. This may involve the appointment of a data librarian—a person who produces a form of on-line catalogue of:

(a) what is available,
(b) who has control over it, and
(c) where it is.

However, it is not clear that a simple catalogue entry is going to be enough. Typically, a single descriptive sentence is not necessarily helpful. Part of the function of any librarian is to bring the detail of the resource to the attention of the persons most likely to be able to exploit it for maximum benefit. So the role of this librarian should be pro-active so that the information facility is actively promoted throughout the organisation.

But the decision whether to create this role has to be taken at both a strategic and a tactical level because it is indicative of the management style within the organisation. The more people are alerted to the range of what is available, the greater the likelihood that one of two things will happen. Either the users are going to get rather frustrated because they are going to gain an insight into the scope of the resources which they could exploit if they had the time or the responsibility, or it is going to allow those users to take decisions which would have been quite out of their range in pre-automation times, and so it will significantly change the classical line management structure which that organisation might have had. The supervisory managers would have been the people within the organisation who achieved the tactical and strategic overview. From this position, they would have looked at the decisions being taken or proposed at the lower levels, and expressed an informed opinion on their propriety. Now staff at an operational level could be given access to information which would tell them exactly what the larger situation is. DSSs and database systems with sophisticated query languages could be made available; proper simulation and modelling facilities could allow them to see whether the decisions which they propose are going to be good decisions. The organisation is therefore allowed to become much more modular than hierarchical, and the extent to which the organisation wishes to allow data decentralisation to also amount to a decision-making decentralisation, is a strategic decision because it provides the greatest change to the culture of the organisation.

4.3 ORGANISATIONAL STRUCTURES FOR MANAGEMENT

4.3.1 Information centres

Within the entirety of the information resource, there are a number of nexus points, ie points within the system where one of the following events may occur:

(a) there will be a human interface,
(b) there will be an interaction between two or more data sets to produce a data transformation,
(c) there will be a manipulation of the data which allows it to perform a different function, ie it differs from the second because the data itself may remain the same, eg as in a database.

Any one of these events may be an information centre in the sense that, through the ultimate human interaction, it will be informing the user, ie through the action of the user's mind, data will be converted into information (see 1.4). In the case of data transformation, which may subsequently inform the user, the user causes the computer to process the data to allow a new form of data to emerge. Taking raw sales data and producing a trial profit and loss account transforms incoherent data into a coherent and summarised form. When the new form is presented to the user, it is more easily understood because there is a consolidated overview of that particular function. In those organisations which have created a large and centralised database that can be interrogated through a software query language or some other software device, users are allowed to get a series of different views of the data. The data is transformed into a different form of information through a difference in perspective for that particular usage.

It must be recognised that the human interaction may be at an operational level rather that at a strategic or tactical level. While it is always the case that the machine will be responding to commands to manipulate or transform the data in some way, the source of that immediate command does not have to be the human user who is ultimately going to use or benefit from the data. The immediate user may be a mere part of the processing activity to pass the data in its refined form up the decision-making structure. Thus, it would not be proper to say that all human interaction is necessarily going to be interaction with a view to gaining information, ie the human who keys in raw data is interacting with the system even though the data may be quite meaningless to the human user. The sales invoice clerk who is keying in data to create sales invoices need not necessarily take either input or output as information. Someone else may pick up the resultant invoice to check it and therefore read the form as information. That data may subsequently be consolidated and summarised into the figures which will go to produce a weekly or monthly profit and loss account. At this point, it may become information for a manager.

Each of the possible transformations or manipulations will take place either at a stand-alone facility (which may interface with a network where other humans operate), or at some place within the system, the place or address being irrelevant, but at the instruction of a remote user. The requirement for an information centre is that there should be hardware, software and user support to allow the user access to the information system. In every organisation, the degree of access allowed to the system as a whole will be determined by the status of the individual user. Hence, a systems analyst who stands at the top of the information processing tree, may use a series of master passwords to gain access to data in all parts of the system. Whereas those lower in the hierarchy may find that their access is limited to only a part of the data.

To be an information centre, the user needs to be able to communicate with the information system in some way. But it does not have to be a physical place, it is a metaphorical concept. Self-evidently, there have to be machines involved so that the data may be accessed or manipulated. Humans have to give commands to initiate and control these activities and this can only be done through interface machines. Equally, the data will be stored at specific addresses within the system. This is particularly true in a networked system where different users may well create separate data holdings in their own part of the system. It does not matter what form the data has, nor where it is. The key determinant is the extent to which it represents a part of the resource available to the organisation as a whole and in a cost-effective way. That which is on the periphery of the organisation is not a centre. Any user could claim to have an amount of data, eg a sales representative touring round the countryside has a volume of data, but it would not be said that the data held by this individual is an information centre because the information in that form is not useful to the organisation at either a tactical or a strategic level. The fact that an individual has data does not make that individual a centre. It only starts to become a centre when others access the data and then begin the process of transforming the data into something useful for better informing the decision-making process. The more potent the transformation, the more useful it becomes to the whole organisation and therefore achieves centrality in that sense.

The information centres are not directly mapped on to the organisation structure. Some data is going to directly map because the classification of the data is going to match the source on a departmental level, eg sales data is produced by the sales staff, etc. What happens to it thereafter need not necessarily be directly mappable. This will arise because the more users that have access to the data, the more people there may be who will process and manipulate that data to produce different views. So there may be a functional specialisation of the data for one individual's immediate purposes, but that need not tie in directly to specific departments. Because as a by-product of one user's activities, information may be produced which is of direct use to a person in another department. It would depend upon how responsibility was attributed for either performing that function or allowing access to it subsequently.

Thus, the concept of the information centre links back to the primary objectives of the organisation. The creation of information centres allows the organisation to integrate the information system into the management structure. This occurs because the creation process is either the mapping of the centres on to the existing organisation, or the adjustment of the management structures to allow staff to better exploit the data and software resources. It gives a framework of reference within which the organisation can see that different processing activities will produce data relevant to different users depending on their status and roles within the organisation. The organisation will therefore want to say that different aspects of the data represent information resource centres for those identified individuals or departments. The organisation may also produce hierarchies of information centres to reflect functional divisions between different organisational levels. Thus, individual departments may generate and maintain data resources, sampling information from other sources to add to or refine their own centres. At a supervisory level, managers may begin the process of abstracting information in a summarised form for monitoring purposes, while senior managers may wish to engage in trend analysis for longer term planning.

To see an information centre in mechanical terms is to misunderstand the concept because, in the final analysis, the organisation is going to make a qualitative judgment about the existence of the information and where it is by looking carefully at where the data is and identifying who can access that information and for what purpose. So the information centre which would be available to a senior manager would be very different from the information centre which would be allowed to a person lower in the managerial hierarchy. Each established centre reflects the type of use and the status of the user(s). The information centres for different status users could be at the same physical location, whether from the same terminal room or even the same terminal on a time sharing basis, but because there are different logical access controls, the access allowed to resources is very different (see 15.2). A clerk would use it at a supervised level, to be followed by a manager who would use it at a quite different strategic level. The number of levels of access will reflect the degree of partitioning either within the centre itself or as between the resources which are made available to the organisation. The extent of the information centre will therefore be measured by the power of the activities which can be undertaken, or by the degree of access which can be gained. It may be a centre where the user simply makes a connection with the data, or more actively makes connections between otherwise separate elements of data.

4.3.2 The management services department

Historically, such departments emerged from the areas of Operational Research (OR) in terms of using quantitative techniques to assist decision-making. Now the department more commonly represents a link between decision-makers and the information system by providing support tools, or by providing the techniques, methodologies or expertise to drive those tools. Thus, the typical management services department is a group of people whose skills lie in identifying problems and then selecting the tools most appropriate for the resolution of those problems. Because the main role lies in the information field, this activity cannot be carried on in a vacuum. The staff have to link with those who have specialist DP functions and systems expertise if they are to comprehensively define the problem, provide the tools that can be used to analyse it, and then facilitate the information coming from the system.

The first issue is to decide at what level within the organisation this team of experts is to operate. If their role is essentially that of servicing the management of the organisation, the managers will initiate work for the management services staff and implement such of their recommendations as are considered appropriate. Alternatively, the department might contain a group of senior managers that generally trouble-shoot, ie they roam through the organisation identifying problems, finding solutions, and implementing those solutions through the line management system.

Originally, this department would have operated at the tactical level, and that may still be the role in some organisations. But many more are now fulfilling a general roving commission —they have the solutions looking for problems. To that extent, the staff have to have seniority within the management hierarchy in order to gain access to all the data about the organisation which will allow them to accurately diagnose its problems and to formulate solutions. They will then either report to the senior managers who are responsible for the defective activities or processes to tell them of the problem and the proposed solution, or they will have been given a management tool kit with which to directly help the organisation. In some organisations they will actually be part of the DP department or the DP department may become a part of the management services department as a part of the total package to cover communications, information systems and decision-support. Their role will also interact with those responsible for the functions of personnel and human resource management because the resolution of the identified problems may involve amendments to the infrastructure of the organisation. Personnel must necessarily be involved in discussions about the structure of the organisation and about how best to use the resources available within the organisation so as to produce the best interaction with the information system.

Thus, in a sense, the management services department is the human equivalent of an automated decision support system. The staff tend to be drawn from an operational background to perform a more significantly strategic role within the organisation. Thus, one of the more usual initial tasks is to provide a series of models of the organisational decision-making structure, particularly on the financial and analytical side of the organisation. This provides the raw materials from which to develop an effective decision support system. A significant proportion of that more numerate processing function is capable of being supported by automated systems and methodologies. OR was always a highly numerate discipline and was susceptible to automation. Indeed, the first major automated decision support systems were probably OR-based, exploiting the machine capacities to extract and manipulate statistical data.

The staff from this department will typically be involved in a feasibility study and in the implementation of the information strategy. They will also assume some responsibility for organising and maintaining appropriate user groups. Within the committee structure, they will have appropriate representation on steering committees, and as a part of their function in helping to manage change, they would need to update user groups to allow proper feed back in both the design and implementation phase. (For a detailed example of the function of a steering group see 11.3.3 and 11.3.5) Indeed, one of their functions might be to lay down a formal structure whereby steering committees interact with user groups, and user groups interact with the workers because, presumably, the user groups are in turn representative of the work force in some quasi-democractic way. So there has to be some form of overall mechanism established for allowing affected individuals access to the user groups, and user groups access to steering committees, and steering committees access to the ultimate decision-makers.

The role of the management services department would be crucial because the underlying rationale is the intention to develop expertise in decision-support and to supply the skills which the users might lack. Thus, in providing support, that department's staff might supply the most appropriate methodologies or techniques of decision-making or they might have access to the information most appropriate to drive those methodologies and techniques. Their input to this structure of representative decision-making should be strong. However, the organisation must set the tone of these groups. The management services staff may be comparatively senior managers. Unless care is taken, the groups may become biased too strongly in favour of the decision-makers instead of being representative of the end users. To prevent the groups from being too large and unwieldy, the management services staff may well have to perform a directly representative function. Their training must aim to make them effective voices on behalf of all those whose interests they are to represent.

In many ways, the function performed by management services for a steering committee matches the role which an external consultant might perform. In both instances, a lay committee will be given professional input about how to solicit information relevant to the decision-making process, and how to make decisions based on that information. The management services staff increasingly play the role of the consultant within the organisation, and representatives of both the management services department and the DP department would be providing two sources of expertise for the steering committees and the user groups. Coming from slightly different directions, a difference of perspectives would emerge. One would be looking at it from the point of view, not of the user, but of the general problem solver and the other would be looking at it from the point of view of the feasibility of the proposed technology in providing the information to solve the problems identified.

If the expertise represented by management services does not exist in-house, the organisation will almost certainly have to buy it in. Coming from outside, the consultant is able to speak the truth, ie to say all those things which an internal person might find it politically embarrassing to say. Thus, the only way in which the management services department can match the external person's level of influence, is if those who run it are sufficiently high in the management hierarchy that they can speak the truth with a reasonable degree of impunity. There is of course no reason why an organisation cannot have an internal department and call upon the services of outside consultants for specialist areas. It would then be the responsibility of the management services department to co-ordinate the activities of both internal and external personnel.

The organisation must also decide whether the function of management services is to be provided by a formally constituted team, or whether suitably qualified individuals should be placed within departments. Such individuals could come together in a steering committee when there are meta-organisation decisions to be taken (ie strategic decisions), but otherwise they would spend the balance of their operational lives helping, supporting and maintaining the management decision-making within their host departments. In the large organisations, the tendency is to create separate departments in much the same way as an internal audit department will achieve a degree of independence within the organisational structure. In smaller organisations, the management services function is there to be performed, and it is often divided among the different departments. Thus, someone in the marketing department will be designated to develop, or placed to provide, appropriate expertise for colleagues, etc.

Given the level of influence which management services would normally be expected to achieve, the organisation must decide to whom that department's staff are to be accountable. In the real world, there are as many solutions as there are types of organisations. The department may be directly accountable to senior management. It is possible that the head of management services might report directly to the managing director. This would represent the situation in which the staff's role would be the most powerful, where they are truly playing the role of consultants within the organisation. In such circumstances, they could have a brief to examine all the major organisational issues. Sometimes the management of the department may assume responsibility for DP and information sciences in a combined department with personnel and human resource management. Indeed, there is a tendency for it to be locked in with other functional areas because, in its own right, it is often not a big department. But even though not numerically strong, whether directly or indirectly, it almost inevitably keeps the performance of the more senior managers under review.

One of the main issues is the effectiveness of the use made of the information resource. No matter how good the initial design, the organisation may experience a form of information log jam effect where the departments generate a lot of very good data at the operational level, but it is not used effectively higher up in the organisation. This arises because the data is not distilled down into a form which will optimally support decision-making. That is sometimes a criticism of the DP department but, more importantly, it may be a criticism of the senior managers who have failed to specify precisely what their needs are. Management services are a form of built-in conscience for the organisation and their function is to prick people into admitting error and to taking suitable remedial action. In taking this action, it represents a built-in critique of the organisation at all levels because, if it is going to propose a solution to a problem no matter where that problem may be located, then it must see problems at a senior level as well as at an operational level.

The precise role and responsibilities eventually adopted by management services must depend on the skills and abilities of the staff who have been recruited into the department and how they have been allowed to go about their work. The department would look to recruit a small number of staff with a high level of expertise. Their expertise would be in the analytical areas. They will retain functional specialisation from their training and initial experience, but they should aim to produce general management skills because, once in the management services department where they stand outside the classical functional restrictions of departments, they should turn themselves into generalists. The level of success achieved will depend upon the amount of rope they have been allowed by the most senior decision-makers. Sometimes the role of management services can become fundamental through the personalities of those involved. If the leader of the department gains influence, say by having the ear of the managing director, that department may end up running the entire organisation. Although it is admitted that this would be relatively unusual because most organisations develop a fairly rigid structure and cannot happily tolerate the form of free-ranging role of the undirected management services department.

The organisation must therefore carefully address the issues of the position to be occupied by the management services department within the organisation, and the role and status which the leader of that department is to have. The result is going to say a lot about the culture of the organisation—both qualitatively to look at the role which the department plays, and quantitatively to look at the number of decisions which the department recommends and which are implemented.

This is likely to be a function of the level of seniority at which the department reports, and at which its recommendations might be implemented.

If the diversity of functions provided by a management services department is mapped on to an organisational chart, it must be recognised that these functions have to be performed if the organisation is to operate effectively. There is always a problem-solving function to be performed in an organisation of size. In a sense, it does not matter what this function is called, nor does it matter where it is located within the organisation so long as it has a general organisation perspective. In practice, all organisations develop some degree of expertise in problem-solving and decision-support. If this is not produced as a separate and identified department, the organisation will tend either to allocate the function to the information system area of data processing, or it will be generally subsumed within the other departments. It would be unlikely that a modern organisation would rely exclusively on buying in the expertise through consultancy.

The problem about placing the function of management services into the technical world of computer departments is that the latter have a tendency towards self-interest, and most DP managers, whether through training or inclination, do not develop organisational perspectives. It is therefore likely that they will not have the most useful contextual view of the organisation when it comes to advising on strategy. Moreover, it is expensive to buy in expertise, not only because consultants tend to charge a substantial sum for the application of their expertise, but also because they have to go through a learning curve so it can take them rather longer to arrive at the same decision as the in-house manager. Hence, it can be significantly more cost-effective to develop in-house expertise so long as it is independent from the DP department which is to support many of its functions. Otherwise they might find it difficult to separate their function from the role of the DP department. The key to the department's success is the ability to keep a proper sense of balance in controlling the interaction between the technology providers and the users. Consequently, alongside the DP department, management services should be the group most closely connected with the management of catalytic function which IT can perform. Controlling and directing the dynamics of change will always be the major problem for management to resolve but better decisions will result from dispassionate advice.

4.3.3 The data processing department

The use of the term data processing department has begun to move out of fashion. Organisations will continue to use the description for some time to come, but it now represents a changing set of functions. Originally, it was there to manage the physical computer resource which was usually a single mainframe machine housed in an environment controlled room, and to provide software support. Because the resource was centralised, it was much easier to understand the function of the ministering department in organisational terms. That function is still there because even though there has been a development of operatorless systems, and the decentralisation of resources through networking has made computerisation more user-driven, the machines still have to be acquired, installed and maintained, and the software still has to be installed and the users trained in its use.

This historical centralisation was in part the source of the concept of the information centre (see 4.3.1). All the data would be collected and maintained in a single location and all the decision-makers would have to address the department which serviced and controlled the delivery systems. With technology-driven changes, the role of the department has shifted towards systems rather than the maintenance of physical hardware. It is also more communications based. It is still involved in systems analysis and design. It has the expertise in the *how* of systems. Whether or not it actually has the skill to say *whether* or *why* will depend upon the calibre of its staff. One of the interesting developments has been in the design of software which is more user friendly. In a sense that has changed the role of the DP department. When computers were being developed, the human interface was extremely technical and required specialist knowledge to achieve any meaningful results. The systems themselves were also predominately batch run and therefore under the more direct control of the specialist DP staff. Today, with the best menu-driven WIMP (Window, Icon, Mouse, Pull-down menus) systems technology to draw upon, and real-time systems for immediacy of response, the DP manager no longer has an interpretive function to perform between the manager and the resource. The manager may directly address and interrogate the resource from his/her own desk, regardless of whether that data is held locally or centrally.

The DP manager has therefore had to develop a more administrative function to ensure that the right packages and services are available to permit the manager to make the best use of the data resources within the organisation. The manager must also be trained to make the best use of those resources. Indeed, training is going to become increasingly important. Thus, for example, the whole philosophy underpinning the development of Fourth Generation Languages (4GLs) has been that the users will be given more control over the development of the software (see 5.10.4). This promise of user-driven systems which can genuinely interact and interwork can only be realised if the lay users have a proper understanding of the potential processing and manipulative power of the hardware which can be exploited by well designed software. This is more than a mere training function. This is a co-ordination function to ensure that all those who are to be allowed to develop software have the appropriate level of expertise and that everyone adopts and adheres to the same basic design standards.

If all the users adopt different standards and protocols, a piecemeal system with no portability will emerge and negate the whole point of automation which is to provide a broad canvas for the exchange of data between the greatest number of involved decision-makers. Maximum portability both of the software itself and of the data within the separately generated packages and systems should be aimed at. The problem lies in the proliferation of packages. If everyone is given the same basic software, although ostensibly the packages are all the same and data will be transferable between them, the enthusiatic amateur programmer may, without proper documentation, produce personalised refinements to the standardised packages which actually inhibit future communications. If the users also produce their own idiosyncratic software from scratch, communications may completely break down. What is required is a mechanism for testing the software before it is allowed to go live within the system. This will help to ensure that it has the maximum compatibility both with what is already held on system, and what is proposed by other users.

EXPERT SYSTEMS

The development of expert systems is becoming an increasingly important issue in the larger corporations. One of the first questions to answer is whether there is any role for the enthusiastic amateur to capture the expertise which is already held by the organisation. No matter what the nature of the information system, whether centralised or decentralised, or the organisational management structure, all organisations are little more than small pockets of expertise which are harnessed for the common good. To achieve the requisite level of co-ordination, departments are being created to manage the formally acknowledged human resources, and knowledge engineering skills are being developed in the area known as **Artificial Intelligence (AI)** to help to capture and support human expertise. The efforts in this direction have become more positive not only because the technology has improved, but also because the increasingly competitive climate makes it essential on two quite different but equally important fronts that the organisation makes the most effective use of all the resources available to it. So the organisation can either see it as a part of the human resource management side that people who have expertise should be exploited to the best advantage of the existing organisation, or it is a way in which the best automated systems to support the organisation can be built by eliciting and incorporating the available knowledge or expertise into the decision support systems and the expert systems which will support the organisation for many years to come (and, of course, long after the given experts may have left the organisation). It also makes that expertise available to a much wider range of individuals within the organisation. Knowledge engineering may therefore be seen as an increasingly important but difficult and specialised function.

THE CONSTRUCTION OF EXPERT SYSTEMS

One of the mistakes most easily made is to believe that computers can be expert in the human sense. In fact, an expert system, so called, is nothing more than a computer system which possesses a set of facts about a particular area of human knowledge, and by manipulating those facts in line with the programming, the computer is able to make useful inferences for the end user. The concept of intelligence has different dimensions but, at the end of the day, the computer cannot be intelligent until it develops a sufficient semantic understanding so that it can convert its own data into knowledge. Until then, it can only be made to mimic intelligence by performing tasks which humans think of as intelligent. Sometimes, the programming can achieve this by elegant means. Thus, simple exhaustive searching, if sufficiently fast, could produce results which might be taken as evidencing intelligence. But it might be considered more intelligent to avoid the search altogether, or to delimit it by prior enquiries.

The way humans think of intelligence will also be determined by the use to which the computer is put. The usual point of distinction is that an intelligent system is one capable of solving problems which cannot be resolved by using crude computational methods, ie there is a distinction between standard data processing techniques and the genuinely expert system. The point made by those who market expert systems is that they will exhibit expert behaviour. In practice, the power of any truly expert system is that some representation of the knowledge used by a human has been achieved in a preprogrammed form which can be used as a basis for computation.

The computer system depends for its effectiveness upon the facts which have been elicited from human experts. These facts, which are often expressed as rules, then form a conceptual representation of the relevant expertise. There are two levels of difference between a human expert and a beginner:

1 a human expert knows more, and
2 a human expert is likely to use the knowledge more effectively.

In the first instance, the actual content of the knowledge base will be unique to each individual who supplies the data, and the explanation of the content will be a personal process. But in learning how to capture and write down exactly what the expertise is, the notational system of concepts which emerges can be applied to other experts' knowledge. Knowledge acquisition, ie the extraction of the knowledge which forms the underlying base of the expertise from the human expert, or knowledge identification by the expert for entry into a shell are the most difficult aspects when developing an expert system of any size. In some domains where the procedures involved are simple and algorithmic, the knowledge can be made explicit fairly easily. A preliminary survey through basic textbooks, followed by confirmatory interviews or discussions with colleagues, will usually be sufficiently effective to permit the creation of a prototype conceptual model which can then be tested.

Generally, the most effective ways for a knowledge (or software) engineer to acquire information from experts are by observation in the field or in-depth interviewing. These methods are inherently slow, a major problem given that experts' time tends to be limited. It can also be difficult to represent the rules which are obtained in this way because observational data is often incomplete and inconsistent, and the observer must continually refer back to the experts for clarification. This substantially increases the amount of time involved, and tests the patience of all involved. The most usual approach is to rely on informal interviews to elicit information which is then converted into empirical rules (usually in a form laid down by the target shell). However, not all expertise is capable of being represented as a rule system, eg areas of medical diagnosis may depend upon extensive practical experience and strategic knowledge which is difficult to verbalise, and the informality of the interview may enhance the incompleteness and inexact nature of the information which is acquired.

Any expert's knowledge is likely to be of different types. It is difficult, if not impossible, to classify knowledge but, it is possible to suggest the following broad categories:

(a) overview knowledge, ie knowledge of concepts and the relationships between different parts of the domain;
(b) knowledge of the routine procedures—this will be backed up by knowledge of key facts which are particular to certain areas of the expertise and of the heuristics, ie the rules of thumb for choosing how to solve a problem; and
(c) classificatory knowledge, ie the ability to make fine distinctions between a number of similar items.

One way for the expert to gain an insight into knowledge held is to write information down. For the objective outsider, an interview of the expert with these classifications in mind can be helpful. This can quickly generate a lot of information that indicates the terminology and the main components of the domain, and is thus a good starting procedure to establish a basic framework. It is also useful to ask the expert to give a one hour lecture which can be followed by later systematic probing interviews where depth is added. But, as indicated above, all interviews have limitations. Although experts have the knowledge, it may not be easily communicated in the interview situation.

It is possible to combine knowledge extracted from several different experts and thereby to overcome the problem of incompleteness, but this may cause severe problems if the experts approach the resolution of problems with different methods. The ideal solution would be to produce systems which could induce rules from all the examples given by the contributing experts. However, the danger with such systems is that there may be a large number of rules generated, or that the one or two rules induced work well with the particular examples given, but do not work well outside the data set.

One of the more recent developments is called **protocol analysis**. This records the behaviour (verbal or otherwise) of the expert and shows how a problem is addressed and solved. The protocol is then converted into a set of productions that moves sequentially through the solution methodology. Its merit is that it goes beyond what the expert can actually tell the knowledge engineer, and permits detailed inference as to what knowledge the expert must be using but either cannot verbalise or may not even be aware of. By reconstructing the solution using the inferred production rules, the expert's knowledge can be modelled. Protocol analysis is preceded by **task analysis**, ie the constraints imposed by the nature of the task are determined. By taping the expert at work, additional or incidental protocols may be elicited, ie informal remarks may provide key insights into the expert's thinking which might not have emerged during a formal interview.

The problem is that this approach is labour-intensive, requiring the transcription and analysis of significant quantities of data and reducing the useful amount of end-product material. A number of multi-dimensional scaling techniques have been used in psychology to show how a particular set of concepts are structured, eg repertory grids can elicit finer grain criteria than formal interviews. By identifying clustering on the dimensions, the system designer can give a structure which more clearly differentiates the domain objects. It can also lead to the development of meta-knowledge, an overview understanding which provides a conceptual framework for the structuring of individual elements or concepts. However, such techniques are extremely specialised and demanding.

The answer for the administrative and commercial sectors lies in the expert system shell. There is an increasing range of expert system shells now available on the commercial market. Most of the shells are supplied in two versions: a larger mainframe system, more suitable for complex tasks, and a smaller version suitable for use on a PC, eg SAVOIR and Micro Expert. Although the ideal system for the creation of software would be subject-led, and not software-led, because this would permit the human expert to structure the information in the most internally consistent and intellectually satisfying way, this presupposes that the experts actually understand their subjects in a way which is suitable for conversion into a knowledge base. It was this problem which could be reduced by allocating a specialist knowledge engineer to each expert, and giving that engineer the task of both representing a form of external objectivity to the creative process involved, and of tailoring the software to the knowledge.

Without this outside assistance, the expert needs a series of prompts from the software itself to indicate the format requirements of the particular system. The danger in this is, of course, that the software will then represent a form of intellectual strait-jacket, restricting the structure of the knowledge and the computational range of the processes which are to be performed. Thus, if the domain expert was, when asked, to clearly state that the method adopted to solve a particular problem was a given series of procedures, a knowledge engineer could either select an appropriate piece of software off the shelf, or create routines which would perform those procedures in their proper context. But if the expert is told from the outset that only a limited number of software procedures are available in the particular shell supplied, it is entirely possible that none of these procedures will match those required within the domain expertise. In such a case, either the expert will be deterred from attempting to create the system, or will distort the real world expertise to meet the constraints of the shell. Neither result is satisfactory, but perhaps some effort is better than none. Even if the expert is unhappy with the result, it may still be better than nothing and assist the organisation.

Because the concept of the shell has been developed to allow newcomers to develop their own expert systems without the need for specialist knowledge engineering skills, the standard shell will provide a means for encoding the domain knowledge and inferencing mechanisms to make use of the encoded knowledge. Most fact-seeking expert systems elicit findings by interviewing the user in an inflexible way. The user has no control over the course of the interaction, which tends to be lengthy and tiring. This pattern may be acceptable for interviewing clients in a professional context, but it is not completely acceptable for the busy professional. However, whether through interview or through self-generated input, the knowledge database can be constructed. Because some shells make it relatively easy to adjust the knowledge modelled, it is even sometimes better for the knowledge engineer to prototype by using a shell before building a bigger system from scratch. However, if a shell is used without expert assistance, there are still problems:

(a) A shell is not self-critical and cannot iterate towards an optimum solution.
(b) Shells cannot be trained to think, so if the user does not know the answer to a given question, the shell cannot rephrase it and will fail to elicit the information.
(c) The correction facilities must be good so that if the user realises that a mistake has been made, it should not be necessary to scrap the program and to start again. It should be a simple matter of going back to the relevant point in the program and changing the wording of the material displayed or amending the switching commands.
(d) There are also fundamental difficulties in basing detailed evidential evaluation on the **Bayesian odds** approach, which is quite common in shell designs.

In the future, knowledge engineers and information scientists are going to be providing software and data systems which allow an organisation to meet the needs of the market place more effectively. The more completely the organisation captures an individual's expertise which is making money today, the longer the period over which that person's expertise can make money for the organisation. In general, selecting which skills to capture is a strategic management decision. The difficulty is that if a computer-orientated person looks at another's expertise and skills, the perspective selected may be the immediate feasibility of automating the whole or a part of that skill, or something may be discarded as unimportant because from the DP person's point of view, it is not a necessary skill, whereas organisationally, it might be considerably more important. The decision should be taken by the human resource managers and it would then feed down to the knowledge engineers who would appraise the feasibility of actually capturing the identified skills.

4.4 THE FUTURE OF THE DATA PROCESSING DEPARTMENT

The present status and role of the DP department is one of change. A consequential redefinition is taking place in the light of the changes taking place in other parts of the organisation. It is going to be interesting to see where the new generation of information managers is going to come from. Up to the early 1980s, most organisations would have considered a computing background essential as the qualification for the post of information manager. Today, it is likely that an increasing proportion, if not a majority, of organisations would say that applicants have to have general management skills with some computer knowledge to meet the demands of the post of information manager. Providing the technical expertise is already in the organisation, the candidate's key ability is to be able to manage that resource while making decisions in the light of the whole organisation's needs. This is a crisis for DP departments because previously they had enjoyed significant power within the organisation, playing the role of the Delphic Oracle, ie they were the only people who could manage the interface between the incomprehensibility of the machines and what the users thought they wanted. So they held real power and they could hide behind the arcane mythology of computing jargon to maintain that power.

Whether or not their training can now be extended to provide them with the sort of general management skills which would enable them to survive in the new organisations is extremely debatable. It is likely that they will move down from their current positions in the more strategic/tactical areas of management towards the more operational side of the organisation, unless their training equips them with much more generalist skills. Some departments may gradually cease to exist as departments, coming down to operatorless systems and a few systems analysts. A lot of people will move over to training and user support which might more properly be found in personnel/human resource management departments. Their power is going to have to be redistributed throughout organisations unless the new managers adopt a more pro-active role to fill the vacuum, changing the functions, the responsibilities and level of the contribution which they make to the organisation. They must become an information centre for what is available in the market both in hardware and software terms. They must become a more detailed source of data about costing, translating their specialist knowledge into more useful data.

They are also going to retain a significant role in the feasibility evaluation for all automation support to information systems. That does require a level of managerial seniority, but the department is likely to be making a different form of contribution—one which is more conceptualised and academic than had previously been the case. Instead of being a sort of nuts and bolts person on particular hardware, the new DP manager's contribution will increasingly be as a form of 'consumers' association' for the organisation to guide in a much more general way about:

(a) what is available,
(b) what is feasible, and
(c) what the costs would be for each possibility.

That is a research-based information function rather experiential. In the past, when organisations were locked into the exclusive use of a particular hardware manufacturer's equipment with its non-portable software, there were very few decisions to make. Today, manufacturers are responding to the pressure to agree upon and implement international standards to produce greater hardware compatibility, software producers are becoming more flexible in providing packages which will run on different hardware, and communications technology now allows distributed processing between the hardware of different manufacturers. The result is that the DP department must move away from single system expertise and into the generality of advice. That will have to be reflected in their training whether in higher education or in-house.

4.5 ORGANISATIONAL INFORMATION SYSTEMS—A CASE STUDY

4.5.1 Objectives

The objectives behind introducing the case study at this stage in the text are to:

1 provide a practical illustration of the information system to be found in most organisations—the previous chapters developed the information system in the form of a schematic model, but this case study is designed to illustrate and elaborate this model by describing the main elements of a practical system (only the more significant features of an information system are covered rather than giving an exhaustive and detailed exposition of each element or sub-system);
2 evaluate the role that various sub-systems play within the total information system and illustrate how they may directly contribute towards the information requirements of other functions within the organisation, ie the integrative and collaborative nature of practical information systems;
3 illustrate how the information systems employed at the operational level can provide the necessary information for both management and strategic decision-making (ie the vertical flow of information between functions);
4 clarify and illustrate the meaning of the term 'database' in the practical situation prior to the more technical development of the term in the later sections on Systems Analysis and Design;
5 identify the role of certain manual and computer-based information systems recognising where these may be appropriately used;
6 introduce the more recent developments in computer applications within the information systems.

4.6 INTRODUCTION

The approach employed in developing this case study seeks to focus on two themes or issues that are central to the successful operation of most business organisations, namely:

PROFIT PERFORMANCE
QUALITY MANAGEMENT

These themes have been selected not only for their importance as key business objectives, but also because they demonstrate the different nature of the data requirements and, hence, of the information systems required to support decisions that will promote each objective. The former theme relies heavily on financial and numeric data typically derived from standard systems, while the latter requires an increasing proportion of non-numeric or textual data which is derived from less structured information systems.

Each theme will be examined at each organisational level of decision-making, namely the short-term (operational), medium-term (managerial) and long-term (strategic). In so doing, the range of the problems, issues and decisions that are likely to be encountered in the organisation will be indicated, and the information required to analyse and take decisions at each of these levels will be highlighted. The case study will also consider the interaction that is required between the following broad functional activities or operations if effective information availability is to be ensured to support decision-making:

(a) Purchasing—Inbound Logistics;
(b) Production/Operations;
(c) Warehousing/Despatch—Outbound Logistics;
(d) Sales/Marketing.

To avoid the duplication of material, only the relevant areas of each function's information system will be addressed. The strategic decisions, by their nature, involve decisions that span the total organisation and its constituent functions and, as such, will be treated separately at the end of the chapter.

4.7 CASE STUDY BACKGROUND

Scribe plc manufactures and sells a range of office furniture products including desks, chairs, tables and specialist computer furniture. The company has been in the business for some 35 years and employs 260 people with a sales turnover in the last year of £5.4 million. The products may be constructed from wood, metals or plastics (or a combination of materials) and they are finished to a high standard of quality. The company's operations involve the purchase of raw materials such as sheet steel, wood, plastics, fabrics, fasteners and other fittings. The production operations essentially involve the preliminary processing of the raw materials and components, assembly of these into the end products and, finally, finishing, painting, polishing and inspection.

The total product range is quite extensive with 16 product groups (group classifications normally being set by function, eg typist/secretarial desks) and a total of 285 individual product items. In order to meet immediate delivery requirements, the company has a policy of maintaining stocks of those product lines which typically have a regular and substantial demand pattern. The delivery policy on such products is to guarantee delivery within seven days of receipt of order should the customer require it. The initial delivery quotation on other product lines will be on a six to eight week time scale, subject to some flexibility to meet the needs of important customers. The company uses a variety of selling approaches. These involve dealing with independent office equipment suppliers, making direct contact with the new office contract market through architects and the building trade, directly mailing catalogues to business and commercial organisations, and placing direct advertising in the trade press and professional magazines.

4.8 PROFIT PERFORMANCE

The overriding objective in most business organisations involves profitability. Scribe plc has suffered a deterioration in profitability in recent years from a 12% ROCE three years ago to 7% ROCE in the latest full trading year. The target originally established by the management team was to increase the ROCE to a rate of 15% by the end of this present trading period. In general, the implementation of strategies to achieve profit performance objectives requires the organisation simultaneously to manage the sales revenues and the costs to ensure that the maximum profit is generated in both the short and the long run. The deterioration of Scribe plc's profit performance has been due to a combination of reduced sales revenues and poor cost controls. This has resulted in greatly reduced profit margins. Clearly, every organisational function has a contribution to make towards achieving this objective. The following paragraphs examine the ways in which the information systems in each major function potentially may contribute towards the improvement of the control of revenues and of costs at both the operational and management levels.

4.8.1 The purchasing function

This function has a particularly evident role in the profit performance of commercially-orientated organisations. Indeed, in the typical organisation, over 50 per cent of the resource inputs are likely to be handled by this function. Scribe plc is no exception with 54 per cent of the cost of finished products being represented by the goods and services acquired by the purchasing department. Improving the profit performance requires not only seeking the most competitive prices, but also ensuring appropriate standards of quality, reliability of delivery and security of the supply sources, while providing accurate and sufficiently detailed information to facilitate effectiveness in planning the subsequent operations of the business.

Operational decisions and activities within the purchasing function involve the acquisition of a variety of inputs from raw materials through to packaging and services. As in most companies, the buyers are required to maintain a list of suppliers for each major input showing delivery times, prices, technical specifications, quality standards, etc. This information needs to be updated regularly and to be readily available to the buyers when required. Although it may be possible to compile lists of the main suppliers, the products supplied and credit terms and to store such data on a computer using a database application, there will be other types of data which would prove more expensive and less effective to store on the computer, eg glossy catalogues or product samples. This collection of information, whether stored manually in a set of filing cabinets or within a computer system (say, using a computer output microform system—see 5.4.3—or optical disk system), would be described as a **purchasing database**.

The usual operation of this form of database will involve the user in seeking access to individual supplier details as and when required. The normally expected result when using an entirely manual database will be the storage of a more comprehensive and detailed set of information, but it may take longer to identify the physical location of the data set and it may not be in a conveniently pre-digested form to allow rapid comparisons to be made between different suppliers. Alternatively, computer-based systems will provide more rapid access to the data, and because the typical database system stores less detailed and more structured information and reports, it is easier to make comparisons between the different suppliers. If the system is only partially automated, the buyer may need to access not only the computer-stored information concerning a possible supplier, but also the other data sources. This would suggest the need for compatibility between the computer-based and the manual database storage, making sure that good cross-referencing is used.

Scribe plc has retained a manual system for storing the product details and price lists of its suppliers. It is referenced alphabetically by supplier name. This has caused frequent problems when it comes to locating alternative suppliers for a given input as there is no cross-referencing by inputs or services provided. In the past, this information has been retained in the memory of the individual buyers as the product of each person's direct experience. The problem implicit in this approach is that the information is not readily available to the other buyers and the departure of the particular employee from the organisation also results in the departure of this element of the organisation's database. A simple computerised database could be established which would generate a list of all the suppliers for each type of input or service simply by listing each product or service and locating against this a supplier code or reference number indicating that they supply such products or services. The manual database could then be used to retrieve the more detailed information required.

The primary financial information within the purchasing department comprises records of each transaction between the organisation and the given supplier. This provides details of the value of the transaction, and will show the timing and stage in completion of the transaction between the two parties. The primary focus of operational decisions based on this information is related to the control of the costs and of the quality of materials and service inputs. Hence, at various stages in the ordering cycle the need may arise to corroborate different financial elements. For example, the unit price, quantity and discount terms from:

(a) the supplier's original quote;
(b) the subsequent purchase order raised by Scribe plc;
(c) the delivery note from the supplier;
(d) the goods received documentation; and
(e) the final invoice submitted by the supplier,

should all be consistent in terms of these details. The purchasing function needs to monitor the accuracy of the data at each of these stages on each order. At present, Scribe plc operates a manual system for the raising of purchase orders and the checking of subsequent deliveries prior to the payment of the suppliers' invoices. There are persistent and frequently significant problems that arise because of changes to the original purchase orders. Such changes may have arisen for a variety of reasons. They may have been initiated by Scribe plc itself, or be the result of unexpected shortages in the supplier's stocks. There may have been an accident or incompetence in the supplier's despatch department, or the goods sent may be a deliberate substitution of replacement items by the supplier at the time of delivery. In each of these circumstances, the reconciliation of the suppliers invoice with the original purchase order invariably requires time-consuming research both to establish the reasons for the variations and to take appropriate remedial action if necessary. This process would prove more cost-effective and efficient if the data were provided through a centralised computer system. This would mean that any changes that arise in the various stages of handling the purchase orders could be amended against a central data source. This system is referred to as a **purchase order system** and it interfaces not only with the purchasing department, but also the accounting and financial control departments and the goods receiving and warehousing departments. Each of the departments involved would be able both to access the purchase order data for a specific order at any time and to input the necessary confirmation or amendment data at the various stages in the purchase order processing.

More recent developments in this field concern the automatic transmission of data from the buying organisation's computer system to the supplier's computer system. For example, Scribe plc would raise an order for the purchase of fittings (eg drawer handles) from a particular supplier. Once entered on Scribe plc's computer system, the computer would automatically locate the instructions for communicating directly with the supplier's computer (ie a set of dialing instructions) through a communications network. Having established the link with the supplier's computer, the order would be transmitted automatically and entered into the supplier's sales order system for processing and delivery. Confirmation of order details, delivery dates and possible stock-outs may be transmitted back to Scribe plc's computer for the attention of the purchasing clerks. This process of **Electronic Data Interchange (EDI)** is already being used in many industry sectors and, in some cases, is being further developed to include the automatic transfer of funds from the buyer's bank account to the seller's bank account on the successful completion of the order. This is known as **Electronic Funds Transfer (EFT)**. The development of such a system by Scribe plc would require significant investment in the analysis and design of a computerised purchase ordering system before such a development could be contemplated. Further investments by the organisation and its suppliers in communications and networking systems and agreements on standard formats for order documentation would also be necessary to ensure the effective use of EDI developments.

Management decisions are concerned with assessing the efficiency and effectiveness of the purchasing function over the medium-term period. This would be assessed not only on the ability to reduce, maintain or control input costs per unit, but also in terms of the ability to ensure appropriate delivery times, while maintaining the quality of the inputs delivered and ensuring the accuracy of the supporting accounting and information systems.

The management and control of the financial position concerning purchases depends upon access to the appropriate information. The financial data necessary to support and control these operations is derived from:

(a) specific quotations from the suppliers;
(b) previous correspondence with the suppliers concerning prices and discounts;
(c) supplier price lists;
(d) credit arrangements and limits agreed; and
(e) the current level of credit owing to the supplier.

The management in Scribe plc, for example, receives monthly statements of the total expenditure on goods purchased classified by different categories, the total credit outstanding to suppliers, the incidence of late deliveries, and production problems or returned goods resulting from inferior quality inputs. This information originates from a variety of sources including the accounting systems relating to accounts payable, the costing and budgetary control systems, and the less formal reports of the purchasing department staff.

It is important to note that the information used to manage the purchasing function comprises both quantitative and qualitative data. The former originates from summaries derived from the purchase order system. The qualitative data originates from the reports and views of the staff involved in the purchasing process, and requires more effective communications systems to capture, record and transmit this information to the management. It is appropriate to observe at this point that the majority of computer systems and applications software packages are designed to handle quantitative (ie numeric) data rather than qualitative (ie textual) data. The major exception to this is obviously the word processing application. But although such applications are designed to manipulate textual data, the capacity to quickly retrieve certain relevant parts of the text stored and to communicate their substance to readers is less efficient than the equivalent systems for the handling of numerical data.

However, the power of text processing software is increasingly significant, and while it will never match that of numeric processing systems, it will nevertheless provide sufficient scope for many routine information retrieval applications in organisations. The use of the Electronic Mail application throughout the organisation would also provide a valuable communication channel for the distribution of memoranda and instructions requiring a wide circulation (see 5.4.1). Further development on this basic data or message transmission system through a network, for example, involve the storage of diaries designed to enable the arrangement of meetings with colleagues when they are not available for telephone arrangements to be made. Additionally, standard reference materials may be stored and accessed as and when required by employees, for example, instructions and procedures concerning sickness, maternity leave, or travel and subsistence rates, etc.

4.8.2 Production operations

The production operations at Scribe plc are subdivided into a number of different departments each carrying out specialist operations, eg upholstery, steel cutting and shaping, etc. The major department is the assembly department which undertakes the assembly of the processed parts and bought-in parts to form the desks, tables and chairs. Following assembly, the products enter the finishing department which applies paint, polishes, etc to produce the finished product. The assembly department comprises some 65 employees, most of whom are engaged in general assembly operations. A minority are engaged in more specialised assembly operations relating to the lower volume items.

Operational decisions within the context of production operations focus on ensuring that the profit performance objectives are related to the productivity of the operational resources being employed. It is quite usual in batch processing systems, such as those used in Scribe plc, to establish the standard costs in terms of the materials, and the machine and labour time requirements for a particular item. Performance may then be measured against these standards and any significant deviations assessed.

Scribe plc operates a computerised manufacturing recording system. The essence of the system is that each type of product is estimated prior to production in terms of the materials, machine and labour inputs, expressed as standard costs. The overheads relating to the batches or individual units are then apportioned. At each stage of the manufacturing process, the production operatives are responsible for the input, via a terminal, of the works order number, the materials used, and the time spent processing the job or batch (including the time taken to set up the particular machine(s) for the job). This data is collated and accumulated against the particular job which may be for a single item or for a batch of similar items.

This data is then employed by the Cost Accountant to evaluate the profitability of each of the orders in relation to the standard data. While the Cost Accountant may access a summary of the cost statements for a particular order or for a particular period in time, the normal procedure in Scribe plc is to produce a print out of all the orders completed at the end of each month—this represents the aggregate performance data for the period. The system is being used to record data on the operational performance of the production department on a real-time basis (ie, as it happens), but the only use being made of this data is the analysis of general performance in production during the period of a month. Scribe plc is clearly not utilising this valuable data resource fully given that it is capable of providing a continuous monitoring of the production system and of indicating whether it is functioning effectively. Further development of the system should therefore enable this same data to be transmitted to the supervisors and production management to enable them to monitor continuously the production system and to detect potential sources of sub-standard performance or other potential problems as and when they arise. Inefficiencies detected at an early stage may be corrected before significant deviations occur. Under the present system, the data would normally only be analysed and the problems identified at the end of each month, when corrective action may prove less effective and/or more costly.

Management decisions relating to the production operations concern not only the day-to-day activities but, more importantly, the evaluation and control of both the effectiveness and the efficiency of the entire production function over a period of time. For these purposes, the cost and, hence, the profit performance may be assessed by type of product and by size of batch. Such assessments may lead to major improvements in the production planning and scheduling processes. In addition, details of plant and individual operative efficiency would be helpful in taking decisions to upgrade the plant or in producing shift rosters to allocate operatives to particular tasks or working groups. At present, Scribe plc's manufacturing recording system concentrates on providing a more generalised financial appraisal of the operations. Yet, as indicated, the data is available within the system to provide other forms of analysis to support the management of the operations, and the whole system clearly contains the key information required to support the management decisions in terms of the efficiency of the operations, machine utilisation and capacity usage.

A typical tool used in the analysis of both the financial and non-financial data is the spreadsheet application. This facilitates the manipulation of data and the comparison of actual performance against budgeted performance. For example, a typical spreadsheet for Scribe plc could have the following structure:

Spreadsheet rows	Elements of the cost structure for a particular product, eg material costs, direct labour, overheads.
Spreadsheet columns	Various products produced by the company, eg chairs, desks, filing cabinets, etc.

Further and perhaps more importantly, it will permit the consequences of current performance to be extrapolated through the spreadsheet to indicate the effects on future periods of production and on profitability in general. While many spreadsheets are viewed as two dimensional, it is becoming increasingly common to consider such tools as providing three dimensional data and, hence, analytical power in three dimensions. This is not essentially a new development, but rather a recognition that data may be structured and analysed in a number of different ways simultaneously. Often this third dimension relates to analysing blocks of data for different time periods:

Third dimension	Analysis of the product cost structures for differing time periods, either historically or in terms of future forecasts and budgets.

Another development that may enhance the use of spreadsheets is the automatic transfer or capture of data from the organisation's existing information systems. For example, Scribe plc could transfer the necessary data from its manufacturing recording system to a spreadsheet which would enable management to undertake the immediate analysis of the performance rather than being required to undertake the more tedious task of manually inputting all of the required data from the computer listings.

4.8.3 Warehousing and distribution

The post-production activities of warehousing and distribution have often been treated as contributing less to the cost and profit performance of the business. However, closer analysis of such activities would indicate that they are equally important in ensuring both the effectiveness and the efficiency of the total business.

Operational decisions must be based upon accurate and detailed records of the stocks available. This interfaces both with the production department for planning the future production of buffer stocks and with the sales department in providing an improved service to customers through shorter delivery times. Scribe plc currently operates a manual system for finished goods stocks by using a series of stock cards for each item. Receipts from production and deliveries from stock are manually recorded. This results in frequent inaccuracies in the stock recording system. If the system were to be computerised, quite apart from enhancing accuracy of data, it would also provide information on excess stocks, slow-moving items and redundant items, all of which could be used by the sales and marketing functions to promote particular products or to reduce prices to remove such items.

Management decisions relating to the outbound logistics are directed primarily towards managing the resources effectively and providing a high level of service to the organisation's customers. The planning, monitoring and control of finished goods stocks is a key element in this process as excessive stocks incur costs for the business in terms of storage space, insurance and financing charges. Insufficient stocks, on the other hand, may be reflected in a poorer quality of service to the customer particularly in terms of delay in delivery. Irrespective of the stock level policy in operation, the efficiency level with which the system of assembling, despatching and delivering orders must operate efficiently if costs are to be minimised and the loss of revenues from poor service are to be eliminated should be identified and adopted as a specific target by the organisation.

4.8.4 Marketing and sales

In many respects, this function may be considered as the most crucial for any organisation in terms of profit performance as it provides the primary interface between the market, the customers and the organisation.

Operational decisions are supported by the sales order processing system. Currently, the sales orders from customers, either coming directly from the customer via the tele-sales ordering service or via the sales force, are passed to the sales order clerks who enter the relevant details into the sales order processing system. This system employs two databases, a customer database containing details of each customer and accessed by a unique customer number for each customer, and a product database containing details of each product, prices, specifications, etc accessed by a unique product code for each product. The sales order clerk is only required to enter the customer code followed by the appropriate product codes and quantities requested to produce the appropriate invoice, despatch notes and entries on the sales ledger for the particular customer.

Scribe plc have been evaluating a Portable Direct Entry (PDE) system for use by their field sales force in completing orders. This system essentially involves providing each sales person with a portable computer system (eg Lap-top) with keyboard, screen and printer. The portable system contains the customer and product databases. The sales person enters the order from the customer directly into the computer at the customer's premises by using a series of menus to guide the input of data, ie the customer's code, the product codes and the quantities. The system will advise immediately on the availability and the expected delivery times for each item, and produce a full invoice listing extended in terms of quantities, prices and totals. The customer checks the details of the order and signs one copy. Details of the customer's credit levels and unpaid invoices may also be displayed if required, permitting the sales person to remind the customer of any outstanding balances or, if necessary, to indicate that no further orders may be accepted until the outstanding balances have been cleared.

At the end of each day, the portable computer system is connected via the telephone lines using a modem to the central computer, and all the details of the orders for that day are transferred to the central computer, automatically updating customer records, sales and stock records, and producing despatch notes for the warehouse to fill on the following day. The main computer will also update the portable system in terms of both the availability of stock items, delivery times or non-stock items and changes in prices, as well as changes in the balances owing and the credit limits for all customers within the sales person's territory.

A key requirement is that the finished goods stock and the production control system are fully integrated to permit the generation of the necessary data for the product database. For example, the sales staff should be in a position to advise the customer at the time of ordering on the availability of items in stock or the likely delivery time from the production schedule.

Management decisions in relation to the sales force are primarily concerned with ensuring the effective and efficient use of the time and effort of the sales staff. The geographic distribution of the sales force and the differing nature of the territories, both in terms of geographic spread and size of potential customers, makes direct comparisons between individuals problematic. The more usual approach is to measure performance against sales targets, either in terms of the number of new contacts made or in terms of the value of orders taken.

In supporting management decisions, the PDE system potentially provides valuable information to aid the management of the sales force, and also to establish sales trends and patterns by customers and products. For example, the data relating to the number of visits undertaken and the sales generated per visit may be used to evaluate the effectiveness of the sales force in general and of individual staff in particular. Similarly, the generation of information concerning the sales generated from particular customers or by groups of similar customers may indicate potential improvements in either sales or marketing approaches to enhance effectiveness and the volume of sales. Additionally, if any changes to marketing and sales promotions are instituted, this system may be used to assist measurement and evaluation to determine their effectiveness. Moreover, the analysis of sales patterns by type of product may be used to enhance the short-term forecasting of the organisation and, hence, the production scheduling, while equally providing valuable information for the development and analysis of all marketing plans and activities.

4.9 QUALITY MANAGEMENT

The management and assurance of quality is arguably the function and responsibility of everyone within the organisation, though certain functions such as purchasing and operations will often have a more significant impact on the overall level of quality by virtue of their role in the overall process.

4.9.1 Purchasing

In relation to the operational, the buyer needs to have access to the quality and performance data concerning the material and service inputs as this may influence purchasing decisions, eg whether to buy from the same source or from an alternative source if quality is inadequate. Similarly, data concerning faulty inputs is required not only to seek credit or the replacement of faulty inputs, but equally to alert the buyers to the nature and scale of the problems encountered. There is a requirement to establish quality standards for the general performance of the suppliers and their relationship to the organisation and also the standards relating to specific material or service inputs. This may be produced in the form of a standards manual which would also specify the precise standards relating to each type of input. There is clearly the potential to store such data on the computer as this would provide a manageable means of updating and retrieving such data.

The management of quality within the purchasing function ultimately relies upon establishing strong initial standards, followed by effective monitoring and control of the quality assurance procedures and standards. The achievement of quality standards data derives from a number of sources within the organisation including:

(a) goods inwards inspection;
(b) production departments during processing, assembly and finishing operations;
(c) quality inspection at completion of production;
(d) customer support services including delivery, installation and after-sales support; and
(e) sales departments, which will report complaints or commendations made directly to the sales office or to the sales personnel in the field.

4.9.2 Production operations

The management and control of quality is practised most regularly in the production stages. However, evidence suggests that many of the systems that have been developed to maintain quality have become ineffective.

An essential prerequisite for effective quality control at the operational level is the establishment of the necessary standards and procedures to ensure that the appropriate quality levels are attained in the end product. Scribe plc, like many other manufacturing companies, has a set of operational procedures and a quality standards manual, copies of which are intended to be available to all staff in the various production departments. In essence, this document represents a database of common procedures and quality standards, together with detailed instructions on how to handle a range of variations from the normal procedures.

Despite efforts by the management to maintain this paper-based system by issuing amendments to the manual at regular intervals, a recent survey of the manuals and their usage indicated that the majority of the manuals were outdated and contained very few of the most recent updates. Further, few of the staff were prepared to refer to the manuals unless there was a dispute about a specific procedure. Of even greater concern was the finding that the general practice and manufacturing approach adopted in the production departments was substantially different from that suggested in the manuals, with operatives modifying the official procedures and tests to suit the circumstances of particular jobs or the equipment being used.

The solution proposed to this problem was the computerisation of the system such that each section within the production department would be able to access the procedures and standards manual through their own workstations. Since all employees would be using the same central data source, this would simplify the communication problem when it came to updates and would help to ensure that all staff were utilising the same procedures and observing the same work practices. But despite a significant investment in extending the computer network, providing workstations in each section and establishing the central database system, the desired benefits have not materialised. It now appears that the issue that those recommending the computer-based system failed to address (as had those who implemented the paper-based system) is the reluctance of the staff to use the system. The longer-term employees prefer to rely upon their own experience and will not willingly adhere to supposedly agreed procedures and standards. The solution really lies in managing and training the staff in the correct procedures, rather than in the development of an effective information system.

From the management perspective, the control of quality in the production stages is essentially one of setting the necessary standards and then monitoring to see whether they are being achieved and that they are providing the necessary quality of outputs. The two keys to effective monitoring are the detection of sub-standard outputs at an early stage and the ability to trace these back to the cause—this allows the necessary corrective actions to be taken. For this purpose, an on-line production monitoring system may provide rapid feedback of potential problems in quality. But this is never enough on its own. Management must consider the nature of the work to be done and modify their expectations accordingly. Thus, it is often the case that inferior quality materials or components will require more time and effort in the machining and assembly processes than normal quality standards. So if it is known that one batch of in-house produced components is of marginal quality, appropriate instructions must be given to the affected operatives in the assembly and finishing sections before work is commenced to minimise wastage.

It should therefore be apparent that the management of quality in the production operations is not simply concerned with monitoring the quality inspection reports which are essentially a record of quality achieved after the event. It is far more important to ensure that quality standards are being achieved continuously. This is likely to involve information flows less concerned with numeric data and more concerned with oral and written reports of a textual nature. For example, the feedback on problems experienced in machining the initial pieces in a particular batch of pre-fabricated metal parts may require changes to the normal procedures or the reworking of those items to ensure that appropriate quality standards are maintained in the finished product. There should also be a review of the source of those parts. If bought-in, the manufacturer should be alerted to the defects so that future batches may be corrected. The goods received department should also be notified so that a more detailed inspection of the next batch may be undertaken when the goods come into the factory. If the batch was produced in-house, production records should be reviewed to determine the cause of the loss in quality.

4.9.3 Marketing and sales

The operational links between the marketing function and the objective of ensuring market effectiveness may be addressed at two levels. First, the purchasing function needs to ensure that sufficient materials will be available to meet the forecast demand and schedule of deliveries to customers. This requires the presence of an effective channel of communications between the marketing/sales function and other functions. Within Scribe plc this system involves the development of a spreadsheet by the marketing and sales departments to generate sales forecasts. The forecasts are presented as monthly forecasts for the next twelve months, and quarterly forecasts for the following year.

Second, the marketing function within Scribe plc has recognised that the purchasing function within the organisation is often the first to be approached in terms of new materials, new processes, changes in the design and colour of fabrics available, etc. There is therefore a strong need to improve the channels of communication between the marketing function which is monitoring and evaluating the needs of the consumers, the design department, and the purchasing department responsible for ensuring the availability of inputs which may be used to satisfy market opportunities. The company is developing a product profiling database and news sheet to overcome some of these problems. The system involves the purchasing department inputting a summary of any new products encountered in their dealings with existing and potential suppliers. These summaries, which are restricted to about thirty lines of text, are stored in a simple database which contains five different product classifications. The marketing and design staff, or other purchasing department staff may access this database and, by using a simple menu, access short reports on the latest developments in the relevant field, eg the type of finishes that may be applied to desk furniture, the quality and range of colours, etc.

4.10 STRATEGIC MANAGEMENT ISSUES

The strategic management of profit performance and quality requires an overview of the organisation and its relationship to the market opportunities that it seeks to exploit. The management team has been considering the concept of **Total Quality Management (TQM)**. For these purposes, quality means meeting the customer's requirements at the lowest cost, first time every time so that:

(a) customers are all those to whom the organisation supplies products, services, information, etc;
(b) requirements are measurable specifications and cover such factors as durability, reliability, accuracy, speed, method of delivery, price, etc;
(c) at the lowest cost means that no time, effort or materials are lost or wasted in the delivery of the product or service so that profitability is maximised.

It is recognised that the primary methodology for achieving quality is to improve the service to customers both internal and external. This means that, for example, the advice from the marketing function to the production function should be treated as a service in the same way that the sales department deals with external customers. Communication has therefore to be considered both internally and externally, with training given to all those who must deal with customers. Accountability has also to be properly established and proper lines of control drawn up to maintain quality of service.

The organisation must therefore set the corporate mission, determining the appropriate business objectives and goals, and developing strategies to align departmental and functional objectives to those of the corporation. The information necessary to support these processes comprises both externally-derived and internally-derived information. Scribe plc, like many other organisations of this size, has failed to develop the externally-derived information systems to support the strategic management process. While there are a variety of governmental and private sector publications providing data on general economic trends, market trends and technological developments, all of which are available at relatively low cost, there is little awareness of these data sources and where they may be accessed. The senior management have tended to rely heavily on their personal perceptions of the external environment without the necessary information to support or validate such judgments.

The internal information used in the current strategic management process is derived from the existing functional sub-systems in the form of regular summarised reports, eg monthly financial statements. But the unique nature of many of the problems encountered at the strategic level usually requires *ad hoc* reports researching and analysing the particular problem and its potential solutions. Usually, this requires the analysis of both quantitative and qualitative data. The differing problems, data and analytical techniques required and the lack of predictability of these requirements usually means that such analysis cannot be handled in the existing information system.

The development of Decision Support Systems and Executive Support Systems would result in a computerised toolkit of analytical techniques that could be used to support strategic management. These toolkits would provide software tools to enable the decision-maker to structure the problem, develop financial or other quantitative models of the organisation, access data from internal and external databases, and perform analytical manipulations on the data using spreadsheets and other techniques. Scribe plc would be required to make a significant investment not only in the hardware, software and information systems to provide these tools but, more particularly, in the education and training of senior management to provide the necessary skills to use these systems effectively.

In relation to the strategic decision-making within Scribe plc, two of the current strategic problems facing the company are outlined, emphasising the nature of the information required to undertake these decisions.

The first problem concerns the strategic development of the relationships with the organisation's suppliers. These will be dependent on:

(a) a general appraisal of the effectiveness and efficiency of the existing relationships; and
(b) the detailed record of delivery, cost and quality over a period of time.

Much of the data may originate from a further summarised form of the data produced at a management level. If the data arising from the database implied a record of production, dislocation or increasing customer complaints due to poor quality of inputs, then the organisation might need to address this strategically to resolve the problems. Hence, Scribe plc has for some considerable time experienced problems with the supply of the upholstery fabrics and materials required for its chairs. Despite changing suppliers more than three times during the last two years, it is still experiencing extensive delays, erratic deliveries and inferior quality from UK suppliers. The costs of these problems, in terms of production dislocation and delayed deliveries to Scribe plc's customers, has resulted in the strategic appraisal of the supply chain. The organisation is considering either purchasing the upholstery materials from overseas suppliers or acquiring one of its existing suppliers and installing its own management to improve the quality and delivery schedules. The data to support the analysis of this latter move would be derived from the quantitative reports accumulated regularly within the management level of the purchasing function. It would also require more qualitative data and assessments concerning the prospective acquisition, including the quality of its promotional materials, its pricing policies and the effectiveness of the sales staff. Much of this data may be available within the purchasing department (because it results from the dealings of Scribe plc's staff with the supplier), but it is unlikely to be formally recorded until requested for this specific purpose.

The second problem the directors of Scribe plc have indentified is the need to improve the efficiency and effectiveness of the production operations, while seeking to minimise the costs involved in holding stocks of raw materials. They would like to adopt a form of the Just-In-Time (JIT) system, though recognise that the diversity and low volume of some of the inputs required may make this total approach unfeasible. A systems consultancy has quoted a figure of £1.2 million for a comprehensive computer system. This system would:

(a) provide automatic scheduling of orders as they are received;
(b) develop forecasts for finished goods stock items;
(c) initiate the acquisition and ordering of raw materials and components required, and provide a schedule of the delivery dates;
(d) produce the necessary paperwork, drawings and schedules for each item or batch prior to production; and
(e) provide monitoring and evaluation data on an enquiry basis.

Although Scribe plc has recognised the potential benefits that such a system could provide, the company has also received advice from an independent consultant that before any commitment is made to any system of this type, the management should formulate and develop their strategies in relation not only to their production operations, but also to their customers and suppliers. For example, the company needs to develop a strategic relationship with its major suppliers such that the interests of all the companies involved are fully recognised within each relationship. This would permit a more effective form of supply in which both companies were protected and developed. The company ought also to review its strategy in relation to its markets and customers. The strategy which seeks to focus on the larger customers, guaranteeing larger volumes of particular products rather than one-off orders from the smaller customers, may provide scope for the development of JIT types of system because it provides greater levels of predictability in supply.

However, it should also be recognised that the profit margins on such high volume business are likely to be smaller than those available in the supply of specialised products to a more limited niche market. Scribe plc would also have to assess the potential risks involved in adopting a JIT system which effectively reduces the stocks held by the manufacturer to a minimum, possibly one or two days supply, while placing heavier reliance on both the supplier and the transportation systems to deliver the right quantities on time and to the correct specification in terms of quality.

4.11 A SUMMARY OF THE ISSUES IN THE CASE STUDY

As observed in this case, the development of the information system is an integral part of the strategic development of, and the decision-making processes within, Scribe plc. But irrespective of the quality or sophistication of a particular computer-based information system, unless it is consistent with the overall strategies and profiles of both the company's operations and its external relations, it will be doomed to failure from the outset. The logic of any planning method demands a clear statement of the mission which the plan intends to achieve. The mission is the embodiment of all corporate purposes and intentions. For this purpose, the company should conduct an audit of all its resources, strengths and weaknesses so that it can better identify its future objectives and match these with the resources. This will then facilitate a consideration of how the company's competitive advantages can be brought to bear on the market opportunities. In evaluating competitive advantage, the managers must inevitably consider quality and the cost advantages which enable the company to extract higher margins than their competitors and to maintain profitability in the face of price turbulence. Note that it is not the sum of resources which determines a company's competitive position. It is the way resources are matched and deployed to exploit the company's competitive advantages.

The key resource issue facing Scribe plc is the need to develop an integrated approach to developing the information system across the whole organisation. The processs of computerising the organisation's information system highlights the interactive nature of the various elements or sub-systems operating in the various functions. The primary danger faced by organisations like Scribe plc is that the piecemeal development of the individual elements in isolation will at best prove significantly more expensive, and at worst be counter-productive in achieving the eventual objectives of effectiveness and efficiency. The first task facing Scribe plc is therefore the generation of an IT strategy. This strategy must span the next three to five years and should clearly articulate the major developments envisaged in the information system and the sequence in which the component elements are to be developed. The remainder of this text is designed to illustrate the approach that should be adopted both at the strategic level and at that of the individual system.

Many of the proposed developments under consideration by Scribe plc would be seeking to make more effective use of the data already available in the organisation, and are essentially concerned with providing wider and more ready access to this data. It is often found, as in the case of Scribe plc, that fuller utilisation of the information resource already available within the organisation can produce significant benefits at relatively low levels of cost or of investment. However, other developments are likely to require more extensive investments in the processes of analysis and design to support the development of software, and in the acquisition of hardware if the necessary progress is to be made to achieve other benefits from the information system.

In taking decisions, it should be recognised that computerisation is not a panacea. Indeed, the solution to many organisation's information needs is often not best served by a policy of computerising all systems. Even in these technological days, it is true that there will always be a number of information systems that may operate more efficiently and effectively as manual systems, eg the detailed supplier database in the purchasing department. The important factor, however, is to ensure both the compatibility and the effective integration of the manual and computer-based systems, aiming to achieve a high level of mutual support between the two facets of the overall system.

The final issue which influences the success of both manual and computer-based systems is the effective use of the systems by the staff involved. The experiences of Scribe plc mirror those of most organisations in that the effectiveness of the use depends upon the quality of the users, both as suppliers of data to, and as receivers of data from, the system. The system must be designed to be supportive of both types of user, and the organisation must be prepared to invest heavily in education and training so that the maximum benefit from the information resource can be achieved both for the individual and, ultimately, for the organisation. This is particularly the case if TQM is to succeed. Total Quality means that everyone is involved, at all levels and across all functions, in ensuring quality in everything they do. The ethos in which the information system is implemented must incorporate participation. Everyone must feel that they have a share in the solution of the problems, with education and training designed to develop awareness and understanding from the top management down to the lowest employee.

SUMMARY

The key points covered in this chapter are that:

1 All organisational planning starts at a level of generality at the strategic level and gets increasingly specific and practical as the plans move towards implementation. Any plans to make changes in the organisation will have to take account of the prevailing culture.

2 Information is one of the major resources available for exploitation by the organisation, making corporate and information strategy formulation highly interdependent. Indeed, it is difficult to envisage an organisation meeting its objectives without specifying and structuring an effective information system.

3 All organisations should consider creating the post of information manager which may be supported by a data librarian. This strategic post would have specific responsibility for information as a capital resource and as a support to the human resource.

4 All organisations should consider whether to adopt a centralised or decentralised decision-making structure.

5 Management services is often the department with the expertise to advise the organisation on how to make the best decisions, either supplementing or supplanting the function of the DP department.

6 Expert systems may assist an organisation to make more of its human resources over a longer period of time.

QUESTIONS *Solutions to questions of an examination standard start on p 395*

Write brief notes on the following:

(a) information strategy;
(b) information technology as a capital resource;
(c) the role of a data librarian;
(d) the construction of expert systems;
(e) the future of the data processing department.

Questions of an examination standard

1 Within all organisations of substance there should be an identified post with responsibility for information management.

Briefly discuss the role of an individual filling this post, indicating the issues which he or she may be expected to address.

2 Your organisation is investigating the value of setting up an information centre.

Briefly report on the concept of the information centre.

3 A management services department represents a link between decision-makers and the information system by providing support tools, or by providing the techniques, methodologies and expertise to drive those tools.

Briefly describe how a management services department may fit into a typical commercial organisation.

SECTION TWO: INFORMATION SYSTEMS DEVELOPMENT

Chapter 5

The Characteristics of Information Technology

CHAPTER OBJECTIVES

The chapter is intended to introduce the detail of the hardware design and acquisitions options, and in particular to:

1 indicate the basis upon which selections between the different system types should be made, ie upon a functional and purposive analysis, and to explore the potential advantages for the knowledge worker in an automated office environment;
2 study the primary forms of the technology available to support the office automation exercise;
3 consider how new systems can be configured, with particular reference to the range of input, output and storage devices currently on the market;
4 perfect an appreciation of the capacities of hardware by considering the range of software available both as operating systems and as applications, and by considering which high-level languages to install;
5 appreciate the options for the development of communications systems and the role generally played by the data communication systems in supporting automation projects.

5.1 SYSTEM TYPES

There are two major factors which will dictate the type of computer-based system which will be chosen from the range of options:

1 the system is to have **functions**, ie the users will require it to perform a number of identified processes, and
2 it should have a desirable **operating mode**, ie it must carry out those functions in an acceptable way.

The typical functions which may be required from a computer-based system can include:

1 the ability to undertake the routine processing of business documents and/or the recording of transactions—ie to act as a DP system;
2 the carrying out of everyday tasks like filing and support of communications between individuals in the workplace—ie to comprise an office automation system;
3 the monitoring and control, often without direct human intervention being necessary except in an emergency, of an industrial process—eg a process control system;
4 the storage and retrieval of facts which, in appropriate cases, will be held in a non-routine manner, eg in a database system;
5 the provision of information and facilities to aid in the design and subsequent production of an article—eg a CAD/CAM system (ie Computer Aided Design and Manufacture);
6 the analysis of information to evaluate alternative strategies—this is usually undertaken by a DSS or an expert system depending on the status of the user.

These functions may be combined within a single software system (eg a database system can include a DSS), and the features which are offered by each system may vary from one application to another. Thus, for example, an office automation system either may, or may not, include a spreadsheet package among its range of features. The precise constitution of each system as marketed will reflect both the programming and the commercial constraints which operate upon the producer.

Each of the system functions listed above may have different attributes and characteristics and these may lead the system designers to require the operating mode to manipulate and process the data in a particular way. Before describing some of the functions in more detail, it is therefore necessary to introduce the four main operating modes.

5.1.1 Batch or delayed processing

This was once the most common form before the development of the more sophisticated modern operating systems. Batch work implies that a series of tasks or jobs, often with different processing requirements and possibly with different users, are submitted for processing during a single and coherent period of run time. The resultant processing is achieved in one of two ways:

1 the data may be input when required but stored in machine-readable form (usually on magnetic media) until the program initiating the batch process is run. This technique, whether using a file as input or output storage, is called spooling. An example would be an invoicing system where warehouse staff input delivery details as and when despatched, but the invoices are printed and the sales ledger updated overnight.

2 the inputs, usually in the form of source documents, are stored until either a requisite quantity or a certain time in the day is reached. An example of this method would be an accounts payable system where suppliers' invoices are collected until input is carried out. The advantage of this method is security as a batch control total (a physical count of the documents) may be compared with a machine-count of inputs, and any discrepancies investigated.

Batch processing is still a common technique within DP systems because of its efficient use of processor time. The two main reasons for this are that:

1 the computer is not slowed down by having to wait for human input, and

2 the programs may be run outside normal working hours, thereby maximising the use of the processor as a resource.

However, batch systems are least effective when the execution of the job needs reference back to the user, either to request prompts (as with a complex database search) or because the data cannot be assembled beforehand (as with telephone orders).

It is possible for a batch system to carry out several unrelated jobs at the same time by using a multiprogramming operating system. This works by partitioning the **Central Processing Unit (CPU)** into discrete sub-units, each processing a stream of jobs, the whole being co-ordinated and controlled by the main operating system. In this way, for example, it would be possible to process and spool each day's purchase orders, invoices and goods inwards receipts and to print out the results overnight. If one of these functions is to be carried out for a department which is geographically separated from the processing site, their job could be inserted into the batch stream by remote job entry. However, no matter how fast and processor-efficient these usually large scale batch processing systems may become, they remain slow and inflexible in meeting the users' changing needs. The reasons for this are that:

(a) printed output in large volume is often printed on a central high-speed line or barrel printer, and is then dependent upon some form of internal or external post system for relay on to the users of the information;

(b) there is little or no opportunity to correct mistakes at run-time because the batch run system is generally not designed to permit the user to interact with the computer in a real way. The result is that incorrect or absent input data may delay the print out until the next batch run which may not be scheduled to take place until the following night, and

(c) the preparation of batch input data can take a long time given that source documentation must be collected and verified before being prepared for input, etc.

5.1.2 Interactive processing

This implies that, from the user's point of view, the processing capacities of the computer are available on demand to either accept input or to make a response while the relevant program is running. This is known as an on-line system. As in batch run systems, the CPU may be partitioned, but an on-line system can be permitted to carry out more processes at one time than it has partitions available. This is achieved through the use of a timesharing operating system which allows each job to own the CPU for a timeslice, before it is replaced by another job in rotation. The processing for each job may not be completed during each slice of time, but details of its state are fixed in memory, to be retrieved when the job is returned to the processor for its next timeslice.

Timesharing makes feasible the use of multi-access operating systems, where a number of users (often hundreds on a large system) may run their own programs and create, edit and delete files. The difference in speed between the user's reactions and the computer system's response may give the illusion (due to timesharing) that his or her program has sole use of the computer. However, in early attempts to perfect these systems, it was found that the larger the number of users, the more slowly the system responds. A typical example of an on-line computer system which appears dedicated to one user would be a bank **Automated Teller Machine (ATM)** or cashpoint. The benefits claimed for systems which use interactive processing systems are that:

(a) since the duplication of data files is minimised, data is more consistent, accurate and easily updated—hence the advantages of a database package;
(b) input to the system is carried out by the user at the point of origin of the data and so errors may be more easily prevented, or detected and corrected; and
(c) there is greater flexibility in the level of interaction which can be achieved between the user and the computer, eg direct access can be allowed to the files which enables complex enquiries to be made, with output being directed to the point where it is needed.

To achieve these benefits, an on-line system will include the following features:

1 sophisticated terminals, possibly workstations, and high-speed output devices;
2 big or multiple processors with large amounts of **Random Access Memory (RAM)**;
3 a database or large direct access filestore;
4 a sophisticated operating system which is capable of controlling many jobs and handling many user requests for service;
5 rapid data communication links to support remote terminals and to interface with other systems; and
6 an adequate provision for security and back-up in the event of system failure.

5.1.3 Real-time processing

This implies that the system is required to respond to changes in its environment as defined by the inputs, as and when those changes occur. The actual timescale involved will vary according to the application, but the aim is usually to provide a response or feedback in such time that corrective action or instruction control may be applied. When used for process control, for instance in chemical production, these real-time systems are said to be embedded, ie their programs do not have to be loaded from disk but are present within the processor at all times to provide the requisite continuity of control. Similarly, applications in the information systems field operate in the real-time mode. These include ticket sales, airline booking and some financial systems. The point of such systems is that they provide up-to-date data rather than a process of instantaneous response and update. In this context, real-time systems are interactive by definition, and are likely to be multi-access in nature.

5.1.4 Distributed processing

This implies the sharing of computer resources across potentially or actually independent systems. In other words, although an on-line processing system may have terminals that are geographically remote from the central processor, these are no more than slave terminals that do not act independently of the processor, and remain part of a single system. Similarly, an on-line system that uses multi-processing, ie two or more processors sharing the jobs of a set of terminals, is a computer configuration, and may be considered a single system. The basis of a distributed system is that it uses a data communications system to create and maintain a network of computers or computer systems, which are equally capable of independent operation or of resource sharing as required. This sharing may range from the simple access of data on a remote file or the transmission of a message or image, to the ability to transfer whole files, programs and processing jobs across systems in a way that is virtually transparent to the user, ie the user does not have to be aware that several different systems have been involved in performing the given task.

The implications of this trend for information systems development are considerable. The distribution of processing in this way is a logical extension of a trend which has come to be known as **user computing**, ie that direct access to resources has been allowed to the individual users. This implies not only a proliferation of computerised functions, but a decentralisation of control over their processing. This trend can be traced through four stages:

1 the development of systems capable of supporting non-DP computing activities for a wide range of users, eg CAD/CAM and process control systems;
2 the proliferation of user friendly hardware and software (in the first instance, usually micro computers with single-user operating systems) which allowed a one-per-desk approach to computing in appropriate organisations;
3 large-scale database systems capable of treating information as a corporate resource to be accessed and used across an organisation's functional boundaries (for instance, finance and production departments both accessing the same data); and
4 distributed computing in which the application of data communications technology to the three stages above enables the development of flexible, independent and yet integrated information systems.

In this cycle, the more unfortunate characteristics of systems development during the first two stages, that is specialisation and lack of integration which represented little more than the practicality of the discarded manual system with each office having the exclusive use of its own files, are overcome. Moreover, the idea of the information system as an image of the real-world system which it serves may be reinforced. Hence, the people responsible for carrying out a given function within an organisation, eg in finance or sales, may now be seen as responsible for creating, storing and processing the data used to support that function while, at the same time and subject to adequate security measures, making it available to other users across the network.

The factors which have influenced the growth of distributed systems include the following, ie that:

1 Economies of scale do not necessarily apply to processors. Large single processor systems incur huge overheads in the form of system servicing and operations costs.
2 Diminishing returns tend to apply in the equation of processing power versus cost. Thus, spending ten times an amount on a single processor will not necessarily increase processor speed and capacity by a factor of ten. Buying ten smaller computers is likely to be more cost-effective.
3 Users are more ready to accept systems over which they have more control. Distributed computing suits the line management view of systems in organisations, and the practicality of involvement and responsibility tends to encourage greater enthusiasm and commitment on the part of the staff.
4 Reliability and robustness may be provided more cheaply by distributing the processing than by taking other measures such as the development of a special computer configuration, and communications costs may be reduced because data can be moved in its most cost-effective form.
5 Organisational information needs to be allowed to grow and change organically in a way which most directly benefits the organisation which it is to serve. It is difficult for a centralised processing system to mirror the perhaps diverse needs of the different classes of user. Hence, the concept of the **distributed system** tends to fit in well with systems theory.

In fact, many organisation-wide information systems still contain a considerable data processing element, ie batch processing with a major (usually printed) output component, with payroll, invoicing and many statistical or reporting applications being the most common. A distributed system of micros may not be the most appropriate or the most efficient way of processing these tasks. Many systems therefore combine a distributed set of small computer systems with a centralised large-scale processing facility (often termed the host computer). The remote processors may be general purpose micros or workstations with additional features to enhance their performance in a particular environment such as sophisticated graphics for CAD/CAM.

It is not only the hardware that may be geographically dispersed in a distributed system, but the data itself may also be shared among the computer systems of a network. This is different from a set of stand-alone computers, each possessing its own files, because the user is able to make accesses across the systems. Such an organisation is called a **distributed database** and it is intended to combine the cheapness, speed and ease of access to local files with the information spreading advantages of an organisation-wide network. The system design usually calls for each item of data to be stored at its most frequently used location, with gateways making it available to other users. But although these systems may bring significant improvements in the quality of organisational decision-making through improved access to relevant information, such systems can prove more expensive to implement and operate than a centralised database, and can suffer from increased vulnerability to breaches of security.

5.2 OFFICE AUTOMATION

The concept of the office as a place where people gather to undertake a certain type of work (information processing) is as old as commerce itself. Offices have been subject to technological developments which have affected their working practices on an increasing scale. Meyer traces the history of office automation through the evolution and development of technological products and techniques which may be summarised as follows:

1870s—the development of the typewriter allows speedier communication and limited copying.

1920s—the invention of the telephone enables both wide and local-area communication in real-time. This is the beginning of telecommunications.

1930s—the use of scientific management (Gilbreth) to analyse and rationalise office practices. This represents the direct ancestor of systems analysis.

1940s—the application of the mathematical techniques developed in World War II (operations research) to the decision-making process.

1950s—the introduction of photocopying facilitates cheap and rapid document production, and the (limited) introduction of EDP speeds up large-scale transaction processing.

1960s—the emergence of Management Information Systems (MIS) provides the background within which office automation can develop.

1970s—the setting up of telecommunications networks allows distant communication between computer systems, the widespread use of word processors speeds up text editing and enables personalised document production, and the emergence of the personal computer starts the trend toward user computing and forms the enabling technology for office automation

1980s—the development of office automation systems which combine data, voice, text and image; and of processing hardware with multi-purpose software packages (graphics, spreadsheets, etc), which exploit the full telecommunications services. Further, the development of DSSs and Fourth Generation Languages (4GLs) which are capable of operation in a distributed computing environment, extends user computing into the areas of decision-making and code generation.

Despite all these changes, however, the basic tasks which take place in office environments remain fundamentally unchanged: offices receive, store, process and communicate business information. In a conventional office, much of this will be in the form of documents, telephone calls and mailed letters, with all the slowness, expense and inefficiencies of duplication and manual filing. Much of the work involved in carrying out these operations is of a routine nature and therefore very amenable to automation. Yet the balance of the work involves non-routine, personal activities and complex social interactions. Office automation should therefore be seen as a merging of the products of technological science with aspects of social science in support of, rather than replacing, normal commercial activities.

Office automation implies the use of computers, office products and communications technology in managing an organisation's information resource. This view of information as a corporate resource suggests the integration of the four means of communication: data, text, image and voice.

5.2.1 The information explosion

One of the most observable features of the macro economic scene in recent years has been the general decline and retrenchment in manufacturing industry which has taken place within many of the so-called industrialised nations. As a form of compensation, the service sector has increased in importance, with the production and dissemination of information becoming by far the most dominant industry and growing to a position of dominance during the last thirty years. Most of this information is textual or narrative in form. It is usually printed and the larger part of the bulk will pass through offices at some time in its life cycle. There is therefore a widening gap between the total amount of information being stored in offices and the information which is stored as part of conventional computerised DP systems. Office automation systems have been developed to handle the information that constitutes this gap more efficiently.

5.2.2 Office automation and productivity

One of the main reasons for the application of IT to the office environment is to increase the productivity of office workers. Studies in the mid-1970s (see *Business Week*, July 1975) appeared to show that improvement in white collar productivity was seriously lagging behind that applying to industrial and manufacturing workers.

The study of companies in the USA over a ten year period showed that industrial performance had risen by almost 90%, compared to an approximate 4% increase in office productivity. During this period, companies reported that corporate expenditure on office functions had increased from 20–30% to 40–50% of total budgets. One of the conclusions which may be drawn from the study is that the office environment has been consistently undercapitalised. Estimates suggest that investment on factory workers was largely on plant and equipment, and has exceeded white collar investment by a factor of ten. The obvious conclusion is that increased investment in the office version of productive plant, ie automation technology, will result in a comparable increase in office productivity. But Hirschheim suggests caution in accepting this conclusion for a number of reasons:

1. it is difficult to measure productivity in an office environment, and to compare industrial and office-based findings;
2. the link between productivity and capital expenditure may not be consistent–the influence of personal factors in the office environment means that, sometimes, the introduction of new technology may result in unrest, industrial action and lower productivity;
3. the relative levels of productivity at the beginning of the study were undefined–it may be that office workers were already more efficient, and therefore improvements through changes in working methods were less likely to be achieved.

Productivity improvements from office automation, where they occur, are likely to affect organisations in the following ways:

1. better utilisation of the workforce by a reduction in staff numbers or by a greater output per person,
2. improved utilisation of time due to greater efficiency,
3. improved quality of management through better decision-making,
4. increased output through better individual performance, and
5. greater effectiveness through the use of information found to be available in the environment.

5.2.3 The knowledge worker

Current thinking identifies a particular role in the modern office—knowledge work. The primary activities of knowledge work as opposed to physical work are diagnosis, decision-making, monitoring and scheduling. A knowledge worker is therefore someone involved in analysing situations, evaluating alternative courses of action, making decisions or recommending procedures based on the use of information. This information may come from internal sources, from the environment or from the knowledge worker's own experience.

In order to combine this creative aspect of problem-solving with the routine activities of the workplace, the knowledge worker must be provided with a support system having the following features:

(a) an information management function which is capable of handling the collection, storage and retrieval of the appropriate information in a speedy manner, eg in a Database Management System (DBMS);
(b) interactive processing functions to perform calculations and to generate alternative solutions, eg in a DSS; and
(c) communication facilities to carry the knowledge worker's output to the right place at the right time, eg in an Electronic Mail System (EMS).

5.2.4 The benefits of office automation

By providing a suitable support environment, office automation systems aim to benefit the knowledge worker in two ways:

1 **Direct benefits** These involve an increase in output or a saving, usually in time and/or labour. Such benefits are usually measurable, and may have a direct, and therefore short-term, effect on cash flow. Direct benefits can include:
   (a) better control over work due to less division of labour,
   (b) fewer conversions from one form of information to another, eg dictation on to tape followed by typing on to paper,
   (c) fewer non-productive activities such as filing, record keeping and updating, etc, and
   (d) better personal organisation due to reduced travel and gathering for meetings by the use of teleconferencing facilities, etc.
2 **Indirect benefits** Benefits in this category are less quantifiable, and may benefit the organisation through longer term profitability and growth. Such benefits include:
   (a) less dependency on other departments for support as with copying, printing, etc,
   (b) less need for procedures and controls to monitor work flow between departments,
   (c) increased job satisfaction due to greater personal effectiveness in carrying out a range of tasks, and
   (d) greater customer satisfaction due to better information products and a more timely service.

5.3 OFFICE AUTOMATION TECHNOLOGY

The basic questions which have to be answered by the specifier of an office automation system are:

1 What functions will the system need to offer?
2 Will the user's hardware be based on a dedicated terminal for each function, or multifunction workstations?
3 What will be the extent of the automation exercise?

Data to answer these questions can be gathered in a **feasibility study** which should aim to indicate the organisation's requirements both as to functions (ie what is required from the system) and as to extent (ie how much of the office should be automated). As a part of the justification exercise, it is also important to identify at an early stage which areas of the organisation are likely to profit most from the automation, ie those that are most likely to achieve the benefits listed in 5.2.4.

5.3.1 Extent of automation

As well as deciding which tasks or which parts of the office are to be subject to automation (this will directly affect the functions found in the system) the nature of the proposed automation should be examined. An office automation project may involve the straightforward mechanisation of the routine tasks currently carried out by the secretarial and clerical staff, in which case the disruption caused within the organisation may be small. Alternatively, the greatest level of benefits may be obtained by transferring routine information processing (augmented by technological means) to professional and managerial staff. Obviously, the extent of disruption will be greater in such cases.

Perhaps the ultimate extent of disruption from an organisational point of view is the growing phenomenon of telecommuting or working from home using office automation technology for communication with customers, suppliers or the workplace. This trend, if continued, is likely to make the office a logical rather than a geographical concept. Some people see this as a natural phasing out of a mode of working introduced by the Industrial Revolution and its replacement with one from the Information Revolution.

The knowledge worker is likely to find the following advantages under the new system:

(a) a complete saving of commuting time or time spent travelling to meetings, conferences, etc;
(b) greater flexibility in working hours—this has been particularly supported by the growth of asynchronous message systems, ie where both parties do not have to be on-line at the same time as is the case with telephone messages. This facilitates the staggering of work patterns;
(c) a significant reduction in the number of interruptions should lead to greater productivity in some tasks; and
(d) reduced reliance on personal contact for communication purposes can benefit the smaller organisation, as for example a self-employed accountant or consultant.

In the case of the employer, the advantages are based on a reduction in operating costs, including:

(a) rental of office space which, especially in large cities, greatly exceeds telecommunications costs;
(b) homeworkers require less in the way of welfare support facilities; and
(c) travelling expenses are greatly reduced.

A number of major organisations (and significantly ICL and Rank Xerox, two leaders in the office automation products market) are using networks of homeworkers to integrate specialist skills.

DEFINING WHAT FUNCTIONS ARE NEEDED

An analysis of an office's data usage and the functions carried out by the manual system (the implications of these steps are explained elsewhere in this book) will suggest a requirements list of functions which the automated system should offer. The system requirements will be suggested by points such as the following:

(a) The experience and aptitude of the office users, and the amount of training they will require. For instance, an office which tended to employ temporary staff, or where the knowledge worker might be a manager rather than a specialist, should opt for a system offering fewer, more simple features.
(b) The nature of the input—its format, variety and volume. This will tend to suggest the devices which will be used to capture the data. Usually, the greater the volume and variety of data, the more specialist will be the technology used to input it to the system.
(c) What the system is intended to do, for instance, routine document processing, information retrieval, evaluation of management decisions, carrying out mail shots, etc. This will have a direct effect on the software. It should be borne in mind that two requirements—word processing and information retrieval for example—could be met by purchasing two different sets of hardware and software (often referred to as dedicated systems). However, with a small compromise, a good personal computer could undertake both functions using separate software packages such as Wordstar and dBase IV or an integrated modular package such as the DEC package All-In-One.

(d) The output requirement identifying the quality, format, range and volume. Some applications may require a high volume of standard letters such as in a credit control operation. Other applications such as management decision support systems, may require both screen and printed graphics, while some tasks may require a high level of presentational output in the form of brochures or information packs.
(e) The interface which will be required with other systems. These may be other offices within the same organisation, other organisations (possibly in other countries) or public information systems such as ORACLE or CEEFAX.

These requirements may be met with different combinations of various devices. Because of this, there may be problems of incompatibility, both within the same office and between office systems. Standardisation as it has been achieved so far, has tended to come through the domination of a particular product supplier such as IBM and the recommendations of the international telecommunications administrative body CCITT (Comité Consultatif International Télégraphique et Téléphonique).

5.4 OFFICE AUTOMATION SYSTEMS

The basic functions which may be required in an automated office can be supplied by the installation of a number of basic systems. Each of these may have different system architecture, ie the devices and software which they use, but the functions or features will be broadly similar. The main categories of office automation systems are set out below.

5.4.1 Electronic mail

Electronic Mail Systems (E-Mail or EMS) are intended to replace the movement of paper messages (internal and external to the organisation) with the electronic transmission of coded graphic or textual information. Such a system should provide the user with the following features:

1 text manipulation facilities to allow the composing, editing and storing of messages;
2 a variety of message formats, for instance formal letters, notepad memos or financial statements;
3 communication over long or short distances (the communications technology that makes this possible is discussed in 5.11);
4 the ability to receive messages in real-time or asynchronously, ie when both the sender and receiver are at their terminals or to be stored in a mailbox for reading later as in asynchronous messaging systems; and
5 the ability to route messages to a single address, a range of specified addresses or to all the users of a local system.

These features are achieved by the following facilities which are commonly found in EMSs although, obviously, the exact range of features will vary from system to system:

MESSAGE COMPOSITION

The facilities offered for message preparation will be similar, in terms of screen handling, etc, to a normal word processor, although those offered by most dedicated word processors will be more sophisticated. An EMS should allow at least the following word processing features:

(a) the deletion of individual characters, or of lines and blocks of text,
(b) the movement and insertion of blocks of text within the message,
(c) the standard text formatting features such as automatic wraparound at the end of a line, margin control, centring, etc.

With some EMSs it is possible to link powerful, dedicated word processors to the mail facility which allows off-line message composition. Text can then be processed and stored on disk, and may be read from storage and transmitted at any time. In this way, a library of standard messages may be built up. Other features which may be offered include:

(a) **Formatting**—a message consists of two parts: a header containing the address and other delivery information (priority, date/time, subject, etc), and a body or text part of the message. Within these restrictions it is possible to have predefined formats for frequently used messages which may have specific detail (for instance, sales or production figures) added when sent.
(b) **A notepad**—for storing points for later composition into messages, and for use as a simple diary or memory aid.

MESSAGE DESPATCH

There are obviously a large number of possible facilities which may enhance the simple sending of messages in EMSs. Here are some of the most common:

(a) **A user directory**—this may vary from a simple list of user names and their address codes which are available through the system, to centrally updated distribution lists for particular subjects (such as updates to cost-centre codes).
(b) **Priority stacking**—which reads the priority code in the message header and orders the receiver's mailbox accordingly.
(c) **Message scheduling**—the sender can specify a particular time and date for the message to be delivered. For instance, an end-of-year close-off warning may be entered in advance.
(d) **External links**—either to other EMSs or to a public information service such as Prestel may be made through a gateway. Some sophisticated systems will carry out automatic routing, choosing between methods of transmission (public telephone network, private leased lines, etc) according to cost, priority and scheduling.

MESSAGE RECEIVING

A good message receiving facility will aim to provide features which assist in the organisation of messages on the receiver's behalf, for instance mailbox management, a feature which distinguishes electronic mail technology from other transmission systems such as facsimile and telex. As with despatch, the possible message receiving facilities which may be offered vary between systems. Normally they will include:

(a) **A mailbox**—this corresponds to a pigeonhole in a manual office. Actually, it is a space in a computer memory which has been assigned to a single user who may have sole access (usually obtained by a password) and identified by a unique address (usually an abbreviation of the user's name). It is normal for a mailbox to provide notification of new mail receipts (usually when the user logs on to the system). In addition, many mailboxes allow scanning, usually providing the user with a list of mailbox contents, showing the details of the sender and subject which are abstracted from the header. Such sophisticated systems permit message selection, either to pick out individual messages or to read the mailbox in a particular order.
(b) **A message forwarder**—this allows a user to automatically redirect messages to other users' mailboxes, either as originals (perhaps when the receiver will be absent for a period of time) or as copies.
(c) **Message filing**—this offers an alternative to deletion after a message has been read. Often the organisation of such files (again a space in computer memory) is left to the user's discretion. Systems usually contain a temporary file (often called a folder) and a permanent file (an archive) to which all messages are ultimately transferred.

Electronic mail is said to offer the advantages of speed and versatility over its conventional rivals, and may be said to combine the best features of telephone and paper communication. However, more extended use and greater knowledge of the costs involved will be needed before the true impact of electronic mail can be judged. Since EMSs often exist within other computer-based systems (including DP systems), the cost may be hard to assess, consisting mainly of software packages such as Messenger or Scrapbook which may be bundled together as a single cost item when purchased, or one of many possible functions when it comes to apportioning variable costs. A cost-competitive alternative may be to employ a bureau such as Telecom Gold's DIALCOM.

5.4.2 Facsimile

Facsimile transmission facilities (or fax) are sometimes offered as part of an EMS. Fax allows the sending of an exact copy of an original (using, for instance, radio transmission or the telephone network) to be recomposed by the receiver's equipment. This is of obvious use with diagrams and pictures, but may also be used with documents, eg to verify signatures. Facsimile systems work by scanning a document and digitally coding the contents which are then transmitted and recoded at the receiving end. There are 750,000 code bits in an A4 sheet, which tends to make fax conversion a slow process, and inconvenient where a single telephone line may be engaged in a fax transmission for long periods. Attempts to overcome these problems include:

(a) **Duplex operation** The fax device can transmit and receive at the same time.
(b) **Telephone reversion** allows another use of the telephone to interrupt the fax connection which is automatically reinstated afterwards.

Other major fax problems involve incompatibility and lack of standardisation between manufacturers of equipment. Now CCITT recommendations which have been agreed within the industry, group fax machines into Groups 1-4, with 1 and 2 being slow, poor quality analogue devices, and 3 and 4 which are high speed, high definition digital types. The Group 3 systems, which will transmit an A4 sheet in less than 1 minute, are proving to be the most popular in the market place and, consequently, it is in these systems that the most development is taking place.

5.4.3 Computer Output Microform (COM)

Essentially, such systems involve the decoding in a COM recorder of computer-generated magnetic media (usually tape) into human-readable images which are then photographed on to microfilm or fiches. Such media are easily stored and retrieved. Some systems use software for fully automated retrieval from a VDU—called **Computer Assisted Retrieval (CAR)**, and may be read or hard copied from a reader/printer device. The importance of COM in an office environment lies in its ability to store and retrieve large volumes of data easily and cheaply. An obvious application is the storing of invoice copies and purchase orders, which are often held for up to seven years and can create considerable cost and nuisance if stored on paper.

5.4.4 Teleconferencing

The advantages to the organisation of being able to conduct presentations, meetings and negotiations without the attendant difficulties of travel and accommodation are obvious. It is reported that over 80% of the Fortune 500 companies have or are planning to install, teleconferencing facilities. Users of such systems report the following benefits:

1 meetings can be arranged at shorter notice,
2 personnel report less disruption to everyday activities, and
3 individuals never feel at a disadvantage on other people's territory.

The first generation of teleconferencing technology was audio-conferencing which is inexpensive and has been available for some time, but poses some operational problems (for instance, lack of visible presence and identification of speakers). Video-conferencing overcomes these problems, but it is far more expensive and, given present levels of technology, potentially requires specialist studio equipment. Both types allow the linking of two or more locations (using a choice of transmission media including satellites), and are likely to become an increasingly important aspect of office automation.

5.4.5 Voice mail

Sometimes called voice store-and-forward, **Voice Mail Systems (VMS)** are the asynchronous counterpart of telephone calls. Such systems allow the sender to record and store a voicegram in digital form, which is stored (usually on a dedicated disk drive) for delivery the next time the addressee uses his or her telephone. IBM, one of the first in this field with **Audio Distribution System (ADS)** is claiming the following advantages for VMSs in general:

— less wasted telephone time as voicegrams tend to have the same precise qualities as a memo,
— fewer interruptions as the messages are stored until it is convenient for the user to receive them, and
— rapid response time as dictation and typing are eliminated.

Despite adverse features such as the one-way nature of a voicegram, the absence of social discourse and the high installation costs, the integration of voice mail into office automation systems seems inevitable.

5.4.6 Private Automatic Branch Exchange (PABX)

It is possible to connect almost any two telephones anywhere in the world by using switching centres or telephone exchanges. Exchanges may be public, ie part of the public telephone service, or private within an organisation or building with links to the public network, hence the term branch. The term **automatic** refers to the fact that PABXs are computer controlled and may be compatible with **Packet Switching Networks (PSN)** and digital transmission systems such as BT's System X, as well as offering the following sophisticated features:

— abbreviated number dialing facilities,
— on-line fault diagnosis,
— audio-conferencing both within and outside the branch,
— call redirection as specified, eg to a deputy,
— call holding, without redial, until a busy number becomes free.

The topology of PABXs is similar to that of many **Local Area Networks (LANs)** which is described in 5.12.1. The feature which separates the two types of system most is data transmission speeds. This means that a PABX can handle fax, voice and printer terminals at around 60 kbits per second, but not interactive disk storage. Therefore, LANs are likely to remain a cornerstone of distributed computing, while PABXs are likely to expand from telephone use to an integrated handling of voice, data, text and image. PABX technology is therefore likely to be central to the development of office automation systems. In fact, LANs and PABXs are not mutually exclusive. The use of protocol conversion and gateways can allow a PABX in an office to be a spur off a LAN within a large building or complex.

5.4.7 Videotext

Videotext (or Videotex) is a generic term for systems which use the concept of data transmission in the form of text and limited graphics, from databases to remote terminals which are usually adapted domestic television sets. Originally intended as a public service extension to public broadcasting, Videotext services are now developing features which may have important applications in the automated office. All Videotext systems fall into two groups which are distinguished by their transmission media—Viewdata which uses the public telephone or cable TV network, and Teletext which uses normal TV channels. The data is actually transmitted in the interval between the conventional television picture lines. While Viewdata allows limited interaction between user and computer (via a keyboard or small keypad), Teletext allows only one-way communication. The main features of these systems, and of the services which use them, are as follows:

VIEWDATA

Pages of information (screen-sized frames of data) are entered on to the Viewdata database via editing terminals. These are in the hands of **Information Providers (IPs)** who buy space by the page in order to advertise, sell services or provide public information. Each part of the database is organised hierarchically as a tree structure of pages, with each page containing routing information for items linked to it. Random access to any page, and forward and reverse paging are possible using the terminal, after the user has gained access by dialing the Viewdata telephone number and keying in a private passcode. The most representative Viewdata service is British Telecom's Prestel, although many private services (some organisation-wide) exist. Developed in 1978, Prestel was expected to have millions of subscribers by the mid 1980s, most of them domestic users. In fact, commercial use of Prestel outweighs domestic use by ten-to-one. Much of Prestel's database of several hundred thousand pages of information is public information, including news, weather forecasts and share prices, but Prestel also supports **closed user groups (CUGs)** which are set up by IPs (usually in the commercial field) and have access restricted to group members. An example would be an airline (the IP) allowing travel agents (the group members) to use the service to check flights and book seats. A CUG may also be used as a private information system by a large organisation with many remote offices. A facility offered in this context is Viewdata Electronic Mail (VEM) which allows user-to-user messaging.

TELETEXT

The concept underlying Teletext services such as the BBC's CEEFAX and IBA's ORACLE in the UK is that of a non-interactive public electronic newspaper. While the system is capable of holding less information than the Viewdata system, it is subject to more routine updates. This makes Teletext very suitable for displaying small amounts of frequently changing information. Although the lack of an interactive facility puts Teletext at an apparent disadvantage when compared to Viewdata, a common application for the system in an automated office environment is the reception of financial information such as share and commodity prices, and exchange rates.

Due to the fact that pages of information are transmitted sequentially in a continuous cycle, and selected pages are stored in memory in the user's TV receiver (by input from a keypad) the access time is slower than with Viewdata. The UK CEEFAX system is currently organised into six 100 page magazines, and waiting for a chosen page to recur in the cycle takes just under a minute on average. A possible future development is of joint Teletext/Viewdata systems with compatible hardware and software. This should give the flexibility to allow the user to tailor the service to the application required.

5.4.8 Public databases

Both Viewdata and Teletext exist to make factual information available to users. However, because of their limited powers of interaction, the usefulness of both systems is bound to be restricted in a commercial environment. It is not possible to match the complex searches or data manipulation facilities available on the standard database system. Thus, while information on all the shares in the Financial Times Stock Exchange 100 index are made available, a user who wanted to compile a list of those shares with a current dividend yield greater than 5% would be obliged to resort to pen, paper and patience. Such a task would need more detailed information and a special method of access called a query language. Such a service is offered by international government bodies and commercial organisations in the form of **public databases**, ie large bodies of information, capable of being accessed on-line via wide area networks or by off-line batch searches.

Currently, the subjects of most public databases can be divided into two categories:

1 **Bibliographic** This category contains information about books and published journals in areas of both general and specialised interest and, by using these databases, it is possible to obtain abstracts from, and citations to, individual publications either by reference to subject matter or to author. Currently, much of the use of such databases is of an academic or research nature.

2 **Factual** Factual databases may be of greater potential commercial use. It is estimated that over 2,000 are available through EURONET DIANE—a continent-wide information system

based on CCITT telecommunications standards. The most common types of factual databases are:

(a) **legal**—containing an index and the full text details of both national and supranational statute law (including EEC laws) and case law which is either classified by subject or held in general files;

(b) **econometric**—databases containing national and regional financial and demographic data, usually indicating trends and, possibly, forecasts;

(c) **commercial**—which may be industry-wide, by product or market, or for individual companies, showing the financial structure, business activities and management/ banking details, and

(d) **scientific**—databases holding technical information or reference tables on a wide range of subjects including patents.

These databases are likely to have the greatest commercial impact because of their obvious applications in product development, marketing, credit control and consumer affairs. Public databases involve the activities of IPs who collect and supply the data, the **operator** or host who creates or maintains the database, and the **transmitter** who provides the telecommunications network. These participants may be a single organisation, or separate organisations acting collaboratively. It is customary for the operator to provide the necessary software package containing the query language and having the correct protocols for compatibility with the host system. It is common to have a micro emulating the host's terminals as this provides dual-purpose hardware and the ability to store and manipulate received data. It is possible to access many public databases using the standard X25 EMS. Where large volumes of data are likely to be produced by a search, it is possible to have the operator print out the results at a remote printing station for despatch to the user by post, thus reducing data transmission costs.

5.4.9 Business graphics

Graphics hardware and software may be used for specialist purposes in an office environment, for instance, Computer Aided Design (CAD) systems in a design office, but the term business graphics is usually taken to refer to the representation of commercial data or statistics, often run on multi-purpose office hardware. Broadly speaking, office graphics applications are of two types:

1 **Statistical** This application is often contained within a multi-purpose office package and stands alongside, sometimes interacting with, the spreadsheet software. Its function is to present numerical data in a visual form, eg as a pie chart, graph or bar chart, with more sophisticated diagrams such as PERT and Gantt charts being made available through specialist packages. Obviously, these applications will accept keyboard input, but for best effect, will require a high quality output medium.

2 **Graphical** In a business context, there is often the need to produce text that includes logos, diagrams or other graphical devices to enhance the message. Alternatively, there can be a need to produce an animated sequence of text including fades, overlays and bright colours to enliven a presentation or demonstration. Both of these situations would require a high quality output medium and a sophisticated method of input. It is customary for such specialist systems as MACDRAW and STORYBOARD to allow screen painting using a WIMP (window-icon-mouse-pulldown) interface.

Since professional quality graphics hardware and software is very expensive, a compromise must often be reached in planning an automated office. When considering screen-based output, a conventional character or alphanumeric VDU will not usually produce graphics output of a high enough quality. For the best results, a purpose-made graphics terminal will be required because they have a bit-mapped display made up of a series of singly-addressed dots called pixels (a word derived from picture elements) and larger in-unit-memory. However, many of the more modern multi-function workstations that are intended for use in office automation systems will produce sufficiently high resolution output for most routine purposes.

For hard copy output, an obvious requirement is that the colours present on the VDU screen must be represented in some way. Some packages will convert colours to a monochrome output of shading and cross-hatched patterns. This can be effective for simple charts, but is obviously limited both in terms of definition and visual appeal. Colour printing can be achieved by using multi-ribbon matrix printers or ink-jet printers with multiple jets for colours. Other types of hardcopy device, such as pen-plotters and graphic camera systems, tend to be too specialised for normal office use.

It is possible to write bespoke programs to produce graphics output rather than to use a graphics package. Traditional high level languages which might already be in use in an office environment, such as BASIC and Pascal, have some built-in graphics capability through the use of sub-routines. More recently developed languages have graphics facilities designed into them, usually as a part of a software system including a WIMP interface. An example of such an integrated system is Xerox's Smalltalk 80 which was originally developed to support the Xerox 8010 intelligent workstation (see 5.6). Smalltalk handles graphical as well as textual or numerical input and allows screen painting, animation and text composition in a variety of scripts to be performed simply by using a mouse to point at display windows on the screen.

5.4.10 Decision support systems

Decision support in an automated office environment refers to the application of IT to the problems met by decision-makers, particularly to problem analysis and evaluation, and to *ad hoc* fact-finding and solution testing. As such, a DSS is intended to support radically different activities from a DP system. The latter uses IT to automate an application with a restricted and routine involvement of the user. A DSS supports, rather than automates, the activity of the application which, in this instance, is decision-making. This is achieved through extensive, and not necessarily structured, user participation. The expansion of DSSs in the office is partly a result of two business factors:

1 a general evolution in the role of middle management which aspires towards more autonomy in decision-making and faster responses to a changing environment through decentralisation; and

2 a redefinition of the role of information in organisations, with the current accent on its importance as a corporate resource and a major weapon in today's increasingly competitive market places.

Both of the factors combine in the term knowledge worker, discussed in 5.2.3. In the hands of such an individual, the first step is for the communication and processing aspects of office automation to obtain, store and manipulate corporate information. The DSS then provides a limited range of analysis tools to make the potential use of that information more effective. To assist in achieving this result, the DSS is likely to have the following characteristics:

(a) a focus on decision-making and the use of IT to support expert human judgment. To this extent, a DSS is less intelligent than an expert system;

(b) the ability to iterate analyses and solutions in an attempt to progress towards an optimum decision outcome within the given constraints;

(c) multi-purpose application to a range of semi-structured problems; indeed, there is no reason in principle why the DSS should not be used in support of functions as diverse as, say, credit control and corporate planning, and at all levels of management; and

(d) a sophisticated and user friendly interface to encourage frequent use of the system and to make the results explicit. These features should be standard in the typical modern multifunction workstation.

DSS REQUIREMENTS

To be effective, the DSS must at least offer the following features:

— applicability to a wide range of problems involving different volumes and types of data,
— a variety of modelling capabilities to support the range of problem-solving applications required,
— flexible human-computer interaction, possibly including business graphics output and input through a non-procedural language, and
— the ability to capture, store and manage large volumes of data in order to support a realistic modelling process.

To supply these capabilities, a DSS is likely to have a framework or architecture including the following components:

— a database of relevant and current data which will represent the central core of the system,
— a DBMS to handle the access and processing of that data,
— a set of software tools allowing the user to interact with the database, and to handle the graphics, selection of model, etc, and
— a flexible modelling package to permit the statistical evaluation and analysis of the data. Such modelling may be of an analytic *what if?* nature or an optimising *what's best?* nature. An analytic model will employ mathematical functions to evaluate the effects of changes made to various parameters. This is the basis of the many popular spreadsheet two-dimensional models such as Lotus 1–2–3 and SUPERCALC. Such packages are adept at answering questions such as, 'What would net profit be if raw material costs increased by 10% with no corresponding increase in selling price?' An example of simple optimising is goal-seeking, which uses backward iteration to calculate parameter values from a given result. Such a model could answer a question such as, 'What combination of raw material costs and selling price would produce a net profit of £x?' A more complex model could support risk analysis based on probability frequencies such as Monte Carlo simulation. Such models are often used in financial markets to make decisions based on simulation results.

CHOOSING DSS SOFTWARE

In an office environment, it is likely that the choice of DSS will be restricted to the software package which is to run on the automated office hardware, usually a personal computer or workstation. The main selection criteria are therefore those related to the majority of the users' requirements and to commercial factors such as:

(a) **Cost considerations** The acquisition cost of a DSS package consists of an initial licence fee (usually per copy) and the usual on-going costs such as vendor support and maintenance which may be included or charged for in a variety of ways.

(b) **Vendor support** Factors which will affect the rating of a vendor include the financial stability of the organisation, their apparent willingness to offer updates or enhancements to the software, research and development activity to produce compatible systems in the future and, perhaps most importantly, the provision of a help line to handle queries.

(c) **Compatibility** The package must be compatible with the operating system of the computer which, in its own right, must have the necessary quality of output terminals and sufficient memory.

(d) **Ease of use** The concept of user friendliness embraces the technical design of the software such as the use of menus, screen layout and editing, and the explanatory aspects such as the user documentation, on-screen HELP facilities and the comprehensibility of error messages. Packages tend to differ markedly in this area of ease of use and should be carefully evaluated before purchase.

(e) **Integration** In an office environment, particularly where a multifunction workstation is in use, it is desirable to use a common database and for the user to be able to move from one function to another without having to log in and out, eg from a spreadsheet to word processing to graphics. This is actually the design trend in the development of DSS packages, but buyers should always acquire the best integrated software currently available.

5.5 TYPICAL COMPUTER CONFIGURATIONS

When looking at the development of computer systems in general over the past thirty to forty years, three things stand out:

1 That computer technology has proliferated. When computers were first offered for sale, because of their size and cost, and perhaps, because of a lack of appreciation of their full potential, the initial market projections were low. Today, hundreds of thousands of computers are in use, and some universities in the USA are even reputed to have more computers than students (although it is not clear that this is necessarily something to be proud of).

2 That the performance levels achievable by computers have improved dramatically—it is estimated that, over the last five years alone, computer equipment has become one hundred times faster, one thousand times smaller, and ten times more reliable, with both capital and operating costs reduced significantly (particularly when related to the amount of storage which is available). Today, the research and development trends are moving in five directions at once, and the rate of change is increasing.

3 That the diversity of the technology has increased—computers have been developed for many different uses in a range of sizes and types. There are also an increasing number of configurations available, ie of the way in which the hardware of the computer system is physically organised.

FIGURE 5.1 **Trends in computing technology**

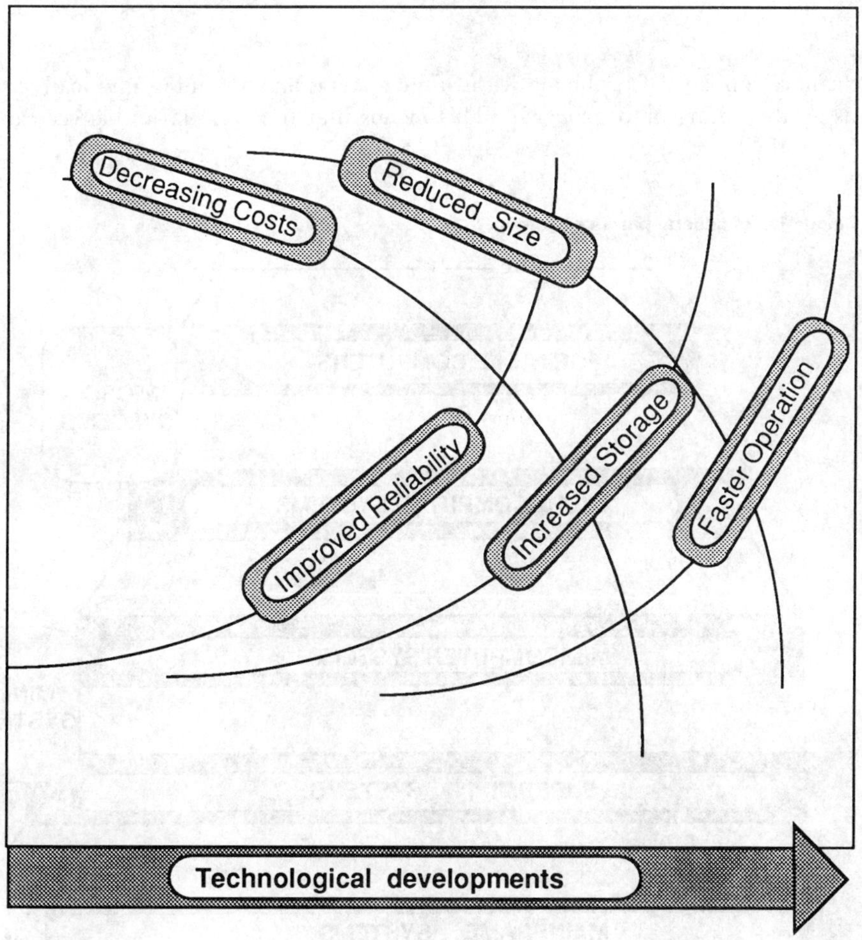

These factors make the overall classification of computer systems difficult. Thus, when seeking to match computer hardware to a particular application, it is possible to approach the task of classifying the resultant system from three different points of view.

5.5.1 The purpose of the system

Most computer systems in use today, particularly those used in business, are described as general purpose systems. In a sense, this also reflects the organisational reality that often the precise reason for acquiring the particular system has not been made wholly explicit. The strength of such systems is that they can be configured or adapted to perform a wide variety of tasks by using different peripherals and software. Special purpose systems are intended to solve particular problems and to perform specific, often limited tasks, eg process control systems. Such systems are, by definition, more specialised, and the preferred design will often sacrifice flexibility to enhance performance, eg to achieve rapid response time in a weapons guidance system.

5.5.2 The size of the system

For these purposes, the word size is taken to refer both to the physical size of the equipment and to its processing power. It is generally agreed that there are four categories of general purpose computer system:

1 microcomputer (commonly micro),
2 minicomputer (commonly mini),
3 mainframe, and
4 supercomputer.

This classification is itself problematic, as large systems are becoming physically smaller, and small systems are becoming more powerful. This means that the boundaries between the different classes are not distinct.

FIGURE 5.2 **Categories of general purpose systems**

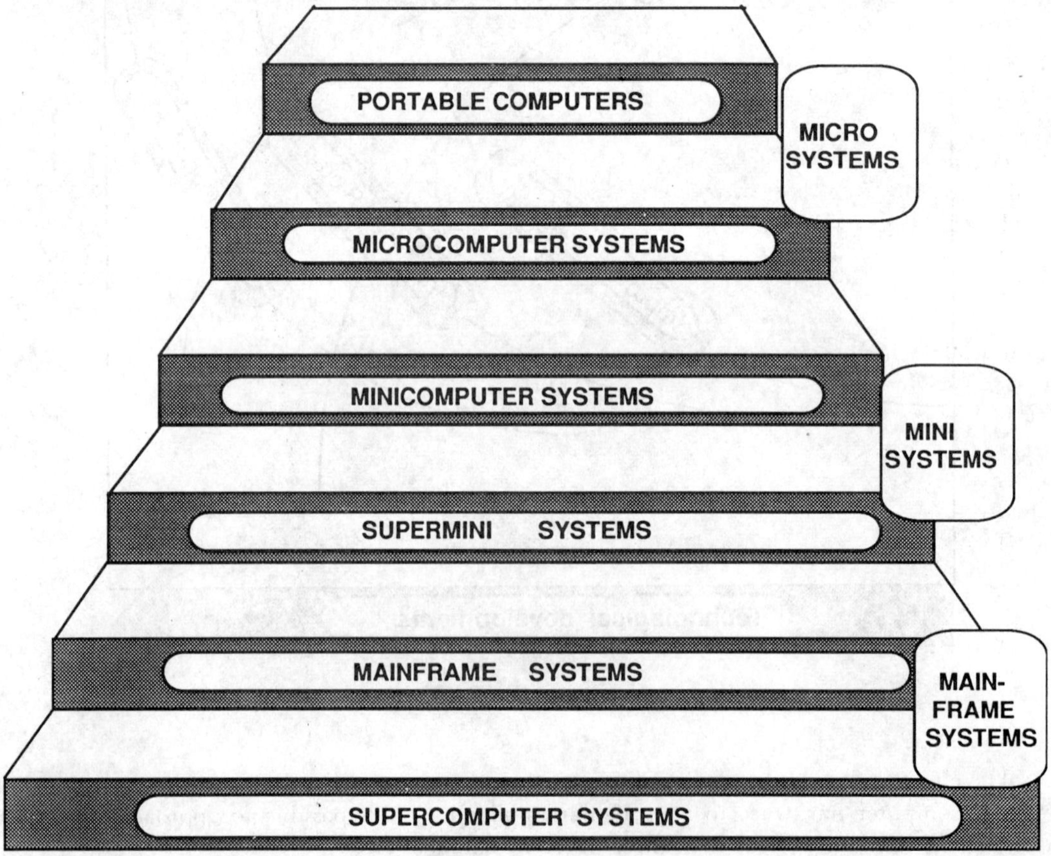

The smallest portable computer currently available is the Seiko 2000, which has the appearance of a large digital wristwatch. A tiny **Liquid Crystal Display (LCD)** shows four lines of ten characters at a time, and a total memory size of 8K allows the storage of 200 lines. Data are input by using a plug-in keypad similar to that of a calculator. The main uses of such devices are as an electronic notepad, a diary or personal telephone pad, but it is debatable whether such a limited device should properly be described as a computer.

Some of the large briefcase-sized machines (the Osborne 1 was the first in 1981) are true small scale computers, ie they can be programmed and they are compatible with floppy disk drives, telephone modems and printers. These computers are proving to have many business uses, eg a salesman may enter customer orders on to a computer system at home base without leaving the client's premises, messages may be composed on an aeroplane for later down-loading on to an EMS, and stock figures may be counted in a warehouse, the main stock record being updated from a cassette tape in the portable computer on return to the office. Such devices are made practicable by advances in low power semi-conductor and flat screen display technology.

Microcomputer systems, often referred to as personal or desk top computers, have achieved widespread use in business and education. Such a system may include a fixed or, occasionally, removable Winchester disk, one or more floppy disks, and a variety of printers, including better quality models which allow the system to be used with appropriate software for word processing and graphics applications. Microcomputer systems are the backbone of most small business systems and are widely used in office automation and process control systems despite the ready availability of special purpose machines. The compatibility and portability of applications software throughout the computer industry has been achieved because only relatively few operating systems are in regular use: CP/M (Control Programs for Microcomputers) and MS-DOS (Disk Operating Software) are the most widely used. MP/M (Multiprogramming Monitor for Microcomputers) is a version of CP/M which allows multi-user microcomputing, and Concurrent CP/M enables a microcomputer system to run several programs at the same time. These features, plus increases in processor power (16 bit machines are now common) have blurred the boundary between micro and minicomputer systems.

Minicomputer systems, now available from most of the major computer manufacturers, were pioneered by Digital Equipment Corporation (DEC). In the late 1960s and early 1970s, DEC's PDP–8 and PDP–11 series were popular for scientific, technical and process control applications. The improvements in peripheral design and attendant reductions in the cost of terminals have made minicomputer systems attractive for business use. The advent of the 32 bit minicomputer, typified by DEC's VAX series, has made such systems a viable alternative to the mainframe machines which have dominated the field of DP systems up to modern times. The minicomputer systems that are popular for general purpose or business applications include DEC's VAX 8000 series, Eclipse C150 and Hewlett Packard HP3000. The more powerful systems, realistically capable of supporting more than 100 users, are termed superminis.

Mainframe systems overlap superminis in terms of price, processing speed and data storage, but extend all of these factors into the range that makes mainframes the province of the largest commercial concerns, usually exploiting the highly capital intensive resource in a centralised processing role. The significant cost of these systems means that more than half the mainframes currently in use are rented from manufacturers or are leased from specialist companies. Major manufacturers include Honeywell, ICL, IBM and NCR. One way of comparing the relative performance of processors is the KOPS (thousand operations per second) rating based on the time taken to process a typical series of program instruction. Where an average minicomputer might have a KOPS rating of 100, and a supermini might be rated at 200, a large mainframe, such as the IBM 3033, would produce a rating of over 5,000, assuming a proportionate increase in the standard internal and auxiliary storage facilities and number of terminals.

For certain specialist processing applications, even this level of processing performance is inadequate. Supercomputers, usually used for advanced scientific and statistical work, can perform in one hour, work that would take a large mainframe one week to complete. The Cray 1, produced by Cray Research, has a KOPS rating of 800,000. The Cray X/MP is five to eight times faster. It has two central processing units (CPUs) each more powerful than a Cray 1. A consortium of Japanese companies are currently in the final phase of a government sponsored project to develop a supercomputer that will be 1,000 times faster than a Cray 1. The significance of this research for business users (or anyone else) is that machines of this type are likely to be instrumental in Japan's National Fifth Generation Computer Project which intends to produce a system with advanced artificial intelligence capable of solving problems which have hitherto required human experience and imagination. There are obvious long term implications in this for large scale simulation and DSS (see 5.4.10).

5.5.3 The configuration of the system

The configuration of the system (also known as the **system architecture**) is determined by the purpose which the system is intended to serve and it is aimed at increasing the system's performance in carrying out that purpose. For instance, process control systems require a high degree of hardware reliability and real-time systems require extremely rapid processor response and, perhaps, concurrent or parallel processing, ie the ability to carry out two or more programming operations at the same time—this may be achieved by a combination of hardware and software.

The configuration of a computer system, at whatever scale of operation, will exploit the concept of modularity. This is the use of common units (architectural components) which may be present in different quantities and combined in a variety of ways. All the components selected for the particular system will be connected by the use of a system bus. This links the processor and memory with the peripherals through interface ports, ie using the RS232 standard. A typical configuration of a conventional microcomputer system would be as shown in Figure 5.3.

FIGURE 5.3 **Simplified microcomputer system configuration**

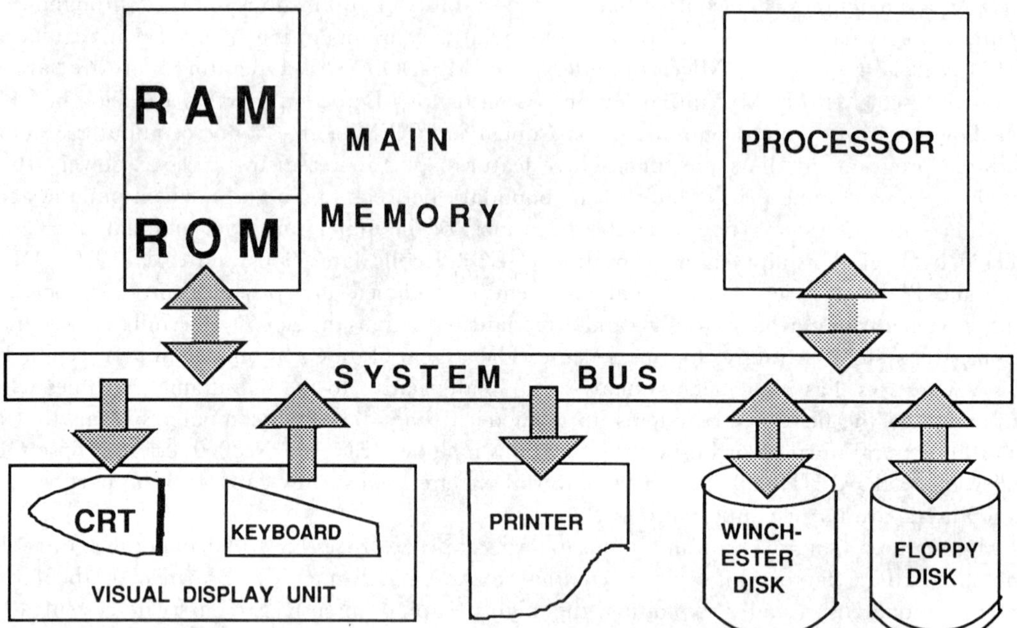

The microcomputer system in the diagram has limited main storage, eg 64k, a single processor and single peripherals, ie a single terminal and backing store. Mini and mainframe systems will have more terminals, more storage and, most importantly, the possibility of different processor configurations, according to the required characteristics of the systems. The major configurations which may be encountered include:

DUPLICATED

In applications requiring a very high degree of reliability, a duplicate processor or other modular components, may be slotted into the system bus, to be switched in immediately when the active unit fails. A similar system is sometimes applied where two workloads of differing priority are to be run at the same time, one of which must be continuous and one which is capable of being interrupted. The low priority processor would leave its normal tasks to take the other processor's work during a period of failure, to resume again when normal operation is restored. An example might be in a banking application where the production of daily management reports may be interrupted to maintain access to customers' records or to safeguard the integrity of an Electronic Funds Transfer (EFT) transaction.

FRONT-END PROCESSOR (FEP)

This is also known as the **tandem** system. Both increased reliability and processing efficiency may be achieved by slotting in a smaller computer, usually a minicomputer into a mainframe system, between the terminals and the main processor. Both processors run constantly, with the FEP passing on part-processed data to the host for completion and output.

LOAD-SHARING

When the workload is extremely variable and continuity is an important factor, two processors may be dedicated to the same workload (hence the difference from a duplicated configuration). During periods of low message traffic, a single processor operates, then as the workload increases to a maximum, both computers share the load equally. Duplicated and load-sharing configurations rely on file-sharing, where all processors read from, and write to, the same storage in order to maintain data integrity and to ensure that the processors taking on workload have access to up-to-date records.

MULTI-PROCESSING

This is often called **array processing** because of the way numbers of processors are connected together. Multi-processing offers the potential of considerable processing power with very good reliability. The concept of linking computers allows the design advantages of flexibility and efficiency over the more conventional stand-alone systems. Sometimes an array will consist of processors carrying out defined tasks:

1. an **input/output processor** to handle data traffic from one CPU to another in and out of internal storage, and to and from a shared-file auxiliary store;
2. a **control processor** to schedule and allocate input for processing and to return output in the most efficient way, under the control of the operating system;
3. a number of **work processors** which carry out the processing. Relieved of the control and input/output work, these processors may operate in the multi-programming mode, running several different programs at the same time, or running the same program at one time, or running the same program on different sets of data.

Since this configuration is designed to operate as a single unit, while allowing the parts to be physically separate, it is called a distributed system, and will usually be found in large-scale applications. Where the computers are capable of either joint or independent operation, the result is called a computer network (this is also called a **cluster** by some manufacturers). This type of distributed processing is becoming increasingly common in business applications using the full range of mainframe, mini and microcomputers. Thus, it may involve minicomputers linked to a central mini or mainframe, or more commonly, a system of equal and independent minicomputers (called a **peer** system) joined by a communications network.

A variety of array processing which is carried out at the device level exploits the newly developed transputers. These are small, single chip processors which may be connected in a number of ways within the same computer. Using a specially developed programming language called OCCAM, transputer systems allow very rapid and flexible processing and they are increasingly finding use in real-time applications and process control systems.

5.6 INPUT DEVICES

The peripherals which may be used to control and communicate with a computer system, or to enter data for processing or storage (called **data capture**) are particularly important factors in the choice of hardware. Input devices form a major part of the **human/computer interface (HCI)** and therefore represent much of the user's view of the system. The choice of input device, and any medium which it uses, must suit the characteristics of the system and the purpose for which the system is intended.

As with computers themselves, input peripherals may be broadly categorised into special purpose (or dedicated) and general purpose devices. Special purpose devices are characteristically used for the routine capture of large amounts of data. It is quite common that the capture process will not be immediately acknowledged by an output or detailed response from the system. General purpose devices typically offer a wide range of features, and may be in physical proximity to an output device. The resulting two-way communication between computer system and human user is called a **dialogue**. The design of this dialogue is an important part of the design of an effective computer-based information system and it should aim to ensure that a constructive and positive attitude is created in the human user (see Chapter 8). An exception to this rule is the case of service points such as ATMs or cash dispensers and EPOS terminals which are for a special purpose, yet which offer a limited dialogue and range of features. The main types of input device which are likely to be incorporated into an information system or commercial application are the following.

VISUAL DISPLAY UNIT (VDU)

These devices are more correctly termed a **visual display terminal (VDT)**, and they combine a display monitor with one or more control devices to allow both input and output, ie the screen allows the user to monitor the input of data from the keyboard or other source, and the screen can also display machine-generated output. It is necessary to specify the type of monitor and control devices in accordance with the use to which the system will be put. Most DP system applications usually require only alphanumeric display—the lowest cost option. These monitors will allow 24 rows by 80 columns of numbers or letters as standard and many offer some or all of the following features to improve screen use in either input or output mode:

(a) **Choice of display mode** In paging mode, data is accepted or displayed on a full-screen basis, ie an empty screen replaces a full screen when the user indicates that the page is full, or a new screen full of data is produced at a signal from the keyboard. This can seem natural to users familiar with ledgers or manual files. The alternative scrolling mode allows new display lines to appear at the bottom of the screen, with the whole display gradually moving up the screen. Some spreadsheet programs require sideways scrolling to display more than 80 columns.

(b) **Reverse video** In which the normal display colour, eg green or black, is inverted. This is useful for breaking up the display of large quantitites of data. For instance, when columns of figures are displayed, every other column may be in reverse video to prevent visual confusion. Also, screen titles, called literals, and instructions, known as prompts, may be reversed.

(c) **Flashing display** This involves a section of the screen blinking, either going blank or going into reverse video for a fraction of a second. This is useful to highlight important data, eg figures over budget or under sales target, and for error messages.

(d) **Cursor controls** These allow the point at which the next character will be input to be moved about the screen more easily than by the use of the space and return keys. Usually, the controls are four keys with arrow symbols to indicate the direction of movement. Such controls are useful where text editing is possible, or where the screen dialogue is in the form-filling mode described in Chapter 8.

(e) **Key functions** These may, in conjunction with the correct software, be programmed to input frequently repeated combinations of characters with a single keystroke.

Some MISs require a graphics display capacity, for which high-definition colour monitors are required. These monitors are most costly because additional computer memory is needed, together with keyboards which incorporate all of the above facilities. In addition, some or all of the following control or input devices should be incorporated:

(a) **Mouse or trackball devices** These use the rolling motion of a ball (a mouse by being rolled on a flat surface, a trackball by being moved manually) to act as a cursor control or to move data about the screen quickly, eg as with a WIMP interface, described in Chapter 8.

(b) **Voice data entry (VDE)** systems employ a modified VDU and microphone to accept vocal input. The simplest speech recognition systems may be programmed to recognise a limited number of keywords. The natural language capacities of computers are still very restricted, but some of the more advanced speech understanding systems are now able to extract a more complex input of combinations of words and numbers from normal speech patterns. The applications for these systems are limited but include high responsibility systems such as those which help to regulate and control air traffic and some of the aspects of financial trading. The advantages claimed for VDE are that operator training can be reduced, that the potential information transfer rate is significant (normal speech conveys between 150 and 220 words per minute) and that the ergonomics of operator activity can be improved because the operator is not restricted to the use of a keyboard terminal for control and input purposes. For such systems to become truly practicable, however, the inaccuracies of interpretation produced by individual speech chacteristics and environmental sounds must be overcome.

(c) **Light pen and touch screen inputs** These use the VDU screen as part of the input medium. A lightpen connected to the terminal is placed against the screen, and a light sensitive device recognises the position by X and Y co-ordinates. A touch screen uses an inlaid screen to accept input through the act of physically touching the screen. Obvious applications in an information systems context include menu-driven programs where a chosen item is touched, and dialogues involving a hierarchy of multiple choice records as with the part numbering systems in some inventory control systems.

The type of VDU terminal described above relies for its intelligence on the time-sharing, multiprogramming operating system of a central processor. The facilities offered and the efficiency with which they operate will always be limited by the system's ability to share resources. Dedicated microcompilers (which may use the control devices described above) may provide excellent facilities and a high degree of responsiveness, but equally tend to offer little in the way of data sharing and their use implies a large-scale duplication of resources. Recent developments in information systems hardware have centred on moving the processing activity closer to the point of input. This is achieved by increasing the attendant storage capacity, and by making use of communications technology (LAN and PBAX, described in 5.12 and 5.4.6 respectively) to allow resource-sharing. This has led to the evolution of the multifunction intelligent workstation.

MULTIFUNCTION INTELLIGENT WORKSTATION

Such workstations or management workstations combine processing, storage, retrieval and communications facilities in a single work place, usually with an ergonomic design appropriate to intensive workstation use. The multifunction workstation is therefore an integrating focus within the concept of the automated office and will offer sophisticated hardware including many of the control devices described above. The real advance over simple VDU input technology, however, comes from the advanced integrated software and the sophisticated HCI and screen handling features. So far, the multifunction workstations in use are targeted at two market segments and price ranges—for management and for operations, the latter being for use by clerks and secretaries, and they are often more complex. Examples of specialist workstations are the ICL Perq, Wang Alliance and Xerox 8010. Workstations can also serve as conventional microcomputers, ie they support various high level programming languages including COBOL and Pascal, and include the Apple Lisa and Macintosh. This type of workstation is commonly used in the management sector.

Development of the multifunction workstation concept began in the early 1970s with the Xerox Star Project. Using their representation in the office market, Xerox aimed to produce a machine which would add sophisticated communications and processing power to a range of office functions already familiar to users. The result was the 8010 information system which used high resolution graphics and a WIMP interface to provide desk-top emulation. A pointer can be used to manipulate common office objects such as in and out trays, filing cabinets, and folders, memos and paper each represented by an icon. The way in which each icon represents the different items seeks to model their behaviour in the real world, and thereby to quickly communicate a sometimes complex concept or function to the user. This advanced graphics simulation was driven by the Smalltalk object orientated language system (see 5.9.2), which was developed especially for the Xerox 8010.

Similarities between the Xerox product and Apple's Lisa and Macintosh systems are possibly explained by the fact that a number of its developers had experience on the seminal Star Project. However, instead of offering facilities for word processing, printing, electronic filing and mail, etc, through an integrated software system, Apple chose to use separate application packages such as LisaWrite for word processing, LisaCalc for spreadsheet and decision support, LisaGraph for business graphics and LisaProject for PERT-type project management. A user was therefore permitted to build up a system and to tailor the functions offered to a particular office environment, for instance, to select and develop applications to support the practice of law or architecture. The Lisa packages were the first genuinely mass-market products to emerge from the general research and development effort. They have now largely been superceded by equivalent Macintosh-compatible packages.

5.6.1 Data capture devices

These devices are intended to allow the input of routine data, often in large amounts, and usually with as little human intervention as possible. Some of these devices use input from a sensor ie an electronic eye or transducer, to measure or count data items, as on a production line for instance. These are termed direct input devices as they create input directly from the object. Other devices derive information from some form of coded data carrying medium either printed on the item or attached to it. The medium and the sensor together with the attendant software make up a data capture system, a classification which includes two broad divisions:

1 document readers, and
2 point-of-sale terminals.

DOCUMENT READERS

These readers have considerable application in business and commerce. In the context of information systems, they are often used for providing input where the data and its source are of a uniform nature and in quantities that make keyboard input impractical. The two methods of document reading in common use are optical and magnetic recognition, and the following systems are found in practice:

1 **Optical readers**—these are usually free-standing peripherals not dissimilar to photocopiers or fax machines. It is quite common to find collating or sorting hoppers included on the output side, and a feed hopper sited on the input. **Optical Character Recognition (OCR)** documents are printed in a special stylised form using standard type fonts. The most common fonts (there is as yet no universally agreed standard) are OCR-A and OCR-B. OCR-A is standard in the USA and is used in four sizes. OCR-B is a European standard and comes in three sizes of character. Most OCR readers can recognise both the specialised fonts, and some will also recognise conventional fonts. Further developments in this area may lead to a more general capacity to accept direct document input in word processing systems. OCR documents may be pre-printed, typed or produced on suitably equipped computer printers. OCR is currently used for Giro credit transfer forms and for turnaround documents such as remittance advice notes and sales order forms.
2 **Optical Mark Recognition (OMR)** systems involve the use of documents which are designed so that a mark or perforation, made in a particular position, represents data. Typically, each possible position is a box in a type of multiple choice array. The box which is applicable is then marked manually or with a special printer. In this way, numbers and dates may be built up or coded with a series of boxes—for units, tens, hundreds, etc, although some practice is necessary to enable a human to make sense of these codes directly from the document. OMR readers must work in conjunction with special software, written to read a particular document, and they are therefore less flexible than OCR systems. OMR is typically used to extract data from survey and questionnaire forms, sales order forms, stocktaking and medical records. One interesting application is employed by one manufacturer of office equipment, whose forms have an exploded view of a machine, each part having a marking box. This provides direct input to the ordering system and avoids the problems and delays which may result from ambiguous descriptions and incorrect part numbers.
3 **Magnetic Ink Character Recognition (MICR)** systems use human-readable characters which are pre-printed in a special ink impregnated with iron oxide. Before being read, the documents are passed through a magnetic field which is picked up by the printed characters. The machine reader recognises the character by its magnetic field pattern, codes it and provides input to the computer. Most models of MICR reader offer programmed sorting facilities, but they are limited in terms of flexibility because of the need to have the characters to be read in the same position on the document, although the documents may vary in size (eg as with cheques). A further limitation is that most systems will only read a single line of data. Two fonts are in common use, E13B which is used mainly on cheques in the USA and the UK, and CMC7 which is used on European cheques and UK postal orders. Because of the need for pre-printing to high quality standards, the use of MICR is largely limited to banking operations, and as input to EFT systems, where the high-speed capability of MICR readers, ie over 2,000 documents per hour, is important.

POINT-OF-SALE (POS)

POS systems combine the features of a sophisticated cash register (eg itemised receipts, coupon refunds, etc) with data capture for an information system. Initially, POS systems were to be found as a part of major applications, eg as in supermarket chains and department stores, but the technology is now being implemented in smaller scale shops as system prices come down. The design of each system, and particularily its data carrying media, will vary both according to the nature of the goods being handled, and to the size of the organisation and its information needs.

Typically, a supermarket will use POS terminals at each service and/or outlet point, each incorporating a laser scanner (ie a static barcode reader), a keyboard with special function keys, a tally-roll printer and an LCD display for customer information. The keyboard is provided both for use with commodity codes, ie abbreviated codes which, when input, will identify items such as fruit and vegetables, which cannot have a bar code or deal with those sitations where the scanner cannot get a clean image from a barcode, and to permit the general housekeeping tasks to be performed, eg operator verification and log-on, session and daily totals, etc. Otherwise the check-out operator will simply pass the bar-coded package over the scanner. The unique barcode will identify the item, enabling the description, price and VAT rating to be looked up, and the stock record to be updated.

There are two European standard barcode formats, ie European Article Number 13 digit code (EAN13) and EAN11 digit code which is intended for use on smaller items and labels. The US format Uniform Product Code (UPC) uses 10 digits and has been in use for a longer period of time. In all cases, a human-readable equivalent of the data (in OCR-B) is printed below the barcode. In EAN13, the first two digits identify the country of origin, the UK being 50, the next five are exclusive to the manufacturer, the following five identify the product/package combination, and the final digit is a check digit. Thus, each manufacturer may register up to 99,999 codable items. The bars may be in various sizes, although larger codes tend to be read more accurately. Similar systems, although the structure of the codes will vary and hand held wands may be used instead of a scanner, are used as part of the circulating system in libraries to indentify books and borrowers, and in other stock control applications. An alternative to barcoding which is often used in clothing stores is the coded swing tag or Kimball Tag, which can be read on a punched card reader, usually at a centralised DP location.

5.7 OUTPUT DEVICES

The most common methods of supplying output information from a computer are:

1 visual display,
2 hardcopy production, and
3 computer output to microfilm (COM).

Audio output is in use as a part of some office automation systems through the voice store-and-forward systems described in 5.4.5, and in the form of synthesised speech which is found in some special purpose systems, but the general application is limited at the present levels of technology.

5.7.1 Visual display

This has already been described in general terms in 5.6 as a part of an input/output terminal—a VDU or multifunction workstation. In an information systems context, the importance of visual display is its ability to represent **transient information**, ie that which is frequently updated or which need not be saved, or that which is complex information such as may be represented by business graphics. Displays may be alphanumeric using a **cathode ray tube (CRT)** to show only the standard range of digital and alphabetic characters (although simple graphics may be produced using such characters) or graphical for more sophisticated graphics applications. The difference between the two types lies in the issue of cost versus performance. Most personal computers now have monitors which will perform either function well. Indeed, current developments in flat screen technology, ie glass plates containing substances which glow when electronically excited, are likely to make truly portable computers more viable in this respect. However, the user must make choices in the display capacities of the VDU, eg whether it will accept colour and, if so, the density of pixels, etc, and in the ultimate hard copy device. Not everyone needs a high resolution graphics capability (see 5.4.9).

5.7.2 Hardcopy devices

These devices include printers and plotters which may be used for a variety of purposes and applications, and they are still widely used in the information systems area—even in the so-called paperless offices. The features offered by hardcopy output devices, their operational performance and, above all, their cost, vary more from type to type than for any other form of peripheral. The range of different types which are available is equally great. The choice of device for a particular application must therefore be made with care. A brief description of the most common types of printer and plotter, together with their salient features, is given under four headings:

1 character printers,
2 line printers,
3 page printers, and
4 plotters.

CHARACTER PRINTERS

These printers, also known as serial printers, are the basic type of device associated with personal computer systems. The method of operation is similar to a conventional manual typewriter, except that the paper, often sprocket-fed, stays put and the print head moves. Two types of printer are in common use: impact and non-impact. Non-impact printers usually produce better quality output; the relevant terms are **letter quality (LQ)** and **near letter quality (NLQ)**. Impact printers are required where multi-part output is to be produced, eg for invoices and delivery notes. These systems will either use carbon interleaved or **no carbon required (NCR)** stationery. The standard forms of printer are as follows:

1 The most basic impact printer is the **dot matrix printer** in which the print head consists in a matrix of tiny tubes containing needles. The needles are fired on to the printer ribbon by solenoids in a pattern corresponding to the shape of the character required. Quality of output can be improved to NLQ standards by using high density matrixes, several print heads or multiple print passes. The latter method tends to compromise the dot matrix printer's greatest advantage which is speed of output where cost is a more important factor than print quality.

2 **Daisy wheel** and **golf ball** printers are capable of printing solid characters in a variety of type faces, as the print heads are easily interchangeable. This is also an important maintenance feature, as is the fact that the solenoid mechanism is much simpler than that in a dot matrix printer. LQ printing and reliability make daisy wheel and golf ball printers almost universal choices for word processing and office automation systems, but the factors of relative slowness and the need to fit an enclosure to suppress noise have inspired many manufacturers to attempt the development of effective non-impact character printers and feasible small system line and page printers.

3 **Ink jet printers** were developed to combine the speed and flexibility of dot matrix printers with an added quietness of operation. The dots which form the characters are formed by tiny jets of ink shot at the paper under electronic control. Early systems which used fields of static electricity to cause the paper to reject droplets which were not required in a particular character proved unreliable. Later models have overcome such difficulties by using self-cleaning jets, different ink and a pumping action instead of static fields to form characters. Although ultimately limited in terms of speed by single character operation and the inability to produce multi-part documents, ink jet printers dominate one important application, eg business graphics. Some models can print graphs, bar and pie charts in up to eight colours, but at considerable expense as special paper must be used. Although ink jet printers are a recent development, it is likely that they will replace the other common non-impact printer, ie the thermal printer, which requires even more expensively coated paper and which cannot print colours.

LINE PRINTERS

Line printers are able to produce a complete line of text in a single printing operation, giving the operational speeds necessary for the bulk printing requirements of a DP system, eg for purchase orders or invoicing runs. The two common types of line printer, **drum printers** and **train printers** are impact types using carbon ribbons and NCR stationery for multiple copies. The other type, **electrostatic printers**, is less common. It also prints one line at a time, and uses wires to electrically charge the paper before passing it through an ink solution to form the characters.

Drum or barrel printers employ columns of complete character sets, usually 132 columns, embossed around the circumference of a rapidly rotating drum. Thus, every print position is capable of being occupied by any given character. A print hammer situated at each print position forces the paper against the drum, through the ribbon, when the appropriate character is in position. As the drum never stops moving (called **fly printing**) the results are often somewhat blurred and irregular. Also the character set cannot easily be changed. Drum printers have therefore largely been replaced by train printers, of which chain and band printers are the types in common use. The principle of operation is the same with both, that a set of characters or type slugs mounted on a chain or flexible band rotates continuously in a horizontal plane across the paper. Hammers at all the print positions (132 is common) fly print through a ribbon as the correct slug passes. The print quality is better than that achievable by drum printers, the character sets are easily changed and train printers are cheaper.

PAGE PRINTERS

Page printers are unexcelled in their print quality, speed and the range of features which may be offered such as double-sided printing, collating and copy multiples greater than seven (the effective limit in impact printers using NCR stationery). Although page printers produce an image one line at a time, their speed of operation is such that the full effect is that of creating a complete page instantaneously. The devices vary from small desk-top xerographic printers used in office automation systems, to large machines resembling printing presses such as the IBM 3800 laser printer which is capable of producing sufficient output to supply the needs of the largest DP system. Whatever the form of the printer, the paper feed may be by a single-sheet hopper system, fan-folded as with normal computer stationery, or on large reels.

1 **Laser printers** form their characters by flashing a low powered laser beam on to a rotating drum, somewhat in the manner of a photocopier. The photoconductive drum surface stores the resulting images, which are transferred on to paper with the use of a dry toner. An almost infinite variety of character fonts may be used, and even mixed in the same line. Logos, tone-block illustrations and graphics may be printed (at present, in black and white although colour systems are under development), giving laser printers a utility which, in many applications, more than justifies their relatively high initial cost.

2 **Xerographic printers** use photocopier technology capable of accepting computer output, and offer many features common in office copiers.

3 **Magnetic printers** use a rotating drum or belt on to which tiny magnetic dots are recorded somewhat like a tape recorder. These character images are coated with toner, against which heated paper is then pressed.

The typical speeds of the various printers are as follows:

Printer	*Type*	*Fonts*	*Typical speed*
Daisy wheel	I	ASCII	2,000 chars. per minute
Dot matrix	I	ASCII, OCR	15,000 chars. per minute
Ink jet	NI	Many	15,000 chars. per minute
Drum	I	Fixed	2,500 lines per minute
Train	I	ASCII, OCR	2,000 lines per minute
Electrostatic	NI	Many	3,000 lines per minute
Xerographic	NI	Any	4,000 lines per minute
Magnetic	NI	Any	5,000 lines per minute
Laser (small)	NI	Any	10 pages per minute
Laser (large)	NI	Any	500 pages per minute

The factors which will most influence the choice of printer will tend to be the following:

— the nature of the document to be printed, eg multi-part invoice set, personalised mail shot letter, etc;
— the volume of output—high volumes usually imply a need for high printing speeds and volume stationery feed;
— the environment in which the printer will operate. An office-type environment would suggest a quiet, versatile printer capable of several character fonts. A centralised DP department might suggest a large, high output line printer;
— the costs involved, both initial costs and cost per copy. A single, high output printer may actually be less expensive than a small impact printer dedicated to each workstation in an office.

PLOTTERS

These have been used in CAD systems where diagrams and working drawings of considerable complexity are produced. The general trend towards cheaper, smaller and faster hardware and the development of business graphics software packages, have made applications in this area possible. Pen plotters come in drum and flatbed types, both of which are capable of producing high quality graphics output by using multiple colour stylus pens. Some plotter systems will produce output in up to six colours, although output is very slow because a separate pass must be carried out for each colour. The inclusion of a digital plotter in the standard information system would be unusual, because the precision of which such a plotter is capable is usually of less importance than speed, so colour ink jet printers are a more frequent choice.

5.7.3 Computer Output Microform (COM)

The use of the term **microform** embraces both microfilm and microfiche, and involves the conversion of digital information into a series of images which are recorded at very high speeds on to microform media. Although the use of microforms for storing large volumes of information, particularly documents such as invoices are accepted (see 5.4.3) the cost of the process will rule out in-house COM for most users. However, there are many bureaux to which it is possible to send a magnetic tape for recording on to microform. On return to the user, the microfilm or fiche may be archived or included in a **computer-aided retrieval (CAR)** system. Such systems typically include a mechanical storage and retrieval unit, controlled by a microcomputer which holds software capable of uniquely addressing each frame. A fiche may be retrieved automatically within seconds upon input of its title or reference number. CAR systems are still relatively expensive, but where actual sight of a document is required (as with delivery note signatures) they are viable for many users.

5.8 STORAGE DEVICES

Most types of computer system will have three forms of storage facility:

1 buffers,
2 main memory, and
3 backing store.

Although the first form is transparent to the user, it is important to the operation of both input and output devices. The latter two types of storage are very significant in the specification process to fit a particular software application to a given computer system.

5.8.1 Buffers

These are temporary storage devices which allow the speed of input and output devices to be matched to the speed of a **central processing unit (CPU)**. Input buffering is essential on most data capture devices (including VDUs) and serves two purposes:

1 the characters typed from the keyboard are accumulated in the buffer to form data blocks. A block is then transferred to the processor at a transfer rate far in excess of that of the terminal or its user, and
2 a CRT screen must be refreshed periodically by retransmitting the screen image contents. This is done from the buffer.

Output buffers are used with all printers and plotters, and operate like input buffers in reverse. In large-scale computer installations, the data buffers will be separate components, and will have a significant effect in increasing the input/output capacity of the system.

5.8.2 Main memory

This is an extension of the CPU and is directly accessible to it. For this reason, it is often called **immediate access storage (IAS)**. Main memory holds three types of contents:

1 the program instructions which are to be executed;
2 the data which is to be processed; and
3 the results of processing awaiting output.

The first form of contents are permanent and will be held in **Read Only Memory (ROM)** even when the power is turned off. The latter two types are volatile and are stored in RAM as they move in and out of the main memory storage. RAM represents the largest part of main memory and it is often used as a measure of the power of a computer, especially with personal computers.

Main memory is composed of uniquely addressable storage locations, each of which can be accessed by a control unit. The capacity of these storage locations varies from one machine to another. Until recently, most microcomputers had locations holding 8 binary digits and were therefore said to have an 8 bit word. Minicomputers often had 16-bit storage locations and mainframes tended to be 32-bit machines. Now these factors no longer apply, and there are even 32-bit microcomputers.

The number of storage locations in main memory (particularly the RAM) dictates the storage capacity or size of the computer. This figure is quoted in **Kilobytes** or **K**, ie groups of 1,024 x 8 bits, and is important in choosing a computer for a particular application. Many micro-based software packages, particularly those offering spreadsheet or business graphics facilities, will occupy up to 256K of RAM. Many recent personal computers have now been designed to provide at least this level of RAM, for instance the IBM PC. The trend in microcomputer design in recent years has been towards producing greater main store capacity, greater word size for more processing power, and faster data manipulation by using a larger bus and a more sophisticated microprocessor. The IBM PC AT uses an Intel 80286 microprocessor chip, which at the time of its introduction, was regarded as having a fast data transfer rate (cycle or clock speed). Intel is working on a still faster chip, the 80486, which would run at over 4 million instructions per second (4 mips), a rate close to that achievable by many mainframe computers.

5.8.3 Backing store

This is also known as **secondary storage** and it is a necessary part of all general purpose and most special purpose computer systems, because no matter how large the main storage of a computer, its RAM is volatile. Therefore, losing power, whether deliberately or accidentally, would mean the loss of the RAM-stored memory contents. Also, even with recent advances in semiconductor production technology, main storage is still relatively expensive. Therefore, backing store is used to hold program and data files ready for transfer to main memory. The trade-off is speed versus cost, as access to pick up (ie read) data from even the fastest backing store will be slow compared to IAS.

To overcome this problem, some special purpose systems use **electronically programmable ROM (EPROM)** which may have semi-permanent data burned into it. Such an application might be the prices of those goods in a supermarket POS system, which are relatively infrequently updated. Price look-up would then be faster than from secondary storage, and would not be affected by the number of users requiring access at any one time. Attempts have also been made to produce storage devices that are mid-way between RAM and backing store, in that they have few moving parts, giving improved access speed and reliability. Devices in this category include RAM disks (actually plug-in auxiliary chips), bubble memory which uses magnetised crystal wafers, and **charge couple devices (CCDs)**, consisting of arrays of electrically charged metal squares. All of these devices would seem to offer considerable potential, but are yet to be accepted in common use. One reason may be cost. Also CCD and RAM disks lose their contents when power is lost.

For a practical data storage device to gain general acceptance under a variety of operational conditions, a compromise must be reached between the following design characteristics:

(a) **Cost**—the initial cost and running costs must be acceptable to the user. It is possible to derive a cost per item of stored data for a given application. This will vary from one type of storage device to another.

(b) **Reliability**—this is important in two ways:
(i) the device should have an acceptable mean time between failure (MTBF) rating, and
(ii) it should hold data without undue risk of loss or corruption.
Obviously, the way in which the device is used will have a radical effect in both these areas.

(c) **Capacity**—the estimation of the number of data items (records) which will be necessary to support a particular application should include provision for future growth. Also the number of devices must allow for sorting operations—normally a minimum of two devices are required.

(d) **Speed**—two factors are open to consideration in this area:
(i) **Access time**, ie the average time taken to find a particular record. This should be suitable for the given application. Normally on-line systems will place a premium on access time.
(ii) **Data transfer rate**—this refers to the speed at which data may be read from, or written to, the storage media on the device. This is obviously important in a batch-mode system.

Devices in which these features are balanced will vary from one system to another, according to the category of computer (micro or mini), the system type (DP or Real-Time) and the processing mode (on-line or batch). A range of typical backing store devices includes the following:

(a) **Tape cassette** units were once used as working storage on microcomputer systems. Their lack of speed restricted their effective use to the home computer market, but a similar design of tape cartridge has an application—**tape streaming**. A streamer tape has no provision for stopping and starting, and is used mainly for back-up copying as part of a security routine.

(b) **Floppy disk** (or diskette) drives are cheap enough to be incorporated into most personal computers, many having two drives, and they have enough speed for most business applications. Floppy disk drives are specific to either single or double sided diskettes in a number of sizes. Traditional diskettes are either 5.25 or 8 inches in diameter, and may be rated up to 2 megabytes in capacity. Since the mid 1980s, a new microfloppy diskette has been adopted by several manufacturers. The IBM System/2 and Apple Macintosh have drives for this type of disk as standard. It is claimed that the system is more reliable, due to better protection of the diskette from contamination. The disks are contained in a plastic envelope, with the access port covered by a retractable plate. Microfloppy drives are sometimes confused with microdrives—a device developed by Sinclair Research for use on the Sinclair Spectrum home computer. This drive uses a loop of magnetic tape wound within a small cartridge. The system has not caught on in business computing circles.

(c) **Winchester** disk drives are robust machines built into many personal computers or, more rarely, available as a stand-alone device. Winchester drives were developed by IBM to overcome problems of limited storage and reliability to which many small-system drives were felt to be prone. Using an air-tight enclosure containing a permanently fixed hard disk with lubricated surfaces allows the read/write heads to move closer to the disk—they touch when the drive stops rotating. This produces greater storage capacity, faster data transfer and improved reliability. Typical Winchester drives may contain disks up to 160 megabyte capacity, and several drives may be linked to one computer via a disk control unit. One disadvantage of using a Winchester for the storage of permanent data, eg customer records, general ledger, etc, is the need for more careful security procedures. Where a floppy disk may be removed and locked away for security, a Winchester disk must be backed-up regularly—usually to a streamer-tape cassette.

(d) **Magnetic tape drives** were once the primary auxiliary storage device for mainframe computer systems. A typical drive unit such as an IBM 2401 will have similar features to a reel-to-reel tape recorder, namely: two reels, one for supply, one for take-up, a set of read/write heads, and a capstan drive assembly. The main differences in operation are that computer tape drives stop and start between blocks of recorded data, and must have vacuum chambers to buffer the resulting tape snatch, and that they use a different size of tape. The 13mm. wide Mylar tapes come in standard reel sizes from 100 metres to 1100 metres long.

With a practical capacity of 20 million characters (bytes) per reel and a data transfer rate in excess of 0.5 million characters per second, magnetic tape is attractive for applications involving mass storage such as DP systems and some MISs. However, the fact that all recorded data must be processed in sequence (sequential access), and that two drives are needed to read and update a tape file on the same run, mean that the most common use of magnetic tape drives is for creating back-up files and archiving from primary disk storage devices.

MAGNETIC DISK STORAGE

This uses changeable disk packs and has become the most popular type of backing storage, with their ability to give direct access to any record by specifying its address outweighing the superior robustness of tape storage. A disk pack unit into which the disk pack or cartridge is loaded will consist of a control unit and a drive assembly which will rotate the disks continuously when in operation. A disk pack will be loaded by the system operator according to processing requirements and will usually contain several masterfiles or a whole database. Replacement of one cartridge by another takes about one minute and it is usual to have a number of identical drives to allow files to be moved between processors in a multi-processor system. An installation with three disk drives may have 10 to 12 packs containing active data in the form of masterfiles, program files, etc, with those not immediately required being stored off-line.

A single disk pack can have a storage capacity of over 100 million characters and a data transfer rate of 300,000 characters per second, depending on the head movements required to produce random and direct access. The speed and capacity of changeable disk pack storage tends to outweigh the fact that the very fine tolerances involved in the read/write operation necessitate a super-clean environment if reliability is to be maintained.

OPTICAL DISK DRIVES

These new devices use a variant of the technology employed in video disks in the entertainment industry and may, in time, supplant the magnetic disk cartridge. A single optical disk the size of a long playing record may have a storage capacity of 3–4 **gigabytes** (15–20 times that of an average magnetic disk cartridge). Access times are much faster because the system relies upon a smaller number of simpler moving parts and, as a result, the achievable data transfer rate of 3 megabytes per second is an attractive proposition. However, the long-term attraction is the promise of increased reliability due both to the simplicity of the read/write operation, which uses a low power laser and photocell, and to the robustness of the disk itself. There is the further advantage that the gap of 2mm between laser unit and disk surface means that air filtration or air tight sealing is not required to prevent head crashes.

But there is a material limitation. Optical disks cannot be erased or overwritten, so updates have to be written to another part of the disk or to a completely new disk. The term is **write once, read many times (WORM)**. Such a drawback has restricted the use of optical disks in business information systems to a few specialist applications where updating is only required infrequently. An example of this is the Ordnance Survey Map database of the UK which is used by motoring organisations to locate and assist the drivers of vehicles which have broken down. A particularly attractive commercial market lies in the exploitation of **interactive video (IV)** in which a video disk player is controlled by a microcomputer to give varied visual stimulus materials according to the user's responses to a computer-driven dialogue. The main market is in vocationally orientated **computer-based training (CBT)** packages. An interesting use of an interactive video information system for non-vocational purposes is the 1986 Domesday Project which provides maps and pictures of life in the UK.

MASS STORAGE DEVICES

These are used where the capacity of the system outweighs the need for speed of access to a particular record, and where cost per record stored is to be minimised. Users are likely to be governments, financial institutions and multinational corporations. The way in which such systems work and the storage medium, will vary from tape cartridge to optical disks, but in all cases, the principle is the same, ie that of automated off-line storage. This has been likened to a juke box.

The IBM 3850 mass storage system consists of banks of cells like honeycombs, each containing a magnetic tape spool holding 50 million characters. A software controlled access arm picks out the required spool and moves it to the read/write station, where the tape contents are written to a conventional disk drive for immediate use. The mass storage volume is then returned to its cell. The standard 3850 layout of 9440 cells gives a total storage capacity of 472 billion (thousand million) bytes. This would enable a single information system to hold census data on most of the world's population.

5.9 SOFTWARE AND PROGRAMMING

Many of the decisions which must be made in the specification and design of an information system are inevitably rooted in the computer hardware and, in particular, in its response and output speed, storage capacity and the likely costs of processing, maintenance, etc. But machines are nothing in themselves. Thus, the ultimate characteristics of the system when installed, and its success in maximising the opportunities offered if the above physical design issues have been properly addressed, will depend to a great extent upon the choices which have been made about the software. Software may be classified by function as either the computer's system software which allows the system to provide services to the user, or the applications software which carries out the user's more detailed requirements.

All the primary functions, ie storing, accessing, retrieving and modifying all the data in the system, whether persistent or transient, are carried out by programs. Program development should be the subject of a design process exactly comparable to that necessary to design the hardware configuration, ie the program development cycle. The aim should be to produce a system which most closely meets the end-users' needs. To that extent, the design process ultimately begins and ends with the user. For this reason, a basic knowledge of software characteristics, alternatives and trends is necessary for a complete appreciation of information systems development.

5.9.1 Systems software

This software comprises programs or routines which are largely hidden from the user, ie they are transparent, yet they help in the process of writing, testing, modifying or running an applications program. Most of the software residing in computer memory is in this category, and is termed the computer's **operating system**. The more sophisticated the computer system, the more powerful and complex the operating system required to manage its resources. At one end of the range, some special purpose systems and some microcomputers may have primitive operating systems with only a few features (these are called monitors), but in general, an operating system could be expected to perform the following functions:

— memory allocation and management,
— multi-user scheduling,
— access control,
— input/output control,
— job scheduling,
— providing utilities and user services,
— interfacing with other systems and devices.

An operating system will contain programs designed to carry out four separate, but fundamental functions, namely:

1 control,
2 utility,
3 translation, and
4 communications.

CONTROL PROGRAMS

These programs are designed to manage the general functioning of the processor, memory and terminal interface. As in human organisations, these programs are arranged in a hierarchy. At the top of the system, the **supervisor or executive program** controls the running of the other programs in the operating system. Most monitor-equipped microcomputers hold the supervisor in ROM. The result is that the system is ready to accept commands from the keyboard or elsewhere as soon as the computer is switched on. Other small computers are made operational by the loading of a system disk containing the program. On larger systems with fixed disks, the machine must be booted up by commands from the control console which cause the supervisor to be loaded into main memory from the backing store. Only when the supervisor is in position and the machine has self-tested can the rest of the system be offered to the user(s).

Within the broad control of the supervisor, a variety of tasks are to be undertaken. Thus, the part of the operating system known as the **job scheduler** will queue and sequence the jobs which are demanding the use of the processor and main memory. Similarly, it is the responsibility of the **file manager** to achieve the interleaving effect of multi-programming (see 5.1.1) Further, the interface with terminals and with the backing store in response to the requirements of any applications program which are being executed, is handled by the **input/output manager**. Obviously, the greater the sophistication of use that is intended for the computer system, the more complex the suite of control programs must be to control the more modern system features such as multi-programming, timesharing and virtual memory. Yet, no matter what the level of sophistication actually achieved, it is generally the case that the detailed functioning of the control programs is not even considered by the naive user —it is invisible or transparent.

UTILITY PROGRAMS

Such programs are also known as **service programs** and they are designed into the operating system by the manufacturer or software house primarily as a support to programmers and, to a lesser extent, to help users when writing, storing and running their programs. The functions most usually provided are:

(a) the loaders—ie those programs responsible for loading programs into main memory;
(b) the linkers—ie those programs designed to link program modules together;
(c) the editors—ie those programs which permit the modification of program code, and
(d) all those routines which sort, merge and otherwise manipulate the data.

TRANSLATION PROGRAMS

This software converts source programs from a high-level language into machine executable code. There are two types of translator:

1 A **compiler** requires the programmer to finish coding the entire program or a free-standing module which is then translated completely into machine code for execution. If the program is error free, it remains in this compiled form, and therefore runs more quickly than programs which have to be interpreted during each run.

2 An **interpreter** which converts and attempts to execute a program one statement at a time. Although the program can be tested as it is being coded, the run time of the completed program will be slower because the translation into machine code has to be undertaken line by line for each run.

COMMUNICATIONS PROGRAMS

This is software which has become increasingly important as the technology to support network computer systems have developed. Many systems now exist, exploiting a variety of techniques, to link different hardware and software into local or wide area networks (LANs and WANs). The result is that many system designers now want the modern types of micro, mini and mainframe computer to communicate one with another. Software is necessary to execute the mere physical linkages and to make the connections which will allow meaningful communications to take place. The communications programs may be required to help select the best transmission medium for a given message, coding and sending the data, and then waiting for, receiving and storing a reply. The control of this interface between two otherwise separate computer systems is governed by a **protocol**—a predefined procedure indicating the message format and the agreed data transfer rate or baud rate. Sometimes communications software can enable two different types of equipment to assume the same characteristics for the purposes of communication, eg a stand-alone micro is allowed to act as a terminal to another computer system. This process is known as **emulation**.

5.9.2 Operating systems

All the main utility and applications programs will be individually identified and stored in the computer's program library. The users can obtain the details of this library through a program directory. In addition to this straightforward function, access to certain programs will probably be security restricted by a piece of software called the **library manager** which also inserts and retrieves programs and maintains the directory. This form of overview function is a part of the operating system.

Operating systems may be **proprietary**, ie specific to a certain manufacturer or computer, and probably protected by copyright, or **portable**. The choice of operating system is critical for the system user as it may dictate the availability of applications software packages and manufacturer support. The current industry trend is towards hardware-independent portable operating systems, particularly in the field of personal computers where mutual compatibility between an operating system and a market leader's software applications products is a strong selling feature. A truly portable operating system will usually consist of four modules:

1 the **nucleus**—this acts as job scheduler and controls both the filing system and the main memory. The design trend is to make it dedicated to a particular microprocessor, but independent of the remaining system hardware;
2 the **storage I/O module**—this handles all access to the backing storage;
3 the **terminal I/O module**—this recognises and holds the characteristics of input and output terminals; and
4 the **user interface**—this will offer a generalised set of commands which can be exploited by the user, together with the appropriate responses including error messages. This should not be confused with the dialogue which is the process of interaction between the user and an applications program.

CP/M AND MS-DOS

The leading operating systems for personal computers are MS-DOS (the proprietary disk operating system produced by Microsoft) and CP/M (control program for microcomputers). The CP/M system was originally developed by Digital Research to provide a set of basic facilities for 8 bit microprocessors based on the Z80 or 8080 microprocessor. It came near to being an industry standard because of the popularity of those processors for manufacturing purposes, and also because many applications packages were quickly developed to run under the CP/M system, reinforcing the market potential. The original system has been developed and now appears in a variety of forms including MP/M (multi-programming monitor for microcomputers) which contains multi-user features, and CP/M-86 which is designed to run on machines using the 16 bit 8086 and 8088 chips.

The processing and storage capacity of the IBM personal computer is based on the Intel 8088 chip, and the manufacturer adopted Microsoft's MS-DOS as the operating system. Because there were no exclusive rights to the exploitation of either the Intel chip or MS-DOS, other manufacturers were able to compete with IBM by creating both a large number of clones or look-alikes, and major new releases of applications software to run on these IBM-compatible machines. IBM has now tried to limit competition by introducing a new proprietary Micro Channel Architecture (MCA) using an Intel 80286 chip in their OS/2 machines. Significantly, the competition is trying to agree an Extended Industry Standard Architecture (EISA) for 32 bit machines based on the Intel 82350 chip and with the support of Microsoft. It will be interesting to see how successful this potential challenge to IBM's market dominance proves to be.

UNIX

The other main contender for operating system domination in the personal computer market has migrated down from minicomputer systems where it has been popular since the late 1960s. This is UNIX, which was developed by AT&T's Bell Laboratories for general purpose multi-programming systems using DEC's PDP/11 minicomputer. UNIX is becoming widely available on microcomputers, particularly the larger multi-user machines based on the 16 bit Zilog Z8000 and Motorola 68000 processors. UNIX claims superiority over the other systems because:

1 It offers better resource sharing and also concurrent processing features. Hence, a user may run a program, edit a file and print another file simultaneously, a feature with obvious attractions in a busy commercial environment. The user interface, called the **shell** in UNIX, operates on the interpreter principle but has particularly rapid response.

2 It offers a powerful range of utility programs as standard for a range of high-level languages including C, BASIC, Pascal, COBOL and FORTRAN.

3 It is particularly suitable for the modern generation of object-orientated languages such as Smalltalk, which has important links with the development of the multifunction workstation in the context of office automation.

The problem is that the industry cannot agree a common standard despite the efforts of the Open Software Foundation (OSF) to promote a peaceful resolution of the conflicting interests of the manufacturers.

VIRTUAL STORAGE OPERATING SYSTEMS

If the modern operating system for mini and mainframe computers is to be competitive, it must be able to support a greater variety of processing modes, eg multi-accessing, multi-programming, timesharing and batch processing with remote job entry (RJE). A number of the common operating systems for larger machines make use of the computer's addressing capability to create the effect known as virtual storage. This is a system for extending the apparent capacity of the main memory for running large application or utility programs. When using the operating system to run in this mode, the computer is often termed a **virtual machine**.

A virtual storage operating system will automatically separate programs into sections, some of which are put into backing store (always disk units for speed of access). The addresses of these sections, and the sections of the program currently being processed, are held in main memory. As the processor moves through the program, the stored sections are called in, processed and put back into storage in a way that is invisible to the user. So seamless is the process that the illusion is created that the storage capacity is larger than it actually is. The sections of program are called **pages** (a fixed size unit of virtual storage) and they are said to page-in from backing store and page-out when being replaced. The execution of virtual storage is therefore called paging. In fact, the limits of capacity are imposed by the machine's addressing capability rather than the number of main storage locations which are available. Problems can arise because some programs are prone to **churn**, ie the excessive swapping of pages between virtual and real storage. A virtual operating system therefore must control this if it is to maintain optimum processing speed and machine efficiency.

A good example of a virtual operating system for large mainframe computers is IBM's multiple virtual storage system (MVS). This powerful system will offer a wide range of utilities and resource management features to over 300 interactive users at any one time, each one having the impression of sole machine use. Effectively, the virtual machine creates the illusion that a number of real computers are available for use. Examples of virtual operating systems which may be found on mini and mainframe systems include OS/VS and CMS on IBM machines, and VMS on DEC machines. At this size of computer, operating systems tend to be dedicated to one machine or the machines of one manufacturer, rather than portable.

SELECTION CRITERIA FOR OPERATING SYSTEMS

The selection of an operating system is crucial because the applications software which the user may want to exploit, may not all be compatible with the same operating system. Further, it must be recognised that most hardware manufacturers make design decisions which limit the availability of operating systems so that the choice of a particular computer is often really a choice of operating system. But it is this control software that gives a computer system its identity and individuality of characteristics. Thus, even when planning the acquisition of a small scale system consisting of a personal computer with applications packages, considerable thought in the choice of operating system is justified. The decision must be seen in the light of the fact that the immediate cost of the software for a typical commercial application, for example, an accounts package such as Pegasus, together with an integrated management package such as Lotus 1–2–3 and a small scale database package such as dBase IV, might equal or exceed the cost of the hardware.

A further factor to consider is that the hardware is more prone to obsolescence. Yet any change to a more advanced computer might make applications software of considerable value redundant if the operating system of the new machine is not compatible. This scenario occurred in a number of instances when some micro manufacturers who had previously followed CP/M, brought out machines with MS-DOS operating systems. Whether as manufacturer or as user, it is important to try and achieve a smooth migration from one generation of technology to another. This would not be so important if industry could agree on standards which would ease the problems of portability. Opinion is divided on what is likely to come closest to an industry standard operating system for microcomputers. Some experts favour UNIX or one of its derivatives such as XENIX, while others await the industry's response to IBM's new OS/2 system.

With mini and mainframe systems, the choice of operating system is more specialised, yet no less important. A key factor in the decision to purchase will be the degree of manufacturer support for a particular system in the form of new releases, ie updates which take account of any software bugs discovered by the users and cured by the manufacturer, and which generally improve performance levels. When surveying the market for software, it is vital to remember that the applications software is likely to be written specifically for a particular generation of operating system, and may need modification or even rewriting if the operating system has been upgraded. Finally, consider that the choice on acquiring a new minicomputer system may be between a new, relatively untried operating system with an expectation of a long life, and an older, well-tried system which may well soon lose its viability. Thus, there may either be work to be done to fit existing applications software to the new system, or existing applications packages may soon be amended to run on the new systems, and the user will be forced to stay with the less effective older packages.

5.10 APPLICATIONS SOFTWARE

This has been likened to the tip of an iceberg, in that it is the part of the software most visible to the user, while the operating system which may be many times larger, is not appreciated and therefore hidden. Applications software performs the functions which the user requires from the system, eg data processing or process control. For the computer user, the range of options involved in choosing application programs exceeds even that of operating systems, and the effects of an incorrect choice are, if anything, more difficult to live with. For this reason, applications program selection and development is a particularly important part of the overall process from the inception to the operation of a system which is known as the systems life cycle.

5.10.1 The criteria of software effectiveness

Although software effectiveness may be achieved in a number of ways, an effective program will exhibit three characteristics:

1 accuracy;
2 flexibility; and
3 performance.

In addition, information systems software will require explicit documentation and a workable HCI.

ACCURACY

This means that the software must be free from errors or bugs. The two common forms of error are **syntax errors**, ie a wrongly spelled command word, and **logic errors** which arise because of the way the program has been constructed. The first category is usually easy to deal with as the interpreter or compiler in the operating system will pick out the more obvious errors and prevent the program from running. A program with logic errors may appear to run successfully, but give inaccurate or unpredictable output. It may be very hard to put such errors right, as correcting one part of the program may introduce errors into other parts. Therefore, software errors may persist for years, or even appear to surface in programs which were thought error free. Attempts to provide accurate software, centre on program design methodologies, of which **Jackson Structured Programming (JSP)** from Michael Jackson Systems is a notable example.

JSP attempts to replace unpredictable creativity in programming with rationality. The philosophy of JSP is that programs exist to manipulate data. The first JSP phase is therefore to define data structures. From these, program structures are developed which may be converted or translated into a target language. The essence of JSP is that it is logical and generalised, ie a program design may be implemented in any high-level language. Accuracy does not therefore depend upon the designer's knowledge of the features of one particular language.

FLEXIBILITY

This means that the software must be capable of handling a range of transactions, and of accepting a variety of input enquiries, while remaining robust under changing operating conditions. The inherent flexibility of a program, together with the quality of its HCI, contribute to the quality of user friendliness, and therefore the system's popularity with users. One way of ensuring flexibility is programming modularity—the separation of program code into discrete sections, each having a special purpose. Modularity is an important aspect of structured programming, as it controls the interaction between program sections, and therefore limits the effect of changes in code on other parts of the program.

PERFORMANCE

This is usually taken to be the efficiency with which the software responds to user enquiries (the response time) and its ability to execute a particular task (run time). The performance characteristics of each applications package not only depends on good program design, eg through the elimination of time-wasting loops from the code, but also the ability of the program to optimally exploit the good features of the system's software and hardware. An important factor in this context is the choice of programming language. Most operating systems, including those for personal computers, will accept a variety of languages, some of which have a higher performance capacity than others, depending on the application. A Pascal program, for instance, will usually execute a particular transaction more quickly than a BASIC program. Also proprietary modifications to languages may offer increased performance. Thus, Turbo Pascal will usually run more quickly than Pascal. Another method of improving the run time of programs involves the modification of the operating system to translate source code into the faster running object code. One of the compiler packages which is often used on a personal computer for this purpose is called Clipper—used in connection with dBase III.

SOFTWARE ENGINEERING

Accuracy, flexibility and performance are ensured in large-scale applications by the use of the discipline of software engineering. Software engineering is a relatively recent concept (the term was first used in 1968) that developed in an attempt to control a perceived software crisis. This situation occurred as newly enthusiastic users and naive programmers jointly attempted to plan and produce increasingly complex applications for their computers to perform, and the level of complexity overwhelmed the capabilities of the processes by which programs were developed. Such processes in the 1960s were based on the assumption that programming was a creative process, generally lacking in methods or principles. The resulting software was often found to have the following drawbacks:

1 it failed to meet the users' real requirements;
2 completion was often delayed;
3 it became usual to run over budget because of poor time estimation;
4 the designers failed to take proper account of the users' lack of expertise and so software was generally difficult to use;
5 control over the design was poor and so it was hard to identify programming errors, and the software was often difficult to maintain; and
6 a large proportion of the software was unreliable.

Software engineering attempts to use similar principles to those used in other engineering disciplines to overcome equivalent drawbacks and to impose quality and usability on software generally. Thus, there was a trend to construct a program product out of proven, reusable modular components. There was work done to ensure that the performance of the product was formally, ie mathematically, specified and tested. But the key step was to recognise that quality cannot be introduced to a system after the event. It must be designed in from the outset.

5.10.2 The sources of software

Applications software may be obtained from three sources:

1 off-the-shelf,
2 from a contractor, and
3 in-house.

OFF-THE-SHELF

Buying software packages is a common approach for well-established applications such as financial accounting, business graphics or small databases. Since the package is designed to perform a specific set of tasks, the potential user's detailed requirements of the application must be carefully mapped on to the features offered by the package. The closer the match, the more successful the package is likely to be in meeting the organisation's needs. Some applications packages are generic in nature, ie they are intended for a broad area of use and come close to having some of the features of a programming language. Examples of this package approach are LOTUS 1–2–3 and dBase IV, which enhance the standard features of the package (spreadsheet and database respectively) by using special language commands or macros. The package approach is almost always the cheapest method of software acquisition especially if the developer can spread the costs over thousands of installations. There is also the advantage of continuing vendor enhancement and support for all the better packages.

FROM A CONTRACTOR

Where no package is suitable for a particular application, and the necessary skill is not available for in-house development, software production may be contracted-out. There are several possible drawbacks to this approach:

(a) the contractor may not have sufficient experience of the application to produce a satisfactory specification;
(b) an extended period may have to be spent in gaining sufficient familiarity with the user's problems to produce good solutions which can make this approach prohibitively expensive;
(c) there may be exclusion clauses in the contract which affect future maintenance and support, or the contractor may cease trading, leaving the user without any help, whether practical or documentary, in the event of difficulty.

It is almost implicit that if an organisation cannot develop its own software, it will not be able to maintain it. Contract programming is therefore perhaps most successfully used as a threshold resource to smooth out the workload on an existing programming team.

IN-HOUSE

In-house software development implies the existence of a programming team, with one or more systems analysts to examine the user's requirements and to produce a programmable specification. The approach has the advantage that this specification, if arrived at correctly, will be precise and specific to the application. For in-house software development to be significantly more successful than other methods, an organisation must have high calibre, reliable and trained staff and the necessary procedures, tools and documentation not only to create the programs, but also to maintain them.

In many organisations, it is likely that a mixture of all three approaches will be used. It is possible to obtain off-the-shelf packages which may be modified or tailored to make them more suitable for a particular application. The software engineering concept of reusability encourages users to create or acquire so-called **library routines** which are, in effect, package modules which may be linked together to form coherent programs. This is a central feature of some recent programming languages, eg Ada. A variation on the theme of in-house development dispenses with the use of a conventional programming team, allowing the users themselves to write programs, using an easily learned user-orientated language called a **fourth generation language (4GL)**. Such languages are a step beyond programmer-orientated languages and allow new methods of program development called prototyping and report generation. 4GLs will be described in more detail in 5.10.4

5.10.3 Program development

Conventional programs, ie those using third generation languages, are developed according to what is known as the **software life cycle** or **program development cycle**. Although the actual constraints of this cycle may vary from one organisation to another, a typical version would include four discrete tasks:

1 **Program design**— which attempts to ensure that the logic and structure of a program are sound and that the program will perform as required. A common design method is JSP. The output from the JSP methodology will be a design specification using structure diagrams and a text part way between natural language and program code called structure text. In this way, the coding requirements are communicated unambiguously (see 5.10.1).
2 **Coding** —converts the specification into a programming language. The details of the coding process will vary according to the language being used, and the choice of language can affect the performance of the system. A brief description of the features of the various languages will be given in 5.10.4.
3 **Documentation**—serves the dual purposes of communication and recording the details of both design and coding stages. Documentation is particularly important for maintenance purposes and where a piece of code may become a reusable module. Its precise functionality must be documented if it is to be used effectively. Ideally, documentation should be produced at each stage of the development cycle and should be updated in line with program maintenance. Often these tasks are neglected, so when the persons who designed and coded the program move on, it is not easy to see how the program works, or even what it is trying to achieve.
4 **Testing**—the testing of software forms a part of a wider testing procedure, and will involve extracting test data from existing files or creating it artificially, to test each program module for errors of syntax and logic. The whole program will then be similarly tested. Ideally, the test results will be included in the documentation for the software.

5.10.4 Programming languages

Next to the choice of operating system, the most important tactical decision which a system developer has to make is programming language selection. An organisation may choose to standardise and use a

FIGURE 5.4 **Program development cycle**

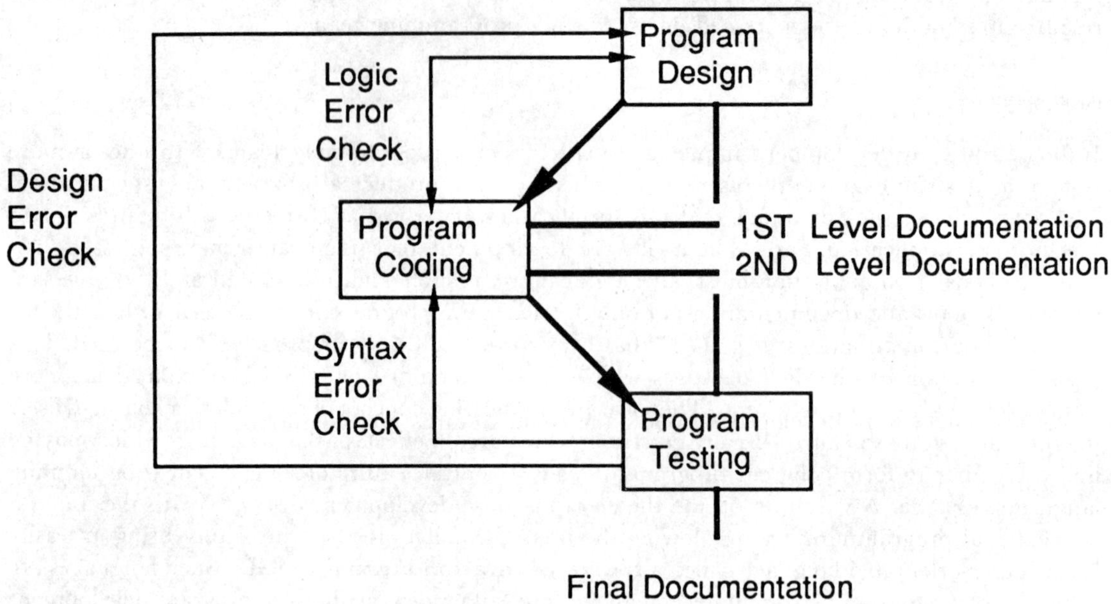

single language, or it may reserve different languages for different purposes, eg one language may be used on the DP system minicomputer and another on the individual managers' personal computers. Special purpose applications, eg process control systems, will tend to use different language types than those for general purpose MIS and DP applications. The programming languages which are available fall into the following categories or levels of coding:

1. machine languages,
2. high-level languages, and
3. fourth generation languages.

MACHINE LANGUAGE

Machine language (or machine code) is made up of the instructions which directly control the computer's own internal code (microcode). Therefore, machine code does not have to be transformed by a compiler or interpreter, and is consequently fast running and efficient. The languages used, the choice of which depends on the type of processor, do not use human recognisable commands and so are difficult to code and to debug.

Assembly languages are written in symbolic rather than numerical code which makes for easier coding. A form of translator called an **assembler** converts the source program into a machine code object program which is automatically syntax checked before loading. Machine efficiency is combined with a greater ease of coding, but assembly language coding is still tedious for programmers compared to a high-level language, and the results are not portable between different processors. Some of the more recently developed languages, such as C, are intended to work in applications where assembly language may once have been used, and provide much higher-level coding. It is extremely unlikely that anyone involved in information systems development would encounter programs written in machine code or assembly language.

HIGH-LEVEL LANGUAGES

High-level languages were developed to provide machine-independence by including features that are relatively abstract, and not limited to one processor design or even to a particular machine.

Effectively, the program specifies what the computer is to do, not how it is to do it. The source program is translated into machine code by the compiler or interpreter which is dedicated to the particular type of machine upon which the program is to run. Such languages are often termed **procedural languages** and are relatively easy to use. Programs can be designed correctly since many procedural languages (Pascal is a good example) have strong features which encourage structured, well designed code, and code can be produced relatively quickly because a number of machine-level instructions may be contained within a single procedural command. Also, a particular application may be coded more easily because high-level languages have features more like human languages and the abstraction means that the programmer can concentrate on writing a problem-orientated rather than machine-orientated code.

As high-level languages developed, it became apparent that specialisation was occuring. Languages began to be designed for particular applications, eg FORTRAN for scientific processing and COBOL for data processing systems. While BASIC, which was originally developed as an educational language, and Pascal are examples of general purpose languages, and they are often used in writing programs for microcomputer systems.

FOURTH GENERATION LANGUAGES (4GLs)

These languages were developed to follow the trend towards user computing which began in the middle 1970s and is still continuing. These languages which have a very high level of abstraction, are often termed **non-procedural** and they are designed to be easy to use. Some 4GLs are close to natural language in terms of the syntax of individual commands. A further advantage is that the languages themselves tend to provide features which are difficult to achieve in a procedural language. The combination of these factors has led to the possibility of non-trivial applications software being developed without the need for conventional programming—and hence programmers. The implication of this is that end users can design their own systems and produce the necessary software. The features which make this revolution possible include:

1 **Prototyping**—this is a systems development technique that uses software in a package of forms, programs and screen painters, to allow the user to quickly produce a simulation of the output required from the finished system. This prototype has the appearance of a completed working system, and it may be tested and subjected to experimentation by the user in a way quite different to that achievable when evaluating a conventional paper-based systems specification. Users are therefore better able to clarify their requirements which may be refined through the subsequent evolution of the prototype. The system will undergo a number of iterations as the user, with probable advice from a systems analyst, finalises the model. The model may then be converted into a functioning system in several ways:
   (a) The whole prototype may be coded in a high-level procedural language. The prototype is therefore treated as a user-friendly specification tool which is later abandoned. This approach is used where maximum efficiency is required from the software.
   (b) Parts of the prototype may be recoded for greater efficiency, for instance, transaction processing programs may be coded into Pascal or C.
   (c) The prototype may have validation, storage and security features built in and then continue to function as the working system.

   Although prototyping is becoming more popular as a systems design approach, there are drawbacks. Yourdon believes that the technique appeals at a facile level, but lacks a sound foundation. He further believes that an alternative development approach using **computer-aided software engineering (CASE)** development tools to augment more conventional methods, may promote equally rapid development. Other disadvantages include the fact that prototyping is an *ad hoc* process, often lacking documentation and testing phases. Moreover, compatibility with other systems, which may be written in procedural languages, may be a problem as prototyping 4GLs are more machine-dependent.

2 **Query languages** These are 4GL tools which may be used in conjunction with a DBMS to enter, update and retrieve information, without having to use conventional programs. It is therefore possible to achieve significantly greater flexibility and speed of use for non-routine applications. Hence, a single question in almost human-language format can produce an answer which would require 50/100 lines of code in a high-level procedural language like COBOL. Examples of query languages include Informix-SQL and Oracle-SQL. Both can provide useful information from an existing database after a few hours' practice.

3 **Report generators** These augment the features of a query language with the ability to format a management report with headings, sections and totals. The user specifies the report

requirements in simple statements, and the software performs the necessary retrieval manipulation and controls the formatting of the output. An example would be Oracle Reportwriter.

4 **Applications generators** These go beyond the answering of questions and the production of reports to allow the creation of complete application programs in a 4GL. The degree of sophistication of these programs may vary from an end user setting up a program to accept data and produce business graphics, to a more experienced 4GL programmer creating software capable of sophisticated file management and transaction processing. Oracle SQL-Forms is an example of a package providing many such features.

5.10.5 The choice of an applications programming language

The choice of a language in which to program a newly developed application can be bewildering as there are so many different languages, each offering certain distinctive capabilities. Yet the choice of language may have an effect on systems development throughout the organisation for the duration of the systems' life cycle. In a large scale DP system or MIS, this may be ten years or more. To resolve the difficulty, software engineers have developed empirically derived sets of features or benchmarks against which the strengths or weaknesses of a program may be evaluated. A typical set of features would be:

— **Portability** This is important because it can imply **machine-independence**, ie the software may be run successfully on different types of computer or even on different operating systems. Most of the popular high-level languages possess this feature, but it is less common among non-procedural languages.

— **Flexibility** This implies that a language is capable of producing good results with reasonable ease in a variety of different types of application; in situations as diverse as statistical processing, business graphics and transaction processing for instance. Most of the early high-level languages, eg FORTRAN and COBOL, are relatively specialised and therefore tend towards inflexibility of application, but the more recently developed languages, particularly Pascal and Ada, have markedly improved levels of flexibility.

— **Ease of use** This is important because a language designed with this in mind enables programmers to code both more accurately and more rapidly, and is therefore less expensive to use in the commercial environment. Other efficiencies can be achieved because better quality training can be provided more quickly, allowing the development of much greater long-term job satisfaction. This satisfaction is likely to arise because the ease of use allows the programmer to concentrate on meeting the users' needs as identified in the specification rather than on resolving the technical problems of programming in the language. Modern high-level languages and 4GLs make a feature of this quality in their design.

— **Documentation** The quality and clarity of the user manual and all other associated documentation adds to the ease of use and enables the programmer to derive the maximum benefit from all the features of the language.

— **Reputation** If the supplier or provider is well known for good support and after-sales service, this will be an important feature.

— **Error handling** All those features which fall under the heading of security considerations should be carefully evaluated.

— **Maximum size** The size of the matrix, files, documents or records which the software may support should be considered in the light of the applications that it is desired to implement.

— **Cost effectiveness** The user must carefully consider both the purchase and the maintenance costs in the light of all the above features.

Other design features which are desirable in a language include the degree to which a program may be structured or constructed in modular units. Good logical structure encourages good design, particularly where structured program design methods such as JSP are being used. Structured code is also easier to read and to modify. Code which is written in modular fashion may be broken down into subroutines which are capable of being reused elsewhere in the same program or in other programs. This can reduce development time and also reduce the number of logic errors in a piece of software. Pascal is regarded as being a language which encourages structured programming, while BASIC is held to have poor design features which can encourage bad coding methods. Newer versions of the language, including True BASIC by the original developer TE Kurtz, go a long way to overcoming these criticisms. BASIC does possess the feature of interactive programming which some programmers prefer as it allows them to enter code into the computer and to immediately receive on-line error messages. The disadavantages are that such languages, which use an interpreter, take longer to execute than compiled languages and may encourage poor design discipline through the temptation to attempt coding by on-line trial and error.

While the features of the language are an important factor in making a choice, it is necessary to examine the potential application and the resources which are likely to be available for the implementation. Factors which will influence this aspect of the selection process are:

1 the performance characteristics of the system,
2 the future policy on systems development, and
3 the system development budget.

PERFORMANCE CHARACTERISTICS

This element refers to the response time, file handling requirements and operational environment. This requires the programmer to have a thorough knowledge of the features of the languages involved to obtain a good match with the application. COBOL, for instance, has good file handling capability, is efficient when processing large volumes of data, and is self documenting. Although COBOL would be ideal for a banking system, it would be inappropriate for use in an airline reservation system. Such a quick-response multi-user application would require a more efficient language such as Assembly Language or C. An attempt to produce a language which would be standard in a range of application types was one of the objectives of the US Department of Defence when they initiated the program to develop Ada.

SYSTEMS DEVELOPMENT POLICY

This would appear to dictate that a commonly used language should be chosen. This approach can lead to stagnation, as many of the most popular high-level languages are also among the oldest. COBOL was developed in 1959 and is still the main language in more than 50% of the large computer centres. It is important to appreciate that even as the technology is changing rapidly with time, so are the requirements of many specifications. ATMs are now a common feature of banking systems, but in terms of language requirements, they would have little in common with existing banking applications such as transaction processing.

SYSTEMS DEVELOPMENT BUDGET

Organisations must, at an early stage of their development, make a policy decision as to the percentage of fixed and circulating capital that can be diverted to the IT budget. This budget must cover the initial cost of the hardware acquisition, the development of suitable systems and long-term maintenance. One of the many problems is that, when organisations are taking their first major decisions in this area, the knowledge and experience of the management team as a whole is at its most limited. Those later responsible for implementing the plans by selecting suitable software can therefore find their budgets artificially limited or unrealistically generous. Proper standards of critical self-awareness must be maintained to ensure that inadequate budgets are aligned to real needs, and that expenditure does not simply match money available.

Fourth-generation languages will need to be evaluated by reference to different criteria than those that will apply to high-level procedural languages. Typically, a 4GL user will look for the features which the language offers such as *ad hoc* reports, queries or spreadsheet work and a short learning curve. Less apparent features which may be sought when assessing a 4GL include the following:

1 **User help** from an on-line help facility which should be comprehensive yet easy to understand;
2 **Different user levels** appropriate to the experience of the user and the nature of the application. The same 4GL could offer features which are of use to both a computing professional and naive user;
3 **Result orientation** which enables the user to specify the details required from the program (the what) while leaving the 4GL to translate the request into a procedure (the how) to produce the report;
4 **User-machine independence** enabling the user to operate the language with a minimum knowledge of hardware and software commands, eg those from the operating system.

5.10.6 Weighted ranking

In order to evaluate and compare alternative pieces of software, whether bespoke programs or applications packages, the National Computing Centre (NCC) has adopted an approach known as weighted ranking.

In this approach, an expert user will review the features such as those listed in 5.10.5 which a piece of software ought to have if it is to perform successfully in a given application. The features are given a weighting (eg 9 = very important, 1 = not important) and the programs or packages are given a score for the way in which their features meet this standard. A total score for each piece of software may then be produced. The technique should prove to be reliable providing that the estimates are reasonably accurate and that the comparisons are conducted properly (eg by using benchmark testing).

5.11 DATA COMMUNICATION SYSTEMS

Data communication (also called **telecommunication**) systems are vital to a number of modern computing applications including MISs and office automation systems. Data communications technology has enabled the development of two central features of modern information systems development:

1 distributed systems, and
2 networking.

5.11.1 Distributed systems

These systems are where the major component parts of the systems, for instance the processors or the backing storage, are geographically spread. Distributed processing as a mode of operation is described in more detail at 5.1.4. The design aim is to reduce the load on a central processor as the number of users increases, or as an application becomes too large. This is achieved by sharing the work between two or more connected processors which, in fact, form part of a single system. Distributed databases are an attempt to place the data to which the user requires access in closer proximity to the user's processes. The aim is to reduce access times and the load on centralised file indexes and DBMSs where a large number of users are involved. An example would be a manufacturing organisation which has a number of factories or depots in various parts of the country. It would be logical to keep the data required to administer each site, for instance, personnel records, accounts and stock control details, at each physical location. The assumption is that each site would make the most intensive use of their own local data. Less frequent access from remote sites, for instance, other depots querying the stock record or a centralised accounting function updating all the depots' price lists would be catered for by the data communications system.

5.11.2 Networking

This may be taken to mean the communication between individual computer systems which otherwise maintain a degree of autonomy. Such networks may link computer systems in different organisations (just as the telephone network does) and may involve widely separated sites called a long haul or **wide area network (WAN)**, or systems within the same site, called a **local area network (LAN)**. The communicating computer systems may vary from personal computers to mainframe systems. Networking allows many of the functions of the automated office to be carried out such as teleconferencing and electronic mail, and also supports many types of MIS. Expensive computer resources may be shared between the users of a network. This may apply to a large scale computer system being timeshared, or to the infrastructure of the network itself. Such an application, where a network operator or carrier allows many users to share the network's facilities, is called a **value-added network or VAN**. Value is added by managing the apportionment of costs among the users.

It is possible to list a number of criteria which a successful network design should meet:

1 **High speed** is necessary to allow the remote accessing and updating of backing storage systems, which are capable of handling large amounts of data very rapidly. This feature is achieved by using a transmission medium which has a high bandwidth, ie a measure of data transfer rate.

2 **Low latency** or delay between sending an instruction or request and that instruction or request being acted on. This is necessary for efficient communication and resource use.
3 **High reliability** is desirable both from the network itself (the hardware and controlling software) and from the point of view of the numbers of messages containing transmission errors. Although networked systems such as electronic mail usually repeat incorrect messages automatically, excessive retransmission adversely affects both bandwidth and latency.
4 **Cost-effectiveness** is important if some network facilities, for instance electronic mail, are to compete with other methods of communication. It must be recognised that network technologies can incur particularly high fixed costs.

The main reason for the wide range of network technologies from which a choice must be made is that few of them meet all of these criteria. Often the first factor in specifying a network design is to decide which of these priorities may be relaxed. Thus, if the intention is to create an EMS, this is unlikely to require a high bandwidth; cost-effectiveness and reliability are likely to be far more important.

The second factor which must be examined is the area which the service must cover. LANs typically connect devices called **nodes** hundreds of meters apart. Such a system will tend to be cheap, fast and error-free. A WAN, in contrast, may cover thousands of kilometers, have slow data transfer rates with high latency, and be expensive to use. Much of this difference arises from the ability to install dedicated communications links or channels when setting up a LAN. Such links will probably be coaxial cable or fibre optic filament. Both of these media provide high transmission quality (18,000 and 30,000 simultaneous messages respectively) with excellent reliability. In contrast, few carriers have been prepared to invest in laying thousands of kilometers of networked cable, and so most WANs rely on existing telephone lines. In the UK, British Telecom has plans to lay over 100,000 kilometers of fibre optic media by 1995.

Many of the existing lines are voice grade only and suffer from a high error rate and narrow bandwidth. This has led to other transmission channels being used for WANs, for instance microwave and satellite transmission. Microwave transmission has a high bandwidth, but relies on line-of-sight communication between repeater stations. Satellites such as Satcom and Comstar, are capable of handling high traffic volumes (typically, 12,000 messages at a time) and can provide point-to-point transmission over 40% of the earth's surface. Although the initial costs of building and launching the satellite and setting up the transmitting and receiving earth stations is enormous, message costs are independent of distance. It would cost no more to transmit a message from London to Rome than London to Paris. Possibly the biggest drawback to the use of satellites for WAN communication is the inherent latency caused by transmission propagation or delay.

5.11.3 Network topology

The principle design features of a network are its topology, ie the way in which the network is configured, and the way in which data is directed through the network—called its **switching mode**. A network may be seen as a number of nodes joined by possible communications or linkages. Where a completely separate physical linkage does not exist between all the nodes, it is necessary to connect communicating nodes by setting up circuits. This is achieved by switches, which may be at the nodes themselves or at separate exchanges, forming paths of linkages on demand between nodes. When the communication period is over, the circuit is dissolved.

CIRCUIT SWITCHING

This is the most basic transmission technique. It is used for **public switched telephone network (PSTN)** services worldwide, and can carry digital data communications. The drawbacks to its use for computer networks are the quality of the lines (narrow bandwidth and slow data transfer) and the general inefficiency of use. For instance, a connection must be made at the start of a session, and disconnected afterwards. This can take longer than the data message takes to transmit. The alternative is to leave the circuit open for long periods of time, with costly idle periods between message bursts. No attempt is made within the system itself to optimise the use of the line. Further, the communicating nodes must have completely compatible equipment using identical data transfer rates. Finally, the circuit switching systems lack any method of detecting and retransmitting messages containing errors. Data communication users can attempt to minimise these difficulties by leasing private circuits between sites with regular message traffic. An example would be a chain of supermarkets linked to a DP centre, or remote manufacturing depots, each wishing to update each other's stock records. Apart from cost/benefit considerations, the choice between private circuit leasing and the use of public circuits is one of traffic volume. A private line can use **frequency division multiplexing (FDM)** equipment to handle transmission rates up to 80 times faster than a public switched circuit.

MESSAGE SWITCHING

Message switching or the store-and-forward technique hands over the task of switching management to the network itself. The user's data is given the address of the destination node and is accepted for transmission even when that destination is not immediately available to receive. The message will be stored at each switching node between the sender and destination, and forwarded as the next node becomes ready. Each node must therefore have enough memory to store a number of messages. The slight delay which may be involved can make message switching unsuitable for distributed real-time processing, but the method is very efficient for most DP or MIS applications.

PACKET SWITCHING

Packet switching is the most common transmission technique for both LAN and WAN use. It exploits the fact that much of the system-to-system communication which goes on takes place in short, high speed bursts. It also takes account of the fact that distributed computing implies a number of concurrent processing activities, all of which may require simultaneous connections. The first of these features is achieved by splitting a message into short **data packets**, each with a destination address. Each packet (also called a **datagram**) may be routed differently by the network management system, and may be received in a different order to that in which they were transmitted. Concurrent transmission is achieved by the setting up of **virtual circuits** through the network. A virtual circuit is established by sending the first header packet of a message which is used to create a route through the system (taking into account usage and cost) which subsequent packets to the same destination will follow. The technique arranges the correct sequence for the delivery of a message in a way that optimises the resource efficiency of the network as a whole. Reliability and availability is assured by the fact that a **packet switched network (PSN)** can route messages around faulty nodes or links. Moreover, because of the flexibility achieved through the use of small packets of data, less buffer memory is required at each node than with message switching.

5.11.4 Protocols

In order to ensure compatibility and to synchronise data exchange throughout the network, it is necessary to impose common conventions or protocols on those who wish to communicate. Protocols must define the format of the datagram and also the functions which are involved in sending and receiving data. These functions, which are carried out using protocols, are conventionally modelled in layers which are often explained by using an example of international diplomacy.

In the model, the individuals on each layer converse according to the conventions of their level. These communications between peers are, for the most part, indirect, the two sides only communicating directly at the lowest layer. An exchange between the two top layers (other than at a summit conference) involves passing messages down through the layers on one side, changing in form at each layer, until direct communication at the lowest levels can be achieved. The message is then passed up the opposite layers. The exchanges at Layers 2 and 3 are virtual; they are observable only as functions, and each function cannot take place until the function below it has been concluded.

FIGURE 5.5 **Diplomatic protocol layers**

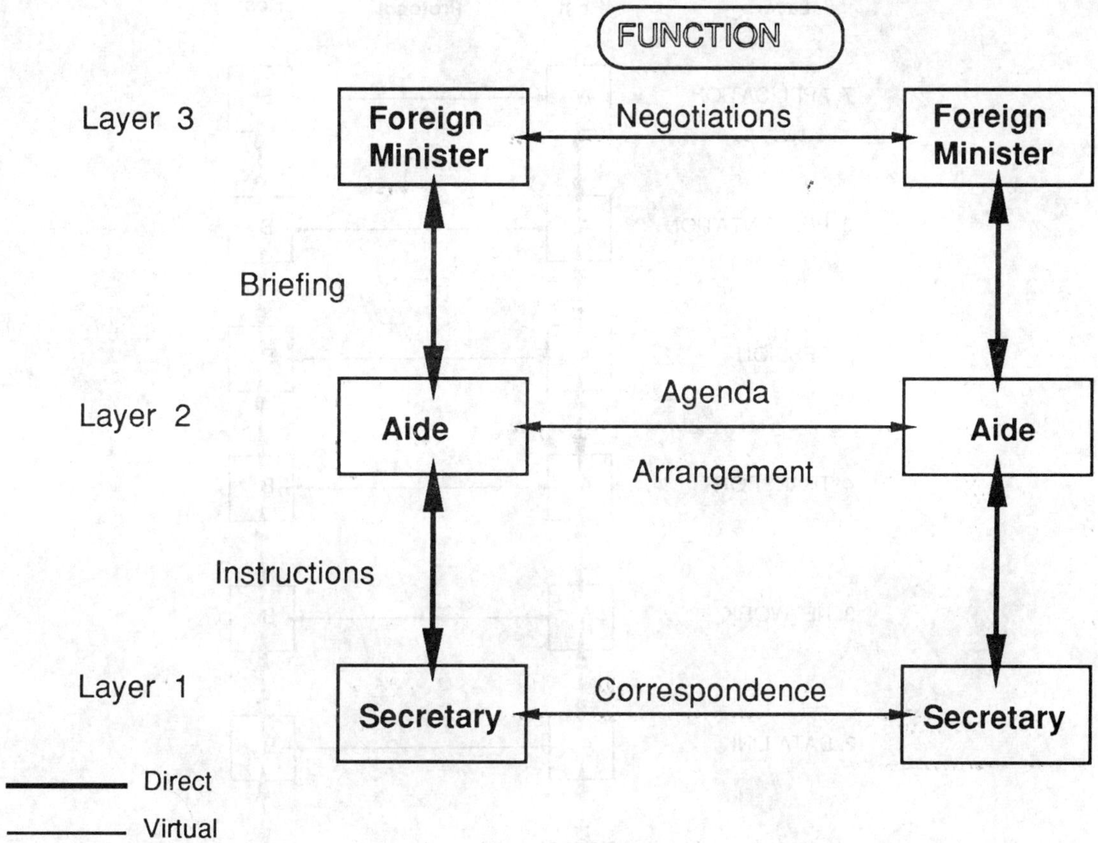

The early development of networks was marked by incompatibility as the grouping of functions into layers tended to be arbitrary. Standardisation was aimed at by the **International Standards Organisation (ISO)** which has produced a reference model for **Open Systems Interconnection (OSI)**. The model used seven layers of functions, shown in Figure 5.6 and arranged as follows:

1 **Physical layer** This handles the transmission of raw data over the chosen communications medium.

2 **Data link layer** This produces reliable communications by handling error detection and transmission speed conversion.

3 **Network layer** This is concerned with the routing of messages and the setting up of circuits by switching.

4 **Transport layer** This layer handles addressing and flow control functions, ensuring that data packets arrive in the correct order.

5 **Session layer** This is the lowest layer which is perceptible to the user. The setting up and termination of communications between a sender and an addressed destination is termed a session. The layer also handles security.

6 **Presentation layer** This layer handles the format in which the data is sent to and from the session layer. This could involve text compression for shorter messages, data encryption for security, and file format conversion for the transfer of large blocks of data between systems.

7 **Application layer** This layer deals with the functions defined by the user, including input and output, processing and storage. There is obviously a great variety of hardware and software configurations which must be able to communicate with each other.

FIGURE 5.6 **ISO/OSI Reference Model**

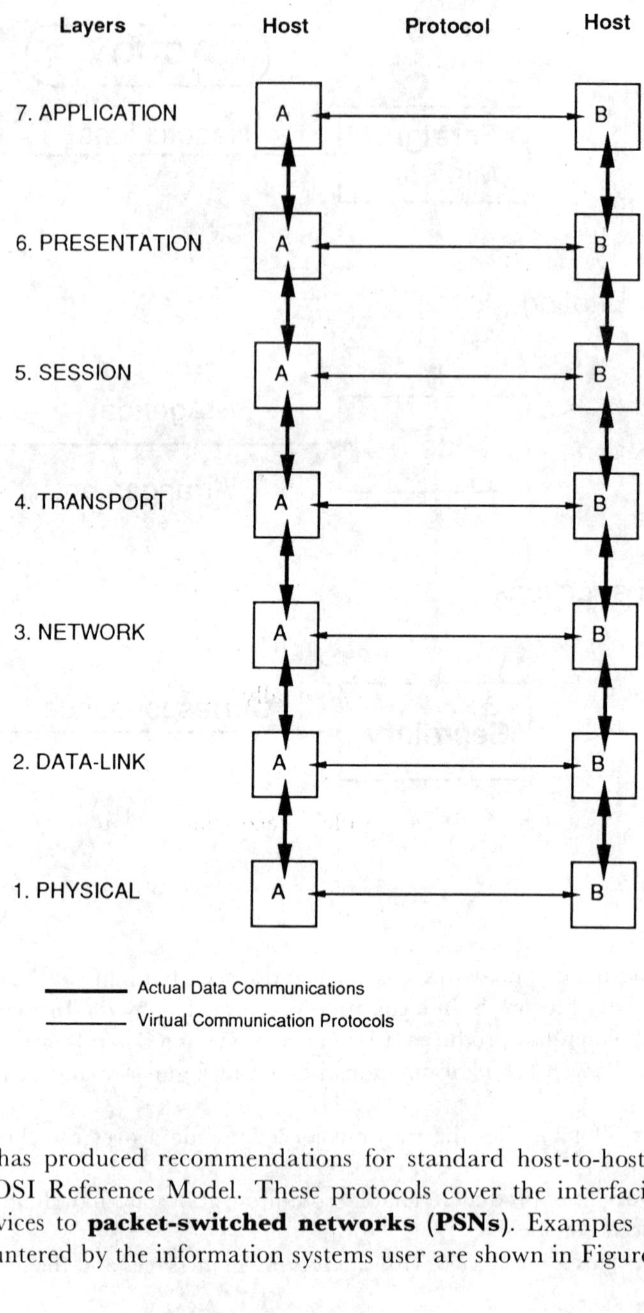

The CCITT has produced recommendations for standard host-to-host protocols based on Layers 1–3 of the OSI Reference Model. These protocols cover the interfacing of terminals and communications devices to **packet-switched networks (PSNs)**. Examples of CCITT protocols which may be encountered by the information systems user are shown in Figure 5.7 and include the following:

(a) **X.25**—This protocol handles the interface of computers, terminals and communications equipment at the user's site with the network's **packet switching exchange (PSE)**. There are three levels in the X.25 protocol, approximately corresponding to Layers 1–3 of the OSI Reference Model. X.25 is close to being a universal standard for public and private networks. There are small variations of the basic protocol, such as British Telecom's version implemented on its packet switched service (PSS), which is more rigidly defined than X.25 at the third level.

(b) **X.75**—This protocol sets standards for the interface between packet switched networks. It mainly covers communication between private and public networks, or international PSN communication. The Euronet-DIANE international network uses this protocol (see 5.4.8).

FIGURE 5.7 **CCITT Network Interface Protocols**

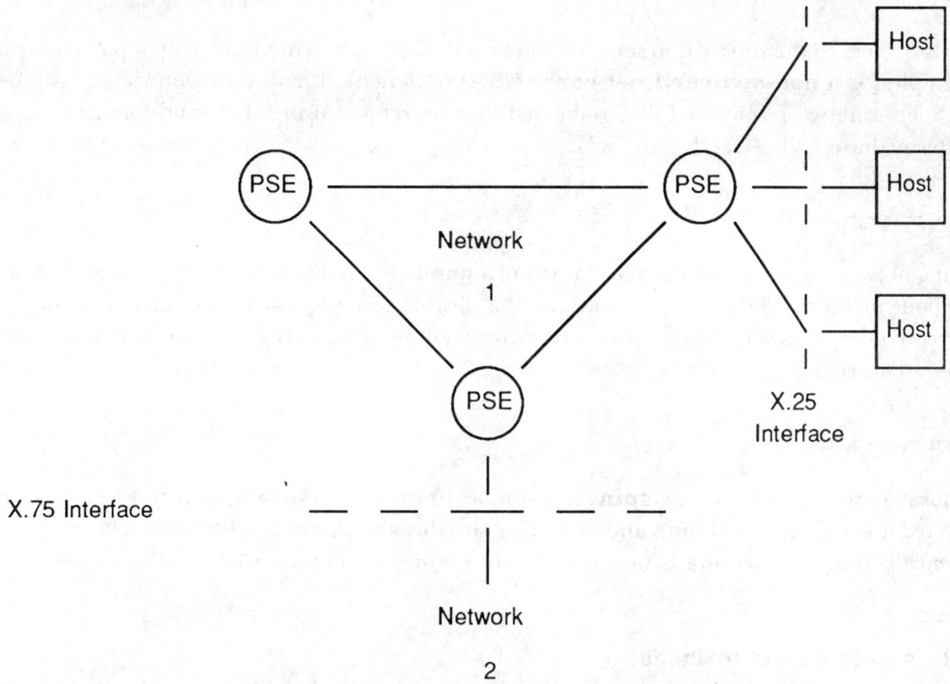

The OSI Reference Model has not been universally accepted as a basis for all types of network communication. This is largely because it was originally developed for use in long-haul communications and its application to WANs or distributed systems is therefore problematic. This is unfortunate as the trend in communications is to the integration of WANs and LANs into single communication systems, through the use of gateways. A further difficulty in achieving this integration is that most land-based networks still rely on voice-grade telecommunication lines using digital-analogue convertors (modems). But, as telephony evolves towards a completely digital network such as British Telecom's System X, the possibility of phasing in new international standards arises. The CCITT is therefore supporting a set of standards for digital interfaces called **integrated service digital networks (ISDNs)**. It is likely that the aim of such a system would be to reduce the reliance on protocols by designing-in compatibility and flexibility to a totally digital network.

5.12 LOCAL AREA NETWORKS (LANs)

A LAN is a communication system allowing data, text, voice and, perhaps, image transmission between specified computers and associated devices, usually within a restricted area. The primary difference between a LAN and a WAN is therefore one of scale, but another important difference is that a user organisation will tend to own a LAN, whereas it will be a subscriber to a WAN. Therefore, compatibility between the individual devices in the network is under the user's control. LANs tend to have the following features:

— **Great bandwidth** allowing high data transmission rates. This readily supports distributed processing, including file transfer and some real-time applications.
— **Low error rates** because of the compatibility between devices and the relatively simple transmission system.
— **Low cost** installation and operation costs as the complex digital-analogue conversion equipment of a public media network is not needed.

There is a confusing number of LAN types and structures, developed by both manufacturers of office automation equipment such as Xerox and Wang, and academic bodies such as Cambridge University. The three important variables in LAN specification are:

1 topology,
2 access control, and
3 transmission medium.

5.12.1 Topology

Topology refers to the physical arrangement of nodes and links which make up a particular network. The simplest is a **non-switched network (NSN)** in which all nodes are connected with dedicated links. Such a network may be fully connected or hierarchical using store-and-forward messaging at the intermediate nodes (see Figure 5.8).

RING NETWORKS

The ring network, also called a **loop**, consists of a number of nodes with receiver devices attached to a continuous medium. Data packets containing a destination address are circulated around the ring. Each receiver examines the message and retransmits those which are intended for nodes other than its own (see Figure 5.9).

BUS NETWORKS

The bus network, also known as **spines**, is similar to the ring system in that receivers and nodes are connected to a single medium, and messages are broadcast with addresses. The major physical difference is that the medium is not a continuous loop (see Figure 5.10).

5.12.2 Access control methods

These methods govern the ability of a particular node on a bus or ring network to broadcast its message in competition with other nodes which desire the use of the medium. The two main strategies are **contention-orientated** and **non-contention orientated control**. The first category allows

FIGURE 5.8 **Types of non-switched network**

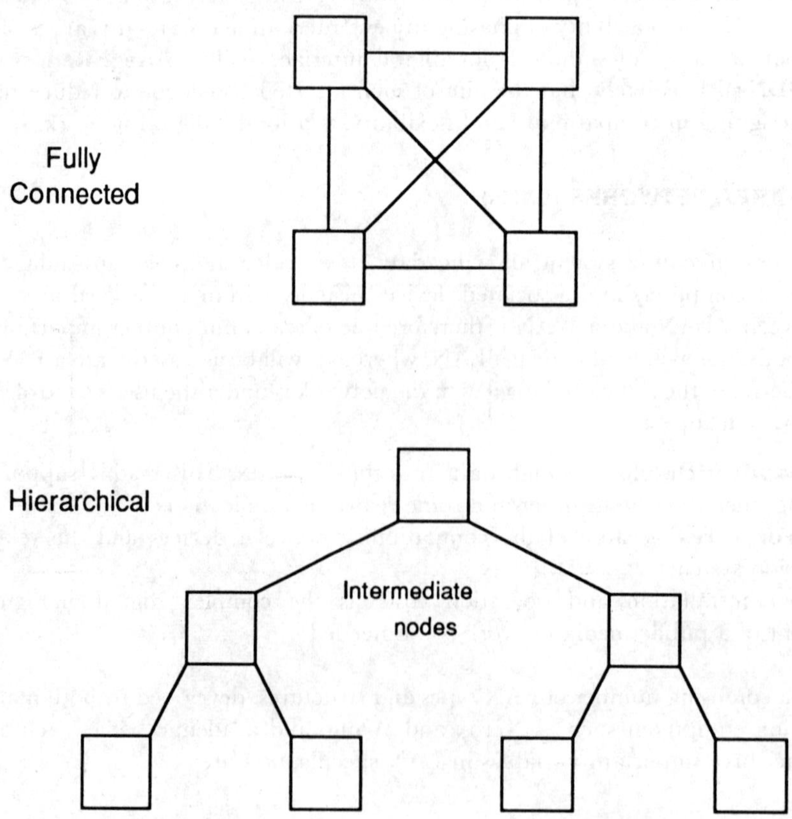

FIGURE 5.9 **Ring network**

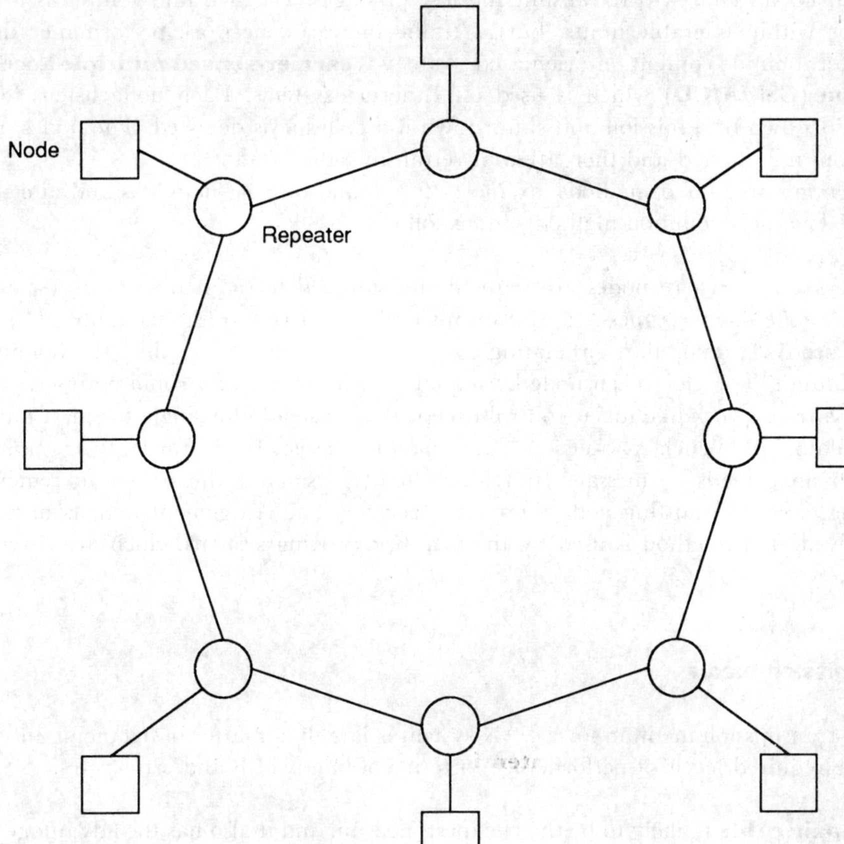

FIGURE 5.10 **Bus network**

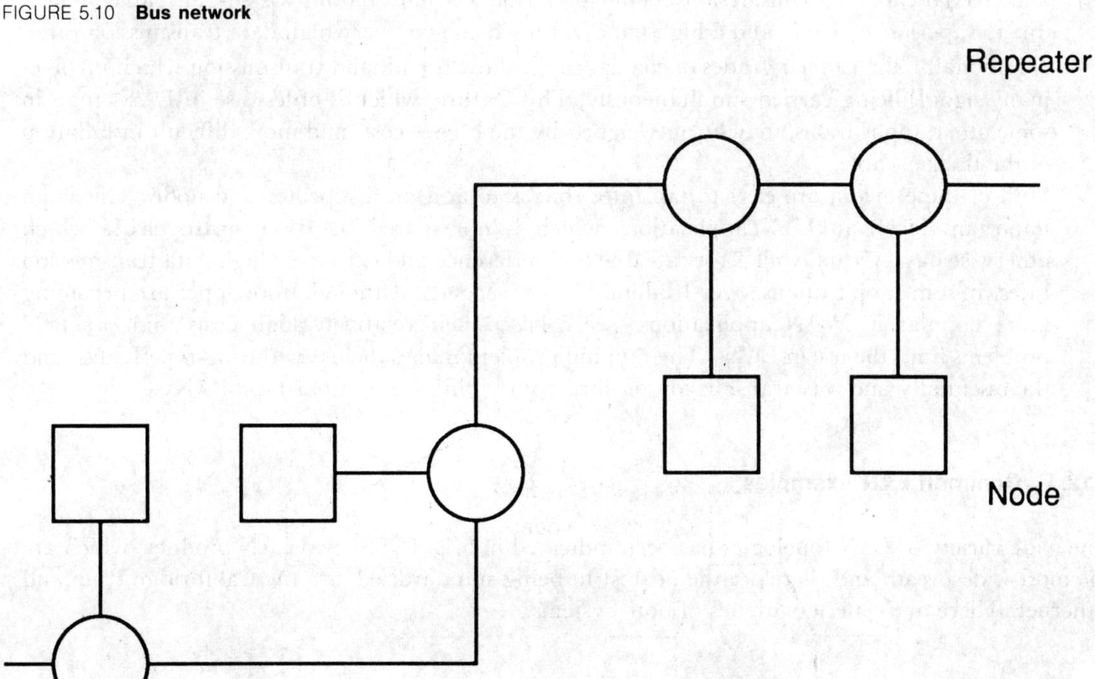

nodes to transmit simultaneously. Such transmissions may collide and, as a result, they are garbled. The system then makes efforts to retransmit the lost messages. When traffic volume is low, such collisions will be within tolerable limits, but as traffic increases, network performance degrades sharply. The most common contention-orientated strategy is **carrier-sensed multiple access/collision detection (CSMA/CD)** which is used on Ethernet systems. Each node listens for other messages during its own transmission and shuts down if a collision is detected. The nodes involved wait for a random time period and then attempt retransmission.

Non-contention orientated methods are most often found on ring networks and aim to avoid retransmissions. The most common methods are as follows:

1. **Polling systems**—where nodes are sequentially sampled to see if they have a message to transmit. A node having a message to transmit is given sole use of the medium.
2. **Token systems** are popular, circulating a special message which enables the holding node only to transmit. Therefore each node has equal priority in a round robin manner.
3. **Slotted systems** work like token control except that, instead of a single token, a number of slots circulate into which packets of data may be inserted by transmitting nodes. The destination node reads its message, but leaves it in its slot for the sender to remove as it recirculates. The transmitting node therefore receives acknowledgement that its message has been received. This method is used by the Cambridge Ring systems which are described in 5.12.4.

5.12.3 Transmission media

The choice of a transmission medium for a LAN system is largely a matter of balancing installation costs against the required levels of performance in terms of bandwidth and error rates.

1. **Twisted-pair cable** is likely to be the cheapest medium and it also has the advantage of wide availability as it is widely used in telephone systems. The disadvantages include a relatively high error rate due to poor anti-interference screening and moderate data transmission rates. Despite these drawbacks, twisted-pair cabling is a popular option for small scale LANs.
2. **Coaxial cable** is a medium which is also widely used in telecommunications for multiplexed trunk channels and the growth area of cable TV. Increased use has brought down cabling costs and coaxial cable has considerably better performance than that of twisted-pair cable. This is due to superior screening and a high bandwidth which gives very high data transmission rates. Additionally, the heavier grades of coaxial cable allow broadband transmission which involves many signals being carried simultaneously. This feature, which is of less use in LANs than in some other applications, may be outweighed by the higher costs and more difficult installation of the thicker cable.
3. Both of these media are easy to tap into, that is to add on a repeater and node. This is an important factor in LAN applications which is not shared by **fibre optic cable** which otherwise has a virtually nil error rate due to interference and extremely high data transmission rates (in some applications, over 1 billion bits per second). Although fibre optics are becoming more popular in WAN applications (see 5.11.2) their relatively high costs and practical problems limit the use in LANs. The tapping problem makes the use with ring-type LANs, and the essentially one-way transmission of fibre optics inhibit use in bus-type LANs.

5.12.4 Common LAN examples

The wide variety of LAN topologies has been indicated in 5.12.1. The two LAN products which are the most widespread, and therefore the nearest to being standardised, are the Cambridge Ring and Ethernet. There are generic varieties of both systems.

THE CAMBRIDGE RING

This ring system concept was developed by Cambridge University in the UK and relies on slotted access control with a standard packet format called a **frame** which includes features to allow acknowledgement and error checking. The basic components of a Cambridge Ring system are:

— the **cable**—usually a twisted-pair;
— **repeaters** which drive the data packets around the ring;
— **stations** which link the nodes or devices to the ring using a connector and which contain a repeater. There is also a station on the ring called a monitor which controls the ring's operation.
— **interfaces** containing the access logic appropriate to the device linked to the station. An interface or access box will usually include some input/output buffering.

FIGURE 5.11 **Layout of cambridge ring**

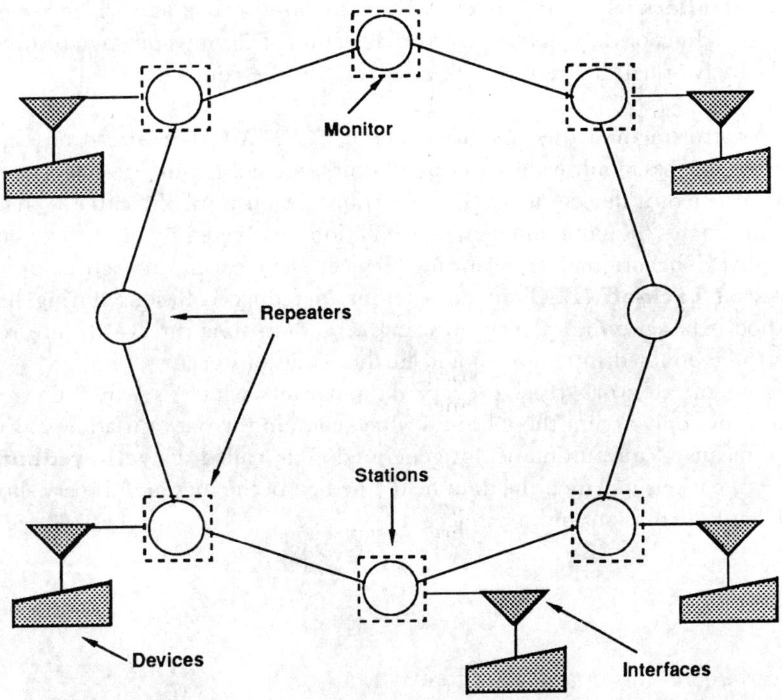

The access control method is based on a circulating slot stratetegy, in which a data packet or frame travels around the ring until it reaches its addressed destination, when it is copied. The receiving station then marks a response field in the frame with a busy or accepted symbol, allowing the frame to carry on around the ring. The station which originally sent the message changes an accepted packet to empty. A packet which is marked busy is retransmitted after a time interval. An unsuccessful retransmission leads to another attempt after a much longer delay.

Error checking is performed by each sending station keeping a copy of its transmitted frames for comparison with corresponding frames as they come back around the ring. In addition, every station on the ring checks the last field of each circulating frame (the parity bit) and, if an error is detected, it puts out an error-report packet addressed to the monitor station. This feature will also register and report breaks in ring continuity.

In spite of its popularity, and its emulation by a number of proprietary LAN products, the Cambridge Ring does not match the ISO/OSI Reference Model. This is less of a drawback in practice than in theory, but it means that communication between Cambridge Ring LANs and WANs must be done through gateways which are capable of performing the necessary address and protocol conversion.

THE ETHERNET

The Ethernet LAN was developed as a joint venture in 1979 by DIX, a consortium involving DEC, Intel and Xerox. The aim was to develop an industry standard LAN based on a bus cable using an access control method based on the **carrier sensed multiple access/collision detection (CSMA/CD)** strategy. The basic components of Ethernet systems are:

1 **The medium** termed the **Ether** as it is completely passive. This is usually a coaxial cable with a device called a terminator at each end.
2 **Transceivers** which are tapped on to the cable with a simple mechanical clamp, making the addition and removal of devices relatively straight forward. Currently, up to 256 transceivers may be attached to one cable in this way. It is the function of a transceiver to handle transmission and receipt of messages, carrier sensing and collision detection.
3 **Buffered controllers** which are remotely wired to a transceiver and which are responsible for handling the coding of data packets, error detection, transmission and retransmission procedures. The networked device is attached directly to the controller.

The access control method used by the Ethernet (CSMA/CD) is based on the listen-while-talking principle. All devices monitor the cable at all times (including during their own transmission). If other traffic is detected, a device delays its own transmission until the cable is free. Should two devices transmit at exactly the same moment, the collision is detected by all devices on the network which become quiet. The original transmitting devices then execute a retrial procedure called **binary exponential back-off (BEB)** in an attempt to reduce collisions during heavy network traffic. The method is based on an algorithm using a random time interval before retransmission, which continues to be doubled in length should further collisions occur.

All devices on the network receive every data packet (which is why Ethernet is called a broadcast medium) but only accept those frames which contain the relevant address. Error detection is carried out by means of an automatically generated code called a **cyclic redundancy check (CRC)**. In addition, packets in which the data field (the text of the message) is very short are held to have been involved in a collision and are rejected.

SUMMARY

The key points covered in this chapter are that:

1 All hardware configurations should be designed to undertake their functions in the way which best supports the operations of the organisation.
2 Office automation has taken place against the background of an information explosion which has posed real problems of productivity for the manual systems, and has led to the creation of the knowledge worker.
3 If knowledge workers are to be effective, the automation systems such as electronic mail, DSSs, etc must be properly tailored to their needs.
4 Input, output and storage devices appropriate to the automation system must be selected. This hardware is largely ineffective unless matched to appropriate software which may be either systems software or applications software.
5 The design of the automation system must match the information strategy and promote effective data flow and communications. It must also match the structure of the organisation in providing either centralised or distributed facilities.
6 Networking, both local and wide area, is achieving fundamental importance in supporting the growth of automated systems. The development of adequate standards and protocols must therefore be a high priority.

FIGURE 5.12 **Layout of Ethernet**

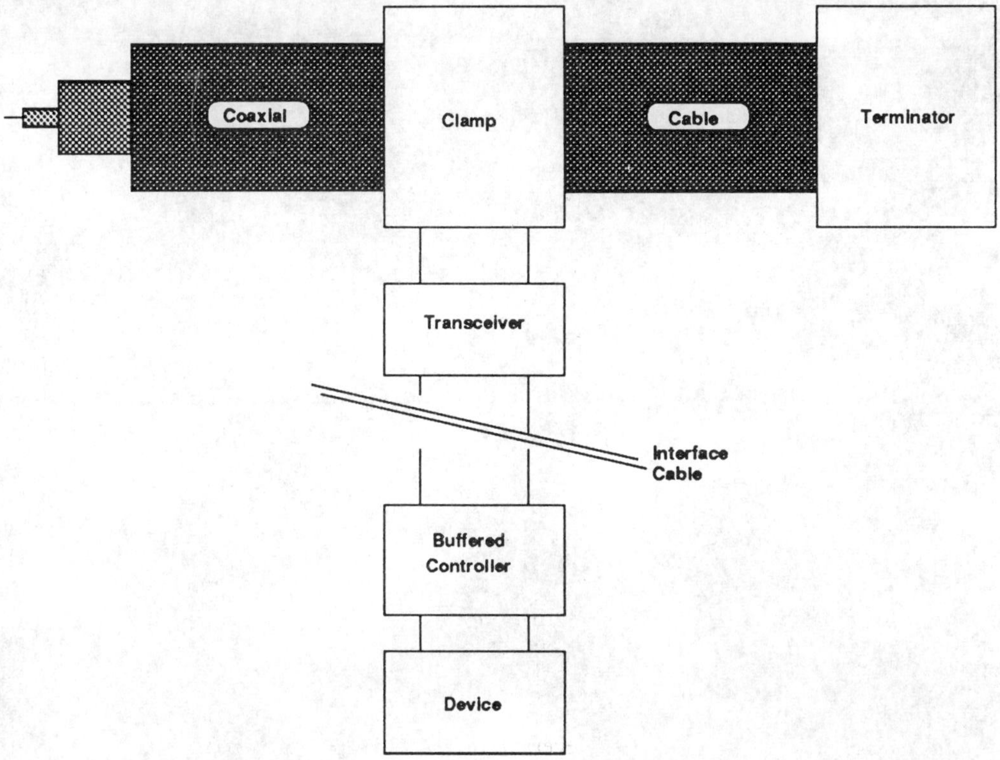

QUESTIONS *Solutions to questions of an examination standard start on p 395*

Write brief notes on the following:

(a) computer system operating modes;
(b) catagories of public databases;
(c) hard copy devices;
(d) applications software;
(e) local area networks (LANs);
(f) the program development cycle.

Questions of an examination standard

1 'Decision support' in an automated office environment refers to the application of IT to the problems met by decision-makers, and in particular to problem analysis and evaluation.

Discuss the requirements for a decision support system (DSS) and the factors involved in the choice of DSS software.

2 The implication of the use of fourth generation languages (4GLs) is that end users can design their own systems and produce the necessary software.

Briefly report on the important features which are associated with 4GL packages.

3 Applications software selection and development is a particularly important part of the systems life cycle.

(a) Discuss THREE main characteristics which an effective applications program will exhibit.

(b) List and briefly describe the benchmarks against which the strengths and weaknesses of a program may be evaluated.

4 Many organisations are assessing the possible advantages of office automation.

(a) Discuss THREE facilities which may be offered by an electronic mail system.

(b) Briefly explain the benefits which may be gained from the use of a teleconferencing system.

Chapter 6
System Development Strategies

CHAPTER OBJECTIVES

Given that the organisation has established an information strategy and defined its data requirements, it is now necessary to consider the more practical issues of developing a system which will begin the process of implementing the strategy. In particular this chapter will:

1 consider the strategic issues relevent to deciding which parts of the information strategy will most immediately benefit the performance of the organisation in meeting its objectives;
2 describe the various stages of the process known as the **systems development life cycle** which will take the organisation from the more abstract strategic aim to implemented reality;
3 evaluate the basis upon which an organisation will select and then justify an automation project, looking in particular at cost-benefit analysis and the standard investment appraisal methods.

6.1 STRATEGIC ISSUES IN SYSTEM DEVELOPMENT

6.1.1 User participation in design

It is most commonly found that the most effective design is deduced from accurately stated users' requirements. This means that to get the greatest appreciation and utility from the design, users should be consulted and, in so doing, it is important to consult with the users who will be most involved in the operation of the implemented version of the system. The difficulty in discussing needs with a lay group of users is that they will often find it difficult to visualise and evaluate ideas without some points of reference. Abstract discussions are helped by having access to simulations and prototypes, or by visiting other organisations where their solutions to problems can be studied. In this way, workers who have not previously been exposed to automated systems can make a real contribution to the debate. But when approaching staff for their views, morale must be maintained. If any jobs are to be lost as a result of the proposed computerisation, the identity of those who are to stay should be known at the earliest possible time, and those who are to be relocated or made redundant should receive proper counselling. This means that the designers must have social skills. They are the catalyst for change and must act responsibly in the role.

For these immediate purposes, it is necessary to propose a more practical definition of an information system. An information system is a mixture of methods of work in a structured work place environment. That environment depends upon a reporting structure for monitoring and controlling its operations. Information system and organisation system design are therefore inextricably linked. It is the task of the designer to identify the organisation's objectives and the roles of individuals and groups in both their internal and external relationships. This information can be elicited through the use of the following techniques:

1 questionnaires—these are limited in what can be asked and, to ensure the consistency of stimulus materials for evaluation purposes, and to save time, no discussion of the questions is possible; but they are an efficient data gathering mechanism
2 interviewing—this represents a strong opportunity for discussion of all the key issues but it is a very inefficient way of using staff time unless only a few senior managers are to be questioned; or
3 group discussions—these are aimed at achieving a consensus view but their value may be limited if not everyone contributes, and they are not necessarily efficient because there can only be one speaker at a time.

With this information, the designer can then propose formal changes to functions and roles. If these proposals are to have substance within the political framework of organisational debate, they must have the support of the senior managers. The designer should then aim to debate the proposals within the most used participation arena. It is not possible to talk to everyone within a large organisation, so the discussions should take place in the most representative forum. This should not exclude the real users in favour of the managers who may lack the necessary level of detailed operational experience. At this point, the organisation must decide the emphasis of the movement for change, ie it should consider whether participation and direction should be from the top down or bottom up. Perhaps as a compromise, the designer should aim for a consensus among the affected managers, and good representative consultation with users.

Nolan suggests that there are six stages of growth in the automation of an organisation:

1 **Initiation**—this is a user-driven move towards automation as a limited solution to a particular problem, and it tends to be autocratic in style.

2 **Contagion**—this is a period of rapid increase in the level of use and cost as departmental systems tend to become part of a central service. Getting control of spending can be difficult at this stage as the managers push for development in their own area and resent the prospect of central direction as meddling and interference. Similarly, because systems are still under local control, it is also difficult to get conceptual control of development —all the enthusiasts just keep on experimenting to solve their own technical problems.

3 **Control**—strong budgetary control with proper planning and cost-benefit justification of developments either emerges or is imposed, and decisions are taken on whether a centralised or decentralised system is desirable. A lot of central management power is used at this point. It is also important to decide whether a DP department is to have responsibility for developing the data processing or whether the users will have the responsibility for exploiting the data resource which is merely serviced by the DP department.

4 **Integration**—planning and control becomes more coherent, as the emerging applications and resources are better co-ordinated. During this period, costs tend to be pushed up because integration frequently means redevelopment. It also brings pressures to break down the existing departmental boundaries and it is the time of greatest change, so the continuation of this period relies upon user support;

5 **Data administration**—at this point, major design issues are to be resolved. For instance, this requires decisions on whether the data should be made to stand independently of the applications. This is a time when the organisation is moving from the management of technology to the management of data as an organisational resource. Which is therefore the more important focus—the data or the information which potentially it represents? User representation is important at this stage to ensure optimum support for management.

6 **Maturity**—a complete application portfolio has now been created, following the form and flow of data within the organisation and supporting all the major management functions. At this point, the organisation should be able to approach future design by directly tailoring development to the known needs of the organisation.

To determine the feasibility of a full information system planning and development exercise, it is helpful to determine the degree of organisation maturity. This will help to prevent the organisation attempting something too ambitious given its level of experience and expertise. At a simple level, the content of the exercise contains the following stages of system development although the precise order may vary from one organisation to another:

(a) conceptual design;
(b) prototyping which br^aks down into:
  (i) screen, ie a lifeless shell to give the users a feel for what the system could look like, and
  (ii) application, i.e. different versions of the possible end-product are produced for evaluation;
(c) programming which must always be done sooner or later;
(d) database design and data architecture which considers:
  (i) the conceptual layout of the data model which is later adapted to,
  (ii) the actual system—ideally the designs will be normative so that the data is transportable from one application to the next;

(e) organisational design—the information system must be integrated into the organisation. Because IT is a catalyst for change (it reallocates resources and therefore tends to redistribute power), the implications of IT implementation for the organisation must be worked out;
(f) objectives analysis—good IT design considers the system from the users' point of view and tries to take account of their needs and objectives.

The design will specify the information system boundaries and the interfaces between the different systems. Each system will perform various processes to achieve identified objects. The best way to identify all of the processes is through the technique of decomposition—HIPO, SSAS, SADT (see Chapter 8). A **process** is a group of logically related decisions and activities required to manage the resources of the organisation. The whole of a system and its component parts must be attributed a priority and a place in the proposed sequence of development. All planning decisions should be taken at a strategic level because the issues involved can only be resolved at an overview level, eg decisions about costs, efficiencies, human resource utilisation, etc.

6.1.2 The first step in a design process is a study phase

Here those who are proposing and sponsoring the project seek to justify the proposals, and the aims and motives of those involved are made more explicit. If the project is accepted, the study team will begin detailing the data flow within each of the process sequences, the team thinking about the shape and form of the organisation following the proposed changes. The team should also identify the current objectives of the organisation, and the facilities and people involved in achieving those objects. Some features of the organisation will be identified as representing vulnerable points, where there will be a risk of loss if the tasks are not properly carried out. Such features should be under the control of the more senior managers, but the degree of control imposed will depend on the frequency of occurrence and the extent to which that feature is organisationally desirable. Some of these features will relate to existing objects, others will allow the organisation the opportunity to aspire towards objects. In each of the processes that are involved, there is a life cycle in operation:

1 the organisation must forecast and plan;
2 it must then implement the plan, say, by developing products or services, or by acquiring raw materials or staff;
3 it then engages in the processes of production and/or supply, and maintenance, ie it must keep the planned output and services going, and must sustain the environment by providing adequate buildings and staff;
4 if the organisation is commercially orientated, it must convert production and/or service provision into income; otherwise it must meet the performance criteria laid down by management;
5 it must circulate equipment and staff—the organisation will depreciate plant and equipment and replace it when necessary; it will also promote and retire staff as competence and age grow respectively;
6 it will reappraise the plan in the light of actual rather than forecasted performance, and decide whether to retain or modify the given processes.

Once the life cycle of each process has been assessed, the organisation should identify the factors in each process which are critical to the success of the process. Self-evidently, greater supervisory management time should be devoted to those factors. It is helpful, in planning the ultimate form of the information system, to discuss each process with representatives of the staff who actually do the work. This will allow a vital comparison to be made between the more abstract senior management's perceptions of the process and the practical working view. Those who undertake this work should be trained in interview techniques so that the maximum of relevant and useful information can be extracted in the minimum time. Those who are consulted should feel free to actively (and constructively) criticise the processes or to make suggestions either for changes to those processes or for new processes. This will allow the study team to address such issues as whether the information arrives where it is supposed to arrive and, if it does, whether it is useful, etc. The interviewees should be asked to identify what information they need to make the process work efficiently.

Following this consultation process, it should be possible to make a preliminary judgment about the quality of the data available to staff at all the points which are considered significant in the information system. It should certainly be possible to identify those parts of the system which do not work at all, or which work too slowly to provide the up-to-date data required for effective decision-making. A further outcome should be the ability to construct a series of **network diagrams** by clustering the data dependent processes into systems. These are organisational decisions which could significantly affect the existing power structures, and therefore require careful handling. Sometimes existing departmental or other power centres have to be disturbed in order to break down process isolation and to achieve proper data flows and process coupling.

6.1.3 Systems architecture

This is the first step towards the creation of a systems architecture. The relationships between the different processes or systems of processes will be ranked according to:

1 the logic of their position in the decision tree;
2 their level of criticality to the success of the organisation; and
3 the risk factor, ie the more critical to the organisation and the greater the risk if anything goes wrong, the more senior the management supervisory role must be. (Risks may arise during development, implementation or operation and, at each phase, the level of risk should be quantified.)

At this point, sometimes difficult design decisions have to be taken. Some processes which depend upon data supplied by other systems may have been directly shaped by the form of the data as supplied. This may have led to distortions and inadequacies in the dependent processes' performance. But the optimisation process may involve considerable knock-on amendments being made to the supplying systems. The cost effectiveness of these consequential amendments will have to be carefully appraised.

6.1.4 Data architecture

At this point, the processes can be placed within a detailed information systems architecture and the primary data flows both real and ideal have been identified. It should then be possible to begin work on creating the data architecture. Databases are collections of related data which are stored together for convenience and which can represent a resource for one or more applications. The different applications may simply present different views of the data through processing. This can be achieved so long as each database has a common structure or a common system of definition. The purpose of this architecture, which should be developed alongside the information system architecture to ensure maximum compatibility, is to allow the users to gain an insight into the different data needs and forms within the organisation and to allow useful relationships to be established between the different data files. If too much data is mixed together in a single database, there may be security problems over access, the attribution of costs on a departmental basis may become difficult, and the quality of the data may become too abstract because of the non-specialised subject matter mixture. Large databases can also be slow to respond and may become too big for the hardware.

The most effective designs call for a clustering of the most used interdependent data files. This produces the most efficient use of computer resources by having the most used data readily available, while leaving the less commonly used data for batch run access or for access at predetermined times when the given database is loaded up. This model should be fleshed out by considering the organisation model. To what extent should the responsibilities for data control and data processing be centralised or decentralised? Should responsibilities be consolidated for some of the processing by specialists or should functionally differentiated processing be allowed to take place in parallel in several locations? This must depend upon the extent to which the tasks are independent, how easily controlled they are and the extent to which the resources will be economically used rather than standing idle for some of the time. This is a problem of economics and logistics which can only be decided at the strategic, tactical and operational levels given the availability of hardware and personnel, and the market needs to be serviced. The organisation will therefore have to consider the costs, revenues and payback periods in the light of:

1 the more detailed budgets and ratios,
2 the hardware and software available,
3 the degree of market share achievable in the commercial sense (if appropriate), and
4 the skills and morale of the staff to be involved.

6.1.5 Centralisation and power structures

If the system is centralised, it will result in increased data communication and no splitting of data, whereas decentralisation means that both the incidence and the data view is split, and data communication is minimal. The problem arises when the wishes of the three levels of choice are different. At a tactical level, it may be preferable to relate the data closely to the operational area, whereas the strategic level leavens operational data with both external and historical data to produce a more distanced view. Thus, operational data processing will require highly formalised data, but tactical decision-making requires data in a form to allow control and analysis of the operational activities. The strategic requirements are to allow modelling and extrapolation techniques to plan for the future.

The design decisions will be based on an attribution of responsibility for decision-making and an analysis of the data required to effectively support each level of decisions. This will also allow the organisation to decide whether the responsibility and authority structures match. The initial justification for centralisation was the cost of the hardware — all processing had to be centralised to achieve economies of scale. To persist in this view is to concentrate on the cost element rather than the benefit to be derived by the individual user. Now organisations can afford to aim for the most effective structures of distribution within a data architecture that will permit the interchange of data for those purposes and processes foreseeable in the immediate future. The solution may be that some parts of the information system must be decentralised, while others should be paralleled or integrated. The emerging pattern will be substantially determined by the degree to which organisational responsibilities are differentiated and specialised.

For each data block, the planners need to decide the pattern of distribution, ie:

1 At which locations is data to be stored and processed?
2 Who is to be responsible for updating data, who should be notified of the update, and who should have access to the updated data?
3 Given that the central data core is not distributed, but represents a resource accessed from different locations, each user will potentially generate a separate data view given local processing: thus, who will be allowed access to the split data views?

At this stage of the planning exercise, the study team should be in a position to offer decisions as to the level of new computerisation appropriate to improve the organisation's information systems. Amending the bureaucracy affects the culture of organisations and potentially shifts power (for more details, see 4.1.1). The critical factors, the risks and the priorities will have been identified in this initial planning phase, and should allow suggestions to be made as to how improvements can be made with the least risk both from an economic and a socio-political point of view. This may include making parts of the organisation more autonomous, but will certainly involve the improvement of vertical information routes and of horizontal resource sharing to permit a greater number of employees access to the best tools for the resolution of local difficulties. The organisation could develop by:

1 buying off-the-shelf packages,
2 paying a software house to customise existing packages,
3 in-house programming, whether by the users themselves with central support or by a special unit which positively consults with the users to be supported.

6.1.6 The basis for preliminary planning decisions

The organisation must start by clearly identifying its **objectives** and the **processes** by which it attempts to achieve them. The problem with using a life cycle approach is that it tends to be a top-down technique and untrained users may be uncomfortable if they cannot relate the study to the level of the organisation with which they are most familiar. Similarly, techniques of functional decomposition may be too limited because they focus on the components rather than the system within which they operate. The best techniques require the planners to think at a level of abstraction and to model the top of the organisation. But no matter where the model starts, there are a considerable number of entities and information sets to be reflected in a complete model and complexity is a constant problem.

The answer therefore lies in separating out the objectives and identifying and grouping the processes which support them. Although this will be a simplified (and some might say superficial) model, it will avoid the problems of the signal-to-noise ratio if too many variables are included, ie it is doubtful that the quality of decisions is improved through the mere addition of more data so long as each item actually included has been verified for relevance. The designers can then consult more accurately with senior management as to the level of information required to support each group of processes effectively. This is achieved because users can more easily understand issues in a model form and so better consultation arises to set the guidelines and strategies for the overall system development.

6.1.7 Implementation planning

As a precondition of implementation, the affected users must have endorsed the declared objectives of the proposed changes. This validation exercise should have been used to produce models of the tasks, processes and resources which are to be created. By doing this, the planners and prospective users are evaluating the change constructively and identifying the most important intended results. If conflicts emerge, it is better to confront them at this stage and to redefine task boundaries and responsibilities on paper rather than leaving it to politically entrenched attitudes when work has progressed to the point where the investment in the implementation effort represents a direct threat to existing responsibility on the ground. If the organisational and administrative disputes cannot be solved through arbitration and compromise, senior management should be involved to make decisions before too many resources have been committed to a contentious project.

This stage of the planning process involves a redefinition of perception. The initial plan, now approved, must be seen as a metaplan to be broken down into its functional components, each one of which must be grouped according to the objectives to be supported and given a priority. The priority is likely to be based on the criticality of the given component as a factor in the success of the organisation. This should allow the planners to gain a sense of the coherence of the different changes to be made, and to produce a framework within which the changes can be most efficiently introduced into operation. It may be useful to group organisational objectives by reference to the five basic categories suggested by Land:

1 **economic**—the organisation hopes to exploit the changes to derive financial benefits;
2 **organisational**—the organisation hopes to achieve practical improvement in its management;
3 **staffing**—the economic and organisational benefits can only be achieved through changes in the practices and attitudes of the staff involved;
4 **third party**—the organisation must be seen as a node in a framework of interactive relations with other parties and organisations, and all internal changes must be monitored by reference to the effect on existing and future relationships;
5 **public policy**—to a greater or lesser extent, all change is aimed at meeting the constraints of the socio-political environment in which the organisation wishes to operate, eg commercial organisations must organise their information systems to comply with the legislation requiring the submission of annual accounts and all must consider data security for the purposes of the Data Protection Act, etc.

Once the basic grouping has been achieved, the plan should be rechecked against the organisation structure to make sure that the implications of the changes remain consistent with the long-term objectives of the organisation. If compatibility is maintained, the planners continue the decomposition and should cluster the component processes into applications, ie the designers should identify those processes which can conveniently be undertaken as a single step (the formation of process flow diagrams will be useful here). In turn, this will permit greater definition of the data architecture and of the data views because it will be possible to see greater logic in the emerging subsystems and to specify the likely form of the data before and after each grouped processing activity. The end product should be a good basis from which to take the strategic decisions of feasibility. The test of feasibility is based on three interdependent issues:

1 Will the staff be willing and able to turn the paper proposals into a working reality?
2 Is it technically possible to make the design operate efficiently?
3 Will implementation represent a good economic return on investment?

6.2 SYSTEMS DEVELOPMENT LIFE CYCLE

6.2.1 Background to systems development

Initially, the early computer-based systems tended to be associated with scientific applications. This arose because such systems were relatively straightforward to design, as the application (which was often highly mathematical) was usually capable of being exactly defined and expressed in formal terms. The complexity and difficulty lay in the production of the software to make the system operational.

In the 1950s, those responsible for selecting projects for automation began to develop more commercial applications for the computer-based systems. These applications were inevitably centred around the data processing functions appropriate to batch-processing systems with their somewhat crude data capture facilities—the emergent mainframe computer technology of the time. But because of the limits of this technology, their impact was usually felt at the operational level of information preparation and decision-making. This trend was reinforced because the prime justification for computerisation during this period was cost-saving, and so the areas which were most usually selected for automation were those which made intensive use of clerical labour, or which offered scope for direct financial benefits. The result in organisational planning terms was that these computerisation projects were often viewed as piecemeal, one-off solutions to current problems rather than long-term strategies in line with an orderly scheme of organisational development.

The difficulty of design and implementation was further exaggerated because the systems had to be developed without the benefit of previous experience or a formal development methodology. The result was that many of the early commercial systems were notoriously unsuccessful as development projects. The symptoms were commonplace. The software product was often delivered late, the programmers underestimated the time required and overran their budgets and, faced with intractable problems and looming deadlines, the eventual botched-together system failed to meet the user's objectives. But, as computer technology improved and the range of applications to which it was applied grew more complex, three factors became apparent to systems developers:

1 that the piecemeal development of systems (or single programs) in response to individual problems should be supplanted by an **integrated systems approach**;
2 that systems development tended to follow a recognised pattern called the **systems development life cycle** which included the same stages irrespective of the application; and
3 that the characteristics of the life cycle could be exploited by using a systems development methodology to plan and control the project through all its stages.

Such thinking led the United Kingdom **National Computing Centre (NCC)** to put forward a seminal systems development approach based on the version of the life cycle which had emerged from their research. This approach, which was first introduced in 1968, is based on the following stages:

(a) feasibility study,
(b) systems analysis,
(c) systems design,
(d) implementation,
(e) review and maintenance.

The approach can be viewed as a serial process in which each phase produces an output in a deliverable form which, in turn, becomes the input to the next phase (the waterfall model), or as a series of iterative cycles in which prior phases can be modified by the results of subsequent phases. Practically, the latter view is probably nearer to the truth.

6.2.2 Feasibility study

In the traditional systems development life cycle, it is the function of the feasibility study to undertake a shallow investigation of the current system and to evaluate its potential for partial or total computerisation. This will involve a **problem analysis** and the production of several outline systems designs or possible alternative solutions to the current problems. These outline plans might include various methods of computerisation or a mixture of manual and computer-based systems.

The alternatives are then compared in terms of their technical, economic and operational costs and benefits, the aim being to produce a recommended solution. This will be the system which has the greatest apparent benefit value. The results of the study are compiled into a formal **feasibility report** to user management, which will then decide whether or not to accept the recommendations contained in it. This is sometimes termed the **go/no go decision**. A positive outcome will lead to the setting of **terms of reference** indicating the scope and constraints for the next phase of the system life cycle.

6.2.3 Systems analysis

This is a detailed fact-finding exercise about the applications area or areas recommended in the feasibility study. This will require the systems analyst to spend a considerable time with the users at various levels of the organisation while building up a file of data about the current situation. Among the techniques which the analyst may use are included:

1 **Interviewing** the users and their managers to obtain a detailed account of the functions which the relevant people carry out, the information which they need to do their jobs, and how they use and update the most common records. This is the most common fact-finding technique in the majority of systems analysis projects. It also represents the greatest area of interaction between analyst and user. The advantage of the technique is that it is flexible and direct, and it also encourages the user to feel involved in the system project. In deciding upon the scale of any interviewing, it should be recognised that interviewing as part of a large project is very resource-hungry. All interviews should therefore be carefully planned to derive the maximum benefit in the time available, the overall process taking the following form:

   (a) **Preparation** in which the analysis team will select the users who are to be interviewed, will examine the facts which are already available, and will prepare a list of areas for examination.
   (b) **Conducting** the interview by asking open ended questions, listening carefully and taking structured notes.
   (c) **Following-up** after the interview by transcribing the notes, comparing notes with others in the team who may be interviewing users in similar areas of the organisation, and producing a summary of the interview. This may be checked with the user.

2 **Observing** the people at work to establish their movements and the number of times when they need to access records, to communicate with one another, or to obtain new work. The technique is sometimes the only one that can be used (eg for industrial processes) but it is very time-consuming. The notorious 'Hawthorne effect', which predicts changes in behaviour when users are observed, may also be a problem.

3 **Questionnaires** perform a similar function to interviews (both are effectively question and answer sessions) but they are usually aimed at fact-gathering from people outside the organisation (eg from suppliers or customers) or where the interview population would be too large. Well structured and properly designed questionnaires which exploit optical mark recognition (OMR) (see 5.6.1) may be directly input for computer analysis. But systems

analysis using questionnaires often suffers from a low rate of returns. This can be partially overcome by making the questionnaire easy to answer. There are three common types of question that may be used:

(a) **Yes/no** questions are easy to answer and to analyse, but offer no real opportunity for shades of meaning.

(b) **Multiple choice** questions have the capacity to produce answers which contain more information, but the question setter requires more skill in drafting the questions to avoid forcing the answers through lack of real choice.

(c) **Open ended** questions remove the element of suggestion and allow almost infinite shades of meaning. They are the most difficult questions to set, and the answers are equally difficult to analyse.

A well-designed questionnaire may contain an appropriate mixture of all of these types of question.

4 **Record sampling** involves the examination of files and documents to find out their contents, their use and their source and destination. Existing computer files may be examined by producing a print out through the use of a special extract program.

Interviewing and record sampling used in conjunction can identify the data that an organisation stores, the information that moves around the organisation and how that information is produced, used and modified. Sometimes the same applications are analysed by different fact-finding techniques to produce a cross-reference check on accuracy.

The results of these activities are recorded using a variety of documents and charts. The systems team then carry out a **problem analysis** exercise based on the data gathered. Areas covered may include:

(a) why current methods and working practices are used;

(b) what alternative methods are available that will achieve the same, or better, results;

(c) what problems are restricting the effectiveness of the current system and what the reasons are for their existence;

(d) what volumes of transactions and data exist, and what rates of increase are likely to apply to them;

(e) what performance criteria are required from the system and how they can be measured.

The emphasis of the detailed investigation and problem analysis phases is on what is to be done to solve the users' problems.

6.2.4 Systems design

The results of the systems analysis stage of the life cycle, modified by the output from the problem analysis exercise, provide the basis for the design of the new system. This phase is both the most creative and the most technical of the whole life cycle. Design will address both computerised and manual procedures in the following areas:

1 **data capture** methods, source documents and data inputs,
2 **program design** and specification,
3 **output design** in terms of screen and print layouts,
4 **file design** of computer and manual file records and data items, and
5 **security** and back-up provisions.

The aim of the systems design phase is to arrive at a detailed statement of how the system is to be made operational. The final steps of the phase are to decide on the hardware and software specification and to put out a tender to suppliers for the necessary items (see 9.2.1).

6.2.5 Implementation

The implementation phase is concerned with putting the systems design into practice. The tasks which must be carried out will include the following software-orientated tasks:

(a) program coding in an appropriate language;
(b) testing the individual programs, suites of programs and the whole system —this will involve the use of packages of test data; and
(c) file set-up and conversion of manual files.

Possibly at the same time as the above, the suppliers' bids in response to the tender specification will be examined. The bid which most closely matches the specification on the most favourable terms will be turned into a recommendation to user management. The hardware (and its environment) will then be selected, ordered and installed.

Implementation goes beyond the physical environment and includes the intellectual. The management must therefore plan for user and operator training, and the creation of documentation such as user manuals. The implementation strategy—the way in which the system goes live—must also be devised. The standard methods are as follows:

1 **Direct changeover** from the old to the new system, with the manual functions being dropped in favour of computerised processes, and manual files being directly converted. This method is comparatively cheap, but carries a high degree of risk, so it is rarely used for critical or strategic systems.

2 **Phased changeover** involves the conversion of manual to computer-based functions in a gradual manner throughout the whole system. This may be done file-by-file or department-by department. The disruption and level of risk is therefore more controlled, and the change may be effected reasonably cheaply, as there will be little, if any, increase in staff. There is no reason in principle why a complete organisation cannot be computerised in this way.

3 **Parallel running** is used on critical systems where the risks and consequences of failure are great. It means that the present system continues to run normally, while the new system functions fully alongside it. Only when a satisfactory performance has been established from the computerised system will the old system be curtailed. This period may vary from weeks to months, depending on the application. The general effect is to minimise the risk of failure at the expense of considerable cost. Thus, it may be necessary to pay overtime premiums for existing staff, or even to take on temporary staff to cover both systems.

6.2.6 Review and maintenance

The degree of success achieved through the use of an implemented computer-based information system will depend on the cumulative success of all the previous stages in the systems development life cycle. Such success can be measured in four ways:

1 The extent to which the features of the system are accepted by the users. Some programs and reports tend not to be used because they are difficult to operate or to understand. This could be a symptom of inadequate work during the systems design phase.

2 Whether the functioning system meets the objectives set for it during the feasibility study phase. This may occur if the running costs of the new system are higher than expected, or the actual direct benefits are lower than was intended.

3 Whether the performance of the new system is adequate for the users' needs, eg in terms of response time, the number of users who may log-on simultaneously, the degree of reliability, etc.

4 The operational integrity of the system. This requires a measurement of the correctness of processing, the accuracy in the functioning of the procedures for setting up batch runs, etc, and the ease with which users can recover from crashes and losses of data. This would include an examination of security and back-up facilities.

These factors are assessed by a major review activity usually involving all of the people involved in the systems project. This is often called a **post-audit review** and it is intended to correct any shortcomings which may be identified under operational conditions and to provide data for subsequent enhancements. All the data arising from such an exercise can and should be recycled to improve the system team's competence in all phases of future projects.

6.3 PROJECT SELECTION AND JUSTIFICATION

The decision to commit resources to transforming all or part of an organisation's operations from a manual or primitive computer-based system to a more efficient computer-based system is termed a **systems project**. The project will follow through the stages of the SDLC and will probably be carried out using a systems development methodology with attendant project management techniques (see Chapter 10). Before this process can be undertaken, however, the need for such a project must be identified, the project must be defined as a solution to this need, and the project must be tested for feasibility within the constraints imposed upon it by the organisation. This is called the **project selection process** and is applied to both piecemeal and total system development. However, although the process is the same, the way selection is applied differs radically between the two approaches.

The **piecemeal** approach will tend to place the project selection process in the form of a feasibility study at the beginning of the SDLC. This is a feature of the traditional methodologies (see 7.1) which originated at the time when a test of technical feasibility was of utmost importance. Since individual systems become obsolete and require replacement in turn, the period of time during which the complete system will be functioning optimally will be short.

The **total system** approach as typified by several of the newer database methodologies places the feasibility later in the life cycle. At this stage, much more is known about the type and size of system which is likely to be implemented. This is important given the number of alternative technical solutions which are available to the modern systems designer.

The project selection process in a total system environment serves to match the implementation of a complete system with the resources of money, manpower and time which may be devoted to that implementation. Only if such resources are not sufficiently available, for instance due to **capital rationing** or a **skill shortage**, would projects A, B and C in Figure 6.2 not proceed simultaneously. Their partition is for the convenience of the project management (see Chapter 10).

It is important for information system developers to appreciate that system development projects are often in competition with other income-generating projects such as improved production machinery or extra retail outlets. When carrying out major investment exercises, top financial management may not be predisposed to favour computerisation against less risky areas of return.

The placement of the project selection process in the two approaches (piecemeal and total system) creates a trade-off between minimising the **sunk costs** if a project should fail an early feasibility test, and acquiring more information through the systems analysis phase.

In Figure 6.3, a project abandoned at A is liable to incur a small cost penalty. A project that reaches point B will incur a heavy penalty if called off, but will benefit in the following ways:

1 there will be more information about the existing system, for instance, size of file storage and processing requirements;
2 the planners will have more detailed knowledge of the resources that will be required to carry out the project; and
3 there will be a greater likelihood of the project meeting its objectives, as these are set closer to actual implementation.

If the project is not likely to be abandoned or heavily modified, therefore it can pay to delay the project selection process, eg as in the CACI Methodology (see 7.2).

6.3.1 Project generation

Under the piecemeal approach, **candidate projects**, ie those which will be submitted for selection, will be generated from a number of sources including:

FIGURE 6.1 **Project development in a piecemeal environment**

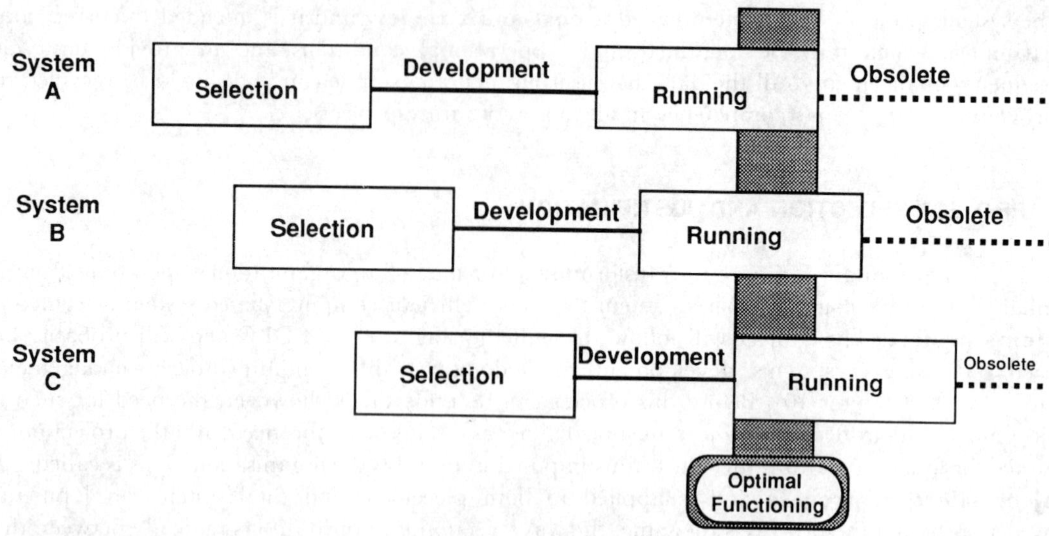

FIGURE 6.2 **Project development in a total system environment**

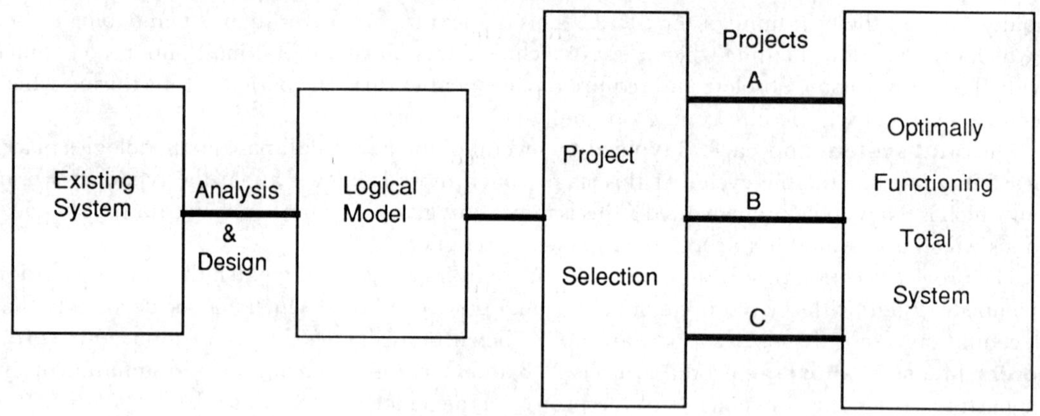

FIGURE 6.3 **Alternative placements of project selection**

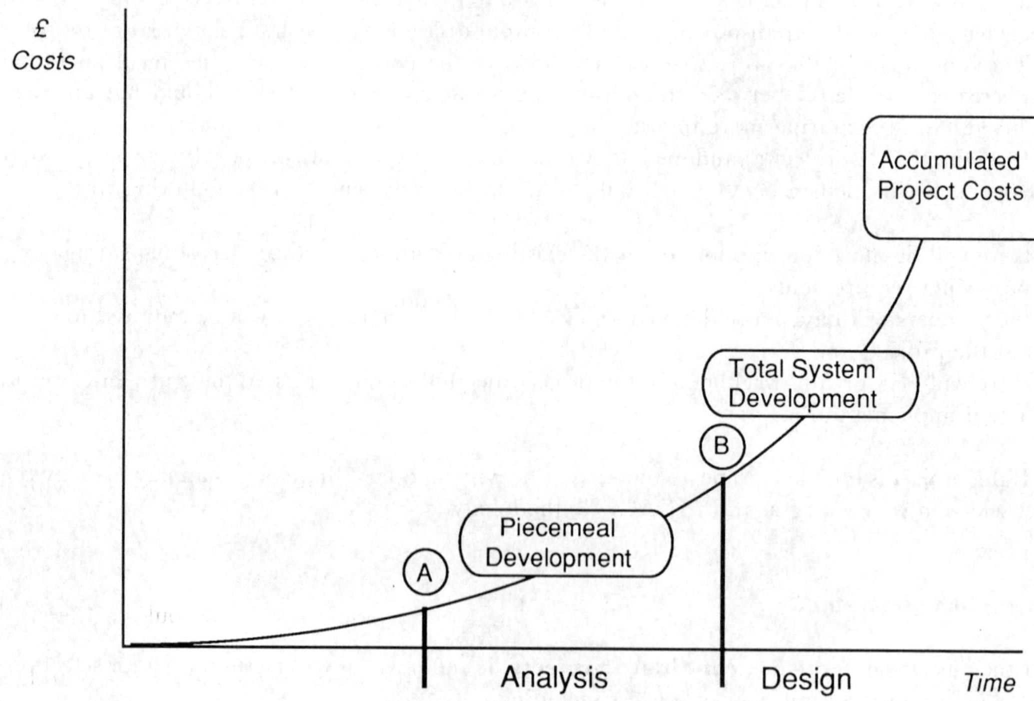

1 the requests from user departments for help in overcoming operational problems in an existing system;
2 the reports from a steering committee which, at the behest of senior management, has been considering ways to improve operational efficiency;
3 input from a formal policy on systems development; and
4 voluntary suggestions made by the computing or systems development group itself.

The effect of collecting possible projects from such sources is that an organisation will have a portfolio of candidate projects which will be continuously tested for selection. Under the total system approach, the initiation of the project will come from strategic management or a steering committee.

6.3.2 The selection process

The process of project selection has been likened to a funnel containing a number of sieves of differing coarseness. They represent the three tests which make up the feasibility study, ie. technical, operational and economic feasibility (see Figure 6.5).

1 **Technical feasibility** This is concerned with matching the system requirements to the performance which could be achieved from available hardware and software. This factor is changing rapidly with technological progress. The technical needs of a system might include:
   (a) the ability to support a certain number of users,
   (b) a certain response time under certain operating conditions,
   (c) the ability to process a certain number of transactions within a certain time,
   (d) the capacity to hold a certain number of records on-line, and
   (e) networking with distant locations.
2 **Operational feasibility** The issues are those concerning organisational and human factors and matters of policy. Operational questions might include:
   (a) the effect of the proposed system on departmental boundaries; for instance, will a new credit control system overlap into traditional sales and accounting areas?
   (b) the changes to manning levels and working practices and how such changes may be managed and absorbed,
   (c) the reaction of individuals both inside and outside the organisation to the proposed system, and
   (d) the effect of the system on the organisation's image; for instance, should a building society with a reputation for friendly personal service replace counter staff with ATMs?
   In reaching decisions, due weight should be given to custom and practice within the organisation, to local and national trade union agreements and to any relevant legislation.
3 **Economic feasibility** This recognises that most business projects, computing or otherwise, must show positive financial returns. For this reason, the economic performance of proposed system projects is regarded as very important by senior management, with one important exception. That is when a project is seen as being part of a technological advance within an organisation that will provide a return in the very long-term, a so-called **loss-leader project**.
   The generic term for this part of the project selection process is a **cost-benefit analysis** and it will usually be carried out with the expert advice of an accountant, who may be drafted into the project team specifically for this purpose. The items which are likely to be encountered during a cost-benefit analysis fall into the following categories:
   (a) **Direct benefits** having an immediate effect on cash flow including the following:
      — reduced operations costs, such as a reduction in clerical staff or overtime payments;
      — reduced systems costs, such as replacing a primitive computer-based system with a more modern one;
      — greater turnover due to increased sales (perhaps as a result of an on-line ordering system) or increased output due to automated production capacity.
   (b) **Indirect benefits** having an effect on long-term profitability. These could include:
      — better decision-making due to better use of information;
      — greater control over operational processes such as stock control and credit control;
      — more freedom to innovate as much of the routine work is automated.

(c) **Development costs** involve the problems of measuring the costs of the existing system and estimating the proposed system costs. This will include the costs of:
— users' time while involved in the fact-finding exercise (this may be considerable for a senior manager);
— systems analysts' and other systems designers' time;
— hardware specification and tendering.

(d) **Implementation costs** are those related to setting up the new system including:
— hardware and software package acquisition; (note that cost patterns can be changed by changing the method of acquisition—see 9.2.2 and 9.2.5);
— commissioning and installation including services;
— staff recruitment and training;
— in-house program design and coding;
— file and database creation.

(e) **Running costs** are those which will continue for the life of the system. They usually make up the greater part of a system's cost; (estimates of as high as 70% have been made). Such costs will include:
— maintenance of hardware, software and services (air conditioning, power supplies, etc);
— financing charges such as loan repayments;
— staff wages;
— stationery and sundries;
— security and back-up.

Cost-benefit can be applied in several ways. It can measure the benefits of a proposed computer-based system as compared to an existing manual system, or it can be used to select the most apparently beneficial from a number of proposed systems (for instance, credit control versus stock control versus sales order entry) where capital rationing applies.

6.3.3 Techniques of cost-benefit analysis

The techniques used in the economic evaluation of computer-based information systems are the same as those used for investment appraisal in other areas of the commercial world. These techniques tend to produce contradictory results, and none of them are universally accepted. Briefly the techniques are based either on marginal costing methods, which deal with a snapshot of a system's performance at a given moment in time, or life cycle costing methods which, more realistically, attempt to measure a system's performance over its working life. A selection of commonly used techniques would be as follows:

1 **Breakeven analysis** can be usefully applied when a proposed system is likely to achieve a direct benefit such as an increase in turnover or production output. The method recognises that computerisation can produce a change in cost pattern. For instance, the cost of processing a customer order (a variable cost) may be less than with a manual system, but the system running costs (fixed costs) may in fact be greater. This is familiar to management accountants as **volume/cost/profit analysis (VCP)**.

In Figure 6.4, outputs to the left of point C do not justify the use of the proposed system (the profit area A, while for outputs above point C (profit area B) the system would be justified. Point C is therefore the **breakeven point**. If the expected average output from the proposed system was indicated by point D, the difference in between C and D would be called the system's **margin of safety**.

2 **Payback period** attempts to measure the time in which the benefits from a proposed system will recoup the initial investment in the system. An organisation which uses this method may have a policy that investments of all kinds must pay back within, say, five years. There are three major drawbacks to the payback method. Firstly, it stresses liquidity at the expense of profitability, and may therefore favour safe, short-term projects (often not a feature of information technology). Secondly, the method fails to take into account the **time value** of money, that is revenues that accrue in the near future are worth most. Thirdly, the payback method is extremely coarse; it is possible to have two projects with completely different cash flow patterns and sizes of initial investment, both giving a payback period of, say, three years.

FIGURE 6.4 **Breakeven graph for proposed system**

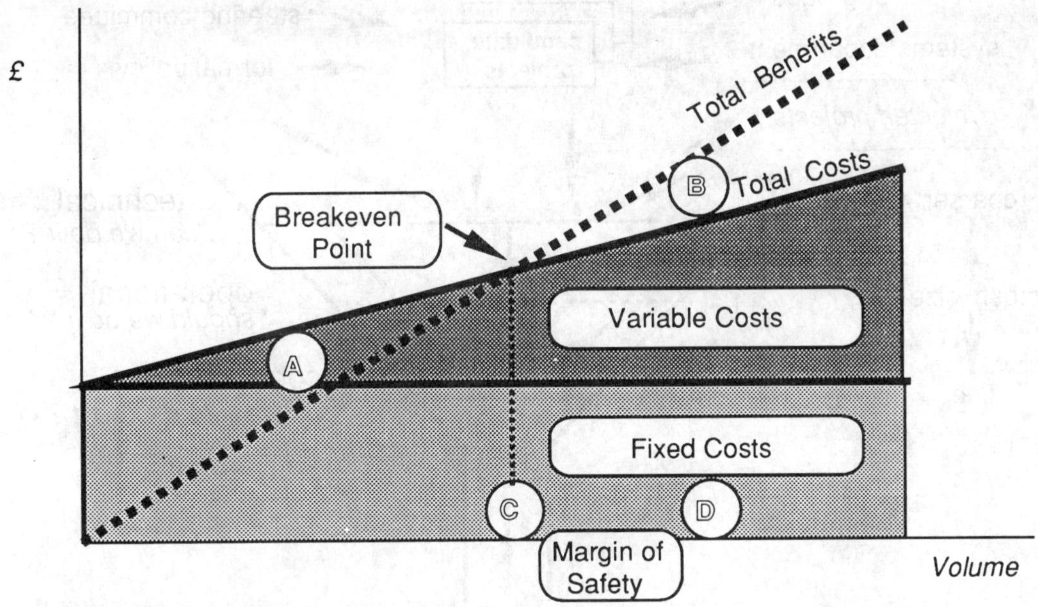

3 **Net present value (NPV)** method discounts future cash flows in line with a present value factor to give all projects, irrespective of their cash flow pattern, a common benchmark of today's value by which they can be judged. The method takes profitability into account by examining revenues for the whole of the project's working life and is less prone to favour short-term views. A development of the net present value is the **internal rate of return (IRR)** method which produces an estimated percentage return which, it is claimed, is more comparable with other forms of investment.

The biggest problem to be overcome during all of the three tests of feasibility is that of predicting the future performance of the system before its design is finalised. This applies as much to the technical aspects such as response time as to the economic aspects such as the generation of a certain cash flow in a ten year time span.

6.3.4 Functions of project selection

The project selection process has two functions:

1 rejecting proposed systems which do not pass the three tests of feasibility, and
2 ranking the remaining projects in order of priority for implementation. What this order is may be a matter for the body in charge of systems policy to decide, eg the steering committee. Often the proposed system which addresses the most pressing functional problems or which performs best in the cost-benefit analysis will be ranked highest. The NCC has developed a method of comparing the non-quantifiable system features such as user interface. It is called **weighted ranking**.

FIGURE 6.5 **Project selection as funnel and sieves**

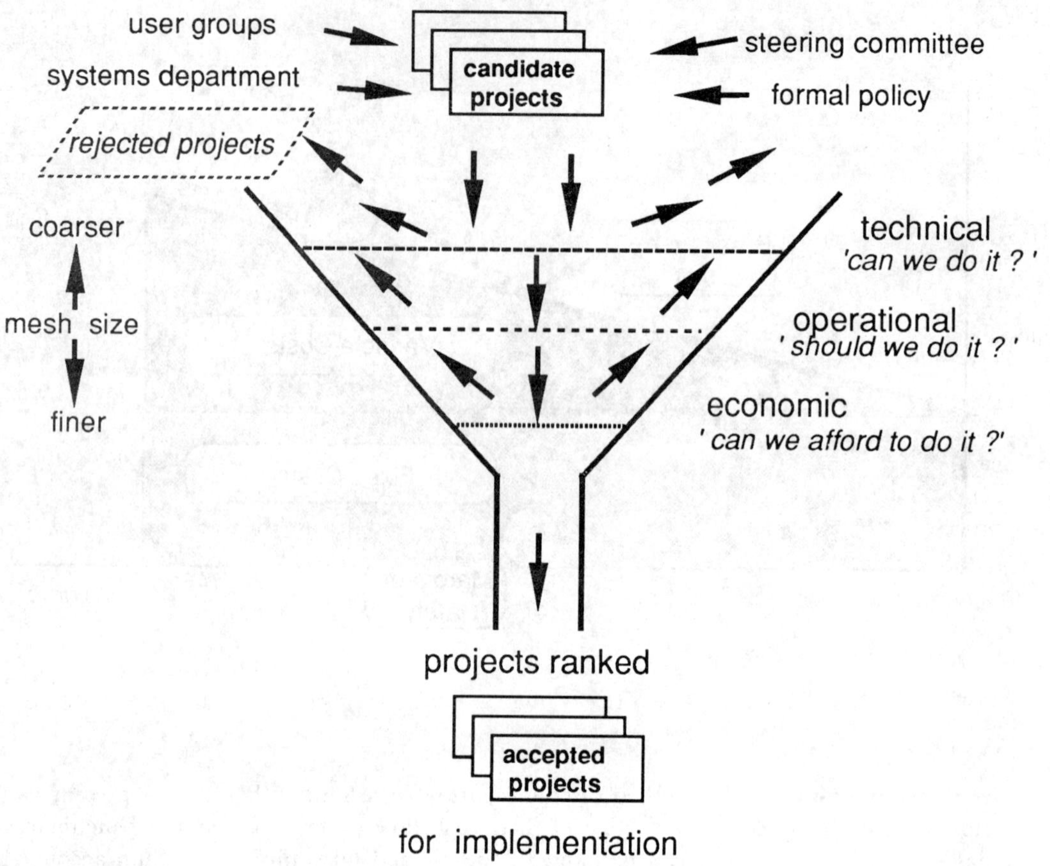

SUMMARY

The key points covered in this chapter are that:

1 The design process will always be strengthened by the addition of good user participation at all stages in the development life cycle.

2 At a strategic level, the organisation must identify its level of maturity in IT terms, and assess the criticality of each of the major process which the organisation undertakes, ie the organisation will determine the extent to which it is dependent upon automated systems and the desirability of that dependence.

3 To get the best out of the information system, the organisation must properly plan the systems and data architecture, and make decisions as to whether to produce a centralised or decentralised system.

4 The systems development life cycle is normally broken down into the following stages: feasibility, systems analysis, systems design, implementation, and review and maintenance.

5 Care must be taken to select the automation projects which will most effectively promote the organisation's objectives at a cost which is economically justifiable.

6 The standard method applied to the selection of projects is cost-benefit analysis. This relies upon identifying all the benefits, both tangible and intangible, and weighing them against the costs (which include the cost of not automating). The standard techniques are breakeven analysis, payback period and net present value.

QUESTIONS *Solutions to questions of an examination standard start on p 395*

Write brief notes on the following:

(a) stages of growth in the automation of an organisation;
(b) centralisation and power structures;
(c) technical, operational and economic feasibility studies;
(d) detailed fact-finding techniques;
(e) implementation strategies.

Questions of an examination standard

1 One of the differences between a traditional systems methodology and one which adopts the total system approach is the placement of the project selection process.

Discuss the arguments for and against the early or late placement of the project selection process in the systems life cycle.

2 A systems project is regarded as having economic feasibility when its benefits exceed its costs.

List and briefly describe the types of benefit and types of cost which may accrue from computerising a typical commercial application.

3 The economic evaluation of computer-based information systems depends on the selective application of investment appraisal techniques.

Briefly describe THREE such techniques which are commonly applied and discuss their advantages and disadvantages.

Chapter 7
System Design

CHAPTER OBJECTIVES

The primary objective of this chapter is to introduce the detail of the system design methodologies, and to address some of the key issues of file and database design. The detailed objectives are to:

1. consider the primary methodologies for system development as being process-driven, data-driven and user-driven;
2. examine the more modern structured school of methodologies which include the process-driven and the data-driven;
3. explore the varieties of file structure and consider which factors control the choice of file organisation;
4. understand the nature of the database and its possible advantages to the modern organisation;
5. consider the difference between logical and physical concepts in constructing a model of an organisation's information needs.

7.1 DESIGN METHODOLOGIES

The NCC and other similarly idealised versions of the life cycle provided a general framework within which systems designers could use procedures, rules and guidelines more effectively. This, in turn, developed into sets of guidelines and standards for systems development which are now termed **methodologies**. A methodology consists of an underlying framework based on a particular approach or philosophy. This theoretical framework will be applied by using a range of practical techniques supported by a set of tools which are contained within the methodology.

Ideally, a methodology should cover all phases of the life cycle but, inevitably, some methodologies are biased towards certain phases or may omit other phases altogether. As a generalisation, methodologies which concentrate on the first two phases identified by the NCC tend to be called **systems analysis** methodologies, while those focusing on phases three and four are often termed **software engineering** methodologies. The difference is mainly one of emphasis and approach. The choice of an appropriate methodology for an organisation has come to be associated with the degree of success experienced in previous software development projects. Those organisations with a need to develop large information systems have therefore developed or adopted a proven in-house methodology. Indeed, the development or adoption of a workable systems development methodology has become a major strategic decision in many organisations.

7.1.1 Categories of systems development

Broadly, the range of established systems development methodologies can be separated into three categories:

1. process-driven development,
2. data-driven development,
3. user-driven development based on **human activity systems (HAS)**.

PROCESS-DRIVEN DEVELOPMENT

This is the approach taken by a number of so-called traditional methodologies, of which the NCC approach described above is typical. The term **process-driven** refers to an emphasis on the

activities or functions which are carried out in the system. The philosophy behind such a methodology is that an improvement in the way things are done, eg by computerising a manual process, will produce a better, more efficient system. The techniques contained in such a methodology tend to concentrate on describing processes and their input-output flows in increasing levels of detail. This is called **functional decomposition** and should result in an understanding of every process at a level of detail sufficient to allow a computer program specification to be written for it.

Critics of the process-driven systems development point out that such techniques, used in isolation, can result in a system that concentrates on the routine, mechanistic activities of transaction processing at the operational level of the organisation. It has also been said that decomposition leads to piecemeal or fragmented systems development with a lack of **enhancement** by the new systems over the old ones.

FIGURE 7.1 **Process-driven system**

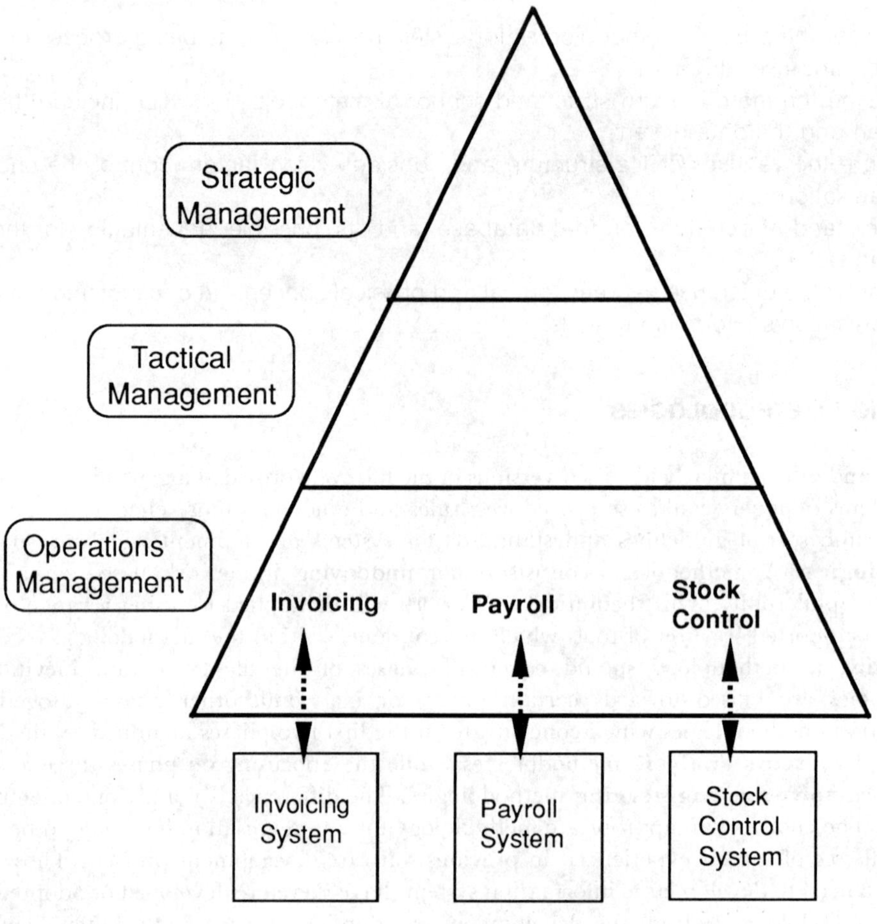

DATA-DRIVEN DEVELOPMENT

The proponents of data-driven development claim that to concentrate on modelling detailed activities or processes is bound to create an unstable system. It is argued that operational details will be more liable to frequent modification and, therefore, the system will be costly to maintain. This is because the methods by which business activities are carried out are transient and likely to change as the business itself changes.

The philosophy behind data-driven development is that the data which a system uses is more constant and will be consistent irrespective of how it is processed. A data model is therefore inherently more stable. The theory then states that a system which is developed by concentrating on the storage and manipulation of data will be more flexible and robust. At its heart, data-driven development is based on techniques that are intended to model the things which are most important to the system, ie:

1 **the entities** or things which are most important to the system,

2 **the attributes** or what the system needs to know about the entities, and
3 **the relationships** or the way in which the entities fit together to make up the system.

Such techniques are typified by the **Entity-Relationship Models (ERMs)** used in the **data analysis** approach developed by Chen in 1976, and used in a number of more modern methodologies.

Data-driven development is frequently associated with the development of large-scale database systems with a DBMS using a non-procedural query language. Information systems having these features are capable of addressing the needs of non-routine decision-making activity at tactical and strategic levels of business, through the use of *ad hoc* reports, DSSs and user-created models.

FIGURE 7.2 **Data-driven systems**

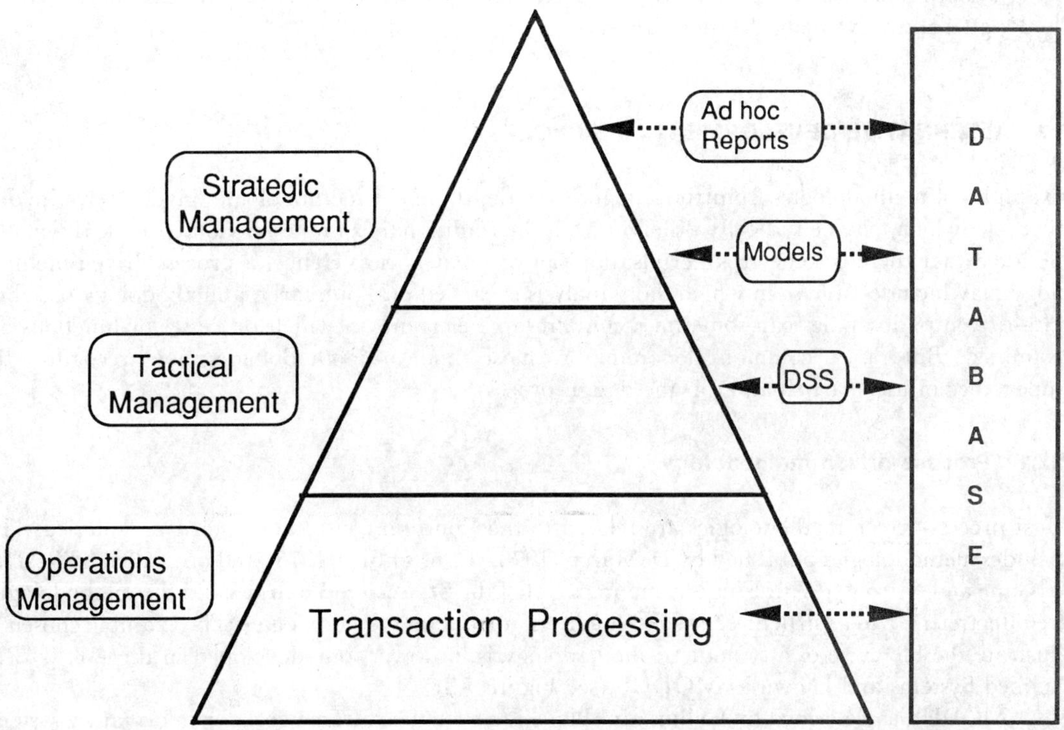

USER-DRIVEN DEVELOPMENT

User-driven development concentrates on the behavioural aspects of information systems design. Technical methodologies which are either process or data-driven, have the computer specialist, usually the systems analyst, as the development driver. The user supplies facts and may be involved quite closely with the project at some stages, but it is the analyst who makes most of the important systems decisions. User-driven systems development seeks to overcome apparent user dissatisfaction with technically developed systems by recognising the importance of user involvement and encouraging active participation in the analysis and design process.

The stress during a project is on the **system team** approach, with users and analysts working in equal partnership. The role of the analysts then becomes that of a technological facilitator, giving advice on a range of design possibilities. The decisions and choices are then made by the user. The philosophy behind such development is that systems only address the users' needs by incorporating those users into the development process. This approach is said to produce systems which are less technologically complex and less reliant on experts. Therefore, they are more likely to be well accepted, flexible and capable of being adapted to meet changing organisational needs.

The techniques employed in user-driven development are typified by **Soft Systems Methodology (SSM)** developed by Professor Peter Checkland which applies systems theory to address the type of fuzzy, poorly-structured or defined problems which are often met in systems analysis. It is argued that modelling processes on data is deceptively convenient, but to understand an organisation, the objectives, attitudes and perceptions of the stakeholders must be understood. This is difficult because of the non-linear unpredictability of human activity systems. SSM attempts to address this problem by using a pictorial representation of the system, called a **rich picture** and a textual description called a **root definition**. The aim is to construct a conceptual model of the system, identifying the users' ideas, problems and behaviour.

The design phase of a user-driven development project lends itself well to the use of prototyping techniques, where the user can employ 4GL tools to experimentally produce a system which has the appearance of a functioning system (screen dialogue, print outs, etc) without the internal functionality (file accesses, program executions, etc). Such a prototype may be produced in a fraction of the time a real system would take. When satisfactory to the user, the technologists add the necessary functions to make the system operational. An extension of the prototyping approach is **evolutionary systems development**, which attempts to recognise that systems change is inevitable (even desirable) and therefore should be exploited. The systems design phase is seen as being a continuous process. Effectively the system is never finished. Obviously the approach requires the long-term involvement of system users.

7.2 ALTERNATIVE DEVELOPMENT LIFE CYCLES

Examples of methodologies from the categories of development methodologies given above involve life cycles which may be radically different from the traditional example previously used. It will also be noted that there is some cross fertilisation between categories. Hence, a process-driven methodology may include a phase in which data analysis is carried out. Similarly, a methodology based on data-driven philosophies can sometimes contain large elements in which processes or functions are examined. But, as a common denominator, most modern methodologies now recognise the importance of user participation in the design process.

7.2.1 Process-driven methodology

Most process-driven methodologies are related to the Yourdon consultancy house in America. This includes methodologies published by DeMarco (1978), Constantine (1978) and one called STRADIS by Gane and Sarson (1979). This is sometimes called the **Structured School** and the methodologies are often referred to as structured systems analysis and design methodologies. The example chosen to illustrate the life cycle of a structured methodology is, however, one developed in the UK by BIS Applied Systems and known as MODUS (see Figure 7.3).

MODUS as described by Collins and Blaye is a structured framework for information systems planning, development and management. The methodology is conveniently broken down into six phases which are as follows:

1 **IS strategy creation**. A strategy for information systems development may already exist within an organisation, or it may be carried out specially as the start of a systems project. In any case, four categories of strategic planning are envisaged:
   (a) broad analysis of information needs in functional areas of the organisation,
   (b) outline of system type and processing facilities for the proposed new system,
   (c) identification of projects and of broad implementation plans, and
   (d) rough forecast of resource and manpower levels.

2 **Feasibility study** The first major project phase looks at the technical and economic feasibility of developing the information system(s) identified in Phase 1. The approach is to include the following steps:
   (a) broad identification of organisational objectives and performance targets, using **Key Performance Factor (KPF)** analysis,
   (b) identification of system requirements in terms of speed, controls and security,
   (c) generation of alternative outline systems which would meet the organisation's requirements,
   (d) selection of the system which best matches the technical framework, and is most feasible economically. Typical cost-benefit analysis tools, eg payback or net present value (NPV) would be used at this phase, and
   (e) recommendations to user management and the development of detailed plans.

3 **Systems analysis** The objective of this phase is to produce a detailed specification for the new system in organisational rather than technical terms. MODUS operates in three areas:
(a) Functional analysis using structured techniques (ie functional decomposition) to describe first the existing, and then the new system in increasing levels of detail. The tools used in this area are **activity diagrams** and **activity summaries**.
(b) Data analysis in which data items (eg purchase orders and stock items) are defined, and their relationships examined. MODUS allows the use of two alternative tools at this stage: **logical data association (LDA)** or **relational data analysis (RDA)**. The former is less detailed, while the latter is of particular use when a large-scale DBMS such as IDMS is planned. Both result in **data structures** for use in Phases 4 and 5.
(c) requirements analysis where the new system requirements are compared to the features offered by the existing system to indicate the need for change. The tool used for this is an **activity/target matrix (ATM)** which is based upon the the results of the KPF analysis.

4 **System design** The activity diagrams and data structures from the systems analysis phase are used to produce program specifications and file/database specifications. Tools used to do this include Structured English, decision tables and decision trees. Attendant documents produced at this stage will include output layouts, security requirements and back-up plans.

5 **Program development** Program development in MODUS follows a common pattern —design, coding and testing. The tools recommended are typically flowcharts and data structures as used in JSP (see 5.10.1). Testing at this stage is applied to individual programs or program modules.

6 **System testing** System testing is intended to prove the reliability of the whole system. MODUS recommends testing for processing accuracy, communications between systems, and security and recovery procedures. The final stage of testing is user acceptance testing under realistic operating conditions.

Not included as separate phases in MODUS, but implicit in the structured approach are reviews at important project milestones. The recommended review method is a **structured walkthrough**— a non-critical team review of progress during or after a phase. There is also provision for a post-audit review of both project success and system effectiveness. The most significant aspects of MODUS as a structured methodology are:

1 the placement of the feasibility study and chosen outline solution before the detailed fact-finding exercise;
2 the use of functional decomposition as a major analysis tool, concentrating on processes or activities at increasing levels of detail;
3 a comprehensive set of techniques, procedures and documentation standards. MODUS is less rigid than some structured methodologies in that some alternatives are allowed, for instance RDA or LDA; and
4 an intention to be applicable to a wide range of systems types and processing modes. The methodology includes a section on design for real-time systems.

Significantly, MODUS is available as a computer-aided systems engineering (CASE) tool in the form of BIS Applied System's IPSE (Integrated Project Support Environment). This computer-based system allows all the guidelines, techniques and document standards of MODUS to be accessed and used by a range of project staff. Their efforts are then integrated into the final systems specification.

7.2.2 Data-driven methodology

Just as the development of process-driven methodologies may be related to one school of thought, so the same names tend to appear throughout the complex and confusing evolution of data-orientated development methods. The two main types of data-driven methodologies are **Information Engineering** introduced by James Martin and Clive Finkelstein in 1981, and subsequently developed into several different versions by subsidiary companies throughout the world, and **Systems Development in a Shared Data Environment (D2S2)** developed by Ian Palmer and

FIGURE 7.3 **MODUS structured methodology phases**

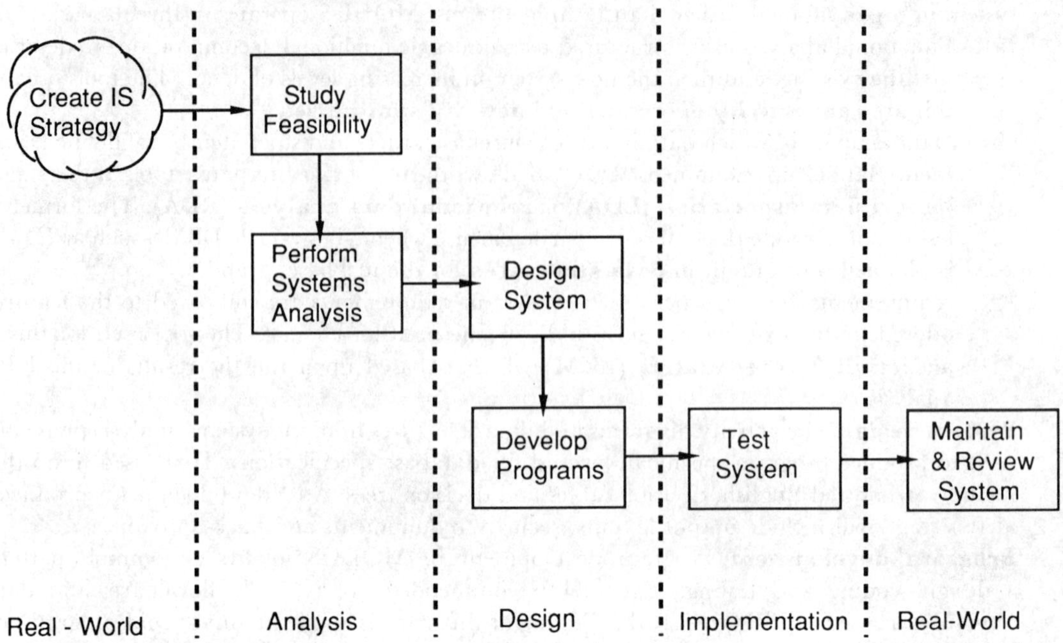

Rosemary Rock-Evans (1981) when working for the CACI consultancy company. Early versions were more simply termed the **CACI Methodology** and this title is still used by many people. Both Palmer and Rock-Evans later joined James Martin Associates to add many of their data analysis ideas to the Information Engineering Methodology. But the CACI Methodology is still used in its own right, and it is chosen as an example to illustrate data-driven methodology in the form as published in 1981, the form which, incidentally, is often used for relational database design.

CACI Methodology features five main phases which, unlike those in structured methodologies, may be undertaken concurrently rather than sequentially, or even in a different order (see Figure 7.4). The broad phases are as follows:

1 **Entity analysis** This phase concentrates on identifying the entities or things that are important to the organisation, the way in which those entities relate to one another, and the facts or attributes that are held about them. The resulting ERM provides both an understanding of the organisation's objectives and activities for planning purposes, and a basis for database design (for more details, see 8.1.4). The documents which are produced to support the model and to provide input to the data dictionary include Entity, Relationship and Attribute forms. In making this analysis it is important that the organisation is analysed and modelled as a whole rather than as separate functions or departments.

2 **Function analysis** This phase examines the processes or activities which occur within the system. These functions act upon or change the state of entities. The phase begins with the drawing of a **function hierarchy**—a functional decomposition chart resembling a MODUS Activity Summary in form. This identifies the make-up of tasks within the system, and is used as a test of completeness. The completed hierarchy can be used to identify common functions—those tasks that take place in different areas of the organisation, but that are basically identical in operation, eg looking up records, changing to the new day's date, etc. A hierarchy modified to take this into account is termed a **function network**. The common functions which are identified may then be eliminated during the implementation phase to reduce the overall amount of duplication.

The function hierarchy has no time or sequence precedence, so in order to record when functions take place and in what order, a set of **function dependency diagrams** is produced from the elementary or bottom level of the hierarchy. A functional dependency diagram is somewhat similar to a **data flow diagram (DFD)** in some other methodologies, except that events which trigger or mark the end of functions are included.

3 **Normalisation** This is a technique for structuring data into ordered groups such that

attributes occur with a minimum of repetition and that the correct relationships between sets of attributes exist. The result is a set of tables or **relations** that represents a refined ERM in that the data held is accurate and stable, permitting access by unique **keys**. The usual standard is normalisation to **third normal form (TNF)**, that is the re-organisation has gone through three stages of normalisation.

4 **Function logic description** This phase of the CACI Methodology serves to describe in detail the operation of all or part of the function dependency diagrams produced during function analysis. The descriptions are usually of actions which take place in relation to entity types, eg create, update, modify and delete. These actions are described in **Structured English**, **decision tables** or **decision trees**. A second exercise called **function logic quantification** examines the frequency with which such actions are likely to be taken in the implemented system (eg one thousand accesses of a given record per hour). This can form the material for a **sizing** operation to find out how powerful the hardware and software of the implemented system will need to be. Function logic description and quantification documents are used for program design, database design and the specification of manual procedures. They correspond to program specifications in other methodologies.

5 **Implementation strategy** The most significant difference between the CACI methodology and the traditional or structured methodologies is the placing of the implementation strategy (corresponding to a feasibility study) at a late stage of the development cycle. The rationale behind this late placement consists of two main points:

(a) Previous (older) methodologies stressed the technical aspects of feasibility studies to reject systems unsuitable for computerisation at an early stage, that is before an accumulation of development costs. Technical developments of late have reduced the importance of this factor as most applications have become amenable to automation.

(b) It is held to be unwise to decide implementation issues (that is, what is to be computerised and how) before a sufficient amount of detail is known about the data and functions used and performed in the existing system. Later decisions are felt to be better decisions.

The implementation issues which are addressed in the CACI Methodology involve decisions being made based on technical, operational and economic criteria, on the drawing up of two system boundaries as follows:

1 The **domain of change** contains sets of functions which are carried out differently, but not necessarily through the use of a computer. The reasons for not changing a manual function might be that its current method is satisfactory or that political reasons for not changing it exist (eg trade union agreements).

2 The **boundary of automation** exists within the domain of change and contains sets of functions which are to be computerised.

Both of these systems boundaries can be physically drawn or mapped on to a collection of all the function dependency diagrams for the whole system. The entity types within the boundary of automation are then mapped on to application files or tables in a database, and their attributes written to the data dictionary which may contain specifications for data validation, security and audit.

FIGURE 7.4 **CACI data analysis methodology**

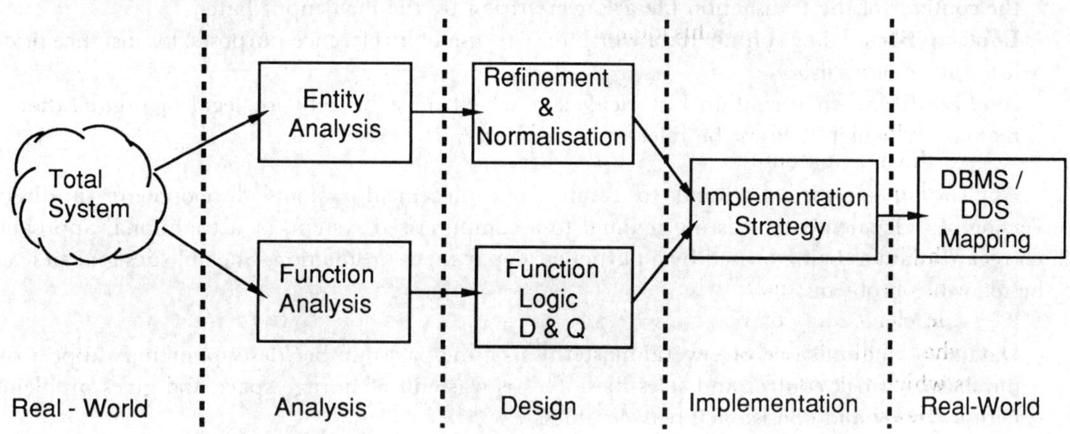

As well as the development of large-scale software and database projects, the CACI Methodology has been used in situations such as the following:

(a) business analysis, policy study and strategy planning,
(b) computer package evaluation based on a comparison between the business entities and functions and those supported by the package,
(c) establishing security and audit procedures by analysis of the data model, and
(d) organisation and method studies.

What makes data analysis so universal is that it takes the **total system** approach, and so produces a multipurpose model of the whole organisation.

7.3 FILE/DATABASE DESIGN ISSUES

Any computerisation project will involve the specification and design of data storage. The choice of storage media (disk or tape) is of less importance than the way the stored data is to be organised and structured. The two storage design issues are whether to use application specific files or a database.

7.3.1 Application specific files

The traditional method of storing computerised data on large-scale systems, and the most common storage method for microcomputer systems is on application specific files. These are files (on any media) in which records are grouped according to a common purpose or dedicated to a single application. There will therefore tend to be a set of files dedicated to each of the major functions of business, for instance:

(a) **sales files**, usually a customer file and a sales order file;
(b) **purchase files**, often consisting of a supplier file and a purchase order file;
(c) **accounts files**, equivalent to the sales ledger, purchase ledger and general ledger; and
(d) **stock file** also containing product details.

File security is maintained by the fact that these files are read from and updated by specific programs, to which access is limited, usually by a password, the programs being in a user account or accessible area.

There are four types of file which are commonly used for storage and data manipulation in an application specific environment:

1 **Masterfiles**—they contain permanent data for use in an application such as sales, purchasing or accounts. Some of the fields on such files will contain virtually static data (eg name and address) or data subject to update (eg sales to date, account balance, etc). The latter will be updated either directly (on-line) or from a transaction file.
2 **Transaction files**—they contain temporary records of values and amounts input from a batch of source documents such as invoices or customer orders. After updating the masterfile(s), the contents of the transaction file are overwritten by the next input batch.
3 **Look-up files**—they contain data which may be used for reference purposes, for instance price lists and mailing lists.
4 **Archive files**—they contain historical data which must be kept for legal or organisational reasons but which will not be referred to regularly.

Application specific files tend to result from piecemeal systems development—a direct conversion of a department's existing manual to a computerised system, or a traditional approach which regards data as being owned by a particular department or function. Such file design can lead to the following problems:

1 Data may be duplicated on several masterfiles, eg the part number/description may appear on purchasing, stock control and sales files. This is wasteful of storage space and gives problems with integrity and consistency between files.

2 Other applications may be allowed intermittent access to a department's specific file, therefore avoiding duplication of processing or manipulation, but this can involve clashes when accesses are tried and lead to increasingly sluggish response times.

3 Different applications may have different access or processing requirements, which may not be compatible. For instance, an invoicing program may access a stock file in sequential batch mode overnight, and a stock control program may access the same file on-line. The two types of application would suggest different types of storage media and organisation. Care must be taken because a choice of the wrong medium may lead to an inferior performance in one of the applications.

A system which is completely application specific will appear to be a number of piecemeal systems, each having its own programs and files, which are owned by a single group of users. There will also tend to be massive duplication of data holdings, and problems with data integrity and consistency between files as the data changes due to processing.

FIGURE 7.5 **Systems using fully application specific files**

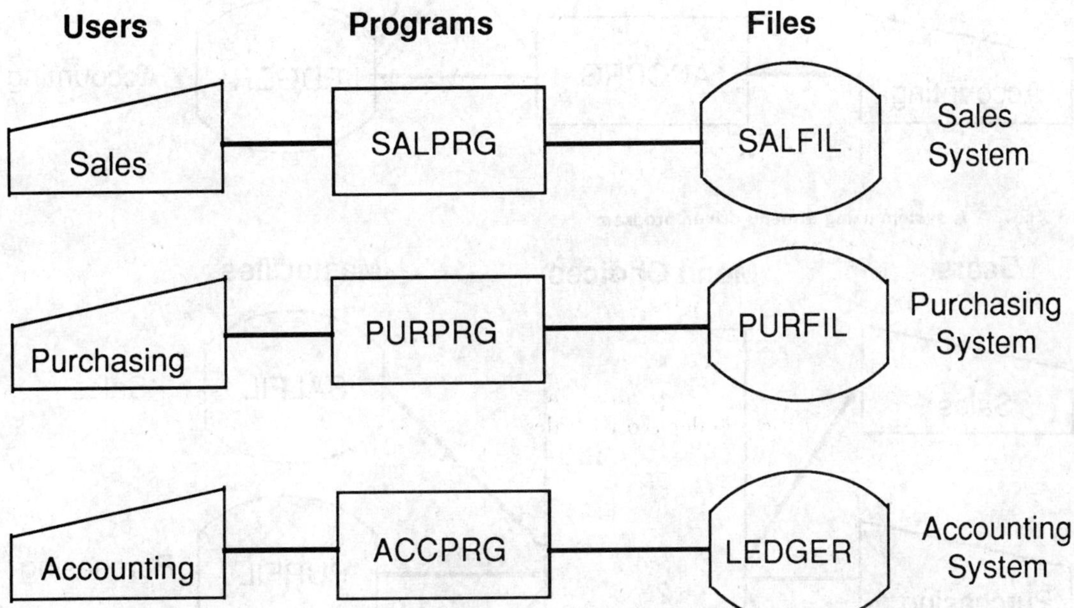

Early computer-based systems were completely application specific. A more modern approach which overcomes many of the problems indicated above is to use a common or integrated file system. Such a system uses files which are capable of being accessed from a number of programs.

From a situation where different application-specific programs access common files (see Figure 7.6), it was a relatively small step to integrate the programs themselves. An example of this integration is in the menu-driven program (see Figure 7.7), within which the user can specify a number of separate functions without leaving a program. Access to menu items will be restricted, usually by password priority. The higher the priority, the more menu choices may be accessed.

7.3.2 File organisation

The way a file is organised (that is its structure and layout) must relate directly to the way in which it is to be accessed, and the processes that will be applied to its contents. File processing activities requiring access may be summarised as follows:

1 **Writing** to a file implies adding new information, such as setting up a new customer record on an existing sales masterfile.

2 **Reading** a record or a whole file involves making an access to examine the record and, possibly, copying the record to main memory without making any alteration to the record. This

FIGURE 7.6 **A system using common masterfiles**

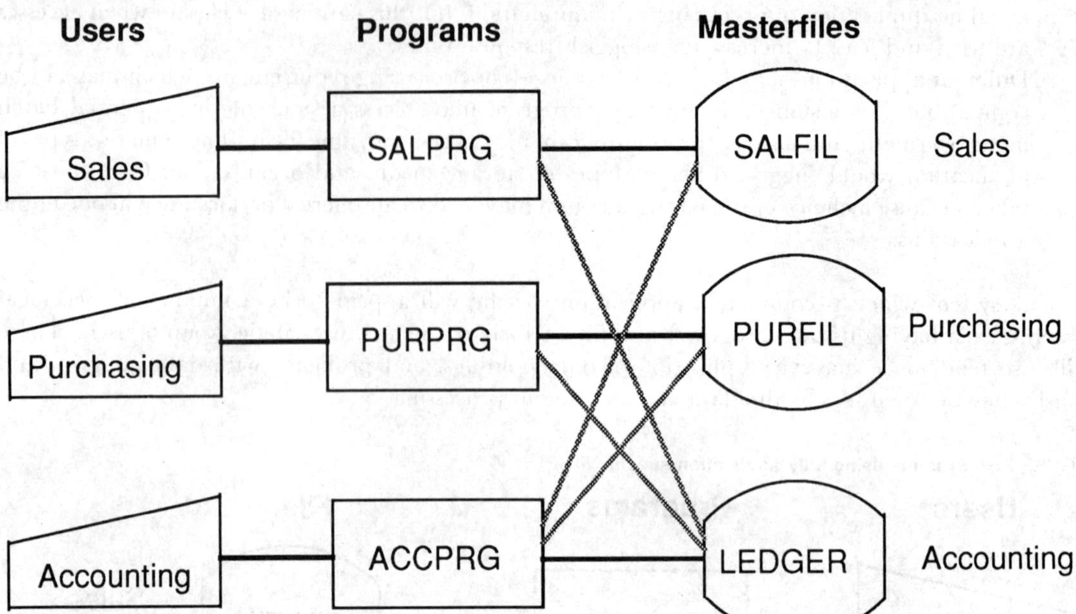

FIGURE 7.7 **A system using a menu-driven program**

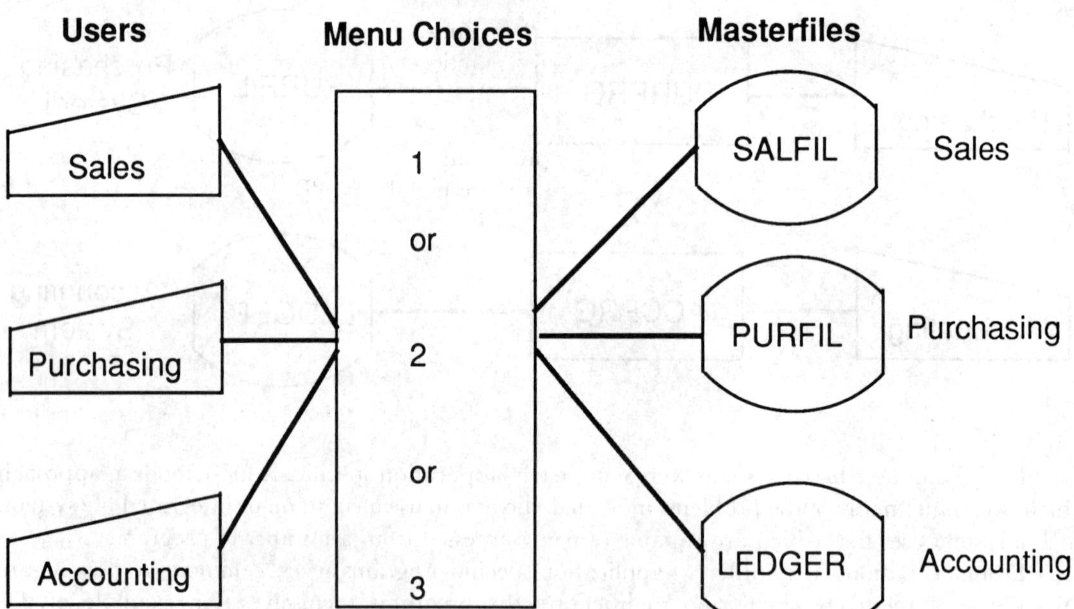

will occur in the case of a stock masterfile being checked for current stock balances during a production scheduling meeting.

3 **Updating** involves destroying an existing, out-of-date record by overwriting it with newer data. A common example is the updating which occurs during a ledger posting run. This will alter selected individual records. All the records on a look-up file, for instance a price list, may be updated in one operation.

4 **Deleting** a record involves removing it from the file. This might be required when a stock line is declared redundant.

Look-up file updates and deletions from masterfiles are usually part of the general process of file maintenance, and they are often carried out by the DP operations staff. Often the files involved will be subject to reorganisation, ie records will be closed up or sorted to a different order.

Other factors which will affect the choice of file organisation are concerned with the file's physical characteristics, such as:

1 **contents** and the order in which they are held, such as alphabetic, numeric or random order;
2 the **use** to which the file will be put, for instance a permanent masterfile or temporary workfile;
3 the **size** of the file, for instance the number of customer records which the file may be expected to contain;
4 the predicted level of file **volatility** which is the percentage of the file represented by records written or deleted during an average processing run,
5 the target **hit rate** which is the average percentage of records it is expected to access for any purpose during a run.

The processing and physical characteristics noted above will tend to dictate a choice of one from four basic types of file organisation: serial, sequential, indexed sequential and random.

SERIAL FILES

Serial files have the simplest organisation of all; a new record is written to the end of the file. No record is kept of the record's location, so as more new records are written to the file, each record is effectively 'lost'. To access a record for a read or update operation, it is necessary to begin at the first record stored in the file. This is known as the **header**. Each record is then read in turn until the required record is found. When searching for all records having a certain characteristic, eg orders above a certain value, a search will be continued until the **end-of-file (EOF)** marker is reached. It is then assumed that all the relevant records have been identified.

Such processing constraints make serial files impractically slow for use as masterfiles or look-up files in DP and MIS systems. However, temporary transaction files and input or output spool files are usually in serial form. Records on such files may be in random order, eg orders on a transaction file, or in the order of some other file, eg as on a spool file of overdue purchase orders taken from a supplier masterfile. Where it is impossible to carry out processing on a serial file, a sort routine using a program and sort file(s) will put the records into a more useful and efficient order.

SEQUENTIAL FILES

Such files contain records in ascending or descending order of some alphabetic or numeric key, eg by customer name or account number. Sequential files may be stored on tape or disk. Tape storage involves slower access and more processing operations (a sequential file must be completely copied every time it is updated, as when a masterfile is merged with a daily transaction file). This means that such files are now restricted to large-scale batch processing environments where space efficiency is more important than speed.

Disk sequential files allow individual records to be updated or deleted and are therefore quicker in operation, but occupy much more space. Such spare space must be designed into a disk sequential file by taking into account such factors as the frequency of record creation and deletion (file volatility) and the expected growth rate, eg the number of new customers expected in a year. A file designer might aim for 50% file occupancy in a customer masterfile in a growing company. This should be taken into account when making decisions on the system size.

INDEXED SEQUENTIAL FILES

These files are sequentially organised, but use a separate, smaller version of the file containing only the keys for the main file records and their location or **address**. This index is referred to before a record search is made, and it is usually small enough to be stored in main memory for fast access. This may be achieved with a very large-scale file by using a partial index called a **bucket** in which the keys to the records at the beginning and at the end of a section of the file are stored. Once the relevant bucket is found by performing a standard search operation on the index, a sequential search of the bucket will find the required record. This is known as **bracketing**.

Access may be gained to the indexed sequential **mass storage** systems by using a **multilevel index**. Such systems hold a highest level master index in main memory, which refers to sub-indexes held in backing storage. These sub-indexes at the file level refer in turn to bucket level. Each of these sub-indexes can be transferred temporarily into main memory as its level is searched. The calculation of the break-even point between the extra time taken to search in backing storage for each index level and the quantity of records which must be searched when the number of indexes is kept low is a technical matter for the file designer. It may be noted that a decrease in the cost of backing storage is being matched by an increase in main memory size as hardware development progresses.

A major problem with sequential and indexed sequential files is the need to cater for **overflow**, ie records which do not fit into the spare space which is designed into the file. These records are placed in a separate overflow area of the file. Standard routines have been developed to store and access these records in a way which is transparent to the program—usually as a utility of the operating system. The two main procedures are **ISAM (indexed sequential access method)** and **VSAM (virtual storage access method)**. ISAM tends to operate more efficiently in terms of storage, whereas VSAM provides quicker access to overflow records. As ISAM leads to overflow chains which may pose file organisation problems, VSAM is generally used for very large or highly volatile indexed sequential files.

RANDOM FILES

Random file use caters for files where single records need to be accessed at random, such as customer records in an on-line sales-order entry system. Files with a random organisation use direct access methods which will locate a specific record without having to read any other records on the file. This is carried out by applying a **transformation rule** or addressing algorithm to the record key to produce the storage address. As with access methods, these procedures are standardised (the commonest uses a **hashing** function).

7.3.3 Choice of file organisation

The choice of organisation, leaving aside other technical design factors, should be based on the system type and purpose. For example, an on-line enquiry system or stock control system needing frequent, rapid direct access to individual records within large files will best be served by a random file using a hashing function for access. Extremely large off-line files may be held most cheaply on magnetic tape, a medium which will not support random organisation. An indexed sequential file may be used in this case, eg with archived files, but there will usually be a break point below which a disk medium, using some other type of organisation, will be more economical.

As a generalisation, the transaction and temporary files in most installations will use a serial organisation, while large files involving off-line batch processing such as invoice files, will tend to be indexed in sequential organisation with ISAM or VSAM. Most files which require direct access, or which are subject to unpredictable on-line processing, will use random files. Most general purpose systems and MISs therefore use random files. Other factors such as file size and transformation methods are for the technical file designer.

7.4 DATABASE IMPLICATIONS

Since piecemeal systems development and fully application specific files were the order of the day, the DP and MIS environment has changed radically. Two major changes that have affected file design are the trend towards on-line systems and the development of database systems.

1 **On-line systems** require quick response times and necessitate a high degree of security and data integrity. The database approach implies that data items may be accessed in a number of different ways by different users. To this extent, the database approach goes beyond the use of commonly accessed masterfiles. The major difference is in the way the data is regarded. The database approach implies that information (and therefore data) is regarded by the organisation as a corporate resource. The analogy which is sometimes applied is that information is something like finance. It is used by many different people for different purposes, but it is owned and controlled by the organisation as a whole. In spite of this centralised control of the database, the use of the data is devolved. Individual departments may be responsible for

providing, and in some cases, maintaining the accuracy of the data, but access to the database will be more free and flexible in the user's terms.

2 **A database** is a collection of data organised in such a way that it can be regarded as a single unit. Important aspects of database use include the following:

(a) **Data independence** means that the item of data is stored for its own sake, and not for any specific use. An employee record, for instance, may be needed for production control, payroll and health and safety purposes. These purposes may be specific, but the use of the data is generalised and not optimised for one particular purpose at the expense of others.

(b) **Controlled redundancy** implies that duplication of data within the database is kept to an acceptable level. The description of a stock item would therefore not appear separately on the purchasing, production and sales system files, nor would there be a need to access application files across system boundaries.

(c) **Data integrity** means that when the facts about a data item change, for instance a stock balance is increased, only one update needs to be made. The possibility of inaccuracies occurring between the same data item on different files is therefore eliminated.

(d) **Flexibility of use** of data is achieved by allowing the data to be accessed in many different ways. Generally, these can be categorised as routine accesses or *ad hoc* (one-off) queries.

All of these features are achieved by the use of a DBMS, a complex suite of software by which the database is maintained and controlled. Most database applications will use a proprietary DBMS package because the cost of producing such a system in-house with acceptable security provision would be prohibitive for most organisations. The features offered by a typical DBMS package may include:

1 **record control**, ie creating, amending and deleting records, the basic functions of file maintenance in a traditional system,

2 **access control** that allows the processing of a complete file, or the retrieval either of individual records by direct access or of all the required records by selective sequential searching, and

3 **security control** which protects against unauthorised access and data corruption, and provides recovery and restart mechanisms after processing interruptions.

The implications of the use of a DBMS are that while security and control of data are centrally maintained, the use of the data is made more flexible, with the facility to enable user-determined access by query languages, etc, as well as the routine applications programs, such as batch run programs in a language such as COBOL.

FIGURE 7.8 **Use of a DBMS**

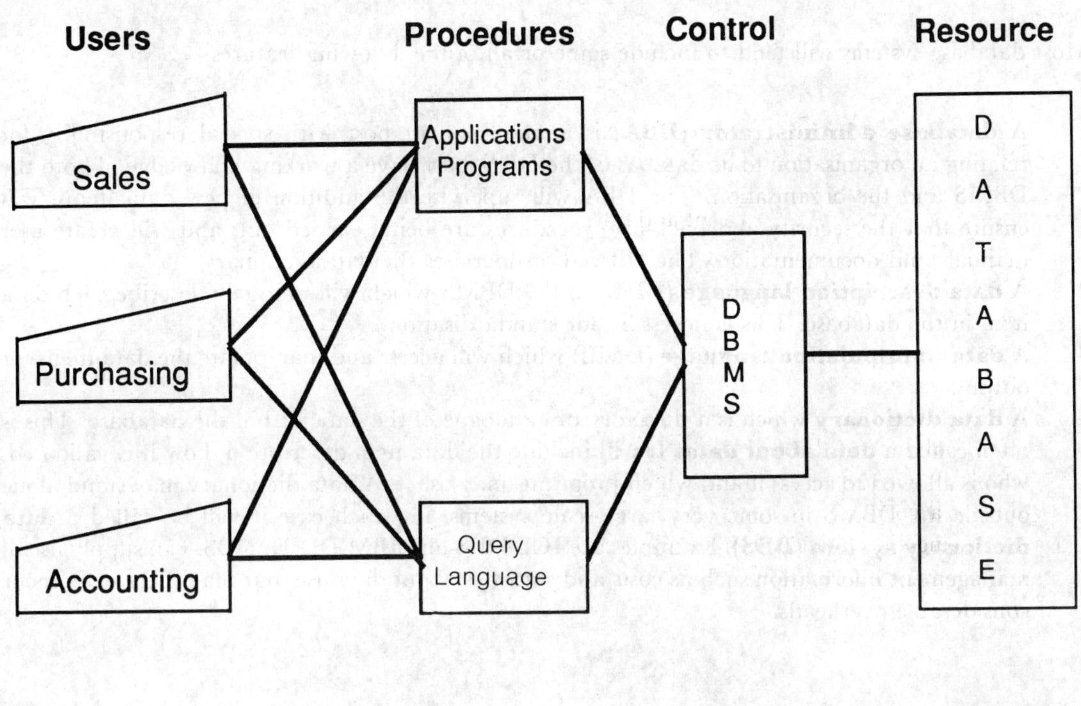

7.4.1 Advantages of a database

Experience of large-scale database use in a variety of organisations during the 1970s pointed out operational problems in the following areas:

1. Systems development projects in a complex environment were difficult to implement. Later systems methodologies, particularly those based on data analysis techniques, were introduced to help overcome this problem.
2. The performance of such systems often proved disappointing as the technology was new and not well understood.
3. High overheads, particularly fixed costs, were needed to support the database environment. The nature of a database implies large backing storage, much of it used relatively infrequently, and expensive security, back-up and recovery procedures due to the increasing dependence of most organisations on their database(s).

In general, technological development and experience have mitigated these problems. The advantages which DBMS suppliers now claim for the user include the following:

1. The view which is achievable through the use of the database reflects the corporate view which managers take of their organisation. This view takes in data from a number of divisions, departments and sections. This enables the use of expert systems and DSSs to augment the query languages in supplying the strategic decision-making needs.
2. Improved standards due to improved data integrity and better system project implementation. This is afforded by the ability to impose procedures and standards more easily in a single-project environment rather than in several piecemeal projects.
3. Faster system development due to the fact that, as organisations grow, more and more functions tend to be subject to computerisation. If the database is set up at an early stage in a series of system projects, subsequent work may concentrate on computerising tasks and functions as the developer is assured that the data is already available.
4. Migration from one technology to another is easier as the database is isolated from the applications (ie is application independent). This means that changes in the hardware or operating system will not cause major re-analysis and reprogramming as would be the case with changing a system with application-specific files from, say, COBOL to Pascal.

7.4.2 Features of a DBMS

Most database systems will tend to include some or all of the following features:

1. A **database administrator (DBA)** is a management post with special responsibility for relating an organisation to its database. The DBA must have a working knowledge of both the DBMS and the organisation. The DBA will supervise the addition of new data items, will ensure that the security and back-up procedures are being carried out, and will create user manuals and documentation. The DBA also supervises the data dictionary.
2. A **data description language (DDL)** in the DBMS which will uniquely describe each data item in the database. This is necessary for standardisation.
3. A **data manipulation language (DML)** which will access and manipulate the data items for output.
4. A **data dictionary** which is a directory or catalogue of the data within the database. This is often called a **data about data**. It will include the data item description, how it is validated, who is allowed to access it and which programs may use it. A data dictionary may stand alone outside the DBMS in some very large-scale systems, in which case it will be called a **data dictionary system (DDS)**. Examples are ICL DDS and IBM DD/D. DDSs can supply useful management information such as costs and statistics about data use, but may themselves incur considerable overheads.

7.4.3 Logical and physical concepts

The development of a database begins with an analysis of the organisation's data needs. The resulting model—the diagrams and documents output from the systems analysis exercise—describes a part of the real world in terms of its data. This is called the **conceptual schema**. Individual user views of parts of this model are called **external schemas**. For instance, the accountants within an organisation will have one external schema, the sales force another, etc. This model is independent of any particular DBMS software and will only change if the data uses of the organisation change.

The conceptual schema must be converted to or mapped on to another model which satisfies the constraints of the DBMS which is to be used for the implementation. This is called the **logical schema** since it represents the logic with which the database is constructed. This is termed the database logical data model, and there are three in current use, ie hierarchical, network and relational:

1 The **hierarchical** model logically links data items by a parent-child relationship which may extend to various levels or generations. An example would be IBM's Information Management System (IMS).

FIGURE 7.9 **Simple hierarchical database model**

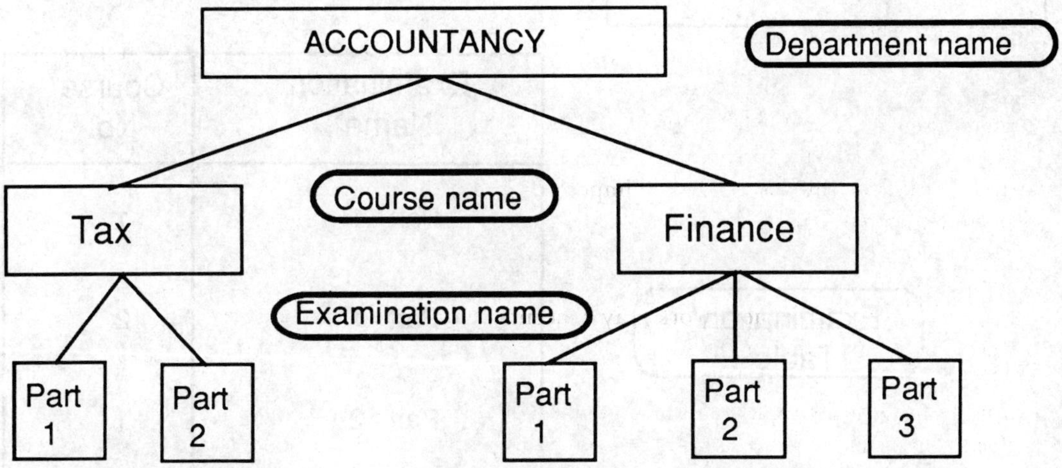

2 The **network** model logically allows a child record to belong to a number of parents. The logical structure will be less complicated than that for an hierarchical model, but the records may require a more detailed description (to associate them with a particular parent).

FIGURE 7.10 **Simple network database model**

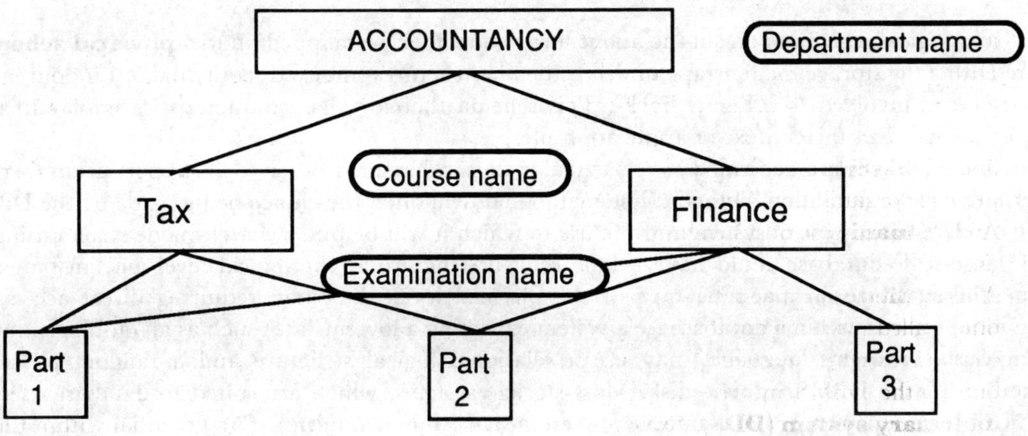

3 The **relational** model operates within a completely different logical concept from the previous two models. The data items are gathered into tables called **relations**. There is no formal structure of links between data items. Database operations are carried out by combining tables in various ways. These ways are explored during the data analysis phase of the systems project, and are carried out by the DML. An example of a relational database would be INGRES which was designed for the Unix operating system.

FIGURE 7.11 **Simple relational database model**

Course Table

Course No.	Course Name
1	Tax
2	Finance

Examination Table

Examination Name	Course No.
Part 1	1
Part 1	2
Part 2	1
Part 2	2
Part 3	2

The logical schema in one of the above forms must then be mapped on to a **physical schema** representing the storage media (tape or disk), the file structures (indexed sequential or random) and the processes involved (see Figure 7.12). This schema therefore has characteristics similar to the factors discussed in the context of application files.

Some DBMSs are dedicated to a particular physical system, others will support a number of alternative file organisation methods. The method chosen, often the choice being made by the DBA, should relate to the type of system and the use to which it will be put. A batch-mode system using a very large-scale database could have a hierarchical structure at the logical level and an indexed sequential structure on magnetic tape at the physical level. A system requiring direct access to individual records within a database (ie a system expecting a low hit rate) such as an on-line enquiry service using a query language, may use a relational logical structure and a random physical structure, obviously on magnetic disk. Mass storage systems, which are suited to database use by virtue of their capacity, are not suitable for responsive on-line enquiries. The potential within these applications for the use of high-capacity laser-disk storage would seem to be enormous, as the technical problems of applying normal file processes to this medium are being overcome.

FIGURE 7.12 **Schematic view of a database system**

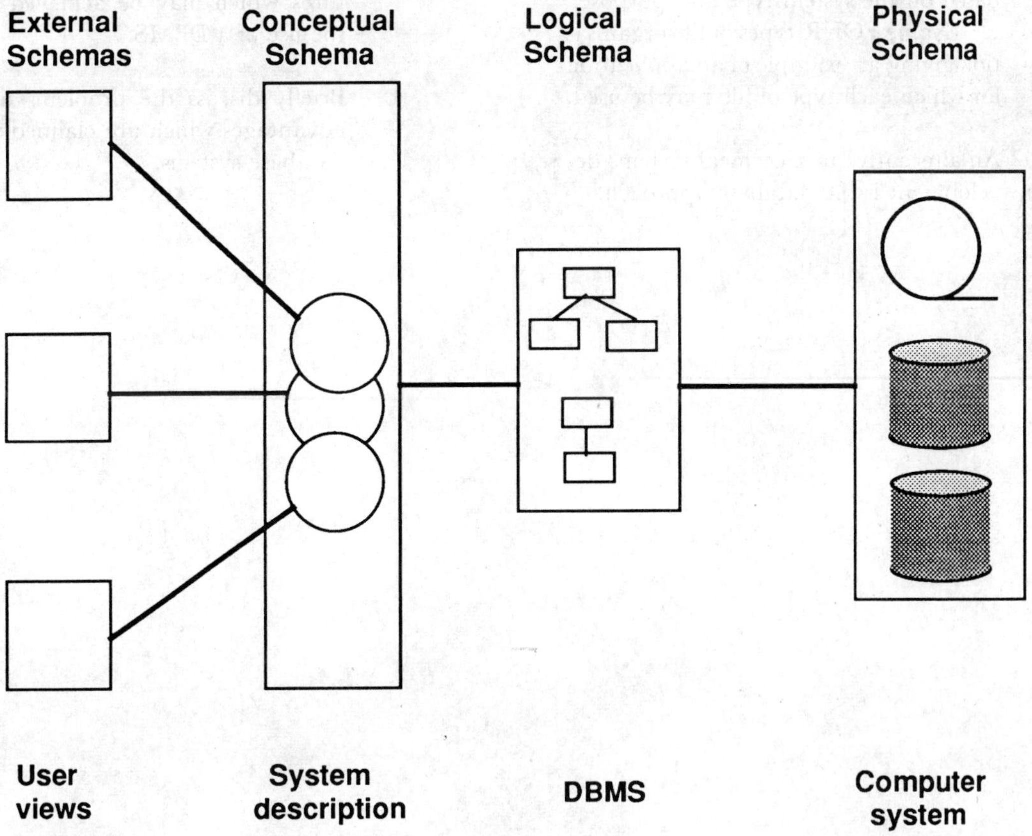

SUMMARY

The key points covered in this chapter are that:

1 The development methodologies are an attempt to scientifically model the things most important to the systems which the organisation comprises, and to show the relationships between each of those things.

2 This modelling is likely to be most informative when there is a high degree of user participation.

3 The more refined the methodology, the more likely it is to become structured in the sense that it identifies separate steps and places them in a coherent framework. The focus of the methodology may be on the processes and activities of the organisation, or be information engineering, ie data-driven.

4 Files may be application specific but care should be taken to avoid piecemeal development, ie to develop software as a part of a properly developed information strategy, and not simply to convert each department's manual system into an automated system.

5 Database systems may help an organisation to centralise its data resources, thereby gaining significant advantages in achieving a strategic view of the organisation's activities and improving standards of data integrity.

QUESTIONS *Solutions to questions of an examination standard start on p 395*

Write brief notes on the following:

(a) user-driven development;
(b) implementation strategy;
(c) entity analysis and function analysis;
(d) file processing activities;
(e) logical and physical concepts.

Questions of an examination standard

1 Process-driven and data-driven systems development methodologies each have their adherents.

Briefly discuss the philosophy behind the two types of development and give examples of both types.

2 The choice of file organisation should be based on the system type and purpose.
Name FOUR types of file organisation giving an example of an application for which each type of file may be used.

3 An alternative to piecemeal systems development is the database approach.

(a) Briefly list some important features which may be achieved by the use of a DBMS.

(b) Briefly discuss the problems and advantages which are claimed for database systems.

Chapter 8
Analysis and Design Tools and Techniques

CHAPTER OBJECTIVES

Having studied the theoretical framework within which design development is to take place, it is now necessary to examine the detail of the tools and techniques which are available to support the practicality of the exercise. In particular, this chapter will:

1 examine the basic tools used to capture the strategic intentions of the organisation and to enable the programmers to produce functional software;
2 review the design techniques employed to facilitate the interaction between the automated system and the users by producing quality output or friendly dialogue;
3 consider the primary procedure specification techniques (both graphical and narrative) to define the operations which the system must carry out; and
4 look more to the future and discuss the extent to which these detailed design and analysis processes can be automated.

8.1 TOOLS AND TECHNIQUES

The tools and techniques which are used by systems analysts have been developed over the years to assist in addressing two basic problems:

1 describing and summarising a mass of highly detailed information such as the results of a fact-finding interview or a set of instructions on how to write a computer program; and
2 communicating and documenting a description or a design to others who may have different skills or levels of knowledge, such as a user member of a project team or a systems analyst who may become involved in designing a replacement system in ten years' time.

Such tools may be said to make up a basic **toolkit** which has evolved through improvement in use. Many techniques have been refined as a result of their promotion by a leading authority. **Entity-Relationship Modelling (ERM)** by Chen, and **data normalisation** by Codd are examples of this. The result is that broadly similar tools appear in slightly different forms in many of the common systems development methodologies. But by examining the detailed content of each methodology, it is possible to categorise methodologies and their tools into traditional process-driven or data-driven. This arises because systems development tools generally fall into three categories of use:

1 Describing the **current physical system**, for instance the formal organisation, the flow of documents between departments and the things that people do to the documents. Examples of tools which are used in this area are the organisation chart and the **systems flowchart**. These are traditional tools and have been in use since systems analysis began.
2 Describing and/or designing the **logical system** whether for the existing system or for the one undergoing development. The logical system is the fundamental set of tasks that exist independently of the administrative conventions of an organisation. For instance, it does not matter whether credit checking is carried out by someone from the sales department or someone from credit control. The important things, if a converted system of limited scope is to be avoided, are the data and the processes which act upon it. A logical system is therefore a system

in its raw state. Examples of logical modelling tools are the **Data Flow Diagram (DFD)**, the ERM and the data dictionary.

3 Designing and describing the **new physical system** and forming the working drawings for the new system, the detailed specification, and the documentation which will describe the system's workings as it becomes invisible in use. This will cover the areas of program specification, data storage design and the human computer interface (HCI). Examples of tools used in these areas include Structured English, data normalisation and dialogue design. A modern variant of the latter is prototyping.

Some common examples of analysis and design tools are briefly considered in 8.1.1 to 8.1.7. Usually these are generic in nature. Where a similar tool is used in another form, for instance a diagram called by a different name in another methodology, this will be mentioned.

8.1.1 Systems flowchart

This is the traditional tool for recording document flows and operations, and where they take place. Figure 8.1 illustrates the NCC flowchart symbols and Figure 8.2 shows an example of their application in a course admission system.

The diagramming conventions are as follows:

1 the participants, whether as individuals or departments, are listed in columns along the top of the diagram;

2 the document flows should begin at the top left hand corner and move documents downwards and to the right. While this is difficult to achieve, input should generally be from the left and output to the right; and

FIGURE 8.1 **NCC systems flowchart symbols**

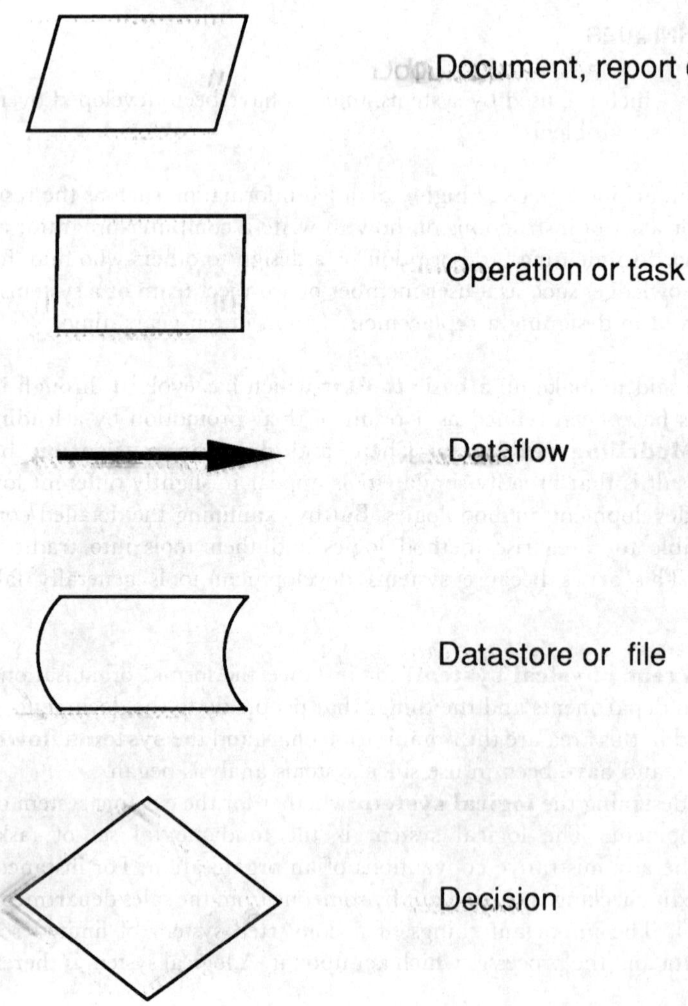

FIGURE 8.2 **Systems flowchart for admissions system**

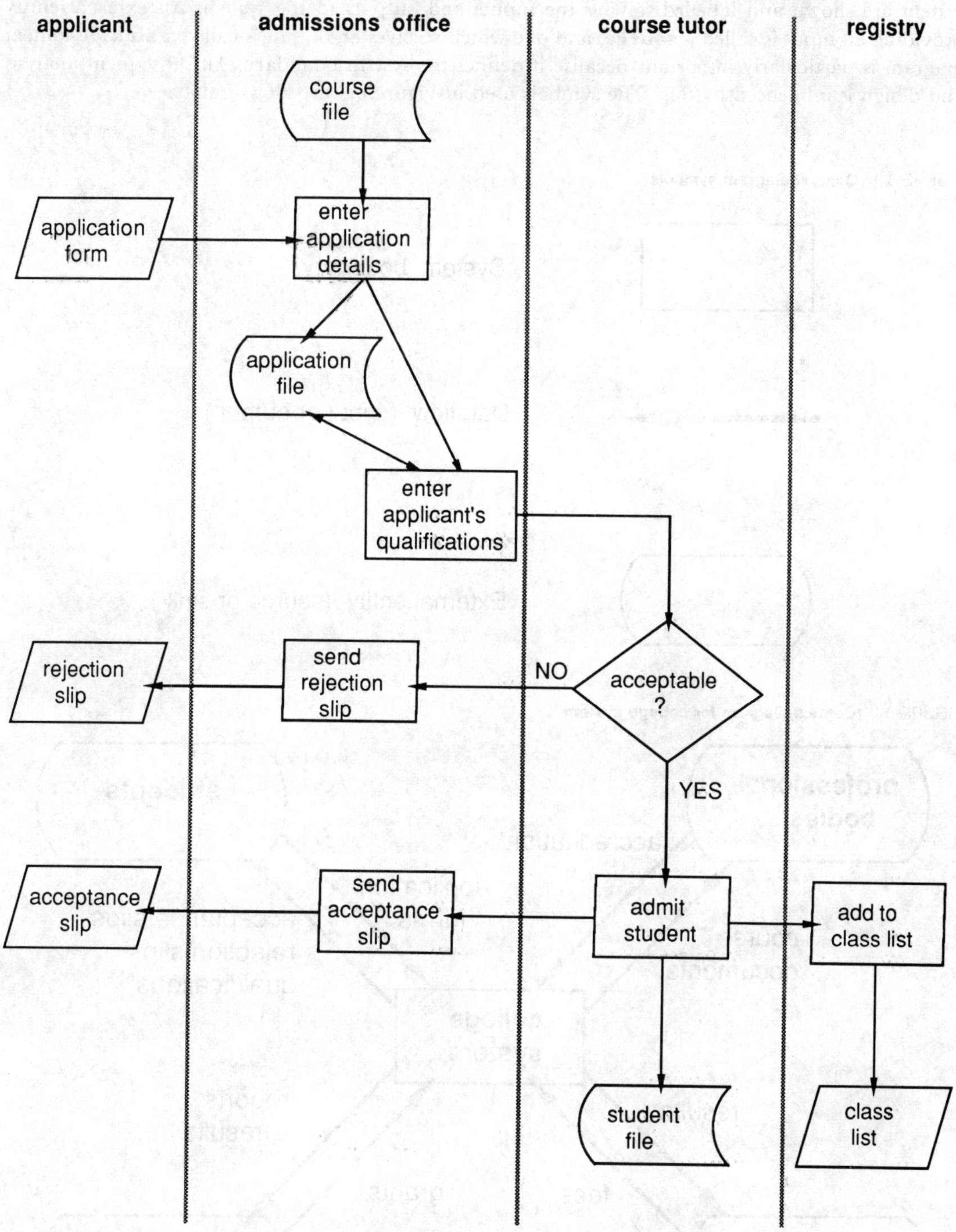

3 the direction of flow should be indicated by arrows.

Systems flowcharts have the advantage that they are intelligible to users and can be used to confirm the analyst's understanding of the users' current system. Problems such as duplicated operations and unproductive data storage may be noticed at this stage.

8.1.2 Context diagram

Several methodologies, particularly those of a structured nature which rely on decomposition, use a context diagram as an initial description of the logical system. BIS Applied System's MODUS is an example. The context diagram simply shows all the **external entities**, ie individuals or organisations outside the system with which it has dealings. The data flows between these entities and the system are shown and labelled, giving the inputs and outputs to the system. An external entity providing an input is called a **source**, and one which receives an output is called a **sink**. A context diagram is particularly important because it defines the system boundary. All subsequent analysis and design is influenced by this. The symbols used in Figure 8.3 are NCC influenced.

FIGURE 8.3 **Context diagram symbols**

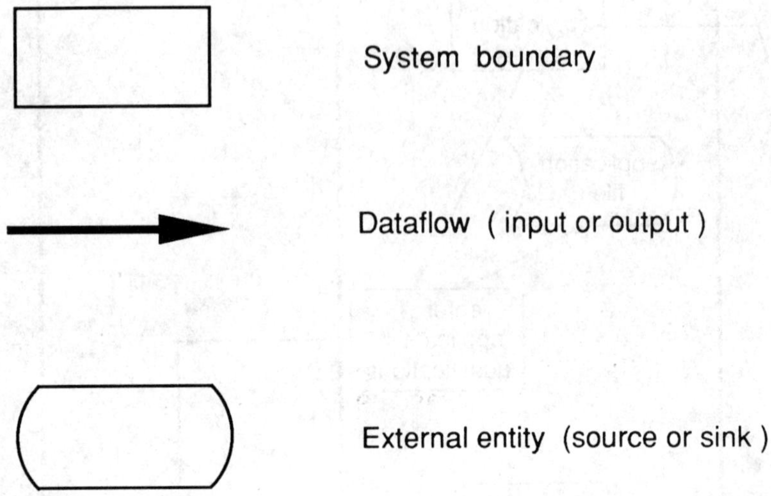

FIGURE 8.4 **Context diagram for college system**

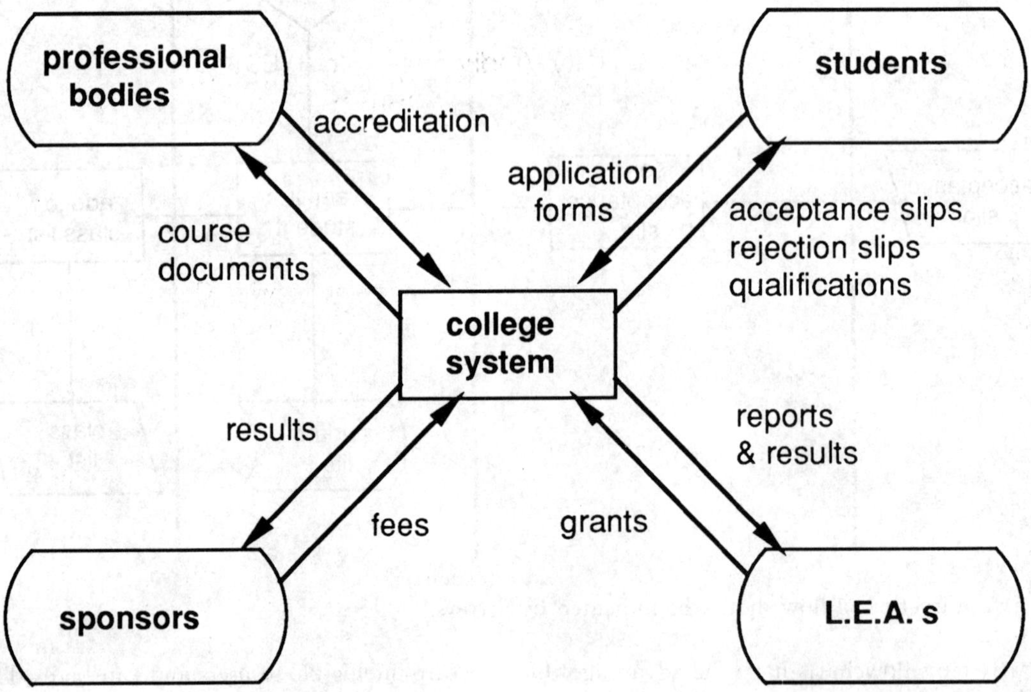

8.1.3 Data flow diagram (DFD)

DFDs form the basis of the decomposition techniques used in most structured methodologies. While the conventions and symbols used may vary between methodologies, the basic purpose is the same, ie to describe the logical flow of data between entities, processes and data stores. When used for decomposition (levelling or explosion) a DFD is done at a high level (level 0) which would be that after the context diagram stage. The next level (level 1) will be able to take one of the processes within the level 0 DFD and explode it, ie draw a DFD of its internal processes. Subsequent levels repeat this process until a level is reached at which the process can be described sufficiently accurately to write a computer program from the description. This is called **program specification** or **minispec**. BIS Applied System's MODUS uses **activity diagrams** which are very similar to DFDs. Figure 8.6 continues the theme of using NCC symbols see 8.6.

FIGURE 8.5 **Data flow diagram symbols**

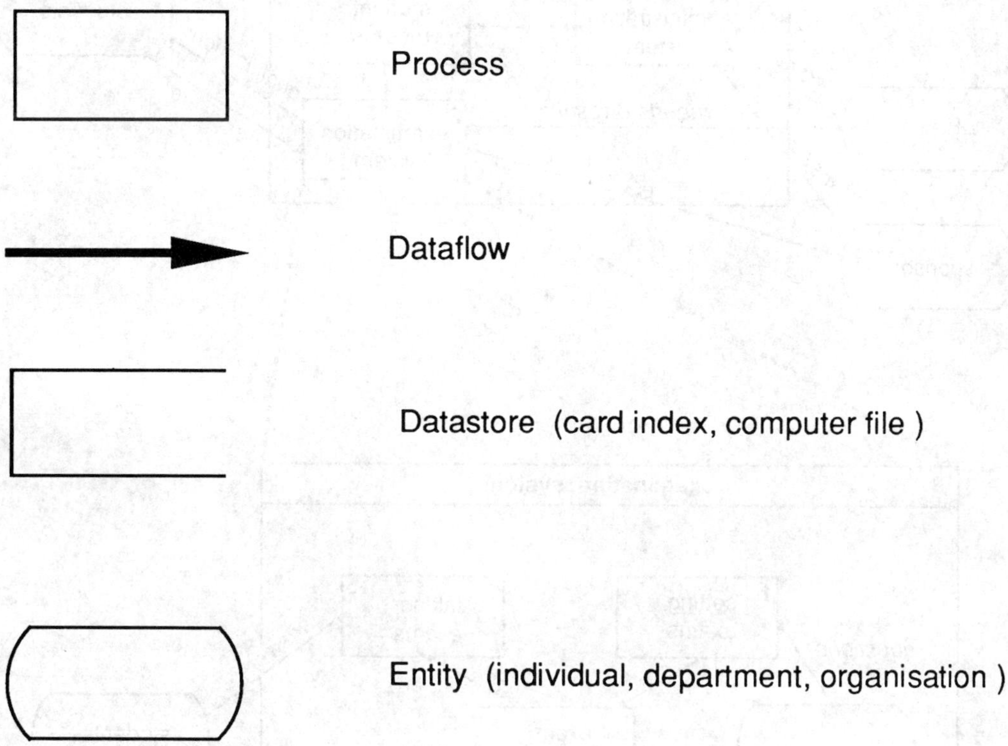

8.1.4 Entity-Relationship Models (ERM)

Entity-relationship modelling is the most important tool within the technique known as **data analysis**. This can be used as the mainstay of a methodology, as with CACI or information engineering (see 7.2.2), or as a support for a process-driven methodology such as SSADM. ERM uses three basic concepts:

1 **entity types** or things which are of importance to the organisation;
2 **attributes** which are facts or data about entities; and
3 **relationships** which are the logical links between entities, in the physical model, these will form the access paths between data items.

An entity type is a generic or classification term such as student. The individual, J Smith, is an entity occurrence which will need to be uniquely identified by one of its attributes called the **identifier** or key, eg customer account number. It is possible to describe the logical system in some detail, for instance the degree of a relationship between entity types may be of three orders as shown in Figure 8.7:

1 one-to-one (1:1) means that an entity occurrence relates to only one other entity occurrence as in the statement, 'student IS ON course';
2 one-to-many (1:n) means that an entity occurrence may relate to one or more occurrences as in the statement, 'course CONTAINS subject(s)' —this is the commonest degree of relationship; and
3 many-to-many (m:n) means that a number of entity occurrences may relate to one or more entity occurrences as in the statement, 'subject(s) HAVE lecturer(s)'.

FIGURE 8.6 **Data flow diagrams at successive levels**

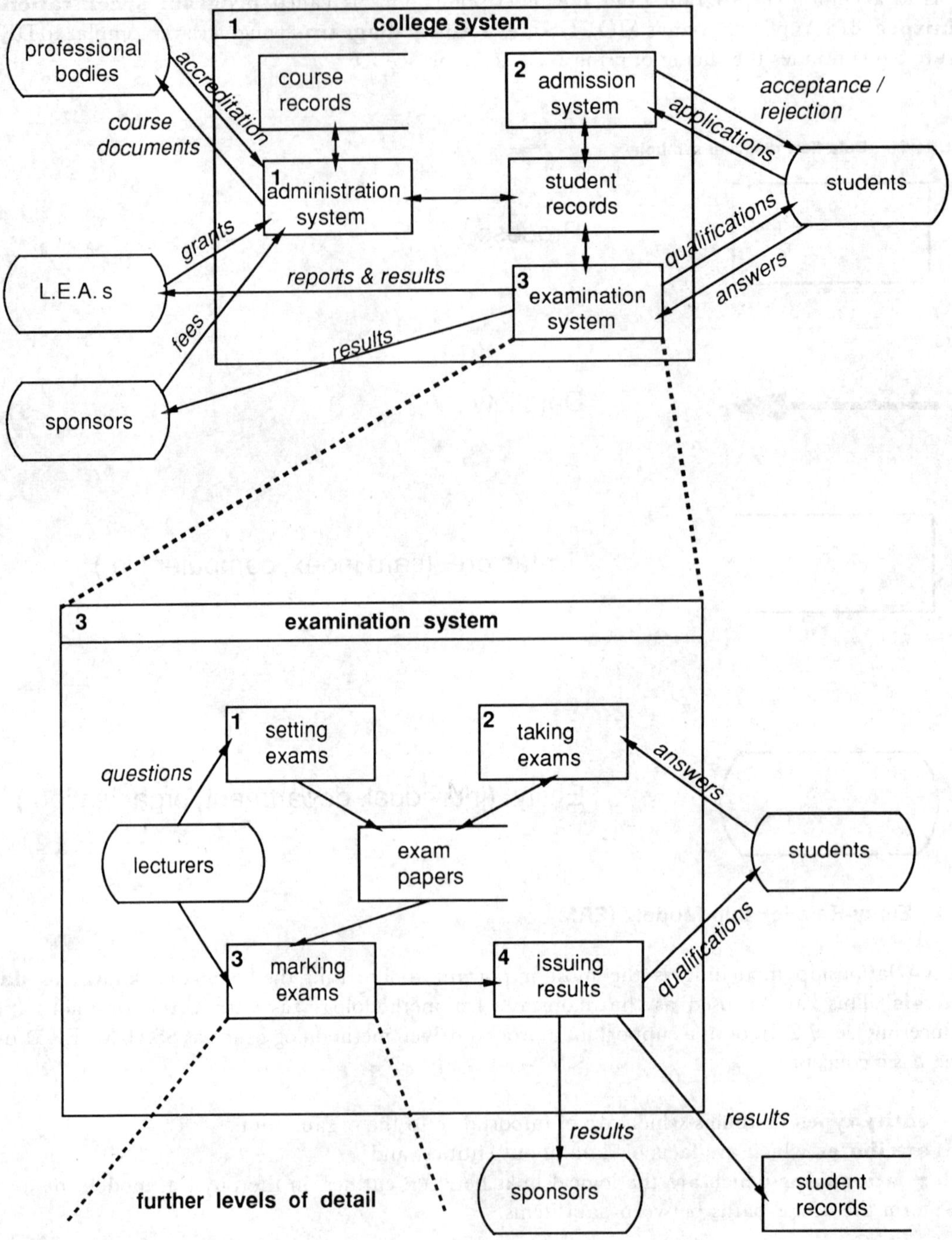

The degree of relationships is important for later systems design as incorrect physical constraints can be imposed by incorrect analysis. For instance, if 'customer PLACES order' were to be recorded as 1:1 instead of 1:n, the system might be designed to allow each customer to place only one order at a time - obviously not what the sales department would want. Also relationships may be expressed in terms of their **optionality** —whether or not all occurrences of an entity type may take place in a relationship. A relationship as illustrated in Figure 8.8 may therefore be:

1 **mandatory** where all occurrences of an entity type must take part in a relationship with another entity type as in the statement, 'course (must) HAVE student';
2 **contingent** where some occurrences of one entity type may take part in a relationship with another entity type, as in 'student (may) ATTEND interview';
3 **fully optional** where some occurrences of both entity types may take part in a joint

FIGURE 8.7 **Degree in relationships**

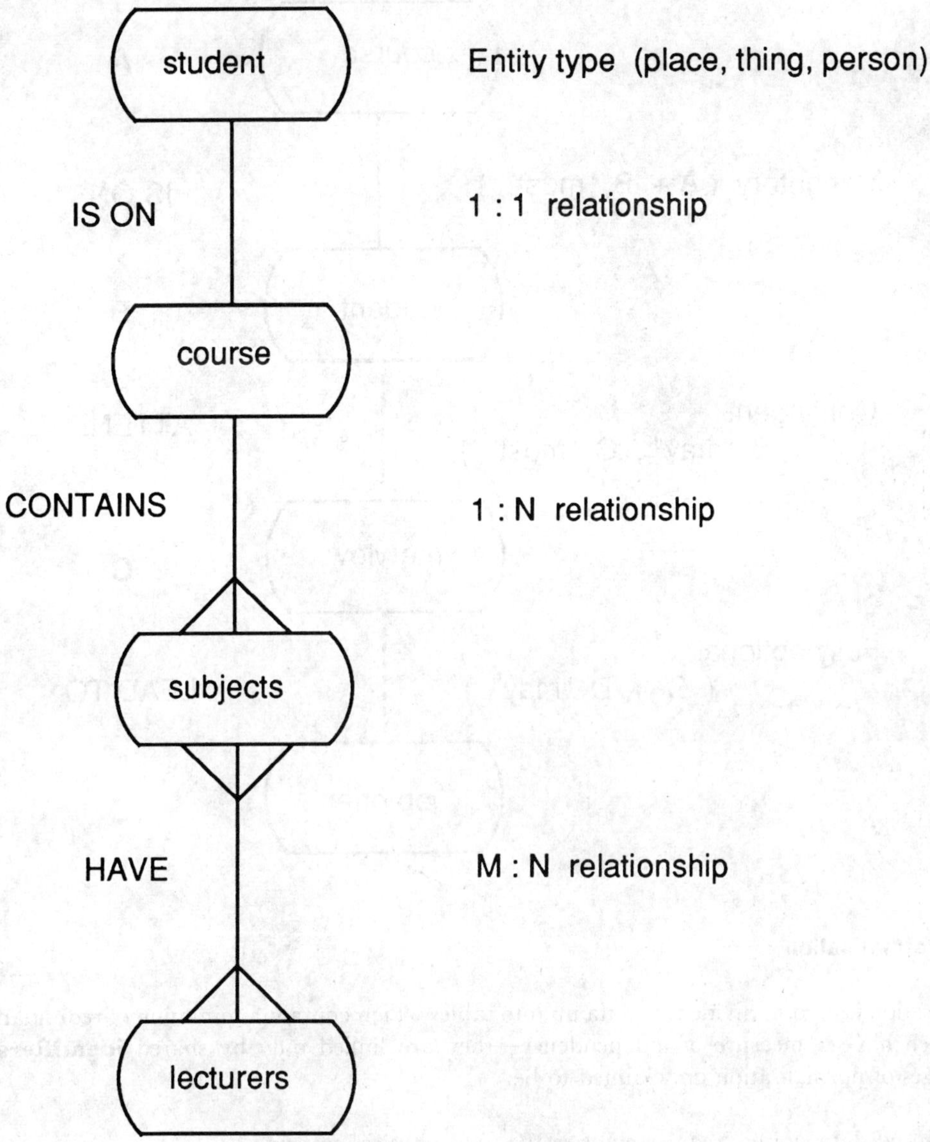

relationship, as in 'interview (may) LEAD TO job offer'. Students may attend interviews which do not lead to job offers, or get a job offer without having to attend an interview.

Optionality has important effects on the design of the system, as it can give an indication of the number of accesses for read or update which may occur between two data items.

Entity-relationship modelling is a process of refinement during which the analysts' and the users' understanding of the logical system may be improved. It is not unusual for a model to go through four or five phases of refinement before being declared satisfactory. The process will include both removing redundant entity and relationship types, and adding intersection entity types to overcome the fact that many DBMSs will not cater for m:n relationships. Somewhat confusingly, this is called **decomposition**. The entity type 'course-module' has been created in the 'college system' model as an **intersection** entity type. This could be prompted by the analyst's experience or by the normalisation process. The finished model has attributes assigned to it (later **normalised** into tables) and is then documented into the data dictionary. The ERM conventions which are used in CACI Methodology are as shown in Figures 8.9 and 8.10.

The attributes which will be assigned to the entity types in the form of **tables** may be derived from the entity-relationship model (the top-down method) or from the more detailed data flow diagram (the bottom-up method). Either will produce a table of attributes.

FIGURE 8.8 **Optionality in relationships**

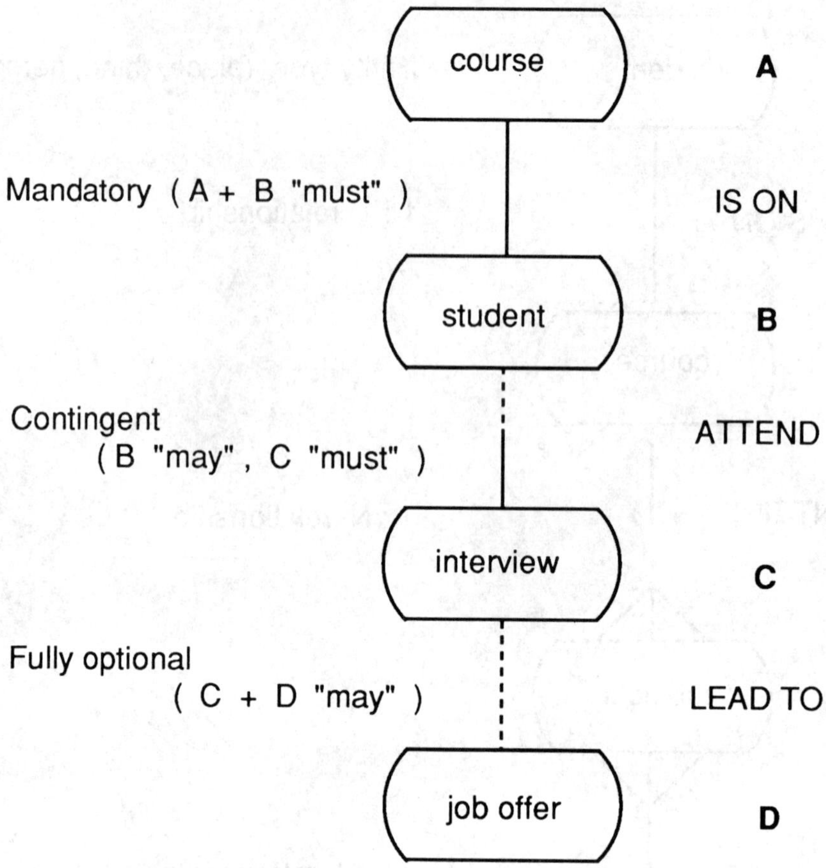

8.1.5 Normalisation

Normalisation is used to divide raw data up into tables which contain a minimum of redundant data and which have a measure of independence—they are linked only by shared **identifiers**. The advantages of normalisation are claimed to be:

1 reduced data storage requirements in the final physical system,
2 access paths in the logical system are rationalised, with possible improvements in response times,
3 processing (ie writing, updating and deleting) of data items should have minimum disruption.

The technique is common in many methodologies (ie structured, process and data-driven) and may be carried out in its own right when setting up a **Data Dictionary System (DDS)**. Normalisation is particularly suitable where a **relational database** schema is to be used.

Normalisation produces sets of tables called **relations**. Each column in the table is called an **attribute**, and each row is called a **tuple**. The items in the attribute columns for instance Business Studies in COURSE table (see the Figures 8.11 to 8.14), are called attribute values. Usually the features desired from normalisation can be attained by three manipulation steps. These are transformation into first, second and third normal form:

1 **First normal form (1NF)** ensures that all the attributes are discrete, ie may stand alone. This is achieved by the removal of repeating groups such as subject details in COURSE table. Ostensibly, this is done by filling in the gaps, but effectively it means that the tuples may be rearranged without losing their meaning (Figure 8.12).
2 **Second normal form (2NF)** involves splitting off into separate tables any attributes that do not depend wholly on the identifier. Thus, by referring to the COURSE table in 1NF, it will be seen that the attributes Subject-Name, Year and Max-Mark depend on the identifier M-Code

FIGURE 8.9 **Entity-relationship model before refinement**

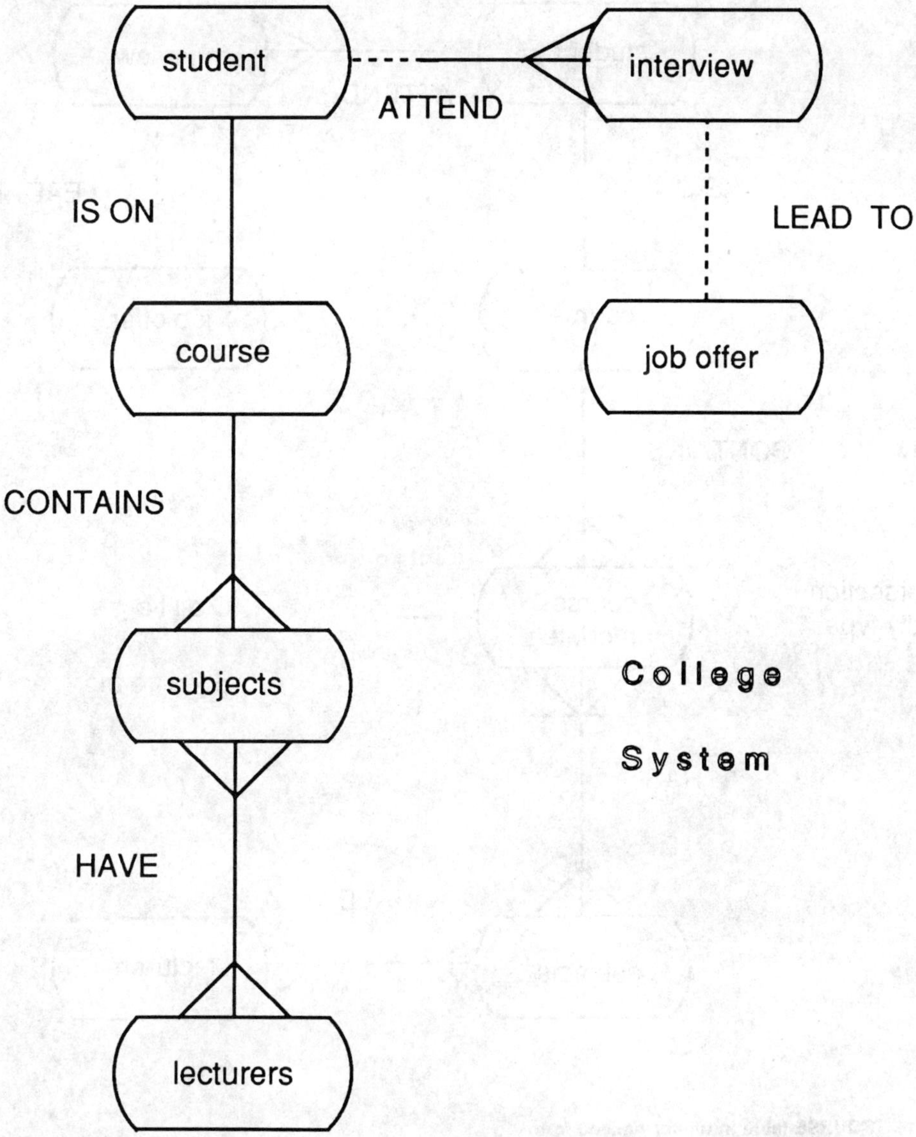

not on Course Code, so a new table SUBJECT is formed. Likewise for the COURSE-MODULE table (Figure 8.13).

3 **Third normal form (TNF)** extends 2NF by making sure that all attributes that are not themselves identifiers (non-key attributes) are independent of one another. Again, this involves splitting off into new tables, as is done with the attribute Year upon which Max-Mark depends. (Figure 8.14)

For more specialised database work, normalisation has been done to fourth and fifth normal forms, but this is beyond the scope of this book. Readers who are interested are referred to books by Date, Fagin and Codd.

8.1.6 Data dictionary

Data dictionaries are closely linked to DBMSs and 4GLs and, as such, are part of the movement called **user computing**. In this context, it means handing over the use of data to the functional departments (accounts, sales, etc) while the DP or systems department assumes responsibility for its control. This control is effected, usually by the **Database Administrator (DBA)** (see 7.4.2), through the use of data about data —this is what the data dictionary contains.

The data dictionary may be a piece of software or may be maintained manually, but in either case, will usually contain at least the following information:

FIGURE 8.10 **Entity-relationship model after refinement**

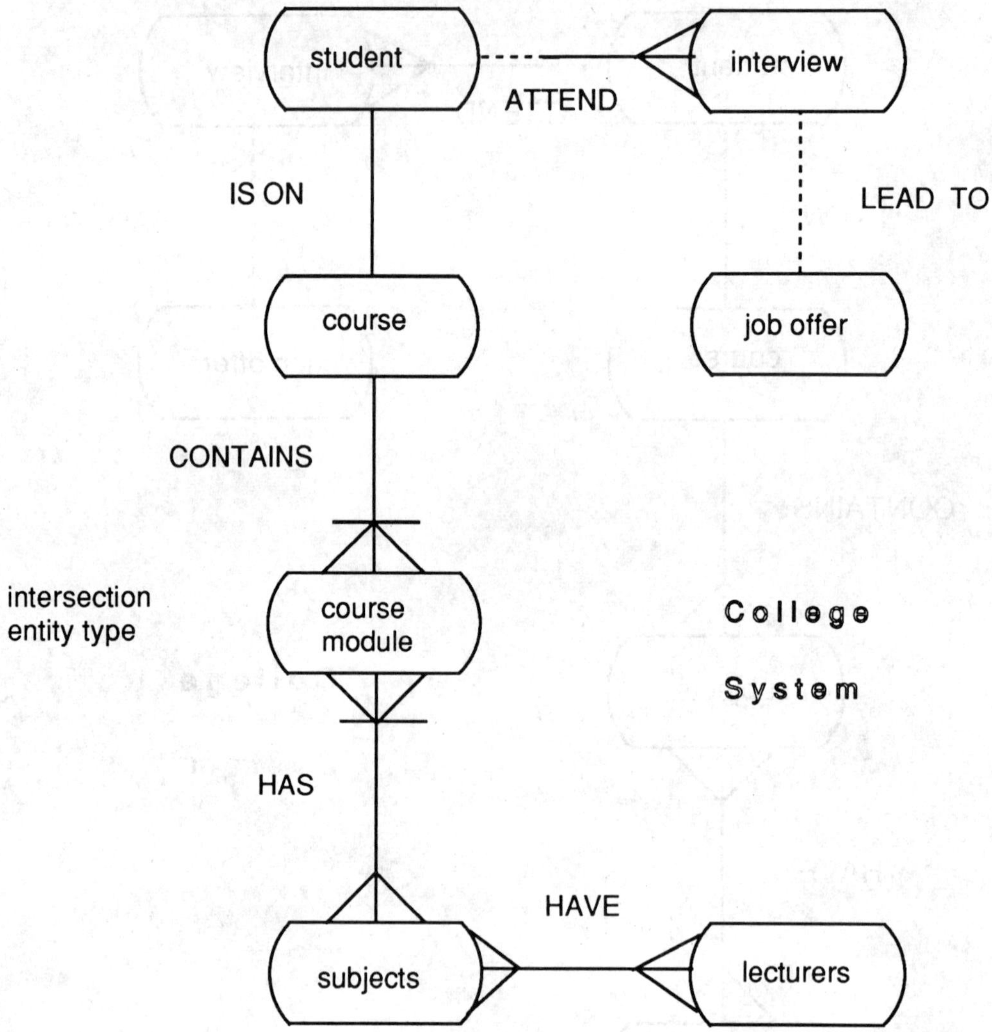

FIGURE 8.11 **COURSE table in un-normalised form**

course table

course code	course name	level	M.code	subject name	year	max. mark
BS10	Business Studies	B.Sc.	BS101 BS102 BS103	Accounting 1 Accounting 2 Marketing	1 2 3	50 100 150
LA10	Law	B.Sc.	LA101 LA102 LA103	Statute 1 Statute 2 Contract	1 2 3	50 100 150
CO20	Computing	M.Sc.	CO201 CO202	Programming 1 Programming 2	1 2	50 100

FIGURE 8.12 **COURSE table in first normal form**

course table (course - 1)

course code	course name	level	M.code	subject name	year	max. mark
BS10	Business Studies	B.Sc.	BS101	Accounting 1	1	50
BS10	Business Studies	B.Sc.	BS102	Accounting 2	2	100
BS10	Business Studies	B.Sc.	BS103	Marketing	3	150
LA10	Law	B.Sc.	LA101	Statute 1	1	50
LA10	Law	B.Sc.	LA102	Statute 2	2	100
LA10	Law	B.Sc.	LA103	Contract	3	150
CO20	Computing	M.Sc.	CO201	Programming 1	1	50
CO20	Computing	M.Sc.	CO202	Programming 2	2	100

1 entity, relationship and attribute descriptions with cross references to functions;
2 process descriptions (events and functions) with details of frequency and timing, and cross reference with entity types;
3 programs which may write, update or delete a data item;
4 data structure, the format (numeric or alphabetic) and length of the data item;
5 ownership of the data item (for instance, security and privacy constraints).

Most commercial DDSs offer considerably more sophisticated features than this, such as operational statistics on the use of access paths and processing activity on data items.

A data dictionary is central to the concept of the management of data as a corporate resource (see Figure 8.15). The use of a data dictionary underpins the setting up and maintenance of most of the analysis and design tools mentioned in this chapter. Since by definition a data dictionary is relatively easy to automate, it is now common to find one at the heart of computer-based systems development tools such as **analyst workbenches** and **integrated project support environments (IPSEs)** (see 8.4).

8.1.7 Data structures

The design of physical data storage (files and databases) is a part of the physical systems design which even the most involved user is unlikely to encounter in depth. The matter is both complex and highly technical, and is usually the province of a specialist file designer in large applications. The following brief descriptions of the main data structures or ways in which records with files are associated, will acquaint the reader with the features of the most common systems; chains, rings, trees and inverted files.

CHAIN STRUCTURES

These connect individual records by way of **pointers**, giving the physical location of the next associated record. The pointer is therefore a part of the record layout and takes up valuable file space. Although long record chains can be formed, when a file has to be reorganised, all the pointers on every record associated with a deleted record must be changed. Similarly, losing a pointer will break the chain, making the remaining associated records irretrievable.

FIGURE 8.13 **Tables arranged into second normal form**

course table (course - 2)

course code	course name	level
BS10	Business Studies	B.Sc.
LA10	Law	B.Sc.
CO20	Computing	M.Sc.

course module table

course code	module code
BS10	BS101
BS10	BS102
BS10	BS103
LA10	LA101
LA10	LA102
LA10	LA103
CO20	CO201
CO20	CO202

subject table

module code	subject name	year	max. mark
BS101	Accounting 1	1	50
BS102	Accounting 2	2	100
BS103	Marketing	3	150
LA101	Statute 1	1	50
LA102	Statute 2	2	100
LA103	Contract	3	150
CO201	Programming 1	1	50
CO202	Programming 2	2	100

RINGS

These resemble chains, but the last added record points back to the first record associated with it. A **one-way** ring points only in one direction and so suffers from breaks in the same way as a chain. A **two-way** ring carries two pointers in the record (a storage overhead) but insures against breakage by the loss of a single pointer on a record.

TREES

These follow the same pattern as hierarchical database logical structures—a parent-child association exists between records. Trees may be **binary**, in which case only two child records are allowed a

FIGURE 8.14 **Tables arranged into third normal form**

course table (course - 3)

course code	course name	level
BS10	Business Studies	B.Sc.
LA10	Law	B.Sc.
CO20	Computing	M.Sc.

course module table

course code	module code
BS10	BS101
BS10	BS102
BS10	BS103
LA10	LA101
LA10	LA102
LA10	LA103
CO20	CO201
CO20	CO202

subject table

module code	subject name	year
BS101	Accounting 1	1
BS102	Accounting 2	2
BS103	Marketing	3
LA101	Statute 1	1
LA102	Statute 2	2
LA103	Contract	3
CO201	Programming 1	1
CO202	Programming 2	2

year table

year	max. mark
1	50
2	100
3	150

FIGURE 8.15 **Elements of data dictionary system**

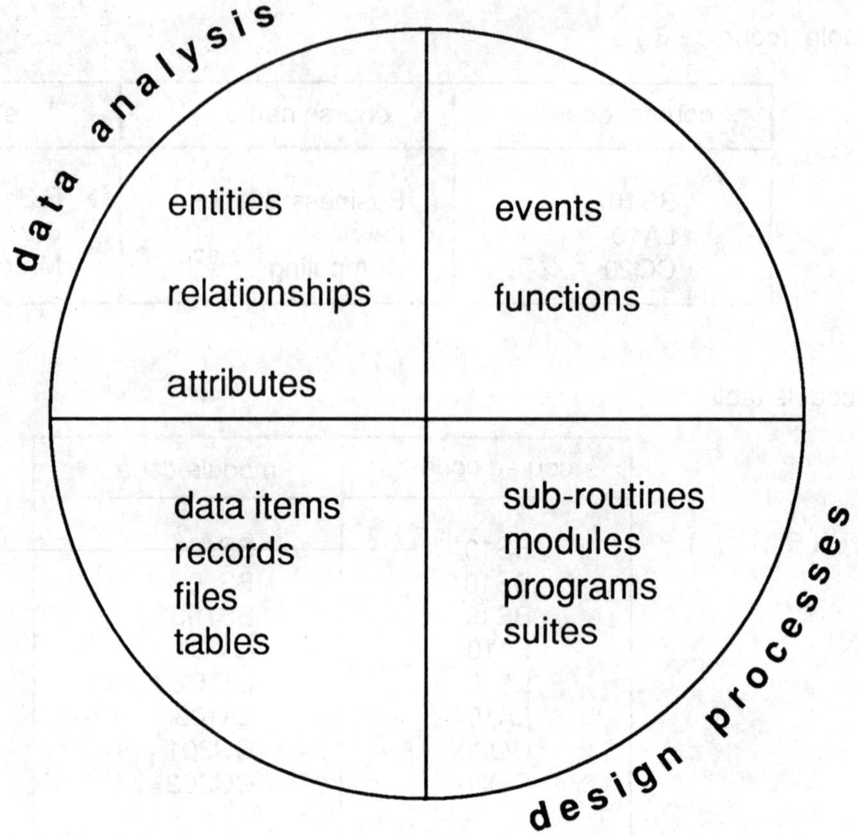

FIGURE 8.16 **File accessed by inverted keyfield**

No.	course	exam
1	tax	part 1
2	tax	part 2
3	finance	part 1
4	finance	part 2
5	law	part 1
6	law	part 2
7	law	part 3

keyfield

inverted to

attribute	No.		
tax	1	2	
finance	3	4	
law	5	6	7
part 1	1	3	5
part 2	2	4	6
part 3	7		

inverted keyfield

parent, **ordinary** which allow any number of child records, or **multiplex** which like a network database, allows a child record to have more than one parent. Binary and ordinary trees impose a more rigid structure, while multiplex trees are more flexible.

INVERTED FILES

These are files which are organised for access by a combination of keys rather than a single identifier.

FIGURE 8.17 **File inverted by secondary indices**

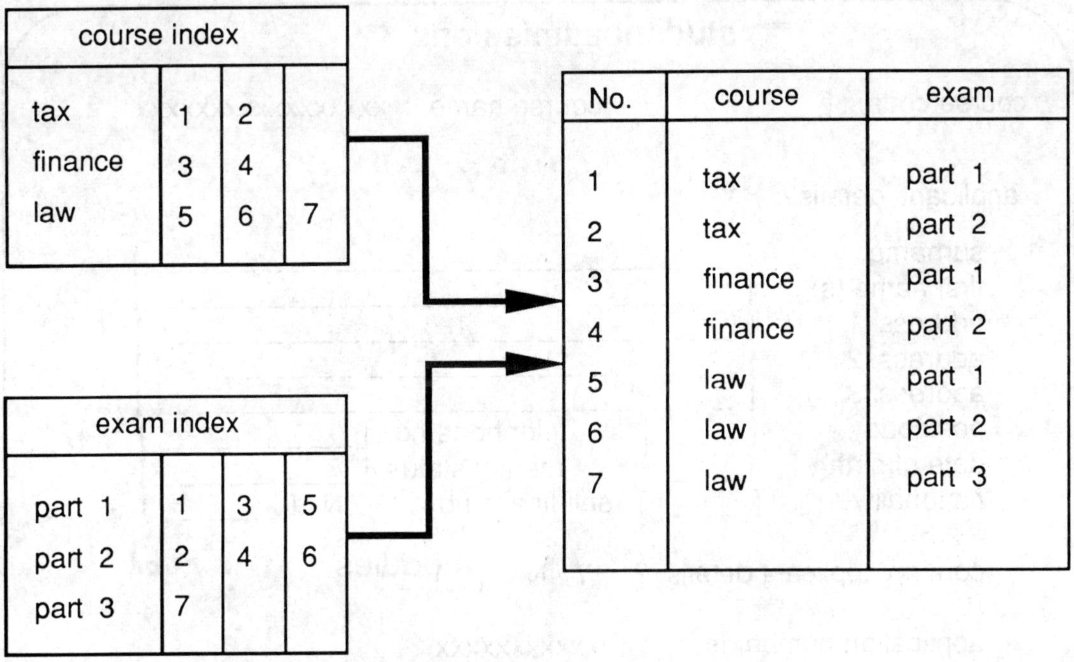

In fact, any of the data items may act as a key. Files may be accessed by inverted keyfield or through secondary indices as shown in Figures 8.16 and 8.17 respectively.

If it is known that access will not be needed by every data item, a set of secondary indices which reference only the used fields may be used. This is known as a partial index.

The type of access which inverted files are designed to offer is one which relies on a combination of attributes identifying a record—for instance, the user may wish to select from a file a student who has passed both Tax Part 2 and Law Part 3. Inverted files form part of several DBMSs, eg ADABAS.

8.2 OUTPUT AND DIALOGUE DESIGN

The aspect of the physical system design with which the user is likely to become most involved is the design of hard copy output, that is computer-generated documents such as invoices and reports, and user-computer dialogue, ie the combination of input and output which enables the user to interact with the computer. Usually, this will be through the medium of a visual display terminal (VDT).

The design of output must begin with a choice of medium; basically between printed hard copy and screen soft copy. The next choice should then be the selection of suitable output hardware (see 5.7). Finally, the physical design of the output of dialogue can take place. The choice of the medium will involve the following factors:

1 How the information will be used—whether as a formal contract document, eg a purchase order, or as a desk report which may be filed and compared with other reports, eg an end-of-month cost-centre analysis.

2 The complexity of the information contained in the report. Physical constraints such as the size of the CRT screen (80 columns X 24 rows of characters) may dictate a larger medium.

3 Period of usage of the report, ie whether the information will be used for a brief period, or will be referred to over a long time. Since computer backing storage carries operational overheads, long-term storage on paper at the user's site may be more attractive.

4 Other outputs from the system. A suite of programs will usually contain a number of reports which will use different media. These reports should have regard for and complement each other, taking into account the other factors.

The matter is slightly complicated by the use of COM which is becoming increasingly common (see 5.7.3), particularly where documents must be stored long-term for legal reasons.

FIGURE 8.18 **Form filling screen layout for admissions program**

```
                     ** student admissions **

course code  : [ ____ ]          course name  : xxxxxxxxxxxxxxxxx

applicant details  :

   surname            [ ______________________________ ]
   first name (s)     [ ______________________________ ]
   address 1          [ ______________________________ ]
   address 2          [ ______________________________ ]
   address 3          [ ______________________________ ]
   postcode           [ ___ ]      telephone no. [__________ ]
   date of birth      [ ___ ]       marital status [ __________]
   nationality        [ ___ ]  self financing ? Y / N [ ____ ]

   confirm applicant details ?    Y / N    [  ]

   application number is  :       xxxxxxxxxxxx

   to enter  ** qualification **  screen key  C/R
                       or
   to leave  ** admissions **  program key  'escape'     [  ]
```

8.2.1 Printed output design

The user may become involved in the design of two types of printed output; pre-printed forms and computer-generated reports.

PRE-PRINTED FORMS

Examples of such forms would include purchase orders, invoices and statements. Their design might begin as draft copies (usually a collaboration by the user and the analyst) which are passed on to a specialist graphic design company to create the necessary artwork. This will then be printed on to continuous stationery. The programmer will then write a program which will control a specified type of printer in the filling in of the variable data on the document. Often a **test mask** will be included in the program (often run from a VDT) to align and start the print run.

REPORTS

These are free-format, but often must comply with organisational standards. It is important at an early stage in output design that the user sees what the finished report will look like. There are two ways to do this: use of print layouts or prototyping. A **print layout** corresponds in terms of rows and columns with the finished report (see Figure 8.19). Many organisations and all the major vendors have their own layout stationery. If the user does not like a particular report layout, it can be changed at this stage more cheaply and easily than when it has been programmed. A typical report design which aims to combine clarity with visual appeal, will adopt the following standards:

(a) Line one contains the run date and time of the report, the sender's name and the page number.
(b) Line two contains the report number and name.
(c) Line three states the time period which the report covers. This is particularly important in

FIGURE 8.19 **Print layout Set adopting standard IBM format**

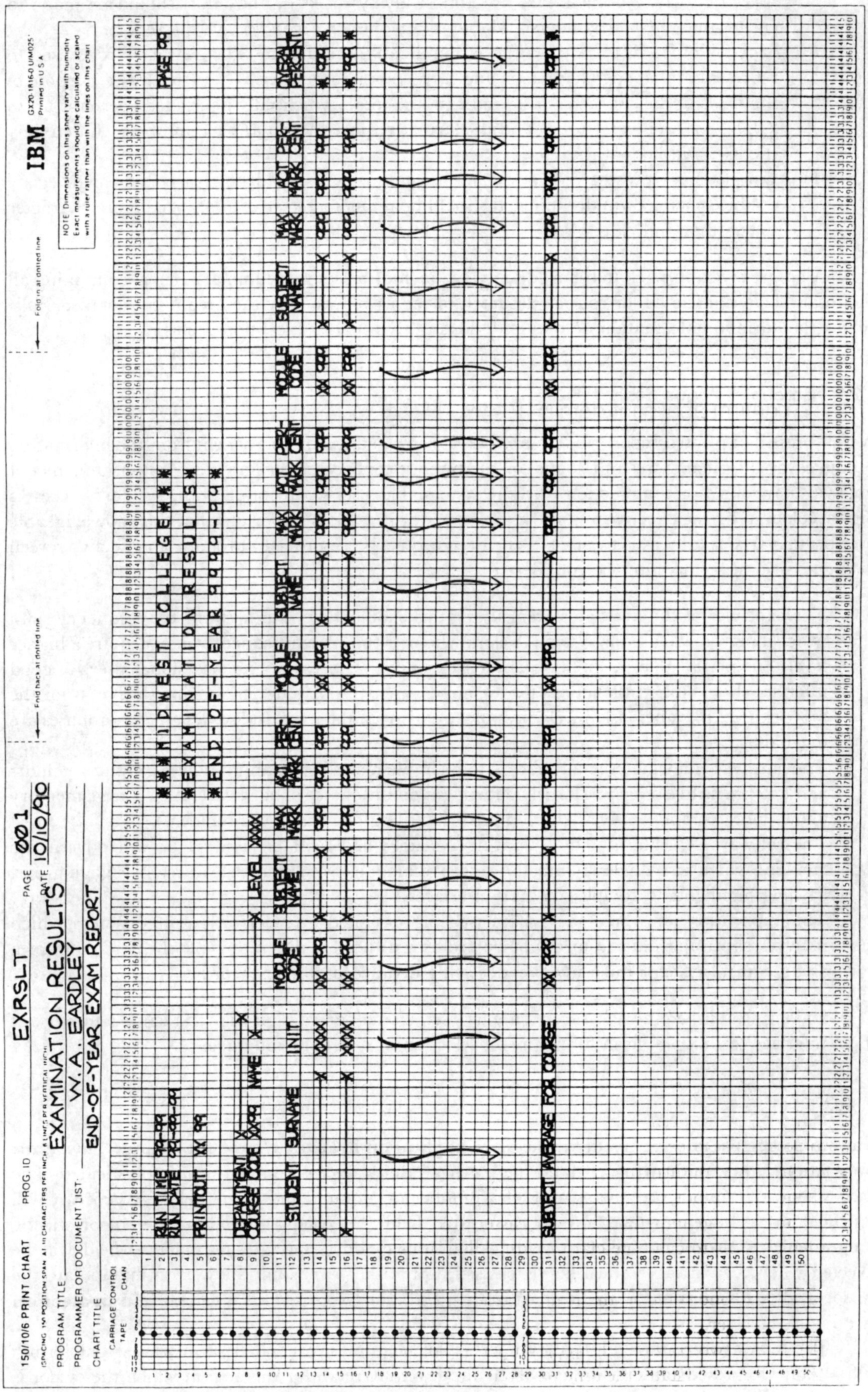

the case of accounting reports, and should clearly indicate whether the dates are inclusive (For month ending ...) or exclusive (Up to ...).

(d) Lines seven and eight contain **literals** (column headings) which should be centred and spaced clearly. Abbreviations are almost always needed, and effort should be made to ensure that these are understandable to anyone who may receive the report.

(e) Line ten onwards gives the information detail in brief form. The character 'x' is used to represent alphabetic characters, and '9' to represent numeric characters. The purpose of the fields of the characters is to indicate the totals which may be needed (perhaps up to £9,999 for an invoice total) and the format required (such as part numbers). Often only the user will know these facts.

(f) Line twenty onwards includes column totals which should be clearly indicated, eg by double spacing or underlining. It should be remembered that totals need more character spaces than individual lines.

A progressive approach to report design is to include a separate summary report containing all the totals. This is intended for routine despatch to the user, who may then request a detailed (full) report should more information be required. This is a variety of exception reporting.

8.2.2 Screen dialogue design

A well-presented printed report can ensure that the user gets maximum benefit from the information produced by a system. Screen dialogue, or the **user interface**, is possibly more important since it involves the user's direct interaction with the system. The user's perception of the system's success is highly coloured by the effectiveness of the dialogue design, so it is important that the knowledgeable user participates as fully as is possible in the design process. In order to produce an effective screen dialogue, several factors must be considered:

1 The expertise of the average system user—this should take into account the frequency with which a person will use the system. A clerk who uses the system frequently may acquire a higher level of expertise than a highly qualified executive who is only an occasional user. A good interface should offer instructions for the novice user, but include time-saving short cuts for the more expert. It is obviously rarely possible to satisfy all the users and so design compromises are inevitable.

2 The hardware on which the interface is to be implemented - the ability to use graphics, colours and touch sensitive screens is largely dependent on the choice of hardware. Also a large memory allows more comprehensive help and error handling facilities to be built in.

3 The software—specifically the operating system which will be used. This will govern the facilities which can be built into the screen dialogue, from simple features like paging and flashing highlights to complex WIMP interfaces.

4 The application for which the system is being designed—a sales order entry system which involves capturing data from customer orders will need a different type of interface from a credit control system which involves accessing detailed customer records.

Having established these features, a modern screen dialogue design will tend to use a mixture of three interface techniques: form filling, menu selection or a WIMP interface.

FORM FILLING

This is an effective interface method where the application involves a lot of data capture, ie names, transaction values, stock items, etc, and the hardware/software environment is unsophisticated. The user is shown an input screen consisting of a number of prompts and blank fields. A **prompt** will instruct the user to input data into the associated field. To accept this input, the cursor will be programmed to move from field to field (called cursor addressing). Usually a new field will be selected when the carriage return key is pressed. Often the user is not allowed to manipulate the cursor —all fields must be covered as part of the validation process. This is called **field protection** (see Figure 8.18).

The bottom of the screen is usually reserved for help messages and error messages. The former will attempt to provide an explanation of the input requirement for the field at which the cursor is positioned, eg the instruction may be given to enter the data in dd/mm/yy format. Often the completed soft copy form will only be input to the file or database after the user has confirmed the contents as correct. A system with buffer storage and page-mode operation is therefore desirable.

MENU SELECTION

This works well with more complex applications, such as systems which integrate the purchasing, stock control, sales and accounting functions. These are made more manageable by the hierarchical nature of menu selection—the user is allowed to select increasingly detailed option choices, each menu screen covering a different function (see Figure 8.20).

The option choices are represented by discrete program sub-routines, capable of independent operation. The individual screens within a menu module may operate in the form filling mode. It is necessary to have help functions, error messages and a 'return to main menu' feature available on screen at all times to allow mistake correction and log-out provision. Menu selection can be made clearer and more effective by the use of colour screens and a WIMP interface.

WIMP INTERFACES

WIMP stands for window/icon/mouse/pull-down and such interfaces are a feature of microcomputer systems, multifunction workstations and/or 4GLs. The WIMP interface is not created by the systems team, but is an environment that allows the user to manipulate the operating system as well as an applications program. One of the reasons for the increase in popularity of the UNIX operating system in office applications is that WIMP interfaces have replaced the difficult commands which UNIX used to rely upon. A WIMP interface removes the need for the user to remember commands and file names, and largely removes the need for advanced key board skills.

Windows are frames or screen compartments which can be dedicated to different applications and can be moved around the screen and changed in size by the use of the mouse and pointer. The user can therefore have several documents on screen at once, and bring into the foreground the one which is being worked on. It is possible to move from one document to another on screen just as one could on a real desk top. The user can file away non-current documents and even dispose of unwanted documents by the use of icons.

Icons are small graphical symbols representing features of the system which can also be selected by the use of the mouse and pointer. For instance, a file is represented by a filing cabinet icon, a word processing facility by a paper pad icon, and an electronic mail facility by an envelope or an in-tray/out tray icon. An attempt has been made to simulate everyday office functions with which the average business user will be familiar— including a waste-paper basket for permanent disposal.

The **mouse** is a device which, when rolled around a desk, will move a pointer or cursor about the screen. According to which icon or menu item is selected (by clicking a button on the mouse) the pointer will accept text, open a window or produce line drawings. A **trackball** performs a similar function but does not require the user to find clear desk space (see 5.6).

Pull-down (or pop-up) menus allow a complete change of function, for instance from word processing to spreadsheet to project management, without apparently leaving the program. The menus for each function are stored in bars, usually at the top of the screen which, when selected by means of the mouse, expand to show all the processes that can be carried out on that function. Again, these can be selected by using the mouse, pointer and click button.

The first commercially viable WIMP interfaces were introduced by Apple Computers with their Lisa, and later Macintosh, microcomputers. These tended to be aimed at the desktop publishing market. The advantages of WIMP interfaces in general, ie helping users who are not computer literate to produce quality documents and screen designs, have led to a move towards this type of interface. The main industry standard WIMP front-ends are Digital Research's Macintosh-like Gem package, and Microsoft's Windows package. Both of these will run on IBM PCs and compatible machines. IBM's new standard operating system OS/2 includes a WIMP interface called **Presentation Manager** which resembles Windows.

Although WIMP interfaces tend to be more prevalent in PCs and multifunction workstations than larger computer systems, they are a feature of many of the 4GLs which allow the user to produce screen dialogue by prototyping (see 5.10.4). The advantage of producing interface prototypes is that they can overcome one of the major problems of systems design—the inability of users to imagine what the interface will look like in operation. Even when users are encouraged to take part in

FIGURE 8.20 **Menu selection interface for admissions system**

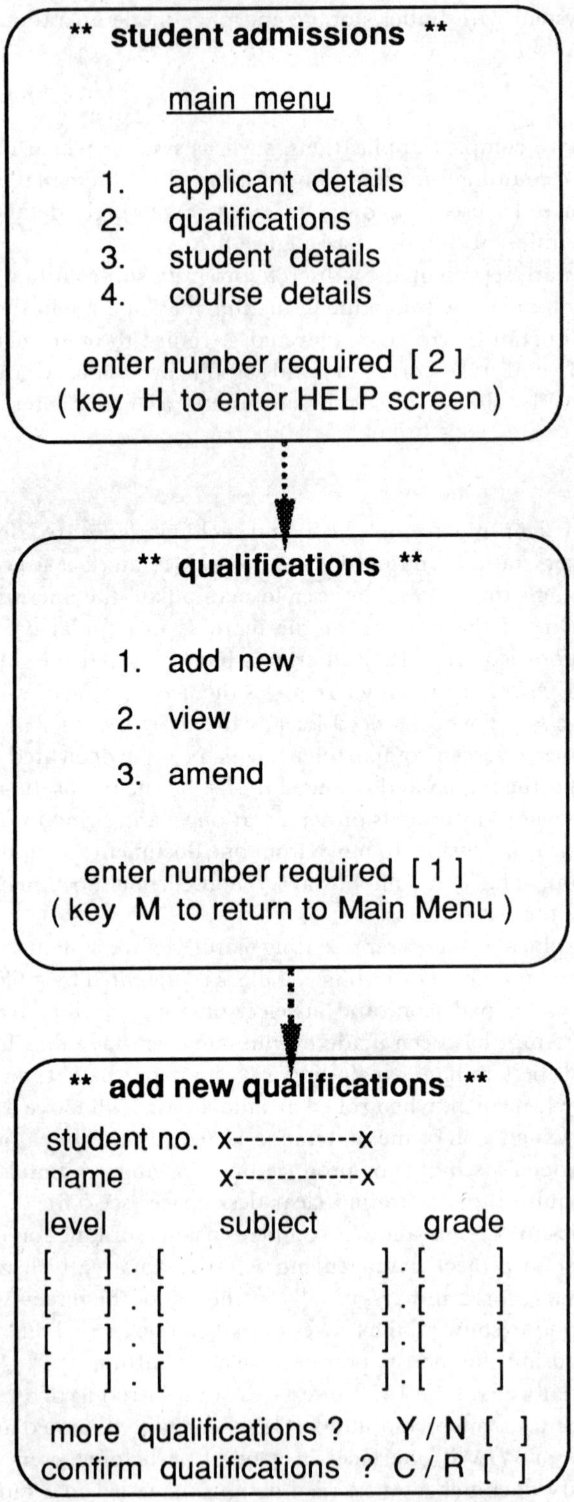

dialogue design by producing their own screen layout sheets, there can be disappointment with the finished interface. Prototyping not only allows the user to see the interface on screen, but can simulate the operation of menus, cursor movement and screen changes in form filling dialogue.

8.3 PROCEDURE SPECIFICATION

The main tools of systems analysis and design, DFDs or ERMs, are central to understanding, describing and documenting a system. However, in common with all the tools and techniques reviewed so far, they are insufficient for specifying the way in which a computer program should be written. Program specifications, also known as **minispecs** or **function logic descriptions**, are created by systems analysts and passed on to the software engineer or programmer along with the system documentation, particularly the screen and print layouts. From this document set, a program or programs can be designed and coded. A specification must therefore contain the following:

1. sufficient detail to describe the operations which must be carried out, ie which records are to be addressed, what the identifier is to be, which fields are to be read or updated;
2. the order in which such operations are to be carried out, and when they are to start and terminate;
3. actions which result from decisions or tests and are mutually exclusive; these are called **cases** or policies.

It should not be assumed that the programmer has any familiarity with the application. A programmer who has considerable experience of working on financial ledger systems may be able to produce a correctly-functioning code from a slack or vague specification, but successful programmers often move on, and the code may have to be maintained by a novice. The three main strands of system specification are as follows:

1. mathematical or formal methods which are capable of extreme precision but which are difficult for non-experts to understand and therefore to approve (formal methods tend to be used for specifying real-time systems with high risk profiles — they may also be used for the rigorous testing of completed programs, called program proving);
2. graphical techniques which represent the basic structure of logic; and
3. narrative techniques which may involve the use of a variety of high-level computer language (a specification language), a variety of natural language, or something in between called **pseudocode**. Specification languages may form the input to application generators, thereby almost completely automating the programming process.

Since formal methods of specification and specification languages are not yet widely used, they are not described in detail in this section. The tools that are included, are those that a user involved in information systems development is likely to encounter. Sometimes a specification will contain a mixture of some or all of these tools, as they all have different strengths and uses.

8.3.1 Graphical techniques

Graphical specification techniques are particularly suitable for indicating under what circumstances a task is to be carried out. They tend to be less useful for describing precisely *how*, as descriptive detail is lacking from all the tools in this category. The main graphical tools are: decision tables, decision trees and program flowcharts.

DECISION TABLES

These are often used for systems with complex logic, ie many decisions and alternative cases which might apply. They are relatively easy to construct and may have a built-in validation process that can check the consistency of the logic with which the table is constructed. Further, some programming languages may be coded directly in the form of decision tables linked by GOTOs or macros, eg Oxtab-COBOL. Some code generation software will accept input from decision tables converted to computer-readable format. The commonest form of decision table is the **limited entry** table. It has a standard format and is constructed as follows:

1. The conditions that can apply within the process logic are listed in any order in the condition stub.
2. The actions which the program must carry out in response to the conditions are listed below in the action stub, again in any order.
3. The remaining empty part of the table is divided into vertical strips called **rules**, which are usually numbered. It is possible to calculate in advance the maximum number of rules which

will apply; a table with three conditions will have 2 to the power 3 = 8 rules, four conditions will have 2 to the power 4 = 16 rules. If the actual number of rules exceeds this number, there is a logic fault. It is possible to fill in the condition entry by careful consideration of the logic, adding Y (yes) or N (no) as applicable. A simple, effective alternative is to begin by filling in half of the rule spaces in the top row with Y and the other half with N. The next row is split into two sections, and again half of each section is filled in with Y and the other half with N. The bottom condition row will therefore have alternating Y and N entries.

4 The action entry is filled in, with X being entered in a rule space if an action would result from the value(s) in the condition entry. An action can result from any number of rules from 1 up to the total.

FIGURE 8.21 **Limited entry decision table**

Stubs	Entries							
condition	**rule**							
	1	2	3	4	5	6	7	8
has 5 GCSE s	Y	Y	Y	Y	N	N	N	N
has 2 A levels	Y	Y	N	N	Y	Y	N	N
part-qualified	Y	N	Y	N	Y	N	Y	N
action								
make HND offer	X	X	X	X	X	X		
make degree offer	X	X			X	X		
offer professional course	X		X		X		X	
send rejection letter								X

The limited entry decision table in course administration describes the policy for course admission at a college (see Figure 8.21). It should be self-explanatory, but points which can be gleaned from the table are as follows:

(a) 5 GCSEs will qualify an applicant for the HND course;
(b) 2 A levels will qualify an applicant for both the degree and the HND courses;
(c) a part-qualified applicant will be offered a place on a professional course in addition to any other course(s) for which they may be qualified.

Note that the table is concise and unambiguous, but somehow lacking in information.

An **extended entry** table is an attempt to include more detailed information. Rules are replaced with conditions, which are often quantified. There are several forms of extended entry table of which one, concerned with examination results, is shown in Figure 8.22. Note that in this example, an X effectively means yes, and a — means no. Extended entry tables have advantages where the conditions are related to one another, as their basic layout is more simple.

DECISION TREES

These are most often used in preference to decision tables where a system does not have too many decision points and each action tends to apply to only one case. In this respect, if not in its

FIGURE 8.22 **Extended entry decision table**

actions	exam marks			
	<35	<40	40 - 69	=>70
record exam failure and notify student	X	X	-	-
arrange exam resit and notify student	-	X	-	-
award exam pass and print certificate	-	-	X	X
enter student for annual college prize	-	-	-	X

complexity, the course admission example used previously would lend itself best to a decision table. Decision trees can be formed from very complex process logic, but this is difficult as their construction tends to be less structured than that of decision tables. Normally, the tree is written (and read) from left to right, with a list of actions being recorded at the extreme right of the tree. It is conventional to structure the decisions so that each only has two outcomes. This can lead to several problems. The program itself may be inefficient if designed in the same way as the tree, and an action may relate to more conditions than the tree can show. This is the case with the example shown, which describes the course admission procedure.

FIGURE 8.23 **Decision tree for course admission**

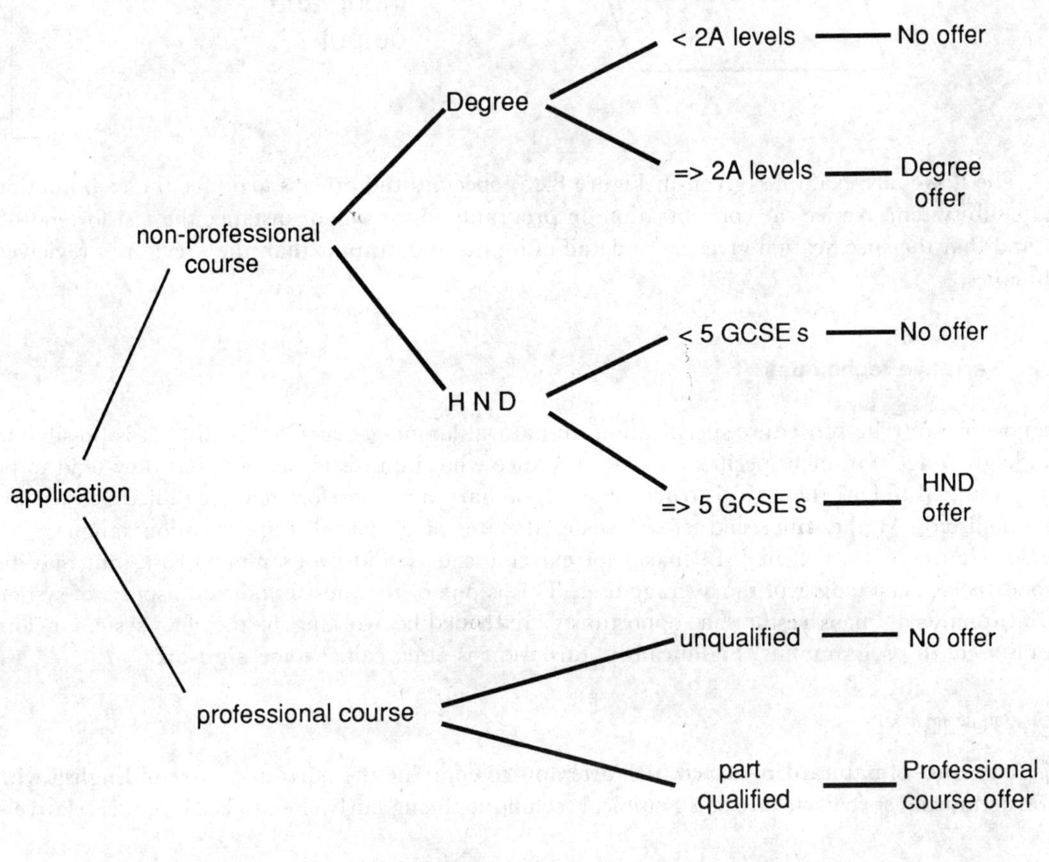

Notice that in the decision tree, to properly represent an applicant receiving offers for more than one course would require more than one pass through the tree, for which there is no provision, or a much more complicated tree structure.

PROGRAM FLOWCHARTS

These are a traditional tool of program design. A better name in the context of system specification would be **logic flowcharts**. Flowcharts overcome the problem demonstrated above in connection with decision trees by including **looping** in the diagram. While this fairly accurately describes the way the program might run in physical terms, it would still not be a satisfactory description of the working of the logical system. The NCC symbols used in this example are:

FIGURE 8.24 **Program flowchart symbols**

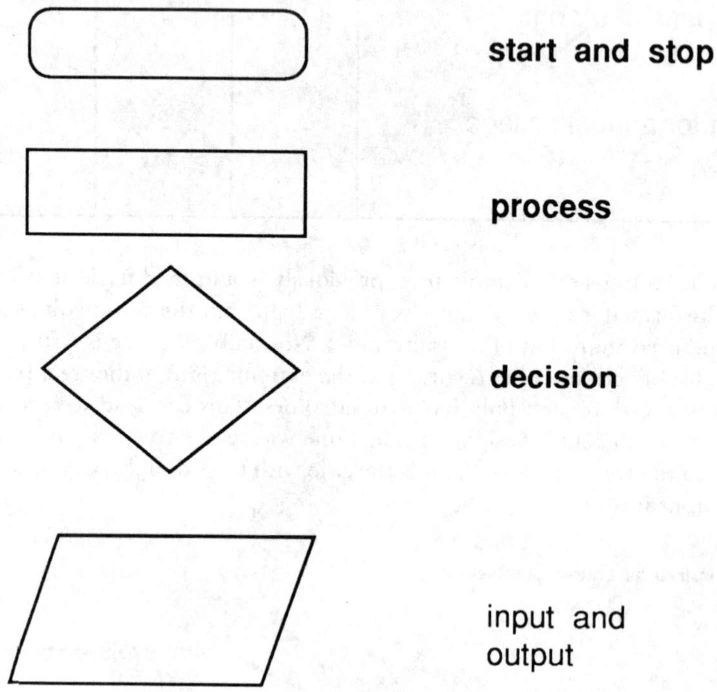

The flowchart example (given in Figure 8.25) specifies the process logic for the examination results sub-system. Notice the concentration on programming steps, for instance the test for end-of-file, and that the specification gives more detail of inputs and outputs than the previously reviewed techniques.

8.3.2 Narrative techniques

It is possible to write procedure specifications in natural languages such as English. It is possible to include great detail in such specifications, for instance what input is to be used, but they tend to be ambiguous and to lack the logical structure of a flowchart, and therefore may be difficult to write a program from. At the other end of the scale, the use of a specialist specification language or pseudocode (structure text in JSP) makes for extreme clarity and programming ease, but may be beyond the understanding of the average user. This is one of the most important aspects of system specification as it may be the last opportunity to check the working of the new system before commitment to programming. Significantly, this event is often called **user sign-off**.

STRUCTURED ENGLISH

This is a subset of natural language which attempts to combine the narrative scope of English with the structure and specific nature of a graphical technique. Being fairly close to English, it is relatively

FIGURE 8.25 **Flowchart for examination results**

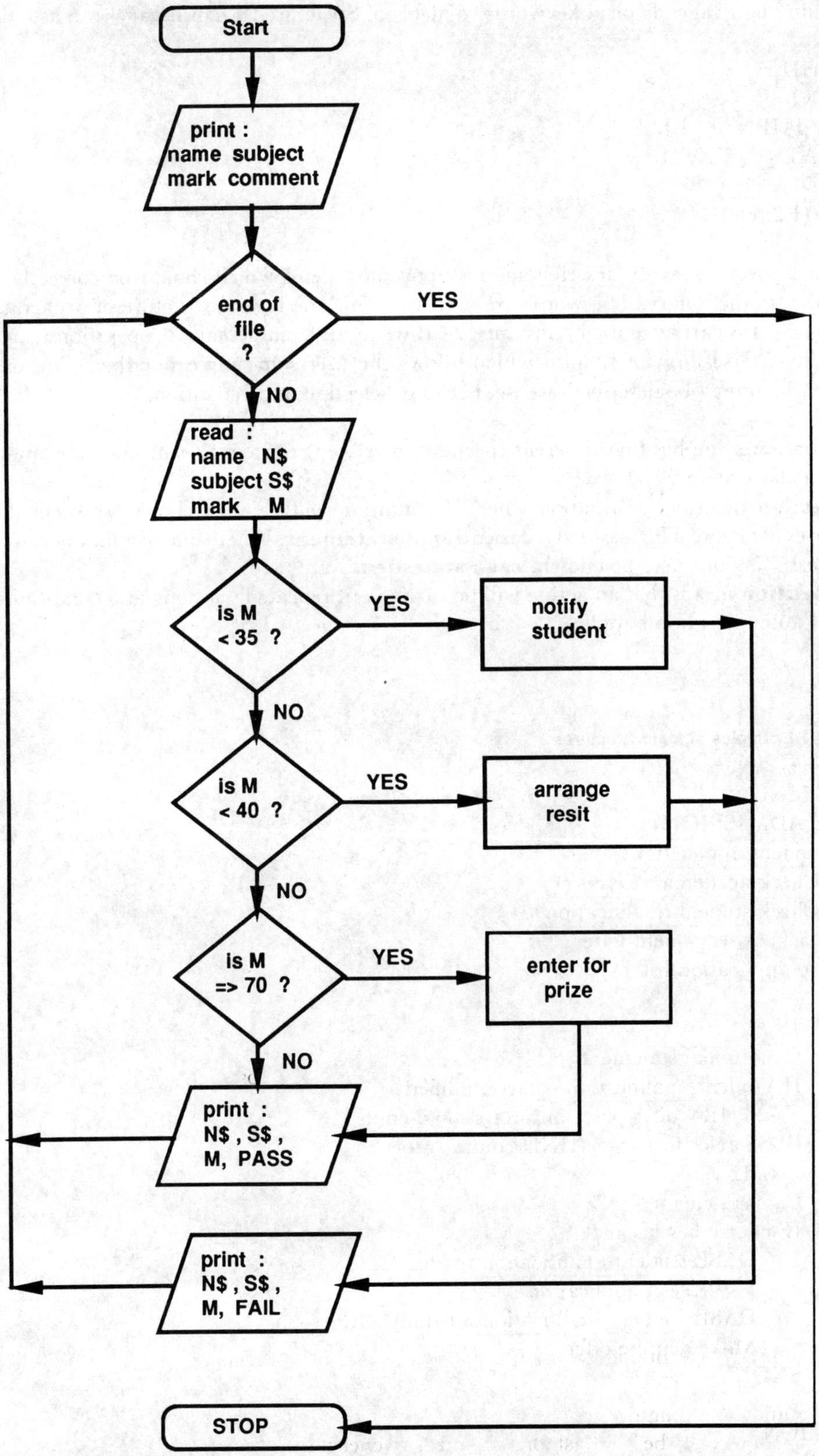

understandable to the user. The technique is based on the use of keywords and logic structures. **Keywords** are words or phrases which have a consistent or reserved meaning, as in a high-level programming language. Typical keywords (dialects of Structured English vary) are as follows:

— DOWHILE
— ENDDO
— IF _ _ _THEN _ _ _ELSE
— REPEAT _ _ _UNTIL
— ENDIF
— CASE (1,2, etc)

Such keywords usually describe actions upon data items which should be correctly specified within the data dictionary. The words are used to define the logical structure of a narrative. The actions which are carried out, for instance read/write and mathematical operations, are usually described in a terse form of English which allows the user some understanding. The basic logic structures which may be described are: sequencing, selection and repetition.

1 **Sequencing** implies that different (perhaps unrelated) processes occur one after another in a particular order.
2 **Selection** describes a situation where a condition will cause a choice between alternative courses of action. This is called a **conditional statement**. Where one of a number of mutually exclusive actions may be chosen, **case statements** are used.
3 **Repetition** means that an action will be carried out repeatedly as long as a condition exists or until a new condition applies.

FIGURE 8.26 **Examples of logic structures**

```
SEQUENCING:
COURSE ADMISSION
    Get student application
        Check academic references
        Check student qualification
    Send acknowledgement letter
    Add to application list

SELECTION
    (a) Conditional statement
        IF student qualification = part qualified
            THEN offer place on professional course
        ELSE refer to Degree/HND course tutor
        ENDIF
    (b) Case statement
        IF course has vacancy
            CASE student qualification inadequate
                Reject application
            CASE student qualification adequate
            Make definite offer
        ENDIF

REPETITION:
DOWHILE student application
    Check course offered
    Send offer letter
    Add to course list
ENDDO
```

The basic features of Structured English are as follows:

1 keywords are always stated in capitals;
2 logic blocks can be named for reference or used elsewhere—again capitals are used;
3 data elements as defined in the data dictionary are underlined;
4 indentation of text (or nesting) is used to show which sub-processes relate to a higher-level process.

In spite of these constraints, Structured English should be written in a way which is understandable to users. DeMarco believes that many users are misled by Structured English specifications as the syntax is subtly different from natural language.

FIGURE 8.27 **Structured English specification for examination award function**

```
EXAMINATION AWARD
DOWHILE student record
    Get examination details
        IF overall performance = pass
            IF average mark > 70
                THEN award distinction
            ELSE (average mark < 70)
                IF average mark > 50
                    THEN award credit
                ELSE (average mark < 50)
                    THEN award ordinary
                ENDIF
            ENDIF
        ELSE (overall performance = fail)
            IF average mark > 35
                IF attendance percent > 80
                    THEN record resit
                ELSE (attendance percent < 80)
                    THEN record fail
                ENDIF
            ENDIF
        ENDIF
ENDDO
```

8.4 AUTOMATED DEVELOPMENT TOOLS

It has been recognised since the 1960s that systems development productivity could be improved by the application of computer technology to the analysis and design process. Early attempts at automation attempted to exploit the fact that many of the functions which were studied in manual systems appeared to be rule-based. Further, since functions tend to form chains of dependency, ie the output from one function becomes the input to another, it should be possible to automatically generate system outputs from specified inputs and *vice versa*. Examples of early automated analysis software tools include TAG (Time Automated Grid) produced by IBM in the late 1960s which attempted to work backwards from print and screen layouts to define the required inputs, and ISDOS (Information System Design and Optimisation System) which attempted to address the whole development life cycle, including code generation. Such projects may have been over-ambitious and hence achieved limited application. This led to the humorous observation that system developers were notoriously unsuccessful at automating their own operations.

A more modern approach to the use of automated development tools is not to totally automate the analysis and design process, but to support the activities of human systems analysis in these areas. There are, broadly, two trends in current computer-aided systems engineering (CASE) tools: integrated project support environments (IPSEs) and specialist workbenches.

IPSEs

An IPSE by definition attempts to provide a set of tools (the environment) with which the whole systems development life cycle may be addressed. The Alvey Foundation, formed to examine the role of the UK in information technology development, recognised the importance of IPSE development as a central component of a future concept of the information systems factory. Most current IPSE systems, for instance BIS/IPSE (BIS Applied Systems) and Phillips' MAESTRO are rated as second generation IPSEs. They contain design databases or data dictionaries. Third generation systems are likely to include some measure of artificial intelligence (AI) for greater automation and flexibility. It is important to appreciate that an IPSE cannot create quality in systems development, but merely support it.

SPECIALIST WORKBENCHES

Usually the term workbench is taken to mean a workstation and set of software tools that are more limited in scope than an IPSE, but capable of higher performance in a few specialised areas. Workbenches tend to be of two kinds: **analysts' workbenches** which support the earlier stages of the development cycle, and **programmers' workbenches** which generally support program design, coding and testing.

Analysts' workbenches may offer generalised features, or be dedicated to the techniques of one particular methodology. A typical system would allow the automatic construction of ERMs, the production of function models or data flow diagrams, and the normalisation of data, and many systems contain report and dialogue design facilities. The most well-known analysts' workbenches are probably Excellerator (by Index Technologies) and Cortex/Corvision's Application Factory.

A programmer's workbench will typically offer features such as a code library and code generator. A **code library** will contain modules of pre-written, pre-tested code which may be re-used and combined in a variety of ways. A **code generator** is capable of producing programs in a high-level language from program specifications (probably in the form of decision tables or pseudocode —a variety of Structured English). Most programmers' workbenches contain diagnostic aids and fault-tracing tools to reduce non-productive time spent on program testing and maintenance. The most widely used system is possibly PDF (Program Development Facility) marketed by Michael Jackson Systems. PDF will produce source code which is capable of being compiled in a variety of high-level languages including COBOL, Pascal and C.

8.5 PROTOTYPING TOOLS

The alternative to systems development methods which follow the conventional systems development lifecycle (SDLC) (see 6.2) is to involve the users in the design process to a greater extent. A variety of this approach is **prototyping** (see 5.10.4) which combines the user-driven approach (see 7.1.1) with the use of fourth generation language (4GL) tools.

Tools which are used for system prototyping (or more simply prototyping the human-computer dialogue) must be user friendly and capable of producing rapid results. Report generators, application generators or screen painters, and even the basic query language, are often used as prototyping tools.

SUMMARY

The key points covered in this chapter are that:

1 The organisation must first define the current physical system, then specify the logical system to underpin the new physical system which is to emerge. The approach may be traditional, eg through flowcharting, or structured, eg through context diagrams or data flow diagrams.

2 All design work depends upon effective data analysis, and entity-relationship modelling is the most important tool at this stage.

3 Data normalisation is fundamental to database design by allowing the designers to show the relationships between data items.

4 The development of comprehensive data dictionaries is necessary to provide a central record of the data elements, their role and characteristics, used by the organisation.

5 No matter how effective the computerised system may be in objective terms, the system will fail in human terms if care is not taken to design the output in the most user friendly form. This applies whether the output is in hard or soft form.

6 The programmer or software engineer requires precise instructions in the form of procedure specifications and system documentation if the best quality of system is to emerge. Graphical techniques are good at showing the order in which operations are to be performed —narrative techniques may include greater detail.

7 The partial automation of the design process in the second generation systems shows greater promise than the more ambitious first generation attempts.

QUESTIONS *Solutions to questions of an examination standard start on p 395*

Write brief notes on the following:

(a) entity-relationship modelling;
(b) data structures;
(c) WIMP interfaces;
(d) graphical specification techniques;
(e) automated development tools.

Questions of an examination standard

1 The Shakespeare Centre is a shopping precinct recently opened by Barsetshire Council. A team has been set up to do a Data Analysis exercise prior to setting up a database to assist in the administration of the centre.

The Centre contains Shop Units, which can be purchased by an Owner if they are Freehold or rented by a Tenant if leasehold. Both types of operator are entitled to the Profits from sales. Each Unit houses a Business which may be a member of the Centre's Trade Association.

The Council pays an annual Grant to the Centre, and takes a return in the form of Rates. Customers make Payment for a wide range of Goods in the Centre

(a) Draw a Context Diagram for the Shakespeare Centre system.
(b) Draw an Entity-Relationship Model based on the above text.

2 The following text describes the function of calculating an invoice total, as described by a clerk:

'When invoicing bulk trade customers I have to work out the discounts which are allowable on each order. Any order over £200 is given a quantity discount of 7.5 per cent. A customer who has been on our books for over 2 years can also earn a 5 per cent loyalty discount, and if records show that they have ordered over £2,000 worth of goods so far this year, they can attract a further 7.5 per cent discount.'

(a) Produce a decision table based on the above text.
(b) Translate the text into Structured English.

3 The user's perception of a system's success is highly coloured by the dialogue design, so it is important that the knowledgeable user participates fully in the design process.

(a) List and briefly describe FOUR factors which should be considered when producing a screen dialogue.
(b) Describe the basic features of the THREE main interface techniques.

Chapter 9

System Implementation and Maintenance

CHAPTER OBJECTIVES

Once the organisation has completed the design phase, it is necessary to move into the next phase which is the implementation of the new system. This chapter therefore considers:

1 the main changeover options to ensure a reasonably smooth transition between the old and the new systems;
2 the issues of system acquisition. The organisation must acquire both hardware and software. This involves consideration of purchasing, renting and leasing agreements and the problems which may be faced in licensing software use;
3 the way in which the system can be tested both during implementation and for the purposes of acceptance testing;
4 how best to train the users and to prepare effective documentation;
5 the services required to support and maintain the new system once it has gone live.

9.1 SYSTEM IMPLEMENTATION STRATEGIES

The first issue to consider is how to make the changeover from the existing set of organisational practices and methods to the new system. This is a question of planning and there are three possible routes for changeover:

1. **Direct**—cold turkey as it is known in the USA. Here the organisation displays such confidence in the new system that the old may be immediately discarded in favour of the new. This is the strategy of greatest risk.
2. **Phased** or pilot running—in this approach, the new system is tested in one department or area of operations. If the test proves successful, the system is introduced to the rest of the organisation.
3. **Parallel running**—in this approach, the new system is run alongside the old until it has proved itself reliable. The old system is then phased out. This method is the most expensive in both systems and staffing terms, but is the most secure.

The method selected in part depends on the **risk profile** that attaches to the particular project, ie if it is a small, low-risk system, eg the introduction of a word processing system in a conventional, non-sensitive office environment, the organisation might opt for a direct changeover. But if it is something like the organisation's equivalent of the installation of a distant early warning system for a nation's defence, the managers will opt for some form of parallel running until it is clear that the new system can safely be left to run on its own. This raises the question about the criteria to apply to quantify the level of risk. There are various factors:

1. the size of the system,
2. the complexity of the system,
3. the newness of the technology,

4 the experience and skills of the users,
5 the percentage of the total budget for IT development that is involved in the implementation of that one system.

Thus, in financial terms, if there are ten projects with one tenth of the budget involved in each project, the level of risk involved in the implementation process is inherently less than having one project with one hundred percent of one year's budget involved. But, in making the choice, it must be recognised that not all systems can be implemented by using parallel running. Hence, if the organisation is not replacing an old system, then the option is to create a back-up system to run alongside the new system—a modified form of parallel running.

The task of producing the risk profile usually falls to whoever is sponsoring the project. This might be one of the senior managers, the steering committee, or the benefiting user department. But, in practice, many less thoughtful organisations tend to have fixed policies on this issue, eg some organisations may always adopt the practice of parallel running regardless of whether it is justified in each case. This amounts to mechanical decision-making and it will only be the successful strategy when the actual circumstances happen to fit the rule. In all other cases, the organisation may be acting quite unreasonably. If the organisation is going to take more objectively justifiable decisions, the question arises as to whether there is a cost-benefit attaching to the changeover options.

In first considering the planning of the implementation, it should be recognised that the greater the apparent benefit which is to be derived from the new system, the greater the pressure which will be experienced by the management to implement that system. Managers must not allow themselves to rush the process because the level of risk will rise if standard safeguards are not applied. In deciding which strategy to adopt, the key factor is the predicted **cost of loss**. The managers must attempt to quantify the costs of failure. This will include development, implementation and maintenance costs on the one hand if the system has to be written off, and the cost of failure on the other through lost orders, lost production, and the possible need to recreate the system itself and/or the data. The rule is that the greater the cost of loss inherent in the prospective system, the more significant the contribution to the risk profile. A system with a high cost of loss would have a high-risk profile. Each organisation must establish the level of criticality in the use of the system and the potential cost of recovering from each disaster (for more detail, see 11.3.7). In assessing the level of criticality, time is one of the most important factors. Some parts of the system may be less critical than others, and a greater time may be allowed to pass before they are restored. But other parts may make such a vital contribution to the well-being of the organisation, that their restoration must be given a high priority. In this evaluation exercise, it must be acknowledged that all information has an intrinsic value—eg a mailing list may be lost. Such a resource will have to be replaced or the loss of orders will have to be made up from another source.

The management must also consider the human aspect. To a certain extent, if a conventional manual system is to be partly or wholly automated by using a parallel run approach, the problem is that the organisation will be required to continue the employment of the staff who are ultimately to be replaced by the machine. This gives rise to real problems of security, motivation, etc. Alternatively, if there is no existing system, the organisation will have to recruit and train the relevant staff. This might be on a temporary basis to run a manual back-up system during the period of testing, or this may be intended as a permanent addition to the staffing. The training issue becomes far more severe if the organisation intends direct implementation rather than parallel running because, in the latter case, there is time to phase in the system and to train the staff. Parallel running also enables the organisation to monitor the performance of the new system more effectively and to produce more relevant data about the comparative benefits of the system (see 6.3.3, 9.2.5, 12.4.1 and 15.3).

9.1.1 What happens at the planning stage?

The management team will discuss the possible strategies and pick the changeover option(s) which most closely fit(s) in with the organisation's needs. In taking decisions about the larger systems, the organisation will probably have to attribute a priority to each of the component elements of the implementation because some aspects of the system may be more important in fulfilling corporate objectives than others. It may be useful to create a data model of the organisation so that, in line with the cost-benefit analysis, more informed choices can be made about the order in which the different parts of the system should be made operational. Self-evidently, the things which are of most benefit to the organisation should be installed first. But it must be recognised that there may be difficulty in attempting whole system development as opposed to piecemeal development. On paper, it is relatively easy to do an idealised and ambitious analysis exercise, to document it by producing a data model, and to arrive at a system which it is impossible to implement in terms of cost because the budget is not big enough. So, if the organisation is to aim at the ideal, it has to impose capital rationing given that computer systems are in competition with other departments for funding.

The probable result is that only a part of the system can be installed at any one time. Those parts of the system which are deferred must then be ranked. The NCC have developed a system which is called Weighted Ranking. This is simultaneously the most easy and the most difficult of concepts. All the affected user departments are contacted and are asked to review the list of those elements left to be installed. Each group of users will then give marks out of ten for each part of the residue, and for the desired quality of the system at each stage in the implementation process in terms of speed of response, size of storage, the extent to which it achieves the users' objectives, etc. The trouble with the system is that it is pseudo-scientific. It seeks to give objectivity to a choosing process based on a series of self-interested opinions. The result is a set of numbers given by a computer following detailed calculations which mere humans might be tempted to take as an authoritative and absolute representation of that which is otherwise mere prejudice and opinion.

The decision-makers then move on to the more detailed planning. There are two elements which tend to run together:

1 testing, and
2 training.

Testing may apply to the program and/or the system. It may also be the formal process of acceptance testing. The former is a part of the systems development life cycle. It first looks for syntax and logic errors in the programs, and then moves on to a second stage which is designed to establish the performance characteristics of the system in terms of:

1 the response time and other similar practical matters,
2 the robustness of the system, ie the testers will try to break the system, and
3 the ease with which the system can be reactivated following failure.

The link between acceptance testing and training is that of the chicken and the egg. Hence, it is the responsibility of the users to undertake the acceptance testing, but if they cannot make the system work, they cannot test it effectively. Thus, before any major computing system is installed, a core of the users must gain a basic understanding of the system's intentions.

The cost of training offered by many manufacturers and suppliers is high and the training itself is often not done well. Part of the reason for this is that some suppliers, in order to make the sale, cut their margin on the system, or the initial margin is not generous. The cost of the training cannot be subsidised out of the sale and is therefore offered at the economic price; but many purchasers are not prepared to pay this price. The result is that much of the training which is thrown in with both hardware and software acquisition tends to be minimal. Generally, it will be unusual for the training to include background information, and refresher courses (which can be so vital to consolidate and extend understanding) will always have to be paid for separately. Moreover, those who market the products need not be the best trainers. The system developers may be too close to their product and not realise what the users will find difficult. The sales staff who demonstrate equipment may not be able to modify their sometimes aggressive selling style to become good teachers. In an attempt to meet the gap in the market, specialist organisations now offer training courses at conference centres or in-house. But courses where the trainees do a lot of work under supervision are labour intensive and therefore tend to be expensive.

If the staff already have the expertise, or training has given sufficient insight to allow work to begin, acceptance testing may be undertaken. Presumably, in their initial requirements specification, the users have laid down the minimum performance standards. If they also provided the designers with test data packs it would be possible for the design team to substantially test each part of the package before it was allowed to go live in the system, although final acceptance testing must always be by the end users in the real world situation. The underlying truth is that no system can be properly judged purely by looking at the results. The literal correctness of the processing or manipulation functions undertaken by the system is only a part of the standards to be applied. The key factor in acceptance testing is the way in which the system works—it is how the system achieves the results which makes the system acceptable or not. Any mechanical approach simply to determine whether the system achieves the results in the way indicated in the requirements specification, and not to take account of the users' response to the system, is potentially doomed to fail. A computerised control system was introduced at one of the Royal Dutch Steel's strip-rolling plant at Hoogovens in Holland, but production fell disasterously because although the system produced excellent results in dry testing, the operators failed to communicate successfully with the system in the real world situation. Similar problems have been reported about air traffic control systems, and were identified by the Kemeny Commission into the Three Mile Island nuclear plant accident as one of the factors contributing to the accident. That is the only way in which problems with the human interface will be identified, ie when real people as opposed to computer designers and programmers are told to make it work. This can be one of the advantages of prototyping because the users can be given an early insight into the look and feel of the future system (see 5.10.3).

The organisation must not only co-ordinate the functions of testing and training, but also must parallel those activities by the creation of documentation. Documentation is used for a variety of purposes:

1. It is a useful reference point for training purposes. In many ways, the ideal systems would always have comprehensive help facilities so making detailed documentation unnecessary, but few products genuinely aspire to this ideal. Whoever is to operate the system will have to develop routines and habit patterns which are efficient, and documentation which supports the acquisition of efficient day-to-day skills is desirable.
2. Once installed, the detailed operation of the system must be described in clearly worded user manuals. This descriptive material will perform two functions:
   (a) It will act as a form of reference manual and describe what the system is. This is likely to be very detailed, and will provide detailed technical explanations of the less commonly used aspects of the system, and of the more advanced uses and facilities.
   (b) It will act as an aid to immediate problem-solving by telling the users, both experienced and inexperienced, how the system is supposed to work. For this purpose, the results of the testing and the detail of the test packs used in dry testing should be included in the system documentation.

9.1.2 Interim summary

The co-ordination of all the tasks of training, testing and the creation of documentation is a part of the overall project management (see Chapter 10). As a necessary precondition to the implementation of each phase of the project, the appropriate environment must be created and the necessary hardware installed. The precise sequence of events is likely to vary in each project, but the necessary constituent elements are:

(a) to acquire: the hardware,
the software, and
the appropriate level of staff competence;
(b) to install: the hardware, and
the software (which may also be seen as an aspect of staff training)
(c) to negotiate or arrange: maintenance, and
services which, in the case of a large system, involves the creation of a protected environment including air conditioning, uninterruptable power supplies (see 13.2.1). Specialist services include consultancy, time-sharing and bureaux facilities, etc).

9.2 HARDWARE AND SOFTWARE ACQUISITION

9.2.1 Acquisition procedure

The hardware is comparatively limited in function as compared to the software which can be designed to achieve great flexibility. The total package required is:

1 the computer hardware itself and appropriate peripherals,
2 the software, both operating system and applications packages,
3 documentation, and
4 maintenance/support.

Following the design phase, the organisation must specify its requirements in terms of hardware together with a suitable support environment, and of software. This is best achieved by identifying the existing data flows and showing how the new system should work. In one sense, the decisions should be taken by those users who will have to make the resultant system work (obviously with guidance from those with technical expertise). But there are dangers:

1 the choices made may not be compatible with those made by other departments and a piecemeal system may come into being,
2 through inexperience, the managers may select a package which is less than ideal, and/or may negotiate terms for supply which are disadvantageous to the organisation, and
3 each department may be struggling to reinvent the square wheel whereas centralisation of decision-making and the pooling of experience can reduce the chances of repeating the mistakes of the past.

The ultimate decision-makers are actually going to answer four deceptively simple questions:

1 What is going to be required?
2 Why is the suggested degree of automation appropriate?
3 When should the new system be installed?
4 Does the organisation have enough competent staff to make it work?

Given that the organisation has identified and justified what it needs in the design phase (eg to reduce costs, to improve the quality of data available to support decision-making, to improve profitability, etc) and has fixed the timescale, it may then issue an Invitation to Tender (ITT), which is known as a Request for Proposal (RFP) in the USA. This document should be sent to as wide a range of possible suppliers as is sensible given the scope of the overall project. It will normally describe:

1 the context in which the new system is to operate,
2 the functions which it is to perform,
3 the proposed timescale of implementation,
4 the performance criteria that will have to be met in terms of volumes of transactions, data handling facilities, output required, etc,
5 the target price, and
6 who to contact within the organisation for further details.

The potential suppliers will also need to know what criteria will be applied to evaluate the proposals and what the proposal deadline is. The serious contenders will exercise their right to ask for more detail of the system requirements or to suggest modifications so that their product(s) might be more acceptable.

In due course, assuming that the market is responsive, a number of tenders will be received. These should be analysed for the features most useful to the organisation's needs. But many suppliers are not that helpful. There is a tendency to send out standardised product information rather than to make a specific response to the immediate Invitation. In such cases, the organisation should seek to identify those products worthy of further investigation on a short-list. It may be possible to arrange for the selected suppliers to attend to give a detailed demonstration of their products, or some form of trial might be arranged —this is increasingly necessary because most acquisitions are software rather than hardware-led, ie based on the ultimate capacities of the system rather than the hardware upon which the applications will be stored and run. Program testing should be run using packs of test data simulating the average and worst case conditions. Such testing, alongside discussions with other users, should allow an informed decision to be made as to whether to adopt the package for trial use and acceptance testing.

The use of the package by those who are ultimately to be responsible for making it work is essential if a detailed understanding of the products is to be achieved. Simply seeing test results produced in a one-off test is not a reliable basis for taking a final decision. Those involved in this last stage must be committed to the process. There must be real effort to make the package work. If the staff are unmotivated, either a decision will have to be made because the deadline has arrived rather than because detailed results are available for evaluation, or the trial will fail. Engaging in the trial must involve the same level of energy as installing and using it productively. Ironically, the right attitude is frequently induced because many suppliers charge for the use of their products during this phase. This addition of cost overheads does focus the mind of the commercial organisation, even though the charges can usually be set against ultimate purchase sums or rental charges payable.

9.2.2 The decision to purchase or lease

Organisations may acquire the hardware by:

1 **Buying** —this may take the form of outright purchase, where title is immediately vested in the purchaser, or the time of the transfer of ownership may be delayed, say until payment has been made. One of the main problems in buying the hardware is that the new owner assumes all the risks of ownership (so maintenance agreements should be made), and the terms of any agreement should be carefully studied to see when the risk of loss is transferred so that the decision can be taken as to whether to insure. The primary advantage of buying is that because the system is owned, the operator has significant freedom to modify the system to meet the requirements of the organisation.

2 **Renting**, sometimes known as direct hire —here legal title in the hardware remains in the manufacturer or supplier during the term of the agreement. Historically, many computers were only available on a direct rental basis from the manufacturer, the philosophy being that manufacturers needed protection from financially unreliable customers. Today, the direct rental customer has to ensure that an adequate environment is provided for the equipment and, when the system is installed, will pay a charge which is divided between the cost of hire and the cost of maintenance. The hire charge will be fixed for a minimum period and will thereafter be subject to review. The service charge is reviewable at any time subject to notice being given. This reflects the fact that maintenance is labour intensive and reasonable increases will always be allowed. If the manufacturer defaults and fails to provide the hirer with the level of availability required, notice to terminate the agreement can be given. The period of notice is to allow the hirer an opportunity to plan the replacement of the service. The other form of rental agreement is for short-term or intermittent use, eg where the user wants to try out a system or to cover during a breakdown or similar emergency. It is common to find rental agreements for smaller pieces of equipment.

3 **Leasing** (usually termed an operating lease) —in principle, legal title remains in the supplier, but the lessee may be given an option to purchase during the term of the lease or at some predetermined time. This is a long-term commitment to the supplier, but it has the advantage that the longer term risk of obsolescence is assumed by the lessor. Further, one of the biggest advantages from the point of view of the lessees is that, because the acquisition is done through the leasing organisations as third parties, the purchasing tends to be done by one or two very big purchasers. They have commercial muscle and can therefore get the best terms, the benefit of which may be passed on to the lessees.

Given the change in the ratio of cost as between hardware and software (decreased cost of hardware, and increased cost and availability of software) the direct rental of the hardware is not as attractive an option as it used to be. The increase in the number of leasing companies has also reduced the attractiveness of the direct rental agreement, and flexible leasing (where the lessee is offered the option to upgrade the system at regular intervals) is becoming the more common form in the commercial world.

If the organisation decides to buy the package, the initial investment costs are high. Thus, either the capital sum paid out must be replaced out of future revenue, or the loan to the organisation must be financed. This cash flow effect must be set against the fact that if the package is kept operational after the end of the payback period, there is a long-term saving as against the continued payment of a rental or hire charge. Whether this is achievable will depend on the degree of obsolescence in the package. Such is the rate of change in the world of high technology, that some aspects of the system may be considered out-of-date within months of acquisition. Moreover, all the risks of ownership and upkeep have to be borne by the organisation so that, even if the organisation immediately pays for the package out of capital, there will still be an increase in overheads through operational, maintenance and insurance costs.

The standard lease runs for between three and five years, with some offering an option to purchase at the end of the specified period. To the extent that no initial capital outlay is required to lease equipment, this option makes automation a more accessible proposition. It also has the advantage that the revenue implications are more regular and predictable, with most rental and leasing agreements including the cost of maintenance in the sum payable. In general, leases are written so that the longer the period of hire, the lower the rental payable. Alternatively, the amount of the rental can be varied during the period of the lease. Thus, the sum payable might be reviewable after a specified period of time, or specific sums might be included for identified periods. It is relatively common to find a higher charge in the initial years while the package is most in use, and a lower sum as the package moves towards obsolescence. But whatever the sums payable, as a part of the organisation's running costs, the rental or leasing charges are tax deductible.

There are several problems in adopting the leasing option, and care must be taken during the period of negotiation with the lessor organisation to ensure either that the best terms are achieved, or that planning can begin at an early stage to avoid the worst effects of the agreement actually made. At a strategy level, there are balancing decisions to be made between the three options of buying, renting and leasing. Organisations do not have to buy, rent or lease the whole system. The management must look at the speed at which the technology is likely to go out of date. For the equipment which is most volatile and tends most rapidly towards obsolescence, it is probably better to rent. Thus, data capture terminals are liable to rapid obsolescence so it is better to rent the terminals, even if the organisation buys the central processors. But this may be offset by the ability to upgrade systems within leasing agreements. In the more flexible operating leases, the lessor initially puts out new equipment at a full rental. As and when upgrades take place, the lessor seeks to find a new lessee for the old equipment at a reduced rental. The organisation ought to develop a plan and discuss it with the leasing organisation before signing. Otherwise it may be difficult to achieve a properly phased development of the affected systems and it will certainly be difficult to get accurate cash flow planning.

If an organisation buys or rents from the manufacturer, it is normal to receive regular system upgrades. This will produce incremental improvements in the quality of service supported by the system, and will go some way towards reducing the damage inflicted by the tendency towards obsolescence. Because the majority of leasing organisations are independent of the manufacturers, they will not necessarily have the technical expertise to upgrade all the systems leased. For example, a number of merchant banks offer this leasing facility to their customers, but are unable to offer any technical back-up or support. Alternatively, if the expertise is available, there may be charges made for the upgrading which make the economics of the improvement marginal. The result in both cases is that the lessee has to operate an increasingly obsolescent system over the period of the lease. Financially, the organisation could be badly placed with high overheads but reducing revenue realised through the use of the system. However, as indicated, many modern leasing agreements allow the lessor to update the equipment, usually through replacement.

If there are technical problems with the package, a whole series of difficulties may be faced by the lessee. Because the lessee is not the purchaser from the manufacturer, none of the standard guarantees and warranties included in the contract of sale are enforceable. The general rule of Privity of Contract states that only the immediate parties to a contract can enforce its terms. Similarly, statutory remedies which might otherwise be available under the Sale of Goods Act 1979, are not available as of right. Some protection may arise by virtue of the Supply of Goods and Services Act 1982, but all prospective hirers of hardware and software should carefully consider their legal position before entering into the agreement. It is therefore important to examine the terms of the lease on package reliability to see whether there are express terms which deal with the rights of the lessees. Moreover, the lessee may well have assumed the responsibility of maintenance during the period of the lease. The result is that there may be an enforceable duty to continue to pay the rental while perhaps paying out substantial sums to repair the equipment. If the lessee tries to opt out of the agreement by seeking to exercise the right of termination, there are often very high (but not penal) sums payable to compensate the lessor for the loss of expected income from the residue of the period under the lease.

9.2.3 Acceptance testing

The tests have to be designed to show:

1 Functionality —does the package actually meet the performance criteria set out in the requirements specification?
2 The appropriate response times and throughput in volume terms achievable with reasonable user friendliness.
3 System compatibility with the existing installation.
4 Sufficient robustness and reliability, with a reasonable ease of service and maintenance if there has been the opportunity to acquire this information—quite often trial periods are not long enough.
5 A satisfactory modularity and facility for future expansion or modification.
6 An acceptable level of cost in terms of both acquisition and operation.

It should be recognised that many organisations find themselves under pressure to get the system operational. Implementation plans can always look good on paper, but even with the help and support of the supplier(s), there can often be a significant shortfall in the amount of time available for acceptance testing. Sometimes, organisations take the decision to omit the testing procedures and fail to detect errors which would have been easy to remedy at that stage, but will prove difficult to remedy once the system is live.

9.2.4 Software acquisition

The software may be purchased, or it may be bundled up with the hardware as a part of the package. In either eventuality, the organisation must address the issue of licensing. A licence is a permission given by the licensor to the licensee to do something which the licensor has the power to prevent or regulate. Licences are either:

1 express, or
2 implied.

Under normal circumstances, if an organisation buys software, it is only buying the medium upon which the software is stored, and it is not buying any other rights. Naturally, if there is no express agreement to allow the use of the software, one will be implied to make commercial sense of the contract which has been made —it would be nonsensical to buy the software product without also having the right to use it. Why then should organisations only get a licence to use the software? The legal problem is that all intellectual property rights, eg copyright, patents, registered designs, etc, are formal legal rights which are capable of ownership independently of the physical means of representing them. Such rights have been designed to give some protection to the creative and innovative members of society. The holder of, say, a copyright has a form of legal monopoly in the exploitation of that right. This allows the creative designers and programmers a reasonable return on their inventiveness during the period of protection. But no particular legal formalities are necessary to transfer these intangible rights and so the problem confronting the owners of the copyright in computer software is to exclude the possibility that the sale of the program also transfers ownership of the copyright. A failure to reserve the copyright in the owner would lead to the loss of the right to continue exploiting that copyrighted material.

The simplest way to achieve this protection is through an express term, or set of terms, which clarifies the respective rights of the parties. This is easily organised where large software packages are to be dealt with, but the situation has become more complex in those smaller, high volume packages which are sold in retail outlets not controlled by the copyright owners. The way of attempting to deal with the problem is through the use of the so-called **shrink-wrap** licence. Thus, the software is supplied in a clear plastic package through which can be seen the terms of the software licence. It is customary for the document to have a warning in large letters to the effect that opening the package is acceptance of the terms which are visible. By this agreement, the software copyright holder attempts to make a contract quite independently of the purchase transaction. Because of the terms most usually included in these documents, it is unlikely that they could be construed as a unilateral contract, and there are difficulties in arguing the case that they could be a binding bilateral contract.

In the case of a formal licence, the licensee must take care to observe the terms of the permission. The standard clauses cover issues relating to delivery and acceptance, the use to which the software can be put, confidentiality, the documentation, restrictions on copying (including archiving), warranties, maintenance and support, training and termination. A breach of the terms will entitle the licensor to terminate the licence and to claim damages for any losses sustained as a result of the breach. If the software as supplied causes loss or damage to the purchasing organisation, the potential liability of the software producers for the economic loss is slightly unclear.

9.2.5 The financial implications of acquisition

A cost-benefit analysis of the project can be a way of seeking to justify the acquisition of the package (also see 6.3.3). As to the **costs**, those who respond to the ITT will supply a part of the costing data. Other costs such as the salaries of the staff who will install and operate the package should also be ascertainable. At an early stage, maintenance costs should be quanitfiable as either the suppliers or independents bid for the contract(s) on larger systems. It is more difficult to quantify the running costs. The basic site costs of space, staff and consumables are likely to remain reasonably stable. Thus, that the same work can be achieved in a reduced proportion of the site is irrelevant unless the now empty space can be used for some other productive purpose. Indeed, there may be a slight loss unless the costs of physically reorganising the use of the space can be recovered. Increases in the overheads are likely to result from the following:

1 structural alterations to house the hardware or to relocate some of the affected staff,
2 installation or enhancement of the building's service infrastructure, eg of the wiring, cabling, air conditioning, etc,
3 additional furniture to house the hardware and appropriate storage facilities,
4 additional security costs which may include additional insurance premiums,
5 the need for specially qualified staff which may lead to increases in staffing costs as there is increasing competition in the market place for competent employees, and
6 the training costs which are likely to be substantial.

The costs of financing will depend upon the method of acquisition selected, but the figures should be reasonably quantifiable. One of the possible areas of difficulty may arise if the package has spare capacity with a Phase II expansion planned. Thus, if a two stage project will call for a total of 150 megabytes of storage, it may be convenient to acquire all the necessary hardware in one package. But if the first part of the project only uses 40 per cent of that capacity, should the whole cost be apportioned in some way, or should the whole cost be written off as Phase I expenditure? It may be convenient to write off all the expenditure against the first project, but in some cases, the more precise allocation of costs may be appropriate. In any event, if the decision is taken to purchase the whole or part of the package, the initial capital requirements may be specified. This is likely to be acceptable for small systems, or where the organisation does not want to go through the process of justifying the project to a bank or other source of finance. But, in the case of the larger packages, the organisation is almost certain to require some form of loan financing. This will allow the organisation to spread the costs over a period, usually of two to five years, but will involve an addition to the overheads in the form of arrangement fees, interest payments, etc.

If capital rationing affects a number of projects over a given period of operation, it is possible to implement more projects if the organisation opts for leasing. With such a strategy, there is a lower initial outlay. But, it treats everything as an increase in the organisation's overheads. This is a short-term view to get the most system installed for the least immediate drain on resources; and, in the longer term, it may be problematical because if there is a lot of leasing, this introduces a significant element of fixed costs in the future. To some extent, a middle line may be taken by acquiring secondhand equipment and software. Here a substantial package may be put together for a more modest outlay. But such has been the rate of technological development, that this may be a strategy of some risk. Thus, depending on the age of the equipment, it may not be reliable, and it may be difficult to find good maintenance cover (in particular, spares may be hard to find). Given that the outlay on an integrated information system will involve the installation of plant and equipment, capital allowances will be available to cover expenditure. Organisations must appraise each option in the light of the current tax regime.

Benefits can be either tangible or intangible. Direct savings can be measured in terms of staff time and other consumables. If the manual system was reasonably efficient, direct savings will tend to be modest. Indirect benefits include factors such as increased cash flow through the more efficient processing of invoices and account statements, the better management of stock and other circulating assets, the better processing of data, etc. These savings are one step removed from the actual benefit. Thus, if responses to mailing lists are kept up to date so that mail shots are targeted on those most likely to respond, more trade may be generated from a lower outlay on stamps. Intangible benefits are more difficult to quantify. The difficulty lies in putting a value on, say, improved access to information or better quality information (see 2.8). If managers spend less time on finding the relevant data to support their decision-making, will the additional time they can devote to the taking of the decisions lead to better decisions? It is obvious that little will improve the decision-making of the bad manager, and that the good manager will only have more time if the use of the new system is properly learned and practised. What is not clear is whether giving a person more time leads to better decisions. All that can be said is that it might do so.

The issue often arises as an abstract question as to what percentage of capital or revenue an organisation should devote to the development of an IT strategy. It is easy to pull figures out of the air and to quote innumerable examples of expenditure to show that, say, between 10 per cent and 15 per cent might be something of a norm. The problem with such approximations is that every organisation's needs are the product of the immediate environmental pressures which have promoted its growth, and figures from one organisation might be completely misleading for another even though both organisations might be in the same market sector. Thus, some organisations might defer expenditure and therefore require a substantial investment for an initial installation. Others might have invested little, but often, and therefore appear to spend comparatively little in each trading period. The scale of investment will always depend upon the potentially unique nature of the organisation.

An additional complication is that, with the growth of user computing, it is becoming increasingly difficult to quantify the precise level of expenditure. When the work was all undertaken by a single DP department, it was quite easy to quantify expenditure. If a value has to be put on every individual's use of IT facilities within an organisation where a distributed system has been installed, the costing becomes more nebulous. Equally, not all the work undertaken by a systems analyst must result in a computerised system. Sometimes, the work will be partly to improve the management environment to enable it to better exploit the proposed automated system. So unless staff complete detailed time sheets, allocating their time between computer and non-computer tasks, it will be difficult to get a precise figure.

9.3 THE ACTUAL SYSTEM

Once the physical hardware and the appropriate services have been installed, the steering committee can proceed to the next step. The hardware must first be tested and the operating system installed. If the new system is compatible with the old, the files and programs can simply be copied from one set of hardware to the other. This must be subject to a proper security audit to ensure that data integrity is maintained during the transfer. However, most new systems have different characteristics and require the user to engage in file conversion. The users must compare the old with the new and determine the precise way in which to reformat the data records to make them compatible with the new system. This is a convenient time for the organisation to review its data holdings. It may well be found that some holdings are redundant and that it is not economical to convert and transfer them. The interest and commitment of the users is of vital importance in this task. Again, proper security auditing procedures are required, firstly to test the conversion process, and secondly to check for data integrity after conversion. An unscrupulous employee could enter new data or modify the old data for the purposes of private gain during the conversion process.

Once the data and software have been installed, and all the necessary database creation or modification work has been done, the organisation should produce the final versions of all necessary documentation. The staff should already be partly trained, and ready to commence work on the new system. It is now appropriate for the new system to go live for the purposes of acceptance testing. During this period staff training is completed on the full system.

9.3.1 Who manages the change and reviews the effect?

It is likely that there will be a formal project team or steering committee to manage the larger exercises. Contributions would also be expected from the system auditor, security advisor and IT manager. But whether the exercise is large or small, it is customary to designate one individual as the **project manager** and to make that person accountable to the overall IT manager for the success or otherwise of the project (see 10.6). Quite often this task will fall to someone in the management services department (see 4.3.2), rather than to someone in the computing/DP department, but because much system development is undertaken on a piecemeal basis, each project tends to be controlled by the department which is going to derive the greatest benefit. So if a credit control system is going to be installed, the credit controller would either directly manage the transition, or be closely involved in monitoring the process. In this respect, the direct responsibility of the DP department has given way to the user department. This is almost inevitably the case for the detailed work of acceptance testing, but it is becoming more common for the whole process.

Then when the system has been live for a specified period of time, a post-implementation audit can be arranged, ie where there is an evaluation and review of performance (see 10.5.6). This sees the system in the context of the organisation, whether merely in a part of the organisation or as a whole depending on the degree of integration. It seeks to answer the following questions:

1. Has the attitude of the staff changed?
2. Has the manner of the work changed?
3. What informational contribution does that system make to the organisation?
4. Has the new system changed the level of the organisation's costs?
5. To what extent does it facilitate an optimisation of decision-making within the organisation?

The general process of acceptance testing will be against the criteria laid down in the requirements specification. The post-implementation audit goes beyond those technical objectives and looks at the broader objectives which either explicitly or implicitly caused the organisation to authorise the project. The difficulty confronted in this auditing process is whether the observer is measuring the success of the system or measuring some other form of success which just happens to show up at the same time. At all times, the management must allow for the so-called **Hawthorne effect**. This effect is an improvement in performance resulting from increased morale. Such an improvement is more likely to be caused by the enthusiasm of the researcher or the sense that the management is constructively interested in the workforce rather than by the actual changes made to the working practices or environment.

There are various methodologies which have been developed to attempt to quantify the successfulness or otherwise of system implementations. Key Performance Factor Analysis is one of the techniques whereby the auditor attempts to identify and set the standards required from the system, but the end-product is usually an organisational standard. In general, if the organisation installs a stock control system, one of the key performance factors would either be in the savings through making staff obsolete or the increased stock turnover. The difficulty is in being able to recognise whether the right facts are being reported to allow the success of the system to be measured. It may be that the management are able to measure an increased stock turnover, but to what is this improvement attributable? A lot of people are going to be encouraging activity within that part of the organisation through a process of appraisal and attempted measurement. If stock controllers are encouraged to use a new system—this might be simply because of its novelty or because supervisors are more in evidence—there may be significant short-term improvements. But as the staff become more complacent through familiarity with the new system, bad habits from the manual system days may reassert themselves. If this can happen, it may point to design defects in the automated system—the system design perhaps ought to have allowed for human frailty and, say, be based on exception reporting rather than on a simple replication of a card-based system which requires human monitoring. In short, the auditing function attempts to measure, in organisational terms, whether the investment has produced beneficial results.

9.4 MAINTENANCE—THE PRACTICALITY

To be accounted a success, the information system must enable the organisation to make a profit or to meet its performance criteria. This can only be achieved if the system is reasonably reliable. Maintenance agreements may offer immediate response and an around-the-clock service. In its simplest form, this may be a help line—a telephone service where a sympathetic expert offers advice to clear up a user's misunderstanding. This form of service is not necessarily helpful. The user may not be able to identify the problem with sufficient certainty to allow the expert to answer the question, or the question may be outside the expertise of the particular telephone operator. Further, because the questioning of the user, the giving of detailed answers and the ministration of comfort all takes time, it can be an expensive service to offer to a large number of users. In such circumstances, it may be more cost-effective for the supplier(s) to offer training courses.

If the extent of the problem goes beyond the help line's capacity, formal maintenance is required, ie there are positive faults to be corrected. But what happens if no-one turns up for hours and then the person who attends is too poorly trained to offer satisfactory repairs? A maintenance agreement is not an insurance policy against loss. The essence of a maintenance contract is that the service provider will maintain the system and remedy defects. That is distinguishable from an insurance policy where the insurer agrees to compensate the insured if some specified event occurs and causes loss.

Originally maintenance was only supplied by the manufacturers. This was logical. Computers were unreliable and needed regular attention. The manufacturers were more knowledgeable about their own machines and, with the experience which they obtained in all their users' sites, they were best placed to provide the service. The contracts were somewhat unfavourable to the customer because once the capital had been invested in the hardware, the customer was trapped into accepting whatever the manufacturer offered. Now that hardware has become more reliable, independent companies offer maintenance, and the market has become more competitive. Some manufacturers have responded by cutting their own prices and improving the service which is offered. Others adopt the strategy of not releasing technical information about their machines and therefore making it more difficult for an independent to maintain them.

The first decision to be made by a computer user is the identity of the service maintenance provider. Small independent companies can provide a highly professional, very efficient service on a local basis. Such firms are much more willing to consider tailoring the service to the user's needs and may offer impartial advice on the equipment generally available on the market. They will also be more likely to offer a total service. Many manufacturers only service their own equipment. In these more modern days of networking, the smaller independent may be prepared to service and maintain all the different hardware on the site. This will cut the administration overheads of the user who, for example, will only need to make one telephone call no matter which manufacturer's equipment needs attention. Because of their size, the price for the service offered is likely to be less than that available from the large manufacturer.

However, just because the service may be cheaper it is not necessarily the best value. As organisations become more technology-dependent, they need to guarantee the availability of the service. To rely on a single service provider may be dangerous as financial margins may be cut down in these competitive times and bankruptcy comes unannounced. It may make more sense for the large user with high criticality of use to employ a back-up firm to provide maintenance. Further, whereas all manufacturers must maintain reasonable standards of care if their overall reputation is not to suffer, there are several cowboy firms in the market place who do not provide the service promised. A part of the difficulty is the cost of maintaining buffer stocks of all the main components. Whereas manufacturers originally would have had no difficulty, small independents may not be able to afford any stocks other than of the most commonly unreliable components. Even the larger companies may now have some problems either because they are reliant on other manufacturers to supply components for assembly, or because they have developed the policy of high stock turnover with the minimum of capital tied up in a buffer stock. Thus, before entering into any maintenance agreement, it is sensible to discuss the service provided with the tendering organisation's existing customers.

There is, however, one factor which may favour the manufacturers. The manufacturers may offer upgrades during the lifetime of the hardware. If these are not undertaken, the resale value of the hardware may be significantly reduced. Because many manufacturers do not release this technical information to the independents, many of them cannot undertake this upgrading work, thereby reducing the capital worth of the equipment. It should also be noted that if a problem emerges which the independent cannot solve, some manufacturers insist upon carrying out all the missing upgradings before solving the immediate problem. This can make the call-out very expensive.

In theory, it is better to engage in prevention and to solve problems before they occur. This would mean that preventative or planned maintenance should be a standard part of the contract, including the planned replacement of components and diagnostic testing of critical systems at regular intervals. Indeed, it may be required by a third party, ie:

1 by the manufacturer as a precondition of a guarantee or warranty,
2 by the manufacturer as a precondition of issuing a certification of maintenance for the purposes of boosting the price on resale or trade-in,
3 by the lessor as a term of a lease,
4 by the insurance company as a precondition to offering cover against loss.

The problem with this system is that it may disrupt the operation of the machine while it is being maintained and repaired. The organisation should therefore consider whether to attempt to negotiate for work to be performed outside the normal office hours. Although this may cost more, it may be better than the disruption. The cost-benefit analysis and risk profile should give the answer as to whether the expenditure is worth while. In the long term, the user should have fewer problems, eg by regularly checking and adjusting the tracking on the head alignment on disk drives, organisations should avoid misregistration problems. It will also get much better information about levels of wear and can make earlier plans for repair or replacement, rather than having to react to an emergency. It should also be recognised that this form of service is relatively costly because service engineering time is paid for regardless of whether any fault is detected in the equipment. As manufacturers produce more reliable equipment, the case in favour of preventative maintenance may weaken and only apply to the peripherals with major moving parts.

If maintenance is on a call-out basis, negotiating the response time is of vital importance. The shorter the response time, the more expensive the service is likely to be, so cost-benefit analysis is essential to justify the level of expenditure. It is also advisable to check where the service engineers are based and to calculate whether that firm can supply the quality of responsiveness required. In taking the decision, it should be remembered that, from their nature within the organisation's information system, batch run systems may tolerate more delays. On-line systems usually require faster response times, and deal with more immediate data needs. The essence is therefore to specify the criticality of each data resource and the level of service which the equipment must maintain if losses are to be kept to a minimum.

This leaves the question of what should happen if the maintenance contractor is in default, ie fails to provide the specified service with due diligence. In principle, the answer is straightforward. There should be a right to call in new contractors and to pass on the cost of the work to the contractors in default. There should also be a right of termination built into the agreement in the event of a serious breach. A period of notice for the termination to be effective may be required.

SUMMARY

The key points covered in this chapter are that:

1 The organisation must select the changeover strategy by considering the risk profile of each project.
2 The training of the staff and the testing of the new system tend to run together. Both depend upon the availability of good system documentation.
3 The organisation must be accurate in specifying its hardware and software needs, and should take care in communicating those needs to potential suppliers through the tendering process.
4 In taking the decision to buy, rent or lease the hardware and software, the organisation must balance the costs of acquisition against the benefits of possession.
5 Acceptance testing and post-implementation auditing are vital measurement steps to determine the degree of benefit accruing to the organisation from the system changes.
6 Unless adequate maintenance arrangements are made, the organisation may be without critical systems for an unacceptable period of time.

QUESTIONS *Solutions to questions of an examination standard start on p 395*

Write brief notes on the following:

(a) possible routes for changeover;
(b) the purposes of documentation;
(c) an Invitation to Tender;
(d) a post-implementation audit.

Questions of an examination standard

1 Testing and training are important

areas of system implementation about which decisions must be made.
(a) Briefly discuss the link between acceptance testing and training.
(b) Give reasons why user training is sometimes not well done.
(c) List and briefly explain some of the factors which acceptance testing is designed to show.

2 The main options for the acquisition of hardware are buying, renting and leasing.
(a) Briefly discuss the features which may be contained in a leasing agreement.
(b) State some of the problems which may be faced by the user when entering into a leasing agreement.
(c) Discuss the advantages which may be offered by leasing compared to the other methods.

3 There is a general trend of change in ratio of cost as between hardware and software; the latter is becoming increasingly costly.
(a) Briefly explain the legal implications for the user of software licensing.
(b) Explain some of the factors which may add to system costs and overheads.

4 To be accounted a success, the information system must be maintainable as well as reliable.
(a) Briefly discuss the forms of maintenance which may be available to a system user.
(b) Explain some of the factors which may be taken into account when considering a maintenance contract.

Chapter 10
Project Management

CHAPTER OBJECTIVES

This chapter considers the management of projects from a number of angles, seeking to highlight potential key issues, the sources of common problems and the potential approaches to their resolution, including:

1 the overall sequence and pattern of activities involved in project management;
2 the primary issues encountered in the process of managing an information system development project;
3 the types of structural arrangements within organisations that are necessary to support an effective project management process;
4 the project management processes and the role, responsibilities and authority of the project manager;
5 an appraisal of the major tools and techniques that may be used to support project management.

Throughout the coverage and development of these areas the emphasis will be directed towards the means for improving effectiveness and efficiency in the project management of an information system's development.

10.1 PROJECT MANAGEMENT: AN OVERVIEW

The ability both to create an effective specification, supported by the analysis, design and implementation stages of the software development life cycle, and to deliver a system to the required standards and within the time and cost constraints imposed, depends on the effective management of the entire development process. A common experience for those organisations that develop their own information systems is that while the system may perform to the required standards, the delivery is often considerably later than the target date and the final costs greatly exceed those included in the budget. Examples of systems taking twice as long and costing twice as much as budgeted are not uncommon. Alternatively, the situation may occur that the system is completed within the alotted time and financial constraints, but is inadequate in terms of its quality and its ability to meet user needs. The major cause of such outcomes is poor project management.

The primary objectives underlying any process of project management, whether related to investments in information systems or to some other capital expenditure project, may be encapsulated under the two headings:

1 **Effectiveness**—ensuring that the project, in this case the system:
   (a) meets the required needs of the users or other objectives established;
   (b) is produced to the specified quality standards to aid the satisfaction of user needs;

(c) integrates within the existing organisational information systems, structures and processes;
(d) is sufficiently flexible to respond to changes in the environment in which the system will operate or the changing requirements of users which may only become articulated and refined during the development process itself; and
(e) provides appropriate support to decision makers at all levels, operational, management and strategic.

2 **Efficiency** — ensuring that the system development project, including the development, delivery, installation and final implementation, are:
(a) undertaken within the manpower resources, cost and time targets or constraints specified at the outset;
(b) efficient in exploiting the human resources of the project team members' and the users' time as fully as possible, avoiding unnecessary idle time, delays or time wasted in undertaking unnecessary tasks or activities;
(c) effective in integrating the activities of those within the project team, and also those interactions and dependencies with other parties outside of the project team including users, suppliers, consultants, or managers;
(d) capable of delivering the resources including hardware, software, services and training on time; neither too late nor too early to cause problems of storage, loss of value due to deterioration, unexpected fluctuations in planned cash flows, or loss of benefits from training due to excessive time required prior to the user applying the knowledge or skills acquired.

In practice, the project management process may involve the management of either a small team of one or two internal systems staff to cover all aspects of the system's development or, at the other extreme, a large group of both internal and external staff many of whom will be specialists in limited features of the system during its development. Irrespective of the scale or complexity of the project management situation, the issues concerned are broadly similar and the practices used to ensure improved effectiveness and efficiency may be applied equally well in all situations.

10.2 PROJECT MANAGEMENT ELEMENTS

The terms **effectiveness** and **efficiency** as defined in 10.1 may be expressed in terms of the key elements of any project, namely:

(a) time,
(b) resources,
(c) costs, and
(d) quality.

The term efficiency relates primarily to the elements of time, resource utilisation and costs (measuring the value of the output produced against the costs and time taken to produce the system). The term effectiveness is concerned more with the quality of the system in terms of meeting the required performance standards and objectives.

10.2.1 Time

This factor represents a key parameter in the project management process. Typically, the objectives of the project will stipulate either a target time for the completion of the development of the system, or the date by which the system should be fully operational. Other intermediate dates or targets may also be specified for the completion of particular component elements or phases in the development process. Failure to meet these prescribed target completion dates may have both direct and indirect consequences for the organisation, some of which may be highly significant. For example:

(a) Losses of potential financial returns, reduced operational efficiency and lost competitive advantages from the system operation itself.

(b) Reduced benefits and potential opportunities if other organisational developments are tied to the project, eg the launch of a new product involving an expensive promotional campaign.
(c) Resources remaining idle, eg specific staff recruited and not utilised, and hardware, software, and the environment facilities all arriving ahead of requirement and increasing the organisation's risk of loss, damage or deterioration.
(d) Delays that may require either the extension of the contracts negotiated with specific programmers or analysts who were hired only for the duration of the project (possibly at increased rates), or the use of overtime working to recover lost time (at higher rates).
(e) The retention of existing computing equipment beyond the anticipated time which necessitates the extension of maintenance contracts and often incurs higher maintenance costs than the new equipment. This may also apply to staffing costs particularly if significant reductions are anticipated as a result of the developments.
(f) Unplanned cash flow effects from either early or delayed purchasing and delivery.
(g) The impact on other system development projects which may either be occurring concurrently with the delayed project, or which are due to utilise either part of the system developed by the current system or the staff employed in its development.

Details of the planning approaches and tools needed to control the time element, resources and costs are provided in 10.7.

10.2.2 Resources

For these purposes, the term **resources** relates to both material and human resources. Thus, material resources will include the hardware, software, consumable materials and support services. Although the acquisition and management of material resources may prove demanding, the management of human resources is usually the key element. The staff involved are likely to differ in terms of their specialisms, skills and experience. There will also be differences in personality and attitudes. Generally, the management of resources involves:

(a) evaluating alternative suppliers of hardware, software and services; negotiating prices, quality standards and delivery times; and progressing orders placed;
(b) recruiting and training the staff for the project;
(c) planning workloads for individual staff, scheduling and co-ordinating the work of the project team, establishing performance targets, and regular monitoring and appraisal of individual staff performance.

10.2.3 Costs

The management priorities for both the time and resource elements will be reflected in the costs for the project. A key performance indicator used by senior management to assess the project during its development phase is the level of expenditure incurred relative to the budgeted expenditure. Managing the costs of a project involves:

(a) Forecasting and estimating the costs of the project in total so that the level of anticipated expenditure can be established for each month or quarter. These costs will normally be subdivided into a variety of sub-headings relating to capital and revenue expenditures, and costs associated with staff, materials and overheads.
(b) Monitoring the actual expenditure in total and under each of the sub-headings within the budget—this will allow the project team to assess the degree to which actual expenditure matches budgeted expenditure. In cases where there are significant variances, the project team will be required to establish the cause and the consequences for the total project costs.
(c) Significant over-spending on a project may require the project manager and the organisation to review either the subsequent stages in the development process, or the initial system objectives and performance standards, with the intention of modifying the more expendable elements to meet the budget limits.

10.2.4 Quality

The task of managing quality differs from the task of managing the elements of time, resources and costs, which are concerned primarily with the inputs, processes and activities involved in developing a system. Quality management is primarily focused on the output of the development process as an operational system. It may be more difficult to measure quality than the three other elements because it may be assessed against more subjective criteria. Thus, the perception of quality may differ depending on the position or role of the individual in relation to the information system. For example, the system designer may perceive a particular system as being of inferior quality in a technical sense as it fails to use the filespace on a disk file efficiently. However, the user of the same system may perceive it as a high quality system as it employs simple and easy to use human-machine interfaces to search for the data required. While different perceptions of quality exist, the important assessment of quality relates to the system's ability to meet the users' requirements. Generally, the management of quality incorporates:

(a) establishing quality and performance standards for the system at the outset, and developing methods for measuring these less tangible elements;
(b) establishing procedures and methods of working which will assist in assuring the achievement of the standards in the final system;
(c) monitoring the system regularly against the desired standards and ensuring that the necessary procedures are being observed.

10.3 MANAGING INTERACTION

Managing each of these elements of time, resources, cost and quality in isolation would impose demands on the project manager. However, in practice the manager needs to manage all four elements simultaneously, and not only do they interact with each other, but they are continuously changing. Further, the four elements may often appear to be pulling in different directions, such that the project's objectives are continually under threat, as illustrated in Figure 10.1.

FIGURE 10.1 **Key issues in project management**

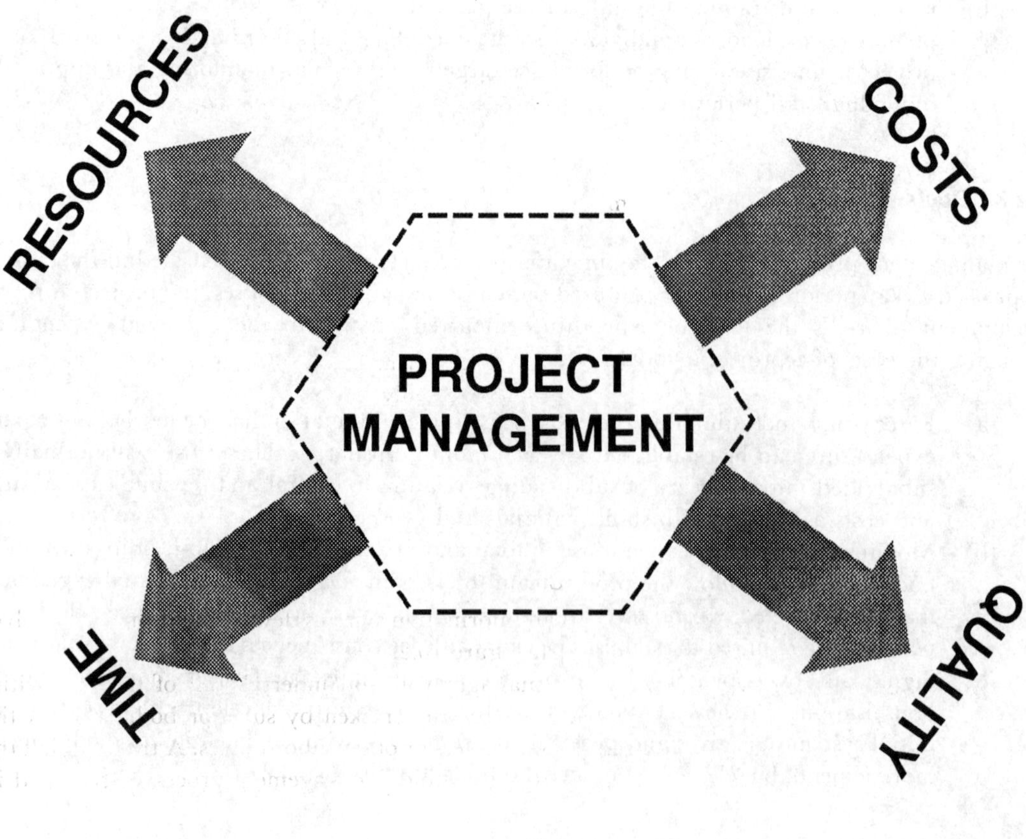

In managing the project, the manager is continuously making judgments and decisions concerning the influence of these elements and seeking to guide and control the development to achieve the objectives. Examples of the type of interaction and the decisions required include:

1 **Managing time** If the project is behind schedule and there is a serious doubt over achieving the target completion date, the manager may resolve this by:
   (a) acquiring extra resources to speed up the completion of the work, or asking existing staff to work additional hours, both of which may intensify the resource management problems and will certainly increase costs;
   (b) either reducing or eliminating particular inspection and testing procedures, and checks which may reduce the time required but at the expense of quality and possibly user confidence in the system.

2 **Managing quality** The decision to establish and maintain high quality standards in terms of system performance and user interface will usually enhance the resources, but the time required to assure this quality level will almost invariably prove more expensive. Some managers would suggest that quality does not necessarily require additional time, resources or cost. They would argue that, providing the staff involved are properly trained and motivated then maintaining high quality standards would be a normal feature of the systems development operations.

3 **Managing resources** Given the opportunity, most project managers would probably prefer to extend the timescale of the project rather than manage periods of peak demand for skilled resources which are beyond the existing complement of the systems team. The hiring of additional temporary staff to cope with the peak workload may not only increase the costs of the project, but may also result in a reduction in quality and generate new problems involving human resource management.

4 **Managing costs** Costs, as can be seen from the previous examples, are inextricably woven into the management of the other three elements. Managing a project by reference to the cost element would involve seeking to reduce or minimise the costs incurred by:
   (a) extending the time required and therefore avoiding the hiring of extra staff or working extra hours;
   (b) utilising less expensive resources where possible;
   (c) decreasing the minimum acceptable quality standards.

The integrated management of these four elements does require the project manager to strike an appropriate balance between them in the ongoing decision-making and control activities. The project manager will usually be held responsible for the project's performance across these four dimensions and will usually be required to report the decisions taken and their effects on these elements to senior management. Often the difficulty facing the project manager is the variation in the perceived importance of these four elements from different areas of the organisation. For example, the management in the potential user department may be particularly concerned with the time element, while the operational users in the same department may be more interested in the quality of the system. The finance director may only be interested in keeping the costs within the agreed budget. The project manager therefore not only requires skills in decision-making, but also in judging the relative importance of these differing perceptions and the extent to which any one of them may be safely ignored. The key danger from the project manager's perspective and, more particularly, from the organisation's point of view, is that concentration on only one or two of these elements at the expense of the other elements may result in significant under-achievement in promoting the total objectives for the system.

10.4 PROJECT MANAGEMENT ACTIVITIES

The management of these four elements within an information systems development project involves a number of major activities which are shown in Figure 10.2.

It should be recognised that the project manager will not undertake all of these activities personally. Some require a strategic input and will be undertaken by superior bodies within the organisation while others will be delegated to team leaders or other subordinates. A treatment of the relationship between organisational structures and the project management process is provided in

FIGURE 10.2 **Major activities of project management**

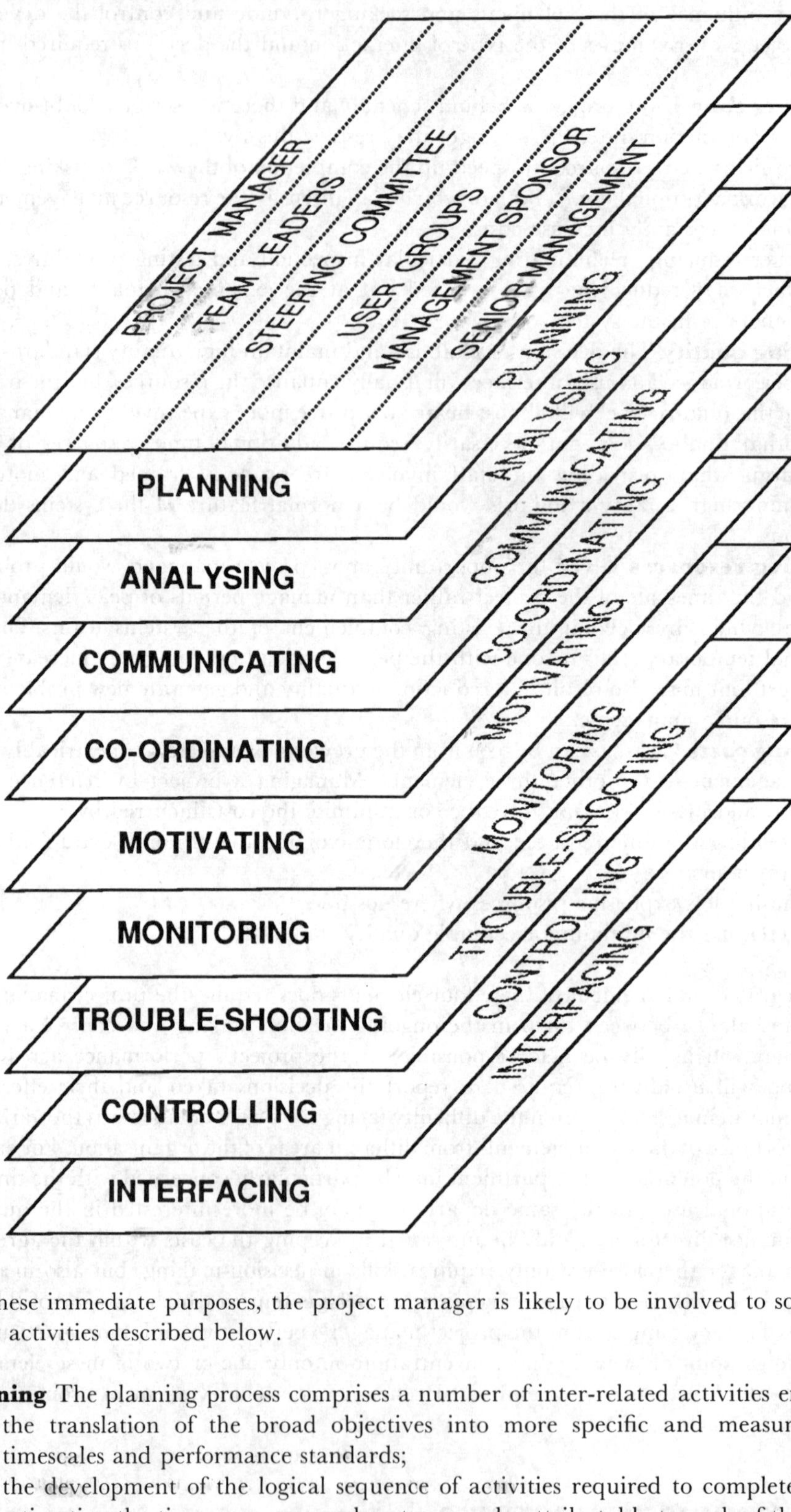

10.6. For these immediate purposes, the project manager is likely to be involved to some extent in most of the activities described below.

1 Planning The planning process comprises a number of inter-related activities encompassing:

(a) the translation of the broad objectives into more specific and measurable targets, timescales and performance standards;

(b) the development of the logical sequence of activities required to complete the project, estimating the time, resources and costs properly attributable to each of these activities; and

(c) the establishment of the necessary structures, procedures and information systems to support the planning process by feeding back data on the progress of the project in terms of time, resource usage, costs, and quality.

Planning is not a single event that occurs once only at the outset of the project, but is a continuous activity involving the reformulation of previous plans to accommodate changes in the situation as a result of:

(a) delays in completing internal activities (this may be due to variables such as staff illness, over-optimistic estimates of the time required, etc);
(b) delays in performance by external agencies, eg late delivery or inadequate quality of supplies of computer equipment, software or support services;
(c) unanticipated problems encountered in the development of the system;
(d) changes in the users' requirements as these become more explicit during the analysis and design process;
(e) changes in the organisational environment in which the system is required to operate, eg a change in the allocation of staff and management responsibilities.

2 **Analysis** This is a general term for a range of activities which includes identifying the cause of a problem, assessing the implications of each problem, searching for possible solutions, evaluating each possibility and selecting the most appropriate for the given situation. This definition of analysis is somewhat wider than that used previously in this text when discussing decision-making. The change arises because it is necessary to functionally decompose the activity into the next layer of component parts. At this level, the analytical methods used are both quantitative and qualitative. Ensuring the efficient and effective use of resources and the adherence to timescales, involves the analysis of:
(a) the primary logical sequence of activities to be conducted and the alternative or contingent sequences that may be adopted either to achieve quicker responses or to deal with unforeseen difficulties;
(b) the effect that any changes in the existing patterns of resource utilisation within the organisation may have on the completion times;
(c) the degree to which modifications to the scheduling of activity and resource utilisation changes the cost profile of the project;
(d) the level of quality that can be maintained in the system if faster target completion dates are adopted.

3 **Communication** A key feature of the project management process, and one that is frequently conducted inadequately, is that of communication. Communication is inextricably linked to the planning and control process and requires effective communication between:
(a) members of the project team itself, between the members of the team and the project's sponsoring department or manager, and between the project manager and project team members;
(b) members of the project team and the affected users to build a degree of mutual collaboration and constructive interaction;
(c) the project management and the management of the organisation to report and review the progress of the project, and to indicate any changes in policy or objectives that may influence the development work; and
(d) the project management and external suppliers of equipment, software or specialist support services to ensure clear understanding of requirements and priorities.

The issue of communications is further developed in 10.6 which deals with the structures and processes required to facilitate effective communications and control within the overall project management.

4 **Co-ordination, integration and co-operation** Planning and managing the co-ordination and integration of the activities and staff of the project both:
(a) **internally** between each other and with other staff in the organisation, and
(b) **externally** with outside suppliers and service support agencies,

is a continuing feature of the management process throughout the project. While the issue of effective communications identified above contributes to this process, often more positive actions are required to ensure effective co-ordination and integration. The larger the project team involved and the more external suppliers and services are used, then the greater the issues of co-ordination and integration become. The term co-operation also relates to the nature of the inter-relationship and integration between staff, though it usually relies more on the inherent culture and personality of those involved rather than on the quality of the planning approach. Most development projects rely heavily on the co-operation of other people, particularly the users involved, and will frequently fail to achieve their desired objectives under all four of the elements (time, resources, costs and quality) if this co-operation is totally absent. Co-ordination and integration involve:
(a) the detailed planning of the contributions to be made by each participant in the process and the dovetailing of their contributions;

(b) regular monitoring of progress in each area or activity and taking the actions necessary to ensure that each component element is progressing in reasonable harmony with affected elements within the structure of the plan;

(c) arranging regular meetings of the staff involved to appraise and review the progress, and to identify the implications of problems or delays encountered in one area on the other areas of development work.

5 **Monitoring, evaluation and control** This group of activities is of considerable importance and will involve all the staff working on the project or associated with the development of the system (see also 2.5). Irrespective of the quality of the initial planning and scheduling activities, or of the quality of the staff and management responsible for undertaking the scheduled activities, it will be necessary to monitor the progress of the development programme continuously, and to identify areas of the programme where actual performance is deviating from that planned in terms of time, resource usage, quality and cost. In addition to identifying such deviations or variances, the project management is also required to undertake an evaluation of:

(a) the cause(s) of each deviation,

(b) the consequences if no action is taken to correct them,

(c) the alternative solutions available and their potential effects on the four key elements, and

(d) the suggested manner for implementing the selected solution.

In many respects the key to effective management of the information systems development process itself is the development of an effective and efficient management information system. The manager requires the appropriate quality of data feedback concerning the progress of the development in terms of detail, accuracy and timeliness. More importantly, the quality of the initial planning process and the use of appropriate methods or tools will facilitate effective monitoring and evaluation of performance in a structured way, and may often provide a vehicle for evaluating alternative actions to resolve or control the situation. Indeed, if the control system is to be given a realistic opportunity to operate effectively, the whole monitoring, evaluation and control process should be made explicit or obvious to those involved in the development operations. Even though the development work is on schedule or even ahead of schedule, the manager should ensure that he or she conveys his or her knowledge of the project status and the status of the individual's contribution to the members of the team on a regular basis. This latter point would also aid the issue of leadership and motivation discussed later.

6 **Trouble-shooting** One of the more onerous and regular tasks encountered in the project management process is that of resolving problems as they arise. This trouble-shooting activity is arguably part of the monitoring, evaluation and control group of activities discussed above, but it has been highlighted separately as it represents a less regulated and more dynamic form of these activities. Because a more immediate response is often required, decision-making will primarily involve the project manager and team leaders rather than the committee structure supervising the project. Indeed, the ability of the project management team to respond effectively to problems as they arise may be an important determinant of the eventual success of the project in meeting the stipulated performance objectives and targets.

Associated with this trouble-shooting activity is the need to consider the delegation of authority and responsibility for managing the various areas of the project. The project manager ought to develop a degree of management decentralisation and encourage the team leaders or development staff to tackle an increasing proportion of problem situations. In delegating this responsibility, the manager also needs to delegate explicitly the authority to make decisions, carefully identifying the limits of each individual's authority. A part of this process of delegation involves the project manager, and indeed other levels of management in the organisation, identifying the key or critical issues and problems, and retaining responsibility and authority for their management. If some degree of decentralisation is encouraged in non-critical areas, it increases the importance of developing and maintaining a good feedback system on the problems that have arisen and the solutions adopted, so that current levels of criticality throughout the project can be monitored.

7 **Quality assurance** An issue which has become of significant importance in the last few years is that of enhancing and ensuring the quality of the system delivered to the users. The first step should be taken during the specification phase of the system's development life cycle, when the quality standards or objectives in terms of system performance are established. These quality

standards are to be made operational by the activities of the systems design, development and programming staff involved in the project. The initial planning of the project should therefore have incorporated the quality dimension into the plans by specifying the timescales allowed, the level of resources to be allocated to specific activities, and the performance targets or standards to be achieved. It is crucial that not only do the staff know the specified standards, but that these are measured throughout the entire process with control actions taken as appropriate to correct deviations. It is often too late to correct deficiencies in the quality of the system once it has been delivered because, although it may be possible to correct operating deficiencies, the cost of doing so and the possible knock-on effects to other elements of the system are much higher.

The confidence of the user may also have been seriously eroded if poor quality interfaces or software performance has been encountered at an early stage, even though the problems are subsequently corrected. This would relate particularly to the situation where the information system being developed required significant changes in staffing, working practices and methods. Human resistance to change is a common feature in many situations, but appears to be more prevalent and vociferous in cases where IT is the source of such changes (see 4.1.1). Inferior quality systems development or implementation provides a golden opportunity to criticise IT in general, and the organisation's systems development team in particular.

8 **Leadership and motivation** Irrespective of the project manager's planning, analytical and co-ordinating abilities, there will usually be a requirement to display effective leadership skills and abilities. The leadership of a team of systems analysts, designers or programmers will require the manager to lead the team and to identify sources of personal conflict, motivate the team during periods when there appears to be a continuous stream of problems, and provide support when the team are under criticism. In essence this highlights a key feature of effective project management that is frequently ignored, as the emphasis is usually placed on the technical expertise of the manager and on the ability to utilise the analytical or quantitative approaches to the management activity. While these attributes of project management are self-evidently essential, they are not sufficient to ensure effective management. Qualities such as good interpersonal skills, the ability to understand different personal perspectives and needs, adaptability in approach to motivating, encouraging or censuring different individuals, and the potential to generate enthusiasm, interest or passion in the task facing the individual or project team are essential to the effective management of a project. It should be noted that it is not sufficient for the project manager alone to be imbued with such qualities, the other management or supervisory levels in the project team also need to display similar qualities to provide a consistent and reinforcing environment and culture.

9 **Managing interfaces** Given the complexity of many organisations within which the systems development and implementation process takes place and the more integrative nature of the systems themselves, an increasingly important role of the project manager is the management of the internal and external interfaces. In situations where the system will span several departments or functions (a not untypical situation), the system interfaces between the departments should be managed to:

(a) Ensure that departments recognise the total benefits arising from the system, and not just those relating to the particular department. The fact that the workload placed on a particular department has increased as a result of the system, eg a requirement to input additional data items which provide information for other areas of the organisation, is frequently a source of contention, and requires effective management if the interfaces are to be maintained on a reasonably stress-free basis.

(b) Prevent departments from seeking to frustrate the development of the project on the basis that it erodes their historical power base in the organisation as the only source of given information.

(c) Avoid the situations where certain users may seek to dictate the parameters, operations and outputs from the system, to an extent greater than their role as either users, providers or processors within the system itself.

Increasingly project managers are being involved in the management of the interfaces between the organisation and its suppliers, and the organisation and its distribution channels or agents. The organisational information systems which are being developed currently are increasingly incorporating these external organisations in an attempt to achieve increased competitive advantage through greater collaboration and the integration of their respective information systems. The role of the system manager in this context is often more demanding than in the internal context where, arguably, the internal structure of authority may be used to enforce a certain degree of compliance. The degree of authority or control that the organisation may exercise over external suppliers or distributors may vary considerably, but will usually be less than absolute.

10.5 STAGES AND LEVELS IN PROJECT MANAGEMENT

The process of project management is a progression through a number of identifiable stages. In addition to this time dimension, it may also be viewed in terms of a series of levels. These levels will operate within each of the stages, performing different roles and having different responsibilities. Figure 10.3 highlights the six main stages or phases of project management and shows examples of the different levels.

FIGURE 10.3 **Stages in the project management process**

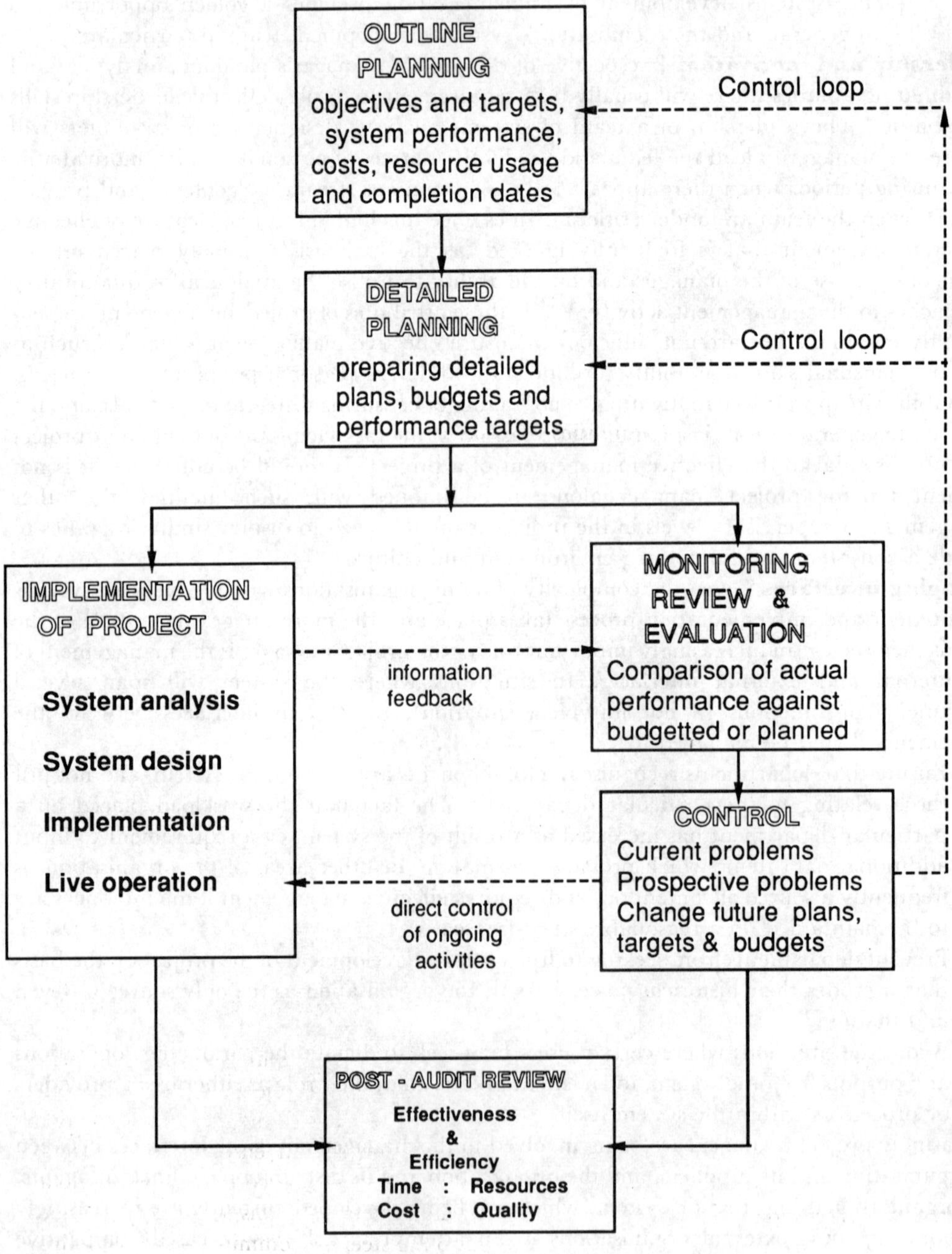

The nine broad management activities outlined in 10.4 will operate throughout each of the phases and to differing extents at each of the levels in the project management structure.

10.5.1 Outline planning phase

This phase covers the period from the initial generation of the system proposal and incorporates:

(a) establishing the objectives and targets for the system in terms of quality,
(b) setting targets for the completion of particular phases,
(c) estimating expenditures for the development and formulating budgets for the expenditure, and
(d) preparing an outline plan of the major stages in the development process and estimating the likely time required for each, and the resources required.

The nature of this process is essentially iterative as a number of proposed plans, objectives, targets and budgets will be prepared and subsequently modified in the light of discussions at differing levels in the project management hierarchy. Following these discussions, agreement will normally be reached on the outline plans and approval given to undertake the next phase.

10.5.2 Detailed planning phase

The detailed planning of the project will primarily involve the project manager and members of the project team, who will endeavour to convert the broad outline plan into a feasible action plan for developing the project incorporating:

(a) a detailed schedule of the activities or tasks to be undertaken, the logical sequence in which these may be performed, and the identification of potentially critical activities or sequences of activities within the overall plan;
(b) an assessment of the resources available to the project and the allocation of particular resources to the activities identified in the schedule above; and the identification of associated issues of recruitment and training of staff to provide appropriate skills to undertake the project, eg staff may be required to attend courses concerning new computer systems, operating systems or applications packages;
(c) a schedule of external purchases of equipment, software or other services required for the system;
(d) detailed budgets covering both internal and external expenditures;
(e) a system for monitoring and controlling the progress of the system development activities in terms of time, resource utilisation, costs and quality standards—the system as developed will itself incorporate an information system to report on these elements but would also include guidelines on the processes to be used in monitoring, reviewing and controlling performance, eg the establishment of steering groups, user groups or meetings of the project team itself would all represent differing processes for monitoring and controlling the project, and would require the formulation of terms of reference, membership, frequency of meetings and the administrative structure to support them.

It would be a mistake to assume that all of the detailed planning must be completed prior to proceeding to the implementation or commencement of work on the project, as many parts of the detailed planning may require further information which is either not readily available or may only materialise as the project proceeds. However, the organisation should ensure that the detailed planning has adequately addressed each of the issues itemised above. The conclusion of the detailed planning phase should typically result in the submission of the detailed plans to the management in the form of the sponsoring department or manager, and to the steering committee if this has already been formed. These detailed plans require consideration, modification and authorisation prior to implementation.

10.5.3 Implementation

The implementation phase in this context of project management refers to the complete cycle of stages incorporating analysis, design and implementation of the information system. The content of each of these stages has been discussed in detail in Chapters 6, 7, 8 and 9, and is not repeated here. In most respects the implementation phase in the project management process represents the operational activities required to produce the required system, and project management is concerned with measuring both the effectiveness and efficiency of these activities, both individually and in aggregate. Figure 10.3 provides a diagramatic illustration of this, showing the implementation phase being paralleled by the phases of monitoring, reviewing and controlling.

10.5.4 Progress review

MONITORING AND REVIEWING

The monitoring and reviewing process may take place at a number of different levels and consequently different time intervals. Irrespective of the level or the frequency of the process, the essential element in common is the measurement of the actual performance on the project against the planned performance. Although this measurement could take account of a variety of criteria, it is customary to limit the scope of the exercise to the four elements identified earlier in this Chapter. Examples of the performance measurement approaches in these elements would include:

(a) **Time** The main test is a comparison of the actual completion dates against their planned completion dates, with management requiring progress reports on current activities to determine whether each element of the project is on or behind schedule for the planned completion dates. Tools to aid this monitoring process (eg PERT or GANTT charts) are discussed in 10.7.

(b) **Resources** It would be common to measure performance under three headings:
(i) the extent to which resources have been made available to the project,
(ii) the percentage utilisation of those resources in promoting the plan, and
(iii) the extent to which the resources are being used efficiently and effectively.
The reference to resources in this context refers not only to the human resources working on the project, but also to the computer resources, accommodation and other supporting services. However, because humans are more prone to error than machines, attention will usually be focused on the human resources to measure their performance and effectiveness.

(c) **Costs** The usual source of information for monitoring the cost performance of the project will be the organisation's costing and budgetary control system. If the project has been established as an identifiable cost centre within the budgetary system, then all the directly identifiable or attributable costs incurred by the project will be collected and reported against the project. The costing system may also incorporate the allocation or apportionment of the indirect or overhead costs to the project. The monitoring and review process will again involve comparisons of the actual expenditure against planned expenditure, though the level of detail in terms of types of costs will depend on the detailed breakdown available within the budget reports. To produce a comprehensive evaluation of performance, it may often be necessary to collect and report other cost data or more detailed data than is available through the standard budget reports, including the range of quotations received for a particular item of expenditure, etc.

(d) **Quality** The regular assessment of quality is often a more complex task than for the other dimensions of performance, particularly in the context of information systems development. In the more usual situations where a product is to be manufactured, quality can be measured in terms of the number of units that either fail intermediate or final quality inspection and testing, or that are returned as faulty by customers within the given period. The measurement of quality in organisations providing services rather than manufactured products is more difficult because it inevitably relies on a more subjective evaluation of performance against the desired standards.

The nature of the interdependent functions of systems analysis, design and implementation is that of a continuous development process with the eventual product or service, represented by the final operating information system, not available until the completion of the project. In this respect, performance measurement needs to relate more to the degree of conformity between the initially agreed standards of quality and the standards actually achieved during the intermediate stages. For example, it can be instructive to monitor the quality of the interviews conducted with users and the resulting reports (see 6.1.1 and 6.2.3), the user's views on the quality of the training courses (see 9.1.1), or the degree to which the documentation conforms to the agreed standards (see 9.1.1). As in the provision of most services, many of the quality performance measures in this area are less objective because they rely upon opinion which may be coloured by self-interest. However, the possible lack of objectivity should not be regarded as an excuse for ignoring the measurement of quality. It is a key element which requires continuous monitoring throughout the entire systems development project, although the nature of the measurement process will vary both in the level of detail and in the form of the output produced.

EVALUATION

An important activity that occurs within the monitoring and review phase, and that is implicit in the above discussion, is **evaluation**. The evaluation process involves:

(a) measuring the progress made during the current reporting period and the cumulative progress to date in meeting the time, cost, resource and quality targets;
(b) assessing the implications of any lack of progress or of current difficulties in the activities being undertaken for the work scheduled to be undertaken in the following reporting period, and for the total project (again in terms of the four elements);
(c) generating a range of alternative actions that may be undertaken to resolve specific problems or delays which have been, or which are likely to be, encountered;
(d) analysing the potential effects of these alternative actions in terms of the four elements, often using differing assumptions concerning the future situation or environment within which the project will develop. This *what if?* type of analysis, or **sensitivity analysis** is a common feature of the evaluation process. It may use computer modelling techniques for the more quantitative dimensions, and the human mind is available (with DSS or expert system help) to handle the more qualitative or subjective dimensions.

10.5.5 Control activities

Control, like the monitoring and review phase, is an ongoing activity throughout the entire system development and implementation phases. It refers to actions which are designed to:

(a) prevent deviations from arising while planned activities are taking place—this is achieved through a continuous process of monitoring and supervising;
(b) correct those deviations from the plan which have been observed in previous reporting periods;
(c) prevent any future deviations from the planned activities or performance standards by instituting revisions to future plans, performance standards, targets and monitoring systems; and
(d) implement any other findings arising from the monitoring, review and evaluation processes.

It should be recognised that control is not merely reactive, ie a series of actions that respond to problems once they have occurred, but it is equally important in the role of controlling current and future activities. Arguably, control is more effective in the pro-active role of seeking to predict potential problems and taking the necessary precautions or actions either to avoid their occurrence or to minimise their effect on the project should they occur. Figure 10.3 illustrates the **closed loop control system** (see 3.1.8) as it applies to the project management process. Control activities may influence the previous phases in the process in the following ways, ie:

(a) make changes in the current operations or activities, eg the re-allocation of an additional member of the project team to a particular activity that is behind schedule, or to cover for the illness of another member;
(b) implement changes to the detailed plans for future activities in the project, eg re-organising the sequence of activities to be undertaken as a result of the anticipated delay in the delivery and installation of a key component in the equipment ordered;
(c) revise the original outline plans, targets, objectives or budgets to reflect significant changes in the project requirements or environment, eg an increase in the requirement concerning the number of workstations that are necessary to support the users in a particular department will increase the budgeted costs for equipment and training, and may require revisions to the timescales and/or the performance standards of the eventual system, say, in terms of the average response time to users which may deteriorate with the increase in the number of workstations on the system.

Each of these control activities or decisions will require some form of discussion and agreement depending on the scale of their impact. Control activities concerning current operations will typically involve the project manager and members of the project team, while changes to the future detailed plans or the project's objectives, targets or budgets will usually require authorisation at more senior levels in the organisation's management hierarchy. These levels and their role in the project management process are discussed in 10.6.

10.5.6 Post-audit review

The final phase in the project management process which is conducted after the completion of the development and implementation of the system is an audit of the complete development process. This audit which addresses both the information system itself and the process of developing the system, ought to assess:

(a) the effectiveness of the completed system in relation to the user requirements and the standards of performance, as either initially specified or subsequently modified, ie the achievement of the required quality;
(b) the efficiency of the system during operation against the agreed performance standards;
(c) the cost of the development in relation to the budgeted expenditure and the reasons for over or under expenditure;
(d) the time taken to develop the system in relation to the target completion date, and the reasons contributing to completion before or after schedule;
(e) the effectiveness of the management processes and structures in managing the project; and
(f) the significance of the problems which were encountered and the effectiveness of the solutions which were produced to deal with them.

The primary purpose behind the post-audit analysis is not the generation of excuses for the poor performance of the delivered system, nor the criticism of the inadequate performance of either the project management process itself or of the members of the project team who were supposed to make it work. The real value to the organisation from conducting this appraisal is to enhance the organisation's experience and learning such that it may:

(a) enhance the organisation's planning and forecasting abilities;
(b) identify problems or issues that may arise in future development projects, and make appropriate adjustments or allowances;
(c) develop the monitoring, control and management processes to achieve greater management effectiveness in future projects;
(d) document the experiences gained to enable future staff not involved in the project to build on the previous experiences.

These benefits may prove significant to the organisation in the future, but their achievement will usually require an open style of debate or a supportive culture in the organisation. Otherwise those directly involved in, or responsible for, the project will react defensively. Those under attack will therefore seek to draw attention away from their own inadequacies or mistakes by attributing the source of the problems to another point in the project development or management system, or by blaming external factors such as late deliveries by suppliers. If the post-audit review is conducted in such a negative fashion, the social and political costs will significantly outweigh any potential benefits. Indeed, the outcome which emerges may prove more harmful to future projects than if no review had been undertaken at all.

10.5.7 Levels of managing the project

Each of the above phases needs to be managed at different levels which match the need to manage the total organisation at a strategic, management, tactical and operational level. In the case of project management these have been subdivided into three levels:

1 **Strategic** This level involves taking a broad view of the total project and of all the major stages involved. The aim is to integrate and co-ordinate the contributions, both direct and indirect, from each area of the organisation and from outside the organisation. While the decision-making is inevitably concerned with the issues of time, resources, costs and quality, the perspective adopted is to view these issues in aggregate terms, eg the total capital expenditure or staffing costs incurred on the project to date in relation to the budgeted levels. Reporting at this level will generally be directed towards the organisation's senior management, and in addition to being in a summarised form, it is also likely to be on a monthly or quarterly timescale to allow the planning, monitoring and control activities to focus on broad issues of performance, timescales or costs.

2 **Tactical** This level is concerned with viewing and managing the project on a short- to medium-term timescale (see 2.7). The actual time horizon of the planning, decision-making and control will depend upon the total scale of the project in terms of resources and time, but it would be usual to review both the work in hand and the work to be undertaken in each of the main activity areas of the project over the coming one or two months. In larger projects, separate teams of development staff may be given specific responsibility for monitoring and controlling the main activity areas of the project. While still concerned with the four basic elements of time, resources, costs and quality, the information used for this purpose is likely to be more detailed and the reporting period will probably be shorter. For example, an evaluation may be conducted of the performance of a particular team of staff during the previous week to measure the progress made, and to identify any problems and the corrective action necessary.

3 **Operational** Management activities at this level are concerned with the more detailed aspect of supervising and controlling the ongoing operations of the development. This will tend to focus on the problems associated with a particular activity and on the direct supervision of staff. The main tasks are resolving any specific technical difficulties encountered, ensuring the maintenance of appropriate standards, motivating the staff, trouble-shooting, etc. While the priority remains the maintenance of effectiveness and efficiency, this is now directly related to specific activities and to individual members of the project team. One of the more important consequences is that the management process at this level will involve less formalised reporting systems—the style usually depends upon a more direct and frequent method of monitoring performance and greater emphasis on inter-personal relationships. An example of an operational management issue would be a debate leading to the selection of the most appropriate method for structuring the organisation's customer database to ensure effectiveness and efficiency both in responding to users' requests and in the utilisation of the disk file space available.

10.6 STRUCTURES FOR MANAGING THE PROJECT

As may be concluded from the above examples, the nature and composition of the management process will be dictated largely by the particular level at which the project is being viewed. There are also a number of differing structures used to perform these management activities at the different levels. A typical structure for the management of the systems development process is shown in Figure 10.4

FIGURE 10.4 **Project management infrastructure**

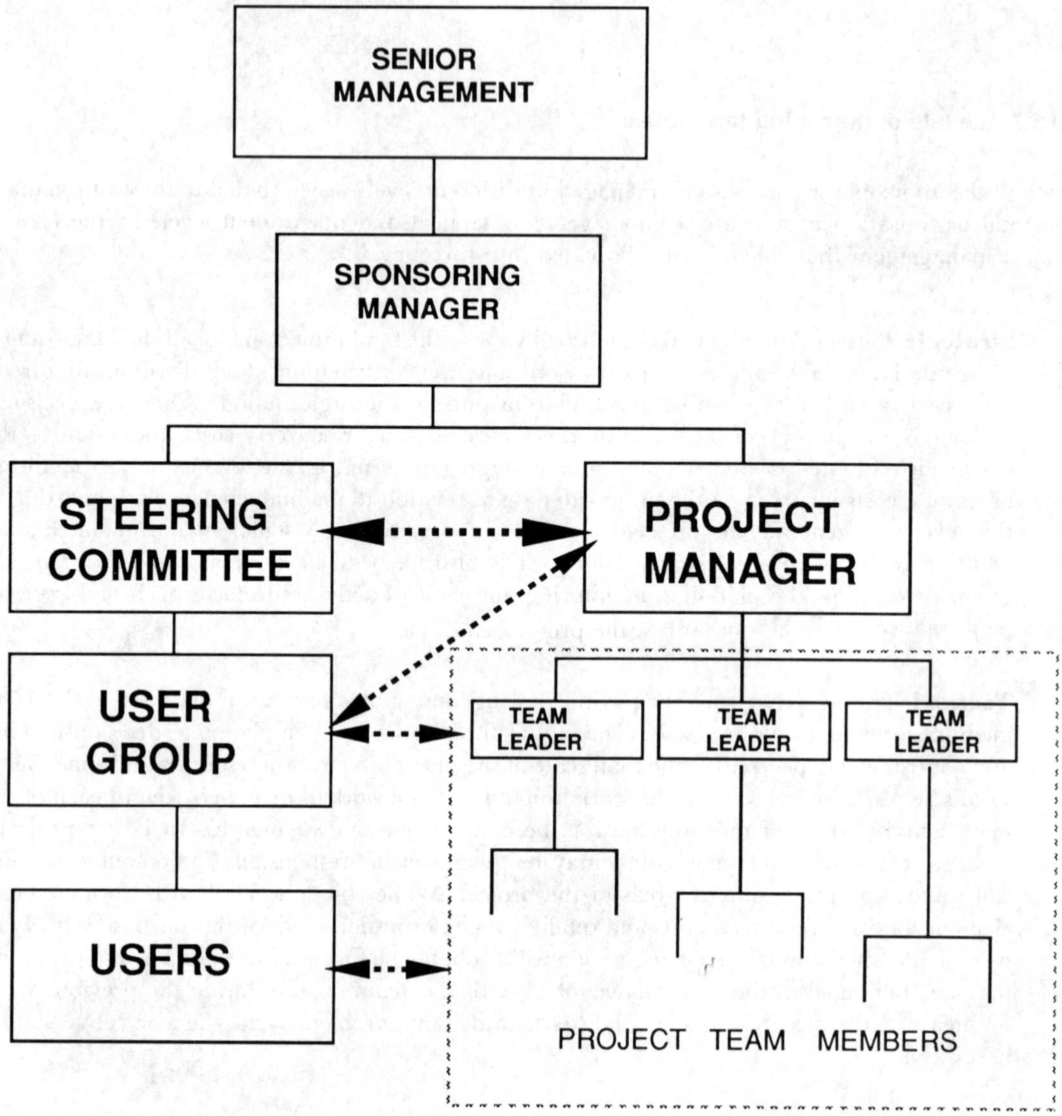

The primary role and responsibilities of each of the major components of this management structure are outlined in the following subsections, together with an indication of the level at which they operate.

10.6.1 Team leaders

It is usually necessary to appoint a team leader whose main responsibilities will be:

(a) planning and organising the work of the members of the particular team on a daily or weekly basis;

(b) continuously supervising the activities of each of the team members;
(c) providing advice or taking decisions on technical difficulties that arise;
(d) co-ordinating and supervising the interaction with user departments and other project teams;
(e) reporting progress to the project manager or user group, and providing advice on possible solutions to the problems which have been encountered;
(f) providing feedback to the team members on any changes in the project that have resulted from decisions at a more senior level; and
(g) implementing any changes to the planned activities and schedules as a result of control decisions.

In larger development projects there may be several project leaders and the project manager should establish a regular pattern of joint meetings between the leaders to assist in the co-ordination of the development work as a whole.

10.6.2 User group

The user group provides a forum for the joint review and appraisal of developments within the project. Ideally, at least one representative from each of the main departments affected by the system(s) targeted by the current project(s) should attend this group together with the project leaders and the project manager. This is frequently a valuable vehicle through which to explore issues and concerns raised by the users, to gauge the strength of user opinion, and to discuss the possible solutions to any problems identified. However, it should be recognised that the user group is primarily an advisory body. It is designed to highlight and discuss the problems that affect the users as the system(s) develop(s). Consequently, although it does not have any executive authority, there must be some degree of responsiveness from the executive management to the issues raised if it is to maintain the support of the users and to provide a useful function in the management process. Thus, in relation to the more minor problems, the project leaders or the project manager may be able to agree a course of remedial action to resolve the issue without further authorisation. More substantial issues which may significantly influence the nature of each project, its objectives, budget or targeted completion date will require discussion and agreement by more senior levels in the management structure. This could be facilitated by reports or recommendations from the user group meetings that are transmitted up to the project steering committee.

10.6.3 Project steering committee

The steering committee membership should comprise representatives from the user departments who are also members of the user group, some or all of the project team leaders, the project manager, and members of the senior management who are either responsible for the systems' development staff or the functional areas primarily affected by the developments in progress. The steering committee provides a key role in:

(a) providing a forum for the discussion of user concerns, where alternative solutions may be discussed at a more senior level with a view to providing recommended courses of action;
(b) reviewing the current status of the project by reference to the dimensions of time, resources, costs and quality;
(c) analysing the cause and effect of any deviations from the plan and evaluating alternative corrective actions;
(d) recommending changes to the project either to correct current or anticipated deviations, or to reflect developments in the users' requirements from the system(s);
(e) providing advice on policy formulation for the operation of the information system within the organisation at the strategic, management and operational levels.

Although the steering committee's function is nominally to provide advice, the committee may have real power and be able to persuade the executive arm of the management to adopt its recommendations. This would be particularly true if the members of the senior management responsible for taking the ultimate decisions participate fully in the work and meetings of the committee. Thus, even though the committee may not have either the responsibility or the authority to make decisions, it will often exert power indirectly, ie through the power of its individual members to impose decisions. To that extent, any failure on the part of senior management to participate in the steering committee will usually relegate its role to that of a mere 'talking shop', providing no valuable contribution to the effective development and management of the information system.

10.6.4 Management sponsor

Senior management must show commitment and involvement in the user group and the project steering committee. Mere participation in these bodies is not enough. There must be tangible evidence of their commitment to the development of improved information systems by:

(a) formally recognising the potential value that this will provide to the organisation,
(b) displaying a real interest not only in the technical aspects of the development but, equally, in its impact in the user departments, and
(c) supporting and encouraging both the project manager and the development team in their work.

The development of information systems, whether for manual or computer-based solutions, will usually involve change. Most organisations and their employees have degrees of resistance to change. If the management of change within an organisation is to be successful and effective, it therefore requires the explicit support of the senior management. One solution is to appoint a member of the senior management, preferably at board level, with responsibility for the development of the organisation's information system, a role which is termed the **sponsoring manager** in Figure 10.4. In larger organisations, one individual may be the IT manager with sole responsibility for overseeing development; while in smaller operations, this role may be combined with other functional roles and responsibilities. An obvious danger in the latter situation is that the systems development role is either relegated to a subsidiary level because of the demands from the other functions, or it is totally ignored. In fact, the importance of information as a corporate resource and its potential to provide significant competitive advantages to the organisation ought to justify the post as a separate functional responsibility within most organisations.

The other important feature of the sponsoring manager's role is to provide a channel of communication either between the project manager and the senior management or between the users and the senior management to report on progress and potential future developments.

10.6.5 Project manager

The project manager may be required to interface with all three levels (strategic, tactical and operational) at different times, although, in the larger projects, the team or group leaders would be responsible for the operational level management of the activities and personnel within their team. The project manager's primary responsibility is to ensure effectiveness and efficiency across the complete project, which involves the following action at each level:

1 **Strategic** At this level, the manager should:
   (a) evaluate and analyse the strategic impact of each proposed system on the organisation's operations, in promoting a competitive advantage and on the other existing or proposed information systems within the organisation;

(b) report to senior management on the results of the strategic evaluation, and quantify the potential costs and benefits that may be derived from each system development;
(c) contribute to the strategic decision-making process of the organisation in terms of the information resource; and
(d) review and evaluate the strategic consequences of the progress achieved in developing the system at regular intervals.

2 **Tactical** At this level, the manager's responsibility is to:
(a) convert the objectives, targets and performance standards agreed for the project into operational plans;
(b) develop the outline and detailed plans for the project, identifying the time, resource and cost parameters, and producing a schedule of activities for the project staff;
(c) monitor the performance of the project against the agreed plans, budgets and quality performance standards, and report progress to both the steering committee and the management sponsor;
(d) liaise with management and staff in the user departments to ensure an effective interface in terms of integration and co-operation between the users and the project development staff;
(e) facilitate a similar level of co-operation with project staff and outside agencies, ie either with suppliers or distributors for the company's main business, or with the specialist agencies supporting the system development project itself;
(f) analyse deviations from the planned performance, evaluating alternative solutions and recommending appropriate control changes to future plans or targets;
(g) develop appropriate information systems to provide the necessary information to monitor and control the project.

3 **Operational** At this level, the manager should:
(a) manage and control the daily activities of the project team members either directly or through the project team leaders;
(b) conduct regular progress meetings with the project staff and team leaders to identify and resolve existing and potential difficulties;
(c) appraise the performance of individual members of the project development staff and seek to assure the achievement of the required quality standards throughout the project development work.

The project manager plays a key role in the effective management of the development process, and although other participants may contribute significantly to this, the project manager fulfills the major role of integrating all the various contributions.

10.7 TOOLS AND TECHNIQUES

There are a variety of tools and techniques which are used in the planning and control of investment projects in other areas of management and which may be equally effective when applied to the management of information systems development. These tools and techniques are primarily concerned with three of the key elements discussed earlier in this chapter, ie time, resources and costs, but it is important to recognise that they are designed merely to support management. No single tool or technique can represent an effective substitute for good management.

10.7.1 Critical Path Analysis (CPA)

The CPA approach to planning and controlling projects is often referred to under other titles, the more common of which are the **Program Evaluation and Review Technique (PERT)** and the **Critical Path Method (CPM)**. Although there are some variations in the detailed approach of each of these methods, the basic assumptions are the same. The stages involved in the CPA approach are as follows.

PROGRAMMING

For these purposes, the term programming refers to the following tasks:

1 The identification and listing of all the major tasks or activities that are to be undertaken in the project. In the initial stages it is often easier to identify only the broad activities rather than to break each of them down into very detailed activities. Figure 10.5 illustrates a **network diagram**. At the initial level, it provides an overview of the total project development process. Subsequently, each of the activities which are shown as arrows in the diagram will be developed into increasingly more detailed network diagrams. The following stages relate to the development of these more detailed diagrams.

FIGURE 10.5 **Network diagram**

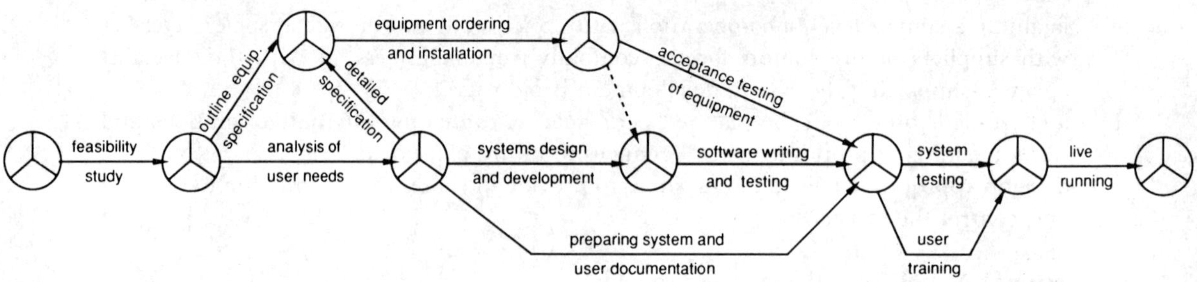

2 The construction of a network diagram that shows the logical sequence of each of the activities listed. The symbols used are an arrow which represents a task or activity with the arrowhead indicating the direction of the logical flow, and circles which represent events. An event is essentially a logical device to connect up the activities and to indicate the point at which an activity starts and finishes. It also ties together all of those preliminary activities which must be completed before the particular activity may commence. For these purposes, activities have durations associated with them, while events are seen as a point in time with no duration. Structuring the logical sequence is often a difficult and time consuming process. It is dependent upon receiving accurate additional information from the key people involved in the project, and relies upon the judgment of which activities are to be completed before the next activity may commence. In practical terms, it is often possible to start a subsequent activity prior to the full completion of a preceding activity. The requirement to allow this to happen is that the interdependent proportion of the work is completed before the subsequent activity can commence. This change in the logical relationship between activities may be represented in the diagram by dividing the earlier activity into two parts (further explained in the subsection entitled 'Evaluation' to follow).

FIGURE 10.6 **Critical path diagram**

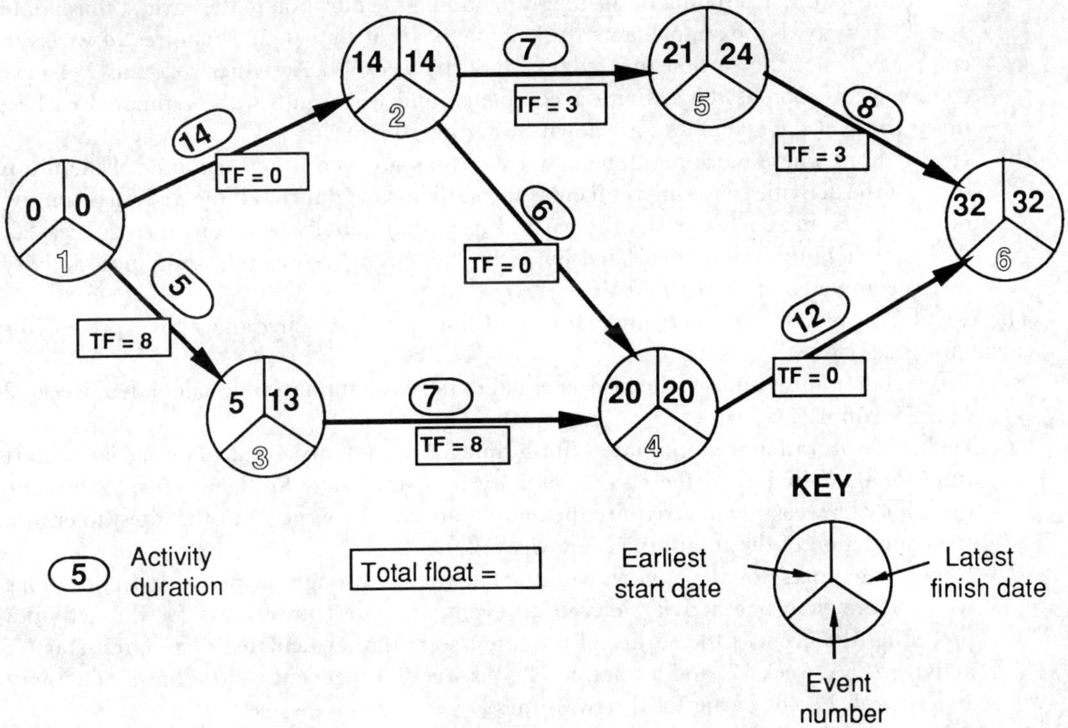

Figure 10.6 provides an illustration of a simple network diagram. The structure of the diagram suggests that activity 4–6 cannot commence until both activities 2–4 and 3–4 have been completed. Even though activity 3–4 may be completed before the other activity, the subsequent activity may still not commence. There are other methods of designing the diagram to show the logic that activity 4–6 may start after a certain proportion of 2–4 has been completed, but this is outside the scope of the present treatment. The correctness of the initial logical representation in the diagram will be examined at later stages in the planning process when attention is focused on specific areas of the plan.

3 The estimation of the time which will be required to undertake each of the activities in the diagram. In the normal project development process these estimates would either be expressed in days or weeks. Certain approaches such as PERT employ a system of estimation based on three time classifications for each activity, ie pessimistic, most likely and optimistic. The three estimates are then aggregated into a single estimate for the *expected duration* of the activity by using a weighting formula of the type:

$$\frac{\text{Optimistic} + (4 \times \text{Most Likely}) + \text{Pessimistic}}{6}$$

The expected duration calculated by this process is then applied to the network calculations as illustrated in Figure 10.7 overleaf. The use of the three estimates will provide some additional data to aid the planning and analysis of the project, though the difficulties in capturing these estimates, the costs of doing so, and the degree of accuracy of the data may suggest that this added value may be significantly outweighed by the costs.

4 The use of the network diagram and the estimated durations for each of the activities to calculate the *earliest start* and *earliest finish* times for each of the activities by:

(a) Starting at the beginning of the network and setting the initial time = 0, progress along each of the paths of activities in the diagram adding the duration to the earliest finish date of each activity. For example, activity 1–2 may start at time 0, and requires 14 weeks to complete, hence the earliest finish date would be week 14. Activities 2–5 and 2–4 may commence as soon as this activity is completed and will result in the estimated earliest finish times of these activities as shown in Figure 10.7.

(b) In situations where more than one activity **enters** an event, then the later of the finish dates of the activities entering is taken as the earliest start date of all the activities coming out of the event. For example, the earliest time that activity 4–6 can start is week 20. Although activity 3–4 is completed by week 12, activity 4–6 cannot start until activity 2–4 is completed at the earliest time of week 20.

5 The calculation of the *latest start* and *latest finish* times by reversing the above process for calculating the earliest times, ie:

(a) Set the latest finish time for the project equal to the earliest finish time calculated, week 32 in the example.

(b) Deduct the duration from this latest finish time for the activity to calculate the latest start time for the activity, in the case of activity 5–6, the latest finish of week 32 less the duration of 8 weeks, would require the activity to start by week 24 at the latest to ensure the completion of the total project by week 32.

(c) Repeat the process for all activities working backwards through the network. In situations where more than one activity **leaves** an event, the latest finish time for the activities preceding the event is the earlier of the latest start times calculated. The latest start of activity 2–5 is week 17, and for activity 2–4 is week 14, hence the latest finish of activity 1–2 is week 14, the earlier of the two times.

A complete schedule of the earliest and latest start and finish times is shown in Figure 10.7

6 The calculation of the *total float* for each activity which allows the determination of the critical path for the project, ie:

(a) Calculate the time available to do the project:

$$\text{Latest Finish Time} - \text{Earliest Start Time}$$

Deduct from this time available the time required to do the activity, ie the duration. The resulting figure is termed the total float for the activity.

$$\text{Total Float} = (\text{Latest Finish} - \text{Earliest Start}) - \text{Duration}$$

The total float for activity 2 − 4 would be calculated as

$$\text{TF} = (20 - 14) - 6 = 0 \text{ weeks}$$

The total float values for the remaining activities are shown in the table in Figure 10.7.

(b) The sequence of activities from the start of the project to the end which has the lowest total float, a value of zero in our example, is termed the *critical path.* This is the longest logical sequence of activities within the project and dictates the overall length of time required to complete the project.

(c) Although the total float in the example used is a value of zero, this is due to setting the latest finish time of the final activities equal to their earliest finish times. However, if a target completion date were used as the latest finish time for the project, then positive or negative values of total float would ensue. For example, a completion date of week 30 would result in a negative value of −2 for the total float on the critical path activities, whereas a completion date of week 38 would result in a positive total float value of 6 weeks on the critical path.

FIGURE 10.7 **Critical path diagram and activity schedules**

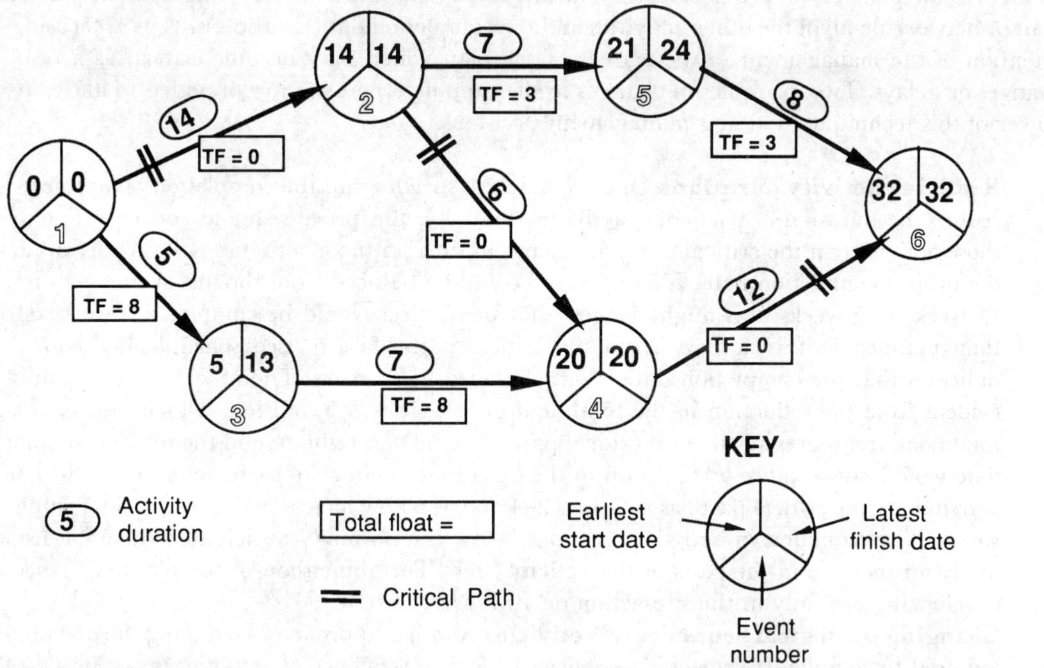

ACTIVITY NUMBERS START EVENT	END EVENT	DURATIONS	EARLIEST START	EARLIEST FINISH	LATEST START	LATEST FINISH	TOTAL FLOAT
1	2	14	0	14	0	14	0
1	3	5	0	5	8	13	8
3	4	7	5	12	13	20	8
2	4	6	14	20	14	20	0
2	5	7	14	21	17	24	3
4	6	12	20	32	20	32	0
5	6	8	21	29	24	32	3

(d) The interpretation of the total float value indicates the degree to which particular activities may be delayed in starting, or extended in terms of their duration without affecting the completion date of the project. Activities 1–3 and 3–4 have a total float of 8 weeks, which means that either the start of these activities may be delayed to week 8 or week 13 respectively, or the total duration of the activities may be increased by a further 8 weeks before the project completion time of week 32 is jeopardised. It is important to recognise that the total float relates to a sequence of activities and not to the individual activities. Thus, if activity 1–3 is delayed by 6 weeks, the total float on the subsequent activity 3–4 would reduce to 2 weeks.

EVALUATION

Following the completion of the network diagram and the calculation of both the activity and project completion dates, and the total float values, it is usual to evaluate the plan against the target completion dates for the project. In most situations, the initial plan will fail to meet the required completion date, and it will be necessary to engage in a process to evaluate the alternative strategies for the reduction of the time required. CPA is a powerful tool in supporting this evaluation of possible changes to the plan, and it provides a rapid means of assessing the effect of changes in one part of the plan or network on all of the other activities and the completion date. It also assists in re-focusing the attention of the management on new areas of the plan which may become critical as a result of changes or delays. Two examples of changes to the simplified network are provided to illustrate the power of this technique in aiding management decisions.

1 **Reducing activity durations** One approach to speeding up the completion of a project is to reduce the duration of particular activities. Initially, this process should concentrate only on those activities on the critical path, as savings in time on these activities will directly influence the project completion date. If activity 4–6 could be reduced from the initial time required of 12 weeks to 5 weeks, this might suggest that the project would be completed 5 weeks earlier than planned as this activity is on the critical path. The revised schedule in Figure 10.8 indicates that the completion date is only reduced by 3 weeks. The reason for this should be evident from the reduction in the total float on activities 2–5 and 5–6, which now have zero total float and represent the new critical path. Any further reduction in the project completion date would now require a reduction in the durations of either of these activities or the earlier activities on the critical path, as activities 2–4 and 4–6 now have a positive total float value of 4 weeks. The reduction in activity durations below the normally anticipated time will usually imply an increase in the costs of the activity itself. This dimension of the planning process is developed more fully in the subsection on PERT/cost below.

2 **Changing the logical sequence of activities** Another approach to reducing the overall time required to complete a project is to review the logical sequence of activities in the initial plan. The purpose is to identify those activities which may be:

(a) undertaken in parallel with other activities that are currently shown as following;
(b) commenced when only part of the logically preceding activities have been completed;
(c) not fully dependent on the completion of all of the preceding activities currently shown in the network.

Again the focus of attention in analysing these possibilities should be focused on those activities on the critical path. In our example, if it were established that activity 1–2 comprised two basic stages, and that activity 2–4 could be started after the completion of this first stage rather than the completion of the entire activity, then the network could be redrawn as indicated in Figure 10.9. The second stage of the original activity 1–2 is now shown as activity 2–7 and is being conducted in parallel with activity 2–5 which also depends only on the first stage of activity 1–2 being completed. The overall effect of this change in the logic would be a reduction of 6 weeks in the project completion time and the detailed effects on the individual activities are shown in the table in Figure 10.9.

REVIEW

The final stage in the application of the CPA approach to project management is the monitoring and review of progress as the plan is implemented. The basic stages of this process involve:

(a) Periodic reports, either weekly or monthly, indicating those activities that have been completed and the date on which they were completed; those activities which are currently in progress, the extent to which they are completed and any revised changes to the time required for the activity; and identifying any changes in the estimates of future activities on the basis of improved information or experiences in conducting the initial activities in the project.
(b) The incorporation of these actual completion times or revised estimates into the network diagram and the assessment of their effect on the project completion date and the critical path.
(c) The evaluation of alternative approaches to the resolution of delays in the project completion time as indicated in the 'Evaluation' subsection earlier, and any necessary attempts to secure agreement to any changes which may be required to activity durations, the sequence of activities, or extensions to the total project completion date.
(d) The provision of revised schedules of activities which incorporate new start and finish dates for all the future activities in the project.

FIGURE 10.8 **Critical path diagram modified for changes in durations**

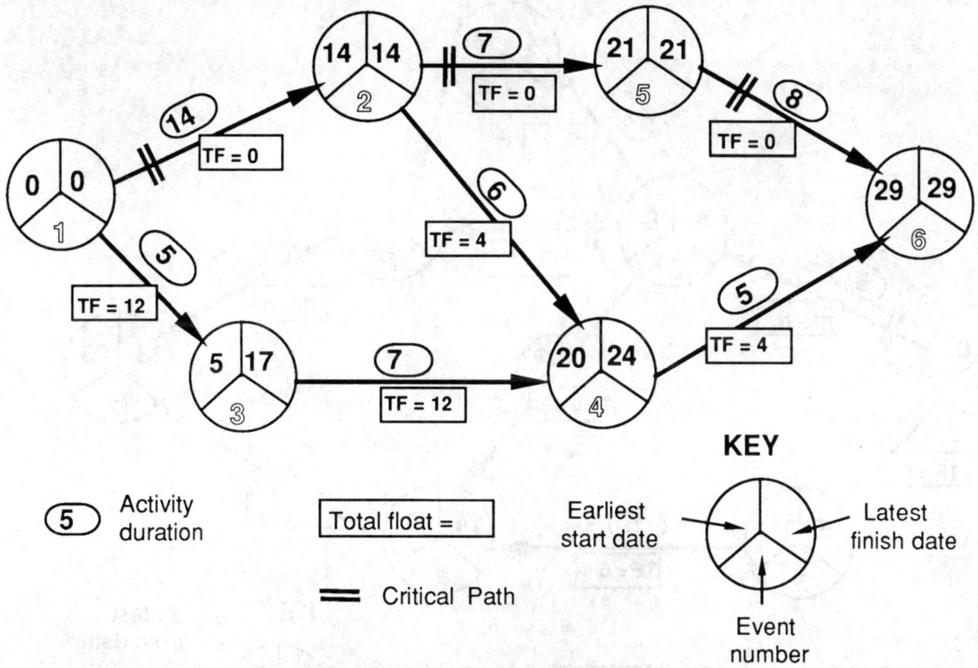

ACTIVITY NUMBERS		DURATIONS	EARLIEST		LATEST		TOTAL
START EVENT	END EVENT		START	FINISH	START	FINISH	FLOAT
1	2	14	0	14	0	14	0
1	3	5	0	5	12	17	12
3	4	7	5	12	17	24	12
2	4	6	14	20	18	24	4
2	5	7	14	21	14	21	0
4	6	5	20	25	24	29	4
5	6	8	21	29	21	29	0

An example of the revised schedule on our simplified project is provided in Figure 10.10. The graphical presentation in the figure is termed a **Gantt chart**, and its purpose is to indicate all of the activities in the project. Managers use shading highlights to indicate the extent to which each of the activities is either on, behind or in advance of the schedule. Consequently, Gantt charts are a useful method of displaying the current state of the project and they are frequently placed on the project manager's wall. They are, however, only really suitable either for the display of relatively small projects with limited activities, or for summarising the activities of a larger project. The major problem associated with the use of this type of chart is that the logical inter-relationships between the component activities or tasks are more difficult to deduce from a chart than from a network diagram. The main advantage lies in the chart's capacity to represent the current state of the project clearly. This latter point is essentially true of all control methods (see Figure 10.10).

FIGURE 10.9 **Changing network logic**

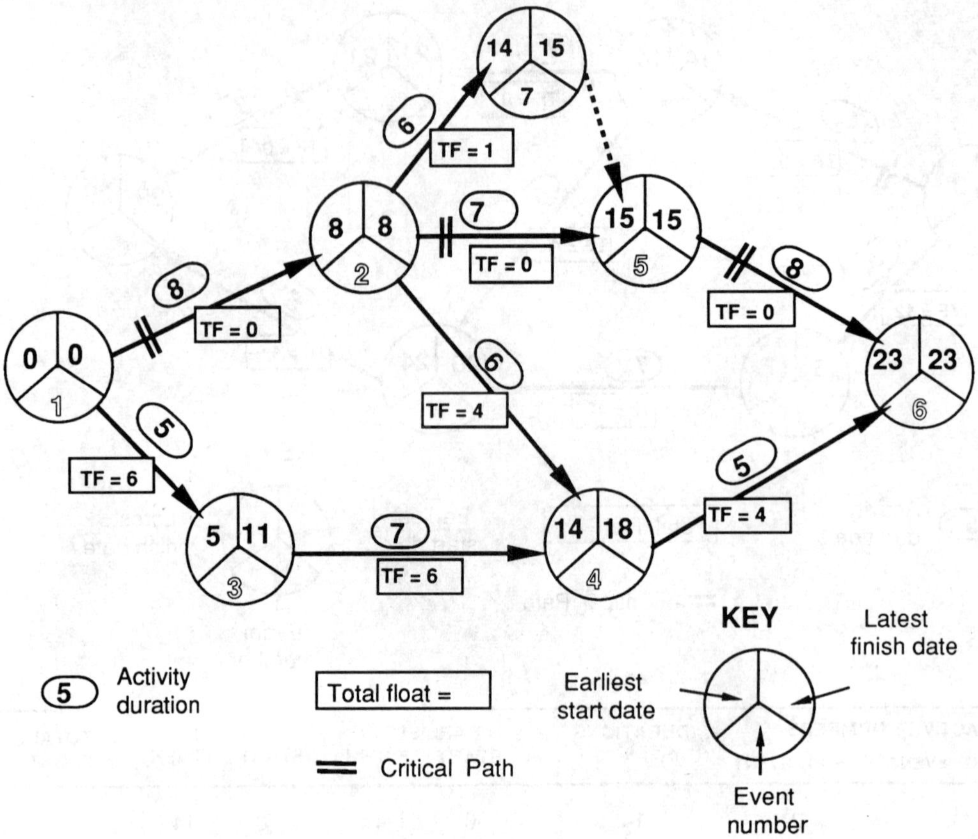

ACTIVITY NUMBERS START EVENT	END EVENT	DURATIONS	EARLIEST START	FINISH	LATEST START	FINISH	TOTAL FLOAT
1	2	8	0	8	0	8	0
1	3	5	0	5	6	11	6
3	4	7	5	12	11	18	6
2	4	6	8	14	12	18	4
2	5	7	8	15	8	15	0
4	6	5	14	19	18	23	4
5	6	8	15	23	15	23	0
2	7	6	8	14	9	15	1
7	5	0	14	14	15	15	1

10.7.2 PERT/cost

The discussion so far has concentrated on the time dimension of the project, although some reference was made earlier to the increased costs which might result from changes in the durations of activities.

FIGURE 10.10 **Gantt chart**

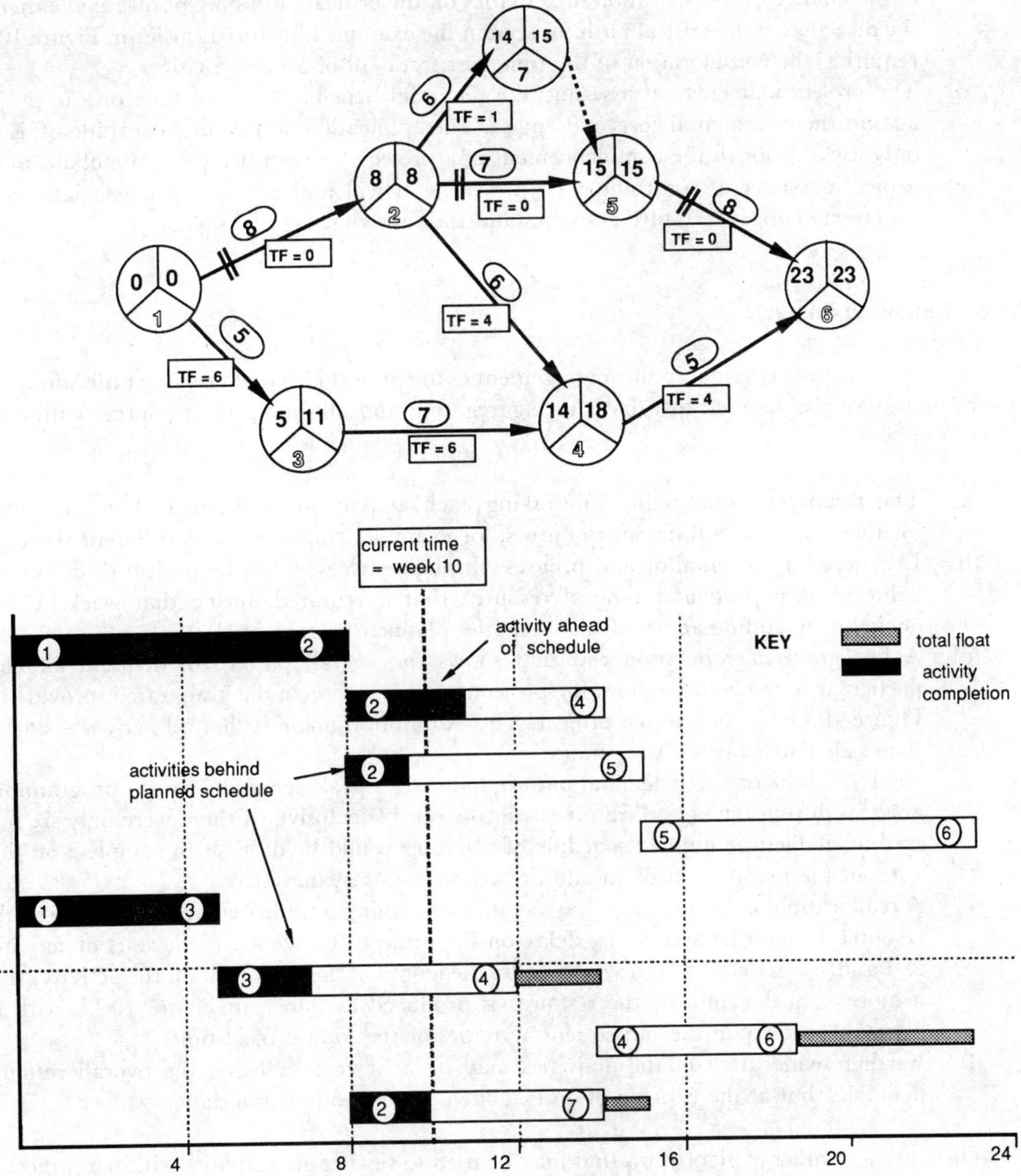

PERT/cost is a further development of the CPA approach which deals with the influence of changes in time on the cost of a project. In summary the approach involves:

(a) Estimating the normal duration for an activity and the normal cost associated with this time period.

(b) Estimating the extent to which this normal duration may be reduced and the additional costs of doing so. The additional costs may arise from the hiring of additional systems staff or the overtime worked by existing staff. However, the additional costs do not always relate to human resources and may, for example, involve additional payments to secure faster methods of delivering the supplies required. Further, not all activities are capable of being reduced in terms of time, and for those where reductions may be achieved, the costs may rise more steeply as successively more time is saved on the activity. In this, the reductions usually plateau at a lower limit in terms of duration and it proves impossible to secure further reductions.

(c) Addressing those activities on the critical path, so that each activity is ranked in terms of the cost of saving one week of time. Starting with the activity that costs least to save a week, and moving down the list in terms of the ranking, produces an assessment of the time that it is possible to save on the total project time and the consequent increase in total costs for each incremental week saved. The process is complicated by the fact that initial changes in the duration of activities on the critical path may result in a change in the direction of the critical path (as seen in the example illustrated earlier in Figure 10.9) requiring the consideration of the time/cost trade-off of other activities.

(d) The project management assessing the potential benefits of saving time on the project against the incremental costs of doing so. The application of the time/cost trade-off is not only useful prior to the commencement of a project, but can become a useful aid to the project manager in controlling the project as it will indicate the costs associated with proposed changes in future activities and the time that may be saved.

10.7.3 Resource analysis

The third key element to consider in the management of the project is that of resource utilisation. The network plan may also be used as a basis for aggregating and allocating the resources within the project.

(a) The resources required in undertaking each activity are estimated. This may often include a variety of different resources, for example, employees with different skills.
(b) It is necessary to monitor and progress through each week of the project duration, the value of each particular type of resource that is required during that week. This is achieved by adding across all the activities planned for that week.
(c) A histogram may be produced that shows the overall pattern of demand for each particular resource throughout the project. An illustration of the histogram is provided in Figure 10.11 for the sample project. The assumption made is that all activities start at their calculated earliest start times.
(d) Analysis of the resource demand pattern indicates a peak demand for eight programmer/analysts during the period from week 8 to week 14 inclusive. If there were only six such staff available, the implied schedule of activities would be difficult to complete on time without the recruitment of an additional programmer/analyst.
(e) A reallocation of the activities may assist in smoothing out the demand for the particular resource without incurring any delay on the project as a whole. If the start of activities 2–4 and 4–6 is delayed by 4 weeks (ie by the length of the total float on the activity) then a more even demand for the resource is produced as shown in Figure 10.11, with no consequent delay in the subsequent activities or the total project time.
(f) Further reallocation of the activities may be achieved, reducing the overall resource demands, but at the expense of an extended project completion date.

There are a number of algorithms that may be used to reschedule activities within a project to achieve a more balanced use of the resources available. Such algorithms are primarily based on the rescheduling of activities within their total float time, and the process is generally termed **resource smoothing**. Although these algorithms may be applied manually, the effort required in applying them to even a small number of activities is usually very high. Fortunately, there are a variety of software packages available on the market which will:

(a) facilitate the input of the network logic, activity durations, cost and resource estimates;
(b) facilitate the calculation of the start and finish times, and total float for each activity, and a highlighting of the critical path;
(c) perform the analysis of time/cost trade-offs, resource aggregation and allocation;
(d) provide schedules of activities to be undertaken by different groups of staff, indicating the target start and finish dates and the resources and costs to be incurred; and
(e) facilitate the input of data on the progress of the project at periodic intervals and the reproduction of the processes and outputs referred to above which incorporate the revised estimates and plans.

It should be evident from the above discussion that the management of the project in terms of planning, evaluating and controlling involves an integrated and simultaneous treatment of the time, resource and cost elements as stressed in 10.3. Changes in one of these elements in a project will

FIGURE 10.11 **Resource analysis**

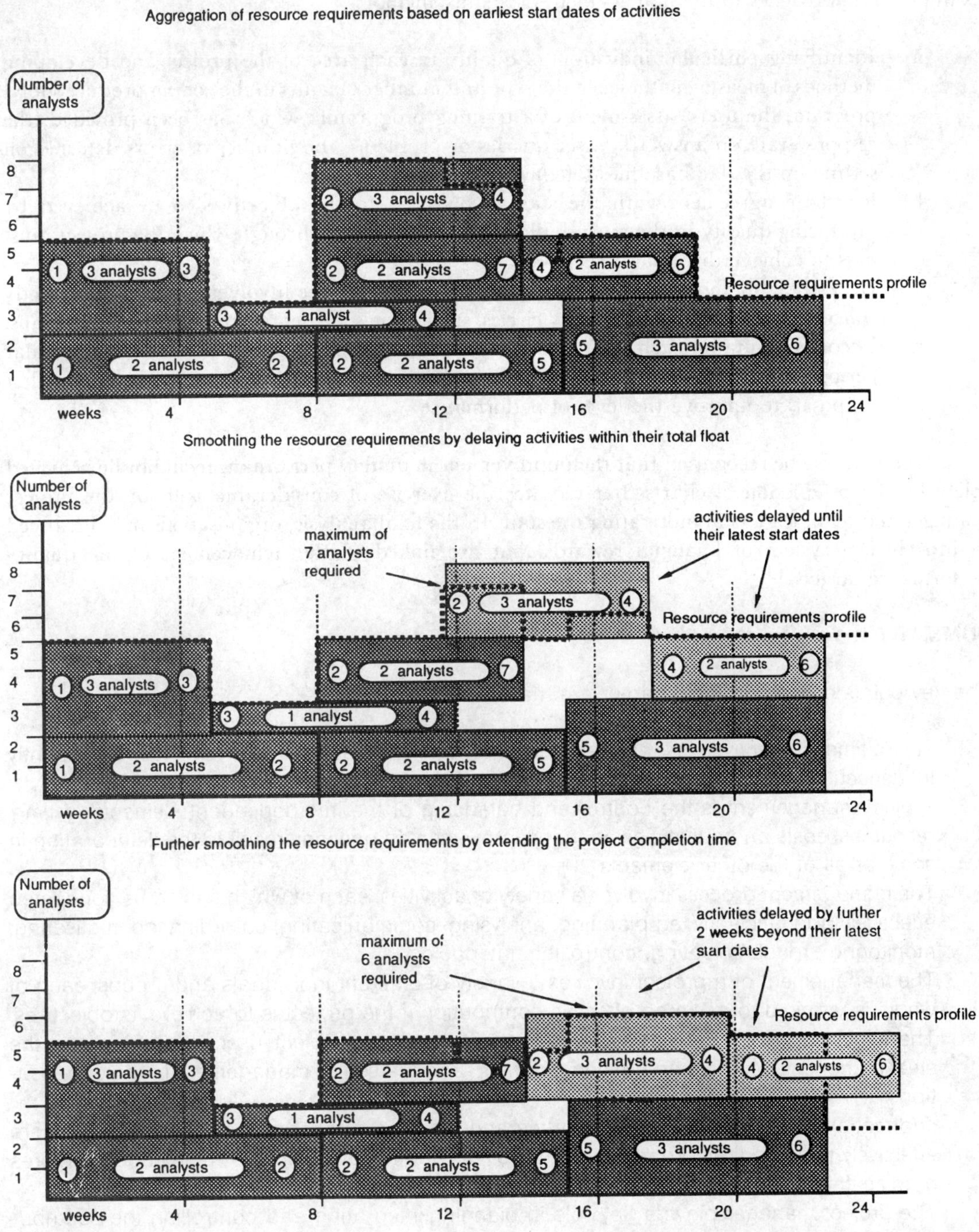

invariably have some effect on either one or both of the other elements. The task of the project manager is to balance these elements and the tools and techniques described in this section are an essential requirement to support this management function.

10.7.4 Quality

The remaining key element identified in 10.2 but not referred to in the previous discussion of support tools and techniques is that of quality. Although quality has always been an element in system development, it is only in more recent years that it has been recognised as an important element that requires effective management in terms of planning and control. Quality control in the manufacturing areas of the commercial sector has developed a range of support tools to aid the planning, measurement and control of quality. Similar tools are less evident in the area of systems development, although increased attention is being given by many organisations to improving performance. Examples of approaches to the management of quality include:

(a) Identifying particular indicators of quality in each area of the project and developing methods of measuring these, eg the type and number of faults in the coding produced for a program, the users' assessment of a training programme which has been provided, the response rate on answering user queries or problems, the number of errors detected on setting up the database files for the system, etc.
(b) Reaching agreement with the staff involved as to the objectives to be achieved by producing quality in the given indicator, and the stages through which the project must pass to achieve this final objective.
(c) Developing methods of improving quality—usually by the involvement of those directly concerned, either through quality circles, suggestion schemes or other appropriate means.
(d) Recording data on each indicator and monitoring the quality level achieved at regular periods, reporting back to the staff involved, and discussing and initiating further proposals to improve the level of performance.

It should also be recognised that the improvement in quality performance will not be achieved solely by the production of charts, but requires the exercise of considerable skills by the project manager and team leaders in motivating the staff. In the final analysis, organisations may be forced to introduce a system of financial rewards that are linked to the achievement of the quality performance targets.

SUMMARY

The key points covered in this chapter are that:

1 The ultimate effectiveness and efficiency of an information system will be significantly influenced by the quality of the project management.
2 Project management is the control and balancing of the interdependent elements of time, resources, costs and quality, given that improvement in one may result in the deterioration in some or all of the other elements.
3 The management process involves a variety of activities, each of which should be conducted effectively and efficiently, eg planning, analysing, communicating, co-ordinating, motivating, monitoring, trouble-shooting, controlling, interfacing.
4 The management of a project involves a variety of different individuals and groups, each of whom is required to make an effective contribution if the project is to achieve its objectives. These include the project manager, the team leaders in the project, users, the user group, the steering committee, the management sponsor, and the senior management in the organisations.
5 Information is an organisational resource and the development of systems to apply it more effectively to solving the organisation's problems and to developing its value added, requires a commitment and contribution from all areas including the senior management.
6 The project manager plays a key role in planning,integrating and controlling the contributions from the various internal and external contributors and he or she is increasingly involved in managing the interfaces between the organisation and its external suppliers or distributors.
7 There are a variety of tools and techniques to support the management of a project, but these are only support tools and they will not replace effective management.

QUESTIONS *Solutions to questions of an examination standard start on p 395*

Write brief notes on the following:

(a) the objectives of the project management process;
(b) project management activities;
(c) stages in project management;
(d) levels in project management.

Questions of an examination standard

1 In practice the project manager needs to manage simultaneously the elements of time, resources, cost and quality. These elements not only interact with each other but are continuously changing.

(a) Briefly explain the role of each of these elements in the project management process.
(b) Give examples of the type of judgments and decisions which the project manager may be required to make.

2 There are a number of organisational structures which are used to perform management activities at different levels.

List FOUR major components of these structures, and discuss their primary roles and responsibilities.

3 Critical path analysis (CPA) is one of the main techniques applied in the planning and control of information systems projects.

List and briefly explain the stages involved in the CPA approach.

SECTION FOUR: CONTROL, PRIVACY AND SECURITY ISSUES

Chapter 11
Control and Security Issues

CHAPTER OBJECTIVES

The primary objective of this chapter is to introduce the concepts of risk and security, and to provide the background essential to an understanding of the function of security in organisation terms. The detailed objectives are to:

1 introduce and explain the role of security systems in contemporary society;
2 provide a series of essential definitions as a foundation for understanding the later detailed material;
3 understand the nature of risk;
4 demonstrate the best way in which organisations ought to approach the formulation of a security strategy and the management of risk;
5 consider the detail of the planning process, and to understand how security planning relates to software development.

11.1 INTRODUCTION

The traditional small office was based on paper systems, with pens and typewriters to provide the words, and telephones to aid communications. Security depended on locking the paper-borne data away in desks, filing cabinets or safes, with access limited to those people recognised by sight. There was an irony in that even the mass of paper itself was a security protection because finding the relevant information often required specialised inside knowledge of the idiosyncracies of the filing system. But as organisations have become larger and more sophisticated, security measures have had to be modernised.

Most governments and businesses now depend upon effective computerised data manipulation facilities and data communications as essential elements in their official and commercial systems. Because of the efficiency, accuracy and speed achievable through the use of computerised methods, organisations are becoming more dependent on their information processing resources. Indeed, automated office systems can bring such considerable advantages and diversity of opportunity, that most organisations are forced to evolve automation strategies if they are to maintain their positions in the market place, or to improve on their results. The increasing competition and growth of expectations in the market place exerts pressure on organisations to improve on planning and investment justification, and to manage change more effectively. This need to react has emphasised the many management problems which exist in trying to run large organisations. Most of these problems arise because of the difficulty of communicating across departmental and hierarchical boundaries. These problems frequently lead to information failures in both directions, ie there can be difficulty in disseminating corporate policy downwards, and those staff involved can find it impossible to cause senior management to appreciate the inadequacies of the organisational systems at an operational level. Moreover, the traditional functional delimitation of departments has been hard to break down. This has resulted in real inefficiencies in achieving adequate co-ordination of effort across jealously maintained departmental boundaries, and although middle and senior management ought to have provided a flexible response to these problems, the conventional line management system has converged at too high a level to provide a dynamic response to problem-solving.

The improvement in technology has had several other consequences. Such is the reliability of the new hardware, that users can confidently expect error-free execution levels in terms of **MIPS (Million Instructions Per Second)**, with many machines now capable of achieving speeds of 20

MIPS and over—a rate that can be achieved on a round-the-clock basis over long periods of time without hardware failure. This remarkable reliability ought to allow faster access to information, to significantly improve manipulation and calculation capacities, and to permit greater sharing of the information, and in these improvements lie the difficulties when it comes to security. Until fairly recently, computer security has not been considered an important issue for the private sector. It was recognised that governments might have secrets to protect, but the commercial world has been slow to acknowledge the vulnerability of its own computer-stored financial and proprietary data. Now that more private sector organisations have recognised the importance of security measures, the technology has progressed and has created new and more intractable difficulties in the redefinition of the work environment.

The modern automated office has passed beyond the mere use of word processors, and provides an interconnected array of word and text processing with extensive use of data retrieval and manipulation facilities and DSSs. But, although much work does still take place in the conventional office, workstations and portable computers can be sited anywhere from a home worker's study to a sales representative's car using a modem on cellular radio. Centralised data facilities are still required for the major data processing (eg on payroll and ledger accounts), but many managerial tasks have now become less structured and are based upon more casual and less predictable computer resource usage. To state the increasingly obvious:

> **problems of computer security can no longer simply be solved by placing a good lock on the door into the computer room.**

Even within the largest organisations, computer resources may be based on microcomputers which can provide effective word processing or spreadsheet-type facilities on a stand-alone basis. Equally, dumb or intelligent terminals can be the gateway to centrally provided capacities. The development of networks and of remote access has enhanced the opportunities for either simple error or fraud, and despite the efforts of regulatory bodies, whether self-policing or governmental, negligence and fraud is on the increase. The machines themselves may have a high level of infallibility, but errors can and do emerge in the control and applications software. Indeed, a great deal of system maintenance is designed to remove software errors and shortcomings. Moreover, if data are incorrectly entered or corrupted, the effects of this inaccurate creation may be spread throughout the computer system within a fraction of a second. It is true that most data errors will eventually be corrected but, depending on the volume of data input, this can often lead to an organisation having to run fast to stay well behind the true facts. This can be critical because the information itself is now recognised as an important and valuable resource in its own right, with data either sensitive or worth billions of pounds (whether as information or as electronic funds transfers).

The blight of data corruption most usually arises through the natural cause of human error and there are many data validation checks which can reduce the worst effects of such unintentional error. But wilful tampering with either the data or the control software can have a fundamental effect on the integrity of the data. In addition to uncomplicated acts of sabotage and criminally motivated damage, some commentators have referred to the increase in computer fraud. Such unqualified comments are misleading. At best it is computer assisted fraud, but it actually remains the simple and perennial problem of dishonesty. In practice, computers may have one or more of the following roles in a criminal or fraudulent activity:

1 the computer itself may be the object of the wrongful behaviour: ie it may be stolen or there may be damage to the hardware or software;
2 the computer may be the means whereby the crime or fraud is to be committed;
3 the computer may be the means whereby the wrongdoer hopes to conceal the crime or fraud.

Indeed it has to be acknowledged that, since the beginning of record-keeping, no-one has managed to develop a security system which can wholly control the devious ingenuity of the criminally motivated, nor prevent all the information corruptions and the consequential losses which can occur. This leads to three general inter-connected propositions:

1 security should never be introduced for its own sake—it must always be provided because it is for the ultimate good of the organisation;
2 good security is a matter of awareness and commitment, ie senior management must be aware

of the problems and have a commitment to providing and enforcing the appropriate countermeasures; and

3 'Whatever is recorded in any individual record has a non-negligible chance of being utterly wrong and absolutely without foundation.' (Grimson & Kugler p32.)

11.2 BASIC DEFINITIONS

This chapter is concerned with the issue of security. This may be defined literally as providing protection against attack, but it is generally taken to refer to a general protection system which stands alongside the ordinary (commercial) operation systems of the organisation, and which is intended to minimise or eliminate the risk of loss. The underlying rationale is the assumption that the organisation intends to maintain the safe and continuous operation of its systems under the control of authorised and well-trained staff. This definition has remained constant even though there has been a form of progression in the security stakes:

(a) from simple data security (securing information inside, firstly, a paper-based environment, and subsequently, a single computer environment);
(b) through to information security (more comprehensive to protect information wherever and however it may be stored);
(c) and leading to the modern security concern of the protection of sensitive knowledge (which can even require the more abstract consideration of how to secure the knowledge inside a person's head —eg confidentiality clauses in contracts of employment).

For all practical purposes, the issue of information security is consistently based upon the following three elements:

1 the weather and other Acts of God as a source of danger,
2 people as a threat, and
3 the information that may be lost or damaged.

It is therefore possible to state that all organisations intend security to perform the following functions:

1 the avoidance or prevention of loss,
2 the deterrence of as many possible threats as possible,
3 the facilitation of recovery once losses are sustained,
4 the identification of the cause(s) of any loss after the event,
5 the correction of known vulnerabilities to reduce the risk of repeat losses.

All five functions must be subject to security in their own right, and one of the concerns of the security department (if any) will be to try to ensure that staff do not discuss security systems with outsiders, eg at conferences.

Initially, three basic concerns relevant to computers may be identified within the broad ambit of security, ie to maintain:

1 the availability of the computerised service itself,
2 the integrity of the data which it processes and stores, and
3 the confidentiality of the data before, during and after processing.

The first two concerns are common to all information systems, but confidentiality may not have the same level of pervasiveness. Thus, organisations may consider that sufficient levels of availability have been achieved when the information systems consistently provide a range of services which, if real time, provide an acceptable response time, or if batch, provide output within an acceptable period. Similarly, true data integrity can be considered achieved if all the data are error free and have not been accidentally or intentionally altered, disclosed or destroyed. The concept of integrity may equally be applied to information systems generally, and will be satisfied when those systems conform to their design specification despite attempts to make them behave differently. To that extent, the concepts of availability and integrity together form the necessary guarantee that the data which is to support the operation of the organisation and its decision-making is accurate, complete and reliable. The concept of confidentiality is more limited and is applied to the need to protect data from unauthorised disclosure.

11.3 FURTHER DEFINITIONS

The following points must also be considered or defined:

11.3.1 Organisation

For these purposes, any reference to an organisation should be taken to include all forms of organisation whether commercially orientated or not, which aims to provide a service for clients or consumers.

11.3.2 Disaster

A disaster is any form of security contingency in any part of the organisation which materially interferes with the ability of the organisation to provide the given service.

11.3.3 Fraud

Fraud may be simply defined as any deviant behaviour which is intended to gain a dishonest advantage by reducing the net worth of the victim in circumstances where guilt can be best concealed. Whereas greed is the usual motivation for the dishonest, instincts of self-preservation dictate that, wherever possible, the loss should be concealed. This will usually be achieved by the alteration of records so that the loss will not be apparent, or the identity of the taker will not be clear and pursuit delayed. This form of manipulation (falsification of accounts) or misrepresentation (falsification of personal or commercial reality) becomes particularly important if a systematic fraud is contemplated, since an investigation will not usually start until a loss is suspected or discovered. It is necessary to remember, however, that the real object of the exercise is to deprive the victim of assets. The manipulation of the records is not usually an end in itself. Collusion is a common element in frauds whereby individuals pool their resources in order to be able to achieve their aims, ie specialist skills might not otherwise be available to the individuals acting independently, or pursuit is restricted because the fraud is institutionalised.

11.3.4 Privacy

Parallel to confidentiality is the issue of privacy. Information is confidential if the holder or the law designates it as such. The modern context for privacy is concerned with rights and civil liberties. At the simplest level, it may be seen as the right of an individual to have some say in which data concerning that person shall be made available to others. People develop expectations as to how things should work, eg they know that the banking system normally maintains confidentiality about transactions, that the policing agencies will be accountable for their use of power, or that the security of the mail can be judged by examining the envelope for signs of tampering. For some of the more important issues, consensus may take many years to emerge, with endless debates both locally and nationally in the political and legislative arena. Often these general, policy-based expectations will transcend the individual elements in a transaction, and take a broader base within society. The rapidity of the change in technology has, however, produced a dislocation in the normal, more staid process of acceptance into the public domain. The new scale of more primitive capacities now available to computers to store and retrieve data, and the range of clever operations which computers can now perform, has brought a number of well-established issues back into focus, eg:

1 Is the storage of information about someone (whether in a computer or not) an invasion of their privacy?

2 Should people be asked to give their consent before information about them is stored on a computer, or why should they care unless they have something to hide?
3 Should information stored on a computer be considered private?

People have been keeping records for centuries, and it might be considered surprising that concern is now being voiced. Put bluntly, why should it matter how the information is kept? The answer lies in the amount of information that can be stored and the ease with which that information can be manipulated and exchanged. It is the amount of information gathering that is now possible. More information about each member of society can now be accumulated and stored than ever before—eg banking records, medical records, itemised telephone billing, etc are all now capable of being consolidated to show what purchases someone makes, where they travel, who they talk to, and how well they are. It is well known that information is commercially traded, eg mailing lists. Suppose that a name is shown as subscribing to a magazine with a particular political bias, is it proper for the law enforcement agencies to infer that the subscriber holds the political view adopted by that publication?

The exchange of information in itself is not worrying. The concern lies in the use to which that information may be put, or how it may be interpreted. The information may be used to decide whether a particular individual should be given a job, or given credit, or called to the police station for interrogation. The introduction of any error into data which is to be widely exchanged, magnifies the extent of the damage. Moreover, even if the error is detected and rectified in one system, it cannot be guaranteed that the data will be changed in all those systems which took that original data. Computer data can be more permanent because it takes up comparatively little space and is cheap to maintain. An error in youth may therefore haunt a person for the rest of life—eg if a false entry appears in school records available to prospective employers, it might be impossible to gain employment. If the record is baldly accurate, but fails to explain the context and justification for what occurred, no one would ever be allowed to start afresh. This places more pressure on teachers to ensure the completeness and accuracy of all the entries.

People want information because they think it will enable them to make better decisions—eg insurance companies or banks need to have some basis upon which to decide whether to insure someone, or to give them credit. However, increased information is only useful if it is relevant and accurate. Relevance is, of course, a matter of judgment. Thus, was it relevant for life assurance companies to know the sexual orientation of the proposer before the incidence of AIDS? Information gathering may be good if it leads to efficiency savings which are passed on to the consumer through better or cheaper products and services. Otherwise, data collection may be a cause for legitimate concern.

In legal terms, general protection is given to the individual through the concept of **confidentiality** which has its origins in Equity. As Lord Denning says in the case of *Seager v Copydex* [1967] 2 All ER 415, 'The law on this subject does not depend on any implied contract. It depends on the broad principle of equity that he who has received information in confidence should not take unfair advantage of it.' The **Data Protection Act 1984** represents a statutory enhancement to the general protections available to the individual, but it is regulatory and not prohibitory, ie it does not prevent computer users from holding information about individuals or disclosing that information to others, but it controls the way this is done. For the purposes of the Act, the following definitions are given:

1 **Data** This is 'information recorded in a form in which it can be processed by equipment operating automatically in response to instructions given for that purpose.' This excludes hand-written records such as index cards and accounting sheets where sequential entries are made periodically. NB: The word 'computer' is not mentioned in the definition, and so the word 'equipment' must be taken to include all forms of device in which information may be processed.
2 **Personal data** This is 'data consisting of information which relates to a living individual who can be identified from that information in the possession of the data user,' The Act does not protect corporations or things, eg production or stock records. The key to its operation is the identifiability of the individual and it covers all factual and judgmental information on age, sex, marital status, race, religion, salary, union membership, creditworthiness, work performance, etc.

3 **Data equipment** includes both the equipment on which data is processed and on which the information is recorded prior to processing.
4 **Data material** includes the documents or other material used with the data equipment, eg technical manuals, hard copies or tapes of source or other codes.
5 **Data subject** is the individual who is the subject of the personal data involved.
6 **Data user** is any person (including a company, building society, etc) who controls the content and the use of data held as part of a collection where the intention is to process that data at some time. Note that it is not necessary for the data user to own a computer. The processing may be performed by a third party such as a computer bureau so long as it is at the direction of the data user.
7 **A computer bureau** is either an individual or a corporate body who provides another with services in respect of data.

At the operational heart of the Act are the eight **Data Protection Principles**. The first seven principles apply to all data users, the eighth applies to both data users and computer bureaux. Personal data must:

(a) be obtained and processed fairly and lawfully;
(b) be held only for one or more specified and lawful purposes;
(c) not be used or disclosed in any manner incompatible with these purposes;
(d) be adequate, relevant and not excessive for their purpose;
(e) be accurate and, where necessary, kept up to date;
(f) not be kept for longer than is necessary for their purpose;
(g) be disclosed on request to the data subject at reasonable intervals and without undue delay or expense, with the individual being entitled, where appropriate, to have such data corrected or erased; and
(h) be kept secure against unauthorised access, alteration, destruction, disclosure or accidental loss.

These principles are enforced through a system of compulsory registration of all data users and computer bureaux, the system being supervised by the Data Protection Registrar and enforced through the criminal law. The Registrar has a number of powers:

1 to accept or refuse registration—only registered data users or bureaux may lawfully process personal data, with unlimited fines available to punish unregistered processing;
2 to issue a range of notices, namely:
 (a) enforcement notices if there is a breach of the data protection principles;
 (b) de-registration notices where enforcement notices have been ineffective; and
 (c) transfer prohibition notices;
3 to enter the premises of data users, search them, and to inspect, examine, operate and test any data equipment to determine whether there has been a breach of the law.

A data subject also has a range of civil remedies to enforce the following entitlements:

(a) to be informed by the data user as to whether any personal data is held relating to him or her;
(b) to be supplied with a copy of that data;
(c) to be compensated for any damage or distress caused by any inaccuracy in the personal data;
(d) to be compensated for any damage or distress caused by the loss or unauthorised disclosure of the data;
(e) to apply for the rectification or erasure of inaccurate data.

There is a defence to the claims for compensation if the data user can show that reasonable care was taken in acquiring, holding or processing the data. Further, a number of exemptions have been granted under the Act, eg on the grounds of national security, or where the user holds the data for purely domestic or recreational purposes.

The Data Protection Act is of direct relevance to the issue of Electronic Data Interchange (EDI) since the information transmitted can be personal data. In the context of **transborder**

data flows, the Registrar may serve **transfer prohibition notices** to prevent the transfer of data to a specified country or countries outside the United Kingdom. Such notices may be issued where any data elements are to be transferred to countries not bound by the European Convention or without similar data protection legislation, and the transfer in question is likely to contravene any of the data protection principles. If such a notice was issued, the transmission of the data would have to be frozen while the Registrar investigated the complaint and/or until the Data Protection Appeal Tribunal had overturned the Registrar's decision. If it proved impossible to isolate the personal data elements from the whole, then all the information transfers from that source would have to be stopped. This would represent an example of supervening illegality to any contract between the transferor and transferee and it would make further performance of the contract impossible.

Within Europe, each country's data protection laws differ in the scope of the protection given to their citizens. Only seven of the twelve Member States have passed data protection legislation. Some of the differences between the actual laws are fundamental. Thus, French law extends protection to manual records, whereas the United Kingdom only covers automated data. Similarly, the Scandinavian countries (Denmark, Norway and Sweden) issue unique personal identity numbers to all their citizens, but in this country, not even football supporters can be required to carry identification cards because of the fear of increased state surveillance. Similarly, the United Kingdom does not include legal persons as data subjects within the definition of personal data, whereas Denmark and Luxembourg give protection to all forms of legal person. Thus, although data about British or Danish companies might be collected and processed lawfully in this country, there would be problems in sending it to Denmark because its receipt might be unlawful in that country. Conversely, data about British or Danish companies could only be sent from Denmark to this country if Danish law were not broken, even though its receipt would be lawful in this country. Illegality under the law of either country (as the law of the place of performance for Private International Law purposes or *lex loci solutionis* potentially makes any contract of transfer unenforceable.

To avoid this outcome, it was necessary for the European Commission to study the question of harmonising the data protection legislation throughout the Community. To some extent, the problems had been recognised. Thus, for example, in 1989 the Council of Europe published a study entitled *New Technologies: A Challenge to Privacy Protection?* which recommended changes in the law on telemetry systems, the interactive media and electronic mail systems. One of the major concerns was to produce much greater transparency in data storage facilities to ensure that data subjects are able to discover personal data holdings throughout a potentially European-wide networked system. As it stands, it would be difficult for any data subject to determine whether there were prejudicial personal data holdings held in other countries where there were fewer protections. This is particularly important given the pace with which the improving technology makes mass data storage, exchange and consolidation ever more feasible. In 1990, the Commission put forward a package of six proposals to deal with data protection and the problems of the 'data havens'—the countries with no data protection legislation:

1 An ambitious draft framework directive, intended to cover 'every situation in which the processing of personal data involves risk to the data subject', and representing the first supranational law on data protection.
2 A recommendation that the Community as a governmental institution adheres to the 1981 Council of Europe Convention on data protection, eg to ensure the protection of personal data transferred to third countries, say, in Eastern Europe.
3 A resolution to extend protection to all personal data held in the public sector that do not fall under Community Law, eg crime and defence.
4 A declaration extending the data protection principles to all personal data held by Community institutions and bodies.
5 A draft directive for the telecommunications sector, especially the Integrated Services Digital Network (ISDN) and the new Value-Added Data Services (VADS).
6 A draft Council decision to adopt a two year plan in the area of security for information systems. This could lead to minimum European standard being developed and imposed on businesses.

In commercial areas, developments such as the UNCID Rules and the EDI Association interchange agreement are beginning to set standards, but the laws of individual states and of the Common Market have not been keeping pace with the EDI explosion. It is to be hoped that the Commission moves swiftly even though some of the implications for business will be significant, eg to include manual data within the protection in all countries, the data subject's consent to the collection of data, etc. The target date for implementation is 1 January 1993 to coincide with the introduction of the Single Market.

11.3.5 Vulnerability

In system terms, it is equally necessary to identify vulnerability, ie those weak points in the system which would allow the system or data to be abused. The following factors increase vulnerability:

1 The computer hardware is open to the staff of many departments and, through the development of remote access, to people from other organisations.

2 There has been a centralisation of hardware or data. This has a number of consequences:

(a) There may be an overdependence on automated systems with the result that, in an emergency, it may not be possible to quickly revert to paper-based systems.

(b) Although there will be fewer people who have access to the data, each one is far more powerful than the privates in the old army of clerks who used to run the paper systems. This reduction in the number of people involved means that there are fewer controls. When large numbers of people are required to perform a given task, fraud requires the collusion of many of those involved. The more individuals who must be recruited, the greater the chance of disclosure.

(c) The centralisation trend concentrates information, making it easier for one person to obtain all the necessary details to perpetrate a fraud.

(d) Centralisation increases the risk through industrial espionage and extortion.

3 The contents of files are invisible which enhances the opportunities for concealment. In a paper-based system, data cannot be altered without leaving some trace and casual inspections might discover an error or an alteration on a page, whereas in a computerised system, there is neither a trace of data mishandling, nor is there the same opportunity for casual browsing as the turning of pages in a commonly used ledger.

4 Computers have a reputation for both reliability and complexity, and the output is often accepted as correct by staff without question. This works to the advantage of a dishonest employee who can commit a fraud in a way which appears normal to colleagues.

5 The centre may be located in a high risk environment, eg in a high crime area or below the flood level of the nearby river.

6 There is a high turnover of staff and those employees who remain have low morale; some might also suggest that there has been a decline in moral standards, making the commission of crime or fraud more likely. It should be the responsibility of management to establish the moral tone of the working environment by issuing, and following, formal behavioural policy guidelines.

11.3.6 Threats

These weak or vulnerable points can only be identified by classifying all the potential threats, ie demonstrating the way in which each threat may represent a potential danger to a component of the information system, the result of which may be damage to the function or purpose of the system. One possible consequence is loss, a highly undesirable result of a threat. Threat analysis should lead to an assessment or quantification of risk.

11.3.7 Risk

In simple formula terms:

$$\text{Risk} = \text{probability} + \text{criticality}$$

ie there is some measure of how often the event might occur plus some evaluation of how great the damage will be if the event occurs. The essential nature of risk is uncertainty, so the responsibility of management is to balance the cost of avoidance against the loss estimated. In seeking to measure risk on the issue of availability, for example, it has to be recognised that, in the ordinary commercial environment, it is not unusual for users to suffer short disruptions. Longer disruptions are less frequent but can be more expensive. The significance of each disruption will vary with the business's dependence on the system. A few hours might be no more than a nuisance, whereas to a commodities firm, even a few minutes could represent a severe loss.

One of the ways in which to classify risk situations is to identify the source, ie:

(a) those situations that have already arisen in-house;
(b) those situations that are known to have arisen elsewhere;
(c) foreseeable situations that might arise in-house.

Although this classification may assist the planners, any form of risk assessment is inevitably educated guesswork because levels of accuracy of prediction cannot be achieved, and if positive numbers are produced by apparently scientific risk assessment calculations, they should not be considered reliable or accurate. In areas where there is significant statistical data, eg motor insurance, risk quantification can be moderately realistic, but security risks are more difficult to evaluate. The measurement process is made more speculative because while some risks may be overt, ie they are manifestly obvious when they occur, many are covert, ie not obvious at all or even suppressed by the victim. Much electronic crime falls into the covert category. Finally, the fundamental aim of all security systems is to provide realistic levels of protection, ie to devise and implement practical safeguards against loss which will represent a reasonable balance between the level of exposure to loss and the cost of the controls necessary to minimise that loss. This cannot change the ideal which is that: 'The best plan for disaster recovery is to prevent the occurrence of disasters in the first place. The cost of prevention is far less than the cost of the cure.' (QED Information Sciences p19.)

The risks to be considered may be spread over a wide range of activity and have different levels of likelihood. The organisation should therefore attempt to estimate the likely annual cost for each probable risk. However, it is difficult to use theoretical savings as a basis for the justification of expenditure. The alternative is for the management to classify the risks as follows:

— For a variety of reasons, some risks will be considered acceptable or to be tolerated (eg the foreseen outcome is considered too remote, or the amount of foreseeable loss is minimal; controls may be considered too expensive or likely to be ineffective). Hence, some managers consider that pilfering has become institutionalised and that it would be impossible to eradicate, say, because of union opposition or lack of staff support.
— Some risks may be covered by a third party (eg through insurance policies or indemnity agreements—these risks are often of a lower probability, but involve high criticality).
— Some risks should be reduced through the introduction of new controls which limit likelihood or criticality.
— Some risks should be avoided altogether.

If the organisation only has one level of security, no matter how effective it may appear and no matter how much may have been invested in it, if it is breached, the whole system is exposed. It is therefore sensible to have several levels of security, each level being integrated with the others.

11.3.8 Protection

This consists of the practical means whereby an organisation can minimise vulnerabilities and reduce the risk of loss.

11.4 SECURITY PROJECT PLANNING IMPLICATIONS

11.4.1 Planning cycles

As a part of the risk assessment process, the organisation must review the likely effects of any disruption and assess the level of expenditure and effort which is justified to minimise the risks of loss. These policy decisions can only be made at a senior management level, and require significant and continuing commitment if the resultant decisions are to be effectively put into effect. All management decisions have to be placed in a proper context, and must be related to a realistic time planning schedule. Within all organisations, there are three major interactive planning cycles:

1 **Physical systems** All organisations occupy buildings. These physical structures tend to have an expected utility of about fifty years. Each building is serviced through the primary services which include the heating, ventilation, air-conditioning and wiring systems. These services have a normal life expectancy of about fifteen years. Within the building, the fabric of occupation is coloured by the lighting system, decoration and furniture. This environment is more dynamic and may experience change on a regular basis.

2 **Information systems** In the same way that a building has a range of different life cycles relating to its structural elements, information systems have different timescales which relate to the level of capital invested in, and the technological capacities of, their various functional components. These components include:
(a) the communications media and network control systems,
(b) the central processing units, workstations and peripherals, and
(c) the software.

3 **The planning systems** Business planning horizons rarely extend beyond a seven year period. Within this overall period, organisations plan at a strategic level, anticipating the future needs of the organisation in its global, social and commercial environment. The planning then moves to a more detailed level and, on a two to four year basis, identifies specific goals and the resources currently available, together with the resources that will be required and the key factors that may affect the ability to achieve those goals. Finally the planning moves to an operational level which actually commits resources to the achievement of very detailed objectives. This part of the cycle may be between six and eighteen months.

In contrast to the life cycles of the physical systems, organisation planning has to be dynamic and constantly updated to reflect the prevailing conditions. However, the planning of information systems cannot be as dynamic because the process is constrained by the life cycles of the component elements. Thus, the wiring system in the building reflects the technology horizons at the time of installation and may not support the desired management decision support goals. The same may be true of the capital invested in the multiplexers and operating software which support the present network. Unless senior management address the needs of the organisation from the buildings up, it is impossible to ensure that each part of the organisation anticipates and supports both the long-term and the short-term needs of that organisation, and only senior management has the necessary overview to achieve adequate planning targets.

11.4.2 Senior management's role in disaster planning

In particular, the whole process of disaster planning must be under senior management control because it directly affects the people who are employed within the physical structures occupied by the organisation, the political framework within the organisation and the special interests entrenched within the existing hierarchy. The result of any plan ought to be change, and because all organisations are based upon people in a working environment, the management of that change must properly address the personnel issues within the overall practicality of the planning cycles.

A recent study of 1,400 UK computer installations revealed that about 50% of those polled had no disaster recovery plan of any sort (Lane & Step p361). This figure should highlight the proposition that disaster planning cannot be properly undertaken without the support of senior management because there are too many diverse interests to be reconciled. Indeed, the probable reasons for this omission are organisational rather than any inherent difficulty in performing the analysis and evaluation. For example, decisions must be taken as to which departmental user functions are deferable in an emergency and for how long—a decision which can only be taken if there is reliable evidence of the cost of that deferment. This cannot be accurately determined unless the users provide basic information which can then be validated. This is a senior management task requiring considerable sensitivity both because it involves making judgments about the merits of the claims made by the affected users, and because it involves determining the relative importance between often competing interest groups. Moreover, without a formal policy which has been thought through from the top down, security and the auditing procedures to support it are likely to be ineffective. Only the most senior of managers can assess the impact of disasters at a macro-organisational level and, without proper macro guidelines, the micro-assessment achievable by individual departments is likely to be unco-ordinated and ineffective. The management should therefore consider:

(a) the full extent and financial effect of each interruption to business services,
(b) the extent of both direct and indirect financial loss likely to arise from the foreseen contingencies, and
(c) the extent of any legal liability which may accrue to all those who may become involved.

The senior management must also accept that there are likely to be real and continuing financial implications for the organisation if an adequate plan is to be produced and kept operational. The plan should have the following elements:

1 an overall statement of policy which makes it clear that responsibility for security is now an integral part of every employee's job;
2 a series of general rules indicating how the policy is to be implemented, eg that information should not be disclosed unless there is adequate value in return;
3 more detailed measures to be taken and responsibilities to be assumed both by individuals and departments within the organisation, and by third parties who relate to the organisation; and
4 mechanisms for the review and change of both rules and measures. Information systems are dynamic and security measures must be kept up-to-date.

At a policy level, every organisation ought to be able to identify baseline controls which can be developed to apply to all aspects of the organisation. One problem, however, is that managers who know little or nothing about computers and the information systems which they support, can overreact and demand security measures from subordinates who have neither the organisational perspective nor the authority to respond effectively. For example, if left to the DP department, the organisation will only get controls for those risks which the DP managers identify, and that department will not be able to ensure that peer departments make the necessary adjustments to their procedures to produce a more secure system. The result can be irrelevant security procedures with the wrong people in charge. It can also lead to unnecessary and uneconomic complexity. The real difficulty therefore comes in designing improvements to these 'obvious' minimum levels. This evaluation should be carried out as a form of cost-benefit analysis to identify and justify security enhancements. For these purposes, a good opening proposition is that:

Security measures are not inherently desirable!

Many of the standard security measures will be expensive to implement and, once installed, can significantly impair performance levels, and can make systems less user friendly and therefore less likely to be used. Then, whatever plans are approved must be given the funding necessary to achieve the expected upgradings in performance; and not only must that funding be given an adequate priority within the overall corporate plan, it must also be built into the staff training schedules so that the desired responses and counter-measures can be thoroughly integrated into the normal organisational procedures, eg most organisations will already have fire alarm procedures, etc. Detailed rehearsals must also be budgeted for, and pushed through against possible opposition—they serve the interests of the organisation as a whole, but may be very disruptive to the immediate working of individual departments and their parochial interests.

11.4.3 The role of the security working party or team

To achieve the best results, each organisation should review its own structure. Every organisation has human resources which can assist in the solution of problems and it is important that the organisation identifies what resources already exist, and plans to produce further resources through a sound education policy and awareness training. This examination may also lead to changes in organisational structure and a reallocation of responsibilities as the worth of individuals or departments is reappraised. Once this process is complete, the organisation should consider whether to set up a fully representative working party to lay down the basic policy for the future. It is emphasised that any review should always be prospective and not retrospective in intent. In taking this step, the security co-ordination role should be a senior and highly visible post.

For these immediate purposes, the security co-ordinator should be responsible both for guiding the pre-planning and for leading the full planning exercise, and senior management must be seen to actively support the role to allow the exercise to retain appropriate credibility. In the long term, the co-ordinator should have the responsibility of:

1 managing all the security systems necessary to protect the organisation's tangible and intangible resources;
2 developing and implementing new security procedures, including the training of staff; and
3 monitoring the awareness and commitment of the organisation at all levels to the declared security policy and investigating all breaches of procedure.

The immediate task of the security team is to set the primary objectives and to identify the fundamental assumptions which will underpin the long-term security plan. The review carried out by this group could start with a historical analysis of the declared record of security performance. The difficulty is that many incidents will not be reported and the scale of the problem may be understated. It may be preferable to ask for that group's best guess as to what can go wrong based upon their own experience. In principle those who are co-opted into the group should understand both the technical and the commercial problems likely to arise, and must represent the interests of all the major departments whose co-operation is essential if the plan is to be made to work.

But in constituting the group broadly, there is a security issue. The problem with teams from several departments is that it teaches each member of the group what the vulnerable points are in each other's departments and what the controls are. If one person, having discovered where there are no controls, then abuses that information, there could be a major disaster. This is not the most secure way of maintaining security within an organisation. The team should certainly be convened but, if there are concerns about the reliability of any member of the group, either its work should be kept at a level of generality, or its work should be dealt with through sub-groups to ensure that the people involved in each area only learn a little about each other's areas.

However it is organised, at a simplistic and overview level, the first task for the team is to consider:

1 Which disasters are to be included in the plan?
2 What are the critical resources and applications within the organisation to be protected?
3 What sort of security strategies are available to counteract each major classification of disaster and, following a disaster, which resources are most critical to the restoration of normal operations?
4 What would be the extent of the possible losses, and the cost of the projected recovery measures?

The team should report directly to the chief executive officer of the organisation and, with this information, the senior management ought to be able to make better decisions.

11.4.4 What are the primary security objectives?

Whether the organisation is governmental or commercial, there are a number of paramount concerns. These include the need:

1 to maintain client/customer services at an acceptable level,
2 to protect the capital investment in buildings and plant,
3 to provide a reasonably safe place of work for all the employees and for those visiting each affected site, and

4 to keep operations running in a disaster situation with less than a specified number of hours loss of essential services and with an acceptable audit trail.

11.4.5 Who should be represented in this planning team?

It is obvious that the security department (if any) must be actively involved. It may also be advantageous to have senior managers or directors sitting on the panel to make them more aware of the essential issues. Thereafter, contributions should be expected from:

1 **The finance department**—detailed costings, appraisals and projections will be required.
2 **The internal audit department** should be actively involved, but their primary function is to review the plan and not to create it. Within an effectively functioning organisation, audit controls are an essential part of the management's drive towards security because they enable the management to achieve proper levels of accountability. The rule should be that every employee should be seen to be responsible for each action taken. Audit controls are more important during a disaster than at any other time. During normal operation, enough back-up information will be available so that, if an application needs to be re-run, the data will usually still be available. During a disaster, all computer-stored input data may be lost. In planning the response, it should be remembered that disasters can be staged to cover up a fraud and to engineer the disruption to audit trails.
3 **The legal department** which may advise on the existing statutory requirements and the possible extent of third party liability in the event of failure to act properly.
4 **The public relations department** to make sure that the best presentation of information to the public is achieved during a crisis, etc.
5 **The industrial relations and/or personnel department** — all aspects of the proposed assignment of duties or redefinition of safety procedures should be properly discussed with those who will be closely involved in the implementation of the plan with the employees and their representative unions. Thus, for example, individual employees will have to be designated as recovery co-ordinators, logistics controllers (ensuring support services are available), and hardware and software controllers who will assess the damage and the likely period of down-time.
6 **Transportation** —it will be vitally important to move both people and equipment during a major incident.
7 **Engineering, production and buildings departments** can give positive guidance as to criticality in their areas of responsibility.
8 **Management services department** to offer a decision-support service (see 4.3.2).
9 **Outside consultants** can be useful because they have a breadth of experience. This will often allow comparisons between the target organisation and other installations which may help to produce a more rapid start by avoiding the more obvious mistakes. In appropriate cases, they may discuss details of other security systems which are already in operation (suitably altered to prevent identification), a practice which can assist the in-house decision-makers to be more objective. On the other hand, in-house efforts to devise security systems keep knowledge within the organisation. It also means that those staff involved will have a better understanding of the plan, can often draw up a more detailed plan than an outside consultant and, because they have invested more effort in it, are more likely to be committed to it. In any event, comparisons with other organisations can be misleading because each organisation will have developed in a different environment and as a response to its own internal and external pressures. The security solutions adopted by other organisations may therefore not be appropriate if simply transplanted into the immediate organisation. Whether there is outside assistance or not, a better overview is normally obtained if the team leader and overall co-ordinator is an internal appointment.

11.4.6 What is the detailed work of the security team?

Whatever the final constitution of the team, it should have a diversity of skills and backgrounds so that, subject to the security considerations referred to in 11.4.3, each possible point of vulnerability can be considered from a different perspective and a more rounded view produced. The more detailed work which the members of the team can then be asked to undertake will be:

1 Gathering information and making preliminary decisions. The first requirements are to obtain and evaluate the following:
   (a) the site and floor plans of the data processing facilities,
   (b) details of the hardware configuration and of any networking,
   (c) details of the placement of existing warning systems and emergency controls, and of medical and first aid facilities,
   (d) details of the software applications and programs, processing requirements and schedules and of the database systems,
   (e) organisation charts and lists of the names, addresses and telephone numbers of key staff,
   (f) a checklist of documentation, and
   (g) details of all subsisting maintenance agreements.
2 Evaluating the alternatives based on the assumption that while all information services should be considered, a full risk analysis is only required for those services deemed critical.
3 Laying down the strategies and creating the plans. The strategies selected must bear in mind the functional requirements which have been identified and accepted as vital by senior management, and which seek to optimise the recovery plans.
4 Engaging in the normal life-cycle review of the plans, leading to an updating where appropriate (if it is assumed that the team will have a continuing function).

11.5 SOFTWARE DEVELOPMENT METHODOLOGIES

An inevitable part of the planning process will be the design of software systems to support management's information needs. The **software development life cycle (SDLC)** and the **software quality assurance process (SQAP)** are tools to prove structure and foundation for the planning and development of application software. The point of these, and similar tools, is to divide the design and implementation process into distinct phases with formal management controls between and during each phase. They have been found to be a good way of controlling costs and schedules, and of ensuring better communication between all the interested parties. The aim is to produce systems which have the following qualities:
1 they should be correct, reliable, efficient, flexible and secure,
2 they should be easy to use, test, maintain and re-use, and
3 in software terms, they should be portable and have the capacity to work with other programs.

The SDLC approach gives a project manager a formal framework within which to:

1 estimate the cost and time likely to be taken to complete the project,
2 make use of industry or government standards and guidelines,
3 assess progress of the project at identified points in the cycle, and
4 control the development through identified decision points throughout the cycle.

11.5.1 The initiation phase

Here the objectives and general definitions of the user's requirements are established. This is based on the initial user definition, ie a statement of what is being done and what needs to be done. This should lead to an understanding of the problem, and allows a formal definition of the scope of the environment within which solutions are to be achieved. It should also be possible to define the functional performance and methodological requirements, and to state the acceptance criteria. An evaluation of the scheme can then be made and, if approved, the preparation of the necessary documents can be initiated to formally commence the development project—ie:

(a) a comprehensive study of technical, operational and economic feasibility of the proposal,
(b) the performance of cost-benefit analysis,
(c) a consideration of which design approach to adopt, and
(d) the generation of the development plan.

This requires user involvement because it is necessary to define the project and its worth. It is usual to produce a **project request document** whereby the relevant users request system development or modification. The next step will be a **feasibility study document** which analyses the objectives and the alternative strategies for reasonably achieving the objectives, backed up by the cost-benefit analysis. These documents should be widely reviewed before the decision is taken to proceed to the next phase.

11.5.2 The development phase

This is broken down into:

1 **The definition phase** where the user requirements are translated into detailed functional and operational requirements. This will involve the definition of data requirements and processing requirements, the definition of functional interfaces (human/machine, system/system, function/function), and the identification of hardware requirements.

2 **The design stage** where the detailed systems and program specification is produced, defining the control and data structures and protocols, including any database specification and test plan. This should be reviewed to ensure that each decision is technically and functionally adequate, and compatible with security requirements. The test plan must be agreed with the user department and those other departments which may be going to share the resource. The nature of the test data must be agreed, and the degree of user involvement in the testing must be set.

3 **The programming stage** where following the acquisition of the required hardware, the software is coded and debugged, and appropriate manuals are prepared. Each major stage should be reviewed to ensure that the detailed design meets the performance requirements in the design specification and to ensure mutual compatibility between the different completed elements.

4 **The test stage** where the software is acceptance tested and the documentation is reviewed. This will involve the installation of the software in the working environment and the training of the affected users and operators. The whole system will then have to be retested in the normal working environment. A review should ensure that the final version conforms to the plan.

11.5.3 The operations phase

During this phase the software is maintained and enhanced as additional requirements are identified. It is subdivided into:

1 **The implementation stage**—this is the time immediately following the release of the software into the full environment on a conditional basis, and should include the removal of latent defects not discovered earlier, and meeting user requirements not specified earlier.

2 **The maintenance stage** will follow permanent release and will either involve ongoing maintenance to correct errors, and to adapt software to meet hardware or support software changes, or will be perfective to improve performance. In planning this stage, it should be remembered that the cost of correcting an error increases with time.

Each review should be carried out by a team that is independent of the development team.

11.5.4 Security within the development life cycle

Much of what needs to be done to incorporate or improve security is not clearly separable from what is needed to improve the utility and efficiency of the application itself, but should parallel it to ensure that there is a separate evaluation of the safeguards within an effective software system. The security activities are to:

(a) determine the sensitivity of the application or the data to be manipulated,
(b) determine the security objectives,

(c) assess the risks,
(d) determine the feasibility of implementing safeguards,
(e) define the most cost-effective security requirements,
(f) implement the security requirements,
(g) develop the test procedures, and
(h) evaluate test results and modify accordingly.

11.6 THE ISSUE OF COMPLEXITY IN SYSTEM DESIGN

A good objective in system design is the avoidance or minimisation of complexity. An excess of complexity may mean that the underlying ideas are difficult to implement and maintain, and the resultant systems may not have sufficiently clear audit trails. However, there are real security issues involved in deciding the degree of system transparency. The difficulty is that the paradigm of user friendliness can quickly amount to abuser comfort. No computer can identify or sense the possibility of hostile intentions in access when the appropriate authorisation appears to be present. Helpful design considerations such as menu-driven systems should therefore be restricted to non-sensitive software. Similarly, access to the documentation and to any embedded training programs should be restricted if they deal with sensitive applications.

However, whatever the sensitivity of the application, there are a number of general rules to be followed. The first is to avoid building unnecessary flexibility into the system. All user interfaces should, wherever possible, be tailored to meet the users' requirements. The more slack and redundancy built into the system, the more the users may have to be trained and the greater the possibility of misuse.

Secondly, human as well as software engineering is vital. Socially and organisationally, life is becoming increasingly complicated. In part, this is due to improved communications and data processing capacities. The effects of decisions made by organisations have also been speeded up so there is significantly less margin for error than in pre-automation times. Unfortunately, the capacity of the human mind has not been enhanced, and managers are no more capable of making wise decisions than they were in the days of the quill pen. It is therefore important to recognise the limitations of the mind and always to design systems that are easy to understand and use. This can minimise the risk of error and enhance the chance that the user will use and respect the system rather than consider it cumbersome and annoying. If complexity is not understood and kept within reasonable limits, individuals will not be the master of the information systems which they create.

Thirdly, the designer should consider the size of the system. The larger the system, the less likely it is that individuals will be able to understand the whole. This creates feelings of uncertainty and leads to errors in problem solving. Sometimes large systems simply grow into being. Others are created from scratch. Complexity becomes a problem of vulnerability when the system is not properly understood and so cannot be changed in an orderly or controlled manner, or protected both because it is not known in detail what the system is doing and because the knock-on effects of each change cannot be foreseen. Yet the pace of technological development has encouraged an increasingly rapid rate of change in information systems. The result has tended to be an inadequately understood system which can be compromised before the users notice that anything is wrong.

If possible, complexity should be avoided at the design stage, using development methodologies which take human limitations into account. Further, positive efforts to understand human decision-taking should be undertaken before too many machine-based technical aids to decision-making are imposed on the organisational environment. Many human decisions are based on approximations and guesswork. Such decisions will not be improved by actually giving the human large quantities of accurate information. Even with this self-knowledge, decisions will not be optimal so systems must be designed to reduce the number of factors presented to the human decision-maker for consideration, yet to ensure that there is minimal risk of error in factor selection. This can be achieved by grouping the essential factors into modules. Even if clear cut divisions can be produced, the problem is then to retain understanding of the horizontal and vertical inter-relationships between each module. The alternative is to make use of the power of the computer to model or simulate the effects of each decision so that the human observer can assess the probable results of each decision. This involves a simplification of each decision so that it can be satisfactorily modelled and the risk here is that the problem is thereby trivialised. Whichever approach is taken, the key is to concentrate on the data and not on the programs and packages which may be highly obsolescent. Data is the resource which has to be protected because the information will not change as quickly as the rules for processing it. Finally, one of the keys to avoid complexity is clear and up-to-date documentation because, if it can be clearly written down, it must be a reasonably accessible system.

SUMMARY

The key points covered in this chapter are that:

1 The control of data quality and integrity has become critical to the operation of the automated office.

2 Security is not just the avoidance of loss, it is the deterrence of future threats and an optimised procedure to recover from a disaster.

3 The organisation must identify where it is most vulnerable, and must assess the probability that given threats will arise and, if so, whether critical operations will be prejudiced.

4 The detailed security planning exercise must be built into the general planning process so that critical issues can be addressed and decisions taken to achieve a desirable level of protection. This involves all the major departments of the modern organisation, and all the major software development projects.

QUESTIONS *Solutions to questions of an examination standard start on p 395*

Write brief notes on the following:

(a) the roles of computers in criminal or fraudulent activities;
(b) the functions of security in organisations;
(c) the classification of risks by management;
(d) complexity in systems design.

Questions of an examination standard

1 It may be said that organisations wishing to benefit from the advantages that an information system may give must be prepared to incur the costs—both financial and organisational —of maintaining system security.
Produce a report as if for the management of a commercial company explaining the factors which increase the company's vulnerability to threats, and the issue of risk.

2 As part of the risk assessment process, the effect of the occurrence of a disaster to the information system should be formally considered at the highest level.
(a) Discuss the role of senior management in the disaster planning process.
(b) List and briefly describe the contents of a disaster or contingency plan for a typical commercial organisation.

3 Disaster planning is best carried out as a team activity, with members from all areas of the organisation under the active sponsorship of senior management.

(a) List and briefly describe the make-up of a security planning team for a typical commercial organisation.
(b) Explain the detailed work of the security planning team.

Chapter 12

Risk Analysis

CHAPTER OBJECTIVES

The primary objective of this chapter is to provide more background information relevant to the security planning process. The detailed objectives are to:

1 understand the nature of the person likely to commit a fraud;
2 gain an insight into the scale of fraud and the reasons for the non-reporting of criminal and fraudulent activity;
3 appreciate the factors relevant to the preparation of cost estimates;
4 understand the range of security decisions to be taken and the contribution which insurance may make; and
5 appreciate the requirements particular to a networked system.

12.1 THE USE OF THREAT SCENARIOS IN RISK ANALYSIS

The successful use of the scenario-based methodologies normally requires positive interaction between the various user departments and risk management experts. The aim of these methodologies is to create a detailed understanding of the issues through a simulation of reality. It is better to involve experts in this process because totally user-based surveys can be highly subjective and superficial. In seeking to analyse the risks, the management should consider who is most likely to be able to damage the organisation's ability to continue its normal operations. This is known as **perpetrator analysis** and defines and quantifies the characteristics of those who may threaten the computer system, and seeks to assess the proclivity of each type of assailant to make such an attack. Some targets will be relatively more attractive to different classes of perpetrator. This will in part be determined by the opportunities available to each class of perpetrator to exploit flaws in the software itself or in the security system, and the levels of knowledge and expertise, and of authority (if any) within the organisation held by those individuals (see 16.3).

Once these targets and the potential perpetrators have been identified, the planners should ask which of the vulnerabilities would be most likely to allow the attack to succeed, and what the relative impact of attack by each class of perpetrator would be. This line of enquiry should direct the mind of the planners to the best safeguards—this process is known as **threat scenario analysis** and can be a vital part of the initial study before entering the more detailed feasibility study, because without this step, detailed security requirements and positive risk control strategies will not have been defined.

It should be remembered that in formulating policy, users may make some of their needs explicit to deal with the errors and difficulties which they know about or suspect. However, users tend to expect that comprehensive controls will be produced without ever mentioning those needs in their discussions. Users need to be made to make their real needs explicit. This is not simply to confirm existing practice because that may be ineffective or based upon manual systems which cannot match the standards achievable by automated means—standards of which they may be unaware. User functions and responsibilities should then be identified in relation to the security system, so that there is a clear understanding of the interaction between different user functions and the security system. This will help to disclose the real needs at each interface because the consequences of error or misuse can be more readily seen, and simple action taken to ensure that high risk activities should be checked and approved from another interface before being allowed to proceed.

The testing of a security system should ensure that procedures are invoked when they are called for, that they cannot easily be avoided, that the audit trails are reliable, and that they represent a reasonable response given the criticality of the protected object. The use of **penetration studies** should also be considered —ie challenge individuals to break the system.

12.1.1 What type of person commits a fraud?

Fraud may be committed by people outside the organisation or by the staff against their employer. It has always been the case that in positions of trust, the dividing line between honest and dishonest behaviour is simply a matter of motivation. An employee may be motivated to act against the employing organisation's interests for a variety of different reasons. These would include:

(a) envy and resentment of the success of other employees or of the employing organisation itself,
(b) frustration that their own high expectations of rewards or recognition have not been achieved,
(c) greed and selfishness (some staff consider this form of extra earning capacity as a perk),
(d) some simply enjoy the intellectual challenge of beating the system, or simply want to have fun.

This presupposes that the wrongdoer has been allowed the opportunity to commit the fraud. Anyone may defraud their own employer or a completely independent third party. The critical factors are the ability to access the relevant building and accounting records, the requisite level of skill, and the time to plan and commit the fraud. This can only be measured on an individual basis. Indeed, one of the ways of identifying the person responsible is by identifying who had both the opportunity of committing the given fraud and of concealing its existence in the given way. Of the possible methods, access is probably the most important. Access to the relevant systems, or parts of systems, may either be authorised by a gullible employer, or it has been engineered by the would-be offender. Indeed, it is clear that the majority of frauds are committed by people who have achieved positions of trust and who then abuse those positions. Further, the would-be offender must believe that there is a reasonable chance of concealing either the existence of the fraud itself, or of the identity of the offender. This act of concealment may:

(a) simply confuse the situation,
(b) divert attention from the dishonest event,
(c) delay its discovery, or
(d) actively prevent the discovery of the identity of the actual perpetrator.

None of these devices can conceal the ultimate truth which is that the organisation has sustained a net loss of worth and, in a well-run organisation, it should not take too long before this truth surfaces. The pattern of fraud is usually incremental as a result of the first successes of the offender, and concealment is a necessary part of a continuing fraud. In this, greed is usually a powerful motivator, subject to the normal feelings of self-preservation experienced by the fraudster. Naturally, concealment will not be necessary if the victim's records will not show the loss of the relevant asset, or there will be no clear record of responsibility. Concealment may also not be considered because it is not possible. The most usual form of concealment is some form of manipulation of the records held by the victim which will hide, or delay the discovery of, the true position. The most usual point of any investigation is the discovery of a loss. In the case of the theft of property, this can be avoided by either the reduction or the inflation of the value of the physical assets so that the accounts appear to balance. This form of falsification actively prevents an auditor from discovering the loss. The falsification may take one of many possible forms, eg in a sale transaction:

(a) A clerk may pocket cash and write the sale to a bad debt account knowing that the loss will be in an acceptable form.
(b) A clerk may pocket the cash and adjust the stock records to minimise the chances of the loss being discovered.

Moreover, the concept of fraud is not limited by the motives listed above. There are a significant number of possible situations where, for example, the frauds can promote the employer's interests, ie may cause damage to competitors or to suppliers, creditors, etc. Staff may also engage in self-delusion, and deny that they intend any direct personal gain, but merely seek promotion or recognition by the employer, or hope to retain their jobs in a limited or declining market. 'There is a close correlation between the ethical standards and management style of a company, the efficiency of its controls, and the scale and frequency of frauds to which it might fall victim. The truth is that corporate fraud succeeds through the weakness of victims.' (Ardis & Comer p16.) The best defensive line is created through:

(a) proper levels of training,
(b) the implementation and enforcement of good controls, and
(c) through a clear deterrent policy operated by the employer in relation to offenders.

This is a management and communications problem. In relation to new recruits, it must be recognised that both dismissed and convicted people are likely to apply for jobs in sensitive areas. Sometimes their motives will be entirely honourable and employers have a role to play in the rehabilitation of those who have offended in some way. However, many are admitted to positions of responsibility because inadequate checks were made into their background before they were allowed into those positions of trust.

If the so-called conspiracy theory is ignored, the statistics also show that a significant number of frauds are collusive. The reasons for this are that it allows low-ability staff to share their resources in such a way that either an opportunity is produced where none would otherwise exist (eg in a sharing of information which would otherwise be kept separate), or that a maximisation of opportunity results (where the commonality of the fraud enhances the returns).

12.1.2 Why do people commit fraud?

The explosion in both the frequency and scale of fraud is caused by:

1 **Economic and political uncertainty** —in times of commercial recession, following boom years, previously honest people or organisations are more likely to consider fraud as a means of ensuring future survival and well-being.
2 **Increasing materialism** —people are becoming more concerned with the acquisition of status symbols, and see greater loss of face in not achieving the external symbols of wealth and position. Further, more will put personal gain ahead of collective interests.
3 **Changing skill patterns** —because of the increasing familiarity with computers which the young have, organisations are increasingly exposed to the activities of a younger technocratic breed of criminal.
4 **Changes in social attitude**—there is less respect for the property of others and more people challenge authority. This trend has been reinforced by a leniency in sentencing policy adopted by the criminal courts in crimes not involving violence. Criminals, particularly first-time offenders (ie people who have not been caught before), have therefore found that there is little or no deterrent policy in operation against the pursuit of fraud.
5 **Frustrated high flyers**—it may be suggested that some computer personnel have a different attitude of mind. Many are highly original problem solvers who find frustration in the more narrowly based management systems, or who lack respect for the managers who have inadequate or outdated technical expertise. The result is satisfaction in breaking the system or exposing the deficiencies of the more senior staff.

12.1.3 How much fraud is being committed?

It is not clear precisely how much fraud is being committed. The statistics based upon reported and prosecuted crime are unreliable. 'Estimates suggest that less than 15 per cent of discovered cases are reported to the police.' (Comer p3.) The failure to report crime may arise for a variety of possible reasons:

(a) not all those involved may recognise that a criminal offence has been committed,
(b) the victim employer may not want to involve the offender in the consequences of prosecution,
(c) the victim may be antagonistic towards the police,
(d) the victim may regard the offence as too trivial to justify reporting it to the police,
(e) the victim may be too pessimistic about the chances of gaining a successful prosecution,

(f) the victim may be too embarrassed to report the offence — eg public confidence might be affected, or the victim might prefer to be deceived than have to be seen as distrustful of colleagues,

(g) the actual victim, the prospective victims or the hardware or software suppliers might not want details of the mechanism of the fraud discussed in public because this might encourage others to try the method, or to 'improve' upon it once the counter-measures and detection systems have been explained,

(h) the victim may be deterred by the threats of the offender, eg the victim has proof that the offender can destroy vital data if the police are involved, or

(i) the offender may have disappeared.

Even if the offence is reported and the offender is traced, a prosecution may still not take place because:

1 The evidence may not be considered sufficiently convincing to justify the expense of a trial —particularly important now that the courts are prepared to award costs to the successful defendant in a criminal case.

2 The law may be unclear and consequently the risk of acquittal high. Sadly, the law has not kept pace with technology.

3 There may be jurisdictional problems—these arise when the offence(s) are committed across national boundaries.

4 The police may consider that a warning is sufficient — particularly when the offender has repaid the value of the loss caused or the amount involved is relatively trivial.

Fraud depends upon motive and opportunity. As indicated in 12.1 opportunity depends on access to the computer and its systems, the skills to identify and exploit the opportunity, and the time to plan and execute the scheme. These features are often a function of the rank of the individual within the hierarchy—often the more senior the person, the greater the opportunity. All frauds have the tendency to diminish the net worth of the victim. In systematic frauds, the precise extent of the losses may be concealed. Frauds concealed in income or expense accounts are closed to the profit and loss account. They result in reduced profit and thus a reduced tax liability for the victim. Because they directly affect profitability, they are easily detectable. Frauds concealed in assets or liability accounts are not closed to profit and loss, do not reduce profits and do not provide tax offsets for the amount defrauded. Such frauds are more difficult to detect. Most current frauds are aimed at financial applications systems within the computer, but increasingly, there is a threat to electronic funds and data transfers.

In some areas of organisational life, fraud is not only tolerated, but has become institutionalised as a perk. The problem is that fraud has either a contagious or a cumulative quality. Hence, if small frauds are not dealt with, they are likely to spread and to grow. Alternatively, losses simply mount up, albeit in smaller amounts. It just takes that little bit longer for the victim to bleed to death. However, many organisations do not take action to control fraud. A wide range of excuses have been tendered in spurious justification of this failure:

(a) Many managers make no serious attempt to quantify the nature of the risks being run, and live in the hope that most of the employees are honest.

(b) Many have the head in the sand view that fraud only happens to other organisations. This opinion is a direct consequence of the first point.

(c) The decision is taken that the controls which would be necessary to bring fraud down to negligible levels will not be cost-effective. This may be an entirely rational decision, based upon realistic estimates of the losses being sustained, or it may be more subjective guesswork.

(d) The management has tried controls and they have proved to be ineffective. This simply proves that it is easy to design ineffective controls. Good security is based on a well-founded appreciation of the risks and sound strategies to keep those risks within acceptable limits.

(e) Because controls are based upon the proposition that employees cannot be trusted, some managers find the imposition and the enforcement of security systems to be socially unpleasant and demoralising. Their preference is therefore not to press for the imposition of controls, or if the controls are introduced, not to apply them rigorously.

(f) Some company managers believe that the auditors will detect all the most serious frauds. This misunderstands the role of the auditors whose primary function is to protect the interests of the members of a company by ensuring that the accounts are a fair and accurate statement of the company's performance, rather than to detect fraud.

(g) Many managers do not have the technical competence to check the work of the newly qualified specialist staff, and therefore feel obliged to consider them honest.

12.2 HOW TO PREPARE COST ESTIMATES

The cost analysis process compares the cost of the proposed security measures with the possible cost of disruption to the organisation. It is relatively easy to estimate the initial and revenue costs of security measures. It is more difficult to estimate actual losses if no action is taken, or the percentages of loss displaced if alternative measures are taken. The fact of the difficulty should not deter organisations from attempting the exercise. The best method of quantifying potential losses is to estimate under the following headings:

1 loss of physical assets, eg buildings, hardware, etc;
2 loss of intangible assets, eg goodwill, software, etc;
3 loss of data and recovery costs;
4 legal costs, eg contractual, late payment penalties, etc;
5 personnel losses, eg death, injury, illness; and
6 financial losses, eg uncollected receivables, delayed cash flow, loss of business, increased costs of working, etc.

The organisation should then undertake a complete asset inventory of facilities, contents and services, and calculate the current and replacement values of the major assets and classes of asset. The next step is to examine the organisation's accounts at a functional level, and to identify the income or services that are directly dependent upon information handling. In this, it is vital to talk to the users. They know the consequences likely to follow a disaster, and it is a good way of interesting all users in the problem of security. Independently, managers should be asked for their perspectives. It is always revealing to compare the views on the same topic from different parts of the administrative hierarchy.

In finalising the evaluation, all the assumptions made as to the probability of each disaster occurrence should be stated, together with the predicted disaster costs, priority of strategy, and the costs of implementation. To justify the effort of assessment, there must be a real probability of each disaster happening, or the losses involved must be significant. Thus, the likelihood of a total loss of major facilities will be of relatively low probability, but disabling fires or the acts of inattentive operators may cause difficulty on a more regular basis. It must be recognised that, cumulatively, the latter type of causes might produce greater losses than one major catastrophe. If the objection is that one cannot accurately assess the probability of any given employee stealing organisation property, this does not justify a failure to take any precautionary measures. Experience must be used to value the probable loss from potentially controllable misbehaviour generally to justify the necessary measures.

If several alternative strategies are conceived, the most cost-effective will be those where the economies of loss outweigh the costs of implementation. For each risk, the probability of each projected loss occurring is increased by the number of vulnerability factors, and decreased by the security measures taken. The question is how to weigh the probability of occurrence as opposed to non-occurrence. If one takes the question of fire in any given room: the more inflammable furniture, materials and equipment stored in the room, and the closer its proximity to a furnace, boiler or other source of fire, the greater the risk unless there are adequate fire walls, alarm and extinguisher systems, etc. By identifying all the evidence upon which the risks of occurrence and damage might be enhanced or diminished, the organisation is better placed to make a more objective assessment of probability in the light of known values, rather than leaving it to a fuzzily intuitive guess.

It is also probable that the measures which offer the greatest displaced losses for the least cost, will be the inevitable preconditions upon which the implementation of the currently less cost-effective measures would be dependent. Hence, a positive statement of support by the most senior executive officer or managing director costs least, but is the essential prerequisite of effective action to follow. Equally, the helpful and flexible responses of a receptionist can be far more beneficial in creating an atmosphere where security procedures are followed, than the lumbering diligence of a guard on a door. Management's task is to consider which measures are most likely to beneficially affect the greatest number of possible threats.

Senior management can be unwilling to commit funds when there is no immediate tangible return or, if funds are committed, it can be difficult to maintain the long-term interest of management in something which has no short-term payback (if it has a payback at all). Even if the decision is taken in principle to commit resources, what is proper provision against estimated losses of, say £500,000? This will in part be determined by the estimated frequency of loss. Thus, if the given disaster is only likely once every 50 years, would an annual budget of £10,000 be cost justified? Computer suites are usually well protected and, from an actuarial point of view there have not been enough disasters to form a trend. Senior management will always ask for the cheapest measures that are consistent with the risks. However, these are mere guesstimates and cannot be binding financial bases for calculating performance. The only criterion is to ensure the survival of the organisation. In hindsight, the level committed may be seen as overspending, but it will have been justified in psychological terms, if for no other reason, because it guaranteed peace of mind in the interim.

In reaching decisions, the probable costs of any disruption given by users will not be directly comparable since each will base their figures upon different assumptions. Some users will plead importance, but will not want to pay for security. Others will underestimate the extent of the likely disruption. Others will ask for unnecessarily high reliability and will make funds available. Objective scrutiny of all the claims is required. This can be achieved through comparisons with other organisations. The problem is that many managers fear the possibility of bias in the advice which they may receive from their in-house computer experts who have already helped to produce this dependence upon the DP resources. Management therefore likes to know what percentage of turnover is usually spent on security in comparable industries. The answer to this question is not necessarily helpful because even organisations trading in the same commodity can be very different. Assessments should always be made on the basis of the organisation as it is.

The loss should first be evaluated without any form of backup— ie on the assumption that current arrangements would not work and should therefore include items such as the costs of recovery and reconstruction of data from original source documentation. The calculation should then cost the loss on the basis that current arrangements would work. Finally, the loss should be estimated on the basis of the desired levels of protection. The time which it will take to recover or to replace the asset or data should be stated, together with all estimates of the additional costs in running the organisation immediately following the predicted disasters. The loss resulting from the inability of the organisation to offer the normal services should be estimated. Replacement costs of hardware and software should be itemised without reference to insurance sums which may be available (subject to the possible payment of increased premiums following a claim). Rebuilding costs and/or relocation costs should be estimated and then all figures index-linked. (In this, it should be remembered that rebuilding may be less expensive than the restoration of damaged facilities.) The calculations should also include generous overtime figures for existing staff, and suitable sums to cover the hiring of temporary staff.

The combined end-product should be a list of proposed and costed measures which are established in a priority ranking order, reflecting the fact that:

1 some measures will be considered absolutely necessary,
2 others will be considered merely necessary, and
3 the remainder will be simply desirable.

Senior management must then make decisions and consider what resources are available for implementation, assigning roles and appointing staff where necessary, but recognising that the active and continuing co-operation of all employees is vital.

12.2.1 Data protection

This planning exercise must be seen against the background of the Data Protection Act 1984, s8, which states, 'Appropriate security measures shall be taken against unauthorised access to, or alteration, disclosure or destruction of personal data and against accidental loss or destruction of personal data.' There is no current definition of what constitutes *appropriate security measures*, but the view of experts will no doubt be highly relevant in setting standards, both within the organisation, and for the computer manufacturing industry. Yet manufacturers have substantial investment in their existing operating systems and will not be motivated to make major changes unless they are seen to be advantageous or necessary for both manufacturer and customer alike.

This means that computer security has to be examined both from a commercial and from a statutory viewpoint. As the penalties for non-compliance can be severe, commercial and non-exempted government departments now have a positive incentive to take adequate security measures which are directly tailored to their individual circumstances.

12.3 THE RANGE OF SECURITY DECISIONS TO BE TAKEN

Each organisation will need to make decisions about:

(a) physical security, ie physical access to buildings and terminals, and controls over the environment of the computer media; and
(b) logical security, ie controls which seek to regulate access to a system or to resources held within that system.

If a serious incident does then arise, recovery will be more effective if there has been adequate pre-planning and the most likely countermeasures or responses have been fully rehearsed beforehand so that all those involved know exactly what their duties and responsibilities are. But this planning exercise should not be limited to the major disasters. It should address all those undesirable events which will affect the performance capacities of the organisation in a real way.

Hence for example, at a purely physical level for loss of system availability, the overall contingency plan is likely to include some or all of the following elements:

(a) Manual fall-back systems to operate during short disruptions and during the initial stages of a major disruption. Information flow has now become critical to the health of most organisations, and sufficient continuity must be maintained if those organisations are not to alienate or lose clients and customers. The ability to maintain cash flow, subject to the normal controls, is also fundamental. The plan should therefore address the issues of customer/client services and financial management so that the commercial competitiveness and/or the reputation of reliability of the organisation can be maintained.
(b) An arrangement with another user or bureau which has compatible systems to use their machine in an emergency. This is called a *hot standby scheme*, but few firms will have a guaranteed level of free machine capacity so this arrangement can represent only a short-term solution and is likely to cover a limited amount of processing.
(c) Plans for commissioning replacement facilities as quickly as possible—the plan might call for the designation of a suitable room as an emergency computer room, and equipping it with essential computer support equipment like air conditioning and suitable telecommunications equipment; or a subscription might be made to a *cold standby scheme* whereby access to an empty computer room is offered to subscribers in an emergency. There are also firms which provide relocatable computer centres —these are prefabricated rooms with built-in facilities but they can take time to erect. Planning is therefore essential to bridge the gap while the new working environment is achieved, so the hot standby schemes may be better value. Copies of essential files and software must survive the disaster for either of these latter schemes to be successful (see 16.6).

At a more mundane level, data processing and user departments should agree upon targets for reliability and availability. This involves deciding:

(a) the number of hours each day during which the service should routinely be operational,
(b) the planned down-time for maintenance, where applicable,
(c) the length of time that the system can be unavailable before the business is seriously affected, and
(d) an estimate of fault frequency, probably based on past experience.

Detailed decisions must also be taken to determine precisely what is to be made available both for normal operations, and in disrupted operating circumstances. For example:

(a) should the service aim to provide the required application programs at all user terminals and subject only to the need to keep terminal response times within acceptable limits, or
(b) should the programs only be available to a proportion of the users at specified terminals, or
(c) should the programs simply be available on the host machine with no reference to terminals?

These examples should serve to illustrate the diversity of matters to consider and explore when any organisation addresses the security issue. The aim of this planning exercise should be to produce detailed manuals which lay down the organisation's detailed disaster recovery plans which have been tested in a series of tests, drills and exercises. These tests and drills will also serve as staff training exercises.

12.3.1 Where does the planning start?

The process should begin by defining the information resource management needs of the organisation as a whole, and determining which range of standardised and compatible equipment will enable the organisation to meet those needs. The creation of information centres, and the development of financial software packages for planning, trend analysis and other management tasks are all useful in producing management information which can be analysed and manipulated. But many managements pay little attention to the issue of information systems security. The first step is to consider what degree of security is required for the different types of information to be held on system. Without deciding which information is sensitive, little coherent planning can take place. Moreover, not all resources are equally important, nor are they equally likely to be harmed. The planning must therefore identify which system functions are supported by which resources, and demonstrate the susceptibility of each element to damage.

In the modern context, it will be rare for the larger organisations to be starting from scratch. Most will already have some form of automated system and it would be commercially inappropriate to ignore the capital invested in existing hardware, and the information which may be stored in its files. However, the appraisal must be objective and, if it is clear that the existing system cannot be upgraded to meet modern requirements, the organisation must make the proper long-term investment decisions. Detailed decisions must also be made about the people who will develop, support and use the new information systems. New staff may have to be recruited with particular skills, and existing staff may have to have further training or be retrained. If the change is to be managed well, the people who must make it work need to feel a sense of involvement in the process of change, and consultation is highly desirable. Indeed, in the first instance, the end users should have responsibility for the security of their data, and if they are unhappy with the security system forced upon them, it is unlikely to work.

If it is ultimately decided that a single mainframe system is to be established, it may be housed in a single building with access restricted to those present in the building. Alternatively, there may be several thousand terminals which are to be established in a variety of locations as a wide area network, or there may be several computer installations linked together as a distributed system. The issue, whatever the system, is to provide cost-effective and operationally effective protection for both the hardware and the information which it processes. The irony is that the computerisation of both public and private sector administrative systems has led to a centralisation of data, and has therefore made each organisation more vulnerable to accidental or malicious acts or omissions.

12.4 WHAT ARE THE MAIN NETWORKED SYSTEMS TO CONSIDER?

The most common use of telecommunications is for voice communications, with the computerised data transmission systems becoming increasingly common. Networks support four basic functions, each one relying on different technical systems:

1 the telephone system which provides a voice link between both internal and external parties (see 5.4.5 and 5.4.6),
2 the data link which allows computer users to interconnect and interact from remote sites and terminals,

3 the electronic mail system which allows text communication between different terminals (see 5.4.1), and
4 image-based systems providing both still and moving image communication between both internal and external parties (see 5.4.4 and 5.4.7).

The design of micro networks relies upon the insertion of interface cards in each machine with appropriate communications software and cable to connect machines together. This is the cheapest way of producing a network but has lower data transmission rates and less satisfactory error rates. Local Area Networks (LANs) are usually self-contained, being designed to operate within the confines of a single site, although it is possible to provide gateways to wide area and public networks (see 5.12). Organisations should not blindly connect machines together but should consider whether there are information flows which would be benefited by a network, or whether the same effect could be achieved by people talking with each other, or by exchanging either pieces of paper or floppy disks. It should also be acknowledged that many early attempts at network implementation were not very successful. Although the hardware and software systems are now more robust, organisations must still plan effectively if the network is to be a productive investment.

The first stage development possibility is a multi-user configuration where several machines share resources. The second stage is a network which may be based on a star-shaped configuration and is centrally controlled (for more detail on network topology, see 5.11.2 and 5.12.1). The security software is inserted into each file server, but if this central unit fails, the whole network will fail. As data moves so quickly through most LANs, traffic management and error checking is vital. Should a collision occur as a result of one or more stations transmitting at the same time, data integrity will be lost. The next option is a ring or loop system which arranges the workstations in a full circle. Signals from each address must pass to the nominated address. Each node on the loop must contain the software security system. The control of the data flows in the ring system is achieved by token-passing, the slotted ring or register insertion. Any one of these systems will avoid collisions and loss of data integrity due to simultaneous transmissions (see 5.12.2).

The alternative topology is the tree or bus system which produces a distributed network of autonomous machines, connected to a common cable bus like the limbs of a tree (see 5.1.4). This has the advantage that workstations can readily be attached to or removed from the bus, but the disadvantage that it can be more expensive to build the network control system into each workstation. However, the system is more robust than either the ring or the star topography and will not fail if one or more workstations break down. Application security software has to be inserted into the workstations themselves. If the receiving station detects that data has been lost, instructions are sent to retransmit the message in its entirety when the line is clear. The other system of traffic control depends upon a token-passing arrangement.

12.4.1 The advantages of a network

The main advantages are:

1 The possible enhancement of communication between users. Paper-based systems are slow if the circulation list includes addressees in geographically dispersed sites, whereas electronic mail and data transfer can be instantaneous, allowing management team consultation to be made more time-effective. Similarly, significant amounts of time can also be wasted on telephone calls when trying to locate key members of the management team, and computer-based messaging systems can dramatically cut such costs.
2 Theoretically, a network can serve a large number of users.
3 The ability of users to share the hardware and software resources (and thereby help to overcome problems of equipment compatibility), but this form of development must be carefully costed because resource sharing can be more capital expensive than the single user systems, and with LANs may lead to greater vulnerability through dependence on centrally located processors. Thus, for relatively high cost items like laser printers, it can be more cost-effective to link users together rather than to provide each user with such a printer. Similarly, software does not have to be duplicated within the pool, but can be stored on the master file server, potentially saving licence fees.
4 With proper planning, it can lead to greater operational flexibility, but what are the physical

office-layout requirements and what staff training may be required to optimise the investment? This is particularly important if intelligent terminals are used, eg if project management tools like PERT (see 10.7.1) are made available to individual user departments, this may significantly improve business efficiency if the staff have been trained in their use.

5 The proliferation of micros has accelerated problems, especially that of unco-ordinated databases, eg each department may keep their own details of customers, suppliers, etc. Cumulatively, this represents a valuable fund of business data and, if linked together, it may provide significant advantages.

12.4.2 Are there likely to be problems?

The possible problems are:

1 The robustness of both the hardware and software. The network must be designed so that if one workstation goes down, there will be no prejudice to the work being undertaken at the others.

2 The adaptation of single user packages (particularly those which have been customised) to multi-user can be difficult. The device of partition locking is a useful way of restricting users to different areas of the disk, but it can be inconvenient if this excludes users from the use of standard packages during solo use, so the practice of record locking may be better, ie users can use the same applications packages, but not on the same set of records. Record locking may be achieved through preventing physical access to the relevant part of the disk, through logical record locking (ie access prevented to a file while one of its records is being updated), or through virtual record locking by flagging the individual records to be protected.

3 The network operating software must check for message integrity, ie to determine whether any data has been lost, say, during a transmission interruption.

4 Not all network operating software has built-in logical access controls. Some form of change controls are fundamentally desirable both on up-dating data files, and on changing software.

5 Whenever organisational changes are made in a working environment, information flows are likely to be affected. This should be carefully monitored and appropriate action taken because although there can be improvements, it can equally lead to bottlenecks, depending on the quality of the planning and the training given to staff.

6 Distributed databases face the probability that they may not be using the most recent information to support management decision-making unless there are regular updating routines.

7 Local database designs and data representation differences will need to be reconciled before linking and data transfer can be made to work. This form of development activity can be expensive.

In making planning decisions, it must be assumed that all information in a network is potentially insecure.

12.4.3 Project planning considerations

The linking of computers and systems must be properly planned at both a physical and a data level. If different pieces of equipment are to interface, they must adopt common standards. This may involve interconnection where two machines are physically connected so that they may exchange information, as opposed to interworking where two or more machines have compatible applications and can work together on the same data. To assist, the **International Standards Organisation (ISO)** has drawn up a set of communications architecture standards called the **Open Systems Interconnection (OSI)** model to lay down a framework for defining the standards for the linking of heterogenous computers (see 5.11.3). The model depends upon a division into seven interdependent layers which call for machine interconnection at seven peer protocol levels:

1 **The physical layer** which defines the practical specifications and procedures to establish and maintain physical connections, ie whereby the data is translated into the form most suitable for transmission.

2 **The data layer** which defines the means of exchanging data with no loss of integrity.
3 **The network layer** which deals with the mechanisms which will permit different systems to be linked together effectively, for instance, where the logical paths between each operating system are planned through packet switching, data routing, etc.
4 **The transport layer** deals with end-to-end and flow control to ensure that communications are orderly and represent an effective use of the network resources.
5 **The session layer** provides the structure for the data exchange by managing the connections between the various systems and applications for the given session.
6 **The presentation layer** takes information from the applications and converts it into a form suitable for common understanding by providing common communications services and protocols, eg for encryption, text compression, etc.
7 **The applications layer** supports the users by providing effective network management tools which will support the packages as they exchange data for processing.

12.4.4 What is available both nationally and internationally?

The Telecommunications Act 1984 broke the British Telecom monopoly and allowed competition in the offer of services on the BT network, eg:

Value Added Network Services (VANS)—the supplier adds functions and capabilities to those neccessary for simple data transmission, such as insurance brokerage systems which link to the major insurance companies, or ICL Tradanet which allows retailers and suppliers to transmit orders, invoices, etc.

Viewdata —VANS will often be available through viewdata/videotex/teletext systems. This is a cheap and efficient way of distributing information stored on computer. Access is by the normal communication links and information is presented in frames, a frame being one screenful of information, 24 rows by 40 columns wide. The public system is called PRESTEL, with an increasing number of systems being made available to private subscribers. The computer immediately accessed can either store the frames or act as a gateway to other computers. The information may be available to the public or to a closed user group. These systems are now being modified to allow for facilities like home banking, but the main use remains in the commercial sector, where a cheap information service can be provided so long as little processing is required, eg in the stock exchange for share prices, and in the travel trade for hotel and holiday bookings. Viewdata systems can also link to the range of telex, teletex, telesoft and electronic mail systems (see 5.4.7).

As to the security design requirements, most viewdata systems use terminal identifiers, ID codes and passwords (normally of up to 16 characters which can define both the user and his or her location). It is a standard operating requirement that the system should enforce account freezing if there are unsuccessful attempts to log-on. In **Closed User Groups (CUGs)**, the **Information Provider (IP)** can control access, with different levels of security given to individual frames. Editing the information is usually only carried out by the IPs who have special passwords. The number of editors needs to be limited and their use of the system privileges should be carefully monitored by the viewdata managers. Similarly, the special utilities which create and delete accounts require further special controls with careful monitoring. The audit trails must also be good.

If all the information is on the same mainframe, the whole database could be at risk if security is broken. However, not to centralise data is to give up the opportunity to integrate the database with other systems, and to give up the more sophisticated access controls that can be produced within a mainframe environment. Fewer users could access a distributed system based on minis. Security has been slightly sacrificed on some of the commercial systems because the preparation of good controls takes time, and time is money. For a firm to introduce a viewdata system means an on-going commitment to training. Any release of software must be tested before it is released otherwise confidence may be affected. At a level of physical security, hardware design and layout planning should reflect the fact that viewdata terminals are often in public places and are therefore vulnerable to vandalism and theft.

Overall, viewdata may be seen as an information service, so system availability is the prime consideration. This means that there should be good back-up and recovery systems, with alternative hardware available in a commercial system.

Text communication This may be represented by the growth of transmissions from one word processor to another which is becoming increasingly common because of the threatened development of the **teletex** standard (see 5.4.7). Teletex has been designed to link word processors together via the telephone network, but adoption and implementation by the manufacturers has been slow. Nevertheless, commercial pressures have persuaded the manufacturers to produce some new inter-machine capacities. One of the problems in the transport of text files has been the use of control characters. Manufacturers have not distinguished themselves in co-operating, although some standards are now emerging, eg DEC's DX transfer specification now allows unrestricted text transfer between Wordstar and DEC's All-in-One integrated office system.

An important feature of a teletex message standard is the **Call Identification Line (CIL)** which identifies the sending terminal, the receiving terminal, and the date and time of the message, thereby providing a reasonable validation of the source of the message. If the right terminal has not been addressed, the message should abort. There should also be a final handshake message to confirm the number of pages sent.

Alternatively, the text may take the form of **electronic mail** —ie an on-line computer system for the electronic exchange of information through a mailbox system (see 5.4.1). The speed and character set limitations of the telex network, have left the market open for the development of good computer-based messaging systems. The public services are Telecom Gold, One-to-One and Mercury Link 7500. Many organisations have comparable internal systems which provide terminal-to-terminal message delivery. The message is normally prepared off-line and transmitted to save the transmission costs of manually typing the message on-line. This is particularly important if a document transfer service is being used and large quantities of text are to be transmitted. Messages can be encrypted on Gold and Link, and all three are passworded. All three commercial systems have good security records.

Voice mail or messaging systems (eg BT's Voicebank) are similar in that each user has a personal voice mailbox which can be accessed by dialing the appropriate telephone number plus an optional password (see 5.4.5). There are some problems:

(a) the sender does not have the opportunity to review and change messages which are usually short,
(b) the system does not work when the recipient is using the telephone,
(c) there is no integration with other systems, and
(d) although messages are usually short, the nuances of speech are retained which is only sometimes an advantage; it may be better to review a written document.

If the **word processing facilities** within an organisation have been centralised, there may be greater problems of security, and the system may become more vulnerable to failure (see 3.3.1). The design may be a dedicated system, ie word processing is the only task performed by the machine, or word processing may be a casual use on either the micro or work station, being built into an applications package such as Lotus 123 or Symphony. It is vital to ensure that there is communication between each part of the system so that a report done casually by one person may be processed by secretarial back-up on a separate system.

There are considerable advantages in standardising on both equipment and software. In the first instance, this will overcome the problems of hardware and software compatibility. It should also make maintenance administratively more convenient, and there should be economies in the negotiation of a single maintenance agreement with one reliable service provider. Further, the education and training programs, which are essential to build up expertise, can be standardised, with the enhanced opportunity to produce the good standard of documentation vital to support new pool users.

For the promotion of security, all users should be taught good disk management habits and good ergonomics. The control of physical access to centrally located terminals should be through a monitored reception area to cut down the risk of outsiders gaining access to confidential documents held on central file. In formulating proper fire precautions, all user departments serviced by the word processor facility should agree the retention periods for each different class of documents so that proper disk management procedures can be laid down. Archiving becomes easier if only a minimum number of documents are to be kept over a longer period of time. A reasonable number of manual typewriters should also be kept as back-up for use in the event of a major systems failure. In addition to the physical controls, centralised systems need logical access controls, and staff must be encouraged to maintain discipline in the observance of the controls.

Desk top publishing/phototypesetting can produce good camera ready copy by using laser printers. It is logical to connect the word processor to the typesetter now that the problems of format compatibility are being solved. Manufacturers have taken security seriously with most systems providing good back-up facilities to minimise the risk of not meeting publication deadlines. The print room in most organisations is usually organised on a limited access basis only. If the typesetter is networked, there should be a proper identification of every user, with good facilities built in to protect the integrity of the data. Where external lines are used, say, to permit a reporter to input data from a lap-held computer, there must be good controls to minimise the risk of data corruption through noise on the line, or from a discontented journalist. It is always advisable to have a final proof read before printing.

Telex and **facsimile machines** (see 5.4.2) have been used for years to allow the rapid transmission of text, pictures or facsimilies of documents. Telex has been improved by the replacement of the electromechanical telephone exchanges by the more versatile **Stored Program Control (SPC)** electronic exchanges. The new networks will permit users to structure their operations in a more cost-effective way through new message management facilities such as the ability to store and forward messages to a single address or to a pre-recorded list of addresses, or to redirect calls, establish multiline facilities or user groups, etc. The teletex service will interwork with telex through the InterStream 3 gateway conversion facility. Much of telex management has now been automated, but many of the concerns remain. Thus, are telex staff trusted not to make unauthorised calls? Can temporary staff gain access to the system? Is it practical to use passwords? Should encryption be used on sensitive information or is it adequate that a message is not sent until an authorised person is in a position to receive it? Are paper copies of telexes kept and, if so, for how long? In relation to the audit trail—are all messages traceable and accounted for?

Facsimile or remote copying machines transmit and receive scanned images of documents through the telephone network. Unlike telex, facsimile machines do not generally interwork with other systems although this is changing. Both are electronic messaging systems and manufacturers should make them compatible. With the general adoption of electronic information processing within the office, the need arises to handle information received from other organisations in physical form, for which no electronic coding is available. These documents can now be handled through imaging and compaction techniques. The security requirements for imaging systems are the standard, ie some form of CIL system to preserve integrity, the possibility of encryption to preserve confidentiality, and an effective audit trail.

Closed circuit television has been in regular use in the security industry for many years, linking different parts of a site or building to a central control position. More recently it has been used to broadcast information around a large site, and to provide a video-conferencing network. The growth of cable TV technology is accelerating the trend.

Tele-conferencing systems have been relatively slow-growing in this country, although teleconferencing is not uncommon in the USA. As high bandwidth digital transmission facilities become more readily available (video transmission of colour motion pictures normally requires encoding of up to 10 MHz, subject to signal compression techniques which may reduce this requirement to 384 kilobits per second), growth in this area of technology must be expected. The underlying network must be reliable so that data is not lost or compromised. Voice conferencing is well proved technology. Audiographics conferencing allows the interpolation of charts and diagrams (ie integrated with facsimile systems), with video conferencing the slowest growing because of the cost of the hardware to transmit the video information, but as the cost falls, this is likely to become increasingly common in office-to-office link-ups, representing considerable savings in travel time and expense. Text conferencing is possible in some electronic mail systems.

12.4.5 What are the methods of communication?

Communication systems depend upon one of the following means:

Analogue transmission This is the norm for transmission over British Telecom telephone circuits, and it means that a continuous range of frequencies is transmitted over the carrier medium. The conversion from binary to analogue and back is performed by modems. Dial-up networks are known as **Public Switched Telephone Networks (PSTNs)**. By and large, these systems provide low speed and low quality, but they are cheap and not inflexible, being cost-effective for small volume transmissions as against the use of leased lines. Their use is essential if people like sales representatives working in the field are to dial in orders. If the volume of transmissions is likely to be significant, organisations usually lease telephone lines, ie private circuits, specially conditioned by the telephone company for data transmission and bypassing the normal switching equipment in telephone exchanges.

Digital transmission This is now preferred to analogue transmission because it is less prone to error and is not limited in speed in the same way. At high speed, the analogue transmission is more easily corrupted because it carries a range of frequencies, whereas digital transmission is simply a stream of pulses sent over the carrying medium.

Telecommunication systems use channels with different sizes to send data at different speeds. Any information can be sent in either analogue or digital form, but the trend to digital is being accelerated because computers are digital machines. Those channels which have been designated as either analogue or digital can only carry information of that type. In designing systems, it is recognised that transmission signal fades and, to maintain data integrity, amplifiers are required to boost signal strength.

Packet SwitchStream (PSS) This is a specialised data service which divides messages into small blocks or packets for transmission purposes. Charges for this service are normally distance independent.

InterStream 2 This allows interworking between teletex terminals accessing the system through PSTN and PSS, while InterStream 3 allows messages to be transferred between the teletex and the telex services.

12.4.6 What are the standard data transmission media?

They are either:

1 **Guided media** which provide a durable physical link between the hardware units. The most usual forms are copper cable for low capacity local connection, and coaxial cable or fibre optics for higher capacity connections. Twisted-pair and multiway cabling is well-established and relatively inexpensive technology and easy to install, but both forms of cable radiate when transmitting data and therefore require security shielding if sensitive data is to be transmitted. Moreover, neither can be used in electrically noisy environments because the signal is vulnerable to interference. It is a sad facet of the emphasis on cost-reduction that modern twisted-pair wire increasingly uses thinner insulation to reduce the overall size of the cable. Coaxial cabling has a higher impedance characteristic but is shielded against eavesdropping through the use of a solid polythene dielectric and a braided copper outer conductor which are effective except in the baseband (unmodulated signalling as opposed to broadband which multiplexes several users onto the same cable) and which are not affected by external electromagnetic interference. Optical fibres are made of glass and are therefore not troubled by the unequal electrical ground potentials and other external sources of interference which may affect the other cabling. They are the most secure from eavesdropping and minimise signal degradation over long distances, but they are relatively expensive and require special connectors and alignment techniques to install (see 5.12.3).

2 **Unguided media** such as microwave and satellite links. Encryption is essential when using such systems because the signals are easily intercepted.

12.5 THE ROLE OF THE INSURANCE COMPANY

One way in which losses can be reduced is through insurance. At the simplest level, insurance policies can guard against:

1 the physical loss of assets through the occurrence of fire and other specified catastrophe perils;
2 those consequential losses which may arise as a result of any specified interruptions to the business;
3 those expenses incurred in recovering from one of the specified disasters, eg repair or investigation costs, etc; and
4 losses arising from the incidence of fraud and employee dishonesty.

Structure and contents insurance comprising fire, property damage and general liability (including all-risk policies against the more extreme contingencies such as flood and earthquakes, as well as business interruption cover and extra expense insurance) remains a reasonably competitive market. The extent of the cover can only be determined by senior management after a careful evaluation of the extent of likely losses in the event of each contingency occurrence, and decisions as to whether the insurance should cover replacement costs, or actual cash value for assets.

However, the market for policies to compensate in the event of fraud (whether computer-based or not) is now becoming more demanding, with increasingly high premium rates and restricted terms reflecting the high risk nature of the cover. In one sense, the problem is that many potential victims do not know what losses they are likely to sustain. But even though the precise mechanics of the ultimate fraud or its scale may not be known, insurers have learned that the only real uncertainty is usually as to the extent of the losses to be expected. Reductions in premiums may nevertheless be negotiated if the organisation is seen to have adequately addressed security problems by formulating sound policies and by installing good safeguards. Such market forces may encourage more hardware and software manufacturers to design more effective security systems from the outset. There are a further three basic types of policy now available from insurers:

1 **Fidelity** —where a breach in the normal standards or duties of care by a current employee results in loss. Guarantee bonds used to be available to cover the activities of named individuals in a position of trust. The market is now moving in the direction of blanket insurance as insurers come to acknowledge that many more employees could now cause loss regardless of their formal position within the organisation. The standard cover excludes liability for the activities of hackers, ex-employees and the employees of any other organisation having access to the system. NB, even part-time or contract staff may not be covered.
2 **Electronic crime** —although all fraud is potentially criminal, it need not be. A crime is an intentional or reckless violation of the criminal law. Fraud causes economic loss to the victim but need not be criminal, eg breach of confidentiality may cause significant loss to the inventor of a process or the originator of information, but it is not criminal in itself. NB, the police only respond to crime, so the victims of non-criminal fraud must look to their own resources for an investigation and pursuit of money or assets lost.
3 **Directors' and officers' liability**—this policy reflects the fact that all directors and senior company officers owe a fiduciary duty to the shareholders, creditors and other interested parties to take adequate care of the organisation's assets.

'In the final analysis, fraud insurance is a large mutual fund into which the better-controlled companies pour in money for the benefit of other insureds. Carriers sit in the middle, hoping that the winners contribute more than the losers pay out and can influence this balance by taking an aggressive attitude towards claims settlement.' (Ardis & Comer p4.) The number of policies negotiated by each organisation should be limited to avoid demarcation problems. Overlaps in the cover negotiated are highly probable (eg cover against damage through fire which has been started deliberately) and this can be particularly important if different carriers are involved. One strategy is to negotiate an all risks policy on specified items of hardware, but this does not necessarily cover computer applications, nor the consequential aspects of computing. In negotiating cover, it should be remembered that hardware may be rendered unavailable for a variety of reasons, eg it may be due to accidental or deliberate damage by an employee, or if air conditioning equipment fails, the main computer environment may have to be shut down; in more extreme cases, access may be denied to the building because of a fire in the neighbourhood, etc.

There are several potential problems which need to be considered:

1 Conventional policies insure on an indemnity basis, ie either the current market price less an allowance for depreciation, or reinstatement, ie new for old. Many organisations insure at

purchase price and expect to upgrade insurance to reflect expected higher replacement costs. In the computer hardware world, real prices have been falling for equivalent capacity. In the event of a loss, the organisation would probably want to improve the installation, but this would fall foul of the rules on betterment unless the issue is specifically addressed in the policy, ie the value of the enhancement is deducted from the insurance monies paid out. A failure to take proper precautions could dramatically affect the ability of the organisation to recover from the disaster.

2 The insured should ensure that the policy includes the breakdown of hardware in the phrase 'all risks of physical loss or damage'. It should also be noted that there may be conditions in the policy requiring that maintenance agreements are in force. In such instances, the insurance cover will only apply to breakdowns not covered by the maintenance agreements.

3 Most policies do not cover software risks, and data risks may be limited. Full cover should include both accidental and deliberate erasure and corruption. However, even then there may be difficulties of interpretation. For example, does cover against consequential loss include the value of the information and all those losses consequential upon its loss, or is it limited to the cost of reinstating the lost data? Theoretically, if data and software have been properly backed up, it will simply be a case of returning to the last archive copy, so the losses should be minimal. But if the back-up copies have been lost, the costs of reinstatement could be substantial. This would particularly be the case if in-house generated software had to be recreated.

4 In addition to the costs of reinstating the data, there are consequences to the lack of computer availability, or the inconvenience which occurs as a result of reduced services. Suppose that the organisation could not meet contract performance deadlines, and was faced by an action claiming damages for breach. Suppose that the organisation cannot fully reconstruct the debtor records, and is faced by a payment shortfall. If the policies are not worded to include all those losses naturally and directly flowing from the event, the loss must be born by the organisation. However, the quantification of those losses is not without difficulty. If the loss of data leads to an increase in the costs of running the organisation or a loss of profit, how are these figures to be quantified, and what is the indemnity period to be? The period agreed must obviously allow the organisation a reasonable opportunity to recover from the disruption, but the insurance market has been slow to recognise the increasing dependency of organisations on computer-generated information, and it is therefore difficult to negotiate all risks cover in this area.

12.6 HOW SHOULD THE MANAGERS APPROACH THEIR DECISION-MAKING?

The legal and practical responsibility for maintaining security lies with the senior management of each organisation. When losses are discovered, they carry the ultimate responsibility. The nature of their responsibility will vary depending upon whether the organisation is incorporated, but to avoid or minimise that liability (whether practical in the sense of dismissal or legal in the form of a judgment in damages), they must be seen to have taken the following steps:

1 To have acted with reasonable diligence to identify and quantify the risks of particular importance to their organisation.

2 To have identified the most vulnerable assets and resources, to have set protection goals, and to have created a formal risk management strategy.

3 To have created implementation policies and assigned sufficient resources to ensure a reasonable likelihood of success.

4 To have monitored the detailed results of the strategy, and to have established a policy of enforcement for all the major security rules and procedures.

5 To have investigated any frauds both within the new regime, and within allied organisations, and to have taken reasonable steps to learn from all identified mistakes and breaches of procedure.

6 To have shown reasonable diligence in seeking to recover money and assets lost.

Each organisation ought to know its own operation well enough to be able to predict both how losses might arise and the extent of those losses, but experience shows that knowledge is rarely used in a systematic way. A mixture of instinct and guesswork is frequently preferred to the detailed investigation and planning exercise.

SUMMARY

The key points covered in this chapter are that:

1. Fraud depends on motive and opportunity. The optimum risk avoidance strategy requires each organisation to analyse its staff profile to determine which members of staff pose the greatest risk to security. Once the potential perpetrators are known, the organisation may either direct them into non-sensitive activities, or exercise greater supervision.
2. The organisation must estimate the potential losses in the event of security breaches and weigh those losses against the cost of installing adequate security measures. The most cost-effective measures will be those which produce the most secure environment in the most vulnerable areas.
3. The organisation must consider both physical and logical security and make contingency plans to deal with the disasters which are most probable and will cause the greatest loss if quick action is not taken.
4. Many organisations are now installing networked facilities. While this may produce significant advantages, the organisation must guard against hardware failure, threats to message integrity, data bottlenecks and unauthorised access.
5. Every organisation ought to consider whether to insure against physical and economic loss arising from a disaster.
6. All managers must be seen to have taken care in making decisions about security.

QUESTIONS *Solutions to questions of an examination standard start on p 395*

Write brief notes on the following:

(a) perpetrator analysis;
(b) data protection;
(c) reliability and availability targets;
(d) the reasons why a prosecution for fraud may not occur.

Questions of an examination standard

1 An organisation which chooses to computerise its information resources must take seriously the possibility of fraud.

(a) Briefly list the factors which may motivate a person to commit fraud.

(b) Describe the steps which may be taken by the perpetrator to conceal the existence of a fraud.

2 The security cost analysis process compares the cost of the proposed security measures with the possible cost of disruption to the organisation.

Describe the factors which may influence the cost analysis process in a typical commercial organisation.

3 The adoption of a contingency plan for an information system will involve an organisation in a range of security decisions.

Explain the decisions which would have to be made by management when installing major security procedures in an organisation.

Chapter 13
Threats to Security

CHAPTER OBJECTIVES

The primary objective of this chapter is to begin the process of considering the extent of the main threats to security. The focus is on the physical threats, with an introduction to the most reliable of counter-measures. The detailed objectives are to:

1 evaluate the threats represented by the weather, electricity, fire, water, temperature and dirt;
2 appreciate the consequences of component malfunction;
3 understand the project planning considerations for the detailed management of physical security;
4 consider the mechanics of physical access control including the use of guards and receptionists, mechanical locking systems and automatic entry control systems such as signature verification, smart cards, etc;
5 consider the problem of equipment theft.

13.1 WHAT ARE THE MAIN THREATS TO SECURITY?

The main threats fall into two primary groupings:

1 Physical threats to the buildings which contain the information systems such as fire, flood, wind, lightning, subsidence, and, in appropriate geographical areas, earthquakes, sand storms, hurricanes, etc.
2 People-based threats—people are at the heart of all security systems and threats. The threats which they pose may be man-made or they may have a political character, eg accidental damage, theft and malicious damage, bomb threats, strikes, riots, war, etc.

The result of either threat may be:

(a) simple damage to the whole or a part of the organisation or its resources,
(b) destruction of the whole or part of the organisation or the total loss of critical resources.

The counter-measures against these threats must therefore be:

(a) People-related measures —which may include ensuring the safety of staff and visitors or the control of movement within a building or part of a building.
(b) Resource-related measures —whether to protect physical assets or to control access to resources.

All these threats may result in the loss of system availability and the destruction of data and hardware. Organisations have always had the problem of protecting their information. In the past this meant the secure storage of physical records in lockable cabinets and safes. In the modern systems, data storage may take several forms. Inevitably, organisations will have hard copy materials, whether from outside sources or generated in-house. For these purposes, hard copy is taken to be material that is readable by a human without the need of computer support, eg material written or printed on paper, or recorded on punched cards, microfilm, etc. Care must be taken at all times, which includes the disposal of hard copy records. If the data is still sensitive, the paper should be shredded or incinerated and not simply thrown out. Prior to disposal, the paper should be stored in a way which minimises the risk of fire yet, ironically, for large scale waste disposal, it is probably better to use a furnace. Information may also be transitorily displayed on VDUs. If sensitive data might be seen by unauthorised individuals, the screens should be kept in a secure room to minimise the risk of disclosure. Magnetic media for the storage of information (ie tapes, disks and drums) can be used repeatedly and, in larger organisations, will usually be stored in libraries. Such storage media are vulnerable to corruption through exposure to magnetic fields (such as those generated by large electrical motors) and to fire (floppy disks have a lower ignition point than paper), so care should be taken in the siting of the storage facility and its construction. Access to the library or storage facilities should be limited to authorised staff and, of course, access to the computers must be controlled.

13.2 PHYSICAL THREATS

13.2.1 The weather and electricity

The weather is the greatest natural threat to most locations. Wind, rain and storms can have dramatic effects on the buildings and their immediate environment both during the winter and, less predictably, at other times of the year. Alongside the physical threat of direct damage, lightning and electrical storms are sources of electromagnetic interference which can materially disrupt power supplies and which, in turn, may indirectly damage equipment through power surges, etc. The electricity supply can be critical. Even nanosecond-long power surges can cause misregistration of data and false logic, actual damage to sensitive circuitry, or system crashes causing the wholesale loss of data. Power supplies can be affected by other environmental factors, eg high demand for power at certain times of the day, damage to power lines or switching gear at a more distant location, etc.

Equipment should therefore be protected against both current and voltage fluctuations. However, full scale power protection can be quite expensive if it includes an uninterrupted and stand-by power supply system which will provide back-up in the event of power failure. **Uninterrupted power supplies (UPS)** use the mains supply to charge stand-by batteries. These batteries power an inverter (direct to alternating current converter) which produces the main alternating power within the organisation in the event of power failures or excessive fluctuations. The alternatives are stand-by generators which will start up automatically in the event of a mains failure (leaving the problem of the time taken to achieve stable power output), or simple battery operation (this may not be able to meet modern power requirements in networked equipment, but will be satisfactory to maintain the telephone system).

13.2.2 Fire

The threat of fire through flames, heat and smoke contamination is well established. The causes vary from careless smoking, through faulty electrical wiring, to the criminally motivated arson attack. The danger posed by fire is not only to the hardware, but also to data records, whether on magnetic storage media or on paper back-up. Fire resistant safes can save a proportion of the backed-up data, but it is better to prevent the fire in first place, or to detect it before it has caused too much damage. As to prevention, the best plans include the following elements to reduce fire risks:

(a) good employee recruitment and training practices (with the possibility of encouraging no smoking in sensitive buildings);
(b) the use of building materials of low flammability and the planning of electrical systems to minimise the risk of overloading—a common cause of fire;
(c) the avoidance of wooden or flammable furniture and fittings; and
(d) the installation of administrative controls over the use and storage of flammable materials (including good refuse disposal practices).

Similarly, automatic heat and smoke detection equipment and extinguishers (including gas flooding systems) should be installed at critical points in the building. When planning the optimum detection system, it should be remembered that fires go through a recognised cycle:

(a) the first stage is normally ignition followed by smouldering;

(b) open flames form, the temperature of the surrounding air rises and the flames then spread the fire by direct contact;
(c) the final stage is the rapid spreading of the fire by heat radiation.

Photoelectric smoke detectors therefore help to detect fires before they are out of control, with thermostats to detect temperature changes as a second line of defence. All sensitive areas should also have manual fire alarms so that alert staff may give a warning.

Small fires can be controlled through the use of hand-held extinguishers if staff are available, with the back-up of hose systems and the automatic systems to deal with outbreaks in vulnerable areas or in the case of the more severe outbreaks. Automatic alarms with adequate sprinkler or gas systems should always be used where sensitive hardware systems are permanently powered up in undermanned environments. To minimise the risks of electrical fires, staff should be trained to always switch off and unplug computer equipment at the end of each working day in terminal rooms.

Water is a cheap extinguishing material but neither water nor foam extinguishers should be used on an electrical fire because of the risk of electric shock —gas or carbon dioxide extinguishers should be used wherever possible. In comparing the two main gas-based systems, the difficulty is that Halon (monobromotrifluoromethane) is expensive but, because it does not displace the oxygen, in small quantities it is not harmful to people, whereas carbon dioxide is harmful to people and 30 per cent by volume CO_2 is required to extinguish a small fire. But 10 per cent by volume represents a harmful level for human beings, so the system cannot be used before the staff have been evacuated. Moreover, although neither system can deal with a fire which rekindles after the gas supply has been exhausted, CO_2 has the virtue of being cheap and plentiful. Subject to storage constraints, CO_2 may therefore offer more comprehensive control capacity at an economic price. Neither gas is harmful to the equipment. Consequently, a reasonable conclusion would be that water systems should only be used to prevent an established fire from becoming a major disaster once other methods have failed. Another possibility, dry powder extinguishers, is also of limited utility because, once released into the office environment, the chemicals may corrode the circuitry. Overall, the staff should be properly trained in the use of the fire fighting equipment and evacuation procedures and, to ensure maximum safety, all emergency exits should be clearly marked and not obstructed.

13.2.3 Water

Water, whether from flooding or fire fighting, represents a significant threat to buildings, and the resources (particularly documentary) stored there. If a building is sited in an area prone to flooding, some form of water defence system such as land drains and dykes, together with structural waterproofing should be considered. Similarly, it would be advisable to avoid ground floor or basement locations for sensitive equipment and storage facilities.

Although basements can be avoided as a site for critical hardware, many wiring and telecommunications distribution systems still come into buildings underground and so the computer or communications network can be disabled by a flood either way. All telephone breakdowns are fatal in a networked or distributed system. One line of defence is offered by British Telecom which offers COMMSURE, a mobile PABX system which is supplied to subscribers. British Telecom also has contingency plans to deal with fire, flood and terrorist activity in its exchanges. These plans depend upon the use of mobile substitutes, operated from large vans which can be driven to the site of the unusable exchange and connected into the lines. However, priority in the restoration of services will always be given to the armed services, police, hospitals, etc. British Telecom can reroute lines in some cases to overcome accidental line breaks, eg in roadworks, or offer replacement dial-up facilities. In designing a network, the organisation should consider whether security can be improved by building in a degree of redundancy. Hence, extra lines can be built into the networking system to reduce and spread the risk. In taking decisions on this and related issues, the organisation should rely on the best evidence. This requires the security department to ensure that all fault reports should be accurate and followed up.

In this planning exercise, the whole range of threats should be canvassed, it being essential to remember that water damage may come from burst pipes and spilled cups of coffee as well as the more dramatic storms. Building design and layout should be considered, and the source of the most likely threats should be identified. Then, whatever the nature of the hardware, it should be sited away from water pipes and leaking roofs. It may also be appropriate to consider the installation of water sensing devices, and good office practice (eg not eating and drinking in sensitive areas and having staff trained to quickly mop up spillages or move the threatened equipment) should minimise other risks which will include the incidence of rust.

13.2.4 Temperature and dirt

Wherever possible, manufacturers' recommendations should be followed in supplying a reasonably stable temperature environment for the equipment. Air conditioning and purifying can be essential to keep mainframe operating temperatures and air quality within manufacturers' tolerances. A failure to keep temperatures down or to extract dust may lead to damage to internal components. In a general office environment, micros and peripherals may require auxilliary cooling systems to supplement their own fan systems. Static electricity can, if not properly controlled, represent as much of a threat as power surges. Organisations should therefore consider using antistatic carpeting, dehumidifiers and ion particle emitters. Further, quite apart from the improvement in working conditions for the ordinary office worker (and possible improvement in morale), it can be essential to filter dust particles and other contaminants out of the air which might damage the disks or disk head readers. If the cost is disproportionate to the risks, vacuum cleaners should be used to suck dust and dirt away (dusting using cloths will only stir up the dust and may promote static). Smoking deposits a film on surrounding objects that holds dust. It should be discouraged.

13.2.5 Hardware threats

General threats to hardware fall under four headings, the latter three being dealt with in 13.4, 13.5 and 15.1 below:

1 component malfunction,
2 theft,
3 physical attack,
4 operator error.

Component malfunction is not always immediately apparent to the operators and so special measures are required. The need is to allow the system to check its own operation and to detect and, where possible, correct the detected errors. Some such systems affect software performance and all affect cost, so few manufacturers have installed such systems. The result is that preventative maintenance tends to be more effective than emergency cure. Generally, equipment with moving parts requires more frequent servicing, and when considering the extent of service and maintenance cover required, the past service record or the experiences of other users should be examined. For these purposes, it is important to record all the faults which arise to get an accurate picture of reliability and to gain a measure of usage. As to back-up arrangements, spare equipment should be provided in the event of breakdown. If the organisation has a sensible policy of standardisation, substituting one piece for another is not a problem. But when it comes to finalising arrangements, a proper corporate plan should be devised. To have a separate agreement for each micro or peripheral in a large organisation is administratively inconvenient and likely to be uneconomic. A reasonable target for management to aim for is a situation where total annual maintenance costs do not normally exceed 15 per cent of annual cost, otherwise the cost of the cover will be out of proportion.

However, no matter what the level of hardware reliability achieved, all organisations should encourage a good data back-up discipline. This means that users should not wait until the end of the day, but should copy anything important at regular intervals, preferably with the back-up stored in another location to the immediate user. The reason for this discipline is that significant losses may arise if data has to be rekeyed. The optimum back-up scheme is termed the parent-grandparent system. This has at least three days' worth of data in rotation. At the end of the first day, all sensitive data files are backed-up with the copy stored off-site. At the end of day two, a further copy is made and stored in a secure location on-site. At the end of the third day, the copy made is kept on-site and the day-two copy is taken off-site. The day-one copy is returned for making the copy on day four. The effect is therefore to have the oldest of the three copies off-site so that in an emergency which destroys the most recent copy, the organisation will never lose more than two days' data.

Floppy disks are insecure both because they are so concealable and therefore easily removed from the work environment, and because they are easily damaged. The surface of a floppy disk can be contaminated by all physical substances, while the disks themselves can be warped by the sun or other heat sources, and the data erased by static and magnetic sources. Given that floppy disks can be unreliable, organisations should look forward to the development of reliable hard disks and optical disks. It is difficult to devise a guaranteed way to prevent staff from taking confidential information home on floppy disks. If micros are used in the system configuration, it is impossible to avoid the use of floppy disks for the storage of information. Risks can be limited by fitting controls to disk drives, but even these are not very practical because the determined thief can still get a print-out and take this home. To a reasonable degree, employers must trust their employees, or if someone is suspect, the employer should monitor access to sensitive information generally. Security products are not a substitute for effective man-management.

Whatever system is being used, a good file and document labelling system is required so that management and control of the information can be kept up to standard. A failure here makes it hard to know where information is, and the organisation may become vulnerable to theft or the activities of malicious employees who deliberately mislabel disks, etc. Disk space management is essential to minimise the risk of a user who is about to save some data suddenly discovering that there is no storage space left. To reduce the risk, users should be trained to delete redundant files as a matter of routine. Staff should also be encouraged in a clean desk policy, ie they should always be trained to tidy floppy disks and other materials away into suitable containers. Shredders should be used for sensitive print-outs and, where appropriate, tape erasers should be used, or disks reformatted or re-used.

13.2.6 Physical communication problems

There are a range of transmission faults which may affect data integrity. These include simple noise on the line, through misconnection, ie data sent to the wrong location, to modem and multiplexer faults. Noise may obscure or destroy the meaning of data being transmitted. Misconnection and disconnection mean that services are disrupted and data delayed or lost. Parity checks, error detection codes and polynomial check codes may detect whether there are end-to-end problems. If such problems are revealed, the solutions are to retransmit the data at slower speeds, to reroute transmission (this relies upon having a degree of redundancy of hardware to be able to substitute different machines), and to engage in cryptography.

13.2.7 Project planning considerations

An accurate appraisal of the local situation is fundamental. Having decided which disasters to plan for, the organisation should identify which are the most probable and which are the most critical, given local conditions. All other disasters should be dealt with as a sub-routine to the main plan. In the modern organisation, the information services are usually critical and vulnerable. As a first step, it is necessary to classify the extent of the damage which might occur and to identify the scale of the action necessary to make an effective response:

(a) The damage might be limited to individual terminal or node areas through a localised fire or other contingency. The counter-measure is to repair or replace damaged hardware, establishing alternative short-term terminal facilities, and reorganising communications in the interim.

(b) The damage to system or support services might be such that many different user departments might be affected. The priority is to restore communications and services as above.

(c) There could be serious damage to the central computer facility. In such a case, all users might be affected, and serious consideration would have to be given to permanently relocating the computer operations.

(d) There might be substantial damage to the organisation's offices which includes the DP department. The result might be little salvageable equipment or space. In determining strategy, it should be remembered that the continued operation of the organisation is the main priority.

(e) There could be regional damage through storms or flood, war or civil disturbances, with widespread loss of power or communications. If the organisation operates on a national or international basis, short- or long-term relocation will be the answer.

The most probable disasters (fire, water damage) will normally be localised in their effect, and will affect only one or two users. A small group would make a temporary move while repairs are made. No specific preparations would need to be made in advance because it is impossible to prepare a detailed response for every event for each group of employees. A response would only be prepared if the event would be critical, ie fire or explosion near the central computer facility, communication links or power supply (this could occur on another floor, but smoke and/or water might cause the damage). Management need realistic advice on which disasters are most likely, to keep their planning exercise in perspective.

If events occur during the day, minor difficulties can usually be dealt with before they become serious—a small fire can be quickly put out, but the same fire over the weekend or at night could become serious before help arrives. In all situations, a rapid evaluation of prospective damage is essential because the organisation may have to authorise responses which involve an element of risk, eg the use of water to extinguish a fire near a sensitive computer facility. Similarly, after the disaster event, full damage appraisal is essential because there can be hidden damage to telephone and coaxial lines, or computer hardware may have suffered damage from water and/or smoke; sifting through the wreckage may reveal damage to offices with document loss, etc. Finally, in planning, it should always be remembered that an organisation relies on the people employed. Their reaction and morale in a disaster are critical to the organisation's recovery.

13.3 PEOPLE AND SECURITY

People are at the heart of all security systems and threats. The threat to an organisation may come from employees or from outsiders. An employee will have direct access to the buildings and records of the employer, whereas outsiders have to take more risks to gain entry unless collusion can be achieved. It may be said with some certainty that a criminal will only exploit an opportunity to gain if there is a reasonable chance of avoiding detection. The probability of loss is therefore reduced if the organisation is alert.

13.3.1 Physical access controls

The fundamental rationale of the task of physical security is to control space. In personnel terms, this requires that the management formally assigns responsibility for controlling space, and takes all measures necessary either to practically control the given area or to make it look as though security is effective. Before networking became established, physical security was achieved by restricting access to the mainframe computer room. As the computer-stored data was concentrated in that one room, physical access controls reduced the risk of an unauthorised person gaining access to the data. It is now considered advisable to design central computer buildings as unobtrusively as possible. But whereas all notices which identify the function of the building should be avoided, there should be security controls sufficiently visible to deter those intruders who are considering unauthorised entry. Further, in planning the site, it is important to secure the support equipment such as air conditioning and power supply as well as the computer itself. The rationale of access control is two-way:

1 it may be used to protect users against inadvertent exposure to known hazards, eg high voltages or radiation, or

2 it may be to protect the installation itself.

Physical access control is designed to allow entry to those people who have a legitimate right to be in the secure area while denying access to all unauthorised persons. The identification and recognition of people is vitally important. Identification means to determine (and hopefully prove) the identity of a person or thing. Humans are good at recognising each other by sight or the sound of their voices. Within an organisation, friends and colleagues do not generally represent a problem.

Face-to-face, people mainly rely on sight, but sound is becoming increasingly important now that the use of the telephone has become a normal method of communicating. Voice recognition technology is becoming more reliable, with voice pattern systems the most effective because they are not dependent upon the machine discriminating between different words. However, recognition by a machine can be an uncertain affair. Whatever the system, the designer must try to minimise the number of false acceptances and false rejections. By way of example, consider how unfortunate it would be if there were a large number of false acceptances at an automated teller machine in a bank wall. The immediate consequence for bank customers would be the increase of bank charges to cover the cost of many fraudulent claims. The prospect of this threat justified the introduction of the **Personal Identification Number (PIN)** system. The correct combination of card and PIN suggests that the withdrawal is proper. If the correct PIN is not entered, the machine can retain the card. Similarly, the card can be withheld if it has been notified as stolen. The designer must also cater for the possibility of false rejections which can be equally annoying or embarrassing if the machine wrongly keeps the card and gives no money when all other sources of cash are closed (see 14.2.3).

For machine purposes, the process depends upon two questions:

1 Has the right identifying sign been used?
2 Does it appear to come from the authorised person?

For the most secure networked or distributed systems, encryption may be proof of sending because only the legitimate sender had the means to encipher the message. The problem is that in a distributed system the keys have to be distributed and this part of the system may be vulnerable. **Public key systems** avoid this difficulty. For these purposes, there are two keys: one enciphers the message, using a special one-way function; a different key must then be used to decipher the enciphered text. User A therefore holds one private key and publishes his other key to all correspondents, together with the appropriate decryption rules. When they receive a message, supposedly from A, they can decipher it using the key. If it makes sense, it should have come from A for the cipher text could only be produced using his or her key. The security of the system depends upon having one-way functions—ie functions which are easy to do one way and difficult to undo. It is easy to multiply two big prime numbers but hard to factorise the result. This is the basis of the **Rivest, Shamir and Adleman (RSA) cipher**. For these purposes, the prime numbers must be about 100 decimal digits long to produce satisfactory security given present mathematical methods. If a better way of factorising large numbers is found, security will be compromised (see 14.5).

The more everyday identification systems rely upon:

1 something remembered such as a password,
2 something possessed like a key or token,
3 a physical characteristic with unique qualities such as a fingerprint,
4 an action performed such as a signature or speaking into a voice recognition system.

Put simply, this means that identification techniques involve identifying a person by something he or she is, or has, or knows, or does, or by a combination of these things.

13.3.2 The methods of access control

One extreme solution to the problem of access control would be to deny access to all the people all the time. This makes the policing activity straightforward since intruders are easy to identify. Equally, there will be different security priorities in operation if the public are allowed access either all the time, or for substantial parts of the day. However, the real problems emerge when access is to be limited to an identified class of person, whether time constrained or not. In these situations, the management has to decide the extent to which:

(a) the class is definable in advance,
(b) the class has a stable and predictable membership,
(c) the membership can be compelled or induced to follow the access rules.

In part, the answers to these questions will depend upon whether access is related to job function rather than to individuals, ie to the DP manager rather than to an identified individual, so that changes of privileges arise with job transfers or redefinitions. A further factor will be the extent to which the organisation depends upon contract staff to supplement in-house personnel, and the frequency with which support staff and engineers come on site for maintenance purposes. Other classes of entrant to consider include the cleaning staff, delivery people and couriers. Some people requiring access will be regular users, needing access as a regular part of their work. Others may only need access on special occasions. When planning access control systems, it must be recognised that it can be difficult to get full co-operation from outsiders because they have no real interest in the site's security needs, but in-house staff can have security procedures written into their contracts of employment and such provisions can be enforced under the standard disciplinary codes. Overall, the security assumptions underlying the adopted access procedures should be based on the proposition that there is a significant risk that, whether deliberately or carelessly, outsiders will disclose the security systems.

There are three basic ways to control a door or gate:

1 by using receptionists and/or guards,
2 by using mechanical locks and keys,
3 by using electronic systems.

In general terms, the security requirements may be of such a high order that precautions must start with a boundary or perimeter fence. Obviously, although this may be desirable, it may not be possible in many city centre sites because of local authority planning constraints. Decisions must then be taken about building access controls. In particularly sensitive environments, each possible door and access point may have to be secured, including windows and air vents. Within the building, areas such as the computer department may require specific access controls. These controls may include some or all of the following: a receptionist, closed circuit television, guard surveillance, keyed locks, and electronic systems using identification cards and pictures—these latter systems to protect doors leading into the most critical areas. A security guard can challenge all those who seek access at strategic points on their need to enter the given area, but people are an expensive way of controlling the environment, and they may be better used in overseeing the correct working of other systems. This is not to dismiss the activity of guarding. Guards are effective if properly trained and motivated, and they can challenge strangers or the apparently unauthorised and call for help if necessary. In laying out the access to sensitive areas, it should be remembered that both guards and receptionists who are stationed at fixed points may need security screens to protect them from attack.

In the most sensitive environments, access to these protected parts of the building should be controlled by the guard or receptionist on a self-locking door or gate, with a remote release under the control of that person. A segregated area in the form of a pen or corridor is a good defence because intruders are unlikely to risk being controlled in this way before possible entry. Elegant forms of trap are available for use in this way. In deciding who to admit, the guard or receptionist must be able to recognise legitimate users, eg from a list with photographs, or where there is a larger number of users, from badges or passes. The production of passes on a routine basis is useful, if only because it checks to see whether a pass has been lost or stolen. Passes should include a photograph and a specimen signature. In case of doubt over a photograph (eg new glasses or hairstyle), sample signatures can be taken and can be compared with the specimen.

Passes should be changed regularly to update the photograph and the sample signature. However, in setting staffing levels and defining duties, it must be recognised that guards are readily distracted and may be diverted from the task in hand unless there are enough people to deal with each problem as it arises. Similarly, telephonists on busy switchboards who are also called upon to act as receptionists are frequently unable to perform the security function well. In part, this will be determined by the number of people claiming the right of entry. If traffic is low, it may be possible to leave would-be entrants outside until their credentials can be validated. If such a step is taken, a comfortable reception area is a good public relations gesture. Otherwise, adequate staffing levels are essential if staff and visitor goodwill is to be maintained.

13.3.3 Signature verification systems

Many documents and transactions are authenticated by signatures. A signature is very personal and, because signatures are not lost in the same way as passes or tokens, they can provide good evidence that a person is as claimed. This is also a socially acceptable way of asking people to identify themselves, with most people who have bank and building society accounts used to performing the activity. But those signing must be able to sign consistently with different pen types and sizes, and it must be remembered that the illiterate have no signature and so it cannot be a universal form of identification. Signatures also change with time and mood. If the signature is to be used for interpersonal identification purposes, it must be produced in front of the person who is to make the comparison with the sample. This method also requires that the sample itself is reasonably tamper-proof. Signatures can also be examined by machine. This is not a straight comparison by way of superimposing one on top of the other because signatures vary too much. However, signature verification can be conducted on a probabilities basis, and the signature approved if there are enough points of similarity. The most modern systems can either take an already written sample for retrospective analysis, or the system can be dynamic.

In the dynamic systems, the test is based on the proposition that producing a signature is a ballistic activity and, once started, each individual tends to do it in the same basic (autonomic) way. The movements of the pen can be analysed and matched to previous efforts. The system will consider five or six examples in file and look for consistency. For example, IBM has developed a signature verification system which uses a pen with transducers to convert the motions made while signing into electronic signals. A mathematical algorithm has been developed which measures the degree of similarity between two sets of these signals. Of the six samples taken, two signatures are designated the primary exemplars and the system always stores the four most recent signatures accepted to allow for the fact that signature styles drift over time. Similarity testing must therefore be continually updated. The characteristics compared are:

(a) segment alignment, a segment being the time the pen is in contact with the paper,
(b) pressure correlation relates segment time to pen tip pressure,
(c) acceleration correlation similarly relates segment time to the motion of the pen as a waveform,
(d) pressure coherence, and
(e) acceleration coherence.

One of the major problems in systems of this type is user motivation. The management must control the natural urge of many employees to experiment with the system to see what changes can be made in the signature and still be accepted. The system described has been designed to operate in an IBM PC and it can be used to protect dial-up telephone access to the IBM VM network, the algorithm being held in a disconnected service machine until the signature has been authenticated. (For more details see Worthington.)

13.3.4 Mechanical locking systems

One view is that good security control is achieved through the use of tamper-proof locks on doors, but this strategy is inconvenient if the door is in regular use. Conventional locks and keys are only suitable for small installations where a few people are employed. The difficulty is that whereas conscientious employees will accept the chore of locking and unlocking a door once or twice a day, they will find it intolerable for a door in regular use. As traffic increases, doors will simply be left open. In unmanned buildings, cheap locks give poor security, and good locks are useless in a poor door because the would-be intruder can easily attack the lock or its fixings to gain entry. Because it requires less skill, most illegal entrants will attempt to force the door rather than to pick the lock. However, it must not be assumed that those who wish to enter are without intelligence, and so all accessible windows and the accessible parts of the roof must be of a similar standard of security to avoid the expenditure on external doors being wasted.

Good locks are expensive, and some modern locks require special machines to cut the keys because complex machining geometry is used in the cutting process. This makes the keys hard to replicate even for a skilled locksmith. If locks have been arranged to permit a master key system, the essential requirement is that it should not be possible to convert an ordinary key into a master key. The master key ought to have more metal or greater complexity than the ordinary keys. The weakness of any locked system lies in the control of the keys. The first concern is the availability of the blanks for both the ordinary keys and for the master key(s). Most ordinary keys are easily duplicated

—a feature which could be considered useful since they are frequently lost or mislaid. Staff also tend to go home with them or leave them in the wrong place unless there are set procedures for dealing with them. When the keys relate to a sensitive area, they should only be issued against a signature, or a tag card system should be introduced to show who has particular keys.

Cipher locks usually have five or more buttons. There are both mechanical and electronic versions of this type of lock. To unlock the door, a code of between three and fifteen digits must be entered, the buttons being pressed in the correct combination to open the door. It is possible to break the code through trial and error, but these locks are relatively cheap to install and will probably be satisfactory for less frequently used routes. Too much traffic and they will probably be abused. The better models will sound an alarm in the event of tampering, and automatically lock the door after a predetermined number of false attempts, requiring a reset by the security supervisor. There should also be in-built precautions to restrict the ability of others to observe the code being punched in, and the locks should be reprogrammable in the event that the code falls into the wrong hands. Forgetful staff must also be persuaded not to jot the code down somewhere close to the door.

13.3.5 Automatic entry control systems

A card reader and lock can control entry by card, carrier, hour and day. These are usually electric locks, with a battery supply which gives extra security in the event of power failure. For additional security, a push button key pad can be provided for supplementary coded input, but this is an inconvenience to staff (it does have the advantage that the codes can be changed for different time windows, so that staff must key in the correct code for the given time of day—a failure would potentially indicate a lack of authority to be in the given area at that time). Some organisations start by developing a comprehensive time and attendance monitoring system. This is particularly useful where flexitime is in operation.

Many systems do offer the option of **time windows** —ie access is only permitted at certain times, eg cleaners are only allowed between specified hours, while ordinary office staff are denied routine access outside normal office hours. The better the system, the more it may be tailored to local conditions. But the management of detailed time profiles creates administrative work. Most employees also value flexibility in their working regime, eg to be able to stand in for a sick colleague, perhaps at short notice. If the responsible substitute cannot quickly gain access because he or she appears to be on the wrong shift, the system is inconvenient. If it can only be overridden by special access, it makes extra work. Moreover, if the system is clock-based, the time may be wrong (even clocks internal to computers do stop or tell the wrong time, particularly after power surge problems or a GMT/summer time change). If people are denied access at the proper time, user confidence and morale is damaged. However, effective staff monitoring and policing is possible using this form of system. All breaches of time discipline can quickly be followed up with the individual's manager. Word then quickly passes round the grapevine that breaches are spotted and time discipline is generally improved. The successful implementation of this type of system requires quick, but sensitive follow-up to each significant incident.

Because the use of key pads is subject to the risk that the entry of codes may be overseen, automatic access control through badges worn by staff may be a more appropriate system. The point of badges and tokens is that they make access dependent upon the production of a special identifier. The manual tokens will carry a photograph and space for signature, but the others will carry information in machine readable form. Conventionally written or photographic information can be altered by an imposter whereas false machine readable information may be more easily detected. Increasingly, identity badges are based on plastic media which have been laminated and, as such, they have become reasonably tamper proof. Whether manual or machine readable, the badge can be clipped to clothing or carried around the neck on a chain. The badges indicate membership of an organisation, and represent passes to particular sites within that organisation. The badge should not show precisely what is authorised so that if the card is lost, a casual finder could not easily utilise it. If the badges are passes, all must wear them prominently. The senior management must set an example in this.

Machine readable tokens may take the following forms:

(a) The simplest tokens are small **punched cards** which can be sensed by mechanical probes, electrical contacts or light. They are cheap but easily replicated. They are becoming more common in hotel systems. They need not be durable because a guest will only use them a few times, the code of the door being changed for the next guest.

(b) **Plastic cards** are coded to infra red by including a lamination that is opaque in ordinary light but transparent to infra red.

(c) **Magnetic cards** incorporate small beads of magnetic material or thin wires or have stripes. The **bead card** is a thick sandwich. The middle layer has a matrix of holes punched in. Small magnetised ferrite beads are then placed within the matrix and form a unique pattern. Such cards can affect data recorded on stripe cards and so should be stored separately by the user. They also have to be encoded during manufacture. As a result, the delivery time may be long, ie months rather than weeks.

(d) The **Wiegand card** uses tiny individual wires for each bit of data that is to be coded. Each wire is about 10mm long. To read the data the card is moved rapidly through a strong magnetic field. The individual wires change state and produce a strong pulse in an adjacent sensing coil. These cards are difficult to replicate and the reader is resistant to vandals because no movable reading head is required.

(e) **Stripe cards** are the most common and form the standard for the bank and credit card industry. These cards suffer from one flaw. The information is easily altered and data can be transferred from one to another by using a skimmer. Although there are security systems which limit the ability to alter the data, in general it remains easily copyable.

(f) **Proximity cards** use radio signals to pass on information between the token and the access controller. The token can be active or passive. The active token transmits a signal continuously. This has the advantage that the user need do nothing other than carry the card to gain freedom of movement. This leaves the hands free, and avoids the necessity of putting the card into a slot or against a reader. They rely on rechargeable batteries and so the card must be left overnight on the premises in its coded slot to be picked up on entry each morning. Cards which are not recharged in this way will not open doors. This type of system is relatively expensive but can be ideal in high security, high density situations. It represents an economical measure for between 20 and 50 mobile staff. The greater the number of staff, the more equipment and space required for overnight recharging. The system is best installed when the building is in construction to ensure that the controllers respond only to those who wish to enter and not to those who walk past. It should be remembered that some cards will transmit through conventionally constructed walls. In congested sites, signal overlaps can therefore be a problem. The alternative passive card responds to a signal issued by the controller. If the controller emits a weak signal, the card must be held near the controller, but it avoids the problem of overlap. This also has the major advantage that because there is no slot, it is effectively vandal-proof.

(g) **Chip cards (smart cards)** are any form of token that includes a microprocessor. These cards retain data and are programmed to disclose it only when the right signals are received. A typical card memory must carry 4K bytes of ROM with 256K RAM (a battery is usually required to maintain it).

Most of these systems need a hand free and so special arrangements must be made for the disabled or those recovering from an injury and who may perhaps be on crutches or in a wheelchair. Moreover, packages and trolleys will need to be moved about the site, and so wide (and high) doorways may be required. Big loads move slowly, so timing on locks and their alarms must be adjustable. The more sophisticated the system, the greater the cost so management must engage in proper cost benefit analysis to ensure that the additional expenditure will represent value for money. All the systems require that authorised staff are in possession of the correctly coded badges for each day and time, and these automatically open the designated doors. However, whatever system is selected, the active co-operation of the staff is essential.

Some systems raise the alarm if the wrong code is used, or the wrong sort of card is inserted or advanced—the card may belong to a different site or not be authorised for that door or time. The primary purpose of this form of alarm is to deter vandals and any others who might seek to abuse the system. Staff must be trained to respond to the alarm constructively. In return, the system must have a little flexibility built in and must tolerate the mistakes most commonly made by the staff (eg if the wrong code is entered, it is usual for at least one false entry to be permitted before the alarm is raised). In a computerised system, the monitoring of staff performance may reveal equipment that is out of adjustment, or it may show the need for better staff training. The system can also report who is in each area and show how they got there—thus revealing tailing—ie where two go through the door or gate together without both registering. If and when comments are made to staff which indicate that their movements have been followed, they must be reassured and must be encouraged not to react fearfully or resentfully at the supervisory capacities of the system.

13.3.6 Planning considerations

The first essential step is therefore to define which areas are to be controlled and to what level of security. The perimeter needs to be defined in terms of physical features such as walls, doors, fences, etc. The designated area may be one zone so that once inside, the user can move anywhere, or there may be a need for a hierarchy of zones to give greater protection to important, or particularly valuable or vulnerable assets. The design should aim for simplicity. Complicated layouts can be expensive and inconvenient to protect. The design should also minimise the level of traffic that is to pass through the various areas. Work should be structured so that most people work within one zone and should not have to pass to other areas on a regular basis. It is obvious that some classes of employee or visitor must be allowed to move around the site, but such individuals should be the exception rather than the norm.

When the floor plan and functionality of each building is being considered, it is vital to consider the siting of toilets, canteens, recreational facilities (if any) and any other commonly accessed facility, so that staff need not move through other sensitive areas on a regular route. Heavy traffic causes queues at controlled doorways which is irritating and wastes time. This may lead to several people passing through barriers together and there is a risk that unauthorised persons might pass through at such times. The design should always cater for the worst cases. If there is doubt, the organisation should undertake a traffic census and get an accurate idea of how many people move around at different periods of the day. The planners should also seek to ensure that the number of doors that need to be controlled is minimised. Quite apart from the cost of installing security equipment, the constant wear and tear makes maintenance and replacement costs higher.

In appropriate sites, strong doors with good locks will be needed. Similarly, turnstiles and air-lock chambers with two sets of doors to prevent follow-through may be considered but they are expensive and their operation may be embarrassing to large people or pregnant women. The presence of these features also complicates emergency planning and may cause accidents. Exit routes have to be planned for emergencies, and emergency doors can often be used to circumvent access controls unless properly alarmed. Audible alarms must be fitted on doors with panic bolts. Glass bolts are useful because it can be seen whether the doors have been opened. Special doors which lead to loading bays and other similar entry points, should be alarmed, as should openable windows and hatches. But all such alarms should have an override switch that can be operated by a responsible person to disconnect the alarm for genuine use, eg during deliveries.

If they are to be fitted, electric locks should always have a mechanical override facility to ensure that the door can be opened in the event of difficulties. Thus, the controller could fail, and batteries might inconveniently keep the door locked for many hours. Similarly, automatic doors must be connected to the fire alarm system so that, in the event of fire, they are released to provide quick and easy release. If both the failure of electric power and the sounding of the fire alarms opens the doors, some other way of securing the doors against intruders must be devised since it is relatively easy to set off a fire alarm or to disrupt power supplies through a deliberately induced short circuit. Equally, if the fire control system is gas-based, the doors must prevent premature return by unprotected personnel, but keep the gas in the required area up to strength so that it will more effectively suppress the fire. One solution is that, once staff have evacuated the area, the supervisor locks the door from the outside which connects with the gas-flooding system. In any event, the premises will need a fire certificate, so early consultation with the fire services at the design stage may produce useful ideas. It is also appropriate to consult the insurance carriers who may have advice on the avoidance of liability if injuries are sustained through the operation of access security systems during a real emergency.

Electrically controlled doors also need to be fitted with automatic closers to ensure that they shut behind each user. This is particularly important in air-lock situations. For these purposes, two-stage closers are needed—ie the door closes fairly gently in first stage to avoid injuring people, with a final extra push to seat the door for locking. These closers inflict heavy wear on doors and they must be provided for in the building design. Further, controlled doors should have an audible alarm which warns if the door is not locked again within a stipulated period of time.

Any access system must be practical or it will fall into disuse, and it must be acceptable to those who have to make it work. To maximise the chances of acceptance, all the users should be consulted before the design is finalised, and some account taken of their views. They must then all be properly trained and the rules for using the system must be positively communicated. Deliberate misuse of any part of the system should be regarded as a disciplinary offence, no matter what the rank of the offender in the managerial hierarchy. All breaches should be monitored and followed up, with a view to making breaches less common. In performing this function, employee goodwill may be more easily maintained if access entitlements are defined in each individual's job description, because there will be less cause for error through lack of clear understanding and therefore less sense of injustice if an employee is disciplined for breach.

It is also essential to have master card or key facilities that allow the security staff quick entry to all parts of the building during an emergency. Similarly, provision must be made for when staff leave, and procedures should be devised for tokens or passes lost or mislaid. In essence, these should forbid the borrowing of another's pass. When staff arrive without their tokens or passes (an inevitable feature of life), the system should make life slightly awkward to reinforce the need to remember the card in future. Finally, it should be recognised that tokens get damaged. The more sophisticated tokens and passes are not cheap. It is therefore important that staff should be discouraged from practices which may more rapidly cause their loss.

13.4 THE PROBLEM OF EQUIPMENT THEFT

The theft of equipment which is often left unattended in offices is becoming an increasing problem. The temptation has become all the greater because office equipment is increasingly portable and now more likely to be compatible with home equipment. It must be admitted that it can be difficult to prevent thefts, and there is a growing underground market for stolen equipment, with many thefts taking place to order. This form of activity is helped because comparatively few organisations consistently carry out checks on staff carrying packages from their premises, particularly where branch offices have few employees. Organisations should estimate the value of equipment likely to be pilfered and the replacement costs (including the loss of productivity and time), and measure those costs against the staffing implications for security personnel on all the main entrances and exits, and the premiums chargeable for insurance.

Real steps to contain the theft problem begin with the creation and maintenance of a detailed inventory with all the equipment and its location logged, and employees identified as responsible for the computers and peripherals in each area. Such ground plans are, of course, a risk to security in their own right because access to the plans would save a thief the trouble of looking for particular items. They should be carefully locked away. Marking serial numbers or ownership with some form of security marker pen may also be useful because it may restrict the abilty of the thief to resell the equipment on the legitimate open market. But if the equipment is leased, a check should be made to see whether the owner objects to identifying codes and labels being permanently fixed on.

The organisation should then consider the installation of a burglar alarm system. Alarms are a way of trying to defend space. Visible systems on doors and windows begin the process of deterring intruders, with more sophisticated measures being taken to protect areas of particular sensitivity. In addition to the standard door/window sensors and pressure sensitive pads placed in rooms or under equipment, there are four basic types of alarm:

1 **The photo-electric** —here any object breaking the beam triggers the alarm.
2 **The microwave** —pulsing microwaves are transmitted throughout the area and monitored, any changes in frequency or occurrence indicating an intruder. Because microwaves can radiate through most barriers, the systems can be unreliable unless used in adequately shielded areas.
3 **The ultrasonic**—ultrasonic sound is transmitted in the same way as microwaves, with any changes in the pulse pattern detecting an intruder. There are problems with their sensitivity to air disturbance and noise.
4 **The passive infra red**—every object radiates heat. The device measures the amount of heat in the protected area and reacts to radical changes in heat level, eg a person walking into the area. These alarms are relatively inexpensive and reasonably reliable.

Any configuration of alarm system can be monitored by computer (the object protecting itself) with warning given to human security staff or to the nearest police enforcement agency through auto-dial taped message.

The most successful crime prevention policies depend upon recognising the risk and taking appropriate action. In this case, the most effective counter-measures depend upon bolting the most portable hardware to the furniture or the fabric of the building. This serves two functions. It firstly makes the theft more difficult, but perhaps just as importantly in psychological terms, it also confirms the fact of the theft to the thief. However, although this may prevent the theft of the equipment, it may not prevent the appropriation of chips and boards from the equipment. Hardware does exist to lock the CPU into place, and both to protect the disk drives and, if necessary, to physically control use. Various manufacturers have also produced security furniture which locks equipment tidily away into cabinets. It is a sound policy to encourage staff to borrow equipment. Personnel should establish procedures which invite the employee to give a satisfactory reason for being allowed to take equipment home. Site security staff must be involved to ensure that authorised staff are not embarrassed by being challenged unnecessarily. This form of regime may encourage a more responsible attitude on the part of the staff, and remove some of the incentives to steal equipment to undertake work at home. Whatever system is devised should be backed up by periodic surveys by the internal auditors. Finally, it should be recognised that whereas locks deter the casual thief, little will deter the determined thief.

13.5 PHYSICAL ATTACK AND INDUSTRIAL ESPIONAGE

All organisations must take account of the increasing danger of vandalism or malicious damage, with sabotage becoming a less uncommon part of industrial action (eg damage being caused to the computer installation during the Coal Board strike in 1984), and in extreme situations, the possibility of civil riot. Government departments are likely to recognise the possibility of attacks from radical or subversive groups (whether terrorist or ideologically motivated). Other large commercial institutions such as banks may also be identified as political targets, as may air passenger and freight companies, etc while the manufacturers of pharmaceuticals and cosmetics come under threat from the Animal Liberation Front and other similar organisations.

Each organisation should consider the location of its more sensitive facilities in the light of the prevailing state of local society. Security experts should advise on the extent to which the site is defensible, the brief including parking areas as well as the buildings. In addition to the more overt attacks, advice should also be sought on the more covert forms of assault. Thus, individuals or rival organisations may seek to disrupt the normal working patterns, eg more overtly through devices like the bomb hoax, and more covertly through false answers to advertisements to tie up the sales force, planting inefficient or disruptive staff in the target organisation, etc. This may be a form of unfair competition which may manifest itself in the forgery of product lines which are of inferior quality, or through psychological sabotage (eg circulating false rumours in the trade, reporting fictitious information to government or debt collection agencies, etc). Rivals may also attempt to blackmail key employees to disclose trade secrets, or to under-perform; or simply try to steal their expertise through headhunting.

This reflects a basic truth which underpins the capitalist ethic of competition. Thus, all commercial organisations would like to be better informed about their competitors and, because of recent developments in technology, industrial espionage has become a growing problem. The main methods are:

(a) unauthorised entry (whether by stealth or by deception) which results in information loss,
(b) surveillance from outside,
(c) the interception of communications,
(d) the poaching or corruption of key personnel, and
(e) the appropriation of sensitive information by employees for exploitation by themselves.

A certain amount of information is available to the public in the form of documents such as price lists, technical specifications and the annual accounts. If this information is considered inadequate, the only available methods for directly acquiring more sensitive information are either to negotiate for its acquisition (which may fall foul of the restrictive trade practices legislation) or to steal it. If the latter strategy is adopted, certain legal anomalies may give an advantage to the potential thief. Thus, the offence of theft is committed if a document or other physical object such as a floppy disk is permanently removed from the premises, but it is not theft to photograph or copy the document—see *R v Lloyd, Bhuee and Ali* [1985] 3 WLR 30 and *Oxford v Moss* [1979] CLR 119. The reason for these decisions is that the law of theft has been designed to protect physical property, and so the definition of *appropriating property* does not include confidential and intangible information. The offence of burglary might also have been thought a possibility because it depends upon unauthorised entry or entry through impersonation. But it requires that the trespasser intends to steal when entering, or steals after entering. This offence can therefore be avoided through the judicious use of a camera. For deception-based offences, the wrongdoer must always deceive a human mind and not a computer. For the purposes of access control to the most sensitive areas, some parts of the criminal law may be invoked by a human rather than a machine checking the credentials of all visitors at a reception area. Indeed, in sensitive areas, it is sound practice that all visitors should be escorted by a responsible member of staff. This will help to control the activities of service engineers and maintenance personnel who are easily impersonated. However, it should be recognised that impersonation is not a crime in its own right although the Official Secrets Act 1911, ss1 and 2 and the Official Secrets Act 1920, ss1 and 7 do create quite wide offences. Entry may be through employment in a legitimate capacity with the intention of boring from within. For these purposes, if a deception is made as to qualifications, etc, the offence under the Theft Act 1968, s16(2)*(c)* will probably be committed. For deterrent purposes, one of the more useful offences is forgery which may be committed even though only a machine is induced to behave in unauthorised ways, eg the Forgery Act 1981, s10(3).

The main counter-measures of good quality alarms and sturdy locks as a deterrent to breaking into inner secure areas have already been discussed. Organisations should also take care of waste paper and magnetic media disposal, and ensure that all photocopiers are clear. It should also be recognised that modern developments like the single strike typewriter ribbon are an invaluable source of information as are old shorthand pads. Moreover, if discarded materials are taken, their loss is unlikely to be noticed, but is still theft if detected. In planning defensive strategies, it should be assumed that many employees are untidy and that missing documents may simply be assumed lost. In their embarrassment, the affected employees may then assist the thief by covering up the loss, eg by generating a substitute document—staff must be properly trained to honestly disclose their own errors.

If entry to the target building is too difficult, the spy may use binoculars and infra red equipment, or laser beams to see who is speaking and to hear what is being said. Computer eavesdropping is dealt with in the next chapter, but bugs planted in buildings can relay the sound of human conversations. The counter-measure of electronic sweeping equipment can detect bugs if they are transmitting, but some bugs can be activated from outside only when required. This limits the chances of detection. As to the interception of communications, any form of communication that uses the public telephone system, the postal system or relies upon broadcast media is vulnerable. Again, it is unlikely that any external surveillance breaks the criminal law in a substantial way unless the spy causes criminal damage in a building while planting the bugs which could be burglary. However, the Interception of Communications Act 1985 creates an offence of intercepting the postal or public telecommunications system. This includes the bugging of telephones because this intercepts the message but not bugging to monitor ordinary conversations.

SUMMARY

The key points covered in this chapter are that:

1. The main physical threats are the weather, fire, water, temperature and dirt. The organisation must also protect the power supplies and take steps to eliminate direct threats to the hardware such as component failure, theft and sabotage.
2. Once the level of danger under each heading has been identified, the organisation must determine the probability and criticality of each substantial threat.
3. No matter how good the physical security, people will always represent a threat. Steps must be taken to exclude non-essential staff from sensitive areas by physical access controls. The first step is to consider the building design and space allocation. Movement within the space is then considered.

4 Access control is achieved through the use of personal vetting, mechanical or electronic systems. The range is from a simple lock and key to sophisticated cards and signature verification systems.
5 All critical hardware and software must be protected from the risk of theft or damage.

QUESTIONS *Solutions to questions of an examination standard start on p 395*

Write brief notes on the following:

(a) protection of power supplies;
(b) classification of the extent of disruption and counter-measures;
(c) methods of industrial espionage;
(d) the problem of equipment theft.

Questions of an examination standard

1 People are at the heart of all security systems and threats.

(a) Explain the importance of physical access controls in maintaining system security.
(b) List and briefly describe TWO methods of access control.

2 The fundamental rationale of the task of establishing physical security is to control space.

Describe the planning considerations which should be taken into account when designing accommodation for an organisation that relies heavily on a data processing system.

Chapter 14
Data Security

CHAPTER OBJECTIVES

This chapter continues the consideration of the theme of the main threats to security by concentrating attention on the threats to the data itself. The detailed objectives are to:

1 understand the scope of the threat to data and the nature of the protection offered by logical access systems;
2 appreciate the strengths and weaknesses of the password and understand how password systems should be administered;
3 explain the nature of file access permissions and authorisation procedures generally, and of flow and inference controls;
4 understand the role of encryption techniques; and
5 appreciate the threat represented by hacking and electronic eavesdropping.

14.1 INTRODUCTION TO DATA SECURITY

The vulnerability of data lies in the following:

(a) indiscriminate searching whether by authorised or unauthorised individuals,
(b) leakage to unauthorised individuals,
(c) inference which breaches confidentiality, and
(d) the ease with which it may be corrupted or destroyed.

Data security is achieved by four basic types of control:

1 **Access** which includes access to both data or software through a terminal or computer.
2 **Flow** which regulates the movement of data from one file to another.
3 **Inference** — statistical databases should not allow a user to extract confidential information through inference. It is difficult to eliminate the possibility altogether. The problem is that in databases, information may be held about many topics. An interloper can pose a series of questions which cause statistical reports to be made which, when correlated, may allow the inference of more detailed information.
4 **Cryptographic** —encodement through encryption may be a way of providing adequate protection.

14.2 LOGICAL ACCESS SYSTEMS

14.2.1 Project planning issues

Just as in planning for the protection of physical assets, where the strategy is based on the creation of defensible perimeters around controlled space, logical access planning requires the establishment and maintenance of perimeters around both the data system at large and, more particularly, around sensitive component elements within the data. The first steps in establishing a logical access system require the organisation to assess the security risks in relation to the systems and applications, and the data held. There are the following dangers to data:

1 It may be inaccurate—the problem is that the systems will apparently continue to function properly, but the answers produced may be seriously distorted on a cumulative basis and, if relied upon as accurate information, will undermine otherwise sensible decision-making.
2 It may be falsified as part of a plan to obtain some advantage to the detriment of the organisation or those dependent upon it.
3 It may be disclosed either to unauthorised individuals or to the public at large.
4 It may be lost before, during or after processing.

Having assessed the risks, the organisation should then classify data by reference to the level of perceived sensitivity. In making these judgments, it is also appropriate to insert caveats and to define the necessary clearances. Classification into categories such as 'secret' or 'confidential' is based upon an attribute of the data, whereas clearance relates to attributes of the users, given caveats such as those groups whose access is discretionary on a need-to-know or similar basis. The information might be based upon:

(a) **Public data** —ie unrestricted and so all may have access to read or copy the data.
(b) **Limited access**—ie private and confidential so that access clearance is to be restricted to specific users, eg in the personnel or finance department.
(c) **Private data**—ie restricted so that the information is only to be made available to identified individuals within the organisation.

It will be observed that the classification and sensitivity decisions relate directly to issues of vulnerability and, once the classification has been determined, the data should be labelled. At a crude level, the resultant classification will assist each organisation to decide who should be allowed access to what, and in which circumstances. To help in this process, the organisation should assess what the targets might be within the system. Whether from within or without, there may be data which is prone to attack or compromise. The planners should then consider who might make such an attack. This is known as **perpetrator analysis** (see 12.1 and 16.3) and it should allow the planners to identify the best safeguards in software terms.

14.2.2 What is the form of a logical access system?

A logical access system will go through three stages:

1 It must identify the user, usually through the use of an ID code.
2 It must authenticate the user, usually through the use of a password system.
3 It must ensure that proper authorisation has been given for the proposed use of the data within the system.

The full access system must therefore have the following features:

1 It must be possible in a fully secure system to uniquely identify and verify each individual user of the system by a logical identifier. Each user's security profile will be expressed as a binary vector for each security domain. There will be one component for each security level and only if the values match will the user be allowed access to the level attempted.
2 It should then be possible to uniquely identify each individual terminal accessing the system by a logical identifier which logs the physical location of that terminal as an additional check to ensure that the user is making access from an expected or required location.
3 In a network, it should also be possible to uniquely identify each individual computer accessing the network by a logical identifier which logs the physical location of that computer. This also helps to verify the propriety of the attempted access.
4 It should then be possible, within the system, to control access to identified data and resources by individual users, terminals and computers. In each security domain, there will be security classification compartments which hold a security key as either a unique or non-unique subset of the data, and this must match with the user profile if access is to be given.
5 It should be possible for auditing purposes to record the access to that data and usage of those resources by both authorised and unauthorised users, terminals and computers.

There could be discrete controls for each separate resource, with separate identifiers for each user on each application. This will be determined in part by the relative sensitivity of the data and the resources, but this piecemeal approach can be difficult to control and administer, with users having to remember different passwords, and probably being out of sympathy with the underlying philosophy. It is therefore better to have a comprehensive, integrated access control system as described above. Moreover, it should be possible to check that the ID with its user profile is not already being used at another terminal, and that the user has the right level of authority to log on at that terminal and to request the use of that resource, ie access to a file, or the use of a procedure or function (eg read, copy, update, create, delete, etc). In short, the system should check to ensure that there appears to be appropriate clearance for the given classification domain(s) for which access is sought, and that authorisation exists for all the read/write/manipulation processes requested in an attempt to minimise the risk to data integrity.

Users of IBM's MVS operating system can incorporate **Resource Access Control Facility (RACF)**, ACF2 and TOP SECRET. Such systems are only effective if properly supported by administration and authorisation procedures (see 14.2.3, 14.2.4 and 14.2.7). The RACF system, for example, allows space for a record of up to 32 passwords for each user so that checks can be made that a user is not simply replicating an earlier password when required to create a new password. Access and utilisation of protected resources must be monitored to detect any violations in security, with appropriate follow-up action and penalties. Some users such as programmers may pose a greater threat because of their detailed knowledge of a particular application or system, or because of their ability to access particular functions. It is therefore useful to limit or control access to system resources. For these purposes, resources can be defined as including:

— terminals,
— application programs,
— system utilities,
— disk files or datasets,
— tape files, and
— transactions within transaction processing systems.

Access controls have the following elements:

1 **Fixed terminal identifiers** —these establish a link between the terminal's logical identifier and its physical location. The terminal ID can then be used to restrict the resources that can be accessed, eg by restricting access to specific functions, to specific terminals or to identified terminals at specified times of the day when supervision is available.

2 **User identifiers and user authorities** —all access control systems depend upon the ability to uniquely identify individuals or groups of individuals. If individual users are so identified, with appropriate logging and reporting facilities available, all activities in the system can be traced back to them. In some systems, it may be an unacceptable overhead to have too many separate users, so overall groupings may be identified with common authorisation. But each group member will still have a separate ID and password. Installations using an integrated access control system can provide a single user ID which will allow access to several resources, but problems can occur when there is no integration or validity checking between an access control system and a transaction processing system (a system which controls the use of computer programs). Special function users are:

   (a) the **administrator** who controls the allocation and authorisation of resources,
   (b) the **operations management staff** who undertake the routine computer housekeeping, administer the magnetic media, etc, and
   (c) the **auditor** who checks the access control system, monitoring selected activities, producing event reports, etc.

   When a key person leaves their post, all passwords and codes should be changed to avoid the future unauthorised use of old privileges.

   With some systems, a user can be authorised to create a group of users who are then logically linked to his or her ID code (this is sometimes known as **propagation**). The authorised user can then delegate the use of his or her specific authorisations to newly identified group members (or revoke earlier authorisations). Extensive use of this facility can cause a problem if propagation policy and authorisation privileges are not clearly identified. Some of the new users will only be allowed access, others will be allowed to subdelegate access rights. The problem in the management of this form of dynamic authorisation system is that it can completely undermine the normal security procedures unless reporting systems are built in to ensure that authorisation is given by a person with suitable authority to an individual with satisfactory clearance.

On a network accessed from geographically separated locations, it is useful to encode the user's name, department, location and telephone number to allow staff to contact that user in the event of difficulty. Access to this information would, of course, be restricted. The processing efficiency of an access control system can be drastically impaired by granting a wide range of programs access to user ID details. This may be done, for example, to allow programs to access the user's name and address fields for addressing print-outs. This can create response time problems, and so should be reserved to times when system use is low.

3 **Passwords** —most operating systems provide passwords to control access to resources both to log on and at several points in the system, eg to control access to transaction processing systems.

14.2.3 The mechanics and administration of passwords

As in any security system there is a trade-off between ease of use and security. Password controls may be inconvenient for the users, yet their co-operation is vital. The incentive to produce a good password system is the simple truth that a system with no password is easy to use but has no real security. In fact, the original purpose of passwords and ID codes was not to protect the data. They were a simple method whereby proper accounts could be rendered on time-sharing systems. In the modern competitive environment, with a high premium on information, organisations are increasingly producing high security systems with extended question and answer sequences which may be secure but which are not easy to use. Further, if applications packages have their own security systems, it should at least be recognised that they should all have the same front end. It is bad enough remembering the different passwords without also having to contend with different protocols as well.

A password or personal identification number (PIN) or formal access protocol represents secret knowledge. The password may be a string of alphabetic, numeric or control characters, a series of numbers, or a sequence of strings which the user enters. The entry is usually in non-echo format so that the characters do not appear on the screen or upon a print-out. The machine checks the input, and if it matches the string(s) stored, access is granted to all files and processes authorised. Thus access is limited to those who have the appropriate knowledge. The alphanumeric format is used in most systems, with upper and lower case being used if a higher level of security is required. A minimum of six characters is probably the optimum length of password, with whatever maximum might be required to strike a balance between the security needs of the organisation and the ability of the user to remember the code. In designing the front end, the user log-on and other password interrogation routines should disable the use of escape and control keys to prevent the user from bypassing the system.

Passwords should always be encrypted one way, ie they should be irreversibly scrambled when stored. The password is then compared in encrypted form. This minimises the risk of disclosure if an unauthorised person obtains a copy of the passwords file, but it does not exclude the possibility. If a user does gain access to the encrypted password file, a more powerful machine might be able to cryptanalyse the file to derive likely passwords. If the storage encryption algorithm is known, the intruder might put suitable words through the algorithm to see whether any of the words match. Only the use of longer, more frequently changed passwords would defeat such attempts. Yet the majority of schemes are allowed to depend upon simple passwords. Most schemes require one short word and, for ease of remembering, users lazily and unimaginatively pick simple words like FRED, SECRET or SEX. Unfortunately, these are often easy to guess.

Words which are allocated by the system administrator have the disadvantage that they are then known by two people, and there could be a dispute if the word is used illicitly. But, in general, assigned passwords are more secure than unassigned. In secure situations, it may be necessary to protect employees by giving them so-called **duress** PINs or passwords, ie a number or word which can be revealed should they be kidnapped or threatened. Such a password apparently allows access to the system as normal, but raises an alarm to indicate that entry is being made under duress. The questions to be answered before using this system are whether the staff would remember such codes over years of non-use; and whether they would be able to use them in circumstances which did not give rise to suspicion. Indeed as victims, they might be in even greater danger if the attacker(s) thought that they had raised the alarm.

Some systems have a routine which generates passwords and notifies the users of each new word through a secure mailing system. If a password has been changed, the system may be programmed to accept a use of the old password but to notify security who can then monitor entry and, if on the premises, apprehend the offender. System-generated words are hard to guess but may be equally difficult to remember and, if a hacker deduces the algorithm upon which the generation is based, the whole system may become insecure. Similarly, systems which depend upon pseudo random numbers are vulnerable to number theory analysis. If the created and assigned password is difficult to remember, the user may write it down which makes it equally vulnerable. Hence, some systems are constrained to produce pronounceable passwords to reduce the risk of amnesia or noting down, but the range of words thus created must be wide. If the password is numeric, one scheme calls for the number to be divided into pairs, and each pair of numbers refers to one of 99 objects which are more easily remembered. This allows the user a choice. If numbers are not easily remembered, the user should be able to remember the objects which can be translated into numbers by reference to a standard list.

However the first password is selected, all users on sensitive systems can be forced to change their passwords regularly —the ideal may be once a month. There should be a check to ensure that the same password is not re-used or that some other obvious word, eg the current month, is not used. To avoid disputes, the best practice probably requires that any password allocated by the system administrator should be changed at the first available opportunity. This is generally desirable because it will mean that no-one other than the user will know the password. Conversely, the administrator usually has the power to overwrite any user's password—a useful facility for the user who forgets the current password, but a power that should be restricted to one or two people. To encourage users to change their passwords at the designated times, some systems allow users to log in using their last expired password, but the only function which they can perform is the changing of the password.

The life expectancy of a password would be infinite, but if broken it is not clear whether the password has been given away or deduced. Passwords may be given for a fixed period, and the quality of the security depends upon the length of that period. Self-evidently, the longer the period, the more likely it is that the password may be compromised. Further, it may be some time before the hacker is detected and, during that time, considerable damage may be done. The defence is to have users notified of their last recorded use of the system. This can be a useful control so long as users always check the accuracy of the information and thereby detect any unauthorised use of the ID codes. For the most secure systems, the use of one-time passwords prohibits breaking by exhaustive search, but a valid user would be locked out if exposure occurs. However, even if an intruder does gain information about one log-in, this will not be helpful for future occasions unless it is known which element changes and upon what rules. If a user is supplied with a list of the next ten passwords, this is a vulnerable paper record which may fall into the wrong hands. The defence is to have the passwords listed in an order known only to the recipient. Disclosure of the list would not therefore reveal the running order. Alternatively, the list could be issued in two parts giving the passwords in two halves.

When an installation buys or rents a system or package, there are standard passwords set up in the system, and usually published in the documentation. These are weaknesses that can be exploited by anyone who gains access to the system so they should be changed immediately. The supplier should also be questioned as to the existence of any backdoor passwords. These are sometimes used to speed up the diagnosis and correction of system problems and can confer global access privileges on the holder of the password. These passwords should either be deleted or changed to those known only by the administrator. Many of the operator commands can be controlled and protected by passwords, or may require the operator to enter his or her ID. This allows a record to be kept of user accesses to commands. Some systems allow the administrator to flag staff who are on holiday or ill, or otherwise away from the organisation. Any attempts to use the ID would be detected and reported as a violation. Similarly, terminals can be locked out by using a password command. The terminal will then remain locked out until the same user resets it by entering the password. The terminal can also be locked out when it has not been used for a predetermined time.

If all the standard IDs and passwords have been changed, the hacker will then attempt the usual names and if all else fails, simply program his micro to permutate alphanumeric characters until entry is achieved. If the password is long, this process will be time consuming and expensive in telephone connect time but if only four characters are used, only 10,000 permutations will not take long to try. If data entry and transmission rate is T characters per minute, the number of characters involved for entry and replying in a log-in attempt is L characters, the length of the password is X characters, and the number of letters and numerics from which the password is selected is N characters, the time taken to break into the password is:

$$(1/2 \times N^x) \times (L/T)$$

For example, in a high speed line T may be 1,200 characters per second, the character set size is 20, password length is 6 characters, and the number of characters in the log-in is 15, the expected safe time is:

$$(1/2 \times 20^6) \times (15/72000) \text{ minutes} = 6667 \text{ minutes} \doteq 4.62 \text{ days (Lane VP p27.)}$$

It is therefore essential either to build in a delay after each unsuccessful log-in attempt, or to construct a trap to log off the terminal or freeze the user ID if incorrect attempts at the password are made. The detailed testing of this aspect of the security system is always advisable. A fixed number of log-on attempts should be allowed when invalid passwords are quoted. A maximum of two or three attempts is not uncommon and seems a reasonable limit to provide for the inevitable misrememberings. But it is admitted that some systems still merely log invalid passwords, while others report details to a security terminal. The better systems feature the automatic suspension of the user's access authorisations if several invalid passwords have been entered. Fast and effective action is essential for good security with access only restored by the system administrator after an investigation. However, in practice in the mainframe environment, security may be maintained because even the most inept of operators would probably notice continual log-in failure, and the cost of attempting all the permutations would deter most amateur hackers if they are using their own telephone lines.

Manual switching through to the computer after voice verification may be appropriate for sensitive systems, with dial-back if necessary to ensure that the call is coming from an acceptable source. However, not all dial-back systems are secure. Hackers can program their micros to simulate the dialing tones that the dial-back device expects to hear prior to recalling an authorised user. The device can therefore be deceived into believing that it has an open line and the hacker gains access to those files set up for the user waiting to be called back. If separate lines are used for the call back, the hacker acquires the dial-back number as above. A decoy program is then run to call the intended user and to capture the account names and passwords.

On a closed user group within a PSS system (see 12.4.4), the software can be amended to record the source of any unauthorised attempt to breach security, and action can then be taken against that installation if it is discovered that proper standards are not being maintained. However, ordinary passwords are not much defence against wire tapping. A legitimate user may be logged-in but not using his or her terminal and channel. This would allow someone else to hook in and gain access. Many systems make some effort to guard against this by closing down any channel where there has been no traffic for a specified period, the user having to log in again after a time out. But, if a user fails to log off properly after an authorised session, the line to the computer and to any files to which the user had access may remain open. By trial and error a hacker repeatedly calls the dial port number in the hope that, sooner or later, an open line will be found. Once connected in this way, new accounts can be created, allocating appropriate passwords and privileges. A hacker who already has a toe hold in a system may write a program that simulates the normal screen format prior to logging on. He or she will dial into this program but fail to properly log off. The next genuine user who dials in will then connect to the decoy program and will enter account name and password. The decoy will then disconnect and return the genuine user to the operating system. This requests the user to log on again. The user assumes that there has been a communications failure and does so. Other hackers write to the telephone exchange on the headed note paper of the target firm requesting that, over a holiday period, calls should be rerouted from the normal dial port number to another number to which the hacker is connected with a decoy log-in program. Other devices rely upon gaining personal information about employees of the victim in the hope that this will reveal likely passwords, eg wife's or children's names, etc.

Greater security is achievable through **handshaking**, which is an extended dialogue sequence rather than the entry of a single password. Here two computers or a user and the computer communicate with each other. The user is given a transform t_u which is known by the computer.

When the user wishes to use the system, the computer sends the user a random number y, and asks the users to reply with the value $t_u(y)$. The transformation might be to add the digits of the number and to subtract the day of the month. This is more difficult to break and secure so long as the secrecy of the transformation is preserved. Alternatively, the computer is given a list of items known only to the user, eg birthdays, the pet's name, etc. When authentication is required, the computer will randomly select from those recorded and ask the user for the information. In high security environments, cards or tokens may be required as a precondition of log-on or, in the most extreme cases, dynamic signature verification systems, retina pattern scanners and fingerprint analysers may be used to identify users.

14.2.4 Transaction or function authorisation

A **transaction** in computer terms means a series of programs which carries out a related piece of processing. The data element involved in this processing is also called a transaction. Some systems will control the use of transactions from specific terminals by specific users, or control the use of terminals and functions by dates or days of the week and within certain time periods. If a user requires access to a function or other protected resource, this can be granted for a limited time period. After the expiration of the set period, the authorisation will automatically lapse. **Profiling** allows the administrator to define common access requirements. Each user can then be linked to a given profile and given the permissions which it contains. Alternatively, combinations of users, terminals and functions can be stipulated for each user. If the system has a copy facility, the administrator can take a proven combination or profile and copy it into a new user's area. Some systems log the detail of each user alongside each transaction or write the detail to a file for later analysis. Some permissions can be qualified, ie to allow permission to make use of the transaction facility, but only up to a specified value of commercial transaction.

14.2.5 Design features of access provision

Some users may be allowed access on the basis of least privilege, ie only allowed to use the privilege to the extent necessary to complete the given job. This limits the damage which may be done by the inexperienced and by those who have yet to prove their trustworthiness. Any default will result in immediate loss of access privileges. This can be a good way of controlling **Trojan Horses** (a Trojan Horse is either an individual or a program which offers a service, but does so in a way which allows the collection of vital information, eg which might allow the impersonation of clients on other occasions). Overall, the designer should aim for economy of mechanism. It is better to implement a relatively simple mechanism which all staff are prepared to use, than to devise sophisticated features that are seldom used. All the mechanisms must be easy to use, but be effective in performing the task of ensuring that every request for access has proper authorisation. Further, security should not depend upon the design remaining secret. If the system cannot safely be described in open literature, it cannot be used with confidence.

14.2.6 File access permissions

All operating systems provide controls over access to disk files. These can incorporate passwords within the logical grouping of files as well as a system of access permissions. Access to either file data or its description can be granted in one of two ways— by quoting the system password for that group of files or the user password. Access modes can be created at different levels within the file organisation systems, such as read, write, exclude (denies access to specifically named users), append (allows users to add information to the end of a file), purge (allows authorised users to release files or groups of files or overwrite the released file data area with zeros), modify (allows authorised users to list or modify file description details, eg file name, organisation, size, access attribute permissions, etc), lock (allows authorised users to deny access under certain conditions, eg time, after a given number of accesses, upon a program terminating abnormally, etc).

Although tape-based systems are now being replaced by on-line disk systems, tape access controls may also be needed both for access, and for housekeeping and maintenance. Access to tape volumes can be granted at user ID and job level under the control of the volume owner or the administrator. Default access is usually owner only. To guard against accidental or deliberate attempts to overwrite a tape, some systems request that the tape write-enable ring be removed when the tape is accessed in read mode. Other systems set the tape drive to read only, without requesting the removal of the ring.

In access hierarchies, high-ranking subjects are automatically given the privileges of lower-ranking subjects. An authorisation list or access control list can limit access to those authorised. Such a system is easy to implement and reasonably effective, although long lists can take time to check, and are not appropriate for accessing every aspect of functions and processes. When a user attempts to gain access, the lists are checked to ensure that the activity is authorised for the particular user. Other software modules will record or journal this activity and may charge for the resources consumed. At the top of the hierarchy, the operator or administrator mode overrides all protections within the operating system. It is the equivalent of a master key in a conventional locking system. At the next level down, users with high privileges can read the lists and directories set up both for their own and for the lower level operations. Those with low level authorisation can only access the files at that level.

Access to systems and resources may be abused within a person's authority level or it may be contrived. Active penetration for commercial espionage and funds transfer frauds usually call for high level skills. Passive breaking applies to people who inadvertently break security and then exploit the information gained. Although hackers are becoming more skilled, few are responsible for substantial losses. The opportunities available to existing employees who are entrusted with access privileges cannot be completely eliminated. Indeed, some industrial spies and committed criminals will deliberately infiltrate the organisation. They succeed because inadequate checks are made into their backgrounds before they are placed in positions of trust. There is also a steady growth in frauds by people who have turned to crime and either extended their legitimate access privileges or contrived unauthorised access. Overall, increases in criminality are encouraged by the lack of security in passwording and through granting high level privileges to too many people.

Access to distribution frames with carefully labelled lines should also be most carefully limited, as should access to the telephone exchange. Controlling access to all the cabling in a building is not practical both because of the cost and the need to allow access for legitimate repair. The practical answer is that all cabling can be ducted with access allowed at service points which can be controlled. To minimise risk of damage through work on the building, network security should be checked before any work is allowed. Ideally, the communications equipment should be located in a room independently of the main computer installation. Some nodes within a network serve as concentrators linking several local terminals and computers through multiplexers, patch panels, etc. These should be specially protected.

14.2.7 Administration or authorisation procedures

The structure of an organisation is not limited at a conceptual level. Each organisation will tend to develop dynamically, and the form of the management system will evolve to meet each organisation's particular needs. Some organisations will have a centralised administrative structure, others will have a distributed structure with some centralised functions. Some systems permit a hierarchical type of administration, others will be modular. Within each management system, the creation and maintenance of good logical access controls requires good software and effective administration. For these purposes, the administration may be centralised in one section or department, or shared between several sections. This may be a division of function at the top of the organisation structure, ie as between the administrator and the internal audit department which scrutinises the whole system, or at an intermediate point, eg as between a DP department and a data control section, etc.

The first part of any control system must address the issue of control of inputs to access control software, eg setting up the logical **identifiers**, or the user IDs and passwords, granting access to time sharing facilities, and to transactions in on-line systems. The authorisation procedures which are established must take account of the value and vulnerability of the resource. If too high a level of authority is stipulated as a precondition of access and too many experienced staff are excluded, the effectiveness of the management which the information system is to support may be substantially reduced. The authorisation levels eventually set must reflect the actual degree of responsibility held, and the normal and most desirable course of events in each work environment. To that end, a profile of the resources which each user will, and should, require access to should be drawn up and implemented. This process should be matched by a training programme which allows the staff to make optimum use of their access to the resources.

Once the system has been designed, the use of pre-printed request forms for resource allocation can be useful in a survey of function and information flow by obtaining basic information of each key individual's job, department and location. The forms should be kept simple, with the amount of written details required from the user being kept to a minimum. More than one form may be prepared for different resources. When the form is received, the administrator should authenticate the application, eg by comparing the signature against samples held. Details of the ID allocated and any initial password(s) should then be transmitted to the applicant by a secure mailing system. If an emergency application is made and circumstances do not appear to permit the usual validation procedures, the administrator should have a fall-back procedure whereby, for example, the applicant's line manager or other approved person authorises the transaction in writing, with the proper documentation to be prepared retrospectively.

The degree of control exercised should obviously reflect the risks involved in the particular resource or assistance requested. Thus, if the user claims that the password has been forgotten, in many systems it will not be possible for the administrator to read the password file because it is one-way encrypted. The only effective remedy would therefore be for the administrator to overwrite the password. Again the degree of control will vary with the nature of the resource for which access is requested. Further, the user's goodwill should be preserved wherever possible because, if the response is unhelpful, the user may be tempted to try to bypass the security controls, eg by asking a colleague if ID and password can be borrowed. Most requests to amend the password will be by telephone. While requests in writing are more secure, the desirable immediacy of response is not achieved. A simple procedure is to log the call and then to call the applicant back once the password has been changed.

Some provision should also be made for the time when the system administrator forgets his or her key password. While this should be a rare occurrence, recovery could be a problem. Some organisations ask the administrator to place the passwords in a sealed envelope which is then locked away in a data safe. Alternatively, a back-up system can be created with access separately passworded and held by another member of staff. This duplication of access may not be wholly desirable from a security point of view.

The second part of the control system regulates outputs from the information system, eg management trail reports—on some systems details of all transactions entered by the security master user are logged and reported on; or activity reports—these can be divided into systems access and exception reports. The first may produce large amounts of print-out and is normally for reference only. The content and layout of reports will vary from one system to another, but monitoring functions must be created to ensure that only authorised users gain access to the resources which they are authorised to access. Unless unauthorised attempts to access resources are brought to the attention of the administrator, the latter may be lulled into a false sense of security. Selective or exception reporting is therefore a useful detective function to log interesting activity.

The effectiveness of security reports is determined by the frequency of report production; the follow-up of detected breaches of security, and the rules which prescribe security systems. The speed with which the system reacts to security breaches is critical. The longer the delay, the less likely it is that the action will be effective. It is much easier to monitor short daily reports than trying to read through a long weekly print-out. If some events are deemed fundamental, they can be reported immediately to a security terminal. However, the nature of the reponse must be carefully thought out to minimise damage to industrial relations. If no action is taken, the system will almost certainly end up compromised. If insensitive action is taken to reprimand all who transgress, regardless of status, function or attitude, the staff will almost certainly resent the system's response and this could again lead to loss of security.

The best route is through a continuous process of staff education. The preparation of guidelines and a code of practice can help to alert staff to the reasons for the various security measures. Once these are understood, the co-operation of the staff can be more readily sought. It is also a good strategy to incorporate these provisions into the contract of employment, and to deal with any breaches through the normal disciplinary procedures laid down in the contract. Detailed consultation with trades unions and staff associations may well be fruitful in securing a code which will gain maximum staff support.

14.3 CONTROL OF FLOW

Although access control can be precise about who should access what, flow controls are necessary to specify the channels along which the information is allowed to flow. Information should be classified as either confidential or non-confidential, and authority levels should be linked to the data thus classified. All information flows are then permitted save the confidential to the non-confidential. These controls can be established to validate all flows as they occur, or when the program is being compiled, ie before the program executes. It can be difficult to classify information and to determine who should have access. In a hierarchical system, for example, information flows down can always be prevented, but not those up the hierarchy. The placement of individuals in the hierarchy therefore assumes significance for each element of information, and may lead to information being hopelessly over-classified.

14.4 INFERENCE CONTROLS

A medical information system may use a statistical database which is supposed to release statistical information without compromising individual patients' data. Unfortunately, summary reports contain traces of the original data, and information about a patient could be constructed from several summaries. For example, if an intruder has the physical characteristics of a patient as to height, weight, age, etc, the query may seek to identify how many people with those characteristics have suffered various illnesses and infer the target's condition. Each query is a logical expression using the logical operators. The reply is a set of records that satisfy the requirements of the expression and is called the **query set**. Interlopers often insert dummy records and then test the size of the query set necessary to obtain precise information. A filter based on the query set size is possible. Where query sets overlap it is often possible to infer information by comparing the two, eg suppose the system contains information of employees' salaries but will not give out an individual's salary. The query could establish the number of men in a given department, the total of salaries for persons employed in that department and the number of employees in that department. If it is known that only one woman is employed in that department, exact confirmation of her salary is now achieved. People may be tracked through age, status or other known variables stored in the databank. The problem with controls is that they may unreasonably limit answers to perfectly legitimate and useful queries. Any controls which are therefore inserted and which distort the data while giving replies, will only be valuable if the loss of confidentiality would represent a significant loss.

14.5 ENCRYPTION

14.5.1 Security risks at terminals

Ordinary users may not have expert typing skills and so an observer may be able to read or guess the password through simple observation. Further, the password must not be displayed at the terminal, ie communication must be in non-echo mode. However, although non-printing characters are used in some passwords, they can be observed in wire-tapping. The countermeasure is encryption of the passwords during transmission but this is an expense to be justified according to the sensitivity of the information to be transmitted. In some systems, the passwords are printed out in logging files produced by the central system, even if they are suppressed by the terminal, so care should be taken to protect those files.

14.5.2 Electronic mail

The two main concerns in the sending of messages are to provide a mechanism for the validation of the content, and for the authentication of the sender. Although special authentication codes (sometimes changed daily) can be included in the message, some degree of encryption remains the best protection against fraud and dishonesty. Thus, for example, digital signatures can be added to the message as a unique identifier; for instance, the Swedish electronic seal system has been used since 1981 to protect banking transactions. The seal is applied to a plaintext message of any length. It is a cryptologically-based hash total of 18 digits which is appended to the message. A secret key of 35 digits is used in the seal algorithm, with the communicating parties free to agree any 35 digit key. The 18 digit seal is then computed using the secret 35 digit key. It uses non-linear permutations and exponential functions and is difficult to break. Similarly, authentication can be achieved by using the public key systems.

14.5.3 Encryption methods

Hardware encryption systems work quickly and effectively and are easy to install, ie every terminal has a black box attached, but this can be expensive if sophisticated hardware is to be fitted to every terminal in a large system. Software encryption methods would potentially be more cost-effective in large systems because the software is installed wherever required in the processing configuration, and it can be adjusted to cater for any peculiarities in each organisation's operating system or data. Standard algorithms are relatively cheap but tend to be slow to operate at the terminal end. This is inconvenient because users require good responsive speeds at the terminal. (Experience shows that public key encryption can be very slow when implemented using micros.) The ideal solution (not yet available on the market) would be true end-to-end encryption based on an algorithm that is fast and small. It should be combined with hardware which has wired-in master keys, and properly sealed to prevent tampering. The combination of hardware and software would be more secure because software remains more vulnerable on its own.

14.5.4 Data encryption

Encryption is the technique or process for deriving enciphered text from plaintext (the term for the readable text from which the encoded message is derived) and it is likely to become very important because more sensitive information is now being transferred (eg electronic funds transfer, corporate planning, marketing and sales information, etc), and hackers are becoming more clever and have more sophisticated computers to aid their access to the data whether stored or transmitted. Thus, the costs of encryption are easier to justify, and the commercial market has developed products which are increasingly effective in preserving data confidentiality. The rationale could not be easier to state. Even if data does fall into the wrong hands, it is useless because it will be unintelligible.

An encryption or decryption process consists of an algorithm and a key. The algorithm is controlled by the key. The procedure is usually symmetrical, ie uses the same key each way. Early systems depended upon a literal code, eg a vocabulary of words is assigned arbitrary values (eg *hidden* might be assigned the value 298, and *meaning* the value 915). If each end of the communications link has the code book, the words can be matched to the code in a process of sending and translation. Self-evidently, the code is broken by discovering a copy of the code book, or being able to independently determine the contents of the message and thereby gain an insight into the vocabulary of the code.

Cipher systems depend upon the processes of **substitution** and **transposition**, either individually or in combination. In basic substitution systems, another symbol replaces the original symbol in the plaintext, but these are too easily broken by using computers because too many features of the original message remain (such as the relative frequency of letters). Similarly, transposition transformations (where the letters are rearranged according to a grid formula) are vulnerable because the original letters are simply jumbled up and may easily be rearranged to form coherent words using the tireless power of the computer. So sophisticated transformations are more commonly based on polyalphabetic or polygraphic substitutions, or upon transposition systems which use different grid sizes.

Computers have made the transmission of data more efficient. The communication protocols devised by the hardware manufacturers were published and networks were initially open to anyone who could gain access. By the 1970s, users were beginning to feel the need for better security. The earliest systems relied upon an algorithm, but once the algorithm is known, all security is lost. The next step is for an algorithm and a key, the purpose of the key being to transform the data. The algorithm should be arranged so that each different value of key produces a radically different transformation of the plaintext. The different values of the key should change the effect of the algorithm so radically that the transformation is entirely different in nature for each value of key. Then if the algorithm is compromised and one value of key is discovered, all is not lost. The secrecy can be restored by using a different key. However, the yardstick of effectiveness is now measured by the effectiveness of the system if the attacker knows the algorithm.

Hence in 1977, the American National Bureau of Standards approved a standard for cryptographic transformations —the **Data Encryption Standard (DES)**. A satisfactory cipher should produce a result which is not detectably different from random, whether regarded as a function of the plaintext or the key, ie it should contain no real statistical information about the plaintext. The DES standard uses a product transformation of transpositions, substitutions and non-linear operations. They are applied for 16 iterations to each block of the message, the result being a 64 bit ciphertext block. The key used is 56 bits taken from a 64 bit key which includes 8 parity bits. Parts of the algorithm do produce regularities which slightly limit the utility of the standard, particularly in the multiple encipherment situation. (For more details, see Davies.) Given increases in the computer power which could be made available to criminal organisations at an economic price, some now argue that a 128 bit key would be better to minimise the risk of decryption.

Further, because the system is known, security depends upon the security of the keys. The weakness in these systems is that they call for the transmission of the key. The problem is therefore to ensure that the key is only transmitted to the legitimate receiver and that the would-be decoder cannot gain access to it. The solution is that the key has to be held at both ends of the link. Distributing the keys securely can be a significant cost overhead. In a network, encryption key management can be a complex and costly overhead, with many having to be created, distributed and stored. Lost or forgotten keys also mean that files of data may be inaccessible, yet users must change the keys regularly. There is no room for complacency because the ciphertext looks unreadable. If someone has compromised the key, months or years of data communications may be read by an intruder.

The so-called **one-time pad** is a classic method of encryption. The data is treated as a string of bits. The key is another random string of bits. The plaintext string and the keytext string are added to produce the ciphertext. The keystring has to be as long as the message and is random, so the ciphertext ends up random. Analysis of the ciphertext produces no information about the plaintext. The computer version is based upon the original paper and pencil version, where both ends of the communication link used the same pads printed with random sequences which were only used once and then destroyed.

Computers allow the cryptanalyst to use techniques impossible by hand. Because the cost of hardware has fallen in real terms, the analyst can now bring far more computational power to decode text economically both in monetary and in time terms. Equally, the encoder can use greater sophistication to hide meaning. The decoder must weigh the economic advantages to be gained from cracking the code against the cost of the decipherment exercise. The encoder must try to ensure that the cost of decoding is high enough to discourage an attacker. The equation of encypherment and decypherment is also affected by the problem that the more sophisticated the algorithm and its key, the more slowly it may process the plaintext. Speed depends upon the key size and the efficiency of the algorithm, and processing time is money.

14.6 HACKING

Hacking is the deliberate accessing of on-line systems by unauthorised persons. Many hackers do not act out of malice, but because it is considered fun. However, breaking into a confidential computer file is morally no different to someone who breaks into a locked office and reads confidential documents. Such views are, however, unfashionable. Indeed, the House of Lords in *R* v *Gold and Schifreen* [1988] 2 All ER 186 has now confirmed that hacking into systems to change or amend records is not the crime of forgery. This leaves the general proposition that the activity of hacking is not inherently criminal with the possible exception of the Telecommunications Act 1984, s5, which makes it an offence to connect any unauthorised apparatus to the licensed telecommunications system. Hackers might therefore be prosecuted for attaching an acoustic coupler or modem.

The threat of hacking has become a more significant danger with the development of micros and modems. To break into a system from the outside, the system must have dial-up connections or be accessible from a system like PSS. Many systems have dial-up facilities as a matter of course because they are distributed systems, or because employees like sales representatives need to be able to access the computer, even from the customers' own premises. Even systems which have leased lines often have dial-up lines as a back-up in the event of line failure, or because the manufacturer's technical support staff want the ability to review the diagnostic or breakdown reports which the machine automatically accumulates. In fact, the practice of remote maintenance represents a security risk and the auditor or administrator should be aware that it is taking place and consider the implications. This will involve issues such as the apparent reliability of the manufacturer's or contract maintenance company's staff; whether disks with sensitive data can be taken off-line during maintenance, and whether the operating system can be reloaded from back-up if unauthorised amendments have been introduced. If it is decided to allow the practice, it is useful to have a manual switch to connect outside lines for remote maintenance purposes rather than to leave such lines permanently open to the main systems. As a pre-condition to switching the alleged engineer through, proper verification procedures can be carried out which will, with luck, eliminate the hackers.

Before a remote hacker can gain access to a computer system, the dial-up telephone number must be obtained. Sometimes a telephone bluff, say posing as a remote user, to the computer department will obtain the number. Some organisations publish the numbers fairly widely in an internal directory within the organisation and risk hacking from ex-employees or the friends and associates of employees. Scavenging the waste paper produced by the installation may show user IDs on the print-outs. The determined attacker will adopt a trial and error strategy. Professional hackers may try bribing employees either for the numbers themselves, or for discarded telephone accounts which show the numbers. Another way of gaining access is through the use of an autodialer. The dialing may be random or dial port numbers may be assumed to be in the same telephone area as the intended victim's voice lines. The hacker programs the micro to try a range of telephone numbers. When a data line is detected (ie after two or three rings, the call is answered with an identifiable computer-generated tone), the system records that number and may then attempt to detect the protocol. Hackers pass on discovered numbers through bulletin boards and electronic mail boxes (ie micros on an auto-answer modem). If a hacker obtains a sign-on screen display, a valid ID and password is normally required to gain access. Standard format IDs laid down by the manufacturers can be tried.

Unmodified computer systems will often accept an unlimited number of tries to input a correct ID without generating a warning or closing off the terminal. Note that once an ID code has been detected, the hacker may telephone the administrator, claim amnesia and ask for a new password. Most systems have standard user IDs and passwords, eg sysman, admin, oper, etc, with similar IDs for engineers, programmers, etc. When the system is supplied, it often has these as standard with passwords set as *password* or the imaginative *XXXXXX*. This information is often freely available in the manufacturer's documentation. If these standard IDs and passwords have not been changed, the hacker has an immediate toehold in the system. Discarded print-outs may also reveal account, program and file names or they may be guessed if the files are functionally named after the relevant aspects of the victim's business. Some hackers have adopted a decoy system to gain information. Having identified the users' communication channels, the hacker sends messages to those authorised users which simulate messages from the main system, eg the log-in frame. When the user attempts to log in, the hacker then has a set of ID codes and passwords. The defence against this is for the main computer to send back a code to the user upon successful log-in. If this code is not received, the user's machine should indicate a possible security breach.

A hacker with the right level of skill can disable the journal or console logs of the main CPU to suppress the records of his or her activities. Another strategy is to disrupt the access control system. The controls may become discredited to such an extent that obvious symptoms of fraud or illegal access are passed off as machine errors, eg if access control software can be made to malfunction so that it denies access to legitimate users, it may be switched off and unauthorised users may then gain access without detection. Similarly, if back-up files can be removed from store, altered and returned, fraud would be achieved when the altered files or programs are loaded onto the prime system. It is particularly difficult to identify the method of fraud after the event. Similarly, some computers have front panel systems which allow direct accessing, and their use frequently leaves no trail on journal records.

14.6.1 Computer viruses

The computer virus is a small program that, once introduced into a system, becomes self-propagating, ie it is designed to spread itself to all parts of the system, and it will disrupt both data and software. The potential for what viruses can do is limited only by the imagination of the programmer. As in the case of its biological equivalent, it replicates itself in such a way that it is impossible to detect its original source, and once a system is contaminated, the only remedy may be to recreate the system from back-up. But some viruses have been programmed to lie dormant for a while. This allows the infection to be transmitted to the back-up copies. In such a case, the entire system can be rendered permanently unusable. Some viruses hide in the optimum places to cause harm, eg the Lehigh Virus lived in the COMMAND.COM file and was activated every time a user typed a DOS command, but the program can include any condition for the virus to apply to decide whether it should reveal itself and what it is supposed to do.

It is almost impossible to protect a computer from a virus. Although software acquisitions can be restricted to reputable suppliers and public domain and demonstration programs avoided, both hackers and disaffected employees can introduce the infection unless access control mechanisms and compliance monitoring is effective. The problem becomes even more intractible in a large network situation. Security experts are beginning to develop vaccine software which may limit or eradicate a viral program, but these programs will not restore corrupted or lost data. Organisations should therefore carefully consider the wording of their insurance policies to determine whether data loss through viral infection is included.

14.7 ELECTRONIC EAVESDROPPING

Line tapping is as easy as conventional telephone tapping. Transmitted signals can be recorded through a radio transmitter and replayed through an appropriate terminal or printer. Passwords will then appear in clear text. Alternatively, devices like the datascope can be connected and will allow text to be read. Wire tapping may lead to one or more of the evils of data insertion, modification and deletion. It may suit the plans of a fraudster to totally block the given transmissions, eg so that a debit to an account is delayed or stopped, or to modify the transmissions, eg thereby reducing the amount of the debit, to engage in forgery or perhaps the increasingly lucrative but simple information gathering. Protection is through encryption because the signal is protected during transmission.

Electronic equipment produces both **Radio Frequency Interference (RFI)** and **Electromagnetic Radiation (EMR)** and eavesdropping the encoded digital information contained in EMR is possible up to 1 km from the target VDU. LANs are particularly vulnerable because, in many cases, the cabling acts as an aerial to enhance the signals. Initially, it was thought that it required sophisticated equipment to decode the signals, but work done at the PTT Laboratories in Holland has shown that all that is required is a TV receiver and the means to synchronise the frequencies of the signals received. The cost of the components required to construct the synchronising device is minimal. Such systems therefore represent a major threat to data confidentiality. Data encryption is no defence because the text will be displayed on the screen in plaintext. The threat may come from a mere hacker who wants an easy way to discover ID codes and systems data, or it may be from professionals who want details of the target organisation's sensitive plans and processes.

To reduce the risk, standards have been developed to define the shielding to reduce the maximum radiation emissions from equipment for use in military or intelligence services. These standards are often referred to by the USA term, TEMPEST. They are not publicly discussed nor can the equipment be offered for sale on the open market, but some manufacturers are now incorporating shielding which is claimed to be of a comparable standard. This is a potentially serious threat to security, but organisations have proved unwilling to spend large amounts of money on counter-measures, eg special metallic foiling on the windows or shielding in front of the VDU screen or other radiating components such as the ROMAG system of laminated materials which helps to divert the radiated signals. The signals produced by flat screen terminals may be more difficult to eavesdrop because a different system of data display is used, or the use of devices to broadcast masking spurious signals may be partially effective. The decision whether to shield the building or the terminals is a simple matter of cost benefit analysis. The variables are the sensitivity of the data, the other consequences of the action taken (eg shielding the building may make the use of radio pagers ineffective), and the cost of the counter-measures.

SUMMARY

The main points covered in this chapter are that:

1 The main threats to data security lie in unauthorised access to data which may result in breaches of confidentiality or corruption and loss.

2 Organisations must first define the security risks and set a sensitivity level for each classification of data. Logical access controls can then be established where necessary to identify and authenticate each proposed user.

3 A password or PIN limits access to those who know the word or number but, to be effective, the system of allocating or selecting that knowledge must be properly administered. The level of protection achieved is only as good as the people who are to make it work.

4 Once the user has logged in, there may be further controls to limit access to files, transactions or functions. This allows the creation of tiers of authorisation within the system, with each member of staff profiled to set an appropriate level of access for their particular job function.

5 Control must also be established over data flow and the ability of users to draw inference from the data stored. One of the main mechanisms of protection is encryption, where otherwise readable text is encoded. Thus, only a user with the correct key may read the data.

6 Hackers now represent a real threat as more systems are distributed and networked. Other dangers are computer viruses and the capacity to electronically eavesdrop.

QUESTIONS *Solutions to questions of an examination standard start on p 395*

Write brief notes on the following:

(a) the elements of access control;
(b) inference controls;
(c) hacking;
(d) electronic eavesdropping.

Questions of an examination standard

1 As in any security system, there is a trade-off between ease of use and security. Password controls may be inconvenient for the users, yet their co-operation is vital to system security.

(a) Discuss THREE ways in which the security of a password may be improved.
(b) Briefly describe THREE ways in which a hacker might attempt to gain unauthorised access to a system and give a counter-measure which could be applied to each.

2 Once successful access control has been established, the next important security measure is data encryption.

List and briefly describe FIVE methods by which data encryption may be carried out.

Chapter 15

Security Design and Operation

CHAPTER OBJECTIVES

This chapter is concerned with the fundamental design and operational features necessary to produce an effective security system. In particular, it considers:

1 what controls should be installed for the control both of the data itself and of the manner of its processing;
2 whether the risks become greater if decision and administration support systems are used to aid the data processing and decision-making;
3 the advantages and disadvantages inherent in the creation and running of a distributed system;
4 whether a microcomputer environment can be made secure and what happens when micros are turned into gateways either to a single mainframe or to LANS;
5 the main methods of fraud and the best ways in which to investigate suspicions of fraud; and
6 regardless of whether the investigation is undertaken by the auditors or some other investigative group, what tests to apply to discover the nature of the fraud.

15.1 INTERNAL DATA CONTROLS

The basic principles for the effective design of data security systems are that:

1 The underlying design criteria should not be secret — there are two reasons for this:
  (a) a new system is improved if its detailed features are exposed to constructive criticism by a significant number of both designers and users,
  (b) so long as the system is effective, the more people are aware of the system, the greater the potential deterrent value (however, if a flaw is detected, the greater the number of people who may get to know about it).
2 Each interface between the software and the users should be kept simple and natural otherwise even the most tolerant of users will be tempted to bypass it.
3 Every access ought to be checked to see if appropriate authority has been given. If access is in doubt, access should be denied because denial is preferable to unauthorised access.
4 The underlying design assumption should be that the final system will have to operate in a hostile environment where it will be exposed to frequent threats. The resulting *worst possible case* system should be reasonably secure.

15.1.1 Human-based accounting controls

Within the overall ambit of the physical and logical access security systems, detailed accounting controls over the data itself and over subsequent management reporting should be built into the various software applications to ensure that the data is properly and accurately processed. At an organisational level, perhaps the most important internal control is the positive segregation of duties among the staff (see 16.4.3). As a general rule, no single employee should have the responsibility for all the stages in the processing of a transaction. The aim is to produce a situation where it would always require at least two employees acting together to make a fraud feasible. The important segregations of duties are that:

1 The tasks of preparation and validation of the input data should be performed independently of any check of the resulting output.

2 Computer operators should not be allowed to amend system software or data, and should be denied access to the detailed program documentation.
3 Programmers and systems analysts should not be allowed unsupervised access to the computer.
4 New programs should not be tested or checked by the team that wrote the code.
5 Neither the operators nor the programmers should have responsibility for the operation of the library of program and data back-up/archive copies and/or of the system documentation.

These rules should be seen against the background of the main advantages of an on-line system which are that all users could be allowed to input data from the terminals in their own departments, and that each user department is potentially able to check the latest state of the data. If adequate security is to be maintained, these advantages may have to be compromised. Hence, the types of transaction that can be initiated and authorised by each department should be clearly defined and limited in the light of the known vulnerabilities. Moreover, all potentially sensitive data should be independently validated before the main system files are updated, ie this may require that all input is to be stored in a collection file and not merged into the main files until proper validation and authorisation checks have been made. The disadvantage of such a safeguard is that users cannot operate in real-time and be allowed access to the up-to-date data. Indeed, it is not unusual in the more sensitive applications to find that only the previous day's situation is available for consultation. This may not be suitable for a significant number of organisation systems where an absolutely contemporary record may be required, eg airline reservation and stock systems benefit from real-time processing.

In many systems, the data may be scheduled to pass through several stages in the input process and errors, whether innocent or fraudulent and usually human, are always possible. One way of detecting errors is by comparing the input to the output, transaction by transaction. This can be expensive in terms of time, but it may be the only effective way to prevent fraud in many situations. As already indicated in Chapter 5, batch controls may be effective but they cannot operate in a real-time system, so validation routines must be built into real-time systems to check each individual entry before the core files are amended. This would be in addition to post-process or post-input batching which allows the operator(s) to check batch totals after a given number of transactions have been processed. Then, if a discrepancy arises, eg if serial numbers are out of order or missing, a manual check can be made. To operate effectively, such a system requires some form of input document, whether form or record, which should be kept in the department which submitted the transaction for processing. Without this, there is nothing to batch and so other compensating controls must be built in.

Hence, if an organisation were to formally design a teleordering system, the following human-based security features would be required:

1 In the first instance, only orders from recognised customers would be accepted (with the additional safeguard that recognition should be given and monitored by someone other than the telesales operator).
2 Then, order values would only be accepted up to pre-accepted credit limits, with deliveries only made to authorised addresses.
3 In general, procedures would have to be established which would create an audit trail back to the originator of the order. This would normally rely on a user ID, date and time, with the customer also required to give some form of password.
4 Phone-back for formal confirmation of the order made to prestored and authenticated numbers. In some organisations, where the unit cost of the items to be manipulated is high, it would be sound practice to tape record all such telephone calls.

With such a system in operation, the organisation could be reasonably confident that errors and abuses would either be detected, or would not cause excessive loss in the short term. The security arises from the degree of protection given to the individual data component elements and the ability to link transactions to identified employees and customers.

15.1.2 Automated controls

Simply creating manual systems which will enhance security is not enough. Organisations must also build in both general and particular software controls. So the first safeguard is that the programs, once validated, should not be changed to reduce the chance of corruptions through software malfunction to data while being input or manipulated. This confirms and consolidates the fundamental objective of hardware security which is to protect the data which may become sensitive information if it falls into the wrong hands. The designers must then turn their attention to the operation of the standard CPU. In real memory protection, the memory should be partitioned into a series of mutually exclusive areas to which access may be separately controlled. When a program is being executed in a controlled area, the program execution should abort if an error is detected. The same effect can be achieved through the creation of a bounds register which keeps track of the events taking place or proposed within a protected area. Some areas can be locked so that sensitive programs can only be executed if the user has a key for access. For these purposes, the system software has overriding rights over all the other software. Since these library-based programs are not fixed to one area, their protection cannot be achieved through memory safeguards alone. The standard security systems therefore use binary execution states or multiple execution states to know whether the computer is executing in a privileged supervisory state or in a non-privileged state. Only a program in a privileged state can issue privileged instructions. Multiple state architecture allows programs to have a hierarchy of privileges and allows the sharing of resources under conditions of mutual mistrust.

Similarly, despite the fact that the more detailed checking systems increase CPU time and reduce run times, individual data element validation by software ensures that the data input is within the predetermined parameters. In real-time systems, data which is rejected can be highlighted on the screen so that the terminal operator can review the item, and if the error has been caused by an obvious keying error, reinput the correct value for the variable. However, it may not be desirable to allow operators to change any of the data (eg because of security implications, or because the operators are not known to be conscientious or alert) and, in those cases, the data should be referred back to the user for validation.

In general, proper controls should be maintained over all data input rejections. Error reports are usually printed out and the record stored pending investigations. Regular review of this suspense file should detect regular errors or offenders. Data verification procedures should be followed to achieve a correct and complete transcription from data to machine readable form. This is particularly important because errors not detected during this phase may cause loss of integrity and produce unreliable data for decision-making.

In general, processing controls are designed to prevent or detect the following types of error:

1. the incomplete or duplicated processing of input transactions;
2. processing and updating the wrong files;
3. processing illogical, incomplete or unreasonable input;
4. loss or distortion of data during processing.

The main methods of verification are:

1. **Visual**, ie to compare the keyed version with source materials; as a method, this is error prone and time-consuming.
2. **Key**, ie to key the data in twice and then to compare the two sets of data.
3. **Internal software checks** for reasonableness, consistency and completeness, listed below.
   (a) **Data format checks** ascertain that:
   — all mandatory fields exist, or
   — the correct number and composition of alphabetic and numeric characters exist, ie that all information fields are complete and that the fields contain data of the expected type, or
   — if it is an updating transaction, the target record is present.
   (b) **Limit or reasonableness checks** ensure that the data is within acceptable bounds, eg if the number of hours worked in a given week exceeds a specified limit, claims for overtime can be investigated.
   (c) **A check digit control** is one in which numbers, usually account or stock reference numbers, are computed in accordance with a special formula to produce an extra digit for validation purposes. This provides good protection against transposition, transcription, omission or addition and the random errors which are likely if the operator is routinely typing in meaningless numbers.

(d) **Crosscasting checks** can be applied so that the computer automatically validates arithmetic.

(e) **Sequencing checks** ensure that the data elements are input in the required order (this is useful if it is coupled with the use of prenumbered stationery, but care is required to recover if an error is discovered in the sequence).

(f) **Batch controls** At an early point in the system, independent totals of documents are accumulated by a control group, and are later matched against totals derived from the processing of the same documents by the DP department. The three most common types of batch total are the following:
   (i) control total—usually a meaningful money total such as the total of credit sales;
   (ii) hash total—a total that need not have any significance other than as a batch total, eg the total of customer account numbers.
   (iii) record count—a count of the number of documents or transactions processed.

The process of data validation is necessary both during data collection and data entry before any of the data is used within the application software, and continuously as new data are generated by the software. Output controls are therefore designed to ensure that:

(a) the processed results are accurate, and
(b) only authorised personnel receive the output.

The psychology of the users is important in this respect. Most lay, but computer-literate users will judge the quality of an information system by its output. Output should therefore be checked as thoroughly as possible before being released to authorised users by the approved distribution routes. If the output was sensitive, the fact and the manner of the distribution should be logged. On receipt, the user should check the output as a matter of routine, and should report any errors. This discipline and the resultant feedback should help to build a more error-free system. (To maintain data security once validated, all data media when off-line should be kept in a secure place—the appointment of a competent data librarian is perhaps an advisable step in the larger organisation where a reasonable quantity of sensitive material has to be stored.)

To some extent, this section has been written from a batch-processing perspective which is more periodic in nature. On-line systems do not require that data from source documents be transferred to machine-readable form before processing takes place. Indeed, it is not necessary that a source document be created for individual transaction elements when an on-line system is used. This difference does not change the security concepts underlying automated control. While recognising that it does become more important to limit access to the terminals and to have password controls on different types of editing functions, effective machine-based verification systems as outlined above remain vital. However, given the potential lack of physical documents, the creation of audit trails assumes primary significance. Thus, it may be expedient that all sensitive transactions and master file changes should be recorded on another set of files, accessible only to authorised personnel so that, in the event of error or fraud, transactions may be reviewed and the master files recreated (see 15.7.14).

15.2 DECISION AND ADMINISTRATION SUPPORT SYSTEMS

The standard contemporary decision support systems include spreadsheet and database packages (for more information, see 5.4.10). The basic problem for all organisations which use these systems for sensitive data manipulations (thus, spreadsheets are frequently used for corporate planning and other confidential applications) is how to guard against unauthorised access and retrieval. Self-evidently, the composite system must do what the organisation needs and must be properly supported by staff and documentation. In one sense, it might be thought ideal that, wherever possible, the component parts of the support system should be designed to look like the organisation's pre-automation forms. This should make it easier for the existing staff to follow the new system. But this may not have been the optimum computerisation procedure (ie simply replicating the paper-system is not necessarily the best way to exploit the power of the modern computer, as discussed in 5.2 and 5.3.1), and it may also lead staff to mistakenly assume they know what to do in all situations rather than to assimilate the training materials on the new and improved facilities.

There must be a positive campaign to encourage good software discipline, no matter what the level of the user, and all those involved must observe proper back-up procedures every time a significant change is made either to the data or to the programming of any macros. For these purposes, all those staff involved must be made to recognise that it is far more difficult to remember changes to a spreadsheet than to plain text. If data is copied down onto a micro or personal computer from a mainframe for processing, it is essential to make sure that only up-to-date and properly consolidated data is used for the ultimate decision-making. Disk space management is also vital, and users should always check whether there is going to be enough room before each program run is started. Similarly, all floppy disks containing software or data must be kept securely. The graphics capacity of these packages is often an integral part of the way in which the system offers support, so senior management must consider the problem of electronic eavesdropping and, in appropriate circumstances, must achieve TEMPEST standards to protect the rooms or buildings within which the systems are used (see 14.7).

Even within the organisation, security can be difficult in a multi-user environment. In unstructured office accommodation, unauthorised staff may be able to oversee the screens or to use the relevant terminals without supervision. Separate terminal rooms with access limited to authorised personnel or with supervised usage may be the answer, or controls should be established within the packages which, in the context of the system, offer an acceptable level of security. Hence, it may be necessary to write macros to protect individual data items within the package, or to inhibit the more sensitive processes.

Administrative support systems include diaries, messaging and reminder systems, telephone, network and other directories, etc. Special function diaries can be created, say, to control room bookings. Some facilities can be provided by creating lists of information using word processor systems or text editors, but modern systems usually have menu-driven friendly systems, integrated with other integrated office systems. It should be the responsibility of the owners of personal diary files to control access to them—legitimately, colleagues and secretaries will require access to scheduling and meetings files to synchronise contacts, but other parts of the systems may have to be properly passworded. Thus, if electronic mail systems are likely to carry sensitive information, the mail boxes must be properly protected. Reminders can be dated, timed and the sender identified, all this data to be displayed if required, to reduce the risk of false data being introduced into the system.

15.3 THE ADVANTAGES AND DISADVANTAGES OF DISTRIBUTED NETWORKS

Many organisations are deciding to take a distributed system approach to the future structure of their data processing (see 5.1.4.). Distributed systems use interconnected, but have separately located computers rather than one centrally located computer. In a distributed system, the separate computers may all have approximately the same status and be capable of doing the same type of processing (a **peer system**), as opposed to a **hierarchical system** which has a main computer with local slaves. A proportion of the processing is therefore carried out locally or is transmitted to a conveniently sited unit which is otherwise not currently in use, and then transmitted to a central facility for collation and redistribution to interested users. Decentralisation of the processing should mean that the system is more responsive to local needs and can be more cost-effective, avoiding the expense of large and complex data manipulation systems. Communication costs will also be lower than on a hierarchical on-line centralised computer system, since less data is transmitted, and more processing is performed locally. Further, distributed systems pose less of a problem in the event of machine failure than do centralised systems because the organisation is not dependent upon a single machine. This does not mean that organisations with distributed systems can afford to be complacent. In addition to the normal standby arrangements, organisations should:

(a) ensure hardware and software compatibility,
(b) make contingency plans to transfer work from the inoperable to the operable machines, and
(c) ensure that there are specific standby plans for any key elements in the system.

However, in planning the network, it should be remembered that not all the components of the system will work at the same speed. Hence, printers are comparatively slow so materials will often have to queue. This can be dangerous if edit facilities can affect the buffered materials. But distributed systems can also reduce the risk of danger from industrial action which, in a centralised facility, might disrupt the entire system. However, the less desirable consequence is that the computer staff are likely to be less cohesive, and some of the smaller, more remote units may even be run by users, or staff who think of themselves more as users than as operators.

The greater the degree of hardware and software compatibility, the more likely it is that the organisation will be able to generate real expertise in the particular systems. This competence is not only of prime importance in-house but, if the hardware and software combination is not uncommon, the organisation's expertise may also be commercially marketable. In a disaster contingency situation, where only a part of the network is damaged, it makes the transfer of processing more straightforward. On the purchasing side, there may be economies of scale available and advantages of administrative convenience. Only a few manufacturers, suppliers and maintenance firms will be required to acquire and service a functioning configuration. This reduces problems of fault diagnosis, increases discounts and fixes legal responsibility and accountability with fewer individuals.

As a general rule, to allow several users within the organisation to buy their own equipment from different suppliers is a recipe for anarchy. Every organisation should therefore formulate an overall buying policy. This will then give a known set of criteria for all departments to follow and should prevent the tiresome task for some central body of having to thoroughly evaluate every computer acquisition request on its merits. This does not mean that departments should normally be allowed to buy equipment without supervision. The organisation must monitor the process to aim at ensuring an integrated system.

At the heart of the strategy lies the identification of the present information flows and an outline of the reasons for introducing the automated systems. The plan will list the existing hardware and software packages, and provide an outline guide as to what will be required. Self-evidently, the projected hardware and software should be limited to a preferred list which can be supported. There should then be a statement which speculates on how the information will flow given the new systems. If any hardware or software is to be used for the first time, the organisation should address the issue of who should run the pilot scheme and be the guinea pig (see 9.1). It is important to consider the departmental perceptions of justice and fair play in the ensuing disruption of departmental efforts through the introduction of new systems. Following the pilot run, proper appraisal of the outcome is essential (see 9.3.1 and 10.5.6). Users must be made to think about what actually happened during the trial, and led to the point where they can more accurately specify what they actually want. If several pilots are being run simultaneously, it is useful to keep a directory of who has what, and to allow the mutual demonstrations of working or non-working systems. If hardware and software from different manufacturers is being used, the planners must specify what communications systems are going to be required. Once the pilot runs and the consultation process is ended, the planners must set target completion dates, identify the costs, and list the benefits both quantifiable and unquantifiable.

The overall organisation strategy needs to be broken down to a departmental level, allowing for logical connections and exchanges between departments as required. The objective of the plan should be to encourage and consolidate the basic and natural information flows between departments. Pilot schemes assume particular importance and utility as an evaluator of future systems. The early experimentation also gets the affected staff well into the planning process which is good for morale. The departmental strategy should only be finalised after detailed consultation and should establish purchasing guidelines. Once the final strategy is agreed, no individual department should be asked for a cost-benefit analysis of the proposed addition to the system. These decisions have been taken by the organisation as a whole. Once the strategy has been finalised, this represents the authorisation for departments to spend money on the approved equipment and software.

However, if the organisation attempts to create a mixed system (ie configurations of hardware from different manufacturers) this can create communications problems, and can be difficult to maintain, particularly if one machine goes down, because the functioning machines may not be immediately compatible to fill in the role of the non-functioning. Moreover, for both maintenance and auditing purposes, it can be more difficult to discover the precise nature of all the processing carried out at each location and the nature of any controls which exist. This means that all the sensitive files must have good data controls which can more carefully monitor access to ensure that data is only updated from approved sources.

In a distributed system, the best control systems operate hierarchically. Thus, local controls should be organised so that the feed of information into the central control system and into peer systems is clearly identified and provides an adequate level of security at each major interface. This will allow the maintenance of a proper data trail whenever data is transferred from one location to the next, and should permit the identification of all those who have been involved at each stage of the transmission. This cannot of itself eradicate errors, but it allows warnings and/or training to be targeted at the staff most at fault. Indeed, mistakes are always more likely to arise if the responsibility for data input is not given to a core of well-trained and motivated staff.

To safeguard information in a distributed system, one of the standard strategies which organisations adopt is that of **intrusion avoidance**. This can be difficult to implement successfully because:

(a) sometimes there is significant geographical separation of the component parts which can make it so difficult to defend all the physical access points, and
(b) the resultant complexity of the configuration can make it difficult to design comprehensive and effective logical access controls.

Further, once the system has been penetrated by an unauthorised person, all the intrusion avoidance controls are useless. Encryption can be used to defend the data once someone has gained entry, but the effectiveness of this strategy depends upon good key management and the processing capacity of the intruder to decrypt the protected data (see 14.5).

Generally, in the design of a distributed system, there is a conflict between data security techniques and techniques for reliability and availability. For instance, if the designer reduces the number of access points for security purposes, there is a corresponding increase in the potential redundancy of parts of the system and perhaps real limits on system availability. However, it is possible to make a virtue out of the difficulty by exploiting the physical isolation between the different components of the system, and thereby reducing the effect of the intrusion, ie the strategy is to produce **intrusion tolerance**. The philosophy is to accept that intrusion is likely at some time during the system's life cycle, and to take those steps most likely to minimise the effect of that intrusion.

The protection is achieved by storing all the sensitive files as scattered fragments which are distributed about the entire system. When a user logs on to an unprotected system at an individual workstation, the user has potential authority over all data which is stored there, or which can be accessed from there. But if the data are stored in a fragmentary fashion, the user must have access granted to the file management system which holds the directory of fragment locations, and which will only permit the reconstitution of the distributed file if proper authorisation is given. Assuming that the fragmentation matrix is complex so that the distribution between sites is significant, and the links between fragments are difficult to determine, intruders will require considerable effort to correlate the data elements, assuming that access can be engineered to all those sites where the data is concealed. (For more details, see Fraga.)

15.4 MICRO SECURITY ISSUES

'The very technology that gave us microcomputers has made them an unguarded bonanza.' (Cronin, p8.) (For a definition of microcomputer, see 5.5.1.) Small businesses have become increasingly dependent on micros and the personal computer as the *golden pliers* phenomenon has increasingly brought down the cost of suitable hardware and software (ie manufacturers have cut the prices but offered more). Yet the advertised virtues of such systems in terms of their accessibility and user-friendly convenience, actually indicate the reality of the security problems. The first step in securing a highly portable piece of equipment is to limit physical access to it. This means that it is not sensible to keep the machine(s) in an open area to which the public might have access, and anything movable should be locked away at night. All the back-up disks should be stored in a secure place. The risks from the staff should also be considered and good office habits should be promoted, eg there should be no eating and drinking near either the equipment or the disks. As in the large systems, fire and power protection should be considered, and disaster recovery plans suitable to the organisation should be drawn up (see 11.4, 12.3 and 13.2). This is in recognition of the simple truth that, regardless of the size of the organisation or of the computer systems which may or may not be involved, all dependence increases vulnerability.

However, in both the design and use of the standard microcomputer, the issue of security is often an afterthought. This reflects the user's more usual and narrow interest which is in the application. Manufacturers therefore tend to install micro operating systems which do not have sophisticated access controls. This matches a general design philosophy which emphasises that micro operating systems should be friendly and allow efficient hardware responses to applications packages. This ignores the security importance of effective memory organisation and disk management, and the underlying need to make it difficult, if not impossible, to alter the operating system files — their integrity is fundamental to the security aspects. All privileged facilities must be protectable. This is particularly the case because, during the last fifteen years, the trailblazing micros have evolved into the new generation of personal computers, which can not only match the performance of yesterday's mainframes, but can act as terminals to other machines via LANs.

The pace of development in hardware terms has forced the development of more sophisticated operating systems which can now permit multi-tasking. But there has been little pressure on the manufacturers or software houses to make the systems more secure. This ought to be given a high priority because many more applications which ought to be secure are now made available on the smaller systems. In single user environments, there may be a reduced need to develop high security barriers, because the single user will require unrestricted access to all the files, software, etc, since efficiency of use is considered more important than internal security. It is therefore important to erect good locking against an intruder and to build something into the applications packages which will slow down access to the individual resources if entry is forced. In multi-user systems, however, the ideal is that detailed file and record locking should be built into the application packages. The least that should be done is for the user to build his or her own front end security menu system which will at least slow down an unauthorised user. It should be noted that minicomputers are not much better in security terms than the micros.

The development of on-line links between terminals and terminal emulating machines and mainframes has represented a major improvement on the old batch processing systems, but because the development of good applications has been slow in the real-time mainframe market, many users have acquired their own desk-top systems where manufacturers have invested heavily to produce bundles of attractive applications packages. In general, the micro-mainframe links are important because they allow the free flow of information up and down the line, ie they move towards an integration of data processing functions even though the hardware involved may have different operating systems. Overcoming the communication and compatibility problems is nevertheless useful because this will give micros access to the mainframe's peripherals and processing capacity—the small machine becomes a gateway to other more powerful facilities. This is achieved through terminal emulation at the lowest level, or through a menu-driven, user friendly software interface at best.

Users should carefully consider whether it is desirable to establish a link between the micro and a mainframe, or whether a link into a LAN is really required. Whichever route is taken, the user should have some system to impose security on down-loaded data to prevent misuse or theft, eg some systems require record definition and formatting as a precondition to data extraction and down-loading—by defining the user's authorisation in this area, and inserting a password requirement, file transfer can be controlled. This can be backed-up through the use of physical systems to prevent copying on to non-approved floppies. Internal software checks on data uploaded to the mainframe can seek to ensure the main system's data integrity. These controls will also help to maintain proper audit trails. When micros which are equipped with removable disk drives or with printers are connected to a mainframe, the user privilege to read a file of data implies the freedom to copy. The only real answer is to have the micros sited in a secure area, with good security supervision over the print-out and disks, and with staff having specific and limited clearance up to the most sensitive levels that they can access.

All the major applications rely on a foundation of system software including the operating system. This is a complex and comprehensive set of program modules which allows the applications software to use the resources of the computer, eg input and output control system, executive program to initiate and terminate application programs, accounting and statistics functions, etc. An operating system must also be able to identify the user and the resources uniquely. The security problem is that penetration of the operating system potentially allows access to all the other resources which it supports and controls. This form of intrusion requires specialist knowledge and appropriate opportunity for access. The answer is a management surveillance function which is able to associate users with the resources in use. In a micro environment, this should be both a physical and a software task. The operating system will have a part of the responsibility for controlling the log-in procedure and access to the procedures, backed up by good disk library facilities which will control the availability of sensitive software with the use being in restricted access rooms. The physical controls over access and the disks is essential because the micro access systems offer poor control over who can use a system. The fundamental difficulty is that, in the absence of a LAN, access is not centrally logged so the user is free to experiment with the resources and to peruse data in an unaccountable way.

In general, the systems are vulnerable during the input phase because data may easily be altered, lost or misinterpreted — internal data controls may be weak and allow users to introduce false data. Sadly, the standard micro systems tend to leave data unprotected or poorly protected, and all systems are vulnerable to program bugs whether accidental or Trojan Horse to subvert the software. Similarly, virus programs can be innocently taken on board but then do considerable damage (see 14.6.1). In a sense, the manufacturers' failure to remedy the inadequacies of the standard operating systems allows the users the opportunity to circumvent all the other controls which may have been introduced.

The maintenance of access controls may become more difficult if a user is using either a micro as a terminal gateway to access a mainframe, or a mini and the mini is linked to a mainframe. Because of the lack of facilities for detailed log-in controls on most micros and minis, it may be easy for staff to gain access to apparently safely passworded files. The problem is that, frequently, the central mainframe will accept any input from an integrated micro or mini as a valid input, ie access to the mainframe is entirely dependent upon controls on the access to the micro or mini. This should be overcome by always requiring log-on procedures when accessing the mainframe even though this will often require the user to log-on twice. The network is only as secure as its weakest link. A further problem faced by the management is to keep track of all the system developments which take place at remote sites. The management must seek to ensure that local programs are well designed and controlled (an argument for central administration), but this may stifle local initiative and flexibility. However, the risks involved in allowing uncontrolled amendments to local systems outweigh the advantages, and so central planning, validation and each implementation of changes being centrally approved are necessary safeguards. The auditor should also ensure the standardisation of all those systems which feed data to the central accounting mechanism so that adequate checks can be made in the overall accounting system. For these purposes, it may be better to make central accounting packages available to remote sites in object code only. This makes unauthorised amendment difficult and is more likely to ensure that all system changes are brought into operation at the same time.

15.5 AUDITING CONSIDERATIONS

The auditing of computer systems is usually done through a computer interrogation program. This program will be based on parameters specified by the auditor, and will perform audit checks on the data, selecting data elements for manual scrutiny and vouching. Auditors may have to become involved in the development of their own software to make enquiry systems work and operate more economically. This reflects the dual aim of the auditor which is to check on the effectiveness of the controls within the systems, and to validate the data which the systems contain (see 16.5). If this interrogation can be carried out from one centralised site, there can be a saving in audit time, a considerable improvement in efficiency and a cost saving. There are two possibilities:

1. files can be transferred from the remote site to the central facility for examination, or
2. the auditor can examine the files at the remote site and transfer the results to the central location. In deciding which strategy to adopt for each audit, it should be remembered that it is cheaper to transmit the results of the check than the whole files, but more on-line time may be required to interrogate the files on site.

A high degree of technical proficiency is required for the work, both in the accounting and in the computing disciplines. Few established internal audit departments have begun a detailed consideration of the security issues, although external auditors are, of necessity, more interested. Awareness of the information system is the first hurdle for auditors. Ironically, the Data Protection Act has actually helped auditors because more managers have been forced to address many of the problems. The auditing function breaks down into the following functional stages:

1 First, the organisation must make an inventory of the hardware and the systems which it contains. It is probably better to involve the auditor in the development of the information system than to expect him or her to validate the system as a whole after it has been put into operation. In this, it is a specific part of the auditor's task to comment on the level of expenditure in providing security.
2 The auditor(s) should discuss issues such as the segregation of duties, user support and training with the management.
3 The auditor(s) must then decide how much of the system will be audited and when the audit will take place. This will inevitably involve a consideration of the security policy drawn up by management. When planning the individual audits, a balance must be struck between the need to maintain proper security and not to alert potential criminals, and the need to maintain reasonable human relations with the management. Thus, a proportion of all the work should be approved by the management of each site and guarantees given as to data security and confidentiality.
4 The auditor(s) should initiate and/or supervise the testing of the physical security systems.
5 The auditor(s) should ensure that logical security systems are working properly and providing proper audit trails.
6 All the inadequacies and defects which are disclosed during the tests and audits should be brought to the attention of the management with recommendations for improvement.

Good communication skills are involved because the auditors must liaise with both the users and the computer professionals to get the reviews performed—and the professionals will know at least as much about the problems of computer security as the auditors.

15.6 METHODS OF FRAUD

The manipulation of computer systems for financial gain must result in the creation of false accounting records. Thus, to conceal a shortage, the book value of assets must be adjusted to correspond with the post-loss reality. This apparent agreement can be achieved either by simply misrepresenting the value, or by manipulating the accounting records. In general, the main methods of fraud include:

1 **False input**—ie to suppress or falsify transaction data before, or as, it is input. This may be achieved:
(a) by entering additional data,
(b) by failing to enter valid data, or
(c) by simply altering the data.
False data can be created at one or more of several points, eg:
(a) at the data preparation stage,
(b) on manual entry,
(c) through the use of false bar codes or some other automated means,
(d) corruptions can lead to non-acceptance of the data by the computer—when rejected into a suspense account, the data can be fraudulently manipulated.
The failure to enter valid data is more difficult to detect because there may be no audit trail to show alterations. The types of transactions may involve the creation of false purchase or sales details, expenses, payroll, etc, and each such transaction is likely to be allocated an entry code which will signal a sequence of events, eg a cash sale code might require the preparation of an invoice, debiting the cash account, crediting the cash sales account and adjusting the stock inventory. The most vulnerable codes are those which allow the movement of goods or funds.
2 **False output** —output can be destroyed or withheld to conceal the impact of the fraud, eg to reduce liabilities or improve performance. The basic devices rely on the fact that output can be reprocessed or reprinted with the originals destroyed or by editing files while they are in the buffer awaiting printing. Output may also be inflated by double printing.

The deceptive loss-making properties of fraud can be aimed at a wide variety of possible targets including shareholders, customers, suppliers, bankers and external auditors. Frauds against shareholders and persons external to the organisation may include producing false accounts simply to conceal losses or to pull in more investment monies/loans where the quality of the investment does not justify it. Frauds against employers may include bribery, extortion (eg threats to poison products or to destroy computer records), pirating copyright or patented information or commercial espionage, manipulation of electronic funds transfer systems or in-house data, or the more crude theft of goods or cheques, etc. The most effective frauds will involve one or more of the following strategies:

1 **The manipulation of master files**, eg the payroll master which will contain details of the employees and their salary and commission rates, or the sales master which contains details of prices, discounts, approval of customers and credit limits. These manipulations may be immediate to cover particular transactions, or long-term. They usually affect pricing and are often collusive with buyers, eg to sell stocked goods at an excessive discount, posting debits to a separate discount file to conceal the loss.

2 **The misuse of suspense accounts** —all rejected and unallocated data are held pending clarification in an edit/error cycle or are posted to suspense accounts. Fraud possibilities arise if entries which should be posted to personal accounts are posted to suspense, or *vice versa*. Similarly, if data held in a suspense account are altered before being inspected and allocated by auditing staff.

3 **The misuse of restricted utilities**—ie those powerful software tools, used by programmers to fix faulty systems and to assist in housekeeping. They are normally (but dangerously) kept on a systems disk and are invoked by using the appropriate password. Utilities can be used for a variety of fraudulent purposes and most do not leave an audit trail, eg as in the use of restricted utilities like SUPERZAP.

4 **The introduction of program patches** -these can divert data into a fraudulent routine based on a conditional jump statement. Such traps can be placed anywhere in the system. The fraudulent programmer must know exactly what the program does, have access and the time and skill to be able to change it, be able to test the patch and conceal it, etc. High levels of skill are required, but the reward is that such patches usually leave no traces and are not detectable by the ordinary auditing techniques. Program patches can be introduced into the software either during the writing, or later during maintenance or updating. The patch may be triggered by a customer name or by any other identified transaction, ie it is a conditional statement requiring a modification of the standard system, either to accept or reject the data, or to manipulate it in some way.

5 **The manipulation of job control (JCL) instructions**—job control or executable programs direct the process of a computer application, ie they tell a computer which program to execute, which data to read and where to make output. JCL is a high level language which interfaces with the operating system and automates much of the work of the operators. JCL instructions are usually held on-line on a systems disk, and may be patched to divert processing to a fraudulent program or master file. Making successful changes to an operating system calls for high skill and time, so the use of this method is rare.

6 **The conversion of assets**—ie the process whereby the manipulation is turned into a gain, eg although the manipulation of accounts may have released goods to an address, these goods must then be sold in a way which does not give rise to suspicion.

The manipulation of incoming data can be the most difficult to identify, eg whereby incoming cheques are omitted from the cash book and ledgers, but either included in the banking returns to cover previous cash shortages, or simply endorsed and negotiated through a third party outside the victim's records. Equally difficult to detect is the conversion of disbursement cheques through the alteration of the payee names or endorsement to third party. Often this type of fraud is supported by the destruction of the cheques after their return through the banking system. Finally, the significant growth in the volume of electronic funds transfers has made the system vulnerable to the one-time smash and grab frauds where the criminal simply changes the destination account number or otherwise alters the payment instructions. It is usual to divert the funds to tax haven countries in which follow-up investigations will be difficult.

It is clear that all companies are exposed to the possibility of fraud but, in statistical terms, only a small number of those frauds will cause significant loss. Insurance should be considered as a safety net for those situations not only where more significant losses are likely to be sustained, but also where the controls cannot be made wholly adequate. In general, insurance will be of marginal assistance, even if it should be obtainable at an economic rate. Thus, insurance should be considered when other forms of risk management seem ineffective and where the consequences of those strategies failing would be unacceptable. There is no justification for purchasing irrelevant cover, or cover for its own sake. Organisations should approach the insurance market with a clear specification of need, or in a spirit prepared to critically evaluate advice received. Carriers are usually prepared to amend and extend coverage to suit the needs of each proposer. It is simply a matter of negotiating what is required.

15.6.1 What to do when a fraud is suspected

If a fraud is suspected, the organisation should maintain absolute secrecy. Unless this is done, the criminals involved will be forewarned, documents may disappear, and witnesses may be discouraged. It is advisable for all organisations to develop a formal policy, laying down the standard procedure to be followed in each of the standard situations. Sadly, many investigations fail because senior managers cannot decide what they would like the immediate outcome to be. The result is to lurch from one crisis to another. If there are no policy guidelines laid down in advance, the investigators should identify what political or other pressures there may be within the organisation against the taking of firm action against the wrongdoers, eg fear of publicity, and plan appropriate counter-measures. In formulating an organisation policy, the first issue to decide, without reference to individual personalities involved, is whether there should be a presumption in favour of the prosecution of identified criminals. The factors to bear in mind are that:

(a) the automatic prosecution of all those detected in criminal activities may be a deterrent to others;
(b) the conviction of the criminals can be used to obtain a compensation order, or shift the burden of proof in any subsequent civil hearing to recover money and assets lost;
(c) prosecution, regardless of outcome, may be a condition of the insurance policy; and
(d) failing to prosecute gives the thief an unfair advantage when applying for another job where the same crime may be repeated.

It must be accepted that fraud trials may be difficult for juries to understand, may lead to criticism of the organisation and its management, and may reveal details of the method of fraud for other criminals to learn from. But to fail to refer the matter to the police for their investigation with a view to prosecution is to encourage more fraud. The Crown Prosecution Service may not prosecute because the police did not have the time or the manpower to investigate, or because the fraud is not considered criminal, or is beyond the local jurisdiction. In such a situation, the victim may attempt a private prosecution in some countries, but there are dangers if a conviction is not obtained because all the costs may have to be borne by the victim, and there may be a subsequent action to claim damages for the now apparently malicious prosecution.

Civil action has two basic aims. The primary aim is the recovery of the value of missing funds or assets; and the secondary aim is the obtaining of injunctions to prevent further abuses. If the victim remains relatively passive, it encourages the criminals and those who have benefited from their activities equally to remain passive. It is often the case that a victim will only obtain restitution of assets if some action is threatened and bargaining ensues. The victim of fraud does have the right to negotiate with the wrongdoers to recover the losses, but the victim must only try to recover the actual value of the losses and not to seek to recover a penalty outside the criminal system as the price of not prosecuting. Equally, the victim must not compromise the rights of any insurer.

In all cases, dishonest employees should leave their employment. The certainty of dismissal is a deterrent to others and sympathy for the criminal's spouse and family should not obscure this long-term truth. Weak policies in this whole area are self-defeating. Care should be taken about dismissal pending the outcome of either civil or criminal proceedings. A useful by-product of the investigations should also be consideration of how the defences may be improved for the future.

When objectives for the investigation have been agreed, the investigation itself may move forward. The victim should consider the mechanics of the suspected fraud, ie:

(a) the number and identity of those involved,
(b) the likely methods of fraud adopted,
(c) which documentary and computerised records will have been falsified,
(d) the scale of the probable losses involved, and

(e) why the fraud was not detected earlier.

The investigation should never be based on the assumption that the alleged wrongdoers have only committed one fraud. The organisation should always plan for the worst possible case. This will enable the investigators to cast the net wide and to engineer the maximum loss recovery. At an early stage, the investigators should identify which points in the investigation are likely to prove difficult, whether from a practical angle or from the point of view of evidence. This should allow them to work out how best to catch the criminals, ie with the maximum chance of evidence of criminality or dishonesty, which may involve trying to catch the criminals in the act or in possession of stolen goods, or doing something outside their normal duties which will tend to corroborate the allegation of dishonesty.

The first priority is to identify what documentary or computerised records might be destroyed and move rapidly to secure them. It is always advisable to take all the physical documents which may appear relevant. Those which prove to be irrelevant can be returned later, but those which may prove to be vital may have permanently disappeared. At this stage, the organisation should seek positive legal advice on whether some specific legal authorisation to search for and seize evidence of wrongdoing is required. It is also necessary to consider the legal effect of taking such documents without sufficient authorisation. The investigators should list which computer records will be needed. These will include:

1 both the detailed hardware and software specifications, eg to show the overall configuration of, and connections to the hardware, and the architecture of the operating systems, communications and network software, etc;

2 in systems where centralised records are maintained, the journal and activity logs, operators' and console logs, time and attendance records should all be secured;

3 all the applications programs which may have been tampered with should be taken, together with library versions and the initial specifications including the flow diagrams, source code and file layouts; and

4 where a micro or personal computer has been used, it is advisable to take everything including the manuals, print-out, disks, etc.

Collection of all this evidence requires careful planning and execution. If employees who work in the data centre or who have direct access to the computers are involved in the fraud, it is possible that they will destroy vital evidence immediately they have notice of the investigation, or will have left programs which will wipe evidence from the computer the moment an investigation is begun. It is therefore necessary to plan how best to recover information from the information system without pre-warning the alleged wrongdoers. A stand-by team of trusted operators (probably consultants or employees of the hardware company) should stand by and move in quickly when the suspects are arrested. For the purposes of evidence, care should be taken to identify precisely where data is located to ensure its integrity and admissibility in court.

If third parties are to be approached during the investigation, a number of factors should be considered:

1 It may be reasonable to assume that they ought to help in the investigation because there is generally some acceptance of a mutual interest between law abiding citizens to defeat criminality.

2 If the allegations involve individuals employed by that third party and, upon investigation, they prove false, there may be a loss of business between the two organisations.

3 Talking to the third party at an early stage and engaging their active co-operation, may avoid the necessity of legal action against that person.

4 It may also comply with contractual or other legally enforceable obligations, eg as to audit.

The victim should consider what resources are available to conduct the investigation, bearing in mind the size and complexity of the fraud suspected. Other parties, eg the Inland Revenue or Customs and Excise, or other organisations may be interested in the outcome of the investigation. A joint investigation may therefore be appropriate, with the emphasis on a speedy outcome.

15.6.2 Methods of investigation

Once the evidence has been collected, the analysis of the documents and computer records must begin. The first step is to identify deviations from the known procedures. All fraud depends to some extent upon modifications to the accepted practice so all possible explanations for each identified deviation should be made. This will be added to the forensic and expert evidence (ie as to how the computer systems work or ought to work, the methods of manipulation, authorship of documents, etc), the interviews with the suspects and other pretext investigations (eg test purchases from a suspected pirate or fence, undercover operations to infiltrate the group suspected, asset tracing, etc). The end product should be the preparation of schedules of evidence so that complex evidence can be easily assimilated. In the case of long-term frauds, schedules of loss should be cross-referenced to the documents.

15.7 AUDITING STEPS

Accounts are designed to show the immediate profitability and net worth of a business. In addition to the information needs of the management, constraints are imposed on the accounting procedures by the need to comply with statutory reporting requirements, professional accountancy standards and the desire of the Inland Revenue to take the proper proportion of tax on behalf of the State. In order to achieve an overview, the organisation must keep proper records of each transaction on a daily basis. These can then be summarised and consolidated into records representing a longer time span until an annual account is achieved. There are a number of interdependent ratios which can then be applied to assist in measuring the performance of a commercial enterprise. Without resorting to illegality, these ratios can be improved through commercial manipulation, eg by arranging to pay off some of its liabilities before the accounts are finalised, the organisation can favourably adjust the *current ratio* which is often used as one of the criteria in deciding whether to offer credit facilities.

Modern accountancy depends upon the double entry system. Hence, for each credit entry, there must be a corresponding debit and *vice versa*. When an asset is removed, a related account should be debited with its worth. The point of any manipulation is therefore:

(a) to conceal the debit by suppressing it altogether,
(b) by creating a false credit, or
(c) by posting it to a safe account.

If debits must ultimately appear, they may either reduce profitability or overstate net worth, eg suppression of sales affects profits while theft of cash reduces net worth, but if the cash shortage is concealed by posting the debits to the accounts of the customers, the loss is hidden in the balance sheet. In all instances, the effect of these concealment methods is cumulative and may covertly destroy the worth of the business. The extent of the problem will be dictated by the number of loosely controlled accounts within the personal and nominal ledger structure, and the number of people having access to them. Within the accounts, the following divisions will be found:

1 **Personal accounts** which relate to individual customers, suppliers, etc.
2 **Nominal accounts** which summarise assets, liabilities, expenses, etc.
3 **Real accounts** which relate to physical assets.
4 **Suspense accounts** which hold entries which cannot immediately be posted to one of the other accounts. The fact that these accounts cannot be immediately reconciled makes them vulnerable to fraud.
5 **Control accounts** which summarise and check on the accuracy of individual postings to ledgers. The assumption is usually that if the control accounts agree, the accounts from which they are derived must also agree.

When attempting to assess the reliability of an organisation's reporting and accounting system, the following records are essential reference materials:

1 stock records which show current inventory;

2 invoices, delivery notes, etc;
3 transportation records, eg routing sheets and drivers' logs;
4 management reports which summarise sales and purchases against targets or previous year's figures; and
5 vouchers, expense claim forms, etc.

15.7.1 Client/customer verification

One of the more obvious methods by which to defraud organisations is to supply goods and/or valuable services on credit to fictitious customers or clients. It is therefore essential to verify the persons, firms and organisations which are listed as receiving value from the organisation. A number of strategies are available to do this:

1 To identify the more obvious frauds, the organisation should compare all the past and present addresses and telephone numbers recorded in the personnel file of employees and ex-employees (including next of kin) with the master file addresses and telephone numbers of customers and suppliers. This will test to see whether employees have, for example, unimaginatively set up fictitious supplier accounts using their own homes or the homes of relatives as the drop address.
2 Using information obtained during the recruitment process, it is advantageous to check the names of the previous employers of key employees against the master file of suppliers - this will help to identify the sometimes dishonest employees who submit false invoices using stationery retained from a previous employment.
3 A more detailed examination of the suppliers' master file entries should then be undertaken to identify accommodation addresses, Post Office boxes and common addresses for supposedly unrelated suppliers. This detects front companies and the form of mail drops characteristically used to support purchase frauds.
4 The investigators should then identify all those customers and suppliers whose names are usually abbreviated and who are held on any master file used for producing disbursement cheques, eg the initials I.B.M are easily altered to I.B.Mainlow on a cheque.
5 Depending on the scale of the verification operation, the investigators could now check master file entries against the entries in telephone directories, street lists and trade directories. The point of the exercise is to look for missing entries, or for different addresses or telephone numbers to identify fictitious customers or suppliers, or false addresses for delivery purposes.
6 A random list of customers and suppliers should be appraised by a reputable credit bureau.
7 It may also be expedient to extract details of those organisations asking for references on ex-employees. These names should be checked against the current customers and suppliers. This may detect the possibility of collusive frauds involving both past and current employees.

15.7.2 Invoice verification

Another common method of fraud is to insert false invoices into the system for payment. To minimise the accounting manipulations which are necessary, the ideal is for the invoices to relate to services rather than to goods or other tangibles which will have to be shown, say, as stock or raw materials —in such a situation, there is a real risk that the discrepancies may come to light in a stock check or through loss of profit expectation. If consequential manipulations are to be undertaken, the aim would be to create a convertible false credit in the supplier's account by inventing purchases, inflating genuine purchases, or by diverting a debit from or a credit to that account, the debit going to a badly controlled account. Alternatively, the manipulations must be related to high risk items such as carbon paper or other consumables which are not usually covered in inventory. Again, a number of investigative possibilities exist:

1 The first step would be to examine batches of paid and pending purchase invoices and to isolate those that do not show a telephone or VAT registration number, or that have an accommodation address. There is a difficulty for any would-be criminal. If a credible false supplier is to be created, the criminal must ensure that the address, and if possible the telephone number, is under control, but that not much other real information is given which might cause an

investigation— eg by way of a VAT return where Customs and Excise would realise that the name and number do not match.

2 The investigators should be suspicious of those invoices which are copies and not originals, or are unfolded (ie where it is unlikely that they have been sent through the post).

3 The investigators should also examine those invoices where the goods are simply described by a code. Although this form of fraud tends to be relatively small scale, it is easy to pass off personal purchases as organisation purchases if the goods are not clearly identified.

4 Any invoice which shows signs of alteration or modification, whether to the value or to the address for payment, is a legitimate target for investigation.

5 By taking an historical approach to the documentation issued by a supplier, it may become apparent that the organisation has received a complete invoice sequence, ie that one supplier's invoices have all been posted to the organisation. There may be a perfectly legitimate explanation for this, but the question is worth asking.

15.7.3 Ledger verification

It is a standard practice to group and consolidate accounts into ledgers. If the organisation simply presumes that the ledgers' basic structure is accurate and that the data which they contain are substantially correct, the auditors merely tracing credits and debits to each ledger from the supporting source documentation, there is very little chance of detecting fraud. Among the steps which can be taken to verify each ledger are the following:

1 The investigators should carefully examine those accounts opened after the appointment of individuals who occupy sensitive jobs, eg those who have responsibility as buyers and/or as authorised signatories to purchase orders and invoices. The forms of fraud to guard against include the possibility that sometimes buyers will introduce suppliers with whom they have worked (and possibly been bribed by) in the past, or will use invoices from the same fictitious suppliers against their new employers, etc.

2 By taking an historical approach to each sensitive ledger, the investigators should look for sudden changes in trends. The reality of fraud distorts the usual organisation patterns and predictions, and even the modest and inventive criminals can seldom guarantee long-term stability and consistency. The best tests would, for example, compare the current year's with one or more of the previous year's purchase ledger and budgetary cost centre records, so that any unusual trends in the volumes passing through an account would become apparent.

3 A range of frauds depend upon the ability of the criminal to intercept cheques as they arrive at the organisation or before they are sent out. To take the former, the investigators should check for purchase credits which have been diverted. Because the organisation is not necessarily expecting the money and may not therefore have included the relevant sum of money in an account, purchase credits can easily be suppressed and the incoming cheques converted into cash. The best way in which to start the investigation is to examine the warehouse and inventory records for goods returned to suppliers, and correspondence in quality control relating to rejected products passed back to suppliers. For the converse, the investigators should examine the file of customer complaints for faulty goods, where it is alleged that credits which should have been passed on to suppliers, have not arrived, etc.

4 Whether generally within the confines of perpetrator analysis (see 12.1) or job sensitivity analysis (see 16.3), or more particularly for these immediate purposes, the investigators should examine the authority levels of employees to place orders, to sign purchase invoices, and to authorise payments out. If it appears that large numbers of approvals have been given by a limited number of individuals close to the authority level, this may give cause for concern. It is entirely possible that the levels are now out of date and need to be reviewed, but the investigators should be alert to the possibility of invoice splitting, ie where fraudulent invoices are artificially split to get otherwise large totals under the supervision limits.

5 Credit cards issued in the organisation's name as well as those used by individual employees and managers are vulnerable. This is particularly so in the area of transport frauds. The first step would be to check the fuel consumption records for all organisation vehicles and to look for patterns of use by all drivers—the consistent use of the same filling station in a distant town may

suggest collusion with the forecourt staff; similarly, re-use of the same credit card on the same day at the same filling station may be an indicator of fraud. Sadly, both the practice of inflating, and of creating entirely fictitious, fuel purchases are an institutionalised method of fraud. Thus, if the credit card voucher is made out for more fuel than is put into the tank, this allows the forecourt attendant to remove the inflated surplus amount of cash which is then shared with the driver.

15.7.4 Tests to detect possible corruption

It is a popular myth that although bribery is common in many Third World countries, it is not a problem in Britain. In fact, it is a common method of fraud and, potentially, it involves all those employees or managers who are in a position to influence a decision in favour of a third party. The organisation is particularly vulnerable in the activities of purchasing and procurement, and one or more of the following strategies should be adopted, the regularity of use depending upon the level of exposure to loss:

1 One starting point would be to take a number of the competitive tenders submitted to the organisation and to carefully investigate the backgrounds of those tendering, whether they were successful or not. The investigators should look for any evidence of common links between the third parties. This tests to see whether there has been any collusion or even bid rigging between the supposedly independent persons or organisations.

2 Even though the best value tender may have been accepted, this does not mean that the best price will be paid. The investigators should select a small number of contracts, particularly where the supplier has no published price list, where charges are on a cost-plus basis or where the contractors' charges are based on third party invoices. There are a number of key indicators of possible fraud which may be found, for instance:
   (a) labour or materials costs which appear to be above the industry norms,
   (b) goods or services which have been supplied outside the normal course of business, substantial time or performance overruns and retrospective emergency extensions to the basic contract prices, or
   (c) supporting charges which are incapable of independent verification.

In this way, it should be possible to identify those cases in which inflated prices have been approved and paid. As in 15.7.3, the investigators should then list the authority levels of employees to place orders and sign purchase invoices. By analysing a random selection of purchase invoices in favour of individual suppliers, it may be possible to detect cases of corruption supported by order and invoice splitting. Thus, an employee with an authority limit of say £5,000 will place orders with favoured suppliers above this amount. The organisation will be invoiced and approved by splitting the charges, usually in amounts just below the authority level.

As a further check against bid rigging, it may be expedient to check the ownership of suspected companies and their associates. It may also be sensible to look for similarities in the way in which the tender documents have been prepared and in the signatures.

15.7.5 Tests to detect the conversion of outgoing cheques

The organisation may be aiming to detect the misappropriation of its own funds, but can also gain information which might suggest that a customer or client is a victim of fraud (whether those suspicions should be communicated to the client/customer is an interesting socio-legal issue). The main tests are:

1 To examine a random sample of cheques supposedly cancelled and returned through the banking system to discover:
   (a) endorsements to third parties which may give rise to suspicions,
   (b) cheques paid through building society accounts instead of the conventional business accounts,

(c) cheques in favour of non-commercial customers or non-standard clients, eg a bank where the cheque might have been used to buy a bankers draft,
(d) renumbered cheques,
(e) cheques which are mere photocopies, which prove not to have been cancelled or which are missing.

2 To critically evaluate the methods adopted by the organisation for the preparation and balancing of the payroll and other payment tapes prior to transmission of the relevant data to the banker. It is relatively common where there are hardware compatibilities, for disks and tapes to be sent to the bank for automatic payment. In these systems, the bank will usually only show a global sum as a debit rather than listing the individual debits, so there is considerable scope for the diversion of funds.

15.7.6 Tests to detect the theft of incoming cheques

This is one of the more difficult frauds to detect, whether the source of the cheques is internal or external to the organisation. Success depends on the organisation's expectations as to the probability of the payment arriving, and as to the manner in which the cheques would be handled upon receipt.

1 If the investigators decide to act without reference to third parties, their first step should be to obtain a selection of original paying-in slips from the bank, and to compare these with retained duplicates, looking for differences between the amount of cash and cheques deposited. Often unrecorded or improperly recorded cheques will be used to conceal thefts of cash, or differences in dates of payment in, or omitted or abbreviated names of payees may be used to delay or endlessly defer the discovery of the loss, eg by adjusting time and manipulating credits on a group of accounts to make it appear that the residual debits on each account are within credit limits. This is part of the more general problem that credits from one customer can be applied to the accounts of others to conceal previous thefts, so it is advisable to trace sample entries to ensure that this is not happening.

2 The investigators should take particular care to verify those paying-in slips which:
(a) only show a global sum and not details of individual credits,
(b) omit to show the payees' names,
(c) are not originals but photocopies,
(d) have no bank stamp of authentication,
(e) appear to have been altered.

3 Finally, the investigators should write to a randomly selected sample of customers asking for details of all payments made to the organisation in a given time period. If the customers are prepared to co-operate (the organisation may have to agree to meet the customers' costs in extracting and supplying this information, or the information can be supplied on a reciprocal basis) and there is no collusion with the in-house criminals, this is a foolproof way in which to detect suppressed income. The investigators may even consider it expedient to visit key third parties to pursue external verification.

15.7.7 Tests to detect frauds in sales and marketing

The standard techniques of fraud in this area of commercial activity are usually based on suppression, the aim being to acquire goods or services without being charged for them or to convert incoming payments. The need is therefore to detect uninvoiced sales, underpriced sales, or the adjustment of posted entries:

1 The first step is to examine the way in which sales orders are obtained and then to trace a selection through to the final invoices and debits to customers' accounts —the creation of false sales credits is a common method of fraud, which to succeed must be passed into the sales ledger. Thieves may not be able to create false source documents to support these entries. Tests of this nature will allow the theoretical expectations to be measured against the reality. It should also be possible to test that there is no second (off-record) sales system by making test purchases and looking for informal sales records.

2 Following 15.7.3, a survey of the master files and sales ledgers may disclose cases in which source data, master files, journal vouchers and suspense accounts have been manipulated — eg accounts where there is a high ratio of credits other than cash —NB that cancelled orders and credit notes are critical signs of manipulation.

3 It is then sensible to check the delivery notes and invoices for any signs of alteration or modification. This should detect one of the more common frauds which is to process an order for a third party customer as if it was an inter-branch transfer of stock; after pricing, the name on the invoice is simply changed. Similarly, frequent adjustments favouring particular customers can be a symptom of fraud.

4 The investigators should then randomly attempt to inspect all those goods which have:

(a) been issued free to other branches or associates,
(b) been sent to remote warehouses or similar facilities for storage,
(c) been placed ready for sale as scrap,
(d) been used for advertising or promotion purposes, or
(e) otherwise left the premises without a third party account being debited.

Such entries in the stock control accounts are well recognised cloaks for fraud, either by writing off the value of the stock, or by making it more difficult to identify stock shortages through not having the goods immediately available for inspection.

5 On occasions, the criminal is obliged to channel income into the organisation before appropriating it. In such circumstances, the income cannot be shown as part of the normal gross receipts of the organisation because its subsequent removal will be too obvious. The investigators should therefore check and verify all the non-standard receipts—eg insurance refunds, claims payouts, bad debt dividends, royalties, etc which would not be shown as receivables in a sales ledger.

6 Care should be taken to investigate alleged sales of unwanted fixed assets, scrapped products and raw materials, with particular reference to sales of shop-soiled goods, and to cash and staff sales. The task is to verify the completeness of each recorded transaction and this may well require that reference is made to the third party buyers whenever they can be identified.

7 Finally, the investigators should carefully read through the correspondence files to look for and follow up all the clear complaints of errors in invoices and statements —these may be signs of frauds.

15.7.8 Tests to detect stock, asset and inventory losses

Inventory control depends on an interlocking documentary system which should show the arrival of specific materials, their place of storage before, during and after processing, and the date and destination of their delivery out. All organisations are at risk at the beginning of this recording process because suppliers or dishonest delivery drivers may deliver short quantities. The recording process is also fallible because many items of value are not included in the standard inventory as assets, eg trade secrets and confidential data, stationery, and the paid-time of employees (which may be stolen through moonlighting or inflation of hours worked). Organisations should install a set of procedures to verify the physical receipt of assets and stock, and reappraise their classification of assets, ensuring that proper day-to-day controls are in place. These controls should be targeted on known vulnerabilities, for instance that physical assets and inventories can be affected by sales suppression, purchase inflation, etc. Annual stocktaking assumes particular importance in this overall process. The main forms of test focus on the following points:

1 The organisation should consider the nature of its operation in the light of past records, and identify those product lines which should have, and which actually have as recorded, the longest turnover periods. There are several possible points involved here. As a statement of the obvious, fictitious stock can never be sold. It will sit as a mere book asset and appear to be under-utilised capital. Similarly, the device of changing the classification of the missing stock to lines known to be very slow moving is a way of delaying the discovery of the loss. The investigators should also beware new product lines which do not appear to sell well or at all, or stock lines held over from previous years, but now out of stock - it will be particularly suspicious if adjustments are made to book stock in the time just before, or as a result of stock checks.

2 It is a sound policy to check that all fully depreciated assets are still held. If it is proposed to

dispose of assets of significant book value as scrap, they should be independently appraised, ie the aim is to detect stock thefts or the concealment of frauds.

3 The investigators should formally audit the schedules of the previous year's stock taking. In particular, they should consider the reasonableness of the alleged stock holdings both in relation to turnover and in relation to storage space available. If the rates of return on capital invested are low on highly portable stock lines, or if the physical volume of stock appears to exceed available storage space, detailed enquiries should be made.

4 To assist in discovering how stock losses are achieved or concealed, it is a good strategy to examine the employees' work records during the critical periods of time. To conceal stock losses, it may be necessary to move stock from warehouse to warehouse so that it can be double counted. This movement must appear as unusual levels of time invested by the staff, or sudden increases in internal transport demands. Similarly, it is expedient to examine the invoices from independent carriers which may show unauthorised stock movements. To mask the purpose, internal records or invoices received may be lost or amended. All such events should be treated as significant. Finally, it is essential to verify those goods which are alleged to be in transit at the time of stock take.

5 Because it can be arduous to physically stock take some of the standard consumables used by most organisations, care should be taken to examine all those accounts which relate to packaging and the other unconventional stocks where controls might be more lax. Unexpectedly high levels of expenditure on such items are probably an indicator of fraud.

15.7.9 Tests to detect fraud in the general accounts

A detailed statistical appraisal of the main component elements of the accounting system may reveal interesting patterns of behaviour from which manipulation and conversion can be inferred. Hence, to take the accounts related to sales by way of example, the statistics may show changes in the accounts of a group of customers whose volumes of purchases have declined against the normal commercial trend but the levels of cancelled orders and returned goods have increased. This may show that customers are now receiving stolen goods, with the balancing credits being written off as returns. In multiple branch operations, it is useful to make inter-site comparisons in the ratio of cash to credit sales. If some sites have unusually low ratios this may be indicative of the suppression of cash sales. Similarly, it can be revealing to examine both the ratio of bad debts to sales, and the percentages of bad debts recovery on a branch by branch basis. Inconsistent ratios suggest suppression of sales. The mechanism of concealment would be in the bad debt accounts or through the conversion of incoming bad debts dividends. At a level of individual employee performance, an examination of the ratio of successful to unsuccessful calls made by the sales representatives can be an indicator of fraud. Of course, low ratios may evidence nothing more than inefficiency or lack of commitment, but they might equally signal a possible conflict of interests. These examples show the basic approach which can be applied to all the general accounting records to identify possible distortions or departures from normal expectations. The methodology is as follows:

1 Following job sensitivity analysis (see 16.3), to identify the most vulnerable transactions, eg:
   (a) any stock reduction with no corresponding debit to a customer's account,
   (b) writing off the book value of goods, debts or stock,
   (c) the creation of special prices or the giving of unusually generous discounts for the product or the volume purchased,
   (d) sanctioning the free issue of samples or demonstration models,
   (e) any adjustments or modifications to the final accounts;

   the investigators should monitor the operation of the organisation for signs of all the most sensitive possibilities, with a controlled response to all those suspicious circumstances which come to light. The enquiries should be most diligent when the assets and cost elements involved would, in normal circumstances, not be closely controlled, eg repairs to office furniture, office cleaning costs, local advertising costs, or those expense accounts for items which are not included in the detailed manufacturing costing systems.

2 Although there can be quite legitimate reasons for specialist accounts held by departments, it is reasonable to ask the departmental managers to justify the separate treatment of the given funds. In this, it is a useful indicator to consider the attitude of the managers involved. Those

who resent outside interference, may have something to hide. However, whatever the reaction, it must be recognised that all such slush funds which hold monies on the margin of the organisation's accounting system, are potentially easy to exploit. A further incentive may be that, because of the account's non-standard and perhaps embarrassing status, the criminal will suspect that the organisation may be unwilling to prosecute.

3 A full analysis of the accounting system should be undertaken to identify all the suspense accounts and to verify a selection of the postings into and out of those accounts. It would be particularly important to check the reliability both of all the personal accounts which receive credits from suspense accounts, and of all the debit items which are transferred to suspense. Indeed, it may be advisable to verify a sample of all inter-account transfers.

15.7.10 Tests to detect fraud in the payroll

Large payroll frauds are uncommon because too many outside agencies are likely to be involved in the verification of the record keeping. Thus, for example, sooner or later the Inland Revenue and the Department of Social Services will require tax returns and pension details for each false employee created. Although the appearance of reality can be maintained for small numbers of inventees, particularly if they are apparently on a part-time basis, larger scale frauds are more difficult. However, one or two modestly paid false employees can be a steady drain on revenues, so the following tests are expedient:

1 The investigators should check the details of the more recently recruited employees. This would involve tracing a random selection of names from the payroll records to the personnel files, telephone directories and voters' registers to detect *straw men.*

2 The investigators should take an interest in patterns of pay adjustment. If groups of employees regularly receive additions to their basic entitlements, this might show improper benefits being diverted to dishonest employees or their colleagues.

3 Behavioural patterns may also be significant indicators of fraud. The investigators should look for employees who do not take holidays, or who only take infrequent holidays. Theoretically, criminals rarely take holidays in case their frauds are discovered in their absence, but in practice, most take extremely expensive holidays. Similarly, if groups of employees go to the same holiday address, this may be nothing more than friendship carried on outside the organisation, or it might be evidence of corruption, with benefits being repaid by favours from a customer.

15.7.11 Tests to detect interference with control machinery

All those processes which enable the organisation to measure the quantity or volume of materials for pricing and valuation purposes, should be treated as vulnerable, eg all the weighbridges, meters, scales, etc used by the organisation to control inventories or the despatch or receipt of goods. The basic method to enforce security relies upon:

1 The identification by the investigators of the possible ways in which these devices can be modified. Each such modification would have certain consequences, some of which would cause loss to the organisation. The responsibility would then be to work out what symptoms to look for in the operation of each device.

2 If employees are experimenting with critical measuring devices, there may be a sign of the interference in the repair and service records—early trials may simply have broken the device or produced too aberrant a set of readings so that the machine had to be represented as broken.

15.7.12 Tests to detect fraud in the transport system

All the aspects of transportation can represent a significant component element in the variable costs of an organisation, whether as a drain on capital or revenue, or as a drag on the profitability of the commercial organisation. One of the problems is that a significant number of situations are not under the direct control of the organisation, but depend upon the accuracy of the reporting procedures from the employees involved. The tests must therefore search for inconsistency in the evidence and other symptoms of fraud.

1 Many frauds can relate to the supply of new vehicles and of spares and replacement parts. It is therefore advisable to check a random selection of vehicles to ensure that they are as described in the sales invoices and inventory. Similarly, checks should regularly be made on the maintenance and service records for reasonableness given the declared age and level of use. One element which is particularly vulnerable is the tyre which can be irreparably damaged while on the road and require immediate replacement. If the tyre is reasonably new, the fraud is either not to replace it at all or, say, to sell the used tyre as a remould through the collusion of the tyre company. The investigators should therefore sample invoices for new tyres and ask for evidence to verify each replacement where there is no independent confirmation of need. In this, note that the tyres for the larger articulated vehicles are expensive. They usually carry serial numbers and it is more likely that they can be traced.

2 The auditors should also verify the general cost justifications for the purchase of new vehicles, tyres, parts and maintenance, tracing a selection of parts to scrap. It is also useful to check the industry norms for, and the actually claimed petrol/diesel of the fleet vehicles—this should help to detect short deliveries of bulk fuel as well as agency credit card frauds (see 15.7.3). As a routine exercise, the routing sheets of the delivery drivers (which, in any event, should be allocated on a random basis) should be scrutinised. The point is to look for alterations of the loads, the drivers and the customers. If a driver is regularly switching routes to a given area, this may be to create better opportunities for fraud.

15.7.13 Tests to detect computer abuse

There is a wide range of possible abuses, from the theft of machine time by employees using their employer's system for their own private gain, to the complete loss of data integrity through fraud or malice. The level of activity in this area depends on the degree of perceived risk. The following represents a sample of possible tests:

1 A detailed appraisal of the methods of control over the issue and use of passwords, and of all the more critical parts of the logical access system could be carried out (see 14.2.2).

2 If there is a real possibility that unauthorised amendments have been made to the more sensitive resources, the auditors should make an object code comparison, seeking to reconcile the source program with the current version to check for any signs of program manipulation.

3 Without alerting the operators who may be actively colluding with the individuals abusing the computer system, the auditors should connect a duplicate printer to the CPU. This will produce a separate console log output which has not been tampered with, for comparison with the operational copy to detect any unauthorised use of resources.

4 For the most extreme cases, covert CCTV coverage of the operations room may reveal the precise nature of any unauthorised use and breaches of procedure.

5 Detailed audits of the back-up library will help to uncover cases of deliberate damage.

6 For internal monitoring purposes, there should be tests to see whether the system is being used by hackers for the playing of games or the setting up of bulletin boards. These tests may also uncover losses of data or the misuse of confidential information, malicious damage, etc. For outside threats arising from the use of dial port lines, the auditors should monitor remote access and check for evidence of unauthorised access or hacking. One of the first signs will be shown on the console logs which will list repeated abortive efforts to log on. If this is shown some months before the date of the audit, it will be wise to assume that the hacker has achieved entry and has taken steps to preserve the privileges obtained within the system—NB because of the passage of time, it may be probable that the back-up media have also been corrupted. In all cases, the victim must take care that whatever action is taken does not prompt retaliation from the hacker until there is positive assurance that any damage can be limited. The first step is to try to identify the hacker without alerting him or her, while discovering which files have been compromised. It can be a good strategy to create a new program which will allow the hacker to obtain traceable goods or services, and to follow those goods or services back to the hacker. Alternatively, the investigators should break into the hacker's files, making it appear that

another hacker has obtained his or her passwords, and allow the two hackers to establish contact. As a final possibility, British Telecom may be invited to trace the hacker on-line, but it must be recognised that this can be a long and difficult process (see 14.6).

15.7.14 Audit trails

Each of the individual tests described in 15.7 must also be placed into a proper organisational context. Indeed, to conduct an auditing investigation only on the basis of constituent elements and without verifying the inter-relationships between the elements for internal consistency, would be to court disaster. The first step is to produce a series of audit trails. An audit or information trail is usually produced by using flowcharting techniques to detail the links between the different elements in a given transaction. The end product can be described as a chain of evidence provided through coding, cross-references and documentation connecting account balances and other summary results with original transactions and calculations. For example, in a manual system individual cash receipts would, in the first instance, be linked to remittance advice notes and to receipts listings, say shown on a till roll or other recording system. Such entries would then lead to the cash receipts journal and be tied to a bank paying-in book and the bank statements which could be the subject of reconciliation checks. Ultimately, there would be postings to the customer's account to show the current state of indebtedness and to the general sales ledger. The preparation of adequate audit trails is important because:

1 it is required by law as a part of the general duty to maintain proper accounting records for reporting and taxation purposes;
2 the management of any organisation needs to be able to trace source documents, eg to enable proper answers to be given to queries from customers or suppliers; and
3 as a part of the reporting requirements under the Companies Act 1985, the Rules of The Stock Exchange relating to member firms' accounts, and the statutes regulating insurance companies, building societies, friendly societies, etc, the auditor should be in a position to certify that the information presented in the final accounts gives a true and fair view of the organisation's trading position, and the only way to be sure is by tracing a representative sample of the source documents.

The auditor should subject the audit trails to extended compliance tests. Documents should be selected from the various stages in the system so that they may be verified in depth (sometimes called *cradle to grave testing*). Thus, an entry for issues of stock in the stock records should be supported by sales order, despatch note, sales invoice, etc, and the sales invoice should be supported by sales order, sales despatch note, entry in stock records, entry in debtor's ledger and subsequent payment, and so on.

In a computer system, the cash receipts data is likely to be transformed into machine-readable form soon after the transaction occurs. In some systems, the data may be transcribed from a remittance advice (a form of source document) to a magnetic tape storage device. The data appears as output in the form of computer print out, representing a combination of a sales journal and a cash receipts journal. The general ledger data may be stored on magnetic tape. In other systems, the data may be transformed into machine-readable form and processed into a general ledger entry as the cash receipts transaction occurs.

In a manual system, the trail may be relatively easy to follow because the recording of transactions is split into discrete actions, but in a computer system there may be breaks in the trail because:

1 data no longer considered necessary may be deleted to save space in the memory;
2 data may be kept on magnetic files only and may therefore not be immediately human-readable;
3 source documents may be sorted by computer, making it unnecessary to hold them in easily accessible order;
4 reports may contain summary information only, giving no reference to source documentation; and
5 transactions may be initiated by the computer program itself, eg in an automated JIT system,

purchase orders may be prepared automatically when minimum specified stock levels have been reached.

Thus, in a computer system a sales ledger may be updated by a sales invoice to create an open entry in the ledger held on computer file. If the sales ledger were to be printed out at this time, the trail would be intact. When the debtor pays the invoice, the computer system is likely to remove the open entry from the file and, if the auditor were then to take a copy of the file, the trail would be broken. If the system has been designed without consultation with the auditor, the solution is either to make more frequent visits to the organisation to be audited, taking more hard copies of the files and reconciling the transaction records, or to attach identification codes to selected transactions with a view both to tracing them through the system, and to obtaining satisfactory evidence that they have been properly processed. If the auditor has been involved in the initial design of the computer system, proper controls and tests upon accuracy can be built in from the outset (see 15.1.2). In a batch-mode system, verification procedures are more straightforward because processing occurs in discrete and sequential stages. In real-time or on-line systems it is often neither reasonable nor practical to take hard copy of every transaction. The answer is therefore to create special audit files where records of the sensitive transactions are recorded.

15.8 DETECTION METHODOLOGY CONCLUSIONS

This last group of methodologies must be seen against the background that some victims are prepared to tolerate small losses, possibly because it is believed the frauds are institutionalised and cannot be stopped, or because it is considered that the organisation will benefit in some way by allowing it to continue. Yet, even on a small scale, condoned crime creates an environment in which employees can begin the process of rationalising major dishonesty—it is the thin end of the wedge.

All of the methods for the detection of fraud which have been listed rely on a series of simple propositions:

1 The one who most needs to conceal a fraud is the one whose guilt would otherwise be obvious.
2 All those thefts which are opportunist in nature have little likelihood of detection unless effective security checks always show the identity of people in each area so that loss can be tied to presence.
3 The more violent smash and grab theft tactics rely either on fast escape and/or on being able to preserve the anonymity of the robbers.
4 Most frauds leave traces which careful auditing can detect. Thus, for example, the conversion of cheques can be achieved in a variety of ways, eg:
   (a) the cheque can be cashed by opening an account in the name of the payee and paying it in for later encashment,
   (b) the cheque can be endorsed as if by the payee and the cheque paid into a safe account, or
   (c) the thief can simply alter name of payee, etc.

   But the cheques, stamped by the collecting bank, will be returned to the drawing organisation in the ordinary course of events. Scrutiny of the cheques can disclose irregularities. But this emphasises the need to separate administrative functions. It would be fatal if the person who diverted the cheque on the way out could dishonestly destroy the evidence after its return through the clearing system.
5 Most long-term frauds rely on collusion. Thus, for example, it is easier to explain account credits or stolen goods if the receiver is already a customer or client of the victim organisation. It is a natural part of a commercial organisation's function to make credits for goods returned. Similarly, it is easier to explain the delivery to, or the presence of goods in, a given warehouse or store if those facilities belong to an existing customer.

SUMMARY

The key points covered in this chapter are that:

1 The best security designs are those which have been exposed to constructive criticism and

review by all who will be involved both in the design and in the use of the system.

2 The best human controls depend upon separation of functions both between individuals and between departments. Automatic controls rely upon checking the arithmetic and the internal consistency of the input.

3 Distributed systems may have significant advantages, but security is a real problem. If intrusion cannot be prevented, the organisation must consider producing an intrusion tolerant system.

4 Although microcomputers have become powerful devices at an economical price, they create significant security problems both as stand-alone machines and as terminal gateways into a distributed system.

5 The auditor's primary duty is to check on the effectiveness of the controls within the systems and to validate the data which the systems contain.

6 Fraud inevitably depends upon the creation of false accounting records. Every organisation is therefore obliged to undertake a series of tests to determine whether fraud may be taking place. If a fraud is suspected, evidence should be collected with a view to prosecution.

QUESTIONS *Solutions to questions of an examination standard start on p 395*

Write brief notes on the following:

(a) basic principles for data security system design;
(b) techniques of input data verification;
(c) the stages of the auditing function;
(d) the most effective strategies for fraud.

Questions of an examination standard

1 'The very technology that gave us microcomputer hardware has made them an unguarded bonanza.' (Cronin)

Discuss the security problems which may face the management of an organisation which seeks to implement a *one-per-desk* policy by networking a large number of microcomputers in various offices throughout the organisation.

2 All organisations which employ a computer-based information system are exposed to the possibility of fraud, and should have a contingency plan or detection methodology prepared.

List and briefly describe the actions which management could plan to take when a computer fraud is suspected.

Chapter 16

Personnel and Back-up Issues

CHAPTER OBJECTIVES

This chapter concentrates on the personnel issues implicit in the development and maintenance of an organisation's security systems. In particular, it identifies:

1. the need for each organisation to establish both a practical and an ethical framework within which security is to be maintained;
2. the fact that the practicality of fraud detection and investigation is a phenomenon which may prejudice labour relations;
3. that job sensitivity analysis can be effective to identify vulnerabilities;
4. the role of the auditor in the modern world of the automated information system; and
5. the main strategies which an organisation should consider to enable it to recover from a disaster.

16.1 THE PLANNING FRAMEWORK

It is a characteristic of modern society that every person, both natural and juridic (eg a limited company is an artificial legal person) has the right to protect his or her property, income, safety and security. Sometimes these protective rights are replicated and reinforced as express or implied duties owed by the employing organisation to its employees, by a local authority to its ratepayers, or by a company to its shareholders. However, no matter what the legal requirements, all organisations have a direct interest in promoting security-based duties to protect both their own capital and revenue, and the safety and economic well-being of their employees. This arises because security is inevitably allied to profitability in the commercial sector, and to efficiency and cost accountability in the public sector.

Thus, as well as setting the framework for a more detailed policy and procedures on security and control, each organisation should set the moral and ethical tone of the employment. This means that, wherever relevant, certain minimum standards should be established in an ethics policy which addresses the behaviour of all the employees in all those situations which might, for example, give rise to:

(a) a conflict of interest,
(b) the opportunity for insider dealing,
(c) the abuse of confidential information, etc.

It must be recognised that written policies in themselves cannot solve even the simplest security problems, but they are important in setting the ground rules and expectations of those involved. More detailed provisions attributing appropriate levels of professional and personal responsibility should therefore be included in all employees' contracts of employment and/or job descriptions, and in any contracts with third parties where there is an identifiable element of risk. For these purposes, it must be remembered that the managing director of a top commercial corporation is just as much an employee as a minor data preparation clerk.

When planning the administration of security matters, the organisation should identify a specific individual who is to have the responsibility for counselling on and maintaining security. This should be a senior management post, visibly supported by the most senior managers. The function should be to advise both horizontally and vertically within the organisation, and to assume overall responsibility for the enforcement of obligations at all levels within the organisation and against third parties. The creation and support of such a post will, for the purposes of later determining and mitigating legal liability in the event of loss, show that the management was acting prudently. However, this appointment should not be in a vacuum. It should be accompanied by organisation procedures for the screening and appointment of staff, the classification and protection of information, the screening of new investments, data protection standards, contingency planning, incident reporting, etc, although their depth and detail will vary with the size and complexity of organisation involved.

There also has to be significant commitment to education and training at every level within the organisation so that the process of change can be properly managed. All those actually or likely to be affected by changes in working practices must understand the new systems and the problems of using them efficiently. Even after basic appreciation input, employees who do not begin using the systems immediately will need refresher courses, and those who have regular practice should be shown how to consolidate and improve upon their skills and be up-dated in any amendments to the systems. It is a good policy to ensure that all relevant staff are well versed in the standard operating procedures laid down within the organisation. This will allow for covering if colleagues are absent from work for any reason, and in the event of an emergency when flexibility of response from employees may be the key to a successful recovery.

It is therefore sensible either to prepare accessible documentation which assumes nothing and is regularly updated, or to provide Computer Based Training systems (CBT) whether stand-alone, or embedded within the operating system or the resources themselves. Staff will then be able to rapidly familiarise themselves with the relevant procedures. But this must be seen against the need, in some organisations, to control and restrict general access to information about the operating procedures. The answer is that all those procedures which are actually in operation should be designed bearing in mind the level of security required in each aspect of the office environment. Hence, levels of security more appropiate to mainframe operations in a sensitive government establishment will not be appreciated in a conventional commercial office. Moreover, whatever the overall system in operation, the staff should understand why things are to be done, what policies underpin those procedures and what the likely effects of applying those procedures will be to them. People are generally more supportive if they understand the reasons for the system. Finally, the organisation should meet the moral and statutory requirements of providing a working environment which is both healthy and safe.

16.2 SECURITY PLANNING FOR PEOPLE

To commit a fraud in an organisation exploiting an information system, the wrongdoer must have access to the computer system. As indicated in Chapter 15, most fraud involves the falsification of input, ie that additional data is entered or suppressed to make accounts appear to balance. One example of opportunist fraud by an employee would depend upon the falsification of transaction codes which would post entries to the wrong accounts. Such a scheme has the merit that often packages have many codes built-in but only a few are used by each customer. By checking in the manual, it is possible to identify unused possibilities which can be exploited. But if the mispostings are identified and traced back, it is easy to explain the entries as an error. The existence of such possibilities produces real risks given that, in many organisations, dedicated keyboards have been replaced by intelligent terminals which can access many more resources, and that high level privileges are frequently granted to too many people. Abuse of access may therefore arise through a simple breach of the trust placed in the given employee, or it may be access by an outsider through skill, eg through dial-up facilities and the breach of the inadequate passwording systems installed to control access. Planning must therefore take account of the known vulnerabilities in the communications systems to tapping and to remote and unauthorised access.

Most frauds have obvious symptoms, and the principal detection strategy relies upon noticing deviations from the norm. In fact, because employees can be driven on by greed, and are forced to manipulate records over a period of time, there are more likely to be signs. Then, once suspicions have been raised, but there are doubts about the precise nature of the fraud (if any), a good rule is to ignore the apparent records and to follow the asset. Similarly, if documents are missing, the person to suspect is the person who would have been suspected had incorrect documents been found. Fraud detection should be a routine part of any business. The main objective of detection procedures is long-term deterrence, with the bonus of recovering a part or all of the assets lost in the immediate fraud detected. To that extent, the investigative process is an aspect of personnel management and should not be seen as a mere by-product of standard auditing. It is a function that requires separate resourcing. Almost all organisations have vulnerable points where fraud is most likely to occur. These critical points should be identified and specially watched. This can usually be done discreetly, eg by analysing trends, and therefore avoiding prejudice to employer/employee relations. But checks should never be restricted to statistical methodologies. Detailed sampling checks should always be made on individual items, regardless of the possible threat to labour relations. If the auditing staff have been properly trained, and the staff to be investigated have a constructive view of the process, there should be minimum friction arising from the disruption.

However, because all audits disrupt the normal working routines, they should be carefully planned to maintain a good level of staff morale and to avoid appearing either provocative or overly paranoid. The manner and attitude of the auditing staff is a critical factor. Those recruited for the task should not be regular employees in the area(s) under review. The expectation is that such individuals are more likely to be objective, to see through plausible excuses, and to avoid friendships which might colour judgments. Once the team has been recruited and the audit planned, it is best to carry out the checks by suprise even though this may introduce a confrontational element between the audit team and the affected employees. Further, the team should not examine too large a part of the organisation over too long a period of time, because this may disrupt the operation too much.

There are two basic types of test that can be performed:

1 **The historical**—it is useful to go back through records held centrally because this avoids overly upsetting the staff under consideration, and it does not disrupt routine operations. But this type of test is limited in its usefulness because it does not detect the live frauds which await concealment.
2 **Proportional and inter-company analysis**—this looks to see how reasonable the entries in accounts are by comparing them with those held in other branches (if the organisation is large enough) or by analysis in the light of historical and/or industry trends. The tests are based on the budgetary records, trial balances and resultant final accounts. A thief cannot guarantee complete regularity of behaviour because the method of fraud is often dependent on opportunity. Inconsistency in behaviour or in the records is a sign of manipulation. To test the quality of the record keeping, information least likely to have been manipulated should be taken as the prime indicator of potential profitability. All other accounts should then be examined to check for deviations and distortions. Where similar companies or branches cannot be found for comparison, the auditors should take average performance figures from the trade (this information is usually available from a trade association or government departments).

It can be useful to suddenly and closely supervise a department in an attempt to produce a fraud-free period of operation for comparative purposes. However, such an exercise is expensive and depends upon having effective auditing staff. If the decision is taken to adopt the strategy, it is important to focus on the critical points in the organisation, using known vulnerabilities and a logic tree approach to show what conditions must exist for fraud to be possible, ie an admixture of the availability of vulnerable assets, poor controls, inadequate supervision and, possibly, suspect staff. It is important to retain these controls for at least 14 days. There are a variety of reasons for this:

(a) thieves often live up to their income and may need to continue the fraud to meet newly acquired commitments,
(b) they may be arrogant enough to believe that the fraud is undetectable,
(c) they may consider the investigation a challenge and enjoy the game of continuing the fraud while under scrutiny, or
(d) they may recognise that if the fraud stops, the operational pattern will change, thus revealing the existence and methodology of the fraud.

Such factors may lead to catching the person in the act. Even if no-one is immediately caught, there is still the prospect of a double benefit should fraud be taking place. This is because the auditing activity is not only likely to produce a deterrent effect through the enhanced chances of detection, but if the fraudulent activities are suspended, reliable comparative data emerges. Subsequent check results in terms of stock losses, sales increases or purchasing decreases, changes in work patterns (eg less overtime claimed), and other changes (eg number of goods damaged or returned for credit) may then be strongly indicative of the method of fraud being employed.

As indicated, organisations should investigate all suspicious situations because this may recover funds, prevent repetition and perhaps as importantly, it may clear the reputation of innocent people who are known to be under suspicion. If potential wrongdoers are identified, the organisation should invite the State to prosecute because it should be the task of society to decide on the guilt or innocence of those suspected. Moreover, only the State has the right to administer the theories of deterrence and rehabilitation through the decision of whether to prosecute and in the trial itself. In fact, a failure of the victim to prosecute gives the wrong signals to other, as yet, undetected wrongdoers and offers no warning to prospective employers of the proven unreliability in job applicants.

But there has been considerable debate as to whether the average person serving on a jury is able to understand or qualified to judge complex fraud cases. The right to jury trial is said to be the corner-stone of the British system of justice, yet the right to sit on a jury is not qualified by an intelligence or even a literacy test. It is therefore suggested that a judge, perhaps sitting with expert lay assessors, would be more effective as a decision-maker and more economical of court time. But, so entrenched is the concept of the jury, that there is little likelihood of any immediate change being made. Moreover, no matter what the composition of the jury, if there is a conviction, it is perhaps indicative of judicial attitudes that sentencing following conviction for non-violent fraud offences is often too lenient to represent a genuine deterrent.

If the prosecution fails, say because the jury fails to understand the prosecution case and thus gives the accused the benefit of the doubt, this may prejudice the other methods for recovering assets lost. Further, even if a conviction is achieved, the passage of time between detection, the criminal proceedings and the civil pre-trial procedure, may make it difficult to then conduct the civil proceedings, eg witnesses may die or leave the country, and they will start to forget what happened, making it difficult to sustain the appearance of credibility under cross-examination in the civil hearing. To add insult to injury, the organisation may also have to carry the salaries of the accused staff on suspension, at least pending the outcome of the criminal case. There is also the possibility of adverse publicity. In reporting both the criminal and the civil trial, the news media may highlight the poor accounting systems and controls which are exposed and this may undermine public confidence in the organisation. However, in many ways, the loss of confidence is actually justified, so the suppression of evidence and the prevention of a prosecution amounts to a different kind of fraud on the public. Indeed, if the truth does eventually emerge, the cover-up may be considered far more damaging.

It is encouraging for the criminal to know that a prosecution is unlikely. Other organisations may be damaged through copycat frauds following a detailed public discussion of fraud methodology and this may encourage a more private means of dealing with identified fraudsters. This form of pressure makes all investigations somewhat contentious and difficult because of both internal and external political considerations. Organisations should minimise the level of internal dispute by having a formalised policy to avoid having to take individual case decisions. If prosecution is the norm, the police should be involved early to ensure that evidence is prepared in a way most likely to be compatible with the Crown Prosecution Service's requirements. The effect of the investigation on employee morale should also be considered. If the decision to investigate is obviously fair, few problems are likely to emerge. But if employees feel they are being unfairly victimised, some trouble is inevitable. The purpose of any major investigation should therefore be explained to the staff at the earliest possible moment consistent with not warning the criminals and permitting them to destroy vital records of their fraud. Overall, there must be no sympathy for the thief who has been wrecking the profitability or service-effectiveness of the organisation.

The organisation must make a decison about the extent to which it is going to introduce security systems. There is an irony in that the more elaborate the preventive or counter-measures adopted, the more the thief may be driven to sophistication to get round the controls. The organisation therefore remains a victim. Further, if the controls are too strong, their inflexibility may well interrupt the otherwise smooth operation of the organisation, but if they are too weak, thieves will be tempted to exploit the situation. Perhaps it is not too naive to hope that fraud is less likely in an organisation which promotes an honest and happy atmosphere. The honesty and vigilance of colleagues will enhance the risks of detection, and a high level of employee satisfaction may minimise motives for fraud. The tone and culture of an organisation is set by the top management. If an organisation is seen to be sloppy and inefficient, there is more of an incentive to steal from it. Effective management policies set standards and assign responsibilities, recognising that security is essentially a line management issue. Each department should be required to budget for security and, in appropriate cases, the costs of any disclosed losses should be charged to the budgets of appropriate managers, with compensatory credit given for losses recovered when considering salary and promotion.

Overall, a reasonable conclusion is that the probability of detection depends upon:

(a) the size of the organisation,
(b) the number of transactions involved,
(c) the scale of the fraud, and
(d) the commitment of the staff at all levels to producing a regime in which the opportunities for fraud are reduced.

16.3 JOB SENSITIVITY ANALYSIS

Upon analysis, it should be obvious that each job in every organisation has a potentially different level of opportunity for fraud. The actual level will depend upon factors such as the ability to gain access to critical resources, the skills of those involved, and the amount of time available to plan and execute the fraudulent plans. **Job sensitivity analysis** is a modification of **perpetrator analysis** (see 12.1), and is a review system to identify risks by examining the operation of the organisation from the point of view of the potential thief. Each security department in all organisations should identify those assets at risk and list them in order of probability of damage or loss, ie decisions should be made as to the likelihood that anyone might want to steal each class of asset—in part this will be determined by how attractive each item will be to thieves; hence, cash has high value, and as a low bulk item, is very attractive. It should then be possible to identify who would have the ability to take each class of asset with a good chance of success. This analysis should include both one-off opportunities and all the standard methods of fraud. This form of evaluation is based upon a series of general propositions, eg that:

1 the more senior the employee, the greater his or her discretion to operate outside normal controls,
2 it is easier for fraud to occur when supervisory managers are under pressure,
3 many subordinates now have greater skills than the managers,
4 branch offices, single occupancy offices or travelling employees represent a greater risk.

Security staff will then look for danger signs from the employees such as:

(a) unexplained wealth which may show itself through high cash spending, gambling, drinking or drug abuse;
(b) social connections with other businesses or organisations which may evidence possible conflicts of loyalty (an inferential sign may be the sudden effectiveness of competitors which might indicate one or more breaches of confidentiality or that there is commercial espionage); or
(c) a general lack of organisation loyalty which may be seen in poor time-keeping, disregard for instructions, dissatisfaction over lack of promotion, or unreasonable self-importance.

If staff who do not conform to the operational norms are identified, the security staff should then consider what reasons have been given for any deviation from the established procedures. This would be particularly important if the given employees have access to high risk procedures, eg those which authorise electronic funds transfer payments, approve contracts or advances to third parties, reconcile bank statements, manage nominal ledger entries, authorise disbursement cheques, etc.

It is then necessary to classify staff by reference to their job status and the criticality of their function. In performing this classification, the security evaluators must compare reality with theory, ie examine the written job descriptions which may have formed the basis of the security system as designed, in the light of the actual tasks performed by each employee once a managerial routine has been established. One element of the review is that some of the staff will be considered to have achieved a professional status, ie they are members of an occupational group, working with computers, with appropriate responsibility as programmers and analysts. As professionals, staff owe a series of interconnected duties:

(a) **to their employers**—in part this will be explicitly contractual, or will be governed by the common law which requires staff to act loyally, etc;
(b) **to their clients**—bureau staff may be hired out to assist client organisations which may be regulated by contract or may be left to the goodwill of all concerned to work out;
(c) **to a fellow professional** in his or her capacity as a professional;
(d) **to society**—if an individual devises a system which damages fellow employees or people in the community, the law may lay down certain minimum standards after the event, but only the professional can, or should, predict likely dangers in advance.

Whether or not individual employees have achieved the dignity of a professional status, ultimately, the growth and development of organisations is dependent upon mutual trust. Trust is required in a series of different relationships, ie both between staff members horizontally and vertically within an organisation, and between that organisation and peer organisations, customers or service-receivers. If computer professionals could not be trusted, the risks of system abuse would be so significant that computers could not be widely used. Although it is accepted that employers could seek to control matters through a contractual framework of disciplinary proceedings, unthinking and routine resort to the big legal stick is always likely to prejudice, and in the long term, sacrifice working relationships. The burden is therefore upon the professional to establish and maintain decision-making or decision-support credibility. This requires that the professionals must remain faithful to their employers and not breach confidentiality, but must maintain proper standards of professional integrity (eg by warning an employer that the proposed amendment to the *status quo* may cause loss to the organisation—this may maintain profitability and may save the employer from possible liability in the civil courts while incidentally protecting the public).

This element of professionalism is of particular importance when the organisation is computerising its information system. Most of those responsible for taking the final decision of whether to buy and install particular computer products will have little direct knowledge of what the operational problems are likely to be, yet the purchase may have a profound effect upon their organisation. Thus, if an organisation buys a good management tool, it may substantially improve profitability and/or efficiency. But if the organisation acquires a system which is defective, it may inflict real damage before the likely effects of the faults are fully appreciated.

The issue is what it is fair to expect the computer designers and manufacturers, the in-house computer managers and the marketing firms to do when it is obvious that there is a lack of expertise in the ultimate organisational decision-makers. Jointly and severally, they have causal responsibility for installing the information system and they may, if they have not used the state of the art standards for their profession, be held legally accountable for any losses which are sustained. This can be particularly important in deciding first, whether there should be litigation, and if so, who should be involved as parties, when the defects in either hardware or software products give rise to breaches in security. The general sale/supply relationship works well when the seller/supplier is honest with the customer during the pre-contractual negotiations. This means that reasonably accurate information has been given to the buyer to permit a properly informed decision to be made as to whether the contract should be finalised. It is obvious that the seller/supplier should not attempt to deceive the customer, but it is not necessarily so clear how much of the truth should be told. The difficulty is that too much information might be just as confusing to the inexperienced buyer, so the real legal issue is the degree of relevance and salience in the information given.

Once the computer hardware is installed, the **systems staff** are in a particularly privileged position because their work gives them a detailed knowledge of many operational aspects critical to the organisation. Moreover, they have considerable freedom of access to both physical and system resources, and become familiar with staff, data and procedures throughout the organisation. All this knowledge and these relationships are essential if the staff are to work towards achieving full system synthesis. Security must start during the design phase so that any risk of threats to the designer or the emerging system are minimised. The most common motives for internal staff to act disloyally are greed, revenge and anger, but other factors like professional arrogance or ignorance can contribute. The results can be positive errors or omissions or general shortcomings in the design, poor documentation, etc. If there is poor control over staff and they are encouraged to work on their own or outside normal office hours, the dangers of both accidental and deliberate threats become more real. To keep proper control, organisational procedures should therefore separate systems staff from programming and operations staff in the the execution of their duties, so that each group will represent a check upon the other, and an intelligently administered supervisory regime is maintained.

In addition to the systems staff, threats from within the organisation by function may be as follows:

1 **Applications programmers**—as for systems analysts and designers, there is a need to take steps to divide responsibilities, set standards, and maintain an effective authorisation system. The possibility of errors or omissions passing through the development stage and into the working programs must be reduced to acceptable levels. In this sense, the programmer is more vital than the analyst. The impact of accidental error can be minimised through detailed testing before the programs are released into the working environment. But following the detection of an error, any amendments to programs can cause difficulty because, at this stage, the software is in a transient state and more vulnerable to accidental damage. Real supervision is therefore necessary to ensure that all the relevant amendment procedures are observed, and that proper records are maintained. Further, it should be a general operating rule that no single programmer should know enough to be able to commit a fraud without a real risk of being discovered; and a programmer should only be allowed access to sensitive data in very special circumstances, eg during the recovery period after a system failure.

2 **Operating staff** receive data for processing and are responsible for disseminating the results to the appropriate users. Any breach in security potentially prejudices data integrity and confidentiality, and may result in the loss of availability of both services and data. Data can be particularly vulnerable in transit and data flow should always be controlled by a responsible person. Data corruption can also easily arise through the careless handling of transmission or storage media, a hardware or software malfunction, incorrect processing, or documents lost or misplaced. One operator working unsupervised can accidentally or deliberately undermine the best security system. Further, the use of the powerful system commands can mask the operator's activities, so independent control must be exercised to minimise the chance that they might be used to influence the system or to wreck the audit trail.

3 **Users** will have a detailed knowledge of the business or operating procedures which could be manipulated to make fraud possible, so their activities must be carefully audited and controlled in the same way as operators.

Threats posed by external staff include:

(a) **Independent contractors**—contract maintenance and cleaning staff can prejudice confidentiality and the availability of services. All externally employed staff who come on to the premises should be supervised as if they were internal staff. Security can be breached by maintenance and other engineers by substituting hardware components, by disabling control mechanisms or by using the powerful software tools on their diagnostic disks to read protected files. All their activities in relation to sensitive equipment and resources should be monitored by competent staff, and any disks containing software used by engineers should be kept under security conditions.

(b) **Third party action**—there could be problems if, for example, the delivery of stationery were to be stopped by suppliers, eg during a strike or other *force majeure* situation (ie one outside the ability of the organisation to control). To provide for such an eventuality and to minimise any loss of availability of service, the organisation should maintain adequate stocks of critical documentation. Similarly, if the electricity supply stopped, say because of a drilling error in road works taking place outside, or the supply was not within hardware tolerances, the organisation would discover whether it had invested in adequate generator back-up facilities.

It is essential for the organisation to select and retain honest and efficient staff, whether on a full-time or contract basis. For these purposes, selection should not be taken to be the same as recruitment. Recruitment attracts applications from either job applicants or service providers, while selection makes the final choice. The costs of choosing the wrong candidate can be enormous. In this, job sensitivity analysis can play a significant part in deciding the level of care required in checking the background and suitability of each candidate. This is achieved because the analysis should have produced an adequate definition of the job to be performed, ie what skills and aptitudes are required, the sensitivity of the job, the highest position the applicant might be expected to reach, etc. The rigour of the checking will be determined by the sensitivity of the job. Application forms may collect information and help to verify the honesty of the candidates—verifying information may be better given to an outside agency to reduce the risk of collusion in the appointment process. In the interview or follow-up to the application form, the applicant can be questioned about any discrepancies which have been discovered. There may be a completely honest reason for the misinformation (eg simple error or misunderstanding about what was required) or it may confirm that the applicant is unsuitable.

16.4 PERSONNEL ISSUES

People represent a threat even if only through their inexperience, incompetence, negligence or curiosity. For these purposes, it is irrelevant that users and their managers may have been made explicitly responsible for maintaining security. If security systems are going to succeed, the active co-operation of all those involved is required at all times during the routine of their work. But people are always a weak link, eg even the most conscientious of employees may forget to log-off or allow an unauthorised person to gain access after temporarily abandoning a terminal or, outside the work environment, talk in an unguarded fashion to strangers (obviously some employees are more likely to be pursuaded than others, eg at conferences or trade fairs, but all should be warned, remembering that employees going through marital or financial troubles are more likely to be distracted from their immediate duties or corrupted).

16.4.1 The dynamics of change

The installation of an information system can represent a significant act of modernisation for any organisation. This can be good for morale if it is properly managed. Employees can draw great confidence from the fact that they are seen to be involved in a progressive organisation, and this can stimulate all those affected to be creative and productive. However, the prospect of change can also be demoralising with staff afraid for their jobs. This is likely to result in a lack of co-operation or even outright opposition to the proposed changes, so the first priority is to establish and communicate a set of organisational goals, with plenty of opportunity built in for consultation and feedback. As an initial step, ideas can be thrown out in an entirely uncritical fashion for comment and evaluation, with everyone invited to comment. If all employees feel that they are well-informed and able to have some influence over their own destiny, they will not feel so threatened by uncertainty. This sense of confidence can be enhanced if, at each critical stage, good training support is offered. People learn through experience. They will accept change more readily if it is implemented in a structured fashion, one step at a time, to allow each person to become familiar with each new phase of the operation before the next step is taken.

Consequently, because change can affect many departments and the third parties with whom the organisation interacts, it is better for all personnel matters to be co-ordinated at a senior level. Adequate liaison with all interested parties during the creation and implementation of plans for change is essential, and because peer organisation may be affected, seniority is vital. From the goal-setting stage, a management team then moves to the planning stage where more detailed consultation with the prospective beneficiaries of the change should lead to the creation of properly defined, costed and scheduled arrangements.

As already indicated, it is essential that a well-respected person should be formally appointed to be responsible for security. Everyone involved in the process of change needs to know who to ask about the risks involved. With a new system, there is a chance to get everything right from the start, so it is important to have a good, security-conscious person in charge during the development stage. It should also be recognised that many end users are being confronted by the reality of computers within a structured information system for the first time, and they will need help. For day-to-day support, they should be supplied with a help-line telephone service (providing a central record of all difficulties and helping to properly target training time). For this purpose, the computer services unit team should have a blend of computer and organisation expertise. If they have a reasonable level of experience, they should be able to quickly allay the usual fears and dispel the standard misconceptions. The appointees should therefore be good communicators and be prepared to service the end users.

16.4.2 Security issues

No matter how good the training, the possibility of accidental error is always present, and this may allow major systems failures to arise. As a result, all reasonable steps must be taken to protect the data. On some occasions, there is the possibility of malicious activity, but it is uneconomic to guard against all the possible causes of data damage except in the most sensitive of activities. The dangers include the insertion of false data. This damages the integrity of the system and may result in fraud and/or the corruption of the data files. Equally, people may read the data and breach confidentiality, or may even steal information so that it is not available for use by the organisation. As a standard precaution, all staff who have access to sensitive data should be vetted, and good clerical and administrative practices should be established in an attempt to minimise risks. In general, human error is more common than deliberate acts of dishonesty. But, since error can conceal the deliberate acts of dishonesty, the reduction of error incidence is essential to maximise auditing effectiveness. It is a typical *wood for the trees* problem. Similarly, when considering physical risks, fire can be accidental or it can be malicious. Thus, once it is acknowledged that all people-based threats cannot be prevented, designers should build in detection systems to allow rapid intervention to limit damage.

All security design must be based upon good psychology and sociology. This is because, in the last analysis, security issues are not simple technical problems. It is inevitable that people will be vital component parts of the system, but they cannot be programmed as if they were machines. In deciding what steps to take, planning teams must consider and reflect upon the fact that people:

(a) may be the source of risk,
(b) may be at risk from others, or
(c) may need protection.

In the first instance, the organisation seeks to implement disaster avoidance measures which are cost-effective in reducing the likelihood of damage while permitting work to proceed in a natural and fluent way. If a disaster does occur, at best the employees' work performance may be prejudiced, at worst the overall system may be prejudiced. Self-evidently, the recovery procedures should seek to limit the extent of that prejudice. When planning the organisation's response to damage which has been caused by an employee, a publicly administered system of deterrent punishment should be considered in the hope that it will either alert the potentially careless to the need to take care, or show the potentially criminal that the costs attendant on detection will outweigh the gains to be made. But, if all else has failed, the system should be changed in an attempt to avoid the problem in the future.

Such steps may be effective in avoiding the effects of the real disasters, but planning needs to take account of the whole spectrum of threats which may be present in the working environment. The concept of employee protection should be sufficiently flexible to include all those factors which may affect the quality of work produced by the workforce. This may include damage to health from causes as diverse as the air conditioning system (Legionnaire's Disease), and the ergonomics of the office lay-out. Staff are vital, if not irreplaceable assets to the organisation, so all should be cared for. Good working conditions, supplemented by the communication of well-structured plans for the protection of staff, help to reduce sickness, absenteeism, and staff turnover, and may also reduce industrial relations problems. Staff morale can also be affected by the intangible quality of the environment, which includes the level of sensitivity with which staff are counselled, appraised or security vetted, threats to privacy if computer-stored data are made available for non-approved purposes, etc. The burden is therefore on the personnel department to co-operate in the production of a safe and paranoia-free workplace.

16.4.3 Functional separation as a security control

Fortunately, most employees are honest, but a standard safeguard is that employees should not be allowed to gain exclusive control over vulnerable functions. Wherever possible, duties should be separated —eg at a practical level, the care of assets and of the records which describe and list those assets should be in different hands. Similarly, separation by function or by transaction ensures that no one person has control over the whole of an administrative system. Indeed, any fraud is more likely to be discovered if jobs are performed jointly or there is some form of job covering or rotation—this is one of the reasons why employees must not be allowed to forego holidays. There are three separate strands of argument:

1 The health of the employee is important and this may be enhanced through rest or a change of activity.

2 Change in personnel helps to uncover frauds which may require continuity of activity or presence to maintain secrecy.

3 However, job rotation will be impractical in many cases because retraining may be uneconomic and inefficient.

The best security controls to protect administrative systems divide sensitive tasks into a series of interdependent steps which must all be performed before the task can be completed. If different people are responsible for each step, this increases the chances of an honest employee noticing the error. Before deciding how functions are to be separated, the security staff should first impose general practical controls, eg account limitations can place ceilings on the amounts which employees can manipulate. Then in sensitive environments, access to information can be restricted on a need-to-know basis, regardless of the rank or status of the staff member(s) who ask(s) for details. Further, it should be considered normal for a person designated as superior in the hierarchy to supervise the work of subordinates so that each employee works under the continuous observation of a supervisor who knows the employee and who may be able to spot unusual behaviour. Given a system incorporating these protections and good functional separation, any employee who wants to break into the whole system should find it impossible to do it alone and will be forced into collusion with other employees. An employee is more likely to abuse a system if it can be done alone because concealment is easier. But in any organisation, there are always some people who must be trusted, eg the security officer or senior systems analyst, and so there will always be employees who can prejudice the system if they want to. But not every employee needs to be in such a position of trust, and ultimate system integrity should be designed to depend upon only a few key people.

In the analysis of the range of administrative tasks performed, it is important to ensure, for example, that responsibilities for the current and archived materials are properly separated. One person should never have access to both because it introduces unacceptable risks of theft, extortion/blackmail or malicious damage, and because it gives that person the opportunity to amend data or programs off-line knowing that the amended material will be innocently introduced into the system the next time a user calls for information from store, and thereby bypasses the logical access controls. It may also be expedient to divide relevant system knowledge among a number of individuals. But this can be a difficult strategy to pursue, both because there may be only a few key staff, and because of the role of the systems analyst which is to gain an overview and therefore to be able to link the disparate parts of the system. Hence, this strategy can really only be followed and enforced where very high security is required for large systems. Further, it is advisable to put third parties (usually the customers) in a situation where they are likely to intervene and either consciously or unconsciously disclose a failure in the system, eg the organisation can introduce promotional prizes based on sales— the prizes have to be claimed by the sellers making a return to a department other than the sales department, thus providing an independent check of sales volumes; or goods to be sold for cash should always be priced at a figure which is most likely to lead the customer to ask for change, thus maximising the chance that the sale will be rung up on the till.

16.4.4 User documentation and training

System manuals and both user and programming specifications can also be a weak link because a potential criminal can quickly discover how the documented system is supposed to work. But without good documentation, serious difficulties can arise. Good and clear documentation and the use of checklists can:

(a) significantly reduce the number of errors and omissions which people make,

(b) ease communication between departments, and

(c) help to ensure operational continuity—a prime objective of security safeguards to deal with problems of equipment failure and personnel turnover.

Thus, one problem which regularly faces the users of stand-alone micros is illness. If there are only a limited number of people trained to use the machines for each function, any prolonged period of absence could produce a serious dislocation of function. Training should therefore always include all those who might be called upon to cover for absent colleagues. If only one or two staff have the expertise, care should be taken to prevent them from either personalising the system, or choosing idiosyncratic places in which to safely store the back-up copies, unless there is very good documentation of what they have done. Any failure to leave accessible information of practice can cause chaos if those staff suddenly leave or are ill, because those who are to replace them will have no idea of how to make the system work. Indeed, the irony is that, without adequate documentation, 'Microcomputers can make people irreplaceable.' (Ellison & Pritchard p50.)

But no-one really likes to write or use documentation so it should be short and precise. It should aim to tell the users in a clear manner how to use the described system and what to do if something goes wrong. An alternative or supplementary strategy is to develop computer systems which have embedded help or CBT facilities which will take people through the proper procedures. But just as documentation must be protected by physical security systems, logical access controls must be designed to exclude unauthorised users from helpful hints on how to abuse the system. All forms of training, whether human or machine-based, help to establish norms of behaviour. A portion of the task training will be in matters specific to security, eg all employees should be told what to do in the case of fire. As to security awareness training, it is a good general rule that, irrespective of whether staff have been, or are likely to be, assigned specific responsibilities, all staff should be educated in security matters.

16.4.5 Reporting the unusual

Training should persuade or condition everyone to respond to anything which is unusual as a security variance. But, if such events are not to be ignored, there must be a procedure for reporting such incidents. It must be recognised that staff will not report all the incidents which occur because friends may be involved. To encourage the proper response, it may therefore be advisable to permit reports to be made in confidence and with no stigma attached to the reporter, regardless of the outcome.

All levels of employee must be encouraged to see themselves as security safeguards, while recognising that it is ultimately the responsibility of senior and middle management to develop an organisation security strategy and to make that strategy work. The practical and technical support of the whole staff will be required if the highest standards are to be maintained. Managers at all levels should make it their business to get to know their staff well enough to detect changes in behaviour and, as a counter-balance, the staff of each section or department should be encouraged to report any incidents which might suggest a deviation in their manager's behaviour. If the system is to work, there must be a top-down management policy of openness about mistakes and losses. Everything should be reported immediately, regardless of the status of the individual(s) involved. In larger organisations, it may be appropriate to use a pre-printed incident form. In the smaller, more intimate organisations, some more informal process which is consistent with maintaining mutual trust and confidence, should be encouraged. The manager with responsibility for security (full-time in large concerns) should monitor and check that all procedures are being followed, and should help to prevent and detect security breaches. The overall aim is to create a secure environment in which employees are aware of their responsibilities and are not tempted to misbehave.

16.4.6 Direct employment policies

As a priority, every organisation should formulate a detailed policy for:

(a) recruitment and selection,
(b) staff assessment or appraisal, and
(c) termination of employment.

It is recognised that the disgruntled, under-utilised or dishonest employees are the most likely to breach security. Good personnel management is therefore essential to maintain morale and to produce effective training. Emile Durkheim formulated the theory of **anomie**. He argued that where a person's aspirations are balanced by opportunities realistically available for achievement, that person is likely to be content. But if there is an imbalance, ie legitimate aspirations cannot be achieved through the channels available, less conventional methods to achieve satisfaction may be adopted and this may include the deliberate causing of loss or damage. This can be particularly important in those cases where well-qualified and intelligent staff are unable to make proper career progress through the organisation because there is a rigid hierarchy and limited promotion opportunities exist, eg where there is a management prejudice against appointing computer technicians to managerial posts.

When considering the initial appointment of staff, the organisation must consider the degree of pre-employment vetting to be undertaken. There are several possible problems:

(a) It may be of dubious effectiveness because a reasonably significant percentage of security breakers are first-time offenders.
(b) If the offender is a professional, a properly constructed identity will be presented for examination and will probably satisfy a standard check of factual consistency.
(c) Even if there are problems, a previous employer may well not wish to disclose fraudulent activity if references are followed up.

It may therefore be sensible to recruit on a probationary system whereby new recruits can be supervised and evaluated for the initial period of their employment before being confirmed in a post where there is to be access to sensitive resources. Generally, the personnel department should monitor the performance and morale of staff for the benefit of both the staff and the employer, and should support the legitimate aspirations and expectations of the staff for maximum career fulfilment and development. In any grievance or disciplinary situation, it is important to create an environment in which the organisation can be seen to deal fairly with alleged offenders. Confidence can be rapidly undermined if staff feel that they are unlikely to receive justice.

Continuing security also depends upon keeping key personnel. If staff are happy and have good promotion prospects with plenty of task variety and stimulation, they are likely to remain. But whatever the conditions under which people work, no employing organisation can assume that its staff will remain loyal. People's attitudes change and, depending on the circumstances, they may become more susceptible to bribery, or they may take information with a view to selling it to a competitior. The law is not necessarily helpful in this type of situation. Subject to the law of confidentiality, it is not a crime to poach employees from a rival organisation even though it may be unethical in that the new employer hopes to take advantage of the employee's expertise (but note that the Prevention of Corruption Act 1906 covers bribes or threats made in the expectation of gaining a benefit, while the Theft Act 1968, s21 deals with the blackmail situation of menaces made with a view to gain —both offences offer some protection to an employee who is offered inducements or the avoidance of pain as the price of disloyalty to the current employer). Each organisation should therefore carefully consider a key person policy which decides how expertise is to be replaced, or how the organisation is to be restructured to compensate for its loss.

Should the sad necessity of employment termination arise, adequate security procedures should be devised. Thus, employees who are to leave should be removed, and subsequently excluded, from all sensitive areas at the earliest possible opportunity. Arrangements should be made for the immediate return of security sensitive items such as manuals, keys and ID badges, and all passwords and logical access authorisations should be cancelled.

The personnel issues may therefore be summarised as follows:

1 Tempered by job sensitiviy analysis, the organisation should have effective pre-employment screening and background checking to reduce the possibility of appointing an untrustworthy person into a responsibility post.
2 All staff should be trained to recognise and act upon deviations in behaviour seen in their colleagues which could be warning signs of likely fraudulent behaviour.
3 There should be strict guidelines following a dismissal or other termination to reduce the opportunity for vengeful behaviour by a disgruntled individual.
4 There should be a well-defined policy on non-disclosure of confidential information.
5 Staff should be given well-defined channels to air their grievances, and there should be regular personnel reviews.
6 Morale is maintained by having a safe and well appointed environment in which to work.

Simple points about lighting (glare from VDU screens), temperature and noise can be very important to people who can vary substantially in what they feel is comfortable, and in the style of office in which they can work well. Wherever possible, each person should be given individual workspace where work can be undertaken efficiently and with minimum disruption.

16.5 THE ROLE OF THE AUDITOR

The traditional role of the auditor has been described as, 'a watchdog, not a bloodhound' (Comer p191). This reflects the assumption that the role is not actively to seek to investigate and detect fraud, but merely to see whether the system appears to be working as designed and producing accurate data. Naturally, if a material irregularity is discovered which would make a significant difference to the reliability of the accounts, the dog will bark to call attention to it. The external audit will normally take place annually, and is designed to allow the auditor to form an opinion as to whether the organisation's financial statements are a fair representation of the state of the operation as at the given date. This audit is undertaken by a professional person of independence and competence other than the preparer of the accounts and the person(s) likely to gain directly from the use of the information. The purpose of the auditor's report on that information is to increase its credibility and therefore its usefulness. (To base a functional definition of auditing simply upon the proposition that the auditor is acting in accordance with statutory provisions misses the public policy issue of the need to provide interested parties with reasonably credible information upon which to base decision-making. Thus, in relation to a company, the directors need to have confidence in the figures before determining future policy, a prospective investor needs to appraise the company before buying shares in it, and a bank to set credit limits before lending money to it, etc).

But, no matter how searching that annual audit may be, the primary responsibility for the detection and eradication of error lies with the directors or senior managers and their internal staff. In practice, the increase in the number of computer systems and the rise in the crime rate is exerting more pressure on the management and, therefore, consequentially upon the auditing profession to look for fraud more actively.

The primary responsibility of internal auditors is to evaluate and identify opportunities to strengthen the administration and the control which it can exercise. For these purposes, a control system sets standards, records performance, compares performance with targets, and takes appropriate action to bring the organisation's performance levels up to standard. The modern auditor therefore has the following functions:

(a) to review the critical applications to ensure maximum data integrity;
(b) to consider proposed software developments to ensure that good data controls and audit trails are maintained—it is more cost-effective that this input should be made at the design stage rather than after the event;
(c) to review the administrative, operational and security procedures in all departments;
(d) to complement the activities of the organisation's external auditors by reviewing financial procedures on a regular basis; and
(e) to review and test disaster recovery plans.

The function of auditing should be authoritative within the organisational hierarchy, and auditors should report directly to the senior management. To achieve the best results, the auditors should be free from local or departmental political commitments, and should have wide experience in review work. The practice of auditing has had to match the evolution of accounting from traditional paper systems to information systems, so the auditor's review of the design, methods and procedures for system modification has become an essential step in producing an environment in which both legal and management requirements are met. The aim is to produce and maintain a sufficient level of overall control so that it is possible to assess the effectiveness of the component controls. This means that it is no longer acceptable for auditors to lack awareness of computer technology and information systems, and there are significant training implications for all accountants who might wish to enter the auditing side of the profession.

Internal auditors should not be content with a yearly assessment of risk, but should review all record keeping systems, including the computerised data store, on a regular basis to ensure the adequacy of the controls. In this, approved members of the audit management team can use the established management information system and decision support systems to manipulate the sometimes large quantities of data through the technique of modelling to detect changes or suspicious trends in the whole. Decision support systems are usually user friendly database management tools, with a good query language through which to interact with the data and to prepare reports on the data environment. Such systems can easily be modified to support the auditing function. The resulting tests could be scheduled on a regular or routine basis, but there are dangers in being too predictable and thereby allowing the criminals the chance to have the data in a good state by the time the known inspection is to be made. Equally, if the tests are too infrequent, they may fail to detect control degradation or the system violations which take place between tests. Alternatively, audit testing could be used to follow up an apparent failure in the controls by attempting to detect the cause or to ensure that previously detected deficiencies have been corrected.

Generally, the auditors seek to ensure data security by:

(a) monitoring computer activity including the exception reports (unauthorised attempts to access files or procedures), console logs (to look for unusual activities), the system management facility which records which operations have been performed, etc;
(b) checking all changes to the system including additions to the system library as well as changes to source codes.

Application software is at the heart of the information system. For this software to operate effectively, security controls are necessary within the software and at the interface between the software and other components of the information system. The security measures implemented must reflect the needs of that system and be consistent with the sensitivity of the data processed by the system. The software most likely to be involved includes the financial and asset management systems, eg payroll, stock management, those systems which provide process support for the organisation's operations, eg CAD/CAM, CIM, etc, and the automated decision-making systems, eg stock re-ordering, maintenance scheduling, etc. In good design, security is built in from the outset. For this to be achieved, a systematic approach to design is required. Moreover, an information system can only be secure if it is a part of an organisation with a positive attitude towards security. It is therefore vital that those in a position of authority should ensure that the standards of best practice are incorporated into the management of the organisational environment. To make the optimum selections of security goals and strategies, and to design effective security safeguards requires a blend of foresight and experience which, when based on a holistic view of the the organisation and its systems, should allow the construction of appropriate security measures to meet the known vulnerabilities.

The design process will go through the following phases:

1 a feasibility study and analysis which identifies which applications and data are most vulnerable and specifies the most appropriate security requirements;

2 the production of a detailed system plan with design interfaces to eliminate specific risks, and management controls to limit those risks that cannot be eliminated —the design phase should end with a structured walk through of the safeguards by a qualified and independent peer group;

3 the production of the software—programming should be supervised and controlled to eliminate, or more realistically, reduce the incidence of errors —wherever possible, there should be tests to see how the system responds to unusual or fraudulent input and how it behaves under unusual conditions; and

4 post-implementation, it is vital to make early checks to ensure that all procedures are being followed—the hope being that a routine of good practice can be established before bad habits have a chance to develop and take root —during this review, further improvements may be developed which can be programmed in at some convenient time, or which can be incorporated into the contingency plan.

Most of the problems which arise with system software can be traced back to those feasibility studies in which there was an inadequate definition of security aims. In taking design decisions, it must also be recognised that automated controls are less costly to operate and more consistently applied than their manual equivalents, but that automated systems must take proper account of those people who are to operate them. More often than not, a compromise will be required to accept slightly less than optimum security in return for a more friendly interface which the employees are likely to accept and operate.

In organisational terms, the role of the auditor has become fundamental. Naturally, the organisation has identified the most probable threats and vulnerabilities. It will be seen that, for deliberate acts, the system will be more vulnerable if it has been inadequately developed and incorporates a poor defensive design. Hence, particularly if access is to be made by many users, unauthorised input controls will be difficult, so there is a positive need for good auditing facilities. There are also dangers in all program modifications and file changes if poorly trained staff are allowed to make them, so it is up to the auditors to liaise with the systems analysts to ensure rigorous testing before the amended software is allowed into the working environment. Both static and dynamic testing of software should be encouraged. Dynamic testing uses test data to compare test results with expected results, but only part of each system can be tested in this way. During the test, the system analyst must judge the extent to which the program has been exercised and attempt to determine whether the unexercised code is an unauthorised insertion.

Once running, the output may not be as expected. The reason is normally human error, clerical procedures being the most error prone. Because the organisation needs good controls over the preparation of source data, there should be detailed discussions between the auditors and the human resource development team to produce a training programme that will promote individual accountability at each data flow interface, and responsibility for the operation of sensitive programs. Each job that connects to the data function is an interface. This will apply whether the connection is human to human, or human to machine. At each interface, the likelihood and consequences of error should be considered. This should include all jobs whether of computer or non-computer staff. No item is too trivial for the attention of the auditor. Hence, control must even be exercised over blank input documents —a good design of documents will encourage proper authorisation, provide an audit trail, and help to ensure that data are accurate and complete. Where appropriate, the organisation should design special documents for special procedures. This should be seen against the general background of the established authorisation procedures, whether by way of simple signatures on a form of approval, or through passwords and ID codes, a proper hierarchy of supervision and control must be established.

16.6 RECOVERY STRATEGIES

In taking decisions, it must be recognised that not all the data processing tasks undertaken by the organisation are critical to the continued functioning of the organisation during an emergency. If the organisation is to act responsibly, it should assess criticality by considering each program or application and asking:

1 What are the legal requirements? —these will be both positive to require the organisation to act, and avoidance-based to limit the potential liability of the organisation to employees and third parties.
2 What do the customers or service-receivers require so that satisfaction and/or loyalty are maintained?
3 What are the public relations requirements to maintain general confidence in the organisation?
4 What are the losses and costs by hour/day, and how long can each source of loss be tolerated before serious damage is caused?

There is no need for the priority list to be absolute, and it will be sufficient to batch the programs and resources in approximate priority groups. A list of priorities must also be drawn up to detail the order in which the data itself is to be restored. This will involve identifying which hardware will be required, and the necessary data back-up and documentation which will include original invoices, etc to support the operation.

16.6.1 The first reaction to a disaster

The organisation must first plan its initial response to any potential disaster situation. During the day, when the majority of the key personnel are likely to be available on site, the decision-making problems should be readily resolved. But, during an off-peak period, when a night watchman, security guard or other employee detects an apparently dangerous situation, detailed decisions must be made as to who should be called in and in what order. Those who first formally attend the scene on behalf of the management, are responsible for appraising the situation and for deciding which sections of the disaster plan to implement. That first team must have the competence to be able to make an accurate assessment of the actual or potential extent of the damage, so that appropriate damage limitation steps can be taken without delay.

But the authority level of that team must be considered. It would be unreasonable to involve the most senior managers for every incident, no matter how trivial. A graduated scale of response will have to be made, depending on the apparent severity of the situation, with more senior decision-makers being called in for the more dangerous events. It may be felt necessary to limit the scope of the action which each grade of decision-maker can authorise, depending upon the level of consequential risk involved. Thus, if the initial response team feel that the extent of the disaster is within their authority levels, all relevant steps can be taken. Otherwise senior management must be called in to authorise the appropriate responses, eg to use water to quell a fire near the main computer installation.

Disaster recovery teams with specific responsibility will be listed for call up, but alternative personnel must always be available in case the first nominated team members cannot be reached. Much work can be achieved if each team engaged on the job is well trained, and can act independently and in parallel. To assist in getting the best results in the more serious disaster situations, a recovery co-ordinating centre should be established where reports can be taken and orders issued. It is better that this should be near the site of the disaster so that immediate management response is achievable. If the most efficient responses are to be made, good communications are essential through all the media involved. Further, in an emergency, simplicity of management communications is essential to get vital messages across quickly.

16.6.2 The option to relocate the organisation

The complete relocation of the organisation to an alternate site is rarely good logistics or economical. Further, it is seldom required. But large organisations cannot ignore the possibility that major disasters may force a move. The first step would be to select suitable office space for relocation if the original site were to be lost. This could be on a temporary basis until the original site is restored to its former glory, or it could be a permanent move. Whether the move is intended as temporary or permanent, no move to a partially prepared site can be carried out quickly. The whole infrastructure of communications, power lines and environmental controls must be installed first.

This work is expensive and it should not be undertaken in advance unless the need for rapid back-up is great or the site could be used regularly for some other purpose. In this, it may be best to plan relocation alongside other plans for the future growth of the organisation. Planners should assess the degree to which the alternative site would be useful in the long term for supporting the expansion of the organisation. This will involve considering whether:

(a) the site can be used for other operations,
(b) employees can get there conveniently,
(c) there are good communications and an infrastructure of road and rail links, and other support services,
(d) there is good parking,
(e) there are good nearby facilities for the supply of food and accommodation,
(f) the site and its environment is safe for the employees and their property.

With competent management on hand, local operations are always easier to organise than remote operations. With this is mind, the creation of multiple DP facilities ought to be considered. The smallest location must always be large enough to carry the critical work of at least one other location during the projected recovery time. This involves the physical dispersion of computer resources into two or more sites with each centre undertaking economically useful work at all times to get the most out of the capital employed. Any additional capacity built in is justified by the additional security given in-house, and by the fact that each computer system has room within which to grow and develop. It is generally accepted that only about 20 per cent of each computer installation's use is critical, so the excess capacity to handle transferred processing can be kept to a minimum. This scheme is likely to be more cost-effective than the creation of ready rooms into which resources can be moved. The difficulty with ready rooms is that this requires that capital is left unemployed and the utility of the resource thus created is dependent upon being able to obtain replacement hardware from suppliers at short notice. The stand-by facility must also be close enough to the original site to minimise the disruption to staff in moving to this new place of work.

In major disasters, transportation can be affected regionally by the weather or public transport may not run for some other reason, eg through strikes. Events which disrupt the movement of people and equipment over a region cannot readily be overcome and it may not be possible to solve the problem in other ways. Hence, overnight accommodation may not be available if it is hoped that staff can live temporarily in the area. If the disaster is entirely localised but the alternative facility is, say, fifty miles away, it is difficult to expect the affected staff to use their own cars to commute. Nor should they be expected to meet the relevant public transport costs without some form of subsidy. Given these constraints, it may be more economical to provide shuttle buses inter-site for those who usually walk to work, have no car, or do not want to use their own cars. This will necessitate the rapid rent of buses or coaches, and vans and lorries, and the recruitment of extra drivers. It may also be necessary to move the catering department or to transport food inter-site so that the sudden influx of people can be fed.

16.6.3 Alternative hardware provision

Commercial computer bureaux (acting as **time brokers**) offer a service by making time available on their own systems in the event of an emergency. The first step is for the organisation to sign an agreement with one of the bureaux and then, as a customer, to receive access codes, information and training so that the organisation's software can be modified to make it portable onto the bureau's systems. Detailed tests will then have to be run to prove system compatibility, and the relevant applications and recent data will be stored on their facilities. At this point, a rental of storage space and support fees become payable. This solution to the problem can be relatively costly to maintain as an on-going commitment, which will include fees for regular system test time. It also involves the expense of system modifications which may be necessitated by any changes in the bureau's operating environment, and if the organisation wishes to amend its own software, the designers will have to allow for the bureau's needs when modifying all the stored applications. However, this strategy is good for the standard high volume payroll and other similar systems.

A number of organisations near large urban areas may decide to pool their resources to save money. These **reciprocal** or **mutual aid agreements** work by allowing one member access to the hardware of another during an emergency, and they are likely to be particularly attractive in those industries which have accepted common hardware standards. Both software and data must be portable between the different members' facilities, and in evaluating the practicality of the scheme, rehearsals can be very helpful even though they can be expensive, and generate unwelcome disruptions to the back-up organisation. But if tests are to be effective, the full critical applications must be put up and made to run realistically. It is difficult to make mutual aid agreements totally reliable. Changes in either system will jeopardise the practicality of the agreement, and changes in management policy may cause the withdrawal of one member without notice so it can be a high risk policy because participants may only discover that promised aid is not available when an emergency arises.

Equipped contingency centres are relatively rare because they are capital-expensive to create and demand for the service is relatively low. If an organisation proposes to use this strategy, it should first ensure hardware compatibility and check all the communications linkages. If the technical problems are overcome, the organisation pays a subscriber fee for the right to use the facility in an emergency. The cost of declaring an emergency may be great because, once the decision is taken to move to the back-up site, the hardware rental fees are payable. The organisation should also carefully consider whether there are any security problems if other organisations are using the facility. The question of the storage of sensitive materials (whether on system or not) at the contingency centre should be canvassed if, say, trade competitors are likely to be using the same resources.

The organisation should also consider the level of availability of the facilities at the centre for rehearsal. It is of fundamental importance that the staff at both ends of the transfer are fully familiar with all the problems which are likely to occur, and detailed training schedules should be drawn up and executed to raise staff awareness to a proper level. Further, the centre itself should disclose the number of subscribers to the scheme so that there can be an intelligent guess made as to the likely odds of another subscriber needing the facility at the same time. The logistics of the transfer should then be calculated starting with simple factual matters such as the distance from the organisation to the centre— recovery at original site may be slowed if key personnel are too far removed in the back-up centre. Finally, as with the bureau system, the planners must recognise that membership of these schemes limits the development of home sites to those changes which are compatible with the back-up site.

Some organisations have constructed **empty rooms** or **shells**. In the event of a disaster, the client organisation is allowed access to assemble a back-up system. This scheme is significantly less expensive than the equipped room system, but suffers from the disadvantage that it is slower to start up. (Co-operative inter-firm provision of empty rooms spreads the costs.) As with the hot stand-by systems, there must be a careful consideration of the number of clients likely to want access at any given time, but overall, such schemes represent a good system for less critical back-up because it is not essential to maintain full system compatibility.

Whatever strategy has been adopted, the organisation should have ensured that there were adequate back-up power systems which allowed the in-house system to be archived and brought down gracefully in the event of a major loss of power during the disaster. This ensures that the most up-to-date data is available for use in the back-up system.

16.6.4 What are the in-house hardware considerations?

Hardware can be easily replaced if it is of recent manufacture or still in stock. Some manufacturers will give priority of supply to those affected by a disaster. However, different suppliers have different policies and it is essential to discuss disaster recovery with the suppliers at an early stage. Some hardware suppliers will, for example, make demonstration computers available to bridge in the event of a disaster. These are usually showcase computers, but they are likely to have poor security, and it is entirely possible that they may have been constantly updated with the most recent software releases, so system compatibility may be a problem.

It should also be acknowledged that it will be hard to replace customised hardware or hardware produced in small quantitites or upon demand, or obsolete equipment. This will inevitably be the case if the manufacturer has discontinued manufacture or has ceased trading. If this fact is recognised during the lifetime of a contingency plan, it should be modified to allow time to find a second-hand system, or to recreate the system using new hardware. When drawing up and maintaining the contingency plan, adequate time should be allowed for the delivery, installation, testing and commissioning of the replacement processors. In this, the size and complexity of the communications network can be a major factor. Although the telephone system may be swiftly reconnected, the supply and fitting of modems, multiplexers, etc may be time-consuming and there may be substantial systems work required to allow for the new configuration, eg for access to become remote during repairs.

16.6.5 What are the data and documentation considerations?

With respect to data, a whole series of decisions must be taken. The first and most serious possibility is that some or all of the source data has been destroyed. This may happen if there is disruption during processing. The organisation should therefore decide:

1 What kind of back-up files should be routinely created.
2 How many generations of back-up are needed to ensure rapid recovery.
3 How much data should be stored in geographically remote sites.

The organisation must aim to produce data which are accurate, complete, timely and authorised; and to create a system whereby, with minimum effort, it is possible to reconstruct transactions from the relevant source documents. With both these facilities, organisations should be able to make decisions based on the best information, to create a good audit trail, and to recover quickly from disasters. The data processing department and user departments have joint responsibility in this respect. The decisions taken are likely to differ from those affecting the programs and applications which have greater stability and, once installed and verified, need only protection from unauthorised or accidental amendment. Self-evidently, great care must be taken during the development and change of software to ensure that nothing is introduced which will prejudice existing or future data integrity.

The organisation should appraise the processes and transactions which it performs and decide which records are vital to its continued well-being. This will range from trade secrets and confidential information, eg marketing and accounting, to ordinary data recording sales and debts. Normally, only a small percentage of data is vital unless the organisation is like a bank, building society or insurance company, which requires absolutely reliable information. Whichever records are designated as vital and their software support must then be declared mandatory and given high priority in the recovery plan.

This should be undertaken alongside **records retention analysis**. In some cases, there are positive legal requirements to retain documentary evidence of transactions, eg for the Inland Revenue, Customs and Excise, etc. Similarly, there will be particular processing requirements (eg to restart processing from source data if the computer malfunctions during processing), which require documents to be preserved. Each organisation should analyse its documentation to identify which documents are critical. It is then advisable to microfilm or fiche the most important and to make arrangements for them to be stored in a remote site. Documents may be moved on a cyclical basis through a series of sites depending on their age, with recovery from those sites to allow the organisation to function and to recreate its computer-based records if there is a disaster at the main computer facility.

User manuals tend to be kept in offices which are fire prone. It is therefore sensible to consider a formal library control system with back-up copies stored at a remote site. This is more cost-effective than the microfilming of all the major manuals. Copies of the disaster plan itself should be distributed throughout the organisation and should be easily available at protected locations. Some copies should be kept at the homes of the key personnel who will be contacted in an emergency. On a lower level of priority, the organisation should consider whether to stockpile supplies of vital letter headings and other similar documents at more than one location, bearing in mind that time can be lost if there are inadequate records of where that stock is located. Paper stocks and forms should be analysed and the routine ordering quantities assessed so that buffer stocks can be kept. Having taken these precautions, organisations should not then make the mistake of storing the supplies in basements or near vulnerable areas because, being paper, the stocks are equally susceptible to both water and fire damage.

16.6.6 Conclusions on back-up strategy

The organisation should plan for the following:

1 The ideal is to preserve the best possible configuration of hardware following the disaster. This will probably mean that the information service will operate at reduced efficiency. This may be acceptable over a period of time for some user departments where there is reduced dependence on computerised information handling, or where reversion to manual systems is still possible, perhaps supported by calculators or personal computers.

2 If limited processor time can be reallocated to priority departments this may allow the organisation to continue efficiently.

3 Manual methods may be better than nothing if there is a choice between operation and no operation.

4 Some departments may not have to perform their work immediately, eg long-range planning, which will allow the reduced processor time to be utilised by priority users.

5 Very few organisations need full and rapid back-up of their entire system.

6 Some applications can wait weeks, others months. These systems do not need to be handled by the same strategies. Some accounting packages could be backed up within hours, others might move to a bureau the next day or be dealt with on a time-share basis as and when required.

7 Other facilities might be made available at a co-operating organisation at low peak, off-shift times. Others might not be run until another facility is prepared or the original site restored.

However, in an emergency, it is people who provide the flexibility, availability and versatility needed to meet an unexpected situation and to adapt the previously made plans to the reality. Everyone must therefore be well trained and have been given an opportunity to comment on the plan as it affects them. People can be expected to work hard if they feel that they are part of the plan—the reliability of staff during a disaster is a problem of motivation. The critical issues are the moving of staff between sites, crowding people into emergency accommodation and requiring them to undertake unfamiliar tasks which should all be considered in detail. Staff should know where to report, how they should get there and what their responsibilities will be. All these personnel matters must be synchronised to the provision of additional power supplies and stand-by communications links so that when the people move, they will be able to continue work effectively. Finally, the plans and training schedule must provide for changes of staff, with consequential reallocation of responsibilities and duties. It may even be appropriate to consider systems of positive rewards during training to engage the interest of all those critical to the recovery process.

SUMMARY

The key points covered in this chapter are that:

1 Long-term profitability relies on installing realistic security systems. This must be more than a paper exercise and must involve all employees in setting and achieving effective performance standards.

2 Because the auditing activity disrupts the operation of the organisation, all audits must be sensitively handled. But the auditor is not a criminal investigator. The primary task is to monitor and verify corporate activity which, incidentally, may reveal symptoms of fraud.

3 The use of techniques such as job sensitivity analysis will assist an organisation to identify both the vulnerable assets and resources, and the employees with the opportunity to cause loss or damage.

4 It is important for all organisations to define the status and role of each member of staff—the more critical roles are the systems staff and applications programmers. Professional staff must be encouraged to achieve state of the art standards. All staff can be protected from themselves through functional separation.

5 The power to make changes within the organisation depends upon ability to persuade the staff to abandon the known procedures.

6 If the organisation is to make an effective recovery from a disaster, appropriately detailed plans must establish initial responses and lay down lines of authority for managing the damage limitation and recovery exercise.

QUESTIONS *Solutions to questions of an examination standard start on p 395*

Write brief notes on the following:

(a) the basic types of security audit check;
(b) job sensitivity analysis;
(c) internal job holders who may pose threats to security;
(d) problems in security vetting at the staff appointment stage.

Questions of an examination standard

1 One of the major problems in information system security planning is the ingenuity and unpredictability of people.

(a) Explain briefly how you would plan to detect breaches of security by audit check.
(b) Discuss the problems which may occur in having the known fraudsters prosecuted.

2 The traditional role of the auditor has been described as that of a watchdog rather than a bloodhound.

(a) Explain briefly the primary responsibility of internal auditors in an information systems context.
(b) Briefly describe the ways in which an auditor will seek to ensure data security.

3 An organisation's success in recovering from a disaster affecting its information system depends on its back-up strategy.

List and explain the methods by which the organisation may make alternative hardware provision.

Solutions to Questions

(Please note these are solutions to the questions of an examination standard found at the end of each chapter)

SOLUTIONS TO CHAPTER 1 QUESTIONS

1 This question concerns the relationship between an organisation's objectives and practical performance criteria. The five dimensions would be:

(1) **Environment**—the things outside the organisation with which it interacts, eg local people, the trade community, the government, etc. To some extent, this is a public relations dimension.

(2) **Competitive edge or distinctive competence**—the way in which the management decide to differentiate its product(s) and/or service(s) in terms of price, quality or reputation.

(3) **Marketing thrust**—how the organisation seeks to promote itself through advertising, sponsoring, etc. A measure of effectiveness may be the size of the client base or turnover.

(4) **Operating efficiency**—this is determined by the ratio of internally-generated costs to income. Ultimately, control of these costs, eg labour, overheads, stock, etc, affects profitability.

(5) **Human factors**—the organisation will seek to create and maintain a humane image for the benefit of employees, consumers generally and potential customers.

Objectives produced will be measured on a timescale, and may be multiple and conflicting. A practical compromise is therefore often necessary. **See paragraph 1.1.1**.

2 This question addresses the concept of the information system as a series of interrelated activities in the following areas:

(1) The reason for which the data is needed or used—this may be a permanent requirement, eg regular postings to an accounts ledger, or be a response to a transient problem, eg to combat the effects of a strike. Not all data needs can be predicted.

(2) How data is captured to meet the given need—the design of the data capture system must reflect the timing and the processing requirements.

(3) How the data is processed—ie how it is turned into information or made useful. This will include storage, access, calculating, sorting and presentation, eg exception reports, level of detail, etc.

(4) The users of the system (or its information) are the people who add value to the data or achieve benefits. If items (1) to (3) are primary data processing, then item (4) onward is secondary information processing. The way in which an accountant will interpret or modify information produced by a computer is an example of this. New developments in information system technology are focussed on this area, eg expert systems.

(5) The results of the user having the information, eg improved knowledge, actions, decisions or any change in behaviour—often these will be intangible. Information has no intrinsic value. Its value lies only in the results which it can bring about.

(6) The control or feedback of results which is applied to the system, often from the user. This may modify the behaviour of the system to better achieve the needs of the user, eg improved methods of stock control.

The model referred to is cyclical. It could be illustrated by a diagram as in Figure 1.7. **See paragraph 1.5**.

3 The question is about the development of information technology, its application to information systems and the resultant effect on organisations. This involves the socio-technical systems, ie the interface between human and computer-based systems. A suitable answer should include some reference to the benefits and dangers:

(1) Benefits:

- greater efficiency, money savings, enhanced human resources, etc;
- better decision-making through higher information quality;
- increased flexibility and responsiveness, eg better use of query languages;
- better user access, eg user computing and user-driven systems development;
- data sharing across organisation boundaries, eg the use of a database;
- increased involvement by the user in information systems development, eg user computing and prototyping;
- better communications, internally and externally.

(2) Dangers:

- data redundancy and lack of consistency due to poor system design;
- installing excessively expensive technology;
- systems which are too complicated for the intended users;
- lack of user involvement in systems leaving the *experts* to take over;
- security problems and the possibility of fraud or accidental information loss;
- sub-optimality, ie parts of the system are managed to achieve their individual objectives at the expense of the whole system—also known as *islands of automation.*

A really thorough answer should attempt to reconcile benefits and dangers by user involvement, total system management and information system strategy. **See paragraphs 1.6.1 and 1.6.2**.

SOLUTIONS TO CHAPTER 2 QUESTIONS

1 This question relates to the general process of decision-making which should be seen as a sequential process, usually undertaken as a group activity and comprising both a planning and a reactive quality. The stages are as follows:

(1) A trigger or event which starts the activity—usually the input of data or information, eg a stock level report or quality control reject.

(2) Problem definition or analysis—the identification of the cause of problems and the separation of cause and effect.

(3) Problem structuring during which a mathematical or conceptual model is constructed, eg linear programming, and the objectives of the decision process are defined.

(4) Information requirement definition—the decision as to the data which must be captured and processed in order to solve the problem.

(5) Information analysis using mathematical techniques, eg regression analysis, or the application of qualitative preferential criteria. One possible result of this stage may be the decision whether enough information of the right quality is to hand or whether further data capture is required.

(6) The decision itself—the selection of a course of action, change in behaviour or commitment of resources.

The decision-making process is often carried out under less than ideal conditions, eg with inadequate information, not enough time or uncertain priorities. **See paragraph 2.1.2**.

2 The question refers to the difference in the decision types (and therefore the information requirements) which apply at different levels in the organisation. Conventionally, a three level model of management is accepted:

(1) strategic or top management,

(2) tactical or middle management,

(3) operational or supervisory management.

It should be stressed that it is the implication of the decision, not the job title, which places the decision-maker at a particular level. The boundaries are therefore not hard and fast. Figure 2.5 would illustrate the model. The character of the decisions could be:

(1) Strategic decisions:

- very long time horizon, eg 5–10 years;

— radical implications for the whole organisation, eg new products new markets;
— very uncertain outcomes, eg adoption of new technology;
— high risk, eg investment in overseas markets;
— non-routine, eg setting up a new company.

(2) Tactical decisions:
— medium time horizon, eg less than 5 years;
— implication for a function under control, eg accounting or production;
— moderately uncertain outcome involving the possible use of forecasting techniques and information technology;
— possible routine decisions, eg quarterly budgets;
— moderate risk as the level of investment is smaller and the decisions are more predictable, eg manning levels.

(3) Operational decisions:
— short timescale, eg 1 day to 1 week;
— routine and specific outcomes, eg achievement of production targets;
— low levels of risk with much decision support;
— predictable, well documented information requirements, eg office procedures. **See paragraph 2.2.1**.

SOLUTIONS TO CHAPTER 3 QUESTIONS

1 The question addresses the organisation at micro level, proposing five layers:
(1) Corporate (relating to strategic management decisions), eg corporate plans, budgets, etc.
(2) Unit level or division, differentiated by product, geography or management structure.
(3) Functional (relating to middle management) including organisational sub-systems, eg financial planning, manpower planning, etc.
(4) Departmental, at the level of tactical activities, eg quality management.
(5) Operational, the day-to-day activities, eg adding to and withdrawing from stock. **See paragraph 3.1.4**.

2 The four factors affecting integration are:
(1) The quality of the data captured; the need for verification and validation; data redundancy and data reduction; problems of noise.
(2) Transmission/reception quality; effect of data capture; coding methods and standards; use of technology.
(3) Channel quality, transmission media, interference, distortion and noise.
(4) Feedback loops, message checking and repetition, batch totals and check digits; data redundancy and possible increase in noise and distortion.

Note should be made of the costs of any measure for maintaining the quality of system integration. **See paragraph 3.1.7**.

3 The question could be answered by naming and describing six elements met in the analysis and design of information systems.
(1) Inputs:
— information quality and content;
— interfaces with other systems;
— the need to capture or produce data.

(2) Processes:
— conversion of input to output;
— system protocols and interaction;
— standards and quality.

(3) Output:
— users' information requirements;
— media choices;
— messages sent to other sub-systems.

(4) Environment:
— other sub-systems;
— monitoring output.

(5) Channels:
— choice of channel/media;
— overcoming interference, noise and distortion.

(6) Feedback:
— use of system control loop(s);
— predicting situations where control is required. **See paragraph 3.2.2**.

SOLUTIONS TO CHAPTER 4 QUESTIONS

1 The question may be answered by considering the role of an individual who would work in the following way:

(1) through a committee structure to co-ordinate activity throughout the relevant part(s) of the organisation;
(2) to develop information resources;
(3) to acquire new information resources;
(4) to control the technology migration, ie the change from one technology or information use to another.

An example of the role might be to investigate and advise on the introduction of a stand-alone microcomputer system (a one-per-desk information system) to replace a previously centralised DP-based MIS. The role of information management is always strategic and continuous, and should therefore be vested in an individual appointed at a senior level. **See paragraph 4.1.4**.

2 The concept of an information centre may be explained by referring to the following issues:

(1) An information centre is a point of interface between the information system and its users.
(2) The job of an information centre is to use data transformation to make information available in its most useful form.
(3) Although an information centre may own the hardware and software, it does not own the data/information.
(4) The information centre should be integrated into the management structure—there could be a single, centralised information centre, or several distributed information centres.
(5) An information centre reflects the nature of its user and the type of use to which it will be put. The same physical information centre would therefore appear different to a clerk and an executive. **See paragraph 4.3.1**.

3 It is first necessary to describe the management services function:

(1) The MS department may contain advisors or experts in particular fields; usually in the functions of the organisation, eg accountancy or in the general area of problem-solving/OR, or the MS department may be made up of managers having actual line authority, rather than just an advisory capacity.
(2) MS staff tend to combine a tactical role with an organisation-wide mobility. They may have open access to all areas, although the MS department may be linked to the DP or systems department.
(3) The MS department may be a formally constituted team or an *ad hoc* body called up for special purposes such as systems development. As such, MS would be an adjunct of the organisation's steering committee.
(4) MS must be seen to be neutral. Often the head of MS will report directly to the managing director.

It can be difficult to decide on the position of the MS department within the organisation and the status of its personnel. It may be said that the functions of MS (problem-solving and decision support) will be carried out in other departments anyway. **See paragraph 4.3.2**.

SOLUTIONS TO CHAPTER 5 QUESTIONS

1 The requirements for a DSS include:
- **(1)** It should handle different volumes and types of data.
- **(2)** It should be capable of solving a wide range of problems.
- **(3)** The HCI should be powerful and flexible.
- **(4)** A 4GL or query language may be desirable.
- **(5)** The data storage/handling capacity should be large.

Factors involved in the choice would include:
- **(1)** Cost including licence fee and running costs.
- **(2)** Compatibility with existing hardware and operating system.
- **(3)** Integration with existing applications software.
- **(4)** Ease of use.
- **(5)** Vendor support.
- **(6)** Future development. **See paragraph 5.4.10**.

2 The important features of a 4GL are based on the idea of user computing, ie:
- **(1)** Prototyping as a method of systems development.
- **(2)** A query language for database interrogation.
- **(3)** A report generator to produce semi-formal reports and documents.
- **(4)** An applications generator to allow user-developed applications.
- **(5)** An advanced interface (eg WIMP). **See paragraph 5.10.4**.

3 The question revolves around the criteria of software effectiveness and benchmarks.
- **(1)** Effectiveness criteria:
  - — accuracy or freedom from syntax and logic errors;
  - — flexibility in handling transactions and absorbing changes;
  - — performance in terms of response time and run time.
- **(2)** Benchmarks:
  - — portability or machine independence;
  - — generalisation or lack of specialisation;
  - — ease of use. **See paragraph 5.10.5**.

4 Users have a direct and positive interest in the benefits and features of office automation.
- **(1)** Facilities offered by an electronic mail system may include:
  - — message composition or basic word processing facilities;
  - — message despatch facilities including a directory, priority queueing and scheduling;
  - — message receiving facilities including a mailbox, message forwarding and filing.
- **(2)** Teleconferencing may allow:
  - — the ability to call meetings at shorter notice;
  - — less disruption through meetings;
  - — no territorial feeling in meetings. **See paragraphs 5.4.1 and 5.4.4**.

SOLUTIONS TO CHAPTER 6 QUESTIONS

1 The question concerns whether to put the feasibility study at the begining of the life cycle, or after the in-depth study. This statement is a trade-off between minimising expenditure if the project is called off (early placement) and better decision-making as a result of more information (late placement). The following points should be made:
- **(1)** early placement reflects lack of confidence (eg in the technology);
- **(2)** the later the study, the more accurate the estimate of design resources (eg data storage size);
- **(3)** late placement means that the project is more likely to meet its terms of reference. **See paragraph 6.3**.

2 Types of benefit may include:
- **(1)** Direct benefits such as reduced costs, or increased turnover or output.

(2) Indirect benefits such as better decision-making, control, or freedom to innovate or grow.

The former affect cash flow immediately, the latter affect profitability gradually. Costs fall into three areas:

(1) development including users' and analysts' time, hardware specification and tendering;
(2) implementation including acquisition and recruitment;
(3) running including maintenance and salaries. **See paragraph 6.3.2**.

3 Commonly applied evaluation techniques include:

(1) Breakeven analysis which recognises fixed or period costs and variable (marginal) or unit costs. The BE point may be derived graphically or by formula.
(2) Payback which attempts to measure the time taken to recoup the initial investment in the system. The method favours safe, short-term projects and stresses liquidity at the expense of profitability.
(3) Net present value uses discounted cash flow techniques. Internal rate of return also exploits the techniques.

The problem with all the techniques is that of predicting the performance of a system which does not yet exist. **See paragraph 6.3.3**.

SOLUTIONS TO CHAPTER 7 QUESTIONS

1 The question addresses the fact that systems development methodologies may be split broadly into two schools of thought.

(1) **Process-driven** This emphasises the activities or functions which are carried out within a system. This leads to a perception of efficiency or a best method of operation which can usually be achieved by computerisation. Processes are understood by identifying their data inputs-outputs and describing them in increased detail (functional decomposition). This philosophy tends to be contained in traditional or structured methodologies and is a feature of piecemeal development and mechanistic DP-type systems.
(2) **Data-driven** Methodologies embracing this philosophy maintain that data should form the basis of systems development because it is stable. Methods of carrying out processes may change, but the data will stay the same. Systems based on an organisation's data resource are said to be more flexible and robust. Data-driven development is associated with database systems and 4GL environments. **See paragraph 7.1.1**.

2 There are four main types of file organisation:

(1) **Serial** A new record is written to the end of the existing file. Each record must be read in turn to access a particular data item. The format is not suitable for masterfiles or look-up tables. It is suitable for transaction files, eg customer orders taken during the day, or a workfile or spoolfile.
(2) **Sequential** Records are stored in ascending or descending order of key, eg account number. Sequential files are prone to frequent reorganisation with high maintenance overheads, but are space-efficient. They are still used in large batch processing environments, often on magnetic tape. A customer masterfile may be in this form.
(3) **Indexed sequential** These are accessed through a smaller secondary file called an index. Overflow must be catered for. IS files may be on disk or tape, and may be used for almost any type of file in a batch processing environment.
(4) **Random** Most often used with on-line systems where records need to be accessed directly, as in an airline booking system. Most major files in DP and MIS are random. **See paragraph 7.3.1**.

3 This question is about database and DBMS use.

(1) A typical DBMS package would feature:
- the ability to create, amend and delete records, ie basic file maintenance and record control;
- the access of individual records or the contents of a whole file;
- protection against unauthorised access and corruption, recovery and restart.

(2) Problems which may be experienced:
- difficulty in developing, installing and maintaining large monolithic systems;
- performance which was below the expected standard;
- high overhead costs and low intensity of use.

(3) Advantages which are sometimes claimed:
- the data reflects the corporate view allowing expert system and DSS use;
- better data integrity and reduced data redundancy;
- faster development of applications once the database has been set up;
- data independence allows changes in technology and changes in application to be insulated from each other. **See paragraph 7.4**.

SOLUTIONS TO CHAPTER 8 QUESTIONS

1 (a) **Context diagram**

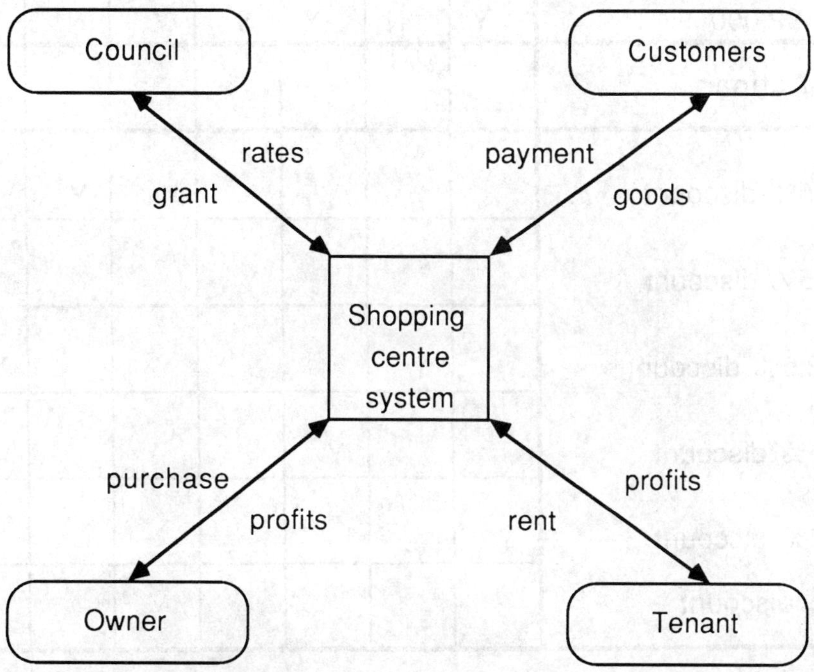

(b) **Entity-relationship model** **See paragraphs 8.1.2 and 8.1.4**.

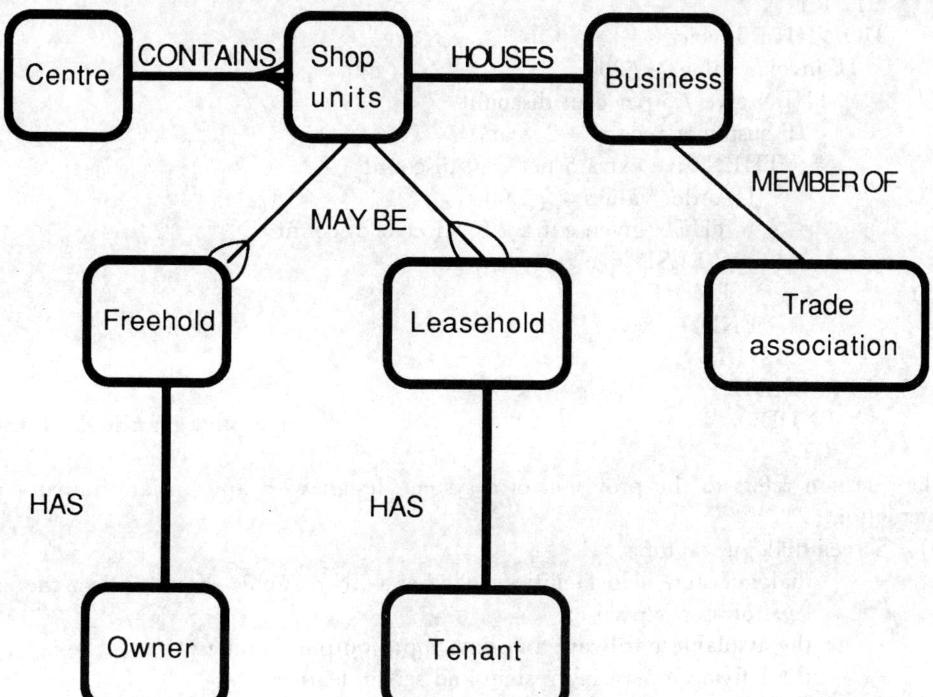

2 (**a**) Decision table

Conditions	Rules							
	1	2	3	4	5	6	7	8
Order value >£200	Y	Y	Y	Y	N	N	N	N
Over two years on books	Y	Y	N	N	Y	Y	N	N
Order >£2,000	Y	N	Y	N	Y	N	Y	N
Actions								
Give 5.5% discount						Y		
Give 7.5% discount				Y			Y	
Give 12.5% discount		Y			Y			
Give 15% discount			Y					
Give 20% discount	Y							
Give no discount								Y

(**b**) Structured English

```
START
DOWHILE invoice
  IF invoice value >£200
    THEN give 7.5 per cent discount
      IF customer record >2 years
        THEN give extra 5 per cent discount
          IF order values >£2,000
            THEN given extra 7.5 per cent discount
              ELSE give zero discount
            ENDIF
          ENDIF
        ENDIF
      ENDIF
    ENDDO
```

See paragraphs 8.3.1 and 8.3.2.

3 The question refers to the provision of a system design with appropriate human-computer interaction.

(1) Screen dialogue factors:

- dialogue and help facilities, together with manuals should reflect the expected level of user expertise;
- the available hardware and data input/output facilities;
- the software operating system and screen features;
- the nature of the application.

(2) Main interface techniques:

- **Form filling**—suitable for mass, routine data capture. The input screen uses prompts and blank fields. There will be cursor addressing and field protection. Instructions and help facilities may be shown in a window or at the bottom of the screen.
- **Menu selection**—menus allow access of multiple applications and are useful for controlling a complex interface. Individual screens may rely on form filling.
- **WIMP**—windows allow the user to control, view and input to screen workspaces. Icons are symbols representing system features. A mouse is a hand operated device which controls the screen features. Pull-down (or pop-up) menus allow features and applications to be selected without the user leaving a screen. **See paragraph 8.2.2**.

SOLUTIONS TO CHAPTER 9 QUESTIONS

1 Both elements in the question are parts of implementation and should be planned for:

(1) The link between acceptance testing and training is a circular one. Users cannot carry out testing until they are familiar with the system.

(2) Training is sometimes not well done because it is a cost which vendors are anxious to cut. Some buyers are reluctant to pay. Many trainers are inadequately motivated and prepared. Training is expensive because it is labour-intensive.

(3) Acceptance testing may evaluate:

- compliance with criteria;
- response times;
- compatibility with existing systems;
- robustness and reliability;
- capability of expansion;
- cost-effectiveness. **See paragraph 9.2.3**.

2 This question is about one method of acquisition.

(1) Features of a lease:

- three to five year's duration;
- possible option to purchase;
- agreement may be tailored;
- may be subject to review.

(2) Problems of leasing:

- achieving best terms;
- possibility of obsolescence;
- developing a replacement plan;
- technological problems;
- lack of guarantees.

(3) Advantages of leasing:

- experience of leasing companies;
- influence of leasing companies;
- low capital outlay;
- may include maintenance;
- controlled outgoings. **See paragraph 9.2.2**.

3 This question concerns the effect of licensing on the user organisation.

(1) Legal implications—the user may accept the terms of a contract by performance, ie by begining to use (or even unwrapping) the piece of software. The contract may control the use of software and the users' right to copy it. A breach of these terms by the user may result in termination of the agreement and claims for damages.

(2) Increases in costs may be caused by:

- necessary alterations to accommodation;
- additional security costs;
- more highly qualified personnel;
- training costs.

Costs will also be affected by the chosen method of acquisition. **See paragraph 9.2.5.**

4 Maintenance is partly a practical and partly a legal matter.

(1) Forms of maintenance:
- a help line which gives problem-solving advice;
- a formal agreement with the manufacturer of the hardware with a call-out provision;
- a third party agreement with a call-out provision;
- preventative maintenance.

(2) Factors in a maintenance agreement:
- the contractor's experience and standing;
- the range of services offered;
- the cost-effectiveness of the service;
- the possibility of upgrades;
- whether maintenance planning is included;
- whether routine work will be done outside normal working hours;
- response time to a call;
- action in the event of default. **See paragraph 9.4.**

SOLUTIONS TO CHAPTER 10 QUESTIONS

1 The question addresses the issues of efficiency and effectiveness in the planning and control of projects.

(1) Efficient utilisation of:
- **Time**—a key parameter. There will be an overall project deadline and, within this, milestones at which specified deliverables will be required. Failure to achieve completion by these dates will incur resource costs.
- **Resources**—may be material or human. Material resources (hardware and software) entail acquisition and production decisions. Human resources require recruitment, management and training decisions and facilities.
- **Costs**—will be influenced by factors 1 and 2. Cost management will entail forecasting and estimating, monitoring and rescheduling project activities to meet budgetary constraints.

(2) Types of judgments and decisions:
- **Time management**—may involve decisions on simplifying project tasks, acquiring extra resources (eg extra staff or overtime) and reducing non-productive activities.
- **Quality management**—often a decision trade-off between cost, time and the effectiveness of the completed system or software.
- **Resource management**—often decisions involve trying to optimise the use of resources with constraints of cost and time.
- **Cost management**—central to decisions on time, cost, quality and resources.

Although listed separately, the management of these aspects should be balanced and integrated. **See paragraph 10.3.**

2 The quesion asks for details on four components:

(1) **Team leaders** A leader of an information systems project team will be responsible for planning and organising, co-ordinating and supervising, advising the team, reporting to sponsors and implementing changes to project schedules.

(2) **User group** The project user group will consist of a cross-section of stakeholders in the project. The component is a vehicle for expressing concerns, resolving queries and discussing solutions. The user group is non-executive, matters for action being communicated to the steering committee.

(3) **Steering committee** This body may be temporary or permanent and will include users and project staff. The committee's role is central in securing senior management involvement, monitoring the effectiveness of planning and resource allocation, and approving changes in the project. Further, the committee will be involved in formulating policy for information systems development and operation.

(4) **Project manager** The person in overall charge of the project will operate at all levels of management and will attempt to achieve maximum efficiency and effectiveness by directing the team leaders in line with the wishes of the steering committee. The project manager integrates all aspects of the project.

Another major component could be the management sponsor of the project who will usually be an executive director. **See paragraph 10.6**.

3 CPA is a sequential approach to project planning and control. The major stages are:

(1) **Programming** The project must be broken down into tasks which may be decomposed into greater detail. The tasks are sequenced by establishing the inter-dependencies and may then be composed into a CPA diagram. An estimate of the duration of each task is made, which may be arrived at by a single estimate or by aggregation as in PERT. The project schedule is then drawn up, eg earliest start, latest finish dates, and the project free time or float is calculated.

(2) **Evaluation** The overall project duration will now be known, as will the critical path (those tasks which cannot be delayed). The project plan may now be examined for possible improvements involving decisions on resource levels and the placement of activities in some other sequence.

(3) **Review** The plan must be kept relevant by constant monitoring and updating. Actual completion dates will be fed into the plan (which may be computerised) and milestone reports and meetings will be conducted. The plan will be amended in line with actual performance. **See paragraph 10.7**.

SOLUTIONS TO CHAPTER 11 QUESTIONS

1 The question refers to factors which must be insured against when designing the physical system. In report form, an answer would contain:

(1) **Vulnerability** This refers to the possibility of a system or its data being wrongly used. Things which place a system at greater risk include the accessibility to hardware, and whether the configuration is centralised or distributed. Further, whether access to files can be made without leaving a trace (as in an access log), and whether the DP centre is located in a high risk area. The recruitment and turnover of staff is also an important factor in increasing vulnerability.

(2) **Risk** Risk analysis attempts to classify and quantify an organisation's exposure to threats. The quantification is based on the probability of an unwanted event occurring, the cost of avoidance and the cost of loss if the event does occur. Risk factors are often classified by source (eg internal/external) or by the method of control (eg acceptance, avoidance or insurance). **See paragraphs 11.3.5 and 11.3.6**.

2 The question seeks to establish the student's knowledge of contingency planning.

(1) Senior management's role is central because a disaster plan should affect most of the people in the organisation and not just the DP staff. It is up to senior management to sponsor and promote the disaster plan. Priorities must be assigned to user functions in the event of reduced system capacity, for example, is sales order entry more important than invoicing? The effect of this on the organisation must be assessed at a strategic level. Moreover, senior management are in the best position to assess the true cost of business interruption, direct loss and legal liability.

(2) A disaster plan should contain the following main elements:

- a statement of policy and terms of reference for each job holder;
- rules on implementing the policy;
- responsibilities and actions to be taken by employees and third parties in the event of a disaster;
- mechanisms for review and update. **See paragraphs 11.4.1 and 11.4.2**.

3 The activites being addressed are those of security planning as a team activity.

(1) The security planning team will involve contributions from:

— finance department—costings and appraisals;
— internal auditors—for review;
— legal department—statutory requirements;
— public relations—press releases, etc;
— personnel department—changes in jobs;
— production department—continued working;
— outside consultants—advice and experience.

(2) The detailed work of the team will be:

— fact-finding and a security audit of the hardware distribution, storage, software requirements and system controls;
— producing and evaluating alternative disaster scenarios, with risk analysis performed for critical applications;
— laying down strategies to cope with the requirements of the disaster scenarios, and producing recovery plans;
— monitoring and reviewing the plans. **See paragraphs 11.4.5 and 11.4.6**.

SOLUTIONS TO CHAPTER 12 QUESTIONS

1 This question requires a knowledge of fraud in computer-based information systems.

(1) A person may be motivated to commit fraud by a variety of factors including:

— the intellectual challenge of beating the system;
— greed and selfishness;
— high levels of debt due to abberant personal circumstances, eg gambling or addiction;
— resentment of the perpetrator's perceived lack of reward;
— jealousy of other employees or the organisation itself.

(2) Fraud may be concealed by some or all of the following methods:

— confusing the situation, eg creating a system crash;
— diverting attention from the actual fraud, eg planting evidence of fraud elsewhere in the system, perhaps implicating another individual;
— delaying the discovery, eg by breaking an audit trail;
— preventing discovery, eg by destroying evidence.

For a fraud to be committed, the individual will tend to believe that the chosen method of concealment will be successful. **See paragraphs 12.1.1 and 12.1.2**.

2 Factors which may affect the cost analysis process could include:

(1) the probability of a disaster occurring, and the likelihood of significant loss—a failure to quantify should not justify a failure to set up counter-measures;
(2) the unwillingness of management to invest in security which can show no positive return under normal circumstances;
(3) the lack of a basis upon which to compare costs;
(4) the fact that some departments may be reluctant to admit their reliance upon the DP function;
(5) a level of uncertainty about the costs and effectiveness of providing system back-up. **See paragraph 12.2**.

3 The decisions which must be made within an organisation that becomes involved in setting up security procedures are in the areas of logical and physical security. The main decision areas would be:

(1) fall-back systems and continued manual operation;
(2) alternative hardware provision;
(3) re-commissioning and restart facilities.

Decisions in these areas would include:

(1) the likely duration of disruption before critical damage to the business occurred;
(2) whether a full service should be provided to a restricted and/or rotating number of users;
(3) whether to allow a partial service to all users;
(4) whether to make mutual arrangements with another user running a similar configuration, or a bureau;
(5) the setting up of emergency facilities. **See paragraph 12.3.**

SOLUTIONS TO CHAPTER 13 QUESTIONS

1 The question addresses the importance of personal factors in system security.

(1) Physical access controls are about controlling space, allowing access to those who have a right. Physical access may be used to protect the installation itself, or to protect users or employees. The concept is therefore two way.
(2) Methods of access control may include:
— automatic entry control systems, eg using machine readable tokens or cards;
— mechanical locking systems using a combination lock, a conventional key or a security guard.

Another method would be signature verification. **See paragraphs 13.3.1/5.**

2 The question refers to security through the physical control of space. Planning considerations in this matter may be:

(1) the definition of the perimeter which is to be controlled—there may be a single zone or a hierarchy of zones with increasing levels of security;
(2) a decision upon the level of security to be implemented—movements between zones should be controlled;
(3) the siting of the commonly used facilities (eg canteen);
(4) the positively required security mechanisms, eg fire control, security doors, etc;
(5) provision for the evacuation of working staff and access for security staff in the event of a crisis.

Planning is vital since testing can only partially prove the effectiveness of security. **See paragraph 13.3.6.**

SOLUTIONS TO CHAPTER 14 QUESTIONS

1 This is a general question about access control.

(1) Three ways in which password security may be improved:
— a duress password is one which causes an alarm (or at least a record) when used—this not only covers the possibility of the password being stolen, but also that the user is forced to use it;
— machine-generated passwords which are communicated to the user through a secure mailing system;
— changing passwords at regular intervals, eg every month.
(2) Three ways in which a hacker might gain access:
— using a microcomputer and a modem (with an appropriate decoy program) to capture the system password on call-back;
— wire tapping or electronically intruding into a legitimately logged-on terminal link—this is particularly likely if the terminal is left unused;
— access to highly secure parts of the system may be gained from less secure parts by inserting a program which simulates the log-on screen—in attempting to log into this, the user reveals his or her password. **See paragraph 14.2.3.**

2 This question refers to the straightforward methods of data encryption for security. The methods are:

(1) hardware encryption—permanent but expensive;
(2) cipher systems using algorithms and a key;
(3) substitution or transposition methods of cipher;
(4) mixed transformation methods, eg DES;
(5) one-time-pad systems using message and key on separate media.

A problem of encryption is simplicity and speed—the more effective the cipher, the slower the transformation. **See paragraphs 14.5.3 and 14.5.4.**

SOLUTIONS TO CHAPTER 15 QUESTIONS

1 The essence of this question is the proliferation of microtechnology without consequent increases in built-in security measures. This creates problems which include the following:
(1) restricting access to public office areas, and imposing fire and damage precautions;
(2) implementing user friendly access controls which invite rather than restrict access;
(3) implementing multi-user micro operating systems which allow access to all files;
(4) encouraging electronic communication links, particularly the ability to tap into a LAN or establish a micro-mainframe link;
(5) developing sophisticated skills in those who use the micros and their operating systems which may be training the next generation of hackers.

A major problem is that of reconciling the concept of the corporate data repository with the relative freedom of user computing. **See paragraph 15.4.**

2 The detection of fraud requires rapid but considered action by management. Actions which may be taken include:
(1) maintaining absolute secrecy to prevent the offenders being warned off;
(2) taking decisions on whether to proceed with a prosecution—this may be governed by a policy (ie it acts as a deterrent) or be dictated by insurance factors;
(3) gaining data on the nature of the suspected fraud, eg the method used, scale of loss, etc;
(4) gathering the relevant computer output and records;
(5) soliciting evidence from third parties, eg Inland Revenue;
(6) analysing the data with a view to producing a schedule of evidence suitable for making a case. **See paragraph 15.6.1.**

SOLUTIONS TO CHAPTER 16 QUESTIONS

1 Audits tend to create disruption and so should involve careful planning.
(1) A security audit plan may include the following:
- staff selection—usually not from the area to be audited, but equally knowledgeable;
- checks which should be scheduled at random with a maximum amount of surprise;
- the location and duration of the check which should be decided, making the task of an appropriate size;
- the selection of the type of audit comparison to be made, eg historical or intercompany;
- carrying out the audit and maintaining controls for several weeks after the event.

(2) Problems in prosecution may occur because:
- a jury may not understand the technical details of the case;
- sentences for non-violent fraud offences may be too lenient to prove a deterrent to others;
- the image of computers may prejudice jury and public opinion against the organisation and in favour of the defendant;
- the organisation may fear adverse publicity through revealing the vulnerability of their systems;
- details of the fraud which are raised in court may inspire copycat crimes. **See paragraph 16.2.**

2 The question is about the methods and practices of auditors in a systems context.

(1) The responsibilities of an auditor include the following:

- assisting in drawing up, reviewing and testing the disaster plans;
- liaising with external auditors during financial audits which involve the organisation's computer system;
- helping to design and review security measures;
- assisting in the specification of software and data storage in the area of controls and audit trails;
- helping to maintain data integrity, eg in collaboration with the database administrator.

The organisation's security auditor should be in a position of authority, possibly in a senior management position.

(2) Data security is about the design and operation of the information system. The auditor will be involved in the development of new applications throughout the system development life cycle.

- The auditor will be particularly involved at the feasibility study phase in the definition of security objectives, at the design stage in developing controls and counter-measures, and at the post implementation stage in ensuring conformity with procedures.
- The auditor will monitor day-to-day operation of the system, including logs and exception reports.
- The auditor will check and approve proposed enhancements and amendments to the system and its software. **See paragraph 16.5**.

3 The ability to restore computing service depends on the replacement of any hardware which may be lost in a disaster. Alternative methods of hardware provision include:

(1) Drawing up a contingency agreement with a bureau (a time broker)—this option will involve detailed testing to ensure system compatibility and may be economically viable only for high volume DP operations.

(2) Arranging a mutual aid agreement with other user organisations having a nearly identical system—although this is potentially cheap and may be superficially attractive, such agreements may be fraught with difficulty. The organisations may be constrained from making alterations, eg a new operating system, in order to maintain compatibility. The disruption to DP operations which would be suffered by an organisation offering aid may be intolerable. Such agreements are therefore difficult to negotiate and maintain.

(3) Maintaining a fully equipped computer centre in duplication of existing facilities (a contingency centre or hot standby). The centre may be shared by several organisations or operated as a commercial venture by a third party on subscription. Although full cost only becomes payable upon exercising the option, there are problems of standardisation and security where data is stored on site.

(4) A similar concept to (3) above is the empty shell or cold standby centre. An organisation using this facility would need special agreements with manufacturers to supply replacement hardware at very short notice. This may prevent the option being used for critical operations, but the constraints on system change do not apply.

All methods of hardware provision rely on successful back-up of data and software in the event of a disaster. **See paragraph 16.6.3**.

ADDITIONAL QUESTIONS

Students are encouraged to attempt these questions. However, the answers are provided only in the manual issued to lecturers. Lecturers may obtain a free copy of the manual by writing to: Sales and Marketing Department, Longman Group UK Ltd, 21–27 Lamb's Conduit Street, LONDON WC1N 3NJ.

1 One of the major problems which confronts information system developers is that of designing systems which are flexible enough to absorb the organisational pressures to produce more information.

List and briefly describe the factors which generate the demand for more information in a typical commercial organisation.

2 A generalisation which is sometimes used to distinguish between data processing and decision support systems is that data processing applies to programmable decisions and decision support applies to non-programmable decisions.

Distinguish between programmable and non-programmable decisions, giving examples of each which may occur in the field of accounting.

3 One of the important decisions which a team engaged in systems development must make involves the defining of the system boundary, and the interface between systems.

(a) **Discuss the importance of defining the system boundary and state four factors which can influence the decision.**
(b) **Explain the essential features of a system interface, giving examples which may be found in an information system in a typical commercial organisation.**

4 Planning may be seen as the process whereby the organisation looks to identify those objectives most realistic for it to pursue.

(a) **Explain the processes by which an organisation might go about creating an information strategy.**

(b) **List and briefly describe the elements which would be contained in the information strategy for a typical commercial organisation.**

5 The organisation for which you work is currently engaged in designing a computer-based system for its accounting applications. Its management is unsure whether the system should operate in batch-mode, interactive mode or a mixture of the two.

Describe the main features, advantages and disadvantages of both operating modes. Give examples of suitable applications for each mode which may be found in an accounting application.

6 It is most commonly found that the most effective system and software designs are those that have been deduced from accurately stated users' requirements.

Discuss the role of the user in the system development process, indicating the steps in the design process at which the user may become involved.

7 User-driven systems development methodologies concentrate on the behavioural aspects of information systems design at the expense of the technical aspects.

Discuss the aims of user-driven development and briefly describe some techniques which may be used in a user-driven development methodology.

8 The main tools of systems analysis and design are not sufficient for specifying the way in which the software to implement a system should be written.

(a) **List and describe the features which an effective procedure specification method must have.**

(b) **Describe two of the main specification techniques, and give the advantages and disadvantages of each.**

9 The choice of implementation strategy is vital to the succesful operation of a computer-based system.

(a) **List and describe the three most common routes for changeover.**
(b) **List and briefly describe the factors which may add to the risk profile of a system implementation.**

10 Each of the phases of project management needs to be managed at different levels which match the need to manage the total organisation.

Discuss the three levels of project management, giving examples of the individuals who may become involved in each, and of the tasks which would be carried out. Your examples should be from an accounting information system project.

11 Most governments and businesses now depend upon effective computerised data manipulation facilities and data communications as essential elements in their official and commercial systems.

Discuss the role of computers in security and the detection of fraudulent activity within a business organisation.

12 One of the ways in which an organisation can reduce the losses which may result from a disaster that affects its computer system is by taking out appropriate insurance.

(a) **Discuss the role of the insurance company in protecting the organisation against loss.**
(b) **List and briefly describe the three basic types of insurance policy which are currently popular.**
(c) **Explain the potential problems which need to be considered when assessing insurance in an information systems context.**

13 The organisation for which you work is carrying out an analysis of the factors which may represent threats to the computer-based information system which is currently being designed.

Categorise and discuss the main threats which should be considered by your organisation.

14 It may be said that the first line of protection for the organisation's information resource is the logical access system.

(a) **Describe the concept of the logical access system, indicating the features which such a system must have.**

(b) **List and briefly describe three types of access control element.**

15 The basic principles for the effective design of data security systems are those based on system controls.

Discuss the role of human-based accounting controls and automated controls in the data security system.

16 People represent a threat to information system security if only through their inexperience, incompetence, negligence and curiosity.

(a) **Discuss the effect which the introduction of an information system may have upon individuals within the organisation.**
(b) **Discuss the organisational measures which could be taken to make personnel security more effective.**

December 1990

Level 2 — Professional Examination

Paper 2.7

Information Systems in Development and Operation

FIVE questions ONLY to be attempted

1 Most large organisations use a 'structured' approach in the development of information systems.

(a) **Outline the main stages in such an approach** (12 marks)

(b) **Describe the tools and techniques available to assist in the analysis of the current system and the design of the new system.** (8 marks)

(20 marks)

2 You are responsible for implementing a payroll system for weekly paid employees, using a bought-in package on a stand-alone microcomputer system. There are 3,000 records (one for each employee) in the current manual system. Each record is held on a card. The information about each employee comprises personal details (personnel no., name, date of birth, grade, section, rate of pay, allowances, deductions from pay, etc) held in the top section of the card. In the body of the card are held a series of line entries, one for each week of the year. As each week is worked the details are entered in the appropriate line; gross pay; tax and national insurance, by reference to the relevant tables; and net pay.

(a) **Fully describe a procedure for transferring data from the manual to the computer to create the master file prior to going live on the new system.** (14 marks)

(b) **Specify the checks and controls to be incorporated into the process to ensure that the computerised master file is accurate, complete, up to date and suitable for running the live system.** (6 marks)

(20 marks)

3 The company for which you work operates a real-time order entry system. Orders and enquiries can be made in person, by telephone or by post. When the system was installed, response time was in the range two to five seconds and the system was performing well. The system has now been running for two years. During the last six months the response time has deteriorated, at peak times it now takes up to 40 seconds to get a response. Staff and customers are unhappy.

What factors would you examine to determine the cause(s) of the problem?

(20 marks)

4 A manufacturing company is considering implementing a production control system. As part of the feasibility study, a cost-benefit analysis is to be prepared.

What factors should be taken into consideration in preparing a cost-benefit analysis? (Use examples, where appropriate, from a manufacturing context).

(20 marks)

5 'Prototyping' is a method of producing application software.

(a) **Explain what is meant by the term 'prototyping'.** (8 marks)

(b) **Give examples of situations where the use might be appropriate.** (12 marks)

(20 marks)

6 **Describe the different levels of management information requirements within a company. Identify examples of information appropriate at each level and describe suitable methods for presenting it.**

(20 marks)

7 It is crucial that the eventual end users of a computer system are in favour of it.

During the development of a system how can a systems analyst seek to overcome the resentment and opposition which may be encountered?

(20 marks)

End of Question Paper

Author's model answers to this examination paper are on page 415.

Authors' model answers to December 1990 Information Systems in Development & Operation Paper

ANSWER TO QUESTION 1

1 **(a)** This question requires a definition of the structured approach to IS development and the description of the main stages in a 'typical' structured approach.

A 'structured approach' is one which follows a logical and disciplined approach from the investigation of the users' needs to the implementation of the computer-based system. Since this is called the systems development lifecycle (SDLC), an approach which covers all of the cycle is often called a 'cradle to grave' method. To produce this full coverage of the SDLC, a structured approach will contain a variety of tools or techniques which are arranged into definite stages. A typical structured approach may have the following stages:

(i) **Feasibility Study** This stage may be optional depending on the size of the IS project and whether the organisation has an IS strategy. A feasibility study will involve problem identification and project identification. The outline system solution will be subjected to tests for technical, operational and economic feasibility. An outline project which passes these tests will proceed through the next stages.

(ii) **Systems Analysis** This stage will involve a detailed analysis of the operations and problems of the current business system. A logical model of the current system (a data model and/or function model) will be drawn up, and from this a requirements specification will be produced. A logical model is one which concentrates on *what* the system does, not *how* it does it. The requirements specification will augment the logical model with additional user requirements ('extra functionality') and with the requirements for physical system features such as control security and audit requirements. Several different technical 'options' may be produced upon which the technical system design may be based.

(iii) **Systems Design** The logical model requirements specification and the chosen technical option(s) will contribute to the technical design. Usually the data model will form the basis of file or database design, and the function model the basis of the program design. A full technical specification will be produced.

(iv) **Development and Testing** The technical design specification will be used to create the program code and to set up the physical files or database. Individual program modules will be tested using simulated data or 'test packages', then whole programs, and then the whole system will be 'acceptance tested' by the users. Sometimes the users themselves may be involved in the development using prototyping techniques or fourth generation languages (4GLs).

(v) **Implementation** When the system has passed its acceptance tests, user training must be carried out and a strategy for changeover from the old system to the new must be chosen prior to 'going live'.

(vi) **Post-Implementation Review and Maintenance** After the changeover period, there will usually be a post-audit or review of the delivered system's performance against the pre-agreed criteria. Enhancements may be suggested at this stage, and maintenance and developments can be continuous.

(b) Several of the structured approaches to IS development (eg SSADM) use a combination of tools and techniques to give a 'multi-dimensional' view of the system. The same tools may be used for both analysis and design. The techniques which are most often used are dataflow diagrams, entity-relationship modelling and entity life histories

(i) **Dataflow Diagrams (DFDs)** DFDs describe the functions, datastores and external entities which make up the system, and they show the flows of data between them. A decompositional approach will be used to go into increasing levels of detail until the detailed operations of the system may be described.

(ii) **Entity-Relationship Modelling** The entity-relationship model or logical data structure (LDS) shows the entities or important 'things' within the system about which data will be stored, and defines the relationships between them.

(iii) **Entity Life Histories (ELHs)** ELHs show the states which an entity can go through from creation to deletion and the functions and/or events which cause the entity to change states.

Other tools and techniques which may be incorporated into a structured approach include normalisation, decision tables and trees, flowcharts and Structured English specification.

ANSWER TO QUESTION 2

2 **(a)** The question refers to the file conversion process which will vary from one system to another depending on the complexity of the files and the choice of media. The process is often extremely labour intensive and the basic project management problems of planning, monitoring and controlling the activities are as important at this stage as at any other. A suitable conversion procedure for the payroll system could be:

(i) Decide changeover strategy and timing. In the payroll application, a direct changeover could be recommended because the system is well structured and an engineered package is being used. The possibility of reverting to the manual system in the case of problems should be considered. An ideal time to implement the changeover would be at the end of the tax year or during a holiday period with many staff on vacation.

(ii) Collate and correct existing (manual) records. In these days, it is unusual to find a payroll system which is based completely on manual records, but this is how the system is described. With 3,000 employee records, this is not a large system, but it is vital that all the records are accurate and up-to-date. People become very annoyed if their salary is incorrect! Since the records are used weekly, few problems will be encountered in this area.

(iii) Data transcription will involve reading the existing records and keying them into the computer. This will form the major part of the procedure, as the single keyboard will prove a considerable restriction if a single file is used. As an example, an input rate of 30 records per hour would take a single person three working weeks to complete the conversion! Alternative approaches would be to use a three-shift input system (one week, but expensive as it requires the payment of overtime or the employment of a bureau) or to hire extra computers, divide the records into three parts, and produce three files which would be combined at the end. To avoid disruption to the existing system, the records could be duplicated (eg photocopied) or the static data (eg personnel number, name, data of birth, etc) entered first and the dynamic data (eg gross pay, tax, national insurance contributions, etc) added later. The final update would be the 'live' data for the week the changeover is made.

It is likely that the chosen payroll package. will contain some built-in functions (eg verification and validation checks) to make the conversion process go as smoothly as it possibly can.

(b) Checks and controls which could be incorporated into the conversion process could include:

(i) A manual check to ensure that all the records are complete and up-to-date. This would probably be done before a normal manual payroll operation anyway.
(ii) User training in the use of the input function of the package could be regarded as a control mechanism, and it should include (documented) instructions for actions to be taken in the event of errors and exceptions.
(iii) 'Change control' procedures should be set up to control and document any non-routine changes (eg grade, section, rate of pay) which may occur during the changeover period.
(iv) Batching controls should be used to check that all records have been input. This would involve dividing the manual record cards into batches (eg of 100 cards) which are input sequentially. The manual total will be compared with a computer-counted total.
(v) Data control checks should be contained within the package. (This may be one of the features for which the package was chosen). Such checks could include control totals, range checks for gross pay, tax and net pay fields, format checks for national insurance number, etc, and check digits for the personnel number.
(vi) Rejected records from the input stage should be collected, corrected and re-input according to strictly controlled procedures.
(vii) A test run (using a duplicate test file) based on the previous week's data could be compared with the result from the output from the manual system, for the corresponding week.

ANSWER TO QUESTION 3

3 What is the point of an on-line order entry system? From the user's point of view, the processing capacities of the computer are available on demand to check stock availability, delivery times, credit limits, etc so that both buyer and seller can confirm the details of each deal on the spot. The flexibility and rapidity of response make an on-line system (as opposed to a batch system) highly desirable. for the purposes of this answer, it is assumed that the organisation has installed a local area network (LAN) to support access to the order entry system from different departments. The generally acceptable response time would be two to five seconds in 95% of all cases in such a system. It is assumed that such responses were obtained during the first 18 months of operation. The marked deterioration has set in during the last six months so the cause must either be the result of a slow degradation which has only been noted during this period or some specific event(s) which occurred during the period. There are three possible causes:

(i) hardware failure;
(ii) software failure; and
(iii) human failure.

These may be operating singly or in combination. The first point to consider is the age of the building(s) which house the computer system and peripherals and the life cycle of its infrastructure of guided media, ie wiring, cabling, fibre optics, etc. If the building is old, it is possible that rain water or some other natural cause might have affected the efficiency of the cabling. As an additional symptom, it would be worth checking to see whether data integrity during transmission has been affected. If electrical equipment which emits electromagnetic radiation has recently been installed, this new source of electrical noise may be affecting cabling where there is thinner insulation..

If the building is well maintained and the guided media were installed together with the computer system itself two years ago, the physical configuration of the communications network should be checked. If there have been any changes to the components of the system, eg modems, multiplexors, etc, these should be identified and their performance verified. Indeed, if any changes have been made to the hardware supporting the network, their possible effect on performance should be evaluated, eg have extra terminals been added. One of the standard security measures ought to be fault analysis. If the organisation has maintained detailed logs, they should be checked to see whether there has been any pattern of line faults or breakdowns which might give a clue to the reduced performance.

Should the physical system prove sound, it may be that the poor performance results from excessive traffic. A check should be made on the total number of transactions being processed when the system was first commissioned and now. If the business itself is new, the level of traffic may have been growing as the business performance improved. It would also be material to consider the type of transactions. If it should appear that the number or complexity of transactions has substantially increased, CPU time might be inadequate and a queuing problem might have arisen, or the traffic management system within the LAN may be inadequate.

The original design specifications should be considered. If this proves to be the problem, there are two possible solutions:

(i) to upgrade the whole system; and/or
(ii) to produce an access timetable to distribute the use more evenly over the working day, and to remove the complex transactions to off-peak periods.

If all the hardware proves to be functioning according to specification, the cause may lie in the software. Again, one should check to see whether any changes have been made, eg the latest edition of the operating system, loaded six months ago, may have bugs which are slowing down the customised order package. Similarly, changes to the software itself may have been made. These should have been fully audited before implementation but errors may be thrown up when the system goes live with real world data. It may be necessary to undertake a full system walk through to test original design expectations against the real world transaction patterns. This might, for example, show that sequential and indexed sequential files have gone into overflow, and that the ISAM (indexed sequential access method) has created overflow chains with the usual file organisation problems resulting. It might show problems with the queuing system because the actual number of users was not anticipated, or the demands on CPU time for complex processing were not expected. All such problems would lead to significant reductions in system performance.

Users play an important part in this investigation. It may be that a facility was built into the software from the outset, eg a sales forecasting package, but the sales department did not start to use it until six months ago. This may have caused unanticipated problems in the functioning of the rest of the system. Indeed, it might only have taken one run of the package to damage the system. Alternatively, one user might have ignored the security system and changed some of the software. It is worth offering an amnesty to get information from such a user as to the detail of what was done.

As response time falls, the risk of machine abuse rises. Users become bored and frustrated, and do not perform well. Ironically, this enhances the appearance of slowness in response time and increases frustration. Staff react to this in a variety of ways. They may literally attack the terminals or PCs, or they may begin to ignore the system and try to find other ways in which to do their work. If the users make lots of mistakes in inputting data, eg because there is a high turnover of staff and training is poor, the additional workload of data verification and rekeying may have slowed the system down.

By reviewing all three elements as potential causes of poor performance, the events which led to the deterioration six months ago will almost certainly come to light. It is probable that the cause will be found to be a combination of several factors which have interacted to slow the system down. The organisation should learn from the experience, and institute a regular monitoring of system performance to identify problems as they arise and not after they have become serious.

ANSWER TO QUESTION 4

4 The investment in a production control system, as in any other investment in an organisation's information system (computerised and/or manual) will compete against the other potential investments for access to the limited capital resources. The key criterion on which choices between alternative investments are taken is the scale, nature and timing of the initial and future commitments in terms of both capital and other resources when compared to the potential profits to be generated. Cost-benefit analysis is a widely used approach to undertaking this form of investment appraisal and typically involves the financial quanification of the costs and benefits involved in each project. A number of financial appraisal methods are available. These methods may help to provide an assessment of the potential profitability of a particular project as well as a basis for comparative analysis across different investment projects (eg payback, net present value and internal rate of return methods). The primary element which determines the resulting quality of the financial appraisal is the accuracy achievable in estimating or forecasting the costs and benefits in financial terms. The factors influencing the accuracy of these estimates are the detailed problems of estimating the costs and benefits particular to each project, together with the more general issues relating to reliability of cost-benefit analysis methods.

The initial determination of the costs for investments such as the production control system may be divided between the Development and Implementation Costs, and the subsequent Running Costs. A further division between costs that are directly attributable to the project and those that are less directly attributable may be helpful. The former costs are generally easier to assess, whereas the latter require greater judgment concerning the impact of the particular project in terms of costs. The following examples under each of these groupings will illustrate this point:

DEVELOPMENT AND IMPLEMENTATION

Direct Costs: hardware, software, buildings, installation system design, programming, file conversion, training and redundancy.

Indirect Costs: disruption to production during the installation of the control system; additional management and supervisory staff time and effort.

RUNNING/OPERATIONAL

Direct Costs: hardware and software maintenance, consumable materials (eg paper), power, staffing, etc.

Indirect Costs: general overheads (eg security, insurance); organisational/operational changes to accommodate the new system; change to the user's work practices and patterns.

In the situation of implementing a new production control system, many of the indirect costs may prove to be significant in scale. Changes to the methods of scheduling and loading of work on to the production lines will often be radical and require the feedback of more data from the operatives than previously.

Benefits may be classified into two broad groups incorporating cost savings/efficiency improvements and added values. Examples of the types of benefits in each of these cases are:

Cost Savings: improved labour and machine productivity, reduced wastage, enhanced quality and reduced raw material storage costs.

Added Values: improved delivery and service to customers, opportunities to develop existing or new markets, application of new technologies (eg JIT), scope for future developments (eg EDI), and improved information for planning, monitoring and control.

The quantification of cost savings is usually easier than the added value factors since the former may be achieved through a comparison between the existing and likely improved performance levels of the manufacturing systems, eg the forecast of stock levels to be required under the new control system as against those required at present. Added value benefits are more difficult to quantify as the forecasting involves higher levels of uncertainty, eg the financial benefits in sales resulting from faster delivery times, the ability of the management to use the information available to improve operational performance, and the capacity of the organisation and the workforce to gain the necessary experience from implementing this new technology to facilitate the adoption of other associated technological developments are all difficult to value.

In general terms, estimates of costs and benefits vary in terms of the degree of uncertainty. In the field of information systems, the degree of uncertainty associated with benefits is significantly higher than those of costs which require fewer judgments in their estimation. It is important that the decision-makers recognise the degree of uncertainty that exists and, where this may be critical to a given decision, take the necessary steps to improve such estimates, eg undertake market research to establish potential customer responses to improved quality and faster delivery. Secondly, the providers of estimates and forecasts within the organisation should be basing all their work on similar planning assumptions, eg for all organisational purposes the forecasts of market growth, cost/price inflation rates, etc should be the same. This is necessary if the organisation is to achieve a degree of consistency in both decision-making generally, and the forecasting costs and benefits in particular. Finally, the identification and estimation of both costs and benefits will usually improve as the project develops. While the initial cost-benefit analysis may be conducted as part of the feasibility study to gain approval for the initial development, the appraisal of the costs and benefits should be continually reviewed at each stage in the systems development. This would either permit the termination of the development if the costs are seen to be outweighing the benefits at any stage or, more importantly, assist in redirecting and redesigning the control systems to ensure the achievement of the full benefits potentially available.

ANSWER TO QUESTION 5

5 **(a)** 'Prototyping' involves creating a simulation of a computer-based system which appears to the user as the finished system would, but which does not update the file(s) or carry out the processing. A full system or part of the system may be prototyped. Prototyping will often be carried out by the users themselves, with the advice of an analyst who is expert in the technique. When the users (and the analyst) are satisfied with the appearance and 'feel' of the sytem, the software will be coded to match the features of the prototype. Prototyping involves the use of fourth generation language (4GL) tools such as a report generator, a screen painter or forms designer and a data dictionary.

(b) The use of prototyping will be especially appropriate in situations such as the following:

(i) Where the users are uncertain as to the nature of the finished system and are lacking in the ability to interpret a logical model 'on paper'. Prototype screen designs may be produced to speed up the development of the human-computer interaction (HCI) elements of the system. This veiw would see prototyping as an alternative to a structured *design* technique.

(ii) Where the present system is somewhat unstructured, and the users' needs are likely to be difficult to capture by conventional analysis techinques. This approach would involve the production of a rough or 'first cut' prototype of part of the system. After evaluation by the user a more refined prototype will be produced, this process being reiterated until the users are satisfied that their requirements have been accurately defined. Mutual understanding and definition of the system grows through this evolutionary approach. This view would see prototyping as an alternative to the *analysis* phase of a structured method.

(iii) Where the finished system will be essentially non-procedural and data-driven. In orther words, a database, data dictionary and 4GL implementation may be successfully developed by prototyping techniques which have the same features — a case of the development method matching the functioning of the finished system. Decision support systems (DSS), executive information systems (EIS) and query based systems are all amenable to the prototyping approach.

Prototyping may therefore be used as an alternative to conventional ('structured') development techniques from either end of the system development lifecycle (SDLC). It may also be used in addition to these tools to make the system more 'real' to the users. The prototype may be evolutionary (ie change to become the 'real' system) or a 'dummy' which will be scrapped and replaced by the final system.

ANSWER TO QUESTION 6

6 The three broad levels of decision-making within an organisation comprise:

Strategic
Management
Operational

The nature of the decisions taken, the processes of analysis and decision-making, and the people involved differ between each of these levels. The information needs and the interface of the information system with the user will also differ at each level.

Operational decisions are concerned with the on-going, daily or routine operations of the business relating to the primary activities of the organisation. Such decisions are typified by short timescales, explicit and specific performance objectives, clearly documented procedures, low levels of uncertainty and risk, and highly predictable information requirements. Operational decisions relating to the Stock Control System, for example, may involve the issuing of stocks to production, verifying physical stock levels, or issuing replenishment orders. Supporting decisions of this type requires an information system that provides accurate, detailed and up-to-date information which may be regularly and quickly accessed. In a manual system, the information would be held on a stock record card, whereas a computer system would provide access via a screen/terminal to information which may be held in a central database. Many of the systems supporting operational-level decisions provide the users with real-time interactive access to highly detailed, accurate and up-to-date information usually through a visual dispaly terminal.

Strategic decisions represent the opposite end of the spectrum to the operational decision in terms of the volume of the decisions and the consequent information support required. This type of decision is concerned with the long-term development and planning for the whole organisation as opposed to specific functional areas or individual operations. Decisions relating to future market or product development, policies and strategies to gain competitive advantage, and proposals to re-organise or change the structure and processes of the business require different types of information. The information needs reflect the long-term nature of the decisions; the need to balance internal and external factors; the more unstructured nature of the decisions faced; the higher levels of uncertainty and risk; and the lower degrees of predictability in the type of decision situation likely to be encountered.

Most systems at this level provide regular and summarised information on the key performance parameters internally together with feedback on key developments in the environment, ie they represent a dual set of corporate intelligence systems. The system needs to be sufficiently flexible and adaptable to respond to the particular decision in hand and to provide the more detailed information required to support longer-term planning. The tendency has been, and still is, to provide this in a hard copy form of presentation. However, the development of decision support systems which are more decision-maker friendly and supportive, and the improved training and skills of senior management present significant opportunities to improve the effectiveness of presentation through computer terminals providing real-time interactive access to the users.

Management or tactical decisions are in the middle of the spectrum both in terms of the nature of the decisions taken and the information support required. These decisions are concerned with the integration, co-ordination and communication between the operational and strategic levels. Such decisions will normally relate to medium-term performance factors, predominantly within one functional area; involve moderate degrees of uncertainty and risk; comprise semi-structured problems for which certain standard analytical approaches may be applied to aid the decision-maker; and have some degree of predictability in terms of the type of decision if not necessarily the detailed elements. The development of policies on finished goods stock-holding, for example, would require the synthesis of the strategic objectives and policies on the financial investment in stocks, the desired levels of customer service (ie the availability of items from stock), and the day-to-day demand patterns from the operational levels. Certain decision support tools, eg economic order quantity models, may be used to support the analysis of such decisions.

The information system, in effectively supporting the decision-maker, must be particularly flexible and adaptable at this level. On the one hand, it must provide regular summarised performance reports monitoring the operations of the organisation, while allowing the opportunity to examine any aspect of this performance in greater detail. On the other hand, it must also provide the appropriate decision support tools and methods to permit analysis and control. The presentation of this information may be in the form of regular hard copy reports, though a system of exception reporting through a screen-based system which facilitates quick and in-depth analysis of specific areas of performance would significantly enhance the effectiveness of the decision-maker.

ANSWER TO QUESTION 7

7 The strength of all organisations ultimately lies in its human resources and it is the responsibility of management to ensure that effective use is made in the deployment of those resources. This involves a process of control and direction where relationships of authority are established and power is exercised. The power structures which develop set the culture and 'feel' of the organisation. The culture may be one of devolved authority where all the key employees are involved in decision-making and are well-motivated, or it may be hierarchical and autocratic where staff feel alienated and unco-operative. If an organisation proposes to change the way in which it works, eg by introducing a computer system to automate some or all of its more routine functions, these changes may be a threat to the existing power relationships. Thus, in proposing these changes, the senior managers must be prepared to address the political issues which underpin the culture, and to steer the project through the maze of entrenched self-interest which is likely to slow down progress.

The first issue which must be considered is that automation may lead to a progressive democratisation of the decision-making activity. This is the usual consequence of sharing more management information and of making the results of earlier decisions more publicly available. This may undermine the reputation and authority of some of the established managers and be a cause of resentment. If it should lead to a downwards migration of authority, it is likely to lead to improved self-esteem among the lower levels of management if they are shown to be effective. The intermediate managerial class will therefore lose a part of their supervisory and control function and this will encourage their resentment unless the whole management structure is redesigned to allow these middle managers a sufficient role of co-ordination and group policy making. This level of organisation redesign is wholly inappropriate for a systems analyst to approach unless with the positive backing of a full strategic management team. Indeed, the whole of the initial planning exercise revolves around critical decisions about the objectives of the organisation and the processes by which it seeks to achieve them.

A detailed process of consultation should then take place so that all the groups likely to be affected by any changes can make a contribution to this strategic formulation. By engaging in this debate, both the planners and the prospective users are evaluating the changes constructively and identifying what the most important results would be for the organisation as a whole. If conflicts emerge, it is better to confront them at this early stage and to redefine objectives and processes rather than to leave it until later when the plans have been agreed at strategic levels and work has already begun to implement them. The most common issues and emotions are the following:

- **(i)** the fear or redundancy — it is always thought that the introduction of technology will lead to the need for fewer people;
- **(ii)** fear of redeployment to another job — this is a part of the general fear of the unkown;
- **(iii)** fear of inadequacy — many people feel that the computer is threatening and that, generally, they will not be able to cope in the new technological environment;

(iv) fear of loss in status — there is often taken to be implied criticism of those who ran the old system so inefficiently that it has to be changed.

If organisational and administrative problems cannot be resolved early, strategic managers are better placed to decide whether to proceed in the face of known opposition. The problems are that if staff do become demoralised and unco-operative, this may lead to absenteeism, retirement, finding other jobs, demotivated levels of performance or hostility to the new system. Committees may be formed with the declared brief of reviewing the proposed plans, but their real purpose is to achieve delay. Indeed, the successful management of change is a challenge to any organisation in breaking down barriers to progress by education and persuasion and, if all else fails, the constructive use of authority.

When strategic plans are complete, the systems analyst should decompose the processes and cluster them into applications, defining the data architecture and views as the logic in the sub-systems emerges. The end-product should be a good basis from which to take the strategic decision of feasibility (the go/no go decision) which is based on three interdependent issues:

(i) Will the staff be willing and able to turn the proposals into a working system?
(ii) Is it technically possible to make the system work efficiently?
(iii) Will it give a good economic return on investment?

If it is a go decision, the process of systems analysis begins, ie a detailed fact-finding exercise about the applications areas. This requires the systems analyst to spend a considerable amount of time with the users at various levels of the organisation while building up a file of data about the current situation. In one sense, this should be seen as a continuation of the consultation process, with users given every opportunity whether through informal dicussion, formal interviews or quenstionnaires, to air their views and to contribute to making the system suitable for resolving their problems. It should be made clear that this investigative process will lead to a problem analysis exercise which is designed to identify:

(i) the existing methods and practices, and their defects;
(ii) the alternative methods and their possible advantages.

The whole process should lead to the basis from which the new system can be designed. The more problems identified by the users that can be solved, the more likely it is that the users' interest and confidence will be maintained. For this purpose, it may be advantageous to have representatives from the affected users on the project management teams so that everyone can be kept informed of progress.

When it comes to implementation, the management must plan for user and operator training, and for the creation of good support documentation. The aim is that all the staff should feel confident about the new system before the changeover occurs. If the staff are able to acutally perform the file transfers and data transcriptions, this will also help to make sure that they are familiar with the new system. It should also produce a more reliable transfer than might be achieved by temporary staff who might not have the same interest in getting the system set up properly. If temporary staff do have to be employed, it would be better for them to run the old system. It will help staff confidence if either a phased changeover or parallel running implementation is adopted. But, as always, staff should be consulted and their morale maintained in whatever way is most consistent with system security. Once the system is installed, there should be a review to test whether the system meets the initial objectives and whether it meets the user's needs. This post-audit review should take account of all the users' comments both with a view to amending the new system, and to building in improvements in the next projects.

Bibliography

AAlders, JCH, Herschberg, IS & Van Zanten *A Handbook for Information Security. A Guide towards Information Security Standards*, (Amsterdam, North Holland, 1985).

Anderson, RG *Information Systems and Technology*, (London, Macdonald and Evans, 1985).

Ardis, Patrick M & Comer, Michael J *Risk Management. Computers, Fraud and Insurance*, (London, McGraw-Hill, 1987).

Avison, DE *Information Systems Development: A Database Approach*, (Oxford, Blackwell Scientific Publications, 1985).

Avison, DE *Information Systems Development: Methodologies, Techniques and Tools*, (Oxford, Blackwell Scientific Publications, 1988).

Barkin, SR & Dickson, GW *An Investigation of Information System Utilization*, (Information and Management, November 1977, Vol 1, pp33–45).

Beer, S *Diagnosing the System for Organisations*, (Chichester, John Wiley, 1981).

Brumm, Penn *The Micro to Mainframe Connection*, (Blue Ridge Summit, TAB Books Inc, 1986).

Camrass, Roger & Smith, Ken *Wiring Up The Workplace. A Practical Guide for Management*, (London, IBC Technical Services Ltd, 1986).

Checkland, PB *Systems Thinking, Systems Practice*, (Chichester, John Wiley, 1981).

Chen, PPS *The Entity-Relationship Model—Toward a Unified View of Data*, (ACM Transactions on Database Systems, March 1976, pp9-36).

Clifton, HD *Business Data Systems*, (New Jersey, Prentice-Hall, Third Edition, 1987).

Codd, EF *A Relational Model of Data for Large, Shared Data Banks*, (Communications of the ACM, 1970).

Collins, G & Blay, G *Structured Systems Development Techniques: Strategic Planning to System Testing*, (London, Pitman, 1982).

Comer, Michael J *Corporate Fraud*, (London, McGraw-Hill, 1985).

Connor, D *Information System Specification and Design Road Map*, (New York, Prentice Hall, 1985).

Cronin, Daniel J *Microcomputer Data Security. Issues and Strategies*, (New York, Prentice Hall, 1986).

Date, CJ *An Introduction to Database Systems*, (Massachusetts, Addison-Wesley Publishing, 1986).

DeMarco, T *Structured Analysis: System Specifications*, (New Jersey, Prentice-Hall, 1979).

Douglas, IJ & Olson, PJ *Audit and Control of Computer Networks*, (Manchester, NCC Publications, 1986).

Driver, MJ & Mock, TJ *Human Information Processing, Decision Style Theory and Accounting Information Systems*, (The Accounting Review, July 1975, Vol 50, pp490–508).

Earl, MJ & Hopwood, AG *From Management Information to Information Management*, collected in *The Information Systems Environment* eds Lucas, Land, Lincoln & Sapper, (New York, North Holland, 1980, pp3–13).

Edwards, Chris & Savage, Nigel *Information Technology and The Law*, (Basingstoke, Macmillan, 1986).

Ellison, JR & Pritchard, JAT *Security in Office Systems*, (Manchester, NCC Publications, 1987).

Fraga, J & Powell, D *A Fault and Intrusion Tolerant File System*, collected in *Computer Security: The Practical Issues in a Troubled World*, (Grimson, 1985, pp203–18).

French, CS *Data Processing*, (Eastleigh, DP Publications, Seventh Edition, 1987).

Galliers, R *Information Systems Planning*, (London, London School of Economics, 1986).

Gane, C & Sarson, T *Structured Systems Analysis: Tools and Techniques*, (New Jersey, Prentice-Hall, 1979).

Grimson, Jane B & Kugler, Hans-Jurgen *Computer Security: The Practical Issues in a Troubled World*, (Amsterdam, North Holland, 1985).

Hirschheim, R *Office Automation: A Social and Organisational Perspective*, (Chichester, John Wiley, 1985).

Hodkinson, Keith & Wasik, Martin *Industrial Espionage. Protection and Remedies*, (Longman Intelligence Reports, London, Longman, 1986).

Jackson, MA *Systems Development*, (New Jersey, Prentice-Hall, 1983).

Johnson, Deborah G *Computer Ethics*, (New Jersey, Prentice-Hall, 1985).

Kent, WA *Simple Guide to Five Normal Forms in Relational Theory*, (Communications of the ACM, 1983).

Land, FF *Evaluation of Systems Goals in Determining a Design Strategy for a Computer Based Information System*, (The Computer Journal, 1976, Vol 19, No 4, pp290–4).

Land, F & Hirschheim, R *Participative Systems Design: Rationale, Tools and Techniques*, (Journal of Applied Systems Analysis, 1983).

Lane, VP *Security of Computer Based Information Systems*, (London, Macmillan, 1985).

Lane, Victor & Step, John *The Formidable—If Not Insurmountable Problems of Disaster Recovery Planning*, collected in *Computer Security: The Practical Issues in a Troubled World*, (Grimson, 1985).

Libby, R & Lewis, BL *Human Information Processing Research in Accounting: The State of the Art in 1982*, (Accounting, Organisations and Society, 1982, Vol 7, No 3, pp231–285).

Longworth, G *Designing Systems for Change*, (Manchester, National Computing Centre, 1985).

MacCrimmon, KR *Management Decision Making*, collected in McGuire, JW *Contemporary Management: Issues and Viewpoints*, (Eaglewood Cliffs, NJ, Prentice-Hall, 1977, pp445–95).

Martin, J *Application Development Without Programmers*, (New Jersey, Prentice-Hall, 1982).

Nolan, RL *Managing the Computer Resource: A Stage Hypothesis*, (Communications of the ACM, March/April 1979, Vol 16, No 7, pp399–405).

Palmer, I & Rock-Evans, R *Data Analysis*, (IPC Publications, 1981).

Porter, ME *Competitive Advantage*, (New York, The Free Press, 1985).

QED Information Sciences Inc *Disaster Recovery: Contingency Planning and Program Evaluation*, (New York, Chantico Publishing Co, 1985).

Ratcliff, B *Software Engineering: Principles and Methods*, (Oxford, Blackwell Scientific Publications, 1988).

Shave, MJR & Bhaskar, KN *Computer Science Applied to Business Systems*, (Massachusetts, Addison-Wesley Publishing Co, 1982).

Sherman, Barrie *The New Revolution. The Impact of Computers on Society*, (Chichester, John Wiley, 1985).

Silverman, B *Expert Systems for Business*, (Massachusetts, Addison-Wesley Publishing Co, 1985).

Skidmore, S & Wroe, B *Introducing Systems Analysis*, (Manchester, National Computing Centre, 1988).

Stowell, FA & Allen, GA *Cooperation, Power and the Impact of Information Systems*, (Systems Practice, 1988, Vol 1, No 2, pp181–92).

Veryard, R *Pragmatic Data Analysis*, (Oxford, Blackwell Scientific Publications, 1986).

Wood, Michael B *Computer Access Control*, (Manchester, NCC Publications, 1985).

Wong, KK & Farquhar, WF *Computer Crime Casebook*, (London, BIS Applied Systems Ltd, 1987).

Wong, KK & Farquhar, WFN *Computer Related Fraud Casebook*, (London, BIS Applied Systems Ltd, 1986).

Worthington, TK, Chainer, TJ, Williford JD, Gundersen, SC *IBM Dynamic Signature Verification*, collected in *Computer Security: The Practical Issues*, (Grimson, 1985, pp129–54).

Yourdon, E *Techniques of Program Structure and Design*, (New Jersey, Prentice-Hall, 1975).

Glossary

Added Value—the term applied to describe the satisfaction of consumer needs or aspirations, ie the consumer's motive to select one supplier rather than another is governed by the perception of the additional value to be derived from the supply of the goods or services, eg value may be added by appearing to provide better quality or currency through the brand name; organisations generally seek to enhance the value delivered as a key platform of their competitive strategy.

ALGOL (ALGOrithmic Language)—a high-level programmimg language based on algebraic principles that is used frequently in developing mathematically based applications.

Algorithm—a sequence of predefined rules, procedures and selection criteria which may be applied to resolve problems with a predictable structure.

Analogue computer—a computing device which operates on data represented in the form of physical measures such as temperatures or air pressures as opposed to *digital* computers which utilise data in a numeric form. Analogue computers are typically used in the monitoring and control of electricity power generation, flows of gas or oil through pipelines and automated manufacturing processes.

Applications software—programs designed to process data for particular user needs, eg payroll application, spreadsheet software, word processing, etc.

Artificial Intelligence (AI)—application of computer-based technologies to mimic certain problem-solving abilities of humans, usually related to structured or semi-structured problem situations.

Automatic Teller Machines (ATMs)—computerised systems employed in banks and other personal financial services institutions to cash cheques, issue cash, and provide other services normally provided by human tellers

BASIC—(Beginners All-purpose Symbolic Instruction Code)—a high-level programming language designed to facilitate the use of relatively simple English-type instructions to create programs. It is common to many machines for use in the on-line interactive mode but, although still widely available, it is being replaced by more powerful and higher level languages, eg Pascal.

Batch processing—aggregating similar types of data requiring similar processing into groups or batches and processing these together rather than individually, thus deriving economies of scale in the processing of the data.

Batch total—a security check to ensure that all records submitted for processing have been processed, and involving either a total of the number of records in the batch or a total across a similar field in each record.

Baud—measure of the speed at which data is communicated along a channel, the number of signal pulses per second.

Buffer—either an insert to separate one block of data from another, or an area of storage which is used to store transitory data, eg the CPU can supply data to a printer device faster than the printer can physically operate, hence the CPU transmits blocks of data for printing to the printer's buffer store and the printer reads the data as required from its buffer store.

CAD/CAM (Computer Aided Design and Computer Aided Manufacture) a generic term applied to the development and design of systems to support design work and to control manufacturing operations.

Cathode ray tube (CRT) visual communications device based on television technology providing the major element of the human/computer interface in modern systems.

CBT (Computer Based Training)—vocational training systems which exploit computer technology to present and explain the instructional materials.

Central Processing Unit (CPU)—main unit of the computer system which holds the software instructions and data, performs the execution of these instructions and controls all the associated peripheral devices. It is also the unit of measurement for the amount of processing time used in the execution of a given program.

Closed system—a system which has no interaction with its environment.

COBOL (COmmon Business-Oriented Language)—a high-level programmimg language primarily designed for the development of commercial or business data processing applications and, despite its antiquity, still used extensively.

COM (Computer Output Microfilm)—computer storage device employing microfilm technology, used primarily for backing and off-line storage.

Conceptual schema—the overall structure of a database expressed in logical terms and used in database design and development.

Console—the interface unit between the user and the computer, typically in the form of a typewriter keyboard but also employing other ergonomically efficient devices, eg mouse or light pens.

CPU—see Central processor unit

CRT—see Cathode ray tube

Data dictionary—a structured file of details (eg contents, structure, location, and relationship to other data elements) relating to all the data held within the system.

Database—a collection of data in the form of records, usually appropriate to more than one user application, which are held centrally and accessed and updated by different users.

Database Management System (DBMS)—software used to build, maintain and control user access to the database files.

Data Flow Diagram (DFD)—diagramatic tool applied in systems analysis and design to indicate logical flows between entities, processes and data structures within a system.

DDS (Data Dictionary System)—software designed to control the operation, maintenance and access to the data dictionary (see above).

Decision Support System (DSS)—collection of data, software, tools and techniques designed to aid decision-makers to analyse problems, and to evaluate and select appropriate solutions.

Decision table—a systems analysis tool applied to the decomposition of problems into potential conditions and the consequent actions.

Digital computer—a computer that processes input in the form of discrete units as opposed to continuous data (see Analogue computer) and performs arithmetic and logic operations on this data—primarily used in commercial data processing.

Distributed Data Processing—a number of devices linked by a network, with each component computer or workstation capable of storing and processing part of the users' requirements in isolation from the network or providing access to appropriate resources within the network.

Electronic Fund Transfer (EFT)—the transfer of financial balances by electronic means through appropriate computer networks (related term EFTPOS—Electronic Funds Transfer at Point of Sale, involves the automatic debiting of each customer's account at the time of purchase without using a cheque).

Electronic Mail (EMS or E-Mail)—communication of messages between users through a computer network.

Encryption—a way of encoding data by using hardware and/or software processes that is designed to enhance the security of data during transmission and storage; it usually requires the reversal of the coding process at the receiving end, **decryption**.

Entities—a term used in context diagrams to refer to individuals, groups or organisations involved in the system, both internally and externally.

ERM (Entity-Relationship Model)—a systems analysis tool designed to assist data analysis in terms of entities, attributes, and relationships.

EPOS (Electronic Point of Sale)—automatic systems for the capture of product and pricing data, using barcodes and electronic sensors to avoid the need to key in prices—used extensively in retailing.

Expert systems—systems designed to apply knowledge and problem-solving rules derived from observation of human processes to mimic human expertise (often termed Knowledge Based Systems).

External schema—the user's view of the structure and contents of the data elements in a database, applied in database construction and development.

Flowchart—diagramatic tool using standard symbols and lines to illustrate the logical flow in the operations of a system or a program.

FORTRAN (FORmula TRANslator)—high-level programming language used primarily for mathematical computations.

Fourth Generation Language (4GL)—term applied to programming or software development tools which are more end-user orientated; automatically generating the necessary program instruction coding from statements describing the structure of the input formats, output reports and storage contents required by the user.

Heuristics—rules of thumb or intuitive approaches to problem-solving.

Hierarchical database—a structured environment for data elements within a database involving a series of different levels and branches within each level.

Human Computer Interface (HCI)—the interaction between the users and the information technologies.

Indexed sequential file organisation (ISAM)—method of storing records within a computer file in a sequential order but which allows more rapid access to individual records via the use of a location index than in the normal sequential storage method.

Information Centre—a location within the organisation at which the users may gain access to information to support their operational needs; in computer systems, this may typically be represented by a computer workstation connected to the computer network.

Input/Output (I/O)—generic term for the processes concerned with the capture and transfer of data to the computer and the subsequent transfer of results to the user.

Interactive—use of a computer system which provides direct and immediate responses to user instructions; often termed on-line access.

Intelligent terminal—computer terminal device which is capable of processing data independently of the central computer to which it is attached; terminals which lack this independent processing capacity are termed dumb or slave terminals.

Internal schema—definition of the internal physical stucture or organisation of the database to be constucted.

KB systems—see expert systems

K or Kb—refers to multiples of 1000 bytes or characters, usually relating to storage capacities of devices or CPUs.

LAN (Local Area Network)—network of computer devices within a close geographical area, usually within the same part of the organisation or building.

M, Mb or Meg—refers to multiples of 1,000,000 bytes or characters, relating to storage capacities of devices.

Management Information System (MIS)—manual or computer-based systems designed to provide management with appropriate information to support planning, decision-making and control of the operations of the organisation.

MIPS—a unit of measurement to indicate the number of instructions that can be executed by the processors comprising the CPU, ie million instructions per second—see also **KOPS**— thousand operations per second.

Multi-access—term applied to computer systems which allow simultaneous access to files or processing by more than one user.

Network—system of communication channels interconnecting users at different locations.

Normalisation—a term applied in relational database design referring to the process of simplifying the logical relationships within the database structure.

Protocol—a set of rules or standards governing the format and methods employed in the transmission of data, necessary to ensure the effective exchange of data between devices within a computer system or users within a network.

Prototype—the initial model of the system to be developed incorporating sample input and output screen layouts, information content and operating guidelines etc; it is used to facilitate user trials and record observations.

Query Language—programming language designed to construct the user's interrogation enquiries in a database system.

Relational Database—database system structured on the basis of the relationships between the data elements and records within the system.

SDLC—see Systems development life cycle.

Sequential access—the method of accessing records on a file involving a record by record search process down the file until the correct record is found.

Spooling—the use of secondary storage devices (eg disk or tape) to act as an interim buffer store between input and output peripheral devices (eg keyboards or printers) to reduce delays in processing due to slow operating speeds of these peripherals relative to the central processing unit, ie it creates a queue.

Star Formation—the computer network structure in which all the devices or users are connected directly on separate channels to the main computer or processing unit.

Systems flowchart—graphical tool used in the analysis and design of systems to display the logical data flows and operations.

Systems Development Life Cycle (SDLC)—the stages involved in the initiation, analysis, development and implementation of an information system.

Tally Systems—typically, hand-held or lap-top data recording devices used to monitor stock levels in retail outlets or details of orders by salesmen—data is down-loaded to the main computer periodically by connecting into the network.

Timesharing—a common variety of operating system within a computer which slices up the central processor time available and allocates access in rotation to each user for the slice of time. The speed at which this sharing of time is effected is typically such that users are unaware of the process in operation, believing they have sole and continuous access—see also Virtual storage.

VANS (Value Added Network Services)—information and data transmission services available over public networks; often of a specialist nature eg share price movements or airline flight and holiday booking information.

Virtual machine—a computer operating system which processes instructions and data as a number of segments (pages), reading and processing each segment as required (paging), and then replacing it in memory. This process makes the machine seem 'larger'—typically used in timesharing systems where pages are processed during each timeslice.

Wide Area Network (WAN)—network connecting geographically separate users, typically employing satellite or micro-wave transmission technologies.

WIMP (Windows, Icons, Mouse and Pull-down menus) relates to a combination of these features in developing the human interface between the user and the computer system.

Workbenches—collection of software and harware tools and facilities designed to support the work of systems analysts, designers and programmers; usually integrated within a single workstation.

Workstation—standalone computer or terminal which provides a combination of hardware and software facilities to support the specialist activities of particular types of users; often related to CAD/CAM application areas.

Spooling [illegible]

Structure [illegible] unit.

[illegible]

Systems Development Life Cycle (SDLC) [illegible]

[illegible]

Time-sharing [illegible]

VANS (Value Added Network Services) [illegible]

Virtual machine [illegible]

Wide Area Network (WAN) [illegible]

WIMP [illegible]

Workstation [illegible]

[illegible]

Index